Communications
in Computer and Information Science   405

Kenli Li   Zheng Xiao   Yan Wang
Jiayi Du   Keqin Li (Eds.)

Parallel Computational Fluid Dynamics

25th International Conference, ParCFD 2013
Changsha, China, May 20-24, 2013
Revised Selected Papers

 Springer

Volume Editors

Kenli Li
Zheng Xiao
Yan Wang
Jiayi Du

Hunan University
College of Information Science and Engineering
Changsha, China
E-mail:
lkl510@263.net
xiaozheng206@163.com
bessie11@yeah.net
dujiayi3@163.com

Keqin Li
State University of New York at New Paltz, NY, USA
and Hunan University, Changsha, China
E-mail: lik@newpaltz.edu

ISSN 1865-0929
ISBN 978-3-642-53961-9
DOI 10.1007/978-3-642-53962-6
Springer Heidelberg New York Dordrecht London

e-ISSN 1865-0937
e-ISBN 978-3-642-53962-6

Library of Congress Control Number: 2013957187

CR Subject Classification (1998): I.6.3-6, C.5.0, C.1.2, H.1.0, J.2

Typesetting: Camera-ready by author, data conversion by Scientific Publishing Services, Chennai, India

Printed on acid-free paper

Springer is part of Springer Science+Business Media (www.springer.com)

Preface

ParCFD 2013 was the 25th of a series of annual international meetings held since 1989. It is dedicated to the discussion of the most recent developments and applications of parallel computing in the field of computational fluid dynamics (CFD) and related disciplines. ParCFD conferences are truly multicultural and international, attracting many researchers across the world with diverse technical expertise either as developers or users of CFD technologies.

Since the establishment of the conference series, computational science, the use of advanced computing capabilities to understand and verify complex problems, has become crucial to scientific research, economic competiveness, and national security. Parallel computing is one of the most important fields in computational science, and parallel computers have become the dominant form of large-scale computing.

However, the emergence of multi-core and heterogeneous architectures in parallel computers has created new challenges and opportunities for applications research and performance optimization in advanced CFD technology.

Previous conference sessions have involved papers on parallel algorithms, developments in software tools and environments, unstructured adaptive mesh applications, industrial applications, atmospheric and oceanic global simulation, interdisciplinary applications, and evaluation of computer architectures and software environments.

This was the first time that the conference was held in China. For a long time, China and the world's major developed countries attached great importance to the development and application of high-performance computing, and they made numerous achievements in this area. "TianHe-2," ranked first in the world recently, and the world's top 10 supercomputer system "Dawning Nebulae" are the representative achievements after years of investment. Also in China, CFD is a main application area in which parallel computers play a key role in solving some challenging problems in the simulation and computation of CFD.

ParCFD 2013 was held during May 20–24, 2013, at Changsha, Hunan, China, and it was sponsored by Hunan University, which is one of the oldest universities in the world, and the National Supercomputing Center in Changsha. The conference received more than 240 papers, and each paper was carefully reviewed by the Technical Program Committee members. Finally, fewer than 120 papers were selected for our conference. This volume comprises 35 excellent papers recommended by the Program Committee members, covering topics such as parallel CPU and GPU implementations parallel algorithms and solvers, multi-disciplinary design optimization, multi-scale and multi-physics applications, and parallel pre- and post-processing. On behalf of the Organizing Committee, we thank all the experts of the Program Committee for their work in reviewing the articles.

September 2013

Kenli Li
Yan Wang
Jiayi Du
Zheng Xiao
Keqin Li

Conference Organization

The 25th International Conference on Parallel Computational Fluid Dynamics (ParCFD 2013) was organized by Hunan University and the National Supercomputing Center in Changsha. It was partly funded by PERA GLOBAL, AlTAIR, and SINOPARASOFT.

Conference Chairs

Chengzhong Xu	Electrical and Computer Engineering at Wayne State University, USA
Keqin Li	Hunan University, China; State University of New York, USA

Conference Co-chairs

Kenli Li	Hunan University, National Supercomputing Center in Changsha, China
Junqian Song	National Supercomputing Center in Changsha, National University of Defense Technology, China
Zeyao Mo	Beijing Institute of Applied Physics and Computational Mathematics, China
Zhengqing Chen	Hunan University, China
Yuxin Ren	School of Aerospace, Tsinghua University, China
Renfa Li	Hunan University, National Supercomputing Center in Changsha, China

International Advisory Committee

Ramesh K. Agarwal	Washington University, USA
Hasan Akay	Atilim University, Turkey
Shahrouz Aliabadi	Northrop Grumman Center for High Performance Computing, USA
Lorena Barba	Boston University, USA
Rupak Biswas	NASA-Ames Research Center, USA
Gunther Brenner	Technical University of Clausthal, Germany
Boris Chetverushkin	Russian Academy of Science, Russia
Anil Deane	University of Maryland, USA
Akin Ecer	IUPUI, USA
David R. Emerson	Daresbury Laboratory, UK

Marc Garbey	University of Houston, USA
Ulgen Gulcat	Istanbul Technical University, Turkey
David E. Keyes	Columbia University, USA
Trond Kvamsdal	SINTEF, Norway
Jang-Hyuk Kwon	Korea Institute of Science and Technology Information, Korea
Jong-Shinn Wu	National Chiao Tung University Taiwan, China
Chao-An Lin	National Tsing Hua University Taiwan, China
Kenichi Matsuno	Kyoto Institute of Technology, Japan
James McDonough	University of Kentucky, USA
Sergey Peigin	Israel Aircraft Industries, Israel
Jacques Periaux	Dassault Aviation, France
Nobuyuki Satofuka	University of Shiga Prefecture, Japan
Damien Tromeur-Dervout	University of Claude Bernard Lyon I, France
Ismail H. Tuncer	Middle East Technical University, Turkey
Gerhard Wellein	University of Erlangen, Germany
Mariano Vazquez	The Barcelona Supercomputing Center, Spain
Kenli Li	Hunan University, National Supercomputing Center in Changsha, China

Chinese Organizing Committee

Chinese Academy of Sciences
China Academy of Engineering Physics
The Specialty Association of Mathematical & Scientific Software
National University of Defense Technology
Tsinghua University
Hunan Computer Federation

Local Organizing Committee

Junqian Song National Supercomputing Center in Changsha National University of Defense Technology China
Li Kenli National Supercomputing Center in Changsha Hunan University China
Zhiwen Zhu Hunan University China

Sponsors

Table of Contents

Simulation Study of Solidification Processes for a Large Scale System
of Liquid Metal Al 1
  Yingqiang Liao, Kenli Li, and Rangsu Liu

Parallel Implementation of Localized Radial Basis Function
Interpolation for Computational Aeroelastic Predictions 11
  Gang Wang, Haris Hameed Mian, Zheng-Yin Ye, and Jen-Der Lee

Solving Seven-Equation Model of Compressible Two-Phase Flow Using
CUDA-GPU 25
  Shan Liang, Wei Liu, and Li Yuan

Parallel Solver for Hypersonic Flow Based on Block-Structured Grid.... 37
  Ding Guo-hao, Li Hua, Liu Jian-Xia, and Fan Jin-Zhi

Medical Image Clustering Algorithm Based on Graph Model 54
  Haiwei Pan, Jingzi Gu, Qilong Han, Xiaoning Feng,
  Xiaoqin Xie, and Pengyuan Li

The Pressure Buildup and Salt Precipitation during CO_2 Storage
in Closed Saline Aquifers.. 66
  Qingliang Meng, Xi Jiang, Didi Li, and Xiaoqin Zhong

Numerical Simulation of the Effects of N_2 on the Solubility Trapping
Mechanism of CO_2 78
  Didi Li, Xi Jiang, Qingliang Meng, and Xiaoqin Zhong

Implementation of the Six Temperature Kinetic Model of Gasdynamic
Laser in OpenFOAM 89
  Gang He, Jin Zhou, and Lin Lai

The Implementation of MapReduce Scheduling Algorithm Based
on Priority 100
  Lianjun Gu, Zhuo Tang, and Guoqi Xie

Efficient Parallel Multi-way Merging on Heterogeneous Multi-core
Cluster 112
  Cheng Zhong and Wei Wei

An Offline Scheduling Algorithm for Certifiable Mixed-Critical
Embedded System 124
  Chengtao Wu and Renfa Li

An Efficient Implementation of Entropic Lattice Boltzmann Method
in a Hybrid CPU-GPU Computing Environment 136
 Yu Ye, Peng Chi, and Yan Wang

Parallelization of a DEM Code Based on CPU-GPU Heterogeneous
Architecture... 149
 *Xiaoqiang Yue, Hao Zhang, Congshu Luo, Shi Shu, and
 Chunsheng Feng*

GPU Parallelization of Unstructured/Hybrid Grid ALE Multi-Grid
Solver for Moving Bodies 160
 WenPeng Ma, ZhongHua Lu, and Jian Zhang

The Analysis of Pile Cap Hydrodynamic Added Mass Considering
the Chamfer.. 172
 Kehua You, Kai Wei, and Wancheng Yuan

Numerical Simulations for DLR-F6 Wing/Body/Nacelle/Pylon
with Enhanced Implicit Hole Cutting Method 185
 Jia Xu, Qiuhong Liu, and Jinsheng Cai

Accelerating High-Order CFD Simulations for Multi-block Structured
Grids on the TianHe-1A Supercomputer 195
 *Chuanfu Xu, Wei Cao, Lilun Zhang, Guangxue Wang,
 Yonggang Che, Yongxian Wang, and Wei Liu*

Large-Scale Parallelization Based on CPU and GPU Cluster
for Cosmological Fluid Simulations 207
 *Chen Meng, Long Wang, Zongyan Cao, Long-long Feng, and
 Weishan Zhu*

Large Eddy Simulation of a Rectangular Lobed Mixer 221
 Qiancheng Wang, Jing Lei, Junhong Feng, and Zhenguo Wang

The Application of Preconditioned AUSM+ in Viscous Flow at Low
Speeds... 232
 Feng Yu, Wu Meng, Qin Jiang, Li Tao, and Huang Hongyan

A High-Order Weighted Essentially Non-Oscillatory Schemes
for Solving Euler Equations on Unstructured Meshes 240
 Li Tao, Feng Yu, Zhu Kaidi, and Huang Hongyan

Unified Computational Aeroacoustic Integral Methods for Noise
Radiation and Scattering with Noncompact Bodies 252
 Fang Wang, Qiuhong Liu, and Jinsheng Cai

Flow Characteristics of Gas-Liquid Phase in New Type of Umbrella
Plate Scrubber 265
 Li Shanhong, Guo Guanqing, Li Caiting, and Tangqi

Three-Dimensional Aeroacoustic Numerical Simulation of Flow Induced
Noise of Mufflers 276
    Yan Yang and Hongling Sun

Dynamic Slack Reclamation with EDL Scheduling for Periodic
Multimode Real-Time Task 287
    Huan Hu and Renfa Li

Modeling of the Pressure Variation during the Inflation Process
of Unsteady Time-Pressure Dispensing............................ 301
    Yu Ji, Jiankui Chen, Haichen Qin, and Yaogen Wu

Performance Analysis and Optimization of PalaBos on Petascale
Sunway BlueLight MPP Supercomputer 311
    Min Tian, Weidong Gu, Jingshan Pan, and Meng Guo

Recursive Kernighan-Lin Algorithm (RKL) Scheme for Cooperative
Road-Side Units in Vehicular Networks 321
    Yao Weihong, Yang Yuehui, and Tan Guozhen

Drag Reduction of a Truck Using Append Devices and Optimization ... 332
    Xiaolong Yang and Zihui Ma

Delayed-VLES Model for the Simulation of Turbulent Flows........... 344
    Yang Zhang, Junqiang Bai, and Chen Wang

Parallel Direct Simulation Monte Carlo Using Graphics Processing
Unit with CUDA 354
    Jie Liang

Internal Leakage Fault Feature Extraction of Hydraulic Cylinder Using
Wavelet Packet Energy 363
    Xiuxu Zhao, Zhemin Hu, Rui Li, Chuanli Zhou, and Jihai Jiang

A Modified Energy Saving Scheduling Algorithm on Heterogeneous
Systems 376
    An Shen and Yuming Xu

Immersed Boundary-Lattice Boltzmann Method for Biological
and Biomedical Flows 383
    *Wen-Hong Zu, Ju-Hua Zhang, Duan-Duan Chen, Yuan-Qing Xu,
    Qiang Wei, and Fang-Bao Tian*

Effect of Shape Parameterization on Aerodynamic Shape Optimization
with SPSA Algorithm 393
    Zheng Wang, Shengjiao Yu, and Tiegang Liu

Natural Frequency Ratio Effect on 2 DOF Flow Induced Vibration
of Cylindrical Structures 403
  Xiangxi Han, Chengbi Zhao, Youhong Tang, Xiaoming Chen,
  Wei Lin, and Karl Sammut

A Grid Reordering Technique for Hybrid Unstructured Flow Solver
Based on OpenMP Parallel Environment............................. 418
  Meng Cheng, Gang Wang, and Haris Hameed Mian

A Novel Method Based on Chemical Reaction Optimization
for Pairwise Sequence Alignment 429
  Danqing Huang and Xiangyuan Zhu

Hydrodynamic Analysis of Floating Marine Structures Based
on an IBM-VOF Two-Phase Flow Model............................ 440
  Nansheng Lin, Xiaoming Chen, Chengbi Zhao, Youhong Tang, and
  Wei Lin

An Improved Fictitious Domain Method for Simulating Sedimenting
Rigid Particle in a Viscous Fluid 450
  Shifeng Wu and Li Yuan

A Divide-and-Conquer Method for Multiple Sequence Alignment
on Multi-core Computers 460
  Xiangyuan Zhu

Hybrid CPU/GPU Checkpoint for GPU-Based Heterogeneous
Systems 470
  Lin Shi, Hao Chen, and Ting Li

A Parallel Chemical Reaction Optimization for Multiple Choice
Knapsack Problem 482
  Tung Khac Truong, Ahmad Salah, Yuming Xu, and Shuangnan Fan

Study of Mesh Generation for Complex Geometries 490
  Dongliang Cui, Bowen Wang, and Meng Li

Numerical Study on Interaction of Ramp-Induced Oblique Detonation
Wave with a Boundary Layer 504
  Yu Liu, Xu Han, Zhiyong Lin, and Jin Zhou

Parallelization of the Local Mesh Refinement on Multi-Core CPU 514
  Hang Chen, Yu Ye, and Ren Lin

Optimized Roles Set Algorithm in Distributed Parallel Computing
System 522
  Wenkang Wu and Zhuo Tang

Application of Improved Simulated Annealing Optimization
Algorithms in Hardware/Software Partitioning of the Reconfigurable
System-on-Chip... 532
    Yiming Jing, Jishun Kuang, Jiayi Du, and Biao Hu

Large-Scale Parallel Computing for 3D Gaseous Detonation 541
    Wang Cheng, Bi Yong, Han Wenhu, and Ning Jianguo

Numerical Simulation about Train Wind Influence on Personnel Safety
in High-Speed Railway Double-Line Tunnel 553
    Limin Peng, Ruizhen Fei, Chenghua Shi, Weichao Yang, and
    Yiting Liu

Parallel Computation of Shaped Charge Jet Formation and Penetration
by Multi-material Eulerian Method................................ 565
    Tianbao Ma, Xiangzhao Xu, and Jianguo Ning

Calculation of Guide Cone Wall Temperature of Concentric Canister
Launcher with Considering Gas Radiation.......................... 577
    Xiaolei Hu, Guigao Le, and Dawei Ma

Numerical Optimization of Structural Parameters on GQ-108C Air
Reverse Circulation DTH Hammer Bit............................. 589
    Zhiqiang Zhao, Lijia Li, Xiangtian Huan, and Kun Bo

Parallel Conjugate Gradient Method Based on Spline Difference
Method for the One-Dimensional Heat Equation 602
    Aijia Ouyang, Wangdong Yang, Guangxue Yue, Tao Jiang,
    Xiaoyong Tang, and Xu Zhou

Author Index... 613

Simulation Study of Solidification Processes for a Large Scale System of Liquid Metal Al

Yingqiang Liao[1,2], Kenli Li[1,*], and Rangsu Liu[3]

[1] School of Information Science and Engineering, Hunan University,
Changsha, 410082, P.R. China
{lyq698828,lkl,liangjie1988}@hnu.edu.cn
[2] National Supercomputing Center of Changsha,
Hunan University Office, Changsha, 410082, China
[3] School of Physics and Micro Electronic, Hunan Universisy,
Changshang, 410082, P.R. China
liurangsu@hnu.edu.cn

Abstract. In this work, for the simulation study of solidification processes by molecular dynamics method for a large-sized system consisting of 5,000,000 Al atoms, a parallel arithmetic program has been proposed. The parallel architecture used in the simulation is MPI+OpenMP model. It enlarges the scale of the simulation system and improves the calculation efficiency. Most importantly, because of remarkably decreasing of boundary conditions effect, the simulation result would be more closed to the real situation of the system with the increasing number of atoms involved in the simulation. In this paper, we adopt many microstructure analysis methods to verify the validity of the simulation, including pair distribution function, bond-type index analysis, atomic clusters analysis and visualizing analysis. From these results, it is clear that the simulation results are in good agreement with the experimental results.

Keywords: parallel algorithm, liquid metals, solidification processes, Molecular Dynamics (MD), computer simulation.

1   Introduction

Molecular dynamics (MD) is a powerful method to solve the classical motion equations of systems comprising a mass of particles, where there exist interacting forces between particles [1,2]. With the advent of computer simulation technology and parallel computing techniques, such as supercomputer, the large scale simulations of some physical processes have been performed by using efficient MD parallel algorithms [3-9]. Meanwhile, the MD simulation has become an effective and common research method for atomic-level theoretical analysis and experimental research in various fields, such as chemistry, materials science, physics and engineering.

In this paper, we change the existing parallel program with PVM parallel architecture, and propose the parallel program adopting MPI+OpenMP model to

---

* Corresponding author.

K. Li et al. (Eds.): ParCFD 2013, CCIS 405, pp. 1–10, 2014.

simulate the solidification processes of liquid metals based on the previous works [10-16] and researches on parallel algorithms in other fields [17-23]. The parallel algorithm enlarges the amount of the simulating system up to 5,000,000 - 10,000,000 atoms comparing with the pervious simulate system consisting of 500 - 50,000 atoms so that the simulation result is more closed to the realities of the system. In the following section, we present the whole processes of MD simulation, and the MD parallel model with MPI+OpenMP is described in section 3. The section 4 presents the main task of paper, demonstrating the simulation results analysis with microstructure evaluation methods such as pair distribution function, bond-type index analysis, atomic clusters analysis and visualizing analysis. All these simulation evaluation results illustrate that the simulation results are corresponding to the realistic situation.

Molecular Dynamics method is an important one to simulate the solidification processes of liquid metals. Given the initial position (coordinate r) and speed (v) of each atom in the systems under consideration, the interacting potential between atoms are known [24, 25], and then the forces acting on each atom can also be calculated, and the new position and speed can be obtained. Thus, we can simulate the dynamic situations and the instantaneous microstructures of the simulation system through circular computations step by step. From these results, the macroscopic thermodynamics properties of the system can be clearly acquired.

In MD simulation, we adopted the VERLET [26] algorithm. The VERLET algorithm is a classical method to solve the motion equations of simulation systems, which is rather mature and widely used. On the basis of VERLET algorithm, given that the coordinates and speed of each atom at a certain time (t), at time ($t+dt$), the displacement is displayed by Eq. (1).

$$r(t+dt) = 2r(t) - r(t-dt) + dt^2 \alpha(t) \tag{1}$$

Where the speed is not necessary to be calculated, but if we want to estimate the kinetic energy, the speed v should be got by the Eq. (2).

$$v(t) = \frac{r(t+dt) - r(t-dt)}{2dt} \tag{2}$$

In Eq. (1) and (2), the calculation of the acceleration a of each atom is equivalent to the calculation of the force f on the atom. We adopt the pair potential approximation to calculate the force f. If we limit the attention to the cases of pair interactions, the force on atom i can be calculated by the following Eq. (3).

$$\overrightarrow{F_j} = \sum_{j,i \neq j} \overrightarrow{f_{ij}} \tag{3}$$

2   Algorithm Analysis and Implementation

In the previous work, we adopted the PVM program with master-slave model run on the YH23M supercomputer. Under this model, the master run on the front workstation of YH23M while the slave nodes are given to the processing machines of YH23M used to calculate the forces acting on each atom. The whole program had been reformed by parallel processing and transformed into the slave programs (see [16]).

However, the performance of PVM program is unsatisfactory when the number of atoms in simulating system is up to 100,000. Therefore, we propose the new algorithm with the MPI+OpenMP programming model. Because the SD (spatial decomposition) method is more appropriate for the CPUs cluster and is widely and common used in some related software, the MPI+OpenMP program adopts SD method. First, the simulation system is assumed to be a big cubic box, and the whole box (entire domain) is split into p sub-box (sub-domain), where P is the number of processor nodes. This assignment method can achieve a good load balancing. During the calculation, the nodes are parallelized by MPI, whereas parallelization within each node is realized using OpenMP, fully utilizing the heterogeneity of the multi-core system among nodes and the shared memory of the multi-core system in a single node. In the first step, the initial position is generated according to the MC random number method in the domain node, and then the related data including neighbor list of each atom will be broadcast to the slave nodes. By this time, the forces calculations in each processor begin. If the atom escapes the current sub-domain, the corresponding neighbor list and related data will be updated through the MPI Send and MPI_ Recv and the next calculation steps are ready. This parallel architecture significantly improves the parallel efficiency with a decrease of communication and computing time, even though the requirement of storage has been increased.

This parallel algorithm program has been run steadily on the Tianhe supercomputer developed by the Chinese National University of Defense Technology (NUDT) in Changsha, Hunan. The master will run on the front workstation of Tianhe; meanwhile, the slave will be given to the processing machines of Tianhe. This program adopts MPI+OpenMP programming with master-slave type and its software programs: Red Hat Enterprise Linux Server release 5.5, MPI+OpenMP compiler version 1.4, and GCC Fortran90 compiler version 4.12.

3   Physics Results and Analysis

As we all know that the pair effective potential function of the generalized energy independent non-local model pseudo-potential theory is widely used to verify the validity of the simulation, which is developed by Wang et al [24, 25]. We use it to simulate the microstructures evolutions during solidification process in a system comprising 5,000,000 Al atoms:

$$V(r) = \frac{Z^2_{eff}}{r}[1 - \frac{2}{\pi}\int_0^\infty F(q)\frac{\sin(qr)}{q}dq] \qquad (4)$$

The function as shown by Fig.1, at 943 K (which is some higher than the melting point of Al, 933 K), we place 5,000,000 Al atoms in a cubic box. Their initial coordinates are obtained randomly. Though getting an equilibrium state at 943K with 80,000 time steps of the system, the system is cooled to some given temperatures at a cooling rate of 1×10^{12} K/s. During the cooling process, for each temperature interval (in general about 50 K), the system state (including the coordinates, velocities, energies and so on) would be recorded separately. From the results, the pair distribution function, the atom clusters, the bond-type index, and visualizing in the system can be analyzed as follows.

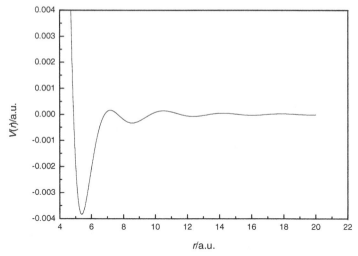

Fig. 1. Effective pair potential V (r) of liquid metal Al at 943 K

3.1   Pair Distribution Function

It is well known that the pair distribution function g(r) can be gained by Fourier transformation of the structure factor S (q) obtained from X-ray diffraction in a system, and has been adopted to compare the theoretical results with the experimental ones of the liquid and amorphous structures for correct inspection of the simulation. Fig.2 shows that the simulation result is in good agreement with the experimental result obtained by Waseda [27] at 943K. This means that the effective pair-potential function adopted here is rather successful for describing the physical nature of the system.

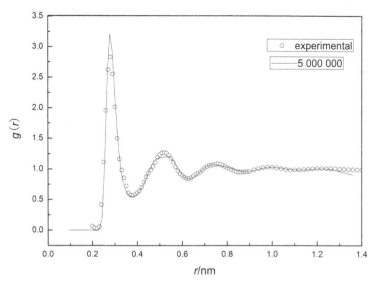

Fig. 2. Pair distribution function g(r) of liquid Al at 943K (Simulation result - solid line; experimental result—small circle)

3.2   Bond-Type Index Analysis

At present, the Honeycutt and Andersen (HA) bond-type index method [28] is a valuable method to identify the microstructure characteristics during the solidification processes. When the local configurations are described by the HA bond-type index method, the 1551、1541、1431 bond-types are closely related to the canonical icosahedrons and defective icosahedrons. In other word, these kinds of bond-types are the characteristic bond-types of a typical liquid state. The 1421 (twelve) bond-type is the characteristic bond-type of the FCC crystal; a set of the 1421 (six) and 1422 (six) and a set of 1441 (six) and 1661 (eight) bond-types are the characteristic bond-type of HCP crystal and the BCC crystal respectively.

Comparing these results with those obtained from the simulation of small-sized system comprising 50000 atoms (as shown in Table 1 of Ref. [16]), there are many differences between them. We find that 1421、1422 bond-types increase slightly, meanwhile the number of that decrease in Ref [16]; 1541、1661 bond-types are also just opposite between this paper and Ref [29]. The changing tendency of the other bond-types of two systems is essentially similar with some difference of their concrete data. In detail, among the bond-types only 1551 bond-type increases remarkably. For the large-sized system, the relative number of 1551 bond-type increase from 18.8% at 943 K to 31.36% at 300 K, while for the small-sized system the corresponding values are 16.95% and 29.256% at the respective temperature. From above analysis, it is just to be explained that the influence of the periodic boundary condition to the simulation results should not be neglected. However, the more number of atomic in systems, the less is affected by periodic boundary condition.

Table 1. Relations hip of relative numbers of various bond-types with temperature (%)

Temperature/k	Bond-types								
	1311	1321	1421	1422	1431	1441	1541	1551	1661
950	6.75	7.05	3.18	6.49	20.71	5.88	15.93	18.80	6.73
900	6.60	6.81	3.14	6.45	20.67	5.84	15.96	19.57	6.85
850	6.45	6.56	3.10	6.41	20.64	5.76	15.97	20.40	6.96
800	6.26	6.28	3.07	6.36	20.54	5.66	15.98	21.55	7.06
750	6.07	6.00	3.03	6.31	20.54	5.53	15.99	22.72	7.12
700	5.88	5.73	2.98	6.27	20.37	5.37	15.96	23.96	7.17
650	5.72	5.47	2.95	6.24	20.26	5.17	15.93	25.22	7.17
600	5.60	5.31	2.90	6.22	20.22	4.92	15.87	26.38	7.04
550	5.52	5.21	2.85	6.20	20.22	4.64	15.78	27.45	6.87
500	5.45	5.16	2.81	6.17	20.25	4.31	15.68	28.58	6.61
450	5.36	5.13	2.81	6.13	20.25	3.96	15.55	29.75	6.32
400	5.27	5.15	2.91	6.08	20.25	3.58	15.40	30.95	5.96
350	5.22	5.12	3.07	6.13	20.20	3.28	15.28	31.82	5.68
300	5.27	5.15	3.21	6.25	20.27	3.07	15.20	32.07	5.42
250	5.40	5.22	3.32	6.42	20.41	2.91	15.12	31.92	5.19
200	5.52	5.30	3.39	6.56	20.54	2.81	15.07	31.69	5.01
150	5.62	5.43	3.43	6.68	20.69	2.72	15.00	31.36	4.84
Tendency	- ①	-	+②	+	-	-	+	++③	-

①- means decreasing ; ②+ means increasing ; ③+ + means increasing remarkably

3.3   Atomic Clusters Analysis

As we known that crystalline materials have translational symmetry and long-range order while there are no long-range orders for amorphous materials. However, some structural models have been proposed over the years. Scattering experiments have demonstrated that the atomic structures of metallic glasses usually exhibit the short-range order (SRO) within one or two nearest-neighbor distances and the medium-range order (MRO) involving several of nearest-neighbor distances.

Highly appealing is that amorphous microstructure composed of a large number of different clusters has been observed by nano-beam electron diffraction [29]. In this paper, we have obtained the relations of the number of basic clusters with temperature as shown in Fig.3, in which the relations of the numbers of the icosahedrons and the defective icosahedrons with temperature are shown with black and red lines, respectively. The icosahedrons and defect icosahedrons basic clusters related to amorphous structure are mainly formed in the solidification process of liquid metal Al.

3.4   Visualizing Analysis

In order to more intuitive observe local atomic packing at 150 K, the three dimensional configurations of 1,000,000 atoms and (111) cross sections pictures are given in Fig.4 and Fig.5. From the (111) cross sections picture, we can find that there are two types of region. The dense regions in which the atoms gather in order and the loose regions in which the atoms distribute in disorder can be sharply distinguished. The dense regions are consisted of tightly bonded atomic clusters, which overlap and form the percolating 'skeleton' of the amorphous structure. In the loose regions, there are indeed some 'vacancies' or 'free volumes', which act as flow defects under mechanical loading.

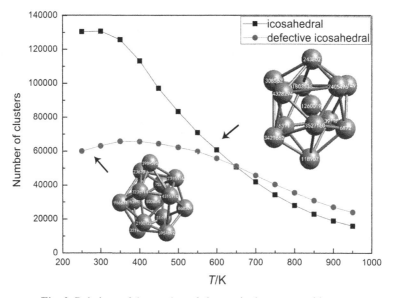

Fig. 3. Relations of the number of clusters in the system with temp

Fig. 4. Three dimensional configurations of 1,000,000 atoms

The larger clusters are consisted of various basic clusters formed in the system. And these basic clusters can be linked each other by vertex-sharing (VS), edge-sharing (ES), face-sharing (FS) or intercross-sharing (IS) models as shown in Fig.6 and Fig.7. From these results, we can get some more complete and larger cluster structures in the actual macroscopic materials, which can not easily be observed in the experiment at present.

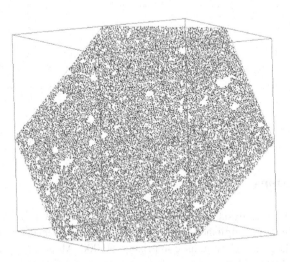

Fig. 5. Three dimensional configurations of (111) cross sections

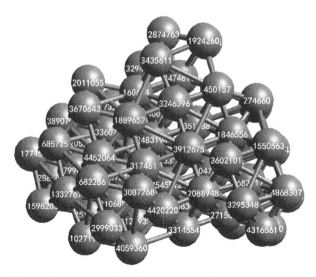

Fig. 6. A larger cluster consisting of several basic clusters formed in the system

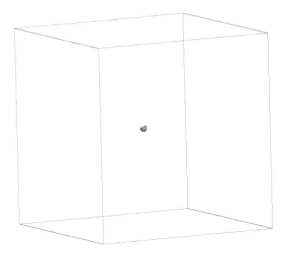

Fig. 7. The position of the large cluster in the cube box

4   Conclusions

Based on the deep analysis of the original MD simulation program, the parallel algorithm has been accomplished, and it successfully performed the MD simulation studies on the large-sized systems comprising 50,000 Al atoms. Under simulation with MPI+OpenMP parallel model, we have got rather satisfied results more closed to the reality. The comparison results between the simulation and the experiment can be seen in the analysis of physic simulation results through many evaluated method as mentioned above. However, we think that when the VERLET algorithm is reconstructed entirely from the parallel algorithm adopting the higher performance super-computers, the total number of atoms involved in simulation system can be enlarged to tens of million, even hundreds of million. Thus, the simulation results will be more and more closed to the realities of materials.

Acknowledgements. This research was partially funded by the Key Program of National Natural Science Foundation of China (61133005) and the National Science Foundation of China (61070057 and 90715029), the PhD Programs Foundation of the Ministry of Education of China (201001611 10019), the Key Project Supported by the Development Foundation, Hunan University "985" Project, and the Program for New Century Excellent Talents in University (NCET-08-0177).

References

1. Alder, B.J., Wainwright, T.E.: Phase transition for a hard sphere system. J. Chem. Phys., 1208–1209 (1957)
2. Allen, M.P., Tildesley, D.J.: Computer Simulation of Liquids. Clarendon, Oxford (1989)
3. Deng, Y.F., Ronald, F.P., et al.: An Adaptive Load Balancing Method for Parallel Molecular Dynamics Simulations. Journal of Computational Physics 250–263 (2000)
4. Murty, R., Okunbor, D.: Efficient parallel algorithms for molecular dynamics simulations. In: Parallel Computing, pp. 217–230 (1999)
5. Taylora, V.E., Stevensb, R.L., et al.: Parallel molecular dynamics: Implications for massively parallel machines. In: Parallel Distrib. Computer, pp. 166–175 (1997)
6. Plimpton, S.J., Pollock, R., et al.: Particle-Mesh Ewald and rRESPA for Parallel Molecular Dynamics Simulations. In: The Eighth SIAM Conference on Parallel Processing for Scientific Computing (1997)
7. Plimpton, J., Hendrickson, B.A.: A New Parallel Method for Molecular-Dynamics Simulation of Macromolecular Systems. S. J Comp. Chem., 326–337 (1996)
8. Plimpton, S.J., Hendrickson, B.A.: Parallel Molecular Dynamics Algorithms for Simulation of Molecular Systems. In: Parallel Computing in Computational Chemistry, pp. 114–132 (1995)
9. Plimpton, S.J.: Computational Limits of Classical Molecular-Dynamics Simulations. In: Computational Materials Science, pp. 361–364 (1995)
10. Liu, R.S., Qi, D.W., et al.: Subqeaks of Structure Factors for Rapidly Quenched Metals. Physics Review B, 451–453 (1992)
11. Liu, R.S., Qi, D.W., et al.: Anomalies in the Structure Factor for Some Rapidly Quenched Metals. Physics Review B, 12001–12003 (1992)
12. Liu, R.S., Dong, K.J., et al.: Formation and description of nano-clusters formed during rapid solidification processes in liquid metals. Journal of Non-Crystalline Solids, 612–617 (2005)
13. Liu, R.S., Dong, K.J., et al.: Formation and magic number characteristics of clusters formed during solidification processes. J. Phys: Condens. Matter, 196–103 (2007)
14. Hou, Z.Y., Liu, R.S., et al.: Simulation study on the formation and evolution properties of nano-clusters in rapid solidification structures of sodium. Modelling Simul. Mater. Sci. Eng., 911–922 (2007)

15. Hou, Z.Y., Liu, L.X., et al.: Short-range and medium-range order in Ca_7Mg_3 metallic glass. Journal of Applied Physics, 083511 (2010)
16. Dong, K.J., Liu, R.S., et al.: Parallel algorithm of solidification process simulation for large-sized system of liquid metal atoms. Trans. Nonferrous Met. Soc. China, 0824-06 (2003)
17. Brown, W.M., Wang, P.: Implementing Molecular Dynamics on Hybrid High Performance Computers-Short Range Forces. Computer Physics Communications, 898–911 (2011)
18. Khan, M.A., Herbordt, M.C.: Parallel discrete molecular dynamics simulation with speculation and in-order commitment. Journal of Computational Physics, 6563–6582 (2011)
19. Liu, Y.L., Hu, C.J., et al.: Efficient parallel implementation of Ewald summation in molecular dynamics simulations on multi-core platforms. Computer Physics Communications, 1111–1119 (2011)
20. Li, J.H., Zhou, Z.W., et al.: Parallel algorithms for molecular dynamics with induction forces. Computer Physics Communications, 384–392 (2008)
21. Mukherjee, R.M., Crozier, P.S., et al.: Substructured molecular dynamics using multibody dynamics algorithms. Intl. J. of Non-Linear Mechanics, 1045–1055 (2008)
22. Parks, M.L., Lehoucq, R.B., et al.: Implementing peridynamics within a molecular dynamics code. Computer Physics Communications, 777–783 (2008)
23. Oh, K.J., Klein, M.L.A.: A parallel molecular dynamics simulation scheme for a molecular system with bond constraints in NPT ensemble. Computer Physics Communications, 263–269 (2006)
24. Wang, S., Lai, S.K.: Structure and electrical resistivity's of liquid binary alloys. J. Phys. F, 2717–2737 (1980)
25. Li, D.H., Li, X.R., et al.: Variational calculation of Helmholtz free energies with applications to the sp-type liquid metals. J. Phys. F, 309–321 (1986)
26. Verlet, L.: Computer experiments on classical fluids. Phys. Rev., 98–103 (1967)
27. Waseda, Y.: The structure of Non-crystalline Materials. McGraw-Hill, New York (1980)
28. Honeycutt, J.D., Andersen, H.C.: Molecular dynamics study of melting and freezing of small Lennard-Jones clusters. J. Phys. Chem., 4950–4963 (1987)
29. Hirata, A., Guan, P.F., et al.: Direct observation of local atomic order in a metallic glass. Nature Materials, pp. 28–33 (2011)

Parallel Implementation of Localized Radial Basis Function Interpolation for Computational Aeroelastic Predictions

Gang Wang[1], Haris Hameed Mian[1], Zheng-Yin Ye[1], and Jen-Der Lee[2]

[1] National Key Laboratory of Science and Technology on Aerodynamic Design and Research,
School of Aeronautics, Northwestern Polytechnical University, Xi'an, 710072, China
[2] Beijing Aeronautical Science and Technology Research Institute (BASTRI),
COMAC, Beijing, 102211, P.R. China
harishameed_33@hotmail.com

Abstract. Mesh deformation and data interpolation using radial basis functions (RBF) in combination with data reduction greedy algorithm has proven to be an efficient method, both in providing high quality deformed meshes and speed up computations. In the present work an in-house hybrid unstructured Reynolds-averaged Navier-Stokes solver (HUNS3D) has been extended to include dynamic mesh motion and aeroelastic behavior prediction. For present computational aeroelastic simulations, RBF interpolation serves as single subroutine and carries out the required data interpolation for both the surface loads and deformations. For mesh motion and displacement interpolation the already developed RBF interpolation methods works reasonably well. But for interpolation of aerodynamic loads the current procedures become expensive in terms of computational time and are greatly influenced by the parameters used in the interpolation. In this paper a more efficient and robust method is presented that localizes the interpolation. This method resembles in concept to the pointwise form of partition of unity method but somewhat differs in its implementation. It is efficient in terms of computational time and can be readily parallelized. Also it reduces the influence of the interpolation parameters on the coupling behavior. The proposed method has been tested by performing static aeroelastic computations in transonic flow over the AGARD 445.6 wing, HIRENASD wing/body configuration and a flexible wing with spar-rib-skin construction. The method has shown its effectiveness in aeroelastic behavior prediction for different aerodynamic configurations.

Keywords: radial basis function interpolation, greedy algorithm, parallelization, mesh motion, computational aeroelasticity.

1 Introduction

Over the recent years computational aeroelastic simulations have gained a lot of interest since significant improvements have been made in the field of computational fluid dynamics (CFD), computational structural dynamics (CSD) and computing

K. Li et al. (Eds.): ParCFD 2013, CCIS 405, pp. 11–24, 2014.
© Springer-Verlag Berlin Heidelberg 2014

technologies [1]. The interaction between theses disciplines is apparent in many problems encountered in aircraft design. Due to the involvement of different discretization techniques such as finite volume, finite element and dynamic mesh approximations; these problems are hybrid in their treatment [2]. To deal with this hybrid nature of the problem two approaches, namely monolithic approach [3, 4] and partitioned approach [5, 6] have been proposed in literature. In monolithic approach, also known as tightly coupled approach [7], the fluid and the structure equations are combined in a single system. Although this method eliminates the coupling requirements between the fluid and the structure part but has proved to be computationally expensive and showed some limitations for analyzing complex configurations [8]. For partitioned approach, also identified as a loosely coupled approach [8], separate equation solving system is used for the fluid and the structure fields. This method results in different fluid and structure meshes and needs some interfacing technique to exchange information between two different solvers. The major advantage of this technique is that it allows the use of variety of existing CFD and CSD codes [9].

Focusing the interest on the partitioned approach, the key problems required to be addressed within this method are dynamic mesh motion and two-way data interpolation. Previously different mesh deformation tactics such as the spring analogy, the linear elasticity analogy, Delaunay graph mapping and interpolation methods based on radial basis function (RBF) have been effectively demonstrated and applied [10-12]. Similarly for two-way information transfer between the meshes several approaches including weighting methods, inverse isoparametric mapping procedure, constant volume tetrahedral (CVT) transformation and boundary element methods have been explained and applied [13-15]. A frequently observed limitation for all the above mentioned data interpolation schemes is the requirement of some explicitly defined connectivity relationship between the two different meshes. To remedy this restriction, Rendall et al. [16] has developed a unified interpolation scheme using radial basis functions. This method has no dependency on the flow solver and it is equally efficient for both structured and unstructured meshes.

In the present work, an in-house hybrid unstructured mesh based CFD code [17, 18] (named as HUNS3D and developed in Northwestern Polytechnical University) has been coupled with an open source finite element solver CalculiX [19] to carry out dynamic mesh motion and aeroelastic behavior prediction. Radial basis function interpolation combined with a data reduction greedy algorithm has been implemented to perform these tasks. This method is robust and efficient is delivering high quality deformed meshes and speed up computations. For mesh motion and displacement interpolation the already developed methods based on RBF interpolation works reasonably well. But for aerodynamic load mapping this method becomes expensive in terms of computational time. The objective of this work is to develop a more efficient and robust method that is based on localization of RBF interpolation in a parallel environment. This method resembles in concept to the pointwise form of partition of unity method for localized interpolation [20], but somewhat differs in its implementation. Previous studies have shown the influence of the interpolation parameters on the results [16]. This parallelized local implementation makes the results almost independent of the interpolation parameters and the computations even faster. The succeeding sections include, brief introduction of CFD and CSD solver coupling, an outline of the RBF mesh deformation strategy, a description of parallelized local implementation and finally the results of static aeroelastic simulation in transonic flow regime for different aerodynamic configurations including AGARD 445.6 wing, High Reynolds Number Aero-structural Dynamics (HIRENASD) wing/body configuration and a flexible wing with spar-rib-skin construction.

2   CFD / CSD Solver Coupling

In the present work partitioned approach has been adopted to perform computational aeroelastic simulations. This method provides the flexibility of using the already developed CFD/CSD solvers with some loss in the accuracy due to coupling procedure [8]. For CFD computations a well developed Reynolds-averaged Navier-Stokes (RANS) based in-house code (HUNS3D) has been used. In HUNS3D, the non-dimensional governing equations are discretized with cell-centred finite volume method on unstructured hybrid meshes composed of hexahedrons, prisms, tetrahedrons and pyramids. Several upwind or central convective flux discretization schemes are available in this flow solver [17]. This code has been parallelized with OpenMP in globally shared memory model. A range of turbulence models is available in the code including the one-equation Spalart-Allmaras (SA) model, two-equation Shear Stress Transport (SST) k-ω model and hybrid RANS-LES (DES) model. For the structure part an open source finite element based solver CalculiX [19], has been used to get the structural displacements. The solver is able to do linear and non-linear calculations with the availability of static, dynamic and thermal solutions. Both the solvers are efficient in their own working domain. The key requirement is to develop an efficient and robust interface for the coupling of the two solvers. Presently, both the mesh deformation and data exchange between the two codes has been achieved by using RBF interpolation. For static aeroelastic prediction following procedure has been adopted.

1. Generate hybrid unstructured CFD mesh. And structured / unstructured CSD mesh.
2. Obtain a steady state CFD solution by HUNS3D.
3. Map pressures at the CFD grid points to CSD element faces through RBF interpolation.
4. Obtain the structural response of the wing by CSD code CalculiX.
5. Map displacements at the CSD nodes to CFD grid points using RBF interpolation.
6. Deform the entire CFD grid by means of RBF mesh motion.
7. Obtain steady state CFD solution for the deformed wing.
8. Repeat steps 3-7 until a specified convergence has been achieved.

The procedure has been shown schematically in Fig. 1.

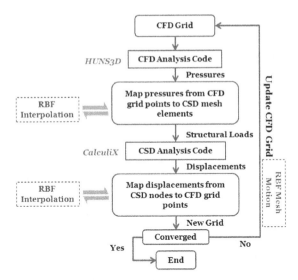

Fig. 1. CFD – CSD coupling procedure for static aeroelastic simulation

3   Localized Radial Basis Function Interpolation

3.1   Radial Basis Function Formulation

The form of required interpolation based on RBFs can be written as [21]

$$F(\mathbf{r}) = \sum_{i=1}^{N} w_i \varphi(\|\mathbf{r} - \mathbf{r}_i\|) \qquad (1)$$

Where, F(r) is the function to be evaluated at location r and will be specified to represent the displacement of mesh points. $\varphi(\|\mathbf{r} - \mathbf{r}_i\|)$ is general form of some kind of RBF adopted, N is the number of RBFs involved in the interpolation and r_i is the location of the supporting centre for the RBF labeled with index i. The coefficients w_i can be determined by requiring exact recovery of the original function at N sample points. In this work, Wendland's C^2 function [22] is selected as the basis function according to the work of Rendall and Allen [23]. This function has the formulation of

$$\varphi(\eta) = (1 - \eta)^4 (4\eta + 1) \qquad (2)$$

Where $\eta = \|\mathbf{r} - \mathbf{r}_i\| / d$, with d denotes the supporting radius of RBF series. The maximum value of η is limited to 1, which gives a zero value to a RBF at a large distance d. For mesh deformation, the supporting centre of RBF is located at the mesh points on the moving surface. The set of sample points used to determine the coefficients w_i is selected as the supporting centers of RBFs. This interpolation problem is described in the following matrix expressions.

$$\Delta\mathbf{X}_S = \mathbf{\Phi}\mathbf{W}_X \qquad (3)$$

$$\Delta\mathbf{Y}_S = \mathbf{\Phi}\mathbf{W}_Y \qquad (4)$$

$$\Delta\mathbf{Z}_S = \mathbf{\Phi}\mathbf{W}_Z \qquad (5)$$

Where, $\mathbf{\Delta X}_s = \left\{\Delta x_{S_1}, \cdots, \Delta x_{S_N}\right\}^T$, $\mathbf{\Delta Y}_s = \left\{\Delta y_{S_1}, \cdots, \Delta y_{S_N}\right\}^T$ and $\mathbf{\Delta Z}_s = \left\{\Delta z_{S_1}, \cdots, \Delta z_{S_N}\right\}^T$
represent the displacement components of the surface mesh points with S denotes the boundary surface. $\mathbf{\Phi}$ is the basis matrix.

$$\mathbf{W}_X = \left\{w_{S_1}^x, \cdots, w_{S_N}^x\right\}^T, \quad \mathbf{W}_Y = \left\{w_{S_1}^y, \cdots, w_{S_N}^y\right\}^T \quad \text{and} \quad \mathbf{W}_Z = \left\{w_{S_1}^z, \cdots, w_{S_N}^z\right\}^T \quad \text{are}$$

interpolation coefficients series need to be determined by solving Eq.(3-5). The displacements of volume nodes are calculated as the following formula

$$\Delta x_j = \sum_{i=S_1}^{S_N} w_i^x \phi(\|\mathbf{r}_j - \mathbf{r}_i\|) \ ; \ \Delta y_j = \sum_{i=S_1}^{S_N} w_i^y \phi(\|\mathbf{r}_j - \mathbf{r}_i\|) \ ; \ \Delta z_j = \sum_{i=S_1}^{S_N} w_i^z \phi(\|\mathbf{r}_j - \mathbf{r}_i\|) \qquad (j=1,2...N_V) \quad (6)$$

Here, NV is the number of volume mesh nodes. The key process of RBF mesh deformation is to setup a RBF interpolation to describe the deformation of boundaries approximately. And the realization of this process is referred by constructing and solving the Eq. (3-5) efficiently.

To simplify expressions, Equations (3-5) are expressed in the following universal form

$$\Delta\mathbf{S} = \mathbf{\Phi}\mathbf{W} \qquad (7)$$

In the above part, N surface points are used to establish the interpolation basis matrix $\mathbf{\Phi}$, which means that the computational cost of solving Eq.(8) is N^3 and a volume mesh update computational scale $N \times N_V$. For small to medium sized meshes, in which the number of surface points is relatively small, the full set of surface points can be taken as the sample points. While for large mesh cases, the number of surface points N often gets to hundreds of thousands. In such cases, the data reduction algorithm should be used to limit the size of RBF interpolation in a reasonable scale. To accomplish this error-driven data reduction greedy algorithm has been used [23]. In this case greedy algorithms are developed to select a reduced set of sample point according to the error incurred by representing the surface mesh deformation with reduced RBF interpolation. This strategy for calculating interpolation coefficients is cheaper than solving the complete system and is more efficient.

3.2   Parallelized Local Radial Basis Function Interpolation

For mesh motion and interpolation of displacement from structure mesh to fluid mesh, the above scheme work reasonably well. But for the interpolation of aerodynamic loads from fluid mesh to structure mesh this scheme becomes expensive in terms of computational time and the results are greatly affected by the choice of the interpolation parameter, such as the support radius. So to make this method efficient for two-way data interpolation, localization is performed by selecting a reduced set of closest aerodynamic points for each structure point. Then for each structure point

RBF interpolation is performed and the pressure value is interpolated from the reduced set. If N_{CSD} are the total number of CSD surface nodes, N_{CFD} are the total number of CFD surface nodes and N_{SET} is the node set of the closest aerodynamic nodes to each CSD node point, then the following algorithm could be used to perform the parallel localized radial basis function interpolation.

do $i = 1 , N_{CSD}$
Initialize:
Select initial set of points (N_{SET})
⟶ *Calculate distance between selected N_{CSD} and N_{CFD}*
⟶ *Select closest N_{SET} for each CSD node point*
enddo

!$OMP PARALLEL DEFAULT (PRIVATE) SHARED (*variables*)
!$OMP NUM_THREADS (*number of threads*)

do $i = 1 , N_{CSD}$
do $j = 1 , N_{SET}$
⟶ *Read N_{SET} for each CSD node point*
enddo
CALL *RBF Subroutine*
enddo

!$OMP ENDDO
1$OMP END PARALLEL

This procedure is not only effective in terms of the reduced memory and processor load but also decrease the influence of the interpolation parameters. Also this localization will enable us to run the data interpolation in a parallel environment. In the present study this part has been parallelized with OpenMP and is very effective in further reducing the computational time.

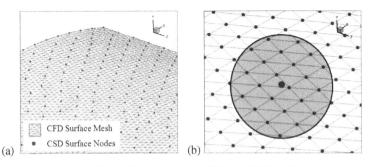

(a)   (b)

Fig. 2. Illustration of wing surface with overlapping CFD and CSD surfaces (a) Zoomed view for a single CSD node point

Fig. 2 (a) shows the overlapping of the CFD and CSD surfaces. The red points are the CSD nodes and the CFD mesh has been shown in blue. Fig. 2(b) shows the illustration of the current methodology. As it can be seen from the figure, that for each CSD node point (marked in red) the program searches for the nearest aerodynamic surface points. The total number of the nearest aerodynamic surface points is left as the input together with the support radius. This number depends on the CSD grid density of the structure mesh. In this way for each CSD node point the corresponding closest CFD grid points are stored in an array. Then the RBF interpolation is performed for each CSD point and the pressure is interpolated form CFD surface to CSD surface. Using this method the computational time for RBF interpolation reduces considerably and the method becomes independent of the value of the support radius.

4   Computational Aeroelastic Test Cases

The present method has been applied to study the static aeroelastic characteristics of three different wing configurations. The results obtained are discussed in this section for each configuration.

4.1   AGARD 445.6 Wing

AGARD 445.6 wing configuration is well known aeroelastic test that is usually referred as a benchmark test case for flutter analysis. However, some static aeroelastic analyses were performed for this configuration [24, 25], the results of which are used to compare the current simulation outcome. In geometric construction this wing has an aspect ratio of 1.65, a taper ratio of 0.66 and a wing sweep angle of 45° at the quarter chord. It has root and tip chords of 0.558m and 0.368m, and a semi span of 0.762m. The airfoil section in the stream-wise direction is a NACA 65A004 airfoil. A weakened AGARD Wing 445.6 is modeled by tetrahedral elements as an equivalent orthotropic material. The aerodynamic and the structure parameters used in this study are given in Table 1.

Table 1. Aerodynamic and Structural parameters - AGARD 445.6 Wing

Aerodynamic Parameters			Structural Parameters				
Mach	Reynolds Number	Angle of Attack (deg)	Longitudinal Modulus (GPa)	Transverse Modulus (GPa)	Modulus of Rigidity (GPa)	Poisson Ratio	Material Density (Kg/m^3)
0.85	5.6×10^5	5	3.151	0.4162	0.4392	0.31	381.98

Fig. 3 shows the rigid and elastic equilibrium state of AGARD 445.6 wing. The final elastic position has been achieved after 14 coupling iterations as illustrated in Fig. 4. Approximately 24% decrease in the lift coefficient has been observed for the current simulation.

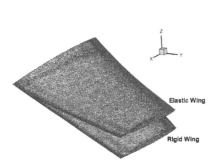

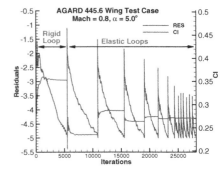

Fig. 3. Rigid and Deformed *(elastic)* states of AGARD 445.6 wing

Fig. 4. Residual and Lift Coefficient convergence

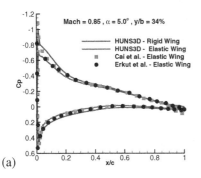

(a)

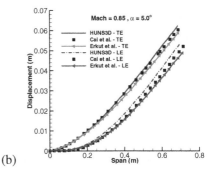

(b)

Fig. 5. (a) Pressure coefficient comparison at 34% wing span (b) Computed deflection normal to wing plane for trailing and leading edges

The pressure distribution obtained at 34% of wing span for the rigid and elastic case is shown the Fig.5 (a). It can be seen from the figure that the pressure distribution for the elastic case is in good agreement with the previously computed distribution. However, some discrepancy was found among the predicted wing deflection for both the trailing and the leading edges, especially at the wing tip (Fig.5 (b)). This slight inconsistency occurred due to difference in the methods used. Cai et al. used monolithic approach for CFD/CSD coupling where as Erkut et al. used partitioned approach with some linear interpolation method for data transfer between the two meshes.

4.2   HIRENASD Wing/Body Configuration

With the aim to fulfil the requirement of some benchmark test case for computational aeroelastic code validation, HIgh REynolds Number Aero-Structural Dynamics (HIRENASD) project [26] was initiated by Aachen University's Department of Mechanics. Experimental testing was performed in the European Transonic Wind tunnel in 2006. This configuration was also included as a test case for the first aeroelastic prediction workshop (AePW) [27]. Therefore, for performing computational aeroelastic simulations this configuration is now regarded as a standard test case. The current method has been applied to study the static aeroelastic response for this wing/body configuration at Mach number 0.8, Reynolds number of 7 million and angle of attack 1.5o. The unstructured hybrid mesh was generated for RANS simulation (shown in Fig.6 (a)) with size of 7.1 million cells. All the computations were performed by employing the SA turbulence model. For finite element (FE) analysis both the hexahedral and tetrahedral mesh (available from the first AePW) were used (shown in Fig.6 (b)).

Table 2. Aerodynamic and Structural parameters - HIRENASD Wing/Body

Aerodynamic Parameters			Structural Parameters			
Mach	Reynolds Number	Mach	Elastic Modulus (GPa)	Poisson Ratio	Material Density (Kg/m^3)	Load Factor (q / E)
0.8	7.0 x 10^6	0.8	181.2	0.31	7910	0.22 x 10^{-6}

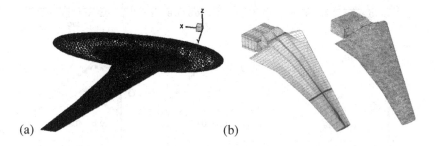

(a)   (b)

Fig. 6. (a) Unstructured hybrid CFD mesh (b) Structured FE mesh *(left)* Unstructured FE mesh *(right)*

The pressure distribution over the entire wing/body surface for elastic case is shown in Fig.7 (a). The wing deflection for the trailing edge of the wing is compared with the deflection predicted by other solvers (FUN3D and elsA). The current computed deflection is in close agreement with the previously predicted one.

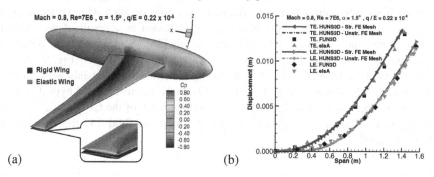

(a)   (b)

Fig. 7. (a) Pressure coefficient distribution for elastic wing (b) Computed deflection normal to wing plane for leading and trailing edges

Fig. 8 shows the comparison of the pressure distribution predicted for both the rigid and elastic case with the measured distribution. The pressure distribution has only small difference for rigid and elastic case, except for the wing tip region where the maximum deflection was 0.0137m. The difference in the predicted and measured pressure distribution, especially at the shock region, is mainly due to low grid resolution. This also caused some difference in the tip deflection.

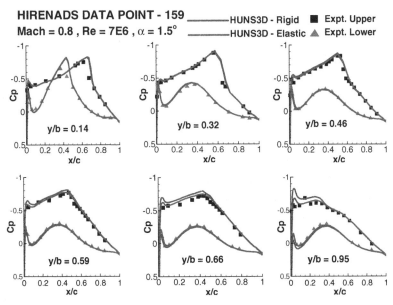

Fig. 8. Pressure Distribution for different span wise stations *(for both rigid and elastic simulation)*

4.3   Flexible Wing Model (Spar-Rib-Skin Construction)

To further investigate the efficiency of the current methodology, static aeroelastic computations were performed for a flexible wing with detailed wing structure (spar-rib-skin construction). This configuration was obtained as a result of aerodynamic optimization study conducted by Newman et al. [28]. Same geometric details, as given by Newman at al. [29] were used to create the CAD model (Fig. 9 (a)). The finite element model was constructed by using the tetrahedral elements with complete structural details, shown in Fig. 9 (b). For CFD analysis, unstructured hybrid grid was generated, with size of 3 million cells. The surface mesh of the CFD model is shown in Fig. 9 (c). The analysis parameters for the both the fluid and the structure are shown in Table 3.

(a)   (b)   (c)

Fig. 9. (a) CAD model (b) FEM model mesh (c) CFD model mesh

Table 3. Aerodynamic and Structural parameters – Flexible Wing

Aerodynamic Parameters		Structural Parameters				
Mach	Reynolds Number	Mach	Elastic Modulus (GPa)	Poisson Ratio	Material Density (Kg/m³)	Load Factor (q / E)
0.85	5.5 x 10⁶	0.85	69	0.31	2700	0.24 x 10⁻⁶

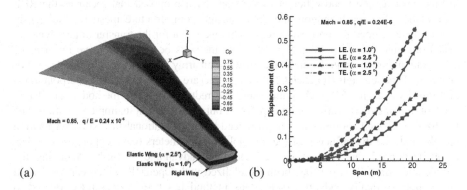

(a)   (b)

Fig. 10. (a) Pressure coefficient distribution for elastic wing (b) Computed deflection normal to wing plane for trailing and leading edges

Static aeroelastic simulations were performed at two angles of attacks (1° and 2.5°). Fig. 10 (a) shows the pressure distribution for the elastic wing surface at angle of attack 2.5°. Fig. 10 (b) shows the wing deflection for both the leading and trailing edge at the two angles of attack. As the angle of attack is increased, the loading on the wing also increases; thus, greater wing deflections are observed. The pressure distribution at different span wise sections for both the rigid and flexible wing is shown in Fig. 11 (a). Maximum difference in the pressure distribution for the rigid and the elastic case occurs at the wing tip, where the deflection of 0.556m was predicted. A qualitative comparison of wing deformation between the current study and the work of Newman et al. [29], for this wing configuration is shown in Fig. 11 (b).

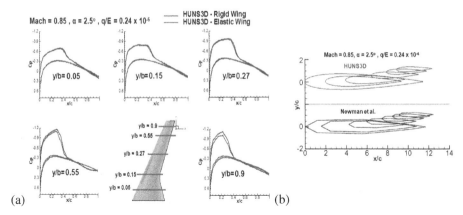

Fig. 11. (a) Pressure Distribution for different span wise stations *(for both rigid and elastic simulation)* (b) Comparison of FE deformation

5   Conclusions

In this paper a robust and efficient method has been proposed that localizes the RBF interpolation. For mesh motion and data transfer from structure mesh to fluid mesh, previously developed methods work reasonably well. But for the transfer of aerodynamic load from fluid mesh to structure mesh these methods become expensive in terms of computational time. To perform the localization, an array is constructed in which a set of closest CFD node points (for each CSD node point) are added. Then RBF interpolation is performed for each CSD node point using the reduced set. The method is similar in concept to pointwise partition of unit approach but is different in its implementation. The localized implementation has not only reduced the computational time for interpolation but also reduced the influence of the interpolation parameters (e.g. support radius). The parallelization of this method has an additional advantage of further reducing the interpolation time. This part has been parallelized with OpenMP, which can be carried out without difficulty and effectively. This method has been successfully applied to perform static computational aeroelastic analysis for three different aerodynamic configurations. The results obtained are in acceptable agreement with the available experimental and previously predicted results.

Acknowledgments. The research was supported by NPU Foundation of Fundamental Research (NPU-FFR-JC201212) and Advanced Research Foundation of Commercial Aircraft Corporation of China (COMAC). The authors thankfully acknowledge these institutions.

References

1. David, M.S., Liu, D.D., Lawrence, J.H.: Computational Aeroelasticity: Success, Progress, Challenge. Journal of Aircraft 40(5) (September-October 2003)
2. Wendland, H.: Hybrid Methods for Fluid-Structure-Interaction Problems in Aeroelasticity. In: Meshfree Methods for Partial Differential Equations. Lecture Notes in Computational Science and Engineering, vol. 65, pp. 335–358. Springer, Heidelberg (2008)

3. Bendiksen, O.O.: Modern developments in aeroelasticity. Proceedings of the Institute of Mechanical Engineers Part G: Journal of Aerospace Engineering 218, 157–177 (2004)
4. Hubner, B., Walhorn, E., Dinkler, D.: A monolithic approach to fluid–structure interaction using space-time finite elements. Computer Methods in Appied Mechanics and Engineering 193, 2087–2104 (2004)
5. Woodgate, M.A., Badcock, K.J., Rampurawala, A.M., Richards, B.: Aeroelastic calculations for the Hawk aircraft using the Euler equations. Journal of Aircraft 42(4), 1005–1011 (2005)
6. Geuzaine, P., Brown, G., Harris, C., Farhat, C.: Aeroelastic dynamic analysis of a full F-16 configuration for various flight conditions. AIAA Journal 41(3), 363–371 (2003)
7. Guruswamy, G.P.: A New Modular Approach for Tightly Coupled Fluid/Structure Analysis. International Journal of Aerospace Innovations 1(1) (2009)
8. Ramji, K., Wei, S.: Fluid–structure interaction for aeroelastic applications. Progress in Aerospace Sciences 40, 535–558 (2005)
9. Manoj, K.B.: A CFD/CSD interaction methodology for aircraft wings. Phd thesis, Virginia Polytechnic Institute and State University (1997)
10. Batina, J.T.: Unsteady Euler Algorithm with Unstructured Dynamic Mesh for Complex-Aircraft Aerodynamics Analysis. AIAA Journal 29(3), 327–333 (1991)
11. Liu, X., Qin, N., Xia, H.: Fast Dynamic Grid Deformation based on Delaunay Graph Mapping. Journal of Computational Physics 211(2), 405–423 (2006)
12. Cizmas, P., Gargoloff, J.: Mesh generation and deformation algorithm for aeroelasticity simulations. In: 45th Aerospace Sciences Meeting, Reno, NV, AIAA-2007-556 (2007)
13. Maman, N., Farhat, C.: Matching fluid and structure meshes for aeroelastic computations: A parallel approach. Computers and Structures 54(4), 779–785 (1995)
14. Pidparti, R.M.V.: Structural and aerodynamic data transformation using inverse isoparametric mapping. Journal of Aircraft 29(3), 507–509 (1992)
15. Chen, P.C., Jadic, I.: Interfacing of fluid and structural models via innovative structural boundary element method. AIAA Journal 1998 36(2), 282–287 (1998)
16. Rendall, T.C.S., Allen, C.B.: Unified fluid–structure interpolation and mesh motion using radial basis functions. International Journal for Numerical Methods in Engineering 74(10), 1519–1559 (2008)
17. Gang, W., Ye, Z.: Mixed Element Type Unstructured Grid Generation and its Application to Viscous Flow Simulation. In: 24th International Congress of Aeronautical Sciences, Yokohama, Japan (2004)
18. Gang, W., Ye. Li, H., Yang, Q.: Studies on Aerodynamic Interferences between the Components of Transport Airplane using Unstructured Navier-Stokes Simulations. Computational Fluid Dynamics Journal 15(1), 191–197 (2006)
19. Dhondt, G.: Calculix (2012), http://calculix.de
20. Rendall, T.C.S., Allen, C.B.: Improved radial basis function fluid–structure coupling via efficient localized implementation. International Journal for Numerical Methods in Engineering 78, 1188–1208 (2009)
21. Rendall, T.C.S., Allen, C.B.: Fluid-structure interpolation and mesh motion using radial basis functions. International Journal for Numerical Methods in Engineering 75(10), 1519–1559 (2008)
22. Wendland, H.: Scattered Data Approximation, 1st edn. Cambridge University Press (2005)
23. Rendall, T.C.S., Allen, C.B.: Efficient Mesh Motion using Radial Basis Functions with Data Reduction Algorithms. Journal of Computational Physics 229(7), 6231–6249 (2009)

24. Cai, J., Liu, F., Tsai, H.M.: Static Aero-elastic Computation with a Coupled CFD and CSD Method. In: 39th AIAA Aerospace Sciences Meeting & Exhibit, AIAA-2001-0717, Reno, NV, January 8-11 (2001)
25. Erkut, B., Ali, A.: Development of a Coupling Procedure for Static Aeroelastic Analyses. Scientific Technical Review 61(3-4), 39–48 (2011)
26. Ballmann, J., Dafnis, A., Korsch, H.: Experimental Analysis of High Reynolds Number Aero-Structural Dynamics in ETW. AIAA Paper 2008-841 (2008)
27. https://c3.nasa.gov/dashlink/static/media/other/HIRENASD_base.htm
28. Newman, J.C., Taylor, A.C.: Three-dimensional aerodynamic shape sensitivity analysis and design optimization using the Euler equations on unstructured grids. AIAA Paper 96-2464 (1996)
29. Newman, J.C., Newmanb, P.A., Taylor, A.C., Hou, G.J.-W.: Efficient nonlinear static aeroelastic wing analysis. Computers & Fluids 28, 615–628 (1999)

Solving Seven-Equation Model of Compressible Two-Phase Flow Using CUDA-GPU

Shan Liang[1,*], Wei Liu[2], and Li Yuan[3]

[1] Computer Network Information Center,
Chinese Academy of Sciences, Beijing 100190, China
`liangshan@sccas.cn`
[2] Academy of Mathematics and Systems Science,
Chinese Academy of Sciences, Beijing 100190, China

Abstract. In this paper, a numerical method which combines a HLLC-type approximate Riemann solver with the third-order TVD Runge-Kutta method is presented for the two-pressure and two-velocity seven-equation model of compressible two-phase flow of Saurel and Abgrall. Based on the idea proposed by Abgrall that "a multiphase flow, uniform in pressure and velocity at $t = 0$, will remain uniform on the same variables during time evolution", discretization schemes for the non-conservative terms and for the volume fraction evolution equation are derived in accordance with the adopted HLLC solver for the conservative terms. To attain high temporal accuracy, the third-order TVD Runge-Kutta method is implemented in conjunction with the operator splitting technique in a robust way by virtue of reordering the sequence of operators. Numerical tests against several one- and two-dimensional compressible two-fluid flow problems with high density and high pressure ratios demonstrate that the proposed method is accurate and robust. Besides, the above numerical algorithm is implemented on multi graphics processing units using CUDA. Appropriate data structure is adopted to maintain high memory bandwidth; skills like atom operator, counter and so on are used to synchronize thread blocks; overlapping domain decomposition method is applied for mission assignment. Using a single-GPU, we observe 31× speedup relative to a single-core CPU computation; linear speedup can be achieved by multi-GPU parallel computing although there might be a little decrease in single-GPU performance. *abstract* environment.

Keywords: compressible multiphase flow, seven-equation model, HLLC, TVD Runge-Kutta, GPU.

1 Introduction

Compressible multiphase flows exist broadly in nature and industry (like bubbles in ocean, cavitation in hydraulic machinery, flows in reactors and cooling

---

[*] Corresponding author.

K. Li et al. (Eds.): ParCFD 2013, CCIS 405, pp. 25–36, 2014.

circuits of power plants). Numerical simulation of such flows is an important
research topic. As the flows are complex and diverse, many multiphase models
with various levels of complexity were proposed in literature, like the seven-
equation model of Baer and Nunziato [1], that of Saurel *et al.* [2, 3], and the
reduced five-equation model of Allaire [4], to mention just a few. Most multiphase models are derived from integrating individual balance equations weighted
by a characteristic function for each phase. This volume average process removes
the interfacial details while introducing additional non-conservative terms. The
resultant multiphase models pose challenge to numerical solutions mainly due
to the complicated characteristics of the equation system and the troublesome
non-conservative terms.

In this paper, we are interested in numerical solution of the compressible multiphase model formulated by Saurel and Abgrall [2, 3]. In this model, each phase
is assumed to have its own velocity, pressure and density, which satisfy respective balance equations. The evolution equation of volume fraction is introduced
from integrating the characteristic function to describe how fluid compositions
change with time. Due to non-equilibrium of velocity and pressure, drag forces
appear between phases causing momentum and energy change. In the case of one
space dimension, the model has seven equations (two sets of mass, momentum,
and energy equations, one volume fraction evolution equation). The advantage
of this model is that it is unconditionally hyperbolic, and can treat a wide range
of applications including non-equilibrium dispersive multiphase flows as well as
free-surface multi-fluid flows [3]. For the latter case, the velocity and pressure of
all phases on each side of the interface must be in equilibrium from a physical
point of view [2, 3, 5], which can be realized by infinite pressure and velocity relaxation process in the model. As the volume fraction only stands for the
constitutive fluid distribution, the material surface is indirectly represented by
location where large gradient occurs. The interface is tracked without considering the details even when the distortion is complicate (cavitation, breakdown
and coalescence of bubbles, etc). Of course, the computational cost is larger than
a free-surface oriented method, e.g., about three times as large as a ghost fluid
method from our experience.

Although this model is unconditional hyperbolic, the numerical solution has
particular difficulties because it is hard to solve associated Riemann problem with a large system of equations, and careless approximations to the
non-conservative terms in the momentum and energy equations and the non-
conservative evolution equation (the volume fraction equation) will often lead to
failure in computation. Therefore, the key in numerical solution is to construct
an accurate and efficient approximate Riemann solver and in the meantime derive corresponding discretization schemes for the non-conservative terms and the
non-conservative volume fraction equation.

Many studies have devoted to numerical solution of compressible two-phase
models in various variants. Saurel [2, 3] used operator splitting approach to solve
their seven-equation model, but the adopted HLL approximate Riemann solver
was inaccurate due to the use of two waves instead of full waves and this led

to excessive numerical diffusion of contact discontinuities. In [6], combining thin layer theorem with special choice for interfacial variables in liquid-solid problem, Tokareva and Toro proposed a HLLC-type approximate Riemann solver which took into account full waves for the Baer-Nunzatio model. Li *et al.* [7] developed a general and simple HLLC scheme for the two-phase model but was confined to subsonic case only, and they used Roe average as the unknown intermediate state of the volume fraction. Tian *et al.* [8] also studied numerical solution of the reduced five-equation by using path-conservative method and a simple HLLC solver. A more thorough effort to construct approximate Riemann solver for the Saurel-Abgrall model was made recently by Ambroso *et al.* [9]. Their definition of Riemann problem included not only convective terms and non-conservative terms, but also source terms associated with gravity and drag forces (the latter refers to so-called velocity relaxation process), while pressure relaxation process was split from them alone. In all the above mentioned work, the multiphase flow equations were approximated by a numerical method, but a strategy proceeded in the opposite way was proposed in Abgrall and Saurel's subsequent work [10], which was able to deal with mixtures and interfaces under a unique formulation. They started from the pure phase Euler equations at the microscopic level, and gave the corresponding numerical approximations via the Godunov scheme and the HLLC flux. After randomization, ensemble average procedures and estimation of the various coefficients of these approximations, the numerical scheme for the averaged multiphase flow equations was derived.

In this study, our objective is to develop a high resolution method for the Saurel-Abgrall two-phase model, which has the simplicity of a standard HLLC scheme and the high temporal accuracy of the third-order TVD Rung-Kutta method, and also is robust to simulate extreme compressible gas-liquid two-fluid flow problems. We advance the solution with the third-order TVD Runge-Kutta method, incorporating the splitting strategy [3] between the hyperbolic parts and the relaxation terms into every sub-step of the Runge-Kutta method. The sequence of the split operators is reordered for robust treatment of free surface flows. To obtain a simple scheme for the two-phase model, we apply the conventional HLLC flux to the conservative part of the two-phase model in a way similar to [7], and then utilize the homogeneity idea of a multi-phase system as proposed by Abgrall to deriving discrete formulas for the non-conservative terms and non-conservative equation corresponding to the HLLC solver used. Our derivation takes into account all cases of HLLC scheme rather than only subsonic case as in [7]. The characteristic boundary conditions for the model are also presented.

Driven by the market demand for real-time, high-definition 3-D graphics, general-purpose graphic processing unit (GPGPU) has been developed for parallel computing decades ago. Many CFD simulations have beed done using GPU.

In order to solve large-scale problems efficiently, the second part of our study is to implement the above numerical algorithm on multi graphics processing units using CUDA. Firstly, every computational mesh point is assigned to a GPU thread, and appropriate data structure is adopted to maintain high memory bandwidth; skills like atom operator, counter and so on are used to synchronize thread blocks. Besides, we use overlapping domain decomposition method for multi- GPU parallel computing. The computation of every subdomain is assigned to a device, the communication between which is done through MPI or Pthread.

2   Seven-Equation Model

For the sake of simplicity, we consider 1D case first. Suppose that two kinds of fluid exist in the system, and there is neither mass transfer nor heat exchange between them. The compressible two-phase model of Saurel-Abgrall [2] can be written in the following form:

$$\frac{\partial U}{\partial t} + \frac{\partial F(U)}{\partial x} = H(U)\frac{\partial \alpha_1}{\partial x} + S_v(U) + S_p(U) \tag{1}$$

where

$$U = \begin{pmatrix} \alpha_1 \\ \alpha_1\rho_1 \\ \alpha_1\rho_1 u_1 \\ \alpha_1 E_1 \\ \alpha_2\rho_2 \\ \alpha_2\rho_2 u_2 \\ \alpha_2 E_2 \end{pmatrix} \quad F(U) = \begin{pmatrix} 0 \\ \alpha_1\rho_1 u_1 \\ \alpha_1\rho_1 u_1^2 + \alpha_1 p_1 \\ \alpha_1 u_1(E_1 + p_1) \\ \alpha_2\rho_2 u_2 \\ \alpha_2\rho_2 u_2^2 + \alpha_2 p_2 \\ \alpha_2 u_2(E_2 + p_2) \end{pmatrix} \quad H(U) = \begin{pmatrix} -u_I \\ 0 \\ p_I \\ u_I p_I \\ 0 \\ -p_I \\ -u_I p_I \end{pmatrix}$$

$$S_v(U) = \begin{pmatrix} 0 \\ 0 \\ \lambda(u_2 - u_1) \\ \lambda(u_2 - u_1)u_I \\ 0 \\ -\lambda(u_2 - u_1) \\ -\lambda(u_2 - u_1)u_I \end{pmatrix} \quad S_p(U) = \begin{pmatrix} -\mu(p_2 - p_1) \\ 0 \\ 0 \\ \mu p_I(p_2 - p_1) \\ 0 \\ 0 \\ -\mu p_I(p_2 - p_1) \end{pmatrix}$$

Here ρ, u, p and $E = \rho e + 1/2\rho u^2$ represent the density, velocity, pressure and total energy per volume respectively, and subscripts $k = 1$ or 2 is related to phase k. α_k is the volume fraction ranged from 0 to 1, and satisfies relation $\alpha_1 + \alpha_2 = 1$. When $\alpha_k = 0$ there is no k-th fluid. Actually, to avoid infinite density and velocity computed by mass and energy conservation equations, $\alpha_k = 10^{-7}$ is used in lieu of $\alpha_k = 0$ at the initial time. μ and λ are the pressure and velocity relaxation coefficients, and p_I and u_I are the interfacial pressure and velocity respectively. Various choices are possible, for example, in the gas-liquid (or solid) problem, $p_I = p_{\text{gas}}$ and $u_I = u_{\text{liquid}}$. Here we follow Saurel's choice [3]:

$$p_I = \sum \alpha_k p_k, \quad u_I = \sum (\alpha_k \rho_k u_k) / \sum \alpha_k \rho_k \tag{2}$$

3   Numerical Method

Based on the operator splitting method given in [3], equation (1) can be decomposed into three parts: the ODE system of pressure relaxation $U_t = S_p(U)$, that of velocity relaxation $U_t = S_v(U)$, and the non-conservative hyperbolic equations $U_t + F(U)_x = H(U)\alpha_{1x}$. In [3], the complete solution of (1) was obtained by the succession of operators:

$$U^{n+1} = L_p^{\Delta t} L_v^{\Delta t} L_H^{\Delta t}(U^n) \tag{3}$$

where L_p and L_v denote the pressure and velocity relaxation operators respectively, and L_H denotes the non-conservative hyperbolic operator. Scheme (3) is only first order accurate in time and higher accuracy can be obtained by adopting Strange splitting or Runge-Kutta method. In this paper, the third-order TVD Runge-Kutta method is used together with operator splitting.

3.1   Hyperbolic Operator

The numerical scheme is based on the idea proposed by Abgrall [5] that "a two phase system, uniform in velocity and pressure at $t = 0$ will remain uniform on the same variables during time evolution".

The considered hyperbolic equations read

$$\alpha_t + u_I \alpha_x = 0 \tag{4}$$

$$Q_t + F(Q)_x = H(Q)\alpha_x \tag{5}$$

$Q = (\alpha\rho, \alpha\rho u, \alpha E)^T, F(Q) = (\alpha\rho u, \alpha\rho u^2 + \alpha p, \alpha u(E + p))^T, H(Q) = (0, p_I, p_I u_I)^T$.

We wish to construct :

- upwind scheme for (4) of the form

$$\alpha_j^{n+1} = \alpha_j^n - \frac{\Delta t}{\Delta x}(u_I)_j^n (\phi_{j+1/2} - \phi_{j-1/2}) \tag{6}$$

- Godunov-type finite volume method for (5) of the form

$$Q_j^{n+1} = Q_j^n - \frac{\Delta t}{\Delta x}\left(F_{j+1/2}^n - F_{j-1/2}^n\right) + \Delta t H(Q_j^n)\Theta \tag{7}$$

3.2   Third-Order TVD Runge-Kutta Scheme

For Eq. (1), the Godunov splitting (3) can be seen as a forward Euler step $U^{n+1} = U^n + \Delta t L(U^n)$ which is the sum of the last two terms of each substep of standard TVD Runge-Kutta scheme. As a naive implementation, we can apply TVD RK3 method to Eq. (1) directly

$$\begin{cases} U^{(1)} = U^n + \Delta t L(U^n) \\ U^{(2)} = \frac{3}{4}U^n + \frac{1}{4}U^{(1)} + \frac{1}{4}\Delta t L(U^{(1)}) \\ U^{(n+1)} = \frac{1}{3}U^n + \frac{2}{3}U^{(2)} + \frac{2}{3}\Delta t L(U^{(2)}) \end{cases} \rightarrow \begin{cases} U^{(1)} = L_p^{\Delta t} L_v^{\Delta t} L_H^{\Delta t} U^n \\ U^{(2)} = \frac{3}{4}U^n + \frac{1}{4}L_p^{\Delta t} L_v^{\Delta t} L_H^{\Delta t} U^{(1)} \\ U^{(n+1)} = \frac{1}{3}U^n + \frac{2}{3}L_p^{\Delta t} L_v^{\Delta t} L_H^{\Delta t} U^{(2)} \end{cases} \tag{8}$$

However, the problem with (8) is that it does not guarantee the pressure and velocity are in equilibrium at the end of each time step. To solve this problem, we reorder the sequence of operators

$$U^{(1)} = L_H^{\Delta t} L_p^{\Delta t} L_v^{\Delta t} U^n \tag{9}$$

$$U^{(2)} = \frac{3}{4}U^n + \frac{1}{4}L_H^{\Delta t} L_p^{\Delta t} L_v^{\Delta t} U^{(1)} \tag{10}$$

$$U^{(3)} = \frac{1}{3}U^n + \frac{2}{3}L_H^{\Delta t} L_p^{\Delta t} L_v^{\Delta t} U^{(2)} \tag{11}$$

$$U^{n+1} = L_p^{\Delta t} L_v^{\Delta t} U^{(3)} \tag{12}$$

(9)(10)(11)are the three sub-steps of the Runge-Kutta method, and (12) is an additional step, and the total computational count is not increased compared with the naive implementation (8).

4   Implementation on GPU

In order to solve large-scale problems efficiently, we present an implementation of the above numerical algorithm on multi graphics processing units using CUDA.

4.1   Implementation on Multi-GPUs

Although single GPU has achieved high performance in many applications, the compute capacity that required for simulating large-scale multi-phase flow problems is far beyond what a single GPU can deliver. Consequently, it is worthwhile to develop multi-GPU parallelization techniques.

In our work, domain decomposition method is used. A 2D grid of $N_x \times N_y$ is divided into m and n parts along its two coordinate directions respectively, which makes the total sub-domain number $m \times n$ (Fig. 1(a)), The computation of each sub-domain is assigned to different GPUs. There are two principles to follow: firstly, $m \times n$ equals the total number of GPUs in use; secondly, the shape of each sub-domain should be as square-like as possible to reduce the amount of information exchanged between GPUs. Indeed, flow field variables of a sub-domain reside in the memory of only one GPU from the very beginning to the end of a simulation, and they will be exported to different files when the simulation ends. A five point difference module, including the target cell and the four cells that adjacent to it in 2D, is needed to support the MUSCL reconstruction; and the reconstructed results of two adjoining cells are used to estimate numerical fluxes in the vicinity of their common cell face. Therefore, as sketched in Fig. 1(b), two layers of auxiliary grids is defined at every boundary of a sub-domain to couple computation. Take sub-domain G1 and G2 in Fig. 1(a) for example, the left two layers of auxiliary grids (invisible) of G2 is updated according to the right-most and second from right layers of initial grids (marked by ×) in G1.

To facilitate communications, the inner-boundary data is passed between devices by means of MPI or Pthread, which is operated in CPU. Considering that most computation is performed in GPU, to avoid explicit data copy between CPU and GPU frequently, mapped pinned memory is used to store auxiliary boundary data, which has two addresses: one at host and the other in device. When boundary computation is finished, each device uploads the boundary data that others need to mapped pinned memory, and then downloads the auxiliary boundary data for next time step computation. As is seen in Fig. 2, there is a little difference in MPI-CUDA and Pthread-CUDA application: in Pthread-CUDA, CPU threads share a common mapped pinned array as Fig. 2(a), and no data transfer is performed; while in MPI-CUDA, data is stored in different arrays which is passed between MPI processes as Fig. 2(b).

The main process is described in Fig. 3. Notice that the entire computation is performed on the GPUs, leaving the CPU almost idle during all stages of the computation except performing data copy and subsequent communication.

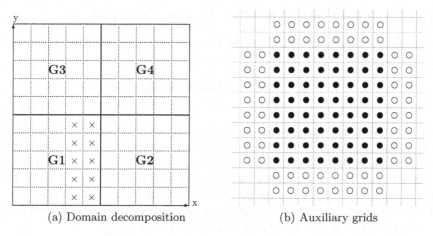

(a) Domain decomposition   (b) Auxiliary grids

Fig. 1. Grid and mission assignment to four GPUs. (a) Decomposition of a domain into sub-domains. A sub-domain is computed by the corresponding GPU; (b) Computation domain for a single GPU. Solid points denote initial cells allocated to the current GPU while auxiliary cells are marked by hollow points.

5   Numerical Results

In this section, numerical tests with several 1D and 2D compressible gas-liquid multi-fluid problems are provided. For 1D cases, we compared our method with the RGFM as well as Saurel's HLL method [2] under the same MUSCL reconstruction. RGFM [11] can capture material interface with little diffusion, but it is not a conservative method. HLL is robust, but too diffusive. We include examples with high density and high pressure ratios to test these numerical methods. 2D problems are simulated with the help of GPU, and speedup of single- / multi-GPU is presented.

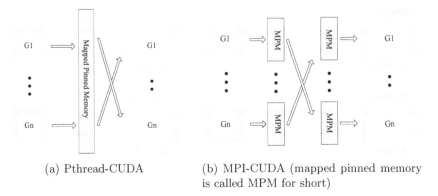

(a) Pthread-CUDA   (b) MPI-CUDA (mapped pinned memory
                            is called MPM for short)

Fig. 2. Data exchange between devices. G stands for grid, and the blue area stands for boundary data that passed between devices.

5.1   Gas-Liquid Shock Tube (High Pressure Ratio)[12]

We consider a shock tube filled on the left side with high pressure gas and on the right side with liquid. The initial data are

$$(\rho, u, p, \gamma, B) = \begin{cases} (1.27, 0, 8000, 1.4, \ 0), & x \le 0.4 \\ (1.0, \ \ 0, 1.0, \ \ 7.15, 3309), & x > 0.4 \end{cases}$$

In this problem, the pressure ratio at the gas-liquid interface is up to $8000 : 1$, while density ratio is $1.27 : 1$. Numerical simulation was conducted to $t = 0.002$. Pressure and density distributions near the material interface are shown in Fig 4. The solid black line is results obtained by RGFM method. It can be seen that there is a density decrease at the interface which might be caused by the non-conservative error of RGFM. Results of multiphase method (the dashed line) look closer to the analytical solution (the solid grey line).

5.2   Underwater Explosion[13]

Material interface is located at $x = 0.5$ initially. The initial data are

$$(\rho, u, p, \gamma, B) = \begin{cases} (0.01, 0, 1000, 2, \ \ \ 0), & x \le 0.5 \\ (1.0, \ \ 0, 1.0, \ \ 7.15, 3309), & x > 0.5 \end{cases}$$

Rarefaction wave with very high speed will appear on the left side. At a very short time $t = 0.000718$, corresponding velocity and density distributions are shown in Fig 5. Results of HLL scheme [2] and present HLLC method are compared. HLL scheme uses only two waves instead of three, and contact discontinuity is heavily smeared out. This might also explain the velocity distribution is abnormal near the interface. Results computed by HLLC scheme are more reasonable and have less numerical diffusion.

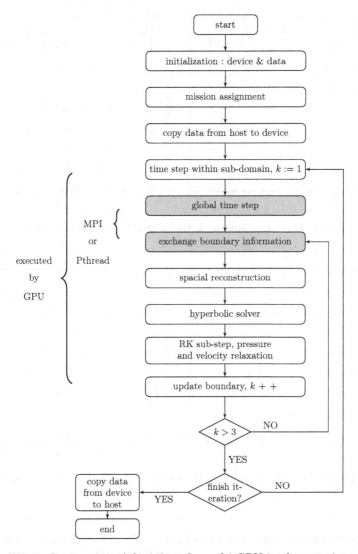

Fig. 3. Computational flow chart for multi-GPU implementation

5.3   Shock-Bubble Interaction

This is a classical problem [14–16]. A 2D bubble filled with helium initially in equilibrium is surrounded by air. Initially the bubble is located at $x = 175$ and $y = 44.5$; its radius is equal to 25. A shock coming from the right of the bubble is characterized by Mach number $M_s = 1.22$. The data are

$$(\rho, u, v, p, \gamma) = \begin{cases} (1.3764, -0.394, 0, 1.5698, 1.4), & \text{postshock} \\ (1, \quad 0, \quad 0, 1, \quad 1.4), & \text{preshock} \\ (0.138, \quad 0, \quad 0, 1.0, \quad 1.67), & \text{inside bubble} \end{cases}$$

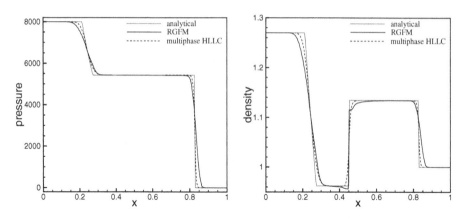

Fig. 4. Flow distributions in Gas-Liquid Shock Tube problem

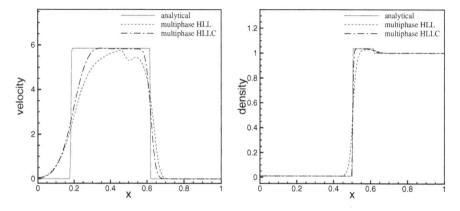

Fig. 5. Flow distributions in the problem of underwater explosion

The computational domain is $[0, 325] \times [0, 89]$, and 1024×256 uniform meshes are used. The simulation is done with the help of CUDA-GPU. Using a single-GPU, we observe $31\times$ speedup relative to a single-core CPU computation from Table 1; linear speedup can be achieved by multi-GPU parallel computing although there might be a little decrease in single-GPU performance, which is shown in Table 2. Our numerical behavior is in accordance with the dynamics of the bubble-shock interaction observed in the physical experiment by Haas [16]. Comparisons are done at different times, one of which is shown in Fig 6. The bubble outline is displayed by volume fraction contour $\alpha_1 = 0.5$. It is seen the results are comparable.

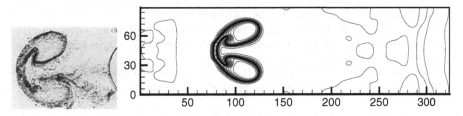

Fig. 6. Comparison of experiment (left) and computed density contours (right) at $t = 674\mu s$ in shock-bubble interaction problem

Table 1. Speedup (GPU *vs* single-core CPU)

grid number	CPU time	GPU time	speedup
128×32	0.097503	0.002830	34.45
256×64	0.358785	0.011469	31.28
512×128	1.434512	0.042854	33.47
1024×256	4.634705	0.167221	27.71

Table 2. Multi-GPU speedup

GPU number	speedup	single-GPU efficiency
1	1	100%
2	1.836	91.83 %
4	3.266	81.64%
8	5.460	68.25%

Acknowledgments. This work is supported by Natural Science Foundation of China (91130019) and 863 programme (2012AA01A304).

References

1. Baer, M., Nunziato, J.: A two-phase mixture theory for the deflagration-to-detonation transition (ddt) in reactive granular materials. International Journal of Multiphase Flow 12, 861–889 (1986)
2. Saurel, R., Abgrall, R.: A multiphase godunov method for compressible multifluid and multiphase flows. J. Comput. Phys. 150, 425–467 (1999)
3. Saurel, R., Lemetayer, O.: A multiphase model for compressible flows with interfaces, shocks, detonation waves and cavitation. J. Fluid Mech. 431, 239–271 (2001)
4. Allaire, G., Clerc, S., Kokh, S.: A five-equation model for the simulation of interfaces between compressible fluids. J. Comput. Phys 181, 577–616 (2002)
5. Abgrall, R.: How to prevent pressure oscillations in multicomponent flow calculations: a quasi conservative approach. J. Comput. Phys. 125, 150–160 (1996)
6. Tokareva, S.A., Toro, E.F.: Hllc-type riemann solver for the baer-nunziato equations of compressible two-phase flow. J. Comput. Phys. 229, 3573–3604 (2010)

7. Li, Q., Feng, H.J., Cai, T., Hu, C.B.: Difference scheme for two-phase flow. Applied Mathematics and Mechanics 25, 536–545 (2004)
8. Tian, B., Toro, E.F., Castro, C.E.: A path-conservative method for a five-equation model of two-phase flow with an hllc-type riemann solver. Computers and Fluids 46, 122–132 (2011)
9. Ambroso, A., Chalons, C., Raviart, P.-A.: A godunov-type method for the seven-equation model of compressible two-phase flow. Computers and Fluids 54, 67–91 (2012)
10. Abgrall, R., Saurel, R.: Discrete equations for physical and numerical compressible multiphase mixtures. J. Comput. Phys. 186, 361–396 (2003)
11. Wang, C.W., Liu, T.G., Khoo, B.C.: A real ghost fluid method for the simulation of multimedium compressible flow. SIAM J. Sci. Comput. 28, 278–302 (2006)
12. Liu, T.G., Khoo, B.C., Yeo, K.S.: Ghost fluid method for strong shock impacting on material interface. J. Comput. Phys. 190, 651–681 (2003)
13. Tang, H.S., Huang, D.: A second-order accurate capturing scheme for 1d invisid flows of gas and water with vacuum zones. J. Comput. Phys. 128, 301–318 (1996)
14. Fedkiw, R.P., Aslam, T., Merriman, B., Osher, S.: A non-oscillatory eulerian approach to interfaces in multimaterial flows (the ghost fluid method). J. Comput. Phys. 152, 457–492 (1999)
15. Quirk, J.J., Karni, S.: On the dynamics of a shock-bubble interaction, Tech. Rep. 94-75, Institute for Computer Applications in Science and Engineering, NASA Langley Research Center, Hampton, VA (September 1994)
16. Haas, J.-F., Sturtevant, B.: Interaction of weak shock waves with cylindrical and spherical gas inhomogeneities. Journal of Fluid Mechanics 181, 42–76 (1987)

Parallel Solver for Hypersonic Flow
Based on Block-Structured Grid

Ding Guo-hao, Li Hua, Liu Jian-Xia, and Fan Jin-Zhi

College of Aerospace Science and Engineering, National University of Defense Technology,
Changsha, Hunan 410073, China

Abstract. According to the instruction of message passing interface (MPI), A parallel CFD solver for hypersonic flow is programmed. The code employs the 3D Navier-Stokes equations as the basic governing equations to simulate the laminar hypersonic flow. The cell centered finite volume method based on structured grid is applied for spatial discretization. The AUSMPW+ scheme is used for the inviscid fluxes, and the MUSCL approach is used for higher order spatial accuracy. The implicit LU-SGS scheme is applied for time integration to accelerate the convergence of computations in steady flows. Ghost cells are applied to treat the boundary conditions, and the physical data at the ghost cells of internal connected boundary are overwritten by the data of adjacent block when each iteration step come to an end. The data communication is carried out by the MPI process. The parallel solver has been run on high performance computers to simulate different hypersonic flows. The numerical results show that the parallel CFD solver has high computational efficiency, and it can be used for the accurate prediction of aerodynamic and aerothermodynamic environment for hypersonic flight vehicles.

Keywords: Hypersonic Flow, Numerical Simulation, Parallel Computation.

1 Introduction

Hypersonic flight vehicle technology is a strategic point for the development of aerospace exploration, and the accurate prediction of aerodynamic force and heat transfer is a precondition for the definitive configuration design, which will affect the trajectory and flight performance to a great extent and it thus becomes a key issue for the study and design of a hypersonic vehicle. In all of the researching methods, the computational fluid dynamics (CFD) method plays a very important role and gets broad application as an essential tool. The CFD method can make up the defect of wind tunnel experiments, it can obtain all-round quantitative information, describe the variation of local and entire flow field with the passage of time in details, easily reconstruct visual image and aid to analyze the structure of flow field. Additionally, the CFD method has an advantage of low-cost and high efficiency.

Hypersonic flows possess the characteristics such as high Mach number, strong flow discontinuities like shock wave, and severe viscous dissipation in the wall boundary layer. The large gradient of physical quantities make the simulation of flow

K. Li et al. (Eds.): ParCFD 2013, CCIS 405, pp. 37–53, 2014.

field very difficult, and the numerical method for hypersonic flow computation requires a high level of robustness, accuracy and efficiency.

In the face of the demand of rapid increase of data amount and reduction of periodic time by a big margin, the limitation of single CPU's performance is obvious in the engineering applications, and thus the parallel computation becomes an inevitable trend in the development to reduce the runtime and expand the solving scale.

The basic idea of parallel computation in CFD application is domain decomposition method, which can be described as follows: Because the numerical simulation of CFD is based on the grid generation and partition, the total computational task can be split into a number of smaller ones with the divide of computational space. Several topologically simpler blocks are obtained, and the tasks are assigned to corresponding CPUs. The geometrical quantities and the initial state of each block are loaded into the memory of each CPU, and then the computational processes are synchronously executed, and controlled by the main process. When the computation of the current iteration is done, the physical quantities or fluxes are exchanged at the interface of adjacent grid blocks with the communications among the CPUs, and the main process gathers entire flow field information to judge the convergence, write the data to storage medium or carry out other operations as necessary.

According to the characteristics of hypersonic flows, this paper presents a parallel CFD solver based on block-structured grid, which exchange the information using the Message Passing Interface (MPI) library functions, and it is tested on high performance computers to simulate different kind of hypersonic flows.

2   Numerical Method

Generally, there are severe viscous dissipation in boundary layers and strong shock waves leading to the large gradient of flow properties in hypersonic flow problems and more complex flow phenomena like shock-shock interaction, shock-boundary layer interaction and eddy may appear, so the numerical method must have high resolution of discontinuity and viscosity. The development of upwind schemes in hypersonic flows is the main trend because of their high accuracy and efficiency.

2.1   Governing Equations

Continuum mechanics provides the basic for describing hypersonic flows of compressible viscous fluids, The corresponding balance equations (mass, momentum, total energy) are the Navier-Stokes equations, and its integral conservation [1] is

$$\frac{\partial}{\partial t} \int_{\Omega} \vec{Q} d\Omega + \oint_{\partial \Omega} (\vec{F}_c - \vec{F}_v) dS = 0 \tag{1}$$

in which $\vec{Q}$, $\vec{F}_c$, $\vec{F}_v$ represent the vector of conservative variables, convective fluxes, and viscous fluxes respectively.

The calorically perfect gas assumption is adopted, for which the equation of state takes the form

$$p = \rho R T \tag{2}$$

where R denotes the specific gas constant.

Thus the number of unknown variables (ρ, p, T, u, v, w) and the equations are closed, and these partial differential equations can be discretely approximated to algebraic equations.

2.2   Spatial Discretization

In the present study, the cell-centered finite volume method based on a structured grid system is adopted, which directly utilizes the integral formulation of the Navier-Stokes equations. Considering a particular volume $\Omega_{i,j,k}$, as displayed in Fig. 1, the semi-discrete form of the equations is as follows:

$$\frac{d}{dt}\vec{Q}_{i,j,k} = \frac{1}{\Omega_{i,j,k}}\left[\sum_{m=1}^{N_F}[(\vec{F}_c - \vec{F}_v)_m \Delta S_m]\right] \tag{3}$$

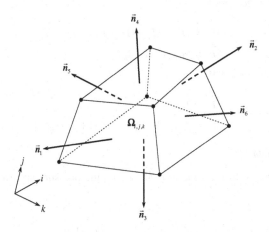

Fig. 1. Control volume and associated interface unit normal vectors for a structured grid

The term in square brackets on the right-hand side of (3) is also generally termed the residual. It is denoted here by $\vec{R}_{i,j,k}$. Hence, Equation (3) can be abbreviated as

$$\frac{d}{dt}\vec{Q}_{i,j,k} = \frac{1}{\Omega_{i,j,k}}\vec{R}_{i,j,k} \tag{4}$$

The convective fluxes are calculated using AUSMPW+ scheme [2] that will be presented in detail below, and the Gauss theorem is used to evaluate the first derivatives of the velocity components and of temperature for the calculation of viscous fluxes.

In AUSMPW+, the convective flux at the interface ($I + 1/2$) of the control volume in Fig. 2 can be recast as

$$\vec{F}_{c,I+\frac{1}{2}} = \bar{M}_{L}^{+}c_{I+\frac{1}{2}}\vec{\Psi}_{L} + \bar{M}_{R}^{-}c_{I+\frac{1}{2}}\vec{\Psi}_{R} + \left(P_{L}^{+}\vec{P}_{L} + P_{R}^{-}\vec{P}_{R}\right) \tag{5}$$

where $\vec{\Psi} = [\rho, \rho u, \rho v, \rho w, \rho H]^{\mathrm{T}}$, $\vec{P} = [0, n_{x}p, n_{y}p, n_{z}p, 0]^{\mathrm{T}}$.

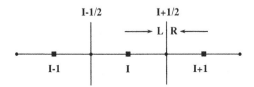

Fig. 2. Left and right state at cell interface

$\bar{M}_{L,R}^{\pm}$ is the Mach number interpolation function that is written as follows:

(i) for $m_{I+\frac{1}{2}} \geq 0$

$$\bar{M}_{L}^{+} = M_{L}^{+} + M_{R}^{-} \cdot [(1-w) \cdot (1+f_{R}) - f_{L}]$$
$$\bar{M}_{R}^{-} = M_{R}^{-} \cdot w \cdot (1+f_{R})$$

(ii) for $m_{I+\frac{1}{2}} < 0$ $\tag{6}$

$$\bar{M}_{L}^{+} = M_{L}^{+} \cdot w \cdot (1+f_{L})$$
$$\bar{M}_{R}^{-} = M_{R}^{-} + M_{L}^{+} \cdot [(1-w) \cdot (1+f_{L}) - f_{R}]$$

where $m_{1/2} = M_{L}^{+} + M_{R}^{-}$.

The Mach number splitting function $M_{L,R}^{\pm}$ and the pressure splitting function $P_{L,R}^{\pm}$ are given by

$$M_{L,R}^{\pm} = \begin{cases} \pm\dfrac{1}{4}(M_{L,R} \pm 1)^{2}, & |M_{L,R}| \leq 1 \\ \dfrac{1}{2}(M_{L,R} \pm |M_{L,R}|), & |M_{L,R}| > 1 \end{cases} \tag{7}$$

$$P_{L,R}^{\pm} = \begin{cases} \dfrac{1}{4}(M_{L,R} \pm 1)^{2}(2 \mp M_{L,R}), & |M_{L,R}| \leq 1 \\ \dfrac{1}{2}(1 \pm sign(M_{L,R})), & |M_{L,R}| > 1 \end{cases} \tag{8}$$

where $M_{L,R} = V_{L,R}/c_{1/2}$ and $c_{1/2}$ is defined as follows:

(i) $\frac{1}{2}(U_L + U_R) \geq 0:$ $c_{\frac{1}{2}} = c_s^2 / \max(|U_L|, c_s)$

(ii) $\frac{1}{2}(U_L + U_R) < 0:$ $c_{\frac{1}{2}} = c_s^2 / \max(|U_R|, c_s)$

$$(9)$$

Here, $c_s = \sqrt{2(\gamma-1)/(\gamma+1)H_{\text{normal}}}$ and $H_{\text{normal}} = \min(H_{\text{total,L}} - 0.5 \times V_L^2, H_{\text{total,R}} - 0.5 \times V_R^2)$.

The function f and w are pressure and Mach number based weighting functions, respectively.

$$f_{L,R} = \begin{cases} \left(\frac{p_{L,R}}{p_s} - 1\right) \min\left(1, \frac{\min(p_{n,L/R})}{\min(p_L, p_R)}\right)^2, & p_s \neq 0 \\ 0, & elsewhere \end{cases} \quad (10)$$

where $p_{n,L/R}$ stands for the value at the same direction interface of the adjacent grids and where $p_s = P_L^+ p_L + P_R^+ p_R$.

$$w(p_L, p_R) = 1 - \min\left(\frac{p_L}{p_R}, \frac{p_R}{p_L}\right)^3 \quad (11)$$

In the discretization of convective fluxes, the left and right state values of a cell interface are utilized to compute the convective flux through the interface. Here The MUSCL (Monotone Upstream-Centered Schemes for Conservation Laws) approach with van Albada limiter [3] is employed to interpolate the left and right state values for higher order, and the formulae are written as

$$\vec{\Phi}_R = \vec{\Phi}_{I+1} - \frac{s}{4}[(1 + \hat{\kappa}s)\Delta_- + (1 - \hat{\kappa}s)\Delta_+]_{I+1}$$

$$\vec{\Phi}_L = \vec{\Phi}_I + \frac{s}{4}[(1 + \hat{\kappa}s)\Delta_+ + (1 - \hat{\kappa}s)\Delta_-]_I \quad (12)$$

where the primitive variables are $\vec{\Phi} = [\rho, u, v, w, p]^T$, the value of $\hat{\kappa}$ determines the interpolation precision, and

$$s = \frac{2\Delta_+ \Delta_- + \varepsilon}{\Delta_+^2 + \Delta_-^2 + \varepsilon}, \quad \varepsilon = 1.0 \times 10^{-6} \quad (13)$$

ε is a small number that prevents division by zero and controls the sensitivity of limiter.

2.3   Time Discretization

The LU-SGS (Lower-Upper Symmetric Gauss-Seidel) scheme [4] is an implicit Newton iteration technique to solve the finite-volume approximation of the steady-state version of the governing equations, which is proposed by Yoon and Jameson, and its basic formula is as below:

$$(D+L)D^{-1}(D+U)\Delta \vec{Q}^n_{i,j,k} = -\vec{R}^n_{i,j,k} \qquad (14)$$

The factors are constructed such that L consists only of the terms in the strictly lower triangular matrix, U of terms in the strictly upper triangular matrix and D of diagonal terms.

The system matrix of the LU-SGS scheme can be inverted in two steps – a forward and a backward sweep, i.e. ,

$$(D+L)\Delta \vec{Q}^{(1)}_{i,j,k} = -\vec{R}^n_{i,j,k}$$
$$(D+U)\Delta \vec{Q}^n_{i,j,k} = D\Delta \vec{Q}^{(1)}_{i,j,k} \qquad (15)$$

with $\vec{Q}^{n+1}_{i,j,k} = \vec{Q}^n_{i,j,k} + \Delta \vec{Q}^n_{i,j,k}$.

The operators L, U and D are defined as

$$L = (A^+_{c,i-1,j,k}\Delta S_{i-1/2,j,k} + A^+_{c,i,j-1,k}\Delta S_{i,j-1/2,k} + A^+_{c,i,j,k-1}\Delta S_{i,j,k-1/2})$$
$$U = (A^-_{c,i+1,j,k}\Delta S_{i+1/2,j,k} + A^-_{c,i,j+1,k}\Delta S_{i,j+1/2,k} + A^-_{c,i,j,k+1}\Delta S_{i,j,k+1/2}) \qquad (16)$$
$$D = \left[\frac{\Omega}{\Delta t} + \omega(\hat{\Lambda}^I_c + \hat{\Lambda}^J_c + \hat{\Lambda}^K_c) + 2(\hat{\Lambda}^I_v + \hat{\Lambda}^J_v + \hat{\Lambda}^K_v)\right]I$$

where the split convective Jacobians $A^\pm_c$ are constructed in such a way that the eigenvalues of the (+) matrices are all non-negative, and of the (-) matrices are all non-positive. In general, the matrices are defined as

$$A^\pm_c\Delta S = \frac{1}{2}(A_c\Delta S \pm r_A I), \quad r_A = \omega\hat{\Lambda}_c \qquad (17)$$

in which A_c stands for the convective Jacobian and $\hat{\Lambda}_c$ represents the spectral radius of the convective flux Jacobian, respectively. ω is a constant number which is larger than 1.0.

$$A_c = \frac{\partial \vec{F}_c}{\partial \vec{Q}} = T\Lambda_c T^{-1}$$
$$\hat{\Lambda}_c = \max(|\Lambda_c|) \qquad (18)$$

and $\hat{\Lambda}_v$ represents the spectral radius of the viscous flux Jacobian.

2.4   Boundary and Initial Conditions

For the problems to be considered in this paper, the inflow boundary conditions are fixed with freestream values, and outflow boundary conditions are obtained using the 1st-order extrapolations. Wall boundary conditions are set as non-slip, isothermal and zero pressure gradient normal to the wall surface. Symmetric boundary conditions set the normal derivatives of all the dependent variables to be zero.

The governing equations are initialized by setting all the dependent variables throughout the domain to the inflow conditions.

3 Parallel Computation Method

According to the mentioned above, the CFD solver for hypersonic laminar flow is programmed. For the parallel computation, further efforts have to be made.

As shown in Fig. 3, the domain decomposition method is a widely used method for program parallelization, and it is very suitable for the CFD parallel computation because the CFD method is based on grid system and the sub-domains in multi-block grid system can be regarded as relatively independent issue.

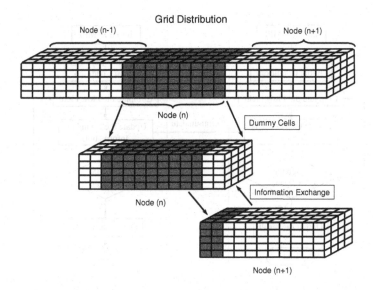

Fig. 3. Schematic of domain decomposition method with dummy cells

To meet the continuity of physical quantities, the adjacent blocks must have overlapping zones, which can be realized by dummy cells. Dummy cells are relative to physical cells, and they are introduced in finite volume method to implement the boundary conditions. In terms of internal connected boundary, the dummy cells are set on the basis of mesh topological relations, and the geometric parameters and physical quantities on dummy cells can be obtained by direct value assignment from the physical cells of the adjacent zone [1]. Then, a similar treatment of all physical cells is allowed, and the calculations of the fluxes between dummy cells and physical cells become easier, that is to say, dummy cells can retain the stencil of the spatial discretization scheme beyond the boundaries, and ensure the program's consistency.

Structured grids are suitable for accurate calculation of viscous boundary layers because of its intrinsic body-fitted feature. The structured grids are stored in a certain order, indexed by multi-dimensional coordinate, and the implicit connection relationship can reduce the storage cost. But the coupling in the cells makes the domain decomposition difficult.

Message Passing Interface (MPI) is an API specification, providing library functions to realize the communications, and is a portable language-independent communication protocol. Using this method, the adjacent blocks can communicate with each other, and the data at the ghost cells can be updated by sending and receiving messages.

Fig. 4 shows that the same processes are running on multi-cores, and the main change in comparison with the single serial process is the addition of the communication module to deliver data, so the modification of the solver code is minor, and the data structures and original modules remain as much as possible. That means the application of MPI in program parallelization can be easily handled, which will reduce the workload of programmers.

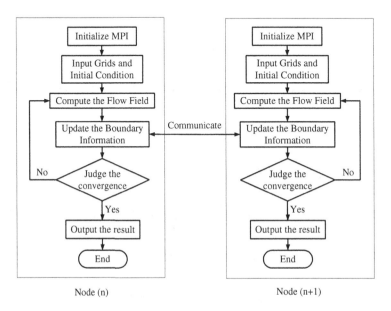

Node (n)   Node (n+1)

Fig. 4. Flow diagram of running processes

4   Numerical Analysis

Three cases are calculated to validate the parallel solver and test the computing performance.

4.1   Cylinder

The radius of this model is 0.038m, and the flow parameters are as follows [5, 6]:

$$M_\infty = 16.34, \quad p_\infty = 82.95 \text{N/m}^2, \quad T_\infty = 52\text{K}, \quad T_w = 294.4\text{K}$$

These represent a low enthalpy flow for which previous computations validate the perfect gas approximation.

Fig. 5 shows the computational grids with $301 \times 101 \times 11$ nodes, and the cell Reynolds number at the stagnation point is 3.9. The grid is split into small partitions up to 4 for parallel computations.

Fig. 6 shows that the flow field structures of strong detached bow shock, wide subsonic flow region near the stagnation line and thin boundary layer. The pressure and temperature increase sharply after the shock. The boundary layer gets thicker along the flow direction on the wall.

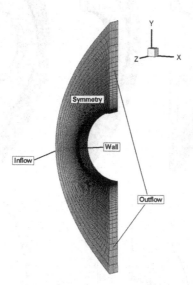

Fig. 5. Computational grid and boundary conditions of the cylinder

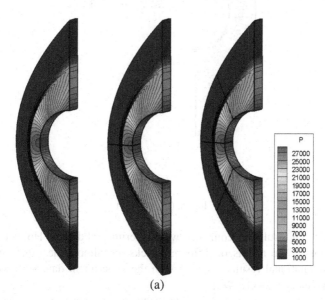

(a)

Fig. 6. Computational results of the cylinder: (a) Pressure contours; (b) Temperature contours; (c) Velocity vectors

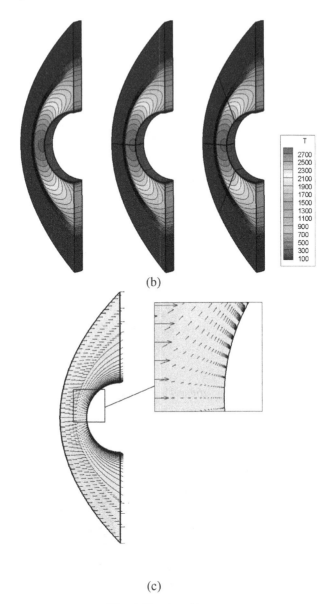

(b)

(c)

Fig. 6. (*Continued.*)

Computational results are compared with experimental data by Holden et al [6]. As shown in Fig. 7, the results of different blocks are almost the same, and the heat transfer computational results coincide with the experiment data very well, and the stagnation value is $5.88\times10^5\,\text{W/m}^2$.

In this case, the accuracy of our code for hypersonic flows is tested and verified, which meets the engineering requirements to solve the shock discontinuity and the viscous boundary layer at the same time.

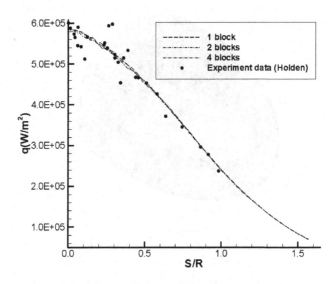

Fig. 7. Wall heat transfer distributions of the cylinder

4.2 Double Ellipsoid

The double-ellipsoid model is tested in FD-07 wind tunnel of China Academy of Aerospace Aerodynamics. The flow parameters of free stream are as below:

$$M_\infty = 7.8, \quad p_\infty = 844.83 \text{N/m}^2, \quad T_\infty = 91.13 \text{K}, \quad T_w = 300.0 \text{K}$$

The computational grids are shown in Fig. 8, the initial grid contains 8 blocks, by further division, two grids of 20 and 32 blocks are obtained.

Fig. 9 (a) shows that the grid amount of the maximum block is near 8 times of the minimum block, so the load on each CPU has great difference, and there is a lot of idle time in the parallel computation. To solve the problem, further division and task redistribution are carried out. Fig. 9 (b) and (c) shows that the load on each CPU are near the balance.

In Fig. 10, we can clearly see the shock waves induced by the double-ellipsoid, the first shock wave is a detached bow shock wave, and the second one is an attached oblique shock wave.

Fig. 11 and Fig. 12 show the comparisons of the numerical result and the experimental data. The computational pressure coefficients of upper and lower surface are both in good agreement with the experiment data. Meanwhile, the contour lines of multi-blocks are continuous and smooth, which shows that the data exchange of the physical qualities using the MPI leads to the desired result, and the way of dummy cell to handle the boundary condition is feasible.

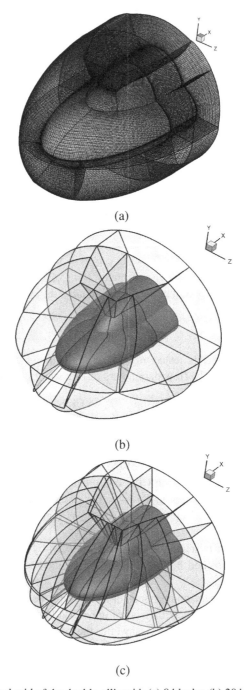

(a)

(b)

(c)

Fig. 8. Computational grid of the double-ellipsoid: (a) 8 blocks; (b) 20 blocks; (c) 35 blocks

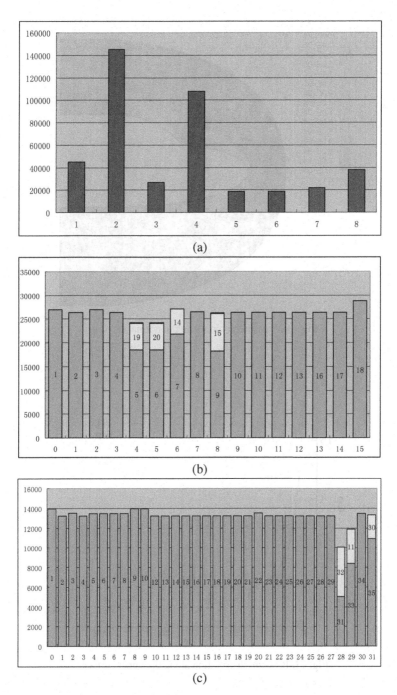

Fig. 9. The load on each CPU based on grid number

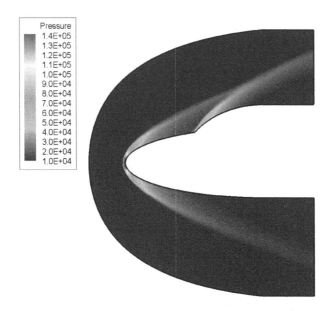

Fig. 10. Pressure contours on the normal section

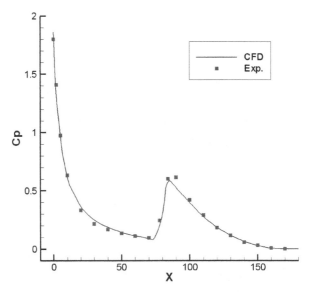

Fig. 11. Pressure distribution along the upper surface

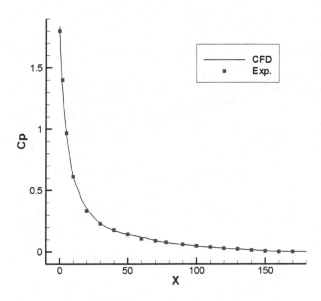

Fig. 12. Pressure distribution along the lower surface

4.3   Internal and External Flows around an Air-Breathing Hypersonic Vehicle

The flow channel of an air-breathing hypersonic vehicle with the design Mach number of 6 is studied here. The computational domain can be seen in Fig.13. The grid size is about 1.57 billion, and is divided to sub-blocks from 128 to 1024. Massively parallel computations are carried out on high performance computers. The pressure contours at the attack angle of zero can be observed in Fig.14.

Table 1 shows that as the CPU number increases, both the cell number on each CPU and the runtime of same iteration steps decrease, and the speedup ratio keeps its growth, but the parallel efficiency firstly increases and then goes down.

As shown in Fig.15, for the parallel computation of coarse granularity, the main factors influencing the efficiency are load balance, the ratio of calculational and communicational quantity, the hit ratio of cache, the acquisition probability of network and the health of computational node. Here, the load balance is met by uniform partitioned operation of the total cells. The calculational quantity is directly proportional to the internal physical cells, and the communicational quantity is directly proportional to the dummy cells. Then the ratio is almost like the relationship of volume and surface area, which is dependent on the direction of partitioned operation on the structured grid. When the partitions grow, the ratio of calculational and communicational quantity generally decreases. Moreover, the hit ratio of cache is enhanced, which can carry the efficiency forward to a certain extent. The interaction of these factors results in the uncertain offset of curve profile of speedup ratio from the theoretical linear values.

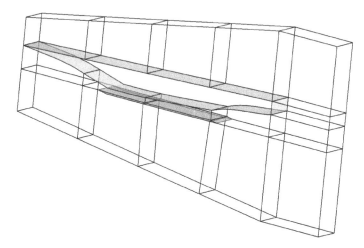

Fig. 13. Computational domain of hypersonic vehicle

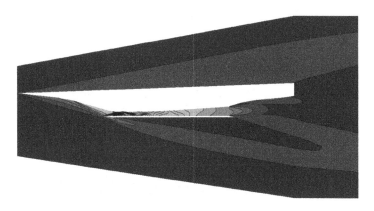

Fig. 14. Pressure contours at $\alpha=0°$

Table 1. The test data of the parallel computation

CPU number	Cell number (I×J×K)	Wall time (sec/20 steps)						Speedup ratio	Efficiency
		Test results					Average		
128	160×960×80	1889.73	1903.50	1915.26	1910.79	1929.65	1909.79	128	100.00%
256	160×480×80	960.18	863.28	880.90	898.52	801.62	880.90	277.5	108.40%
512	160×240×80	468.38	421.11	429.71	438.30	391.03	429.71	568.9	111.11%
1024	80×480×40	241.70	209.04	222.10	209.04	206.86	217.75	1122.6	109.63%
2048	160×60×80	125.45	112.79	115.09	117.39	104.73	115.09	2124.0	103.71%
4096	40×480×20	65.73	59.10	60.31	61.51	54.88	60.31	4053.5	98.96%

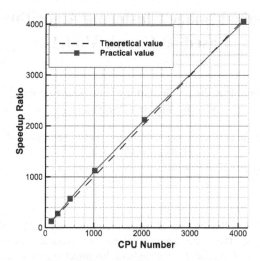

Fig. 15. Curve profile of speedup ratio

5   Conclusion

In this paper, the CFD method for solving the hypersonic flow is developed based on the characteristics of hypersonic flow, the AUSMPW+ scheme and MUSCL approach is introduced for higher order spatial accuracy, and the LU-SGS scheme is applied for acceleration of the solution of steady state. The parallel programming is realized by using the MPI library functions, and the information can be exchanged among the CPUs.

The results of thee cases shows that the CFD parallel solver presented in this paper has high accuracy for the solution of hypersonic aerodynamic force and heat problem. Meanwhile, the parallel computation can speed up the global convergence process and reduce the work time, which is very important for the massive tasks.

References

1. Blazek, J.: Computational fluid dynamics: principles and applications, pp. 5–25, 76–77, 93–95, 110–113, 116–119. Elsevier (2001)
2. Kim, K.H., Kim, C., Rho, O.H.: Methods for the accurate computations of hypersonic flows I. AUSMPW+ scheme. Journal of Computational Physics 174, 38–79 (2001)
3. Van Albada, G.D., Van Leer, B., Roberts, W.W.: A Comparative study of computational methods in cosmic gas dynamics. Astronomy and Astrophysics 108, 76–84 (1982)
4. Yoon, S., Jameson, A.: Lower-Upper Symmetric-Gauss-Seidel Method for the Euler and Navier-Stokes equations. AIAA paper 87-0600 (1987)
5. Lee, J.H., Rho, O.H.: Numerical analysis of hypersonic viscous flow around a blunt body using Roe's FDS and AUSM+ schemes. AIAA paper 97-2054 (1997)
6. Holden, M.S., Moselle, A.R., Riddell, F.R.: Studies of aerothermal loads generated in regions of shock/shock interaction in hypersonic flow. AIAA paper 88-0477 (1988)

Medical Image Clustering Algorithm
Based on Graph Model

Haiwei Pan, Jingzi Gu, Qilong Han, Xiaoning Feng,
Xiaoqin Xie, and Pengyuan Li

College of Computer Science and Technology, Harbin Engineering University,
Harbin 150001, China
panhaiwei2006@hotmail.com, jingzigu@yahoo.cn

Abstract. The algorithm of medical image is an important part of special field image clustering. There are many problems of technical aspects and the problem of specific area, so that the study of this direction is very challenging. The existing algorithm of clustering has requirement about shape and density of data object, and it cannot get a good result to the application of medical image clustering. In view of the above problem and under the guidance of knowledge of medical image, at first, detects texture from image, and T-LBP method is put forward. Then divides the preprocessed image into many spaces, and calculates LBP value of spaces. At last build spatial sequence LBP histogram. Based on the LBP histogram, the clustering method of MCST is proposed. The result of experiment shows that there are good result at time complexity and clustering result in the algorithm of this paper.

Keywords: Medical Image, Clustering, LBP, MCST.

1   Introduction

In recent years, with the development of computer technology, the technology of human medical imaging is more and more widely used. CT and other medical images are used as one of the most important methods in medical diagnosis. Medical image consists of a great number of features and abundant characteristic information that make it difficult to be classified by hand. Therefore, the research about medical image has become a new trend, including the technology of medical image clustering [1], classification, association rules and retrieval [2-7]. Image data mining [8] is the mining of image data of implicit knowledge, which includes the internal information of the image and the relation between images. Therefore it can help doctors to diagnose on the basis of the given information.

Image preprocessing is an important step of image clustering, and the result of preprocessing will directly affect the result of clustering. Different preprocessing transformations should be performed according to the different needs of image, such as region of interest detection, texture detection [9-12], wavelet transform operation. Canny contour detection algorithm will be used to preprocess images.

K. Li et al. (Eds.): ParCFD 2013, CCIS 405, pp. 54–65, 2014.
© Springer-Verlag Berlin Heidelberg 2014

Besides, Karen Simonyan proposed a medical image real-time query algorithm [13] by which users could select ROI [14], and a similarity region is returned by querying ROI. Moreover, the returned image has been ranked by the similarity. In the research of image retrieval, many feature extraction methods could be good examples and applied to clustering field. In [15] the authors proposed a method of image retrieval which is based on sketching. A matching image is returned at real time through sketching an image. The higher similarity the image is, the higher the image ranks. Then, clustering of data mining is an important research direction. At present, there are a large number of image segmentations using clustering methods. Different single images are clustered and divided into different areas. A segmentation clustering method based on graph is proposed in [16], in which the border area of image is regarded as a sub-graph, and segmented consequently after clustering. This algorithm preserves the details of the low changing regions and neglects the details of high changing regions.

Feature extraction of images LBP is an important method for image feature extraction. Devrim Unay introduced the rotation-invariant feature extraction method of LBP [17]. Timo Ojala introduced a method of feature extraction, which is about the simple and efficient analysis method of rotation invariant feature in gray-scale images based on LBP [18]. The paper describes the algorithms of calculating LBP using different radius, and different numbers of points. Devrim Unay also described the value of image LBP on medical image for Space Division [19]. Choose image center as the center of the circle, and divide it into different regions. Choose image center as the origin of coordinates, and divide the image into several parts with the same type. Then each block has a histogram. Merge these histograms into a histogram of the whole image in accordance with the order to each block.

The method, which computes with large space and more time, proposed by Devrim Unay needs to calculate the LBP value of the entire image. This paper has proposed the T-LBP method that used texture in response to the above question, which simply needs to take the LBP values of texture points. This method greatly reduced the number of calculative points, and reduced the amount of calculation and time. Existing clustering algorithms required for shapes of data and density. In this paper the medical clustering method of minimum spanning tree (MCST) not only has no requirements for clustering shape, but also performs well for the clustering of different levels of loose degrees in the same data set data.

The first section of the paper describes the background and related work; the second section describes the T-LBP method for texture; the third section introduces clustering algorithm based on graph model; the forth section is experiments part and the fifth section is summary.

2   LBP Method Oriented Texture

Data mining of medical image needs the knowledge of image processing in order to preprocess the medical image, and lots of preprocessing work has to be done before clustering image. In this paper, interested region will be extracted after clearing away cerebral cortex, and setting the image into the same size and format will be executed. Figure 1 (a) is a brain image showed in CT. It will cause a bad quality to get contour by original image, because the half circle on the middle bottom of the image is not the information of cerebral cortex, which will cause a bad effect. Therefore, extracting the region of interest will be the first step, and further useful information of brain should be saved, figure1 (b). Then detect the contour of figure1 (b), whose result is figure1 (d). As a result, important contour information of brain will be gathered after these operations.

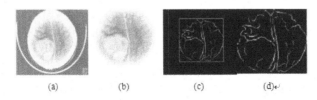

(a)   (b)   (c)   (d)↵

Fig. 1. The Brain CT. (a) original image;(b) grayscale image of region-of-interest;(c) texture image;(d) corrected texture image.

Definition 1. The set M={g_c (x, y) | g_c(x, y) is pixel of the point (x, y) in grayscale image} is defined grayscale image set. The set N={g_c' (x, y) | g_c' (x, y) is pixel of point (x, y) in images after texture detecting} is defined point set of texture image. H (g_c (x, y)) is pixel of any point g_c (x, y) in M.

Definition 2. The set P={ g_p (x', y') | |x'-x|=1 |y'-y|=1 (x, y)∈M} is defined eight neighboring points set of any point g_c (x, y) in M.

Index of texture image is established after preprocessing. Each image corresponds to a queue that stores the texture coordinates. Queue stored in a texture image in the set N points of horizontal, and vertical location of texture points in the set N are stored in the queue.

The purpose of T-LBP method is to compute the LBP value of texture. The texture image can be got after detecting image. The method is as follows: The image sets M and N are known. The point g_c' (x, y)∈N, the point g_c (x, y) ∈M. g_c(x, y) and g_c' (x, y) are in the same position on the two image in the condition that both horizontal ordinate and vertical coordinate are equal. The method of calculation is shown as the formula (1). The set P is eight neighboring points of the points g_c(x, y) in set M. The point g_c' (x, y) in texture image N is corresponding to the point g_c(x, y) in M which the horizontal ordinate and vertical coordinate are equal. g_p(x',y') ∈M, and g_c'(x,y)∈N. In the formula (2), the value of s is 1 when the value of e is equal or bigger than 0, the value of s is 0 when e is equal or less than 0. If the difference between gray value h (g_p (x', y')) of point in set P and the gray value h (g_c'(x, y)) of the point g_c' (x, y) is greater than 0, the value of s is 1. If the difference is less than 0, the value of s is 0. So we can get a string of binary encoding. And this binary encoding is the LBP value of g_c'(x, y).

$$LBP = \sum_{p=0}^{p=7} s(h(g_p(x,y)) - h(g_c'(x,y)))2^p, g_p(x,y) \in M, g_c'(x,y) \in N \quad \cdot \qquad (1)$$

$$s(e) = \begin{cases} 1, e \geq 0 \\ 0, e < 0 \end{cases} \cdot \qquad (2)$$

In this method, LBP value of texture is taken based on relationship between texture images and grayscale images. As shown in figure 2, T-LBP method simply calculates the LBP value in the position of black texture, while [19] needs LBP value of the whole grayscale image. So the calculation of T-LBP method is less and saves the time. The time complexity of calculating LBP value of whole image is o (8n), where n is the number of pixels of grayscale images. The time complexity of T-LBP is o (8t), where t is the number of texture points. Through analysis, we can see that the average of the number of texture points is about one-tenth of the grayscale images in the number of columns. So the number of required calculating points in T-LBP method is one-tenth of the radian images. So time T-LBP method has lower time complexity, it's about o (4/5n).

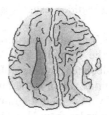

Fig. 2. Grayscale texture image

3   Clustering Algorithm Based on Graph Model

This paper refers to a T-LBP method for feature extraction. By this method, a CT picture of brain is checked and then divided into several parts. Partition strategy is that the center of this picture is seen as the center of a circle. Then this circle is divided into some fan-shaped areas. It is divided according to the detection of texture. Then according to the texture line of the texture image, it needs to find the neighborhood gray value, which will be compared with the texture point of gray value. And then the LBP histograms of texture image are calculated.

The existing clustering method cannot be used in the case of fewer parameters to get the results of any shape and different densities. In response to this problem, this paper proposes the clustering of medical clustering method of minimum spanning tree (MCST). In this paper, the clustering method is not required about cluster shape and density, so it can get clusters of any shape and density.

3.1   Feature Extraction

The partition of image space can restrict the characteristics of the region of image. The similarity is compared between the images according to the characteristics of the corresponding region. Now the feature extraction method will be introduced. CT image is divided into different areas to get the space partition of the image. At first, it can be divided into different circular area when we regard the center of the image as the center, and the texture image is divided into circular area with the order from the inside to the outside. Secondly, fan-shaped areas are divided, which the center of the image is treated as the center. Suppose the image numeral order is from the inner to the outer ring, and sequentially mark number from the top of the positive x-axis, as figure 3.

Fig. 3. Partition texture image

According to the different regions after partition, the vector of the different dimensions can be obtained by the formula. This vector is seen as the basis of similarity calculation. Vector calculated by the following formula (3). m is the number of the divided circular regions, and n is the number of the divided fan-shaped area. FUN (m, n) is consisted by m * n histograms. The splicing process is set histogram on coordinate system in order from Hist [1] to Hist [MN]. In formula (4), value(0,…,255) means 0,…,255 is horizontal ordinate, and the points on the horizontal ordinate is gray value. T-LBP values of every pixel are got and put on the horizontal ordinate, and then Y-axis pluse 1. The value of the sum (number) is the number of the total texture points. The sum is divided for the purpose of normalized histogram, and more accurate calculation results are got.

$$FUN(m,n)=\text{Hist}[1]...\text{Hist}[mn] \quad . \tag{3}$$

$$\text{Hist}[x]=\frac{\text{value}(0,...,255)}{\text{sum(number)}} \quad . \tag{4}$$

The image is divided into different small areas in image space division. This allows the expression of the extracted feature more accurately without causing interference. If LBP is extracted from an entire image, the gray is grayscale information of the whole image, the limit is more relaxed and expression of image is not accurate enough. After image space is divided, we only need to compare the T-LBP features of the corresponding region.

3.2   Graph Model

The method based on the principle of the nearest neighbor data, the adjacent objects are in one class, and the distance objects are not in the same class. This paper based on the method of minimum spanning tree divides the data set G into different sets, with a high similarity in each set and a low similarity in different sets. We use S to present the sets after the division, S(C1,…,Cr). Graph theory is a kind of effective method for solving the clustering problem. The weights between the points in data sets can be seen as similarity.

Graph theory is already a kind of mature theory. The algorithm about graph theory has good characteristics, and the application of the graph theory is a kind of effective method to solve the clustering problem. In order to construct a graph G= (V, E), the data object is treated as the point, and the relationships between objects is treated as the edges in the graph. V= {$v_1...v_n$} is the set of points, and v_i in V is a object. E={e_{ij}|1 ≤ i ≤ n, 1 ≤ j ≤ n and i ∈ V, j ∈ V} is the set of edges of the graph. e_{ij} is the edge constructed by point v_i and v_j. v ∈ V is the element to be clustered. There is a weight of similarity w (v_i,v_j) between v_i and v_j. In the process of graph clustering, an image denoted as V, the relationship of images denoted as E, and the weight of edge W is the similarity of the two images. Suppose that the num is the area number after space division. Hist[i] present the LBP histogram of ith area. Take the 256 gray values as X-axis of Hist[i], and the number of texture LBP value in a gray value as Y-axis. As shown in figure 4, image denotes a brain CT image, and Hist[1]... Hist[mn] denotes the histogram from area 1 to area m*n. Because the CT image is gray image, and the gray scale range from 0 to 255, so histogram of the horizontal ordinate is gray value from 0 to 255, Y-axis r is the number of the gray value.

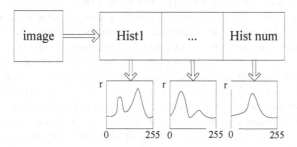

Fig. 4. Histogram constitution

The distance between each histogram is as follow formula (5). Dis (G_i (Hist [x])), G_j (Hist [y])) is the distance between the xth area histogram in G_i image and the yth area histogram in G_j image. Where G_i(Hist[x]) represents the xth histogram in the ith image, G_j(Hist[y]) represents the yth histogram in the jth image. Variable index is from 0 to 255 pixels. r is the Y-axis value of the corresponding pixels points. This value is T-LBP value after the normalization.

$$Dis(G_i(\text{Hist}[x]),G_j(\text{Hist}[y]))=\sqrt{(G_i(\text{Hist}[x])-G_j(\text{Hist}[y]))^2}$$
$$=\sqrt{\sum_{index=0}^{index=255}(r_{i,x}[index]-r_{j,y}[index])^2} \tag{5}$$

Weights w (v_i, v_j) calculate by the distance between the ith image and the jth image according to the corresponding area. The distance of the division of each small area is the difference of small area histogram. As formula (6), w (v_i,v_j) denotes the distance between image i and j. Variable x, y denote the area from 1 to num, and G_i(Hist[x]) represent the xth histogram in the ith image. The distance of each image is the distance of correspondingly histogram.

$$w(v_i,v_j)=\sqrt{\sum_{x,y=1}^{x,y=num}(G_i(\text{Hist}[x])-G_j(\text{Hist}[y]))^2} \tag{6}$$

3.3   MCST Clustering Algorithm

This paper uses the minimum spanning tree method based on graph to clustering. S is the classification of G. Set $C \in S$, and C is the subgraph of G. Graph $G' = (V, E')$, and $E' \in E$. In most cases the elements in the same set are similar, and the elements in different sets are not similar. That is to say, the weight of edges between points in the same subgraph is the lowest, and the weight of edges between points in different subgraph is the highest. For each subgraph C, the similarity in each subgraph is the maximum of minimum spanning tree (MST), as shown in formula (7). $G_i(\text{Hist}[x])$ in each object represents the xth histogram in the ith image, and the number of divided area is num. G_i and G_j are in the same set C.

$$Int(C) = \max \sqrt{\sum_{x,y=1}^{x,y=num} (G_i(\text{Hist}[x]) - G_j(\text{Hist}[y]))^2} \cdot \qquad (7)$$
$$G_i \in C, G_j \in C$$

$MInt(C_1, C_2)$ is the minimum similarity between subgrab C_1 and C_2. In this paper $\tau(C) = k/|C|$, k is a given parameter, and $|C|$ is the number of elements in the subgraph. This item is added for making the algorithm more robust, because the value of $Int(C)$ is 0, if there is only one element in set C. At this time, there is edge between subgraph C_1 and C_2, then merge them. All outlier point will be assigned to the other set. That is to say, there will be not outlier in clustering results. Here to add $\tau(C) = k/|C|$ overcome this shortcoming well and adjust the clustering algorithm well. We will mention it later. The values of parameter k can be adjusted according requirements. When it becomes bigger, it means that the condition of clustering is loose, and the number of elements in a class is relatively larger. Otherwise, it means the condition of clustering is strict, the number of elements in a class is fewer, and classes of clustering are small. k can be adjusted according actual requirements to make the clustering result meet the requirements. As shown in formula (8).

$$MInt(C_1, C_2) = MIN(Int(C_1) + \tau(C_1), Int(C_2) + \tau(C_2)) \cdot \qquad (8)$$

The similarity between each subgraph is the shortest distance of the points in the two sets. The value of $Dif(C_1, C_2)$ is ∞, if there is no edge between the two subgraph. As shown in formula(9), C_1 and C_2 are the different subgraph, $v_i \in C_1, v_j \in C_2$, and v_i and v_j are in the edge set E. G_i, G_j belong to different subgraph C_1 and C_2 respectively.

$$Dif(C_1, C_2) = \min \sqrt{\sum_{x,y=1}^{x,y=num} (G_i(\text{Hist}[x]) - G_j(\text{Hist}[y]))^2} \cdot \qquad (9)$$
$$G_i \in C_1, G_j \in C_2$$

Now introduced the MCST clustering algorithm:

```
Input: G = (V, E)
Output: S = (C₁,…,Cᵣ)
1. Sort the edger in graph G according increasing order,
get the set O= (o₁,…,oₘ).
2. S⁰ as the initial clustering, and every point vᵢ is
the initial set.
3. According to q = 1... m repeat step 3.
4. The qth edge in the sequence connect the point vᵢ and
point vⱼ, and oᵩ= (vᵢ,vⱼ).
```

```
5. Construct Sᵍ according to Sᵍ⁻¹
If (vᵢ and vⱼ are not in Sᵍ⁻¹, and w (oᵍ) is smaller than
the similarity of subgraph which the two points belong
to in respectively) Then {merger the two subgraph}
If (Cᵢᵍ⁻¹ contains the subgraph of Sᵍ⁻¹ and vⱼ belongs the
subgraph Cⱼᵍ⁻¹){If (Cᵢᵍ⁻¹•Cⱼᵍ⁻¹ and w(oᵍ)•MInt(Cᵢᵍ⁻¹,Cⱼᵍ⁻¹))
Then {merger Sᵍ⁻¹ and get Sᵍ}} Else {Sᵍ=Sᵍ⁻¹}
6. If (after merger Sᵍ, it has not rings)
Then {Merger Cᵢᵍ⁻¹, Cⱼᵍ⁻¹ and oᵍ= (vᵢ,vⱼ), get a new
subgraph set}
Else {According to the objects belongs to Cᵢᵍ⁻¹ and Cⱼᵍ⁻¹,
generate minimum spanning tree again, and generate a
new subgraph.}
7. Return S=Sᵐ
```

The original data set in this algorithm is image set, it doesn't limit the density and shape between the object of data set, and well overcome the influence of outliner. If there are both loose data and dense data in the initial data set, the cluster algorithm can make the dense data and loose data cluster together respectively. So it doesn't limit the density of object. Each division is computed with the method based on minimum spanning tree, and the relationship of objects is distance of object which is also the similarity. So it doesn't limit the shape of original data set. We can adjust the strictly degree of cluster according to the value of k. While it requires looser, the value of k is bigger. Otherwise, the value of k is smaller.

4   Results and Discussion

According to the error rate of the results of medical image clustering, whether the result is good or not can be judged. The following is the error rate calculation. As formula (11), where p is the number of images misclassified, and q is the total number of images.

$$e=\frac{p}{q} .\qquad(11)$$

The method of space-based LBP feature extraction[19] is to divide the CT image into different areas. At first, it can be divided into different circular area when we regard the center of the image as the center. Secondly, fan-shaped areas are divided, which the center of the image is treated as the center. As shown in figure 5. This method make the image is limited to the different regions. According to the division of the area object the gray histograms are calculated for each region, and gray histogram is obtained from the image's grayscale LBP value. According to the gray histogram of the corresponding area of each image, the similarity is compared and calculated.

Fig. 5. Space Grayscale Graph

4.1   Analysis of Clustering Time

Here is the T-LBP feature extraction based index and traditional feature extraction of image LBP on one hundred images. Experimental results show that the average number of texture points in texture image is one tenth of the number of grayscale image points. So when T-LBP feature is extracted, the calculation of the number of points is one-tenth of the number of whole image points. The computation time of T-LBP features extraction is less than the entire image features extraction. Figure 6 is time chart of extracting two features, where the X-axis is the serial number of the image. There are 100 images, numbered from 1-100. The ordinate is time, and the unit is microseconds. The points of T-LBP are the time distribution of T-LBP feature extraction, and the ALLLBP are the time distribution of entire image LBP feature extraction. It can be seen from the figure the time of AllLBP feature extraction is about 10 microseconds to 12 microseconds. The experiment demonstrates reduced the time complexity of the feature extraction by an order of magnitude using the T-LBP method.

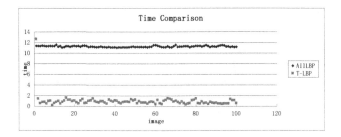

Fig. 6. The picture of time comparison

4.2   Analysis of Clustering Results Error Rate

All of the following experimental results shown in the line of T-LBP are error rate curve of using MCST algorithm after feature extraction using the T-LBP. The line of ALLLBP is the error rate curve of using MCST algorithm for clustering after entire gray image feature extraction. Where the X-axis is the value of k in MCST algorithm, the Y-axis is the error rate.

The following are T-LBP features of image and LBP features of the entire image using MCST method for clustering, and error rate comparison. Through the image library we simulate images, and then there are 100 images, which include real images and simulate images. The images includes five layer brain images. Clustering results are as follows Figure 7. When the T-LBP method is used for feature extraction, and then 0 <k <0.048, the error rate is higher and gradually reducing. At this time the value of k is small and density is high. The number of clusters is larger. With the increase of k, internal cluster distance increases, and the number of the objects is more. When k=0.048, the minimum error rate is 0.04, which is far less than the error rate of AllLBP clustering. At this time the value of k is the most appropriate for this group of pictures. When k> 0.048 error rate increases, the number of clusters is reduced, intra-class distance gradually increases, and pictures which are not in the same class are clustered together. Therefore, the error rate gradually increases. LBP feature extraction of the whole image AllLBP curve probably has been maintained at about 0.7. So the error rate of T-LBP feature extraction methods is far lower than the error rate of the whole gray image feature extraction.

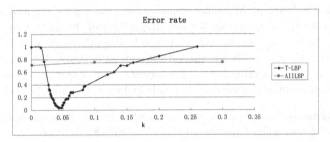

Fig. 7. Error rate 1

As the result can be seen from figure 8, the group of images uses the T-LBP method for feature extraction. When 0 <k <0.056, the error rate is higher and gradually reducing. At this time the value of k is small, and density is high, the number of clusters is larger and smaller distance with the same class. With the increase of k, internal cluster distance increases and the number of the objects increase. When k=0.056, the minimum error rate is 0.09, which is far less than the error rate of AllLBP clustering. At this time the value of k is the most appropriate for this group of pictures. When k> 0.056, error rate increases the number of clusters is reduced, intra-class distance gradually increases, and images which are not in the same class are clustered together. Therefore, the error rate gradually increases. LBP feature extraction of the whole image AllLBP curve probably has been between 0.7 and 0.9, when k=0.056, the error rate of T-LBP feature extraction methods is far lower than the error rate of the whole gray image feature extraction.

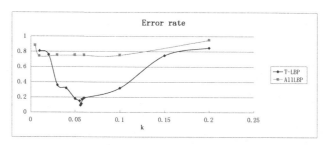

Fig. 8. Error rate2

5   Conclusion

In this paper, image feature is extracted, and images are clustered with the feature. There are many feature extraction method, T-LBP method is used in this paper. MCST method is based on Minimum spanning tree, and a good clustering result can be got by changing the parameter k value. Regardless of the data of any shape and density, the processing results are very good. Regardless of the data sets are concentrated or loose, the MCST method can handle it better. This method is also good at Outlier. The clustering method put forward in this paper can be used as a part of the automatic medical diagnosis system to help doctors examine the patient.

Acknowledgements. The paper is partly supported by the National Natural Science Foundation of China under Grant No.61272184, 61202090, 61100007; Natural Science Foundation of Heilongjiang Province under Grant No.F200903, F201016, F201024, F201130; The Program for New Century Excellent Talents in Universities(NCET-11-0829); The Fundamental Research Funds for the Central Universities under grant No.HEUCF100609, HEUCFT1202; The Science and Technology Innovation Talents Special Fund of Harbin under grant No. RC2010QN010024.

References

1. Haiwei, P., Li, J., Wei, Z.: Incorporating Domain Knowledge into Medical Image Clustering. Applied Mathematics and Computation 2(185), 844–856 (2007)
2. Ritendra, D., Dhiraj, J., Jia, L.: Image retrieval: Ideas, influences, and trends of the new age. ACM Computing Surveys 40(2), 5–60 (2008)
3. Michael, J.S., Dana, H.B.: Color Indexing. International Journal of Computer Vision 7, 11–22 (1991)
4. Liu, G., Yang, J.: Image retrieval based on the texton co-occurrence matrix. Pattern Recognition 41(12), 3521–3527 (2008)
5. Quellec, G., Lamard, M., Cazuguel, G., Cochener, B., Roux, C.: Fast Wavelet-Based Image Characterization for Highly Adaptive Image Retrieval. IEEE Transactions on Image Processing 21(4), 1613–1623 (2012)

6. Xiaoqian, X., Lee, D.J., Antani, S., et al.: Spine x-ray image retrieval using partial vertebral boundaries. IEEE Transaction on Information Technology in Biomedicine 12(1), 100–108 (2008)
7. William, H., Sameer, A.L., Rodney, L., et al.: SPIRS: A web-based image retrieval system for large biomedical databases. International Journal of Medical Informatics 78(1), S13–S24 (2009)
8. Jiawei, H., Kamber, M.: Data Mining: Concepts and Techniques, 2nd edn., pp. 396–399. China Machine Press, Beijing (2006)
9. Cosmin, G., Nicolai, P.: Contour Detection Based on Nonclassical Receptive Field Inhibition. IEEE Transactions on Image Processing 12(7), 729–739 (2003)
10. Arbelaez, P., Maire, M., Fowlkes, C., et al.: Contour Detection and Hierarchical Image Segmentation. IEEE Transactions on Pattern Analysis and Machine Intelligence 33(5), 898–916 (2011)
11. Catanzaro, B., Su, B.-Y., Sundaram, N., et al.: Efficient, high-quality image contour detection. In: IEEE International Conference on Computer Vision, pp. 2381–2388 (2009)
12. Wang, B., Fan, S.: An Improved CANNY Edge Detection Algorithm. Computer Science and Engineering, 497–500 (2009)
13. Simonyan, K., Zisserman, A., Criminisi, A.: Immediate Structured Visual Search for Medical Images. In: Fichtinger, G., Martel, A., Peters, T. (eds.) MICCAI 2011, Part III. LNCS, vol. 6893, pp. 288–296. Springer, Heidelberg (2011)
14. Bradski, G., Kaebler, A.: Learning Opencv. In: Yu S., Liu R.(trans.) Tsinghua University Press, Beijing (2009) (in Chinese)
15. Cao, Y., Wang, C., Zhang, L., et al.: Edgel Index for Large-Scale Sketch-based Image Search. In: IEEE Conference on Computer Vision and Pattern Recognition (CVPR), pp. 761–768 (2011)
16. Felzenszwalb, P., Huttenlocher, D.: Efficient Graph-Based Image Segmentation. International Journal of Computer 59(2), 167–181 (2004)
17. Unay, D., Ekin, A., Cetin, M., Jasinschi, R., Aytul: Ercil Robustness of Local Binary Patterns in Brain MR Image Analysis. In: Proceedings of the 29th Annual International Conference of the IEEE EMBS, pp. 2098–2011 (2007)
18. Ojala, T., Pietikäinen, M.: Multiresolution gray-scale and rotation invariant texture classification with local binary patterns. IEEE Transactions on Pattern Analysis and Machine Intelligence, 971-987 (2002)
19. Unay, D., Ekin, A., Jasinschi, R.S.: Local Structure-Based Region-of-Interest Retrieval in Brain MR Images. IEEE Transactions on Information Technology in Biomedicine, 897–903 (2010)

The Pressure Buildup and Salt Precipitation during CO_2 Storage in Closed Saline Aquifers

Qingliang Meng[1], Xi Jiang[2], Didi Li[1], and Xiaoqin Zhong[1]

[1] Department of Safety Science Engineering & State Key Laboratory of Fire Science,
University of Science and Technology of China, Hefei, Anhui 230026, China
[2] Engineering Department, Lancaster University, Lancaster LA1 4YR, United Kingdom
{qlmeng,lididi,zhongxq}@mail.ustc.edu.cn,
x.jiang@lancaster.ac.uk

Abstract. The storage of large-amount CO_2 captured from coal-fired power plant in deep saline aquifers can be an effective and promising measure for reducing emissions of greenhouse gases. High rate and long-term CO_2 injection into the geological formation may cause multi-scale phenomena such as pressure buildup in large scale, CO_2 plume in medium scale and salt precipitation in small scale. In this study, parallel computations are performed to determine the three-dimensional spatial effects during the injection of CO_2 into closed systems. The study is aimed at investigating the propagation of pressure buildup, the development of CO_2 plume and the impact of precipitation on the process due to the evaporation and capillary pressure. The results show that the region of elevated pressure is much larger than the CO_2 plume size and the two types of salt precipitation close to the well both lead to the injectivity degradation and the declined transportation.

Keywords: CO_2 storage, Pressure buildup, Salt precipitation, CO_2 plume.

Nomenclature:

d	diffusivity (m^2/s)
$\mathbf{g}$	gravitational acceleration (m/s^2)
k	magnitude of permeability (m^2)
$\mathbf{k}$	permeability tensor (m^2)
$\mathbf{q}$	Darcy flux (m/s)
s	saturation
S	source/sink term (kg/s)
t	time (s)
V	mesh volume (m^3)
X_i	mass fraction of i component

Greek symbols

μ	dynamic viscosity (Pa·s)
ρ	density (kg/m^3)
Γ	surface area of connected mesh interface (m^2)
Σ	summation
τ	tortuosity
∇	gradient operator

K. Li et al. (Eds.): ParCFD 2013, CCIS 405, pp. 66–77, 2014.
© Springer-Verlag Berlin Heidelberg 2014

Subscripts/superscripts

c	capillary
i	index
s	solid
α, β	fluid phase

1   Introduction

Geological carbon dioxide (CO_2) sequestration in deep saline aquifers is potentially the most promising method for reducing greenhouse gas emission from fossil fuel combustion into the atmosphere [1-2]. In this method, one of the primary mechanisms of securing CO_2 at underground conditions is that low-permeability caprock will prevent the injected CO_2 from leaking to the surface and the CO_2 would diffuse in the permeable, porous zone for an extended period of time. In certain geological situations, a storage basin may be composed of a number of compartmentalized reservoirs laterally separated by impervious seals, which acts as a closed system [3]. In this case, any native brine and injected CO_2 cannot escape from the aquifer, and a significant pressure buildup will be produced.

High rate and long-term CO_2 injection into the geological formation may cause multi-scale phenomena. When large volumes of CO_2 are injected into this system, a significant pressure buildup will be produced, leading to the reduction in the volume of native brine and enlargement of the pore space, through compression of the fluid and rock material, respectively [4]. The elevated pressure can quickly propagate and accumulate in the whole field, which is a large scale phenomenon. At the temperature and pressure conditions of deep brine formations (for temperature higher than 31.1°C and pressure higher than 7.38 MPa [2]), injected CO_2 will be in a supercritical state (scCO_2). At supercritical conditions, CO_2 has different properties than in either the liquid or gaseous phase. The most notable and relevant in this problem are the high-density characteristic of liquids, and occupying the entire available volume, like a gas [2]. Since the density of scCO_2 is lower than that of the native aqueous phase, it will tend to accumulate at the top of reservoir and spread out along the top caprock driven by the gravity force and injected pressure gradient [2], as schematically shown in Fig. 1(a). However, the CO_2 plume size is much smaller than the regional scale of elevated pressure [3]. The injection of dry scCO_2 will displace the resident brine immiscibly, combined with the dissolution (evaporation) of water into the flowing CO_2 stream. The evaporation may eventually lead to the aqueous phase dry-out and salt precipitation in the vicinity of the injection well [5]. However, the size of precipitation region is just a small fraction of the plume. This salt precipitation results in decreased porosity and permeability. Consequently, the well injectivity will be degraded and the transportation will be declined.

For the multi-scale phenomena under investigation, numerical simulations are effective tools to obtain insight into the physics of complex flows; especially the complicated multiphase flow phenomena, such as advection and diffusion, mixing, phase appearance/disappearance, dissolution and precipitation of chemical species, geo-chemical reactions, and the large spatial and temporal scales in this problem [6]. In order to numerically evaluate the feasibility and reliability of CO_2 disposal, large amounts of computational meshes and detailed physicochemical models are needed, leading to a large computational challenge. Parallel computations are increasingly used in computational studies of complex flows for engineering applications. In order to capture the essential flow physics and evaluate different spatial scales in the problem, three-dimensional (3D) parallel computations combined with a domain decomposition approach are performed in this study.

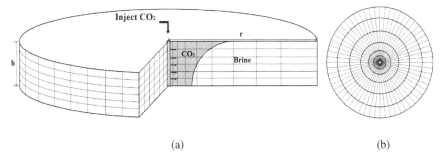

(a)   (b)

Fig. 1. Schematic representation of (a) CO_2 injection into a closed aquifer via a vertical well and (b) top view

2   Introduction

2.1   Computational Domain

The physical problem is CO_2 injection and propagation, via a vertical well, into a confined saline aquifer, as indicated in Fig. 1(a). The storage formation, located at a depth of approximate 1200 m below the ground surface, is 100 m thick with a radius of 40 km. The computation domain of the aquifer is discretized into 1000 grids in the radial direction, 60 grids in the axial direction and 100 grids in the vertical direction. The wellbore radius is selected to be 0.15 m. The grid size increases logarithmically from the injection well, with the finest grid locate close to the wellbore and the coarsest at the far side boundary of the computational domain in the radial direction. As a result, the majority of the grids are located within a 10 km radius of the injection well. Every circle in the radial direction is divided into 60 gird blocks uniformly except the wellbore, while the targeted formation is divided into 100 layers vertically. The total number of the meshes is 5, 994, 100. All the boundaries are assumed to be impermeable to both supercritical CO_2 and brine except the well bore boundary.

Table 1 lists the assigned values of the hydro-geological properties, which are typical conditions for a homogeneous brine aquifer suitable for CO_2 storage. The aquifer is initially fully brine-saturated, with a hydrostatic fluid pressure distribution. Isothermal condition is considered with a uniform temperature of 45 °C. An injection period of 30 years with 100 kg/s injection rate is chosen for the simulation to access the spatial distribution of pressure buildup, the CO_2 plume and solid salt precipitation over time.

Table 1. Hydrogeological properties of the storage formation

Initial conditions	
Temperature	$T=45°C$
Pressure	$P_{ini} \approx 120\text{-}131$ bars
Salinity	$X_s=0.15$
Dissolved CO_2 concentration	$X_l=0.$
Formation properties	
Horizontal permeability	$k_h = 10^{-12}\,\text{m}^2$
Vertical permeability	$k_v = 10^{-12}\,\text{m}^2$
Porosity	$\phi=0.12$
Pore compressibility	$D = 4.5\times10^{-10}\,\text{Pa}^{-1}$

2.2   Governing Equations

The governing equations for the mathematical description of geological carbon storage are similar to those used to describe oil, water, and gas flows through porous reservoirs [1]. For isothermal problems, only the mass conservation equations for CO_2, water and salt are considered. The integral form of mass equations for an individual ith species or component can be given as [7]:

$$\frac{\partial}{\partial t}\int_{V_n}\phi\sum_\alpha\left(\rho_\alpha s_\alpha X_i^\alpha\right)dV_n + \int_{\Gamma_n}\sum_\alpha\left(\rho_\alpha X_i^\alpha \mathbf{q}_\alpha\right)\cdot \mathbf{n}d\Gamma_n$$
$$-\int_{\Gamma_n}\sum_\alpha\left(\phi s_\alpha \tau_\alpha d_i^\alpha \rho_\alpha \nabla X_i^\alpha\right)\cdot \mathbf{n}d\Gamma_n = \int_{V_n}S_i dV_n \tag{1}$$

where $\mathbf{n}$ is the normal vector on the surface element dS_n (assumed pointing inward into the mesh n). $\mathbf{q}_\alpha$ can be defined by Darcy's law [8]:

$$\mathbf{q}_\alpha = -\frac{kk_{r\alpha}}{\mu_\alpha}\left(\nabla P_\alpha + \rho_\alpha \mathbf{g}\nabla z\right) \tag{2}$$

Equation (1) is closed by four terms representing the time rate of change of mass at a fixed location, convective and diffusive transports, and source/sink term of mass respectively [1].

The problem is closed by constitutive relationships and supplementary constraints for saturations, component compositions and pressures. For instance, assuming the fluid saturations fill the media would lead to:

$$\sum_{\alpha} s_{\alpha} = 1 \quad . \tag{3}$$

The difference of pressures between two phases satisfies the relation [8]:

$$P_{\beta} = P_{\alpha} + P_{c,\alpha\beta} \quad . \tag{4}$$

Equation (4) shows that the fluid pressure in phase β is the sum of the gas phase pressure P_{α} and the capillary pressure $P_{c,\alpha\beta}$. The Van Genuchten model is used to calculate the capillary and the relative permeabilities for the two-phase flow [9].

The permeability reduction due to solid salt precipitation is calculated using a tubes-in-series model [10]. This permeability is reduced to zero at a finite porosity. The ratio of permeability k to original permeability k_0, can be given by:

$$\frac{k}{k_0} = \theta^2 \frac{1 - \Gamma + \Gamma/\omega^2}{1 - \Gamma + \Gamma\left[\theta/(\theta + \omega - 1)\right]^2} \quad . \tag{5}$$

Here,

$$\theta = \frac{1 - S_s - \phi_r}{1 - \phi_r} \quad . \tag{6}$$

which depends on the fraction $1-S_s$ of the original pore space that remains available to fluids and on the parameter ϕ_r. Γ is the fractional length of the pore bodies, and the fraction $\phi_r = \phi/\phi_0$. The parameter ω is given by

$$\omega = 1 - \frac{1/\Gamma}{1/\phi_r - 1} \quad . \tag{7}$$

The values for parameters ϕ_r and Γ are set both as 0.8, which many numerical studies have taken [11, 12].

2.3   Numerical Approach and Parallel Algorithm

Equation (1) is discretized in time using an implicit finite difference scheme and in space using an integral finite difference method, which lead to a set of coupled nonlinear equations. Newton/Raphson iteration is used to solve these equations. The temporal differencing is based on an automatic scheme used to track the process accurately and effectively, by changing the time steps according to the variations of solutions between adjacent time steps. The computational domain is decomposed into a number of subdomains using the METIS software package [13]. MPI is used for the parallel implementation. Parallel simulations are performed on 360 processor cores in National Supercomputing Center in Tianjin simultaneously. Each process is responsible for each sub-domain for updating thermo-physical variables, sending and receiving messages to assemble mass conversation equations, and solving the linear equation systems.

3   Results and Discussion

The results are obtained from 3D simulations with the effect of permeability reduction due to salt precipitation taken into account. The snapshots shown in Fig. 2(a1-a3) correspond to the pressure buildup, gas saturation and solid saturation at the end of the 30-year injection period. The region of elevated pressure is much larger than the CO_2 plume size, while the solid saturation only occurs in the zone of single gas phase. The pressure buildup contour lines shown in Fig. 2(a1) in the CO_2 plume region are inclined, which is due to the buoyancy and nonlinearity inherent in the two-phase flow processes [3]. While the contour lines away from the CO_2 plume region are mostly vertical, indicating a horizontal brine displacement. The radius of CO_2 plume is about 6 km and the plume is concentrated at the top portion of the aquifer in Fig. 2(a2), as a result of the buoyant CO_2 accumulation below the impervious caprock. The size of the salt precipitation region is about 150 m wide, as shown in Fig. 2(a3).

There are two kinds of precipitation near the well, non-localized salt precipitation of smaller values and localized salt precipitation of large values shown in Fig. 2(a3) [11]. The non-localized solid saturation is from 0.08 to 0.04, corresponding to the permeability reduction from 60% to 30% in Eq. (5). The highest solid saturation in the localized salt precipitation region amounts to 0.20, which results in a near-zero permeability. The two types precipitation are both due to the evaporation of dry gas phase, while the biggest difference between them is that the capillary-driven backflow of brine toward the injection well continuously supplies the precipitable solids for the localized precipitation. Both of the two kinds of salt precipitation will lead to the injectivity degradation and declined transportation.

Due to the density difference between the injected CO_2 and native brine, the buoyant CO_2 can flow upwards and accumulate below the imperious caprock, as indicated in Fig. 1(a). For the physical problem under investigation, it is necessary to study the variation of pressure, gas saturation and solid saturation (In analogy to pore occupancy by multiple fluid phases, the fraction of pore space occupied by solid precipitate is termed as the "solid saturation".) with time at the aquifer top. Fig. 2(b1-b3) shows the radial profiles of pressure buildup (compared to the initial hydrostatic pressure), gas saturation and solid saturation at different times throughout the injection period.

The pressure buildup shown in Fig. 2(b1) near the well shows nonlinear behaviors. Simulation results predict an initial jump followed by a quick decline and then a gradual increase in near wellbore pressure over time. This phenomenon can be understood as follows. At the beginning of the injection phase, CO_2 has to first displace the resident brine, which needs to satisfy a certain threshold pressure. In this period, viscous force dominantly acts on the lateral CO_2 plume, corresponding to the initial jump of pressure. When there is enough room for CO_2 to migrate upwards, some of the gas would flow upward because CO_2 is less dense compared to the brine with the injection of more CO_2. As more and more CO_2 accumulates at the bottom of the caprock, gravity override [14] would occur due to the viscous difference between the two fluids, and the CO_2 could be injected easier and the native brine could be displaced quickly. Consequently, the pressure would decrease as vertical flow becomes important. However, this decrease process of pressure would stop when the pressure pulse reaches the outer boundary. The pressure of the entire field will increase due to the effect of confined boundaries. Turning point in every curve in

Fig. 2(b1) can be observed, corresponding to the phase transformation points from gas-liquid two phase to a single aqueous phase.

The displacement of brine process can be shown by the gas saturation profile at different times, which presents an outstanding characteristic with presence of sharp moving fronts, as shown in Fig. 2(b2). The dry-out zone (a zone where all the liquid phase has been removed by the evaporation of dry supercritical CO_2) and the two-phase zone increase with time. The values of gas saturation increase at a fixed radial distance with time, which indicates the upward flow of gas phase. The zone of solid saturation in Fig. 2(b3) extends with the increase of distance for single gas phase. The solid saturation decreases with the increase of distance from the injection well because the liquid phase saturation decreases under the injection pressure gradient.

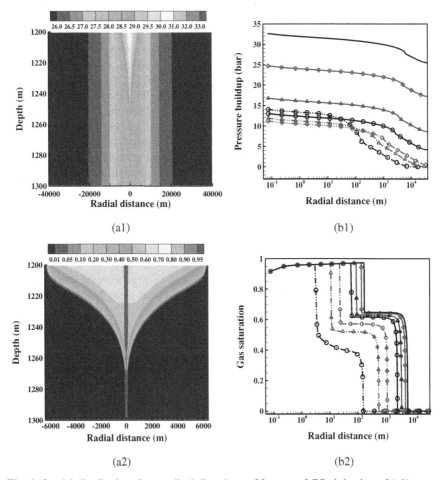

(a1)   (b1)

(a2)   (b2)

Fig. 2. Spatial distribution along radical direction at 30 years of CO_2 injection of (a1) pressure buildup, (a2) gas saturation and (a3) solid saturation (Note that the figures are shown in different coordinate length scales); profiles along the aquifer top at different injection times for (b1) pressure buildup, (b2) gas saturation and (b3) solid saturation (Note that the figures are shown on logarithmic length scales).

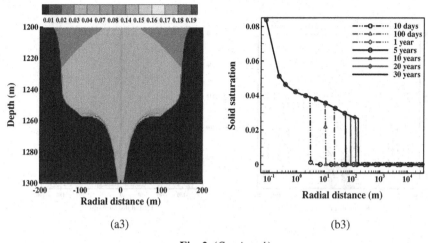

(a3)   (b3)

Fig. 2. (*Continued.*)

The formation of the localized solid saturation is a dynamical process, which needs to satisfy three conditions. The first condition is the existence of a single dry gas phase, which can quickly evaporate the water in brine. The second condition is that the formation location of the localized precipitation is relatively fixed under the effects of forces. Under this condition, the salt from the vicinal brine can accumulate continuously until the zone is clogged (i.e., the permeability is zero). Due to the density difference between the supercritical CO_2 and the brine, the bottom CO_2 will rise and the sharp of CO_2 plume will be a funnel. At the same time, injection pressure gradient and capillary pressure gradient will contribute to the movement of CO_2 and brine. As a result, high solid salt precipitation takes place near the wellbore. And the precipitation is advanced with the movement of gas phase. The last condition is the continuous backflow of brine due to the capillary pressure, as shown in Fig. 3. When the counter-flowing brine encounters the dry CO_2 in the gas phase zone, the precipitation will form quickly and accumulate on the front. Meanwhile, the reduction of permeability impedes the brine flowing into the well and promotes the upward flow of gas phase.

Fig. 4(a) shows the temporal evolution of gas phase saturation, the salinity of the brine and the solid saturation, to illustrate the process of the non-localized precipitation, which clearly indicates the three different periods for the non-localized precipitation near the wellbore. The three periods are the incubation of solid saturation period, the increasing solid saturation period due to the evaporation of gas phase and the solid saturation with a constant value, respectively. During the first period, the NaCl mass fraction decreases due to the volume increase of the aqueous phase upon CO_2 dissolution. As the gas phase saturation increases, the brine becomes

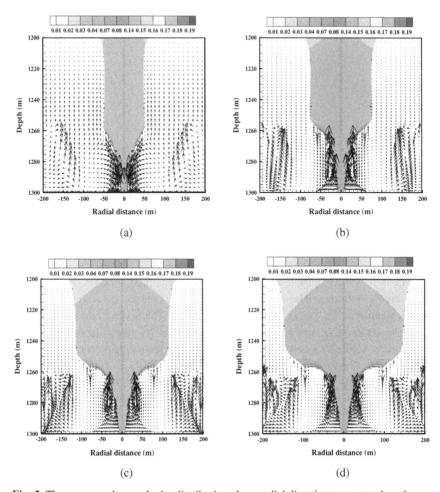

Fig. 3. The aqueous phase velocity distribution along radial direction superposed on the contour maps of solid saturation at (a) 5 years, (b) 10 years, (c) 20 years and (d) 30 years. Note that the figures only focus on near injection well region.

salt-saturated and solid salt start to precipitate in the second period. Because the brine is saturated, the salt can be quickly precipitated, and the brine is displaced by CO_2, corresponding to the quick increase of gas and solid saturations and the fast decrease of salinity. During the third period, the values of gas and solid saturation are constant.

Fig. 4(b) shows the time evolution of gas phase saturation, the salinity of the brine and the solid phase saturation, indicating five different periods for the localized precipitation near the dry out zone. Unlike the process of non-localized precipitation, there are five periods for the localized precipitation, i.e. the incubation of solid saturation period, the increasing solid saturation period due to the evaporation of gas phase, the solid saturation with a lower constant value for the evaporation, the

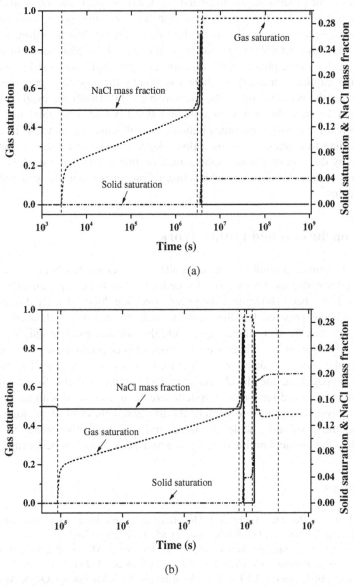

(a)

(b)

Fig. 4. The time evolution of gas phase saturation, solid salt saturation and NaCl mass fraction in (a) the non-localized precipitation region (b) the localized precipitation region

increasing solid saturation for the capillary pressure and the solid saturation with a higher constant value for the capillary pressure, respectively. The first three periods are similar to the process of non-localized precipitation, while the duration of the third period is different. For the localized precipitation, the time for precipitation with a lower constant value is short due to the backflow of brine. The backflow of fluid will increase the solid saturation and decrease the gas phase saturation. In the fourth period, there are three phases in the domain (i.e., gas, liquid and solid phase). At this period, the capillary pressure gradient overcomes the injection pressure gradient, which drives the brine to supply the precipitable solid. Under the evaporation of gas phase from the well, the evaporation/precipitation front becomes thick and extended. In the core of the localized precipitation zone, the maximum value is near 0.20, corresponding to a near-zero permeability. Hence the aqueous phase is trapped in it, indicated by the sum of gas and solid saturation that is less than one. Once the solid saturation reaches to 0.20, the composition of phases are not changed and the fifth period begins.

4   Conclusions and Future Work

Numerical simulation combined with parallel computation has been carried out in a saline aquifer with closed boundaries for understanding the complicated CO_2 injection problems. It has been shown that the gravity override due to density difference leads to the nonlinear pressure buildup near the well, the region of elevated pressure is much larger than the CO_2 plume size, while the salt precipitation only occurs in the zone of single gas phase. There are two types of precipitation formed near the well leading to the injectivity deterioration and the transportation decline. The evolution of pressure propagation, the development of CO_2 plume and the formation of solid saturation in open and semi-closed systems are being compared with the results from the closed system. In order to capture the dynamic behaviors of geological CO_2 in saline aquifers, sub-grid scale dynamics may be modelled using an upscaling approach of the physical problem on a given time scale, which is being carried out.

References

1. Jiang, X.: A Review of Physical Modelling and Numerical Simulation of Long-term Geological Storage of CO_2. Applied Energy 88, 3557–3566 (2011)
2. Bachu, S.: CO_2 Storage in Geological Media: Role, Means, Status and Barriers to Deployment. Progress in Energy & Combustion Science 34, 254–273 (2008)
3. Zhou, Q., Birkholzer, J.T., Tsang, C.-F., Rutqvist, J.: A Method for Quick Assessment of CO_2 Storage Capacity in Closed and Semi-closed Saline Formations. International Journal of Greenhouse Gas Control 2, 626–639 (2008)
4. Mathias, S., González Martínez de Miguel, G., Thatcher, K.: Pressure Buildup during CO_2 Injection into a Closed Brine Aquifer. Transport in Porous Media 89, 383–397 (2011)
5. Pruess, K., Müller, N.: Formation Dry-out from CO_2 Injection into Saline Aquifers: 1. Effects of Solids Precipitation and Their Mitigation. Water Resources Research 45, W03402 (2008)

6. Zhang, K., Moridis, G., Pruess, K.: TOUGH+CO2: A Multiphase Fluid-flow Simulator for CO$_2$ Geologic Sequestration in Saline Aquifers. Computers & Geosciences 37, 714–723 (2011)
7. Helmig, R.: Multiphase Flow and Transport Processes in the Subsurface: A Contribution to the Modeling of Hydrosystems, pp. 85–91. Springer, Berlin (1997)
8. Jacob, B.: Dynamics of Fluids in Porous Media, pp. 119–125. McGraw-Hill, New York (1972)
9. Van Genuchten, M.T.: A Closed-Form Equation for Predicting the Hydraulic Conductivity of Unsaturated Soils. Soil Science Society of America Journal 44, 892–898 (1980)
10. Verma, A., Pruess, K.: Thermohydrological Conditions and Silica Redistribution near High-level Nuclear Wastes Emplaced in Saturated Geological Formations. Journal of Geophysical Research: Solid Earth 93(B2), 1159–1173 (1988)
11. Kim, K.Y., Han, W.S., Oh, J., Kim, T., Kim, J.C.: Characteristics of Salt-Precipitation and the Associated Pressure Build-Up during CO$_2$ Storage in Saline Aquifers. Transport in Porous Media 92, 397–418 (2012)
12. Alkan, H., Cinar, Y., Ülker, E.B.: Impact of Capillary Pressure, Salinity and In situ Conditions on CO$_2$ Injection into Saline Aquifers. Transport in Porous Media 84, 799–819 (2010)
13. Karypsis, G., Kumar, V.: METIS. A Software Package for Partitioning Unstructured Graphs, Partitioning Meshes, and Computing Fill-Reducing Orderings of Sparse Matrices, V4.0. Technical Report, Department of Computer Science, University of Minnesota (1998)
14. Okwen, R.T., Stewart, M.T., Cunningham, J.A.: Temporal Variations in Near-wellbore Pressures during CO$_2$ Injection in Saline Aquifers. International Journal of Greenhouse Gas Control 5, 1140–1148 (2011)

Numerical Simulation of the Effects of N_2 on the Solubility Trapping Mechanism of CO_2

Didi Li[1], Xi Jiang[2], Qingliang Meng[1], and Xiaoqin Zhong[1]

[1] Department of Safety Science Engineering & State Key Laboratory of Fire Science,
University of Science and Technology of China, Hefei, Anhui 230026, China
[2] Engineering Department, Lancaster University, Lancaster LA1 4YR, United Kingdom
{lididi,qlmeng,zhongxq}@mail.ustc.edu.cn,
xijiang@ustc.edu.cn

Abstract. Parallel computations are carried out to investigate the effects of impurity on geological storage of carbon dioxide. The CO_2 streams captured contain a variety of impurities. It is indicated that impurities in the CO_2 streams have an effect on all types of geological storage mechanisms. Dissolution trapping occurs when injected CO_2 transported by molecular diffusion dissolves into the formation water. The density of the formation water would increase in response to dissolution of CO_2 and cause an instability. In the long term, the downward convection would be triggered and may greatly accelerate dissolution rate of carbon dioxide. This dissolution-diffusion-convection process could increase storage security and permanence. However, nitrogen would lead to a density reduction of the aqueous phase when dissolved in the formation water. The onset of convection would be delayed and the dissolution rate may be affected when co-injecting CO_2 with N_2.

Keywords: CO_2 Storage, Impurity, Convection, Numerical Simulation.

Nomenclature

D	diffusivity of gas in aqueous phase (m^2/s)
$\mathbf{g}$	vector of gravitational acceleration (m/s^2)
k	absolute permeability of the formation (m^2)
K	equilibrium constant
K_H	Henry's constant
M	molecular weight
V_n	mesh volume (m^3)
V_i	partial molar volume of dissolved gas (m^3/mol)
P	pressure (MPa)
$\mathbf{q}$	Darcy flux (m/s)
t	time (s)
T	temperature (K)
x	component mole fraction in aqueous phase
y	component mole fraction in non-aqueous phase
z	component mole fraction in the total system (assumed to be known)

K. Li et al. (Eds.): ParCFD 2013, CCIS 405, pp. 78–88, 2014.
© Springer-Verlag Berlin Heidelberg 2014

Greek symbols	
β	mole fraction of non-aqueous phase in the system
ϕ	porosity
φ	fugacity coefficient
ρ	density (kg/m^3)
μ	dynamic viscosity (Pa·s)
Subscripts	
aq	aqueous phase
i	component index
n	grid element index
w	water

1   Introduction

Carbon dioxide (CO_2) capture and storage (CCS) in geologic formation has been considered as an important option to effectively reduce anthropogenic emissions of CO_2 into the atmosphere [1-3]. The CO_2 streams captured contain a variety of impurities, such as N_2, O_2, Ar, SO_x, NO_x, H_2S, H_2, etc. Purity requirement of the CO_2 streams would greatly increase the cost of capture, which is one of the current challenges to large-scale CCS deployment. Impure CO_2 geological storage might be a cost-effective way to cut down the total cost of CCS by dramatically lowering the requirement of CO_2 capture [4]. Furthermore, one of the important barriers to large-scale CO_2 injection projects is forming regulations or guidelines that specify the required purity of the injection streams [5]. Consequently, the possibility of co-injecting CO_2 with other gaseous compounds, the so-called impurities, is currently considered for economic reasons [6] and regulation reasons.

There are concerns over negative effects of impurities on all types of geological storage mechanisms. Solubility trapping occurs when injected CO_2 transported by molecular diffusion dissolves into the aqueous phase. Dissolution of CO_2 would increase the density of the aqueous phase at the interface of the layers by 0.1–1%, depending on salinity of the brine [7]. The density increase is gravitationally unstable, and can give rise to downward convection of CO_2-rich brine from the phase boundary. When the small perturbations grow, a pattern of the saturation (for immiscible displacement) or concentration (miscible displacement) that looks like fingers would form, and the phenomena are therefore called fingering [8]. Such buoyant convection may greatly accelerate the rate at which CO_2 is dissolved and removed from the interface [8-11]. Dissolution into the aqueous phase and eventual sequestration as carbonates are highly desirable processes as they would increase permanence and security of geological storage [12-14]. Because of its practical importance for CO_2 storage, the process of dissolution-diffusion-convection (DDC) has been studied by many investigators. Both short-term and long-term behaviors of the process have been considered by several numerical simulations [15-17].

Dissolution of CO_2 could give rise to a density increase, leading to the convection mixing. When CO_2 is co-injected with other gases, the onset time for convection, the dissolution rate of CO_2 and other indicators of the behaviors of solubility trapping would be different from injecting pure CO_2. However, few studies have focused on the impact of the impurities on the DDC process. H_2S is shown to decrease the aqueous phase density [10], but there are few papers focusing on the effects of N_2, which always occupies a large proportion of the impurities [11] and is different with CO_2 chemically and physically. In this study, parallel computations are carried out to investigate the effects of N_2 on the solubility trapping mechanism of CO_2 to obtain a better understanding of geological storage of CO_2.

2   Modelling Approach

2.1   Problem Setup

Fig. 1 is a simple sketch of the problem investigated. At typical subsurface temperature and pressure conditions of geologic storage, CO_2 and N_2 injected are less dense than the aqueous phase in situ and tend to rise to the top of the permeable formation due to buoyancy and accumulate beneath the impermeable caprock [3]. An interface would form between the CO_2-rich phase above and formation water below. It is assumed that the interface is rather flat for simplicity, as shown in Fig. 1 (a).

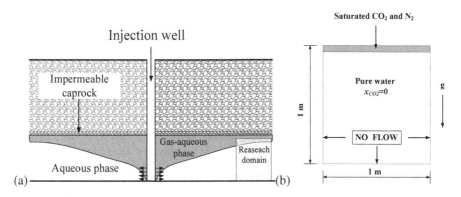

Fig. 1. Sketch of the problem, (a) schematic of the solubility trapping model and (b) applied boundary conditions

A vertical cross section beneath the two (gas-aqueous) phase zone is selected as the computational domain, and the size of the domain is 1 meter high and 1 meter wide. The fluid properties, typical at the depth of 1000m, as specified in Table 1, correspond to pure water (no salinity) at conditions of temperature $T = 318.15K$ and pressure $P = 10MPa$.

Since the two phase interface is in contact with the overlying gas phase, the top boundary is assumed to be saturated with dissolved CO_2 and N_2. The saturated concentrations of CO_2 and N_2 at the top boundary are supposed to be related to the compositions of CO_2 and N_2 in the injection phase (feed gas).

Table 1. Fluid properties

Property	value
Salinity	0
Pure water density	994.56 kg/m^3
Pure water viscosity	0.5947×10^{-3} Pa·s
CO_2 diffusivity	2×10^{-9} m^2/s
N_2 diffusivity	2×10^{-9} m^2/s

The partitioning of the gas species and H_2O among the aqueous and gas phase can be obtained by solving the Rachford-Rice equation

$$\sum_i \frac{z_i(K_i-1)}{1+\beta(K_i-1)} = 0 .$$

(1)

The equilibrium constant of H_2O is obtained from the approach of Spycher et al [18], while the equilibrium constants of CO_2 and N_2 are defined as follows

$$K_i = \frac{K_{H_i}}{P\phi_i} \quad i = CO_2, N_2 .$$

(2)

Henry's constant as a function of temperature and pressure could be obtained from the correlation established by Akinfiev and Diamond [19]. The fugacity coefficients of components are obtained from the volumetric properties given by the Peng-Robinson equation of state.

Once the Rachford-Rice equation has been solved for β, the compositions x_i and y_i can be subsequently calculated as:

$$x_i = \frac{z_i}{1+\beta(K_i-1)} \quad y_i = K_i x_i .$$

(3)

Four different compositions in the feed gas and corresponding dissolved gas compositions (saturated CO_2 and N_2 concentration at the top boundary) are shown in Table 2. The bottom, left and right boundary conditions are assumed to be no flow, i.e., no fluid flux flows across these three boundaries, as shown in Fig. 1 (b). A perturbation of 4% of the permeability of the formation is added to trigger the convection.

Table 2. Compositions of gases dissolved in water for various concentrations of CO_2 and N_2 in the feed gas composition

Heading level		Water-gas ratio	Dissolved gas composition	
CO_2 (%)	N_2 (%)		CO_2	N_2
100	0	12.82	2.031583×10^{-2}	0.0
98	2	12.75	1.985452×10^{-2}	3.587533×10^{-5}
95	5	12.65	1.923644×10^{-2}	7.643890×10^{-5}
90	10	12.50	1.824413×10^{-2}	1.321329×10^{-4}

2.2   Governing Equations

In this paper, temperature is assumed to be constant so that the energy conservation equation could be neglected. The mass conservation equations in the integral form are given by [2]

$$\frac{\partial}{\partial t}\int_{V_n}\phi\rho x_i\,dV_n + \int_{V_n}\nabla\cdot(\rho x_i\mathbf{q})\,dV_n = \int_{V_n}\nabla\cdot(\phi D\rho\nabla x_i)\,dV_n \quad i=1,3 \ . \tag{4}$$

There is no source/sink term in the model, so that the mass conservation equations are made of three terms, i.e., the accumulation term, the convective and diffusive term. $\mathbf{q}$ is given by Darcy's law [2, 7]:

$$\mathbf{q} = -\frac{k}{\mu}(\nabla P - \rho g) \ . \tag{5}$$

The system is closed by the equation of state

$$\sum_{i=1}^{3} x_i = 1 \ . \tag{6}$$

The aqueous phase density taking into account of dissolved CO_2 and N_2 is given by [20]

$$\frac{M_{aq}}{\rho_{aq}} = \frac{x_w M_w}{\rho_w} + \sum_{i=1}^{2} V_i x_i \ . \tag{7}$$

2.3   Numerical Method and Parallel Algorithm

The governing equations are a set of coupled nonlinear equations and could be solved by Newton-Raphson iteration. The mass conservation equations are discretized in space using an integral finite difference method by introducing appropriate volume averages. Time is discretized using an implicit finite difference scheme. In order to resolve concentration gradients, the sizes of vertical grid blocks near the top boundary are chosen to be rather small, specifically, smaller than the thickness of the diffusive boundary layer obtained by linear stability analysis [12]. Larger grid sizes are used in the regions far away from the diffusive boundary layer. Horizontal grid sizes are partitioned to be smaller than the critical wavelength [7]. A sufficiently small time step size is used to capture the onset time of convection and an automatic time step scheme is adopted to solve the problem effectively.

The computational domain is partitioned into several subdomains, the number being equal to that of given processor cores used in the parallel computations. In order to balance computational work, the number of grid blocks on each processor is roughly the same. Each processor is in charge of the linearized equations of its corresponding subdomain independently. The entire equation system is solved by all processors via communication between neighboring processors. Data between neighboring grid blocks assigned to different processors could be exchanged through communication between a pair of processors. The parallel algorithm makes it possible to solve the problems efficiently.

3   Results and Discussion

3.1 CO_2 Dissolution Rate and Inventory

The dissolution rate of CO_2 at the top boundary is an important indicator to describe the DDC process and could be represented by CO_2 mass flux flowing into the simulation domain [12]. The sensitivity of the CO_2 dissolution rate to N_2 mole fraction in the feed gas is explored. Fig. 2 and Fig. 3 show the CO_2 mass flux and inventory changes versus simulation time, respectively. In Fig. 2, at the early stage (for example, $0\sim1\times10^5$s for 100% CO_2), the dissolution rate declines with time as $1/t^{0.5}$, which suggests that the transport of CO_2 away from the top boundary occurs only by molecular diffusion. After that, the convection takes place, and the dissolution rate experiences an increase. As can be seen in Fig. 2, CO_2 mass flux decreases with increasing concentration of N_2. Furthermore, the onset time of convection increases with increased N_2 mole fraction. Consequently, the increase of N_2 concentration will lower the total inventory of dissolved CO_2 into the aqueous phase. For example, when N_2 mole fraction in the feed gas is 5% and 10%, the reduction of inventory at $t = 1.0\times10^7$s could be 7.4% and 13.2%, respectively, as shown in Fig. 3. It should be noted that in Fig. 3, after 6.15×10^6s, the inventory of pure CO_2 is exceeded by that of 98% CO_2. Since the difference of N_2 mole fractions in these two cases is rather small, the excess may be caused by the non-ideal phase behavior of multicomponent fluids and the chaotic nature of the convection process.

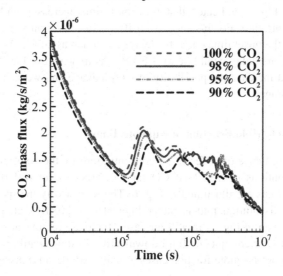

Fig. 2. Simulated CO_2 mass flux at the top boundary

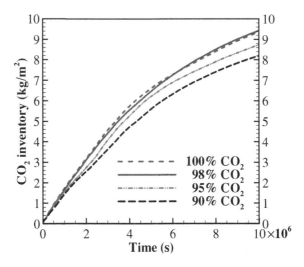

Fig. 3. Simulated total CO_2 inventory

3.2   Onset Time

The sensitivity of onset time for convection to the mole fraction of N_2 in the feed gas is examined. CO_2 mass flux provides a rather sensitive indicator for the onset time [12]. Moreover, it is suggested that the product of CO_2 mass flux and the total dissolved CO_2 inventory remains to be constant for purely diffusive process, which makes it very sensitive to the onset time of convection. Fig. 4 shows the results of the product for four cases and Fig. 5 illustrates the variation of onset time with different N_2 concentrations. Fig. 4 indicates that the onset time increases with increasing dissolved N_2 concentration. For instance, even if N_2 concentration is moderate, say, 5% in the feed gas, the onset time could be delayed as much as 14.8%. When N_2 mole fraction is doubled, the delay would be over 30.2%, as indicated in Fig. 5. The delay of onset time would increase the possibility of CO_2 leakage and weaken the security of CO_2 geologic storage.

3.3   Dissolved CO_2 Mole Fraction in Aqueous Phase

To investigate the influence of different N_2 concentrations on the convection process, snapshots of distributions of dissolved CO_2 at $t = 2.0 \times 10^5$s for different N_2 mole fractions in the feed gas are illustrated in Fig. 6. The reason why the specific time is chosen is that the dissolution rate is rather high at $t = 2.0 \times 10^5$s after convection happens, as can be seen in Fig. 2. In all four cases, there are regions at the top of the domain to deliver CO_2-rich aqueous fluid downward, but downward convection has advanced less in higher N_2 mole fraction cases as expected, because dissolution of N_2

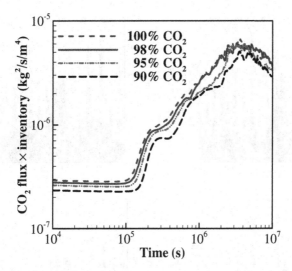

Fig. 4. CO_2 mass flux times total inventory

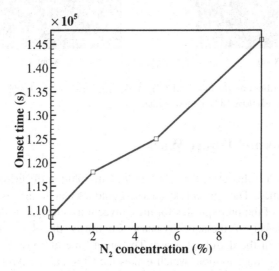

Fig. 5. Variation of onset time with different N_2 mole percentages in the initial feed gas

in the aqueous phase would suppress and delay convection. At about X = 0.45m, the patterns of the fingers in Fig. 6 (c) and (d) are different from the other two cases. According to linear stability analysis, the dimensional critical wavelength is inversely proportional to the density increase in the aqueous phase [21]. The higher the N_2 mole fraction, the smaller the density increase and the longer the critical wavelength. In that case, the number of the fingers would decrease with increasing N_2 mole fraction, as can be seen in Fig. 6. This indicates that, the changes of N_2 concentration do have an effect on the formation and growth of the fingering.

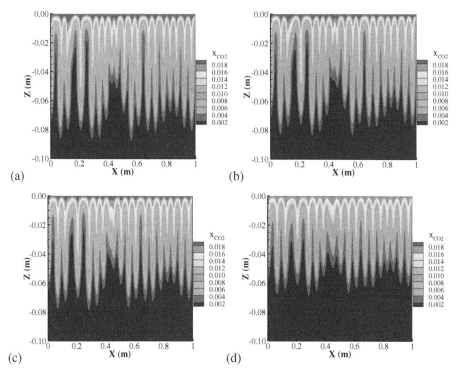

Fig. 6. Simulated distributions of dissolved CO_2 mole fractions for (a) 100% CO_2, (b) 98% CO_2, (c) 95% CO_2, and (d) 90% CO_2 in the feed gas

4   Conclusions and Future Work

Parallel simulations of the effects of N_2 on the dissolution-diffusion-convection process were performed. The convective activity could accelerate the dissolution rate of CO_2 greatly. One of the prerequisites for the convection to happen is that dissolved CO_2 increases the density of the aqueous phase. Contrarily, dissolution of N_2 would decrease the density of the dissolved phase. The onset time of convection would be larger with higher N_2 concentration, which makes the CO_2 leakage through fractures or faults more likely. The CO_2 dissolution rate per unit area of the reservoir decreases with increasing N_2 mole fraction in the feed gas and thus the total CO_2 inventory would be reduced. The impact of N_2 on the DDC process seems moderate, partially because N_2 has a much lower solubility than CO_2. In the future, the effects of other impurities, like SO_2 and H_2S, which are more soluble than CO_2, will be considered. Furthermore, parameters that may also play a part in the dissolution-diffusion-convection process like diffusivity will be investigated.

References

1. Metz, B., Davidson, O., de Coninck, H., Loos, M., Meyer, L.: IPCC Special Report on Carbon Dioxide Capture and Storage. Cambridge University Press, Cambridge (2005)
2. Jiang, X.: A Review of Physical Modelling and Numerical Simulation of Long-Term Geological Storage of CO_2. Appl. Energy. 88, 3557–3566 (2011)
3. Bachu, S.: CO_2 Storage in Geological Media: Role, Means, Status and Barriers to Deployment. Prog. Energy Combust. Sci. 34, 254–273 (2008)
4. Wei, N., Li, X.C.: Numerical Studies on the Aquifer Storage of CO_2 Containing N_2. In: 10th International Conference on Greenhouse Gas Control Technologies, vol. 4, pp. 4314–4322 (2011)
5. Ellis, B.R., Crandell, L.E., Peters, C.A.: Limitations for Brine Acidification due to SO_2 Co-injection in Geologic Carbon Sequestration. Int. J. Greenh. Gas Con. 4, 575–582 (2010)
6. Gaus, I., Audigane, P., Andre, L., Lions, J., Jacquemet, N., Durst, P., Czernichowski-Lauriol, I., Azaroual, M.: Geochemical and Solute Transport Modelling for CO_2 Storage, What to Expect from It? Int. J. Greenh. Gas Con. 2, 605–625 (2008)
7. Pau, G.S.H., Bell, J.B., Pruess, K., Almgren, A.S., Lijewski, M.J., Zhang, K.: High-Resolution Simulation and Characterization of Density-Driven Flow in CO_2 Storage in Saline Aquifers. Adv. Water Resour. 33, 443–455 (2010)
8. Elenius, M.: Convective Mixing in Geological Carbon Storage. PhD Thesis. Univ. of Bergen (2011)
9. Riaz, A., Hesse, M., Tchelepi, H.A., Orr, F.M.: Onset of Convection in a Gravitationally Unstable Diffusive Boundary Layer in Porous Media. J. Fluid Mech. 548, 87–111 (2006)
10. Ji, X., Zhu, C.: Predicting Possible Effects of H_2S Impurity on CO_2 Transportation and Geological Storage. Environ. Sci. Technol. 47, 55–62 (2013)
11. Ennis-King, J., Paterson, L.: Rate of Dissolution due to Convective Mixing in the Underground Storage of Carbon Dioxide. In: Greenhouse Gas Control Technologies, Kyoto, vol. 1, pp. 507–510 (2002)
12. Pruess, K., Zhang, K.: Numerical Modeling Studies of the Dissolution-Diffusion-Convection Process (2008)
13. Ennis-King, J., Preston, I., Paterson, L.: Onset of Convection in Anisotropic Porous Media Subject to a Rapid Change in Boundary Conditions. Phys. Fluids 17, 084107 (2005)
14. Farajzadeh, R., Salimi, H., Zitha, P.L.J., Bruining, H.: Numerical Simulation of Density-Driven Natural Convection in Porous Media with Application for CO_2 Injection Projects. Int. J. Heat Mass Tran. 50, 5054–5064 (2007)
15. Lindeberg, E., Bergmo, P.: The Long-Term Fate of CO_2 Injected into an Aquifer. SINTEF Petroleum Research, NO-7465 Trondheim, Norway (2003)
16. Lu, C., Lichtner, P.C.: High Resolution Numerical Investigation on the Effect of Convective Instability on Long Term CO_2 Storage in Saline Aquifers. Journal of Physics: Conference Series 78, 012042 (2007)
17. Farajzadeh, R., Ranganathan, P., Zitha, P.L.J., Bruining, J.: The Effect of Heterogeneity on the Character of Density-Driven Natural Convection of CO_2 Overlying a Brine Layer. Adv. Water Resour. 34, 327–339 (2011)

18. Spycher, N., Pruess, K., Ennis-King, J.: CO_2-H_2O Mixtures in the Geological Sequestration of CO_2. I. Assessment and Calculation of Mutual Solubilities from 12 to 100 °C and up to 600 Bar. Geoch. Cosmochim Ac. 67, 3015–3031 (2003)
19. Akinfiev, N.N., Diamond, L.W.: Thermodynamic Description of Aqueous Nonelectrolytes at Infinite Dilution over a Wide Range of State Parameters. Geoch. Cosmochim Ac. 67, 613–627 (2003)
20. Battistelli, A., Marcolini, M.: TMGAS: A New TOUGH2 EOS Module for the Numerical Simulation of Gas Mixtures Injection in Geological Structures. Int. J. Greenh. Gas Con. 3, 481–493 (2009)
21. Xu, X., Chen, S., Zhang, D.: Convective Stability Analysis of the Long-Term Storage of Carbon Dioxide in Deep Saline Aquifers. Adv. Water Resour. 29, 397–407 (2006)

Implementation of the Six Temperature Kinetic Model of Gasdynamic Laser in OpenFOAM

Gang He, Jin Zhou, and Lin Lai

Science and Technology on Scramjet Laboratory,
National University of Denfense Technology, 410073 Changsha, China
15116400360@139.com

Abstract. In order to calculate the vibrational non-equilibrium flows in gasdynamic laser nozzles, a six temperature kinetic model is implemented in the open source CFD toolbox OpenFOAM. A new solver using central-upwind scheme is developed to solve the 2-dimensional coupled equations. To validate the new solver, numerical analysis of small signal gain coefficient in two minimum-length contoured nozzles at corresponding condition is carried out. The results obtained are in satisfactory agreement with the published experimental data, showing the validation of the solver. Profiting from the excellent parallel performance of OpenFOAM, numerical results could be quickly obtained to predict and refine the performance of the gasdynamic laser devices.

Keywords: OpenFOAM, gasdynamic laser, non-equilibrium flow, central-upwind scheme, six temperature kinetic model.

1 Introduction

In a gasdynamic laser (GDL) nozzle, a mixture of high pressure, hot gases (such as CO_2, N_2 and H_2O) is accelerated to hypersonic speed rapidly to create a population inversion, thus the gases mixture turns into a laser medium. The flows in the nozzle are vibrational non-equilibrium, in which complex processes of energy exchange occur between the translational and vibrational (T-V) modes, as well as between the vibrational and vibrational (V-V) modes. Small signal gain (SSG) is an important figure of merit for GDL, and it is also a direct measurement of the population inversion. The higher the SSG is, the easier laser action can be obtained in the gases mixture [1]. Simulating the non-equilibrium flows and calculating SSG is a good way to evaluate the performance of GDL nozzles and investigate the energy exchange processes in the nozzle.

1.1 Background of Simulation

A useful alternative time-dependent technique which solves the unsteady, quasi-one-dimensional conservation equations of the vibrational non-equilibrium flows in steps of time was presented by Anderson [2]. The steady-state solution approaches at large

K. Li et al. (Eds.): ParCFD 2013, CCIS 405, pp. 89–99, 2014.

time steps. In this form, the equations are hyperbolic for all flow conditions and no stability difficulties are experienced around the nozzle throat [3]. As development in CFD (computational fluid dynamics) field, the vibrational non-equilibrium flows can be calculated using the method mentioned above by developing CFD program, therefore two or three dimensional calculation could be carried out and more details of flow fields can be obtained. Because of the large time steps for unsteady simulation and large scale of grid points, the parallel method of CFD should be taken into account.

OpenFOAM is a good choice for developing program to solve the vibrational non-equilibrium flows. It is an open source CFD toolbox written in C++ language, using object oriented programming. The method of parallel computing used by OpenFOAM is known as domain decomposition, and the parallel running uses the public domain openMPI implementation of the standard message passing interface (MPI) [4]. There have been much R&D (research and development) done based on OpenFOAM [5-8], just as what this work does.

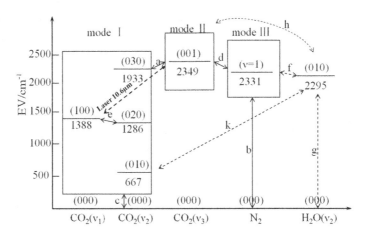

Fig. 1. Vibrational energy-level diagram for CO_2-N_2-H_2O system

1.2   Kinetic Model

Because of the limited knowledge of the complex energy exchange processes in the GDL nozzles, a reasonable kinetic model which takes into account main features of them is necessary. There have been several kinetic models reported and applied to predict the performance of GDL system [9], such as two-vibration-three-temperature model, three-vibration-three-temperature model proposed by Anderson [1], and three-vibration-four-temperature model proposed by Yan Haixing [10]. The two-vibration-three-temperature model has been used generally for it is simpler than other models, with the most important energy exchange processes considered, while the three-vibration-four-temperature model is more complex and can include more important kinetic processes. The numerical results obtained by them don't agree well with the experiment data [10]. One common characteristic of them is that vibrational modes of H_2O molecule and the vibrational-vibrational energy exchange processes between this mode and others are neglected, while the six temperature kinetic model is not, see Fig 1. This model was used to predict the performance of a high power fast axial-flow CO_2 laser successfully [11]. This work discusses the implementation of the six temperature kinetic model in OpenFOAM to calculate the vibrational non-equilibrium flows in gasdynamic laser nozzles.

2   Governing Equations

The unsteady conservation equations for vibrational non-equilibrium flows are as following:

Continuity equation

$$\partial \rho / \partial t + \nabla \cdot (\rho U) = 0 \ . \tag{1}$$

Momentum equation

$$\partial (\rho U) / \partial t + \nabla \cdot (\rho U U) = -\nabla P \ . \tag{2}$$

Energy equation

$$\partial [\rho (e + \frac{1}{2} U^2)] \Big/ \partial t + \nabla \cdot [(\rho (e + \frac{1}{2} U^2) + P)U] = 0 \tag{3}$$

State equation

$$P = \rho R T \ . \tag{4}$$

Vibrational energy transport equations

$$\partial (\rho e_{vib2}) / \partial t + \nabla \cdot (\rho e_{vib2} U) = \rho * S_{vib2} \ . \tag{5}$$

$$\partial (\rho e_{vib3}) / \partial t + \nabla \cdot (\rho e_{vib3} U) = \rho * S_{vib3} \ . \tag{6}$$

$$\partial (\rho e_{vibN}) / \partial t + \nabla \cdot (\rho e_{vibN} U) = \rho * S_{vibN} \ . \tag{7}$$

$$\partial (\rho e_{vibH2}) / \partial t + \nabla \cdot (\rho e_{vibH2} U) = \rho * S_{vibH2} \ . \tag{8}$$

Where ρ is the flow density, U is the velocity vector, P is the pressure, e is the internal energy of the gases mixture, T is the gas kinetic temperature. e_{vib2} and e_{vib3} are the vibrational energies of v_2 and v_3 mode of CO_2 molecule, e_{vibN} is the vibratioanl energy of N_2 molecule, and e_{vibH2} is the vibrational energy of the v_2 mode of H_2O molecule. S_{vib2}, S_{vib3}, S_{vibN} and S_{vibH2} are the source terms of the above modes respectively, which describe the complex energy exchange processes between vibrational energy levels:

$$S_{vib2} = 2X_{CO_2}R_{co_2}\theta_2\{[\sum_M \psi_M Z_{CM} P_{CM}^{v_2:1\to0}][e^{-\frac{\theta_2}{T}}(1+\hat{e}_2)-\hat{e}_2]$$

$$-\frac{3}{2}[\sum_M \psi_M Z_{CM} P_{CM}^{v_3:1\to0,v_2:0\to3}]\cdot[e^{-\frac{\theta_3-3\theta_2}{T}}(1+\hat{e}_3)(\hat{e}_2)^3-(\hat{e}_3)(1+\hat{e}_2)^3] \tag{9}$$

$$+\frac{1}{2}[\psi_{H_2O}Z_{CH}P_{CH}^{v_2:1\to0,v_{H2}:0\to1}]\cdot[e^{-\frac{\theta_2-\theta_{H2}}{T}}(1+\hat{e}_2)(\hat{e}_{H2})-(\hat{e}_2)(1+\hat{e}_{H2})]\}$$

$$S_{vib3} = X_{CO_2}R_{co_2}\theta_3\{[\sum_M \psi_M Z_{CM} P_{CM}^{v_3:1\to0,v_2:0\to3}][e^{-\frac{\theta_3-3\theta_2}{T}}(1+\hat{e}_3)(\hat{e}_2)^3-(\hat{e}_3)(1+\hat{e}_2)^3]$$

$$+[\psi_{N_2}Z_{CN}P_{CN}^{v_3:1\to0,v_N:0\to1}][e^{-\frac{\theta_3-\theta_N}{T}}(1+\hat{e}_3)(\hat{e}_N)-(\hat{e}_3)(1+\hat{e}_N)] \tag{10}$$

$$+[\psi_{H_2O}Z_{CH}P_{CH}^{v_3:1\to0,v_{H2}:0\to1}][e^{-\frac{\theta_3-\theta_{H2}}{T}}(1+\hat{e}_3)(\hat{e}_{H2})-(\hat{e}_3)(1+\hat{e}_{H2})]\}$$

$$S_{vibN} = X_{N_2}R_{N_2}\theta_N\{[\sum_M \psi_M Z_{NM} P_{NM}^{v_N:1\to0}][e^{-\frac{\theta_N}{T}}(1+\hat{e}_N)-\hat{e}_N]$$

$$-[\psi_{CO_2}Z_{CN}P_{CN}^{v_3:1\to0,v_N:0\to1}][e^{-\frac{\theta_3-\theta_N}{T}}(1+\hat{e}_3)(\hat{e}_N)-(\hat{e}_3)(1+\hat{e}_N)] \tag{11}$$

$$+[\psi_{H_2O}Z_{NH}P_{NH}^{v_N:1\to0,v_{H2}:0\to1}][e^{-\frac{\theta_N-\theta_{H2}}{T}}(1+\hat{e}_N)(\hat{e}_{H2})-(\hat{e}_N)(1+\hat{e}_{H2})]\}$$

$$S_{vibH2} = X_{H_2O}R_{H_2O}\theta_{H2}\{[\sum_M \psi_M Z_{NM} P_{NM}^{v_{H2}:1\to0}][e^{-\frac{\theta_{H2}}{T}}(1+\hat{e}_{H2})-\hat{e}_{H2}]$$

$$-[\psi_{N_2}Z_{HN}P_{HN}^{v_N:1\to0,v_H:0\to1}][e^{-\frac{\theta_N-\theta_{H2}}{T}}(1+\hat{e}_N)(\hat{e}_{H2})-(\hat{e}_N)(1+\hat{e}_{H2})]$$

$$-[\psi_{CO_2}Z_{CH}P_{CH}^{v_3:1\to0,v_{H2}:0\to1}][e^{-\frac{\theta_3-\theta_{H2}}{T}}(1+\hat{e}_3)(\hat{e}_{H2})-(\hat{e}_3)(1+\hat{e}_{H2})] \tag{12}$$

$$-[\psi_{CO_2}Z_{CH}P_{CH}^{v_2:1\to0,v_{H2}:0\to1}][e^{-\frac{\theta_2-\theta_{H2}}{T}}(1+\hat{e}_2)(\hat{e}_{H2})-(\hat{e}_2)(1+\hat{e}_{H2})]\}$$

Where X_{N2}, X_{CO2}, X_{H2O} are the mass fractions of species, and ψ_{N2}, ψ_{CO2}, ψ_{H2O} are the molar fractions. θ_2, θ_3, θ_N, θ_{H2} are the characteristic temperature of the vibration modes.

$$ZP = 1/\tau \tag{13}$$

τ is the relaxation time which characterize the rate of energy exchanges between the vibration modes. The parameters used to calculate τ are taken from reference [11] [12].

The relationship between e_{vib}, $\hat{e}$, and T_{vib} can be described as:

$$e_{vibi} = g_i X_M R_M \hat{e}_i = \frac{g_i X_M R_M}{e^{\frac{\theta_i}{T_{vibi}}} - 1} \tag{14}$$

When the steady-state solution reaches, SSG could be calculated by the translational and vibrational parameters:

$$SSG = \frac{\lambda^2}{8\pi\tau_{21}} g_v \cdot \Delta N \tag{15}$$

g_v is the Voigt function which takes both Doppler-broaden and collision-broaden transition into consideration [13]:

$$g_v = \begin{cases} \dfrac{1}{\Delta v_D/2}\sqrt{\dfrac{\ln 2}{\pi}}*(1+\displaystyle\sum_{i=1}^{6}a_i y^i)^{-16} & (y \le 2.4) \\[3mm] \dfrac{1}{\pi\Delta v_p/2}[1-(2y^2)^{-1}+3*(2y^2)^{-2}-15*(2y^2)^{-3}+105*(2y^2)^{-4}] & (y>2.4) \end{cases} \tag{16}$$

$$y = \frac{\Delta v_p/2}{\Delta v_D/2}(\ln 2)^{1/2} \tag{17}$$

$$\Delta v_p = 4.184(\sigma_{CO_2}\times10^{14})p(\frac{300}{T})^{0.5} \times$$
$$(\psi_{CO_2}+1.134\frac{\sigma_{N_2}}{\sigma_{CO_2}}\psi_{N_2}+1.312\frac{\sigma_{H_2O}}{\sigma_{CO_2}}\psi_{H_2O})\times10^9 \tag{18}$$

$$\Delta v_D = \frac{2v_0}{c}\sqrt{\frac{2RT\ln 2}{\mu}} \tag{19}$$

Where Δv_p is the Collision-broadened laser transition, and Δv_D is the Doppler-broadened laser transition, σ is the collision cross section of the molecules.

ΔN is calculated as following [10]:

$$\Delta N = (0.992045 N_3 e^{24.12} - N_1) \frac{43.735}{T} e^{-235.5/T} \qquad (20)$$

where N_3 and N_1 are the number density of CO_2 molecules in the υ_3 and υ_1 vibration modes respectively.

3   The GasdynamicFoam Solver

GasdynamicFoam is a newly developed solver to solve the vibrational non-equilibrium flows using OpenFOAM. The new solver is based on the standard solver rhoCentralFoam provided by OpenFOAM, which is a density-based compressible flow solver based on central-upwind scheme of Kurganov and Tadmor [14].

GasdynamicFoam uses the same framework of rhoCentralFoam, but only Eq. (1-4) are solved in it, so when developing the vibrational non-equilibrium flow solver, there is a need to add Eq. (5-8) to GasdynamicFoam. In order to solve the non-equilibrium flow in OpenFOAM, transformation must be made to the energy equation, as described bellow:

$$e = e' + e_{vib1} + e_{vib2} + e_{vib3} + e_{vibN} + e_{vibH1} + e_{vibH2} + e_{vibH3} \qquad (21)$$

$$e' = (\frac{5}{2} X_{CO_2} R_{CO_2} + \frac{5}{2} X_{N_2} R_{N_2} + 3 X_{H_2O} R_{H_2O}) * T \qquad (22)$$

Combining Eq. 3 and Eq. 21,

$$\frac{\partial[\rho(e' + \frac{1}{2}U^2)]}{\partial t} + \nabla \cdot [(\rho(e' + \frac{1}{2}U^2) + P)\bar{U}] = -\sum_{i=1}^{3}[\partial(\rho e_{vibi})/\partial t + \nabla \cdot (\rho e_{vibi}\bar{U})]$$
$$-[\partial(\rho e_{vibN})/\partial t + \nabla \cdot (\rho e_{vibN}\bar{U})] - \sum_{i=1}^{3}[\partial(\rho e_{vibHi})/\partial t + \nabla \cdot (\rho e_{vibHi}\bar{U})] \qquad (23)$$

It is assumed that the v_1 and v_3 vibration modes of H_2O molecules are in equilibrium with translation and rotation. And according to the six temperature kinetic model, the v_1 and v_2 vibration modes of CO_2 molecules are in equilibrium. Thus,

$$S_{vib1} = \alpha * S_{vib2} \qquad (24)$$

$$\alpha = \frac{\theta_1}{\theta_2} * \frac{e^{\frac{2\theta_2 - \theta_1}{T}} * e_2(e_2 + 1)}{[(1 - e^{\frac{2\theta_2 - \theta_1}{T}}) * e_2^2 + 2e_2 + 1]^2} \quad (25)$$

Combining Eq. 23, Eq. (5-8), and Eq. 24,

$$\frac{\partial[\rho(e' + \frac{1}{2}U^2)]}{\partial t} + \nabla \cdot [(\rho(e' + \frac{1}{2}U^2) + P)\bar{U}]$$

$$= -\rho * [(1 + \alpha) * S_{vib2} + S_{vib3} + S_{vibN} + S_{vibH2}] \quad (26)$$

$$-[\frac{\partial[\rho(e_{vibH1} + e_{vibH3})]}{\partial t} + \nabla \cdot [\rho(e_{vibH1} + e_{vibH3})\bar{U}]$$

Eq. 26 is the form of energy equation calculated in the GasdynamicFoam solver. Therefore we could express this equation in the OpenFOAM program:

```
solve
(
        fvm::ddt(rhoE)+ fvc::div(phiEp)
        ==
        - ((1.0+alpha)*SourceC2+SourceC3+SourceN+SourceH2)
        - (fvc::ddt(rhoevibH1)+fvc::div(phievibH1))
        - (fvc::ddt(rhoevibH3)+fvc::div(phievibH3))
);
```

In the code, E is the visual total energy. According to the assumption mentioned above, e_{vibH1} and e_{vibH3} are calculated using gas kinetic temperature and the transport equations of them are treated as source terms.

e' in Eq. 26 is regarded as the visual internal energy in the OpenFOAM program, According to the definition of it (in Eq. 22), we could set the specific heat at const volume (Cv) of the gases mixture as:

$$C_v = \frac{5}{2}X_{CO_2}R_{CO_2} + \frac{5}{2}X_{N_2}R_{N_2} + 3X_{H_2O}R_{H_2O} \quad (26)$$

Because the vibration energy is only a tiny percentage of total energy, the non-equilibrium source terms would not affect the flow field much. Therefore we treat these source terms explicitly.

The central-upwind scheme is implemented to the convection terms of Vibrational energy transport equations as well. Just as the standard solvers of OpenFOAM, this solver uses the domain decomposition method and openMPI implementation of standard message passing interface (MPI) for parallel running as well. We have used the version 2.1.1 of OpenFOAM to develop the new solver.

4   Numerical Model

To examine the new solver, we simulate the vibrational non-equilibrium flows in two minimum-length contoured nozzles. The area ratios of the two minimum-length contoured nozzles are 20 and 50, with throat height 1 mm and 0.356mm respectively. The nozzles are assumed to be two-dimensional and inviscid. The computational domain is discretized to 100×700 quadrilateral grid.

Since the nozzles are symmetrical, we only calculate half of the nozzle divided by the center line. The boundary type (defined in [4]) of the nozzle boundaries are shown in the following table:

Table 1. The boundary type of the boundaries

Boundary type	P	T	U	$e_{vibi}(i=2, 3, N, H_2)$
Inlet	total pressure	total temperature	zeroGradient	fixedValue
wall	zeroGradient	zeroGradient	zeroGradient	zeroGradient
outlet	zeroGradient	zeroGradient	zeroGradient	zeroGradient
symmetry	symmetryPlane	symmetryPlane	symmetryPlane	symmetryPlane

5   Results and Discussion

5.1   SSG Field

Fig 2 shows the SSG field simulated in the two nozzles at corresponding condition as an example. The two figures show that, SSG rises quickly with rapid expansion of the nozzles, indicating that population inversion is established by complex energy exchange processes. It is clearly seen from the figures that, SSG is not so even at y direction of the nozzles, indicating that the assumption of the quasi-one-dimensional flows is limited and can only be used to analysis the performance of the nozzles qualitatively. Two-dimensional calculation can provide more information to investigate the kinetic processes and refine the performance of the GDL nozzles.

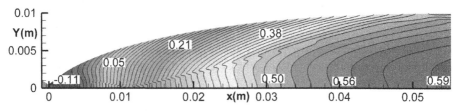

(a)   Area ratio 20, total temperature 1800 K, total pressure 20 atm, molar fraction of H_2O vapor 0.01

Fig. 2. SSG field simulated by GasdynamicFoam

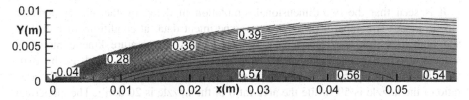

(b) Area ratio 50, total temperature 1800 K, total pressure 37.5 atm, molar fraction of H_2O vapor 0.1

Fig. 2. (*Continued.*)

5.2   Validation of the GasdynamicFoam Solver

To validate the GasdynamicFoam solver, comparison is made between the two-dimensional calculation carried out by GasdynamicFoam and the experiment results [15] at location 12.7 mm downstream of the nozzle exit, see Fig 3.

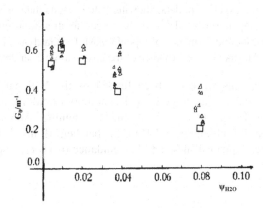

(a) Area ratio 20, total temperature 1800 K, total pressure 20 atm,   Δ experiment results

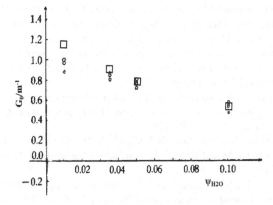

(b) Area ratio 50, total temperature 1800 K, total pressure 37.5 atm,   ○ experiment results

Fig. 3. Comparison between the simulation and the experiment results, □ numerical results

It is seen that the two-dimensional simulation modeled by the six temperature kinetic model is comparative against the experiment data, at conditions of both low and high area ratio nozzles, indicating that the six temperature kinetic model is successfully implemented in OpenFOAM. But numerical results modeled by two-vibration-three-temperature model agree well with the experiment data when the area ratio of the nozzle is 50, while the area ratio of the nozzle is 20 don't. The numerical results modeled by three-vibration-four-temperature model are just opposite to the two-vibration-three-temperature model. Thus we think the six temperature kinetic model is more suitable for GDL than the other two.

6   Conclusion

The six temperature kinetic model is implemented successfully in OpenFOAM through the newly developed solver GasdynamicFoam. The model is used to model the complex energy exchange processes in GDL nozzles. Numerical results of GasdynamicFoam are comparative against the experiment data, showing better results than ones modeled by the two-vibration-three-temperature model and the three-vibration-four-temperature model. Profiting from the parallel performance of OpenFOAM, the GasdynamicFoam solver can be used to predict and refine the performance of the gasdynamic laser devices efficiently.

Acknowledgements. This work has been funded by the National Natural Science Foundation of China under grant 11202234. The authors would like to thank Ms Zhao Juan, staff of the Research Center of Supercomputing Application, National University of Defense Technology (NUDT), for her help to install the OpenFOAM program onto supercomputer Tianhe and her guidance of supercomputing technique affairs.

References

1. Anderson, J.D.: Gasdynamic Lasers: An Introduction. Academic Press, New York (1976)
2. Anderson, J.D.: A Time-Dependent Analysis for Vibrational and Chemical Nonequilibrium Nozzle Flows. AIAA J. 8, 545–550 (1970)
3. Jones, A.T.: Time-dependent solutions of the vibrational non-equilibrium flow of CO_2-N_2-H_2O-O_2 mixtures in gas dynamic lasers. J. Phys. D. 9, 1193–1206 (1976)
4. OpenFOAM, OpenFOAM user guide (2012)
5. Kassem, I.H., Saqr, M.K., Aly, S.H., et al.: Implementation of the eddy dissipation model of turbulent non-premixed combustion in OpenFOAM. International Communications in Heat and Mass Transfer 38, 363–367 (2011)
6. Favero, J.L., Secchi, A.R., Cardozo, N.S.M., Jasak, H.: Viscoelastic flow analysis using the software OpenFOAM and differential constitutive equations. J. Non-Newtonian Fluid Mech. 165, 1625–1636 (2010)
7. Alexander, K., Yu, L.: New adaptive artificial viscosity method for hyperbolic systems of conservation laws. Journal of Computational Physics 231, 8114–8132 (2007)
8. Erik, A., Gennady, M., Silvia, N.: Rebuilding of Rothe's nozzle measurements with OpenFOAM software. Journal of Physics: Conference Series 362, 1–10 (2012)

9. Lei, J., Lai, L., Wang, Z.G.: Study on kinetic model of combustion driven CO_2 gas dynamic laser. In: 37th AIAA Plasmadynamics and Lasers Comference, San Francisco, California, USA (2006)
10. Yan, H.X.: Non-equilibrium nozzle flow calculation in a gasdynamic laser. J. Acta Mechanica Sinica 4, 274–287 (1978)
11. Siserir, F., Louhibi, D.: Vibrational and translational temperatures model for a fast-axial flow CO_2 laser. In: 37th AIAA Plasmadynamics and Lasers Conference, San Francisco, California, USA (2006)
12. Yan, H.X.: The vibrational relaxation process in CO_2-N_2-H_2O laser system. Chinese Journal of Lasers 6, 1–8 (1981)
13. Gross, W.F., Bott, J.F.: Handbook of chemical lasers. Wiley, New York (1976)
14. Greenshields, J.C., Weller, G.H., Gasparini, L.: Implementation of semi-discrete, non-staggered central schemes in a colocated, polyhedral, finite volume framework, for high-speed viscous flows. Int. J. Numer. Meth. Fluids 63, 1–21 (2010)
15. Vamos, S.J.: Small-signal gain measurements in a high area-ratio nozzle shock temmel GDL. In: AIAA 12th Aerospace Science Meeting, Washington D.C, pp. 1–6 (1974)

The Implementation of MapReduce Scheduling Algorithm Based on Priority[*]

Lianjun Gu, Zhuo Tang, and Guoqi Xie

Key Laboratory for Embedded and Network Computing of Hunan Province,
Changsha 410082, China
gulianjun110@sina.com

Abstract. Nowadays cloud computing has become a popular platform for scientific applications. Cloud computing intends to share a large scale resources and equipments of computation, storage, information and knowledge for scientific researches. Job Scheduling problem is a core and challenging research issue in the current cloud computation area, and the aim is to the reasonable control of the job execution sequence as well as the allocation of computing resources, making the job total completion time of the shortest and resources are fully utilized. Data locality is one of the main factors to influence scheduling algorithm. The paper proposed an improved scheduling algorithm based on priority, after taking full account of data locality (IPDSA), which can distinguish the user's job levels, so as to reduce the job execution time and avoid losing into locally optimal solution. The experimental results on the Hadoop platform show that the new scheduling algorithm can reduce the job average execution time, and raises the rate availability of resources.

Keywords: Cloud computing, Hadoop, MapReduce, Priority, Data locality.

1 Introduction

In recent years, as a new high-performance computing model, cloud computing has been focused by the majority of researchers and scholars, even that many companies also have provided their own platform, such as the Eucalyptus of University of California, Hadoop platform of Apache, as well as MongoDB of 10gen ect. Hadoop is an easier development of distributed computing and parallel processing of large-scale data platform, which is currently the most widely used open source cloud computing software platform [1]. Hadoop is mainly composed of two parts of the HDFS (Hadoop Distributed File System) and MapReduce engine. HDFS is the open source implementation of Google File System (GFS) [2]; MapReduce is the open source implementation of Google MapReduce [3].

MapReduce [4] is a programming model and an associated implementation for processing and generating large datasets that is amenable to a broad variety of

---

[*] This work was supported by the National Natural Science Foundation of China (61103047), SKLSE Open Foundation (The Open Foundation of State Key Laboratory of Software Engineering, China, and SKLSE 2012-09-18).

real-world tasks. We focus on the problem of scheduling MapReduce work in this paper. Before describing this scheduling problem in detail, we provide a brief overview of the MapReduce. The structure of MapReduce is based on the master-slave architecture. A single master node monitors the status of the slave nodes and assigns jobs to them. A task assigned to slave nodes has three phases of processing: the map stage, the shuffle stage and the reduce stage. Fig.1 shows the overall flow of a MapReduce operation.

- In the map stage, the mapper takes as input a single <key, value> pair, and produces as output any number of new <key, value> pairs. It is crucial that the map operation is stateless—that is, it operates on one pair at a time. This allows for easy parallelization as different inputs for the map can be processed by different machines.
- During the shuffle stage, the underlying system that implements MapReduce sends all of the values that are associated with an individual key to the same machine. This occurs automatically, and is seamless to the programmer.
- In the reduce stage, the reducer takes all of the values associated with a single key k, and outputs a multiset of <key, value> pairs with the same key k. This highlights one of the sequential aspects of MapReduce computation: all of the maps need to finish before the reduce stage can begin.

Since the reducer has access to all the values with the same key, it can perform sequential computations on these values. In the reduce step, the parallelism is exploited by observing that reducers operating on different keys can be executed simultaneously. Overall, a program in the MapReduce can consist of many rounds of different map and reduce functions, performed one after another.

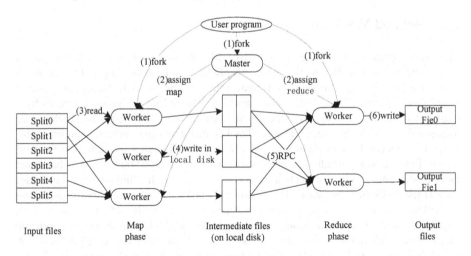

Fig. 1. Scheduling model of MapReduce

The main goal of job scheduling is to achieve a high performance computing and the best system throughput. Traditional job scheduling algorithms are not able to provide scheduling in the cloud environments. Data intensive applications often involve large distributed data sets, whose size can be assumed to be much larger than that of the codes used in the whole processing procedure. There are several main factors that affect scheduling issues such as data locality, synchronization, priority and fairness constraints; data locality is one of the main factors. Therefore, map tasks are often scheduled to the nodes nearest to the involved data, i.e., Improve data locality, which can help reduce the network traffic as well as the data transmission latency, thus achieving high system performance in a distributed computing environment. Nowadays, the MapReduce scheduling algorithms mainly include FIFO (First Input First Output), LATE (Longest Approximate Time to End), Fair Scheduler and Capacity Scheduler. Basic features such as data locality, user priority, fault tolerant and fairness is all considered by these algorithms. Moreover, few algorithms have considered multi-aspect of priority scheduling.

Priority of jobs is an important issue in scheduling because some jobs should be serviced earlier than other those jobs can't stay for a long time in a system. A suitable job scheduling algorithm must consider the priority of jobs. To address this problem some researchers have considered priority of jobs scheduling algorithm [5, 15, 16]. These researches have focused on a few criteria of jobs in scheduling. In cloud environments we always face a wide variety of attributes that should be considered.

In this paper, we have designed and implemented a new job scheduling algorithm, which is based on Hadoop, as far as possible to obtain the minimum computation time of each working node.

The rest of the paper is organized as follows. Section 2 describes the related work of this article. Section 3 presents our new scheduling algorithm. Section 4 evaluates the performance of our new scheduler. Finally, we conclude in Section 5.

2   Related Work

The performance of a parallel system like MapReduce system closely ties to its scheduling algorithm, the works about MapReduce scheduling algorithm focus on data locality, sharing, fairness and fault tolerant ability. Scheduling in Hadoop MapReduce is centralized, and worker initiated. Scheduling decisions are taken by a master node called JobTracker, whereas the worker nodes, called TaskTrackers are responsible for task execution. The JobTracker maintains the currently running jobs, states of TaskTrackers in a cluster, and list of tasks allocated to each TaskTracker. Every TaskTracker periodically reports its state to the JobTracker via a heartbeat mechanism. The contents of the heartbeat contain a flag indicating whether the sender TaskTracker should be assigned additional tasks. The reasonable scheduling algorithm is crucial to improve the efficiency of large-scale data processing in a distributed cluster system. Many scholars have conducted in-depth research on MapReduce scheduling algorithm, raising a lot of scheduling algorithms. A scheduling policy is used to determine when a job can execute its tasks. The default Hadoop scheduler schedules jobs by FIFO where jobs are scheduled sequentially. [6] proposes a fair scheduling algorithm for data-intensive jobs and interactive jobs on the cluster, as much as possible the resources on average to each job scheduling.

Dynamic Proportional Scheduler [7] provides more job sharing and prioritization capability in scheduling and also results in increasing the share of cluster resources and more differentiation in the service levels of different jobs. Data locality is a key performance factor of task's completion time in Hadoop. To achieve data locality, for each idle server, the scheduler greedily searches for a data local task in the head-of-line job and allocates it to the server [8]. However the simple policy leads to limited data locality; meanwhile the completion time of small jobs is increased. To enhance both fairness and data locality of jobs in a shared cluster, Matei Zaharia et al proposes the delay scheduling algorithm [9] to address the conflict between data locality and fairness. However, the method takes fairness withered as the cost and it doesn't fit for the jobs which have large size or few slots per node. This assumption is too strict, so delay scheduling does not work well when servers free up slowly. Quincy [10] maps the scheduling problem to a graph data structure according to a global cost model, and solves the problem by a well-known min-cost flow algorithm. Quincy can achieve better fairness, but it has a negligible effect on improving data locality. In [11], the authors improve data locality through building a relationship between application and nodes to place data reasonable. [12], [13] focus on supporting deadline constraints in traditional parallel computation models which differ from the two-phase computation and unique dataflow of MapReduce jobs. In [13], the authors use a P2P approach, extended the MapReduce architectural model making it suitable for highly dynamic environments where failure must be managed to avoid a critical waste of computing resources and time [14], [17]. In the two-stage assembly flowshop scheduling cloud theory-based simulated annealing algorithm, and prove that the algorithm makes the total running time and a decrease in the average running time. Polo et al. [18] and Phan et al. [19] designed the scheduling methods to satisfy the performance requirements of jobs. Sandholm et al. [20] proposed the method enabling users to control the resource allocated by adjusting their spending.

To meet the corresponding requirements of the job in the cloud environment we propose the MapReduce Task Scheduler for (IPDSA) algorithm. The IPDSA algorithm takes the job priority (JobPriority), the ability of computing nodes (wp) and the distance between compute nodes and the master node into account.

3   Problem Description and Modeling

3.1   Model Description

Without loss of generality, the model is based on the following principle:

1. Master node as far as possible in a related map block computing node to arrange a map task. If this fails, try in the compute nodes near the map block where the arrangement map task, so will be able to do it's utmost to ensure that the input data read in the local or nearby taken in order to ensure the utilization of network bandwidth.
2. Different configuration of computing resources calculated performance is different.
3. The transmission time of the data in the network is related to transmission medium and the transport mechanism, and this paper only considers the difference of transmission medium, and other factors will not consider.

In the existing scheduling algorithm, determine the priority level is always from the job priority parameter, only consider the job priority to determine the order of execution of the jobs is not accurate, one-sided, because there is no consideration of data locality, working node calculation ability, once considered data locality, worker priority and other issues, decision becomes more complex. Based on the original job priority parameters, we introduce two parameters: the priority of the worker node (wp), the interval of compute nodes and the master node (Distance). As the follows chapters, the above three parameters is considered to establish a new priority calculation model.

Definition 1: we set a few constants in order to calculate the job priority. jobSize indicates the size of the submitted job. taskNumber shows that job contains the number of tasks. averageTaskSize represents each task average execution length. PriorityValue indicates job weights. WeighValue indicates the number of task based on job weights.

The average execution length of each task in the job:

$$averageTaskSize[i] = \frac{jobSize[i]}{taskNumber} \tag{1}$$

where i represents the i-th job. In all the jobs of a scheduling, the total amount of data of the job processing S:

$$S = \sum_{i=1}^{n} S[i] = \sum_{i=1}^{n} averageTaskSize[i] * weightValue[i] \tag{2}$$

Typically, the number of map tasks much more than the number of reduce tasks, due to the differences of node processing capability in each cluster, the vast majority of the task's size is set to blockSize, therefore, we consider the MapTask processing capacity for Testability in the entire cluster. Every time the amount of data of the job scheduling:

$$S = Max(num * jobNum * blockSize, taskAbility * blockSize) \tag{3}$$

where, *jobNum* indicates the number of jobs in the job scheduling, *num* represents the average number of tasks per job (If each job once only performs a data block). job[i] corresponding value S[i] and total value S ratio is equal to the corresponding value priorityValue[i] and total value priorityValue ratio:

$$\frac{averageTaskSize[i] * weightValue[i]}{S} = \frac{priorityValue[i]}{\sum_{i=1}^{n} priorityValue[i]} \tag{4}$$

We obtain the value of weightValue [i]:

$$weightValue[i] = \frac{S * priority[i]}{averageTaskSize[i] * \sum_{i=1}^{n} priority[i]} \tag{5}$$

Definition 2: The distance between the computing node and the master node is called d_i. The network transmission time of information is proportional to the distance between the node and the master node, every meter transmits information time is called γ.

Definition 3: The priority of work node should first consider the type of node. Some work node (such as working node P) is mainly used to deal with short job, such as query function; Some work node (working node Q) is mainly used to dealing with the long job, such as historical data analysis, etc.; When working nodes P and Q to apply for tasks, work node P should take precedence over Q to perform tasks, *wp* value is bigger, the corresponding task priority is higher, the calculation model is as follows:

$$wp = \begin{cases} MaxValue \\ \alpha f(x) + \beta g(y) \end{cases} \tag{6}$$

where x indicates the last time work node asking for the number of the task, the greater its value, the working node load is lower, the ability to deal with the task is stronger, when having idle task, this node can receive the task first. y indicates the task success rate. The greater its value, the ability to deal with tasks is stronger, so it will give priority to execute the idle task.

When work node local task list is not empty, *wp* can be set to the maximum: *MaxValue*, this work node performs a local task, otherwise in accordance by Eq. (2) obtain corresponding task. *f(x)* and *g(y)* are monotone increasing function.

Combined with the analysis of the above parameters, we obtain the final priority decision model as follows:

$$\begin{cases} \text{Pr}iority = k_1 * Job\,\text{Pr}iority + k_2 * wp + k_3 * d \\ \sum_{i=1}^{3} k_i = 1 \end{cases} \tag{7}$$

3.2 Algorithm Description

In this paper, we will continue to use the parameters set by LATE algorithm. It's to find out the most needed backup by way of calculating the rest time to complete the task and data locality in the requested node rack.

In Fig.2, we define three queues: DynamicQueue, BackupQueue and ReadyQueue, which DynamicQueue to maintain the executing job; BackupQueue is maintenance for load level adjustment from DynamicQueue to remove the executing job; ReadyQueue is to maintain the user submit job.

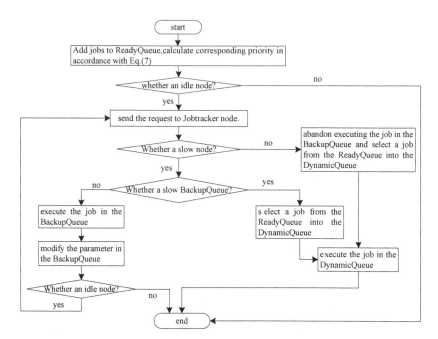

Fig. 2. The process of the algorithm

The pseudo-code of IPDSA algorithm is as follows:

```
R=Φ /*R is ready queue*/
B=Φ /*B is backup queue*/
D=Φ /*D is dynamic queue */
for each node i of the N slave nodes do
     compute the priority of each node
     wp[i]=get the task's on node completion time on node
end for
for each job i of the M jobs do
     compute the priority of each job
     update job's priority in queue R
     resort the jobs in queue R
end for
upon receiving a heartbeat from node i:
while node i is an idle node,
   if node i is a slow node then
      waive the job in B
      select the first job from queue R into queue D
   else if B is not empty then
           execute the first job in queue B
```

```
        else
            execute the first job in queue R
        end if
    end if
        update job's priority in queue B
end while
```

4   Experiments

We have implemented our scheduling algorithm in Hadoop-1.0.0. In this section, we describe the environment to evaluate our scheduling algorithm and discuss the experiment results.

4.1   Experimental Environments

In this subsection, we introduce the details of the experimental environment. The experiment is being completed under the condition of Hadoop platform. Fig.3 shows the topology of the cluster used to deploy the implementation of our method. As the topology shows, the cluster was constituted of eight slave nodes, and each node was connected by Gigabit Ethernet.

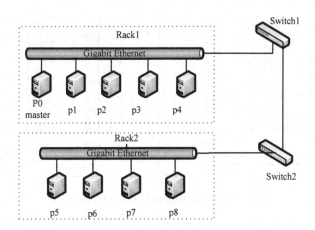

Fig. 3. Topology of the cluster used in our work

The version of Hadoop is 1.0.0 and the version of JDK is 1.6.0_43. In the experiment, the Hadoop HDFS default blockSize parameters is 64 MB, but due to the limitation of physical devices, modified to 32 MB. We run experiments in the above cluster with 9 nodes, designating one node (p0) as NameNode, master and JobTracker, the other 8 nodes (p1-p8) as DataNode, slave and TaskTracker. The operating system is Linux (kernel version 2.6). The configuration information of the corresponding node is following below.

Table 1. Hadoop cluster parameter configuration

Node	Configuration	Distance/m
p0	Core 3.2 GHz, RAM 4.0GB	0
p1	Core 2.81 GHz, RAM 2.0GB	18
p2	Core 1.8 GHz, RAM 2.0GB	5
p3	Core 2.5 GHz, RAM 6.0GB	8
p4	Core 2.1 GHz, RAM 2.0GB	4
p5	Core 1.91 GHz, RAM 2.0GB	13
p6	Core 2.1 GHz, RAM 4.0GB	10
p7	Core 2.4 GHz, RAM 4.0GB	2
p8	Core 2.2 GHz, RAM 2.0GB	11

4.2   Experimental Results

Two classic benchmarks, Sort and WordCount, are used to evaluate the performance of our scheduling algorithm. The two benchmarks are always used to evaluate the performance of MapReduce schedulers, such as LATE [17] and Phoenix [18]. For each test, every benchmark is run ten times and the average execution time is used as the result.

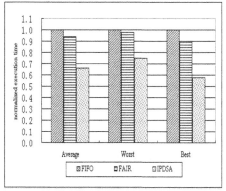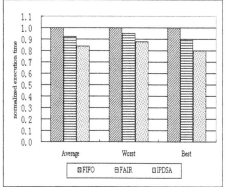

Fig. 4. Execution time of Sort and WordCount

Fig.4 shows the performance of Sort and WordCount in FIFO, FAIR and our scheduler. We show the worst-case and best-case gain from both schedulers. On average, my scheduler significantly improves the performance of Sort, with the performance gain up to 35%. Through our analysis, we can see the performance is satisfactory to our expectations. Because the number of map tasks in our environments is much bigger than the number of nodes.

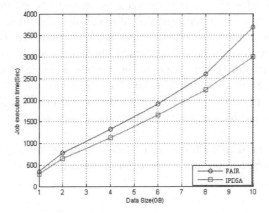

Fig. 5. Job execution time of different data size

All the above jobs are executed with the same input data sizes of 1GB, 2GB, 4GB, 6GB, 8GB and 10GB. We have conducted the same set of experiments with the same input data using Fair scheduler and my scheduler. The results are plotted in Fig.5. It is observed from the results that as the input data size increase, the execution time of jobs will also increase.

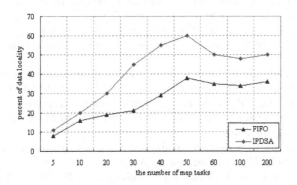

Fig. 6. The Map task's data locality

We run WordCount program to measure the proportion of the data locality. The result is shown in Fig.6 as follow. From Fig.6, we can see that the proportion of data locality of nodes with my scheduler is higher than the nodes with FIFO scheduler. So we can draw the conclusion that my scheduling algorithm can improve the data locality.

5   Conclusion and Future Work

Schedule strategy is an important part of a distributed system. The improved scheduler proposed in the paper takes into account the job character, data locality and node character. Performance evaluation results demonstrate that the improved scheduler based on priority decreases the data movement, speeds the execution of jobs, so improving the system performance. Although this algorithm has advantages compared to other scheduling algorithms, it also has limitations. On the one hand, the heterogeneous environment is very complicated, there are a lot of factors can affect the overall performance of clusters, we only consider some simple factors, and how to build a more accurate calculation model based on priority have further research value. On the other hand, the priority calculation model is a simple weighted, and these weights coefficients are hard to take, the need for a large number of experimental verification.

Current and future research efforts include further bettering the improved scheduler based on priority in the optimization of the computational model and reliability.

References

1. Lin, Q.: The cloud computing model based on Hadoop. Modern Computer, 114–116 (2010)
2. Chemawat, S., Gobioff, H., Leung, S.T.: The Google file system, http://labs.google.com/papers.gfs.html
3. MapReduce, http://www.mongodb.org/display/DOCS/MapReduce
4. Dean, J., Ghemawat, S.: MapReduce: Simplified Data Processing on Large Clusters. In: Proceeding of the 6th Symposium on Operating Systems Design and Implementation (OSDI 2004), pp. 137–150. USENIX Association (2004)
5. Bansal, S., et al.: Dynamic Task Scheduling in Grid Computing Using Prioritized Round Robin Algorithm. IJCSI International Journal of Computer Science Issues 8(2), 472–477 (2011)
6. Zaharia, M., Borthakur, D., Sarma, J.S.: Job scheduling for multi-user mapreduce clusters. In: Proceedings of the 5th European Conference IEEE, pp. 145–161 (2009)
7. Sandholm, T., Lai, K.: Dynamic proportional share scheduling in hadoop. In: Frachtenberg, E., Schwiegelshohn, U. (eds.) JSSPP 2010. LNCS, vol. 6253, pp. 110–131. Springer, Heidelberg (2010)
8. Tatebe, O., et al.: Grid datafarm architecture for petascale data intensive computing. In: CCGRID 2002. IEEE Computer Society, Washington, DC (2002)
9. Zaharia, M., Borthakur, D., Sarma, J.S., Elmele-egy, K., Shenker, S., Stoica, I.: Delay scheduling: a simple technique for achieving locality and fairness in cluster scheduling. In: EuroSys 2010: Proceedings of the 5th European Conference on Computer Systems, pp. 265–278. ACM, New York (2010)
10. Isard, M., et al.: Quincy: fair scheduling for distributed computing clusters. In: SOSP 2009, pp. 261–276. ACM, New York (2009)
11. Xie, J., Yin, S., Ruan, X.J., Ding, Z.Y., Tian, Y.: Improving MapReduce performance through data placement in heterogeneous hadoop clusters. In: IEEE International Symposium on Parallel & Distributed Processing, Workshops and PhdForum, pp. 1–9 (2010)
12. Lin, X., Lu, Y., Deogun, J., Goddard, S.: Real-time divisible load scheduling for cluster computing. In: 13th IEEE Real Time and Embedded Technology and Applications Symposium, RTAS 2007, pp. 303–314, 3–6 (2007)

13. Yu, J., Buyya, R.: A budget constrained scheduling of workflow applications on utility grids using genetic algorithms. In: Workshop on Workflows in Support of Large-Scale Science, Proceedings of the 15th IEEE International Symposium on High Performance Distributed Computing (HPDC). IEEE CS Press (2006)
14. Marozzo, F., Talia, D., Trunfio, P.: Adapting MapReduce for Dynamic Environments Using a Peer-to-Peer Model,
http://grid.deis.unical.it/papers/pdf/CCA08.pdf
15. Yang, L., et al.: A new Class of Priority based Weighted Fair Scheduling Algorithm. Physics Procedia 33, 942–948 (2012)
16. Kyriaki, Z.: Multi-Criteria Job Scheduling in Grid Using an Accelerated Genetic Algorithm. J. Grid Computing 10, 311–323 (2012)
17. Torabzadeh, E.: Cloud Theory-based Simulated Annealing Approach for Scheduling in the Two-stage Assembly Flowshop. Advances in Engineering Software 41(10), 1243–1258 (2010)
18. Polo, J., De Nadal, D., Carrera, D., Becerra, Y., Beltran, V., Torres, J., Ayguad´e, E.: Adaptive task scheduling for multi-job mapreduce environments. Technical report UPC-DAC-RR-CAP-2009-28, Departament d'Arquitectura de Com-putadors, Universitat Polit´ecnica de Catalunya (2009)
19. Phan, L.T., Zhang, Z., Lo, B.T., Lee, I.: Real-time mapreduce scheduling. Technical Report MS-CIS-10-32, Department of Computer and Information Science, University of Pennsylvania (2010)
20. Sandholm, T., Lai, K.: Dynamic proportional share scheduling in hadoop. In: Proc. IPDPS Workshops, Atlanta, GA (2010)
21. Zaharia, M., Konwinski, A., Joseph, A.D., Katz, R., Stoica, I.: Improving mapreduce performance in heterogeneous environments. In: 8th USENIX symposium on operating systems design and implementation, pp. 29–42. ACM, New York (2008)
22. Ranger, C., Raghuraman, R., Penmetsa, A., Bradski, G., Kozyrakis, C.: Evaluating mapreduce for multi-core and multiprocessor systems. In: HPCA 2007: Proceedings of the 2007 IEEE 13th International Symposium on High Performance Computer Architecture, pp. 13–24. IEEE Computer Society, Washington (2007)

Efficient Parallel Multi-way Merging on Heterogeneous Multi-core Cluster

Cheng Zhong and Wei Wei

School of Computer and Electronics and Information,
Guangxi University, Nanning, Guangxi, 530004, China
chzhong@gxu.edu.cn, wei_2001_iew@163.com

Abstract. Data merging and sorting are often applied to the scientific and engineering applications such as computational fluid dynamics and computation geometry. By constructing a data sending matrix, solving the data exchange range and determining the data exchange order among compute nodes to reduce the communication overhead, this paper proposes a load-balance data distribution strategy among nodes, and designs a communication-efficient parallel multi-way merging algorithm on the heterogeneous cluster with the multi-core compute nodes which have different computation speed, communication rate and memory capacity. The experimental results on the heterogeneous cluster with multi-core machines show that the proposed parallel merging algorithm obtains high speedup and has good scalability.

Keywords: Parallel merging, Parallel sorting, Multi-core architectures, Heterogeneous cluster, Thread-level parallelism.

1   Introduction

Data merging and sorting are often applied to the scientific and engineering applications such as computational fluid dynamics, computation geometry and database system. Many parallel merging and sorting algorithms on the traditional parallel systems were introduced in [1]. Based on the randomized sampling method, Helman and JáJá [2] designed a parallel merge sorting algorithm on clusters of SMPs. Ding et al [3] proposed a parallel merging algorithm by fixed sampling and evaluated its performance on the massively parallel processors systems. Giusti et al [4] studied dynamic load balancing among processes in parallel merge sorting on homogeneous clusters by forecasting workload. Jeon and Kim [5] proposed a parallel merge sorting algorithm with load balancing, which gives the index exchange method to decrease the communication overhead. Recently, some parallel merging and sorting algorithms have been developed on multi-core architectures. Govindaraju et al [6] used the bitonic merge to develop a high-performance graphics coprocessor sorting algorithm. Gedik et al [7] designed a bitonic merge algorithm using the SIMD bitonic sorting on the Cell processor. Chhugani et al [8] implemented an efficient sorting algorithm on multi-core SIMD CPU architecture by multi-way merge technique. Hao et al [9] proposed a partition-merge-based cache-conscious parallel sorting algorithm for chip

K. Li et al. (Eds.): ParCFD 2013, CCIS 405, pp. 112–123, 2014.
© Springer-Verlag Berlin Heidelberg 2014

multiprocessors. Hultén et al [10] organized the merge procedure by applying pipeline mode to reduce the number of memory access, and optimized the on-chip-pipelined merge sorting on the Cell/B.E. Satish et al [11] implemented a bandwidth oblivious SIMD sort algorithm on CPUs and GPUs systems respectively. Zhong et al [12] presented a non-periodic multi-round data distribution strategy and designed an efficient and scalable parallel sorting Multisets algorithm on multi-core systems. By applying two-round probing strategy, Zhong et al [13] proposed an efficient multi-round scheduling divisible loads algorithm with return messages on the heterogeneous multi-core clusters with unknown system parameters.

To develop a communication-efficient parallel multi-way merging algorithm on heterogeneous multi-core cluster systems, the key issue is how to distribute properly the ordered data sequences to the compute nodes among heterogeneous multi-core cluster to balance their loads and reduce data exchange and communication overhead during parallel merging. The main contribution of this paper is to present a load-balance data distribution model and an ordered data sequences partitioning algorithm on the heterogeneous cluster with multi-core compute nodes that have different computation speed, communication rate and memory capacity, and design a communication-efficient parallel multi-way merging algorithm by optimizing the communication order among compute nodes. The remainder of this paper is organized as follows. Section 2 gives a load-balance data distribution model and a communication-efficient parallel merging algorithm on the heterogeneous multi-core cluster. Section 3 evaluates the experimental performance of the presented algorithm. Section 4 concludes the paper.

2   Parallel Merging on Heterogeneous Multi-core Cluster

We assume that the given k ascending ordered data sequences are $S_1[1 \cdots n_1],\ldots,$ and $S_k[1 \cdots n_k]$ respectively, $n = \sum_{a=1}^{k} n_a$, the heterogeneous multi-core cluster is consist of $k \times num$ compute nodes which have different computation speed, communication rate and memory capacity. All the compute nodes on the heterogeneous cluster are partitioned into k groups which each group has num compute nodes. The b-th compute node in the a-th group is denoted by $ND_{a,b}$, $b=1 \sim num$, $a=1 \sim k$.

2.1   Partitioning the Ordered Data Sequences

Sequence S_a will be distributed to num compute nodes in the a-th group. Each compute node stores a data segment in sequence S_a. We assume that the data segment on compute node $ND_{a,b}$ has $F_{a,b}$ elements, $b=1 \sim num$, $a=1 \sim k$. If $b=1$, $F_{a,b}$ data elements are $S_a [1..F_{a,1}]$, $a=1 \sim k$; if $b>1$, $F_{a,b}$ data elements are $S_a [\sum_{c=1}^{b-1} F_{a,c} +1.. \sum_{c=1}^{b} F_{a,c}]$, $b=2 \sim num$, $a=1 \sim k$. We find $k \times num$ partitioned positions in sequence S_a and denote the d-th partitioned position by $g_{a,d}$, $d=1 \sim k \times num$, $a =1 \sim k$. Hence, $g_{a,k \times p} = n_a$ and $g_{a,0} = 0$, $a =1 \sim k$.

In order to help people to understand the partitioning sequences method better, Figure 1 displays an example of partitioning 3 ordered data sequences on a heterogeneous multi-core cluster with 6 compute nodes.

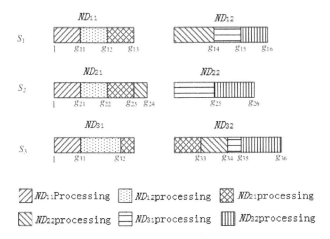

Fig. 1. Partitioning 3 ordered sequences on heterogeneous multi-core cluster with 6 nodes

We distribute k ordered data subsequences $S_1[g_{1,d-1}+1\cdot\cdot g_{1,d}],..., S_k[g_{k,d-1}+1\cdot\cdot g_{k,d}]$ with size $L_{e,f}=\sum_{a=1}^{k}(g_{a,d}-g_{a,d-1})$ to compute node $ND_{e,f}$, and denote the capacity of main memory in node $ND_{e,f}$ by $M_{e,f}$, $e=\lfloor d/num\rfloor+1$, $f=d$ mod $num+1$. The transmission rate from compute node $ND_{a,b}$ to $ND_{i,j}$ is represented by $B_{(a,b)(i,j)}$, $j=1\sim num$, $i=1\sim k$. We assume that compute node $ND_{e,f}$ can merge $D_{a,b}$ data elements by executing the thread-level parallel merging algorithm using SIMD instructions [14] in a unit time and it takes $H_{a,b}=L_{a,b}/D_{a,b}$ time to complete merging its local ordered subsequence, $b=1\sim num$, $a=1\sim k$. Let H_{max} denote the required time to merge the given k ordered data sequences on the heterogeneous multi-core cluster. Hence, $H_{max}=\max\{H_{1,1}, H_{1,2},..., H_{k,num}\}$. Partitioning the given k ordered data sequences on the heterogeneous multi-core cluster should satisfy the following equations:

$$0\le L_{e,f}=\sum_{a=1}^{k}\left(g_{a,d}-g_{a,d-1}\right)\le M_{e,f}, f=1\sim num, e=1\sim k \qquad (1)$$

$$\sum_{a=1}^{k}\sum_{b=1}^{p}L_{a,b}=n \qquad (2)$$

$$H_{a,b}\le H_{max}, b=1\sim num, a=1\sim k \qquad (3)$$

$$\max\{S_1[g_{1,d}],...,S_k[g_{k,d}]\}\le\min\{S_1[g_{1,d}+1],...,S_k[g_{k,d}+1]\}, d=1\sim k\times num \qquad (4)$$

We can obtain size $L_{e,f}$ of the data sequence to be distributed to node $ND_{e,f}$ by solving equations (1)~(3), $f=1\sim num$, $e=1\sim k$. According to $L_{e,f}$ and equation (4), we can determine the exact partitioned position by executing the following ordered data sequences partitioning algorithm on the multi-core heterogeneous cluster.

2.2 Constructing Data Sending Matrix and Partitioning Sequences

Based on the idea of the data partitioning algorithm on SMP machine [15], we give an ordered data sequences partitioning algorithm on the heterogeneous multi-core cluster to find the exact partitioned position for k ordered data sequences according to the given ordered sequences partitioning model in section 2.1. We use $V[a][b]$ to represent the index value of one specific element in sequence S_a and this element is the last one in the subsequence which is stored in compute node $ND_{a,b}$, and use $LB_{a,b}[i]$ and $RB_{a,b}[i]$ to denote the left and right boundary positions of the region in sequence S_a which is searched by node $ND_{a,b}$, $b=1\sim num$, $a=1\sim k$. The searched partition position $G_{a,b}[i]$ is sent to compute node $ND_{1,1}$ and it is stored in array *split* $[1\cdot\cdot k][1\cdot\cdot k\times num]$, $i=1\sim k$, $b=1\sim num$, $a=1\sim k$.

Algorithm 1. Partitioning Ordered Sequences on Heterogeneous Multi-core Cluster
Begin
for all compute nodes $ND_{a,b}$ where $a=1$ to k and $b=1$ to *num* do in parallel
(1) Node $ND_{a,b}$ executes initialization: $LB_{a,b}[i]=1$, $RB_{a,b}[i]=n_i$,$G_{a,b}[i] =$
$(\sum_{c=1}^{b} L_{a,c}) / k$, $i=1\sim k$;
(2) for $i=1$ to k do
(2.1) if $V[a][x-1]\leq G_{a,b}[i]\leq V[a][x]$ then
        The element with the partitioned position $G_{a,b}[i]$ is corresponding to the $addr_1$-th element in node $ND_{a,x}$, $addr_1=G_{a,b}[i]-V[a][x-1]$, $x=2\sim num$;
    if $V[a][y-1]\leq G_{a,b}[i]+1\leq V[a][y]$ then
        The element with partitioned position $G_{a,b}[i]+1$ is corresponding to the $addr_2$-th element in node $ND_{a,y}$, $addr_2=G_{a,b}[i]+1 -V[a][y-1]$, $y=2\sim num$;
(2.2) the $addr_1$-th element in node $ND_{a,x}$ and the $addr_2$-th element in compute node $ND_{a,y}$ are sent to node $ND_{a,b}$ and stored in $test1_{a,b}[i]$ and $test2_{a,b}[i]$;
    endfor
(3) while (true) do
(3.1) $maxNum=\max\{test1_{a,b}[1],...,test1_{a,b}[k]\}$; $minNum=\min\{test2_{a,b}[1],...,$ $test2_{a,b}[k]\}$; the index of element $maxNum$ in array $test1_{a,b}$ is denoted by ma and the index of element $minNum$ in array $test2_{a,b}$ is denoted by mi;
(3.2) if $maxNum<minNum$ then exit while-loop;
(3.3) $LB_{a,b}[mi]=G_{a,b}[mi]+1$; $RB_{a,b}[ma]=G_{a,b}[ma]-1$;
(3.4) $deltaMax=(RB_{a,b}[ma]-LB_{a,b}[ma])/2$; $deltaMin=(RB_{a,b}[mi]-LB_{a,b}[mi])/2$; $delta=\min\{ deltaMax , deltaMin \}$;
(3.5) $G_{a,b}[ma]=RB_{a,b}[ma]-delta$; $G_{a,b}[mi]=LB_{a,b}[mi]+delta$;
(3.6) Find the corresponding elements with partitioned positions $G_{a,b}[ma]$, $G_{a,b}[ma]+1$, $G_{a,b}[mi]$ and $G_{a,b}[mi]+1$ by applying the same way in step (2), and store these elements to $test1_{a,b}[ma]$, $test2_{a,b}[ma]$, $test1_{a,b}[mi]$ and $test2_{a,b}[mi]$ respectively;
    endwhile

(4) Send array $G_{a,b}[1 \cdots k]$ to compute node $ND_{1,1}$, and node $ND_{1,1}$ copies
$G_{a,b}[1 \cdots k]$ to $split[1 \cdots k][q]$;
$q=a \times num+b$;
endfor
End.

In Algorithm 1, since one execution of the loop wants to compare num data elements and step (2) executes the loop for k times, step (2) requires $O(k \times num)$ time. Step (3.1) executes k comparisons, and step (3.2) executes $2 \times num$ comparisons. To refer to the analysis in [15], we can know that if the ordered data sequences are evenly partitioned and distributed to all the compute nodes, the loop in step (3) is executed at most $\log(n/(k \times num))$ times. By applying the given sequences partitioning model in section 2.1, the given k ordered data sequences can be evenly partitioned and distributed to all the compute nodes on heterogeneous multi-core cluster. Hence, the computation time complexity of Algorithm 1 is $O(k \times num+(k+num) \times \log_2(n/(k \times num)))$.

In step (2), one execution of the loop wants to request and return 2 data elements respectively, it means that step (2) requires $4k$ communication cost. One execution for step (3.6) wants to request and return 4 data elements respectively. Because the given k ordered data sequences can be evenly partitioned and distributed to all the compute nodes, the required communication cost are $4\log_2(n/(k \times num))$ in step (3). Hence, The communication cost of Algorithm 1 is $O(k+\log_2(n/(k \times num)))$.

2.3   Solving Data Exchange Range among Compute Nodes

All the partitioned positions for sequence S_a are stored in array $split[a][1 \cdots k \times num]$. $S_a[low \cdots up]$ is a subsequence of sequence S_a, and it is stored in compute node $ND_{a,b}$, where $low = \sum_{c=1}^{b-1} F_{a,c} +1$, $up = \sum_{c=1}^{b} F_{a,c}$, $b=1 \sim num$, $a=1 \sim k$. According to the above information, we can know that compute node $ND_{a,b}$ will send/receive what data elements to/from other compute nodes in the data exchange process.

Figure 2 describes six possible positioned relationships about subsequence $S_a[low \cdots up]$ and the logical data segment in sequence S_a between adjacent partitioned positions $split[a][d]$ and $split[a][d-1]$, where $left=split[a][d-1]$, $right=split[a][d]$, $d=1 \sim k \times num$, $b=1 \sim num$, $a=1 \sim k$.

We construct a vector $SV_{a,b}[1 \cdots k \times num]$ for compute node $ND_{a,b}$, where $SV_{a,b}[d]$ is a two-tuple of $(start, count)$ and it denotes that compute node $ND_{a,b}$ sends $count$ elements in its subsequence from the $start$-th element to compute node $ND_{e,f}$, $e=\lfloor d/num \rfloor+1$, $f=d \bmod num+1$, $d=1 \sim k \times num$, $b=1 \sim num$, $a=1 \sim k$. We can determine the value of $SV_{a,b}[d]$ for 6 partitioned positions: if $left<low$ and $right<low$, then $SV_{a,b}[d]=(0,0)$; if $left<low$ and $low \leq right \leq up$, then $SV_{a,b}[d]=(0, right-low+1)$; if $low \leq left \leq up$ and $low \leq right \leq up$, then $SV_{a,b}[d]=(left-low+1, right-left+1)$; if $low \leq left \leq up$ and $right>up$, then $SV_{a,b}[d]=(left-low+1, low-up+1)$; if $left>up$ and $right>up$, then $SV_{a,b}[d]=(0,0)$; and if $left<low$ and $right>up$, then $SV_{a,b}[d]=(0, low-up+1)$; where $d=1 \sim k \times num$, $b=1 \sim num$, $a=1 \sim k$.

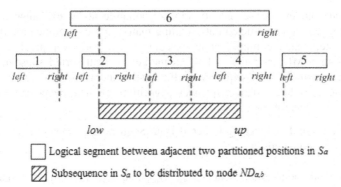

Fig. 2. Six position relationships about subsequence S_a in compute node $ND_{a,b}$ and logical data segment between adjacent two partitioned positions in S_a

Therefore, data sending matrix $SM[1 \cdots k \times num][1 \cdots k \times num]$ can be generated by merging $SV_{a,b}[1 \cdots k \times num]$, $b=1 \sim num$, $a=1 \sim k$. Notice that element $SM[r][s]$ is a two-tuple and compute node $ND_{\lfloor r/k \rfloor +1, r \bmod num +1}$ will send $SM[r][s]$ to compute node $ND_{\lfloor s/k \rfloor +1, s \bmod num +1}$, $s=1 \sim k \times num$, $r=1 \sim k \times num$. The data sending matrix construction is completed by compute node $ND_{1,1}$.

2.4   Selecting Communication Order among Compute Nodes

During the data exchange among compute nodes, if several compute nodes want to send data to the same compute node at the same time, it may produce conflict. Hence, it is necessary to arrange properly the communication order to reduce the conflict among the compute nodes on the heterogeneous cluster.

We solve the amount $N'_{(a,b)(i,j)}$ of the data that compute node $ND_{a,b}$ sends to compute node $ND_{i,j}$ and calculate the required sending time $X_{(a,b)(i,j)}=N'_{(a,b)(i,j)}/B_{(a,b)(i,j)}$ by $SM[1 \cdots k \times num][1 \cdots k \times num]$. In each round communication, the node-pair $(ND_{a,b}, ND_{i,j})$ with larger value of $X_{(a,b)(i,j)}$ is selected to communicate with each other, and there is no join set between the selected two pairs of compute nodes to avoid the conflict and reduce the communication overhead for data exchange on the heterogeneous cluster.

We assume that the communication with w rounds is required to complete the data exchange on the heterogeneous cluster. A pair of nodes participating in the i-th round communication is joined to set O_i, $i=1 \sim w$. Compute node $ND_{1,1}$ can construct a communication order set $OR=\{O_1,O_2,\ldots,O_w\}$ among compute nodes on the heterogeneous multi-core cluster.

2.5   Parallel Merging Algorithm on Multi-core Heterogeneous Cluster

The parallel merging ordered data sequences algorithm on multi-core heterogeneous cluster is made of the following three steps. First step computes the amount of the data which is distributed to each compute node by applying the given sequences partitioning model in section 2.1, and it executes Algorithm 1 to search the partitioned positions, constructs the data sending matrix and determines the communication order among compute nodes. In the second step, all compute nodes exchange data each other according to the constructed data sending matrix and communication order set. In the third step, each compute node executes the thread-level parallel merging algorithm using SIMD instructions [14] to merge its local sorted subsequences in order to obtain a final sorted sequence on the heterogeneous multi-core cluster. The parallel merging ordered data sequences algorithm on heterogeneous multi-core cluster is described as follows.

Algorithm 2. Parallel Merging Ordered Data Sequences on Heterogeneous Multi-core Cluster

Begin

(1) Compute node $ND_{a,b}$ sends $M_{a,b}$, $D_{a,b}$ and $F_{a,b}$ to compute node $ND_{1,1}$, $b=1\sim num$, $a=1\sim k$;

(2) Compute node $ND_{1,1}$ first solves the length $n_a=\sum_{b=1}^{p} F_{a,b}$ of sequence S_a and the indices of subsequence S_a [$\sum_{c=1}^{b-1} F_{a,c} +1 \cdots \sum_{c=1}^{b} F_{a,c}$] on compute node $ND_{a,b}$, and calculates $V[a][b] =\sum_{c=1}^{b} F_{a,c}$ and amount $L_{a,b}$ of the data which are distributed to compute node $ND_{a,b}$, $b=1\sim num$, $a=1\sim k$;

(3) Compute node $ND_{1,1}$ sends $V[1\cdots k][1\cdots num]$, n_a and $L_{a,b}$ to compute node $ND_{a,b}$, $b=1\sim num$, $a=1\sim k$;

(4) Compute node $ND_{a,b}$ executes Algorithm 1 to find k partitioned positions in given k ordered data sequences, assigns the positions to its local array $G_{a,b}[1\cdots k]$, and sends $G_{a,b}[1\cdots k]$ to compute node $ND_{1,1}$, $b=1\sim num$, $a=1\sim k$;

(5) Compute node $ND_{1,1}$ merges $G_{a,b}[1\cdots k]$ ($b=1\sim num$, $a=1\sim k$) to a array $split$ $[1\cdots k][1\cdots k\times num]$, and constructs data sending matrix $SM[1\cdots k\times num]$ $[1\cdots k\times num]$ and communication order set OR by $split[1\cdots k][1\cdots k\times num]$ and $V[1\cdots k][1\cdots num]$;

(6) Node $ND_{1,1}$ broadcasts $SM[1\cdots k\times num][1\cdots k\times num]$ and OR to the other nodes on the heterogeneous multi-core cluster;

(7) All the compute nodes exchange data each other according to the assigned communication order after they has received $SM[1\cdots k\times num]$ $[1\cdots k\times num]$ and OR;

(8) Each compute node executes the thread-level parallel merging algorithm using SIMD instructions [14] to merge its local subsequences to form a final sorted sequence on the heterogeneous multi-core cluster. The data in the final sorted sequence are distributed and stored orderly on compute nodes $ND_{1,1}\sim ND_{k,num}$.

End.

In Algorithm 2, step (1) requires $O(k\times num)$ communication overhead. Step (2) requires $O(k\times num)$ computation time. The communication overhead in Step (3) is $O(k+\log_2(n/(k\times p)))$. Step (4) requires $O(k\times p +(k+p)\log_2(n/(k\times p)))$ computation time and its communication overhead is $O(k+\log_2(N/(k\times p)))$. Step (5) requires $O(k\times num)$ computation time. The communication overhead in step (6) is $O((k\times num)^2)$.

Step (7) requires $O(k \times num)$ communication overhead. Step (8) requires $O\left(\left(\dfrac{k\log m}{m}+\dfrac{k\log w}{p\times w}+\dfrac{t_{me}}{4r\times\log k}\right)\times n\log k\right)$ computation time [14], where m is the size of data blocking in L2 cache for multi-core processor, w is the size of data blocking in L1 cache for multi-core processor, r is the number of parallel threads, and t_{me} is the required time to execute SIMD k-way merge.

Hence, the computation time complexity of Algorithm 2 is

$$O\left(k\times p+(k+p)\log_2(n/(k\times p))+k^2 m+\left(\dfrac{k\log m}{m}+\dfrac{k\log w}{p\times w}+\dfrac{t_{me}}{4r\times\log k}\right)\times n\log k\right)$$

The communication cost of Algorithm 2 is $O(\log_2(n/(k\times p))+ (k\times num)^2)$.

The storage space complexity of Algorithm 2 is $O(k^2 \times num)$.

Algorithm 2 distributes the partitioned subsequences to each compute node according to its computation speed, communication rate and memory capacity, and it can balance the loads among compute nodes such that all the compute nodes can finish the data merging at the same time. On the other hand, it can determine the appropriate communication order according to the communication link rate between any two compute nodes and the amount of the data to be transmitted, it uses the given communication order to exchange data among compute nodes to reduce the waiting delay, and its communication cost is low.

3   Experiment

The heterogeneous multi-core cluster is consists of the compute nodes. Table 1 lists the system parameters of the compute nodes. The running operating system is RHEL5. The programming language and parallel communication library are C, OpenMP and MPI respectively. Each node executes the thread-level parallel merging algorithm using SIMD instructions [14] to obtain its merge speed $D_{a,b}$, and the compute nodes exchange the data each other to get communication rate $B_{(a,b)(i,j)}$ for each link.

Table 1. System parameters for compute nodes on the heterogeneous multi-core cluster

Processors	Capacity of L1 cache	Capacity of L2 cache	Capacity of main memory
Intel quad core	32KB×4	12MB	2GB
AMD dual core	64KB×2	1MB	1GB
Intel dual core	32KB×2	4MB	2GB
Intel single core	32KB	2MB	512MB

We evaluate the execution time, speedup and scalability of Algorithm 2 using the different combination of the number of compute nodes, processing cores and threads.

Figure 3 gives the execution time of Algorithm 2 with increase of the number of running compute nodes and the size of the input ordered data sequences.

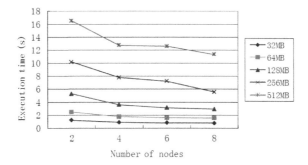

Fig. 3. Execution time of Algorithm 2 with increase of running compute nodes

We can see from Figure 3 that on the one hand, the required merge time of Algorithm 2 will be gradually decreased along with increase of the number of running compute nodes. On the other hand, when the number of running compute nodes is gradually increased, the required execution time of Algorithm 2 will be slowly decreased. This is because the amount of data exchange among compute nodes will be increased and its required communication time is relatively large at this time.

When the number of running threads is equal to the amount of running cores on each compute node, Figure 4 displays the required execution time of Algorithm 2 running 4 compute nodes and multiple cores with increase of the size of the input ordered sequences.

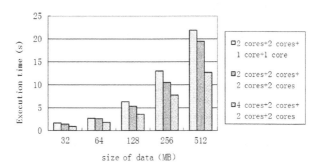

Fig. 4. Execution time of Algorithm 2 running 4 nodes with different combination of number of running cores

For the given input ordered sequences with different size, Figure 4 shows that when Algorithm 2 is executed on the multi-core heterogeneous cluster with 4 compute nodes, the more the number of running cores, the less its required execution time.

When the number of running threads is equal to the amount of running cores, Figure 5 gives the required execution time of Algorithm 2 with increase of the size of the input ordered sequences.

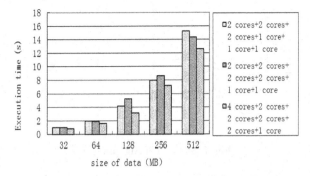

Fig. 5. Execution time of Algorithm 2 running 6 nodes when the number of running threads equals amount of running cores

As shown in Figure 5, when Algorithm 2 is executed on the multi-core heterogeneous cluster with 6 compute nodes, the required time will be somewhat increased with increase of running cores sometimes if the size of the input ordered data sequences is relatively small. The reason is that the communication overhead among the running compute nodes and cores way be increased and the size of the data to be assigned to each core will be reduced with increase of running cores, at this time, the increase of communication overhead may be superior to the saved time of parallel merge. On the other hand, we can also see from Figure 5 that when the size of the input ordered data sequences is large, the more the running cores, the less the required execution time. It means that Algorithm 2 is suitable for merging the large-scale ordered data sequences on the heterogeneous multi-core cluster.

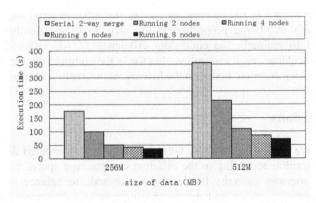

Fig. 6. Execution time of Algorithm 2 and serial 2-way merge algorithm

For the input ordered data sequences with size 256MB and 512 MB, Figure 6 displays the required execution time of the serial two-way merge algorithm and Algorithm 2 on the heterogeneous multi-core cluster with 2, 4, 6 and 8 compute nodes respectively. The obtained speedup of Algorithm 2 is given in Figure 7.

Clearly, we can see from Figure 6 that Algorithm 2 is faster than serial 2-way merge algorithm, and Algorithm 2 is efficient.

We also see from Figure 7 that Algorithm 2 obtains high speedup.

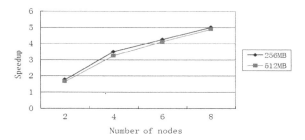

Fig. 7. Speedup of Algorithm 2

Figure 8 shows the equivalent efficiency curve of Algorithm 2.

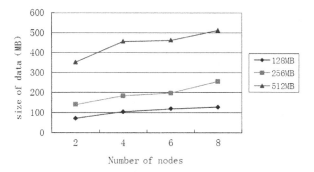

Fig. 8. Equivalent efficiency curve of Algorithm 2

As shown in Figure 8, the increase of size of the input ordered sequences to be merged is weakly sub-linear proportion to the increase of the number of running compute nodes to maintain the equivalent efficiency of Algorithm 2. Therefore, Algorithm 2 is scalable and it can utilize effectively the computation capability of the gradually increasing compute nodes on the heterogeneous multi-core cluster.

4   Conclusions

In this paper, we propose a data distribution strategy and an ordered data sequences partitioning algorithm according to the different computation speed, communication rate and main memory capacity for each compute node to balance the computing loads among compute nodes, and design and implement a communication-efficient parallel multi-way merging algorithm by constructing a data sending matrix and determining the optimized communication order among the compute nodes on the heterogeneous multi-core cluster. The presented parallel merging algorithm obtains high speedup and it has good scalability. Power consumption is one of important issues for multi-core computing. The next work is to develop an efficient and saving-power parallel merge algorithm on the hybrid multi-core CPU and GPU clusters.

Acknowledgments. This work is supported by the National Nature Science Foundation of China under Grant No. 60963001.

References

1. Chen, G.L.: Design and analysis for parallel algorithms. Higher Education Press, Beijing (2009)
2. Helman, D.R., Joseph, J.: Sorting on clusters of SMPs. In: Proceedings of the 12th International Parallel Processing Symposium, pp. 561–582. IEEE Computer Society Press, Los Alamitos (1998)
3. Ding, W.Q., Ji, Y.C., Chen, G.L.: A Parallel Merging Algorithm Based on MPP. Journal of Computer Research and Development 36(1), 52–56 (1999)
4. Giusti, A.D., Naiouf, M., Chichizola, F., et al.: Dynamic Load Balance in Parallel Merge Sorting over Homogeneous Clusters. In: Proceedings of the 19th International Conference on Advanced Information Networking and Applications, vol. 2, pp. 219–222. IEEE Computer Society Press, Los Alamitos (2005)
5. Jeon, M., Kim, D.: Parallel Merge Sort with Load Balancing. International Journal of Parallel Programming 31(1), 411–434 (2003)
6. Govindaraju, N., Gray, J., Kumar, R.: GPUTerasort: High Performance Graphics Coprocessor Sorting for Large Database Management. In: Proceedings of the 2006 ACM SIGMOD International Conference on Management of Data, pp. 325–336. ACM Press, New York (2006)
7. Gedik, B., Bordawekar, R.R., Yu, P.S.: CellSort: High Performance Sorting on the Cell Processor. In: Proceedings of 33rd International Conference on Very Large Data Bases, Vienna, Austria, September 23-27, pp. 1286–1297 (2007)
8. Chhugani, J., Nguyen, A.D., Lee, V.W., et al.: Efficient implementation of Sorting on Multi-core SIMD CPU architecture. In: Proceedings of 34th International Conference on Very Large Data Bases, Auckland, New Zealand, August 23-28, pp. 1313–1324 (2008)
9. Hao, S., Du, Z., Bader, D., et al.: A Partition-Merge Based Cache-Conscious Parallel Sorting Algorithm for CMP with Shared Cache. In: Proceedings of International Conference on Parallel Processing, Vienna, Austria, September 22-25, pp. 396–403 (2009)
10. Hultén, R., Kessler, C.W., Keller, J.: Optimized On-Chip-Pipelined Mergesort on the Cell/B.E. In: D'Ambra, P., Guarracino, M., Talia, D. (eds.) Euro-Par 2010, Part II. LNCS, vol. 6272, pp. 187–198. Springer, Heidelberg (2010)
11. Satish, N., Kim, C., Chhugani, J., et al.: Fast sort on CPUs and GPUs: a case for bandwidth oblivious SIMD sort. In: Proceedings of the 2010 International Conference on Management of Data, Indianapolis, Indiana, USA, June 6-11, pp. 351–362 (2010)
12. Zhong, C., Qu, Z.Y., Yang, F., Yin, M.X., Li, X.: Efficient and Scalable Thread-level Parallel Algorithms for Sorting Multisets on Multi-core Systems. Journal of Computers 7(1), 30–41 (2012)
13. Zhong, C., Li, X., Yang, F., Liu, J., Yin, M., Huang, Y.: Scheduling Divisible Loads with Return Messages on Multi-core Heterogeneous Clusters with Unknown System Parameters. International Journal of Advancements in Computing Technology 4(7), 110–120 (2012)
14. Wei, W.: Study on Parallel Merging Algorithms on Multi-core Systems. Master Degree Thesis, Guangxi University (2011)
15. Francis, R., Mathieson, I., Pannan, L.: A Fast, Simple Algorithm to Balance a Parallel Multiway Merge. In: Proceedings of 5th International PARLE Conference, Munich, Germany, June 14-17, pp. 570–581 (1993)

An Offline Scheduling Algorithm for Certifiable Mixed-Critical Embedded System[*]

Chengtao Wu and Renfa Li

Key Laboratory for Embedded and Network Computing of Hunan Province,
Changsha 410086, China
chengtao_wu@163.com

Abstract. In modern embedded platforms, safety-critical functionalities that must be certified correctly to high level of assurance co-exist with less critical software that are not subjected to certification requirements. These caused many scheduling problems. Nowadays, many researches focused on promising techniques for meeting the following two goals: (1) being able to certify the safety-critical functionalities under very conservative assumptions, and (2) ensuring high utilization of platform resources under less pessimistic assumptions. In this paper we propose an offline scheduling algorithm called OSS for certifiable mixed-criticality systems on a uniprocessor platform. Compared to previous proposed algorithm CBEDF, OSS can supply better schedulability.

Keywords: mixed-criticality, certification, offline scheduling, uniprocessor.

1 Introduction

Modern safety-critical embedded platforms have recently begun to address the challenge of the resource share between safety-critical functionalities that must be certified correctly to high levels of assurance and less critical software that are not subjected to certification requirements. Suppose ABS (high-critical system) and infotainment system (low-critical system) for vehicles share computing resources. The jobs for the infotainment system can cause deadline miss of the jobs for the ABS system by occupying the shared computing resources longer than expected. This situation can cause incorrect control of the vehicle, which may result in severe safety problems such as car accidents. In such Mixed-criticality Systems, to avoid these safety problems, we need some new methods.

Recent years, many papers related to the mixed-criticality systems have been published. In[1], mixed-criticality System was first defined:" Mixed-criticality is the concept of allowing applications at different levels of criticality to interact and co-exist on the same computational platform". Vestal[4] introduced the scheduling

---

[*] This work was supported in part by the NSFC (Grant No.61202102, 61173036), Department of Science & Technology of Hunan Province, China (Grant No. 2011GK3131), and Department of Education of Hunan Province (Grant No.CX2011B137).

K. Li et al. (Eds.): ParCFD 2013, CCIS 405, pp. 124–135, 2014.

problem of multiple criticality system firstly by identifying and formalizing the problem. He assumed that a task may have multiple worst-case execution times, each of which assures a different level of confidence. Vestal's algorithm is proved as the optimal for traditional FP scheduling on uniprocessor by Dorin at [9]. By showing that neither FP nor EDF scheduling of MC tasks on uniprocessor dominates the other, Baruah and Vestal proposed a hybrid algorithm by combining the benefits of both FP and EDF policies[10]. Niz[3,12]proposed a zero-slack calculation algorithm, the zero-slack calculation algorithm minimized the utilization needed by a task set by reducing the time low-criticality tasks are preempted by high-criticality ones.

Certification of mixed-criticality systems has been the latest hotspot. S. Baruah [5,13] showed that reservation-based scheduling approach is pessimistic in terms of utilization of resources for the mixed-criticality systems. To improve the utilization, they proposed an effective scheduling algorithm (OCBP) which is a priority-based scheduling algorithm for the mixed-criticality systems that use "Audsley approach"[11] to get the lowest priority job recursively. They showed the effectiveness of the algorithm on dual-criticality systems by finding upper bound of speedup factor for each algorithm. After that, they extend their work to multi-criticality systems by deriving a quantitative processor speedup factor [8].

Follow S.Baruah's System model, many new algorithm were proposed. Dario Socci[7] proposed a static priority scheduling algorithm called MCEDF. MCEDF is an optimization to EDF by swap the priority of some safety-critical jobs with non-safety-critical jobs. The swap enhance the schedulability of safety-critical jobs in the precondition that do not hurt the schedulability of non-safety-critical jobs. In [6], Taeju Park proposed a dynamic algorithm CBEDF. CBEDF divide jobs into safety-critical queues and non-safety-critical queues, safety-critical jobs predetermined their execution time through a offline handle, non-safety-critical jobs insert into the slacks in the slack remained by safety-critical jobs. Park also proved that CBEDF can dominate OCBP.

2   Dual-Criticality System Model

In order to certify a system as being correct, the certification authority (CA) mandates certain assumptions about the worst-case behavior of the system, in this paper, we care about the execution time: The Worst Case Execution Time. CA is typically far more conservative than the assumptions that the system designer would use during the process of designing, implementing, and testing the system if subsequent certification is not required. The difference in pessimism between designer's assumptions and CA mandate could be used to add non critical activities and increase utilization. However, while the CA is only concerned with the correctness of the safety-critical part of the system the system designer is responsible for ensuring that the entire system is correct, including the non-critical parts.

To simplify the System model, in this paper, we assume that there is only one certification authority, so a job has two different WECT at most.

2.1   Job Model

A dual-criticality instance $I = \{J_1, ..., J_n\}$ is composed of n dual-criticality jobs, where each job J_i is characterized by a 5-tuple of parameters: $J_i = \{ X_i, A_i, Di, C_i(LO), C_i(HI)\}$.

X_i: Criticality of J_i. HI indicates a safety-critical and LO indicates a non-safety-critical job.

A_i : Release time of J_i.

D_i : Deadline of J_i. We assume that $D_i \geq A_i$.

$C_i(LO)$:Worst-case execution time of system assumed by designer.

$C_i(HI)$:Worst-case execution time assumed by CA, if X_i=LO, $Ci(LO) = Ci(HI)$, if X_i = HI, $Ci(LO) \leq Ci(HI)$.

2.2   Scheduling in Mixed-Criticality Systems

Mode. To a HI job J_i, if it completes its execution in less than $C_i(LO)$, we say J_i is in LO mode, else if did not complete execution in $C_i(LO)$ times, J_i will switch to HI mode, and system will assign $C_i(HI)$ times to J_i.

Behavior (γ_1, ..., γ_n). Each job J_i executes for some amount of time, γi, at runtime. The γ_i units of time should be executed on its scheduling window $[A_i, D_i]$ to meet its deadline. A behavior of an instance is a collection of γ_i for all the jobs.

Definition 1. To instance I, if all jobs J_i can complete its execution at $C_i(LO)$ when I execute at a Behavior (γ_1, ..., γ_n), we say the system is LO schedulable.

Definition 2. To instance I, if all HI jobs can complete its execution at $C_i(HI)$ when I execute at a Behavior (γ_1, ..., γ_n), we say the system is HI schedulable.

Definition 3. Instance I is MC schedule's only if it can both LO schedulable and HI schedulable at a Behavior (γ_1, ..., γ_n), now we use an example to express it.

Load. In[2], [5], K.Baruah frist proposed the concept of load in mixed-critical system: Load means the maximum usage rate over all the time intervals. LO-criticality load, $Load_{LO}(I)$, and HI criticality load, $Load_{HI}(I)$, of a dual-criticality instance I are defined by the following two formulas:

$$Load_{LO}(I) = \max_{0 \leq t1 \leq t2} \frac{\sum_{J_i : t1 \leq A_i \leq D_i \leq t2} C_i(LO)}{t2 - t1}$$

$$Load_{HI}(I) = \max_{0 \leq t1 \leq t2} \frac{\sum_{J_i : t1 \leq A_i \leq D_i \leq t2} C_i(HI)}{t2 - t1}$$

Definition 4. If instance I is MC schedulable, $Load_{LO}(I) \leq 1$, $Load_{HI}(I) \leq 1$.

Example 1. Instance I comprise HI job J_1, J_3, and LO job J_2

$J_1 = \{HI, 0, 2, 1, 1\}$

$J_2 = \{LO, 1, 5, 2, 2\}$

$J_3 = \{HI, 0, 5, 2, 3\}$

We scheduling I in the following Behavior:

Step 1: execute J_1 at [0,1), then skip to Step 2.

Step 2: execute J_2 at [1,2), then skip to Step 3.

Step 3: execute J_3 at [2,4), if J_3 finish at 4, we skip to Step 4, else we skip to step 5.

Step 4: execute J_2 execute at [4,5].

Step 5: continue J_3 execute at [4,5].

The two different scheduling procedures are showed in S_{LO} and S_{HI} in Figure 1, according to Definition 3, I is MC schedulable.

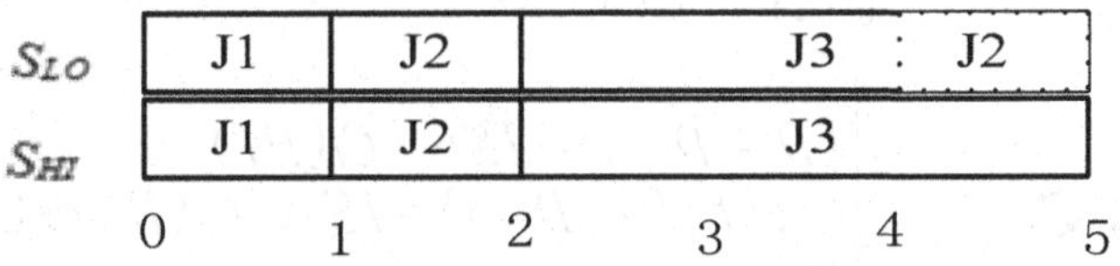

Fig. 1. Two different scheduling way of instance I

2.3   The Basic Idea of CBEDF Algorithm

CBEDF is a dynamic algorithm in uniprocessor mixed-criticality system based on Baruah's model. In CBEDF, Park introduced 2 new parameters named Empty Slack and Remaining slack.

Empty Slack(ES). If there are available units of time when all HI jobs are reserved their $Ci(HI)$ units of time, then we call the available units of time empty slack.

Remaining Slack(RS). At runtime, a HI job J_i finishes execution earlier than its deadline. Then, the time interval between $Ci(LO)$ and $Ci(HI)$ is available for other non-safety-critical jobs, we call this slack is remaining slack.

As is shown in Figure 2, job $J_1 = (HI, 0, 4, 2, 3)$, System execute J_1 at[1,4], so [0,1] is the empty slack of J_1, if J_1 finish execution in 2,then [3,4] can assign to other jobs, so [3,4]is the remaining slack of J_1.

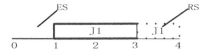

Fig. 2. Empty slack and remaining slack

The first step: separate I into 2 queues, one for HI jobs, the other for LO jobs, and sort the queues according to job's deadline.

The second step: Offline Empty Slack Location Discovery for HI jobs, suppose $I_{HI} = \{J_1,...,J_n\}$ is the queue for safety-critical jobs, so, for J_i: $ES_{Ji} = D_i - A_i - C_i(HI)$, however, the empty slack can be used by other HI critical jobs, Thus, the empty slack size is decreased by the other HI critical jobs. Consequently, calculating empty slack size should consider the decreased size. We can calculate the empty slack size for each HI critical job with following equations:

$$
IS_{Ji} = \begin{cases} (D_i - D_{i+1}) + IS_{Ji+1} + C_i(HI) \\ \quad , if\, (D_i - D_{i+1}) + IS_{Ji+1} + C_i(HI) > 0 \\ 0\,, if\, i = n \\ 0\,, ohterwise \end{cases}
$$

$$
ES_{Ji} = \begin{cases} (D_i - D_{i-1}) - IS_{Ji} - C_i(HI) \\ \quad , if (D_i - D_{i-1}) - IS_{Ji} - C_i(HI) > 0 \\ 0 \\ \quad , ohterwise \end{cases}
$$

The third step: Scheduling at Runtime, there are 4 possible cases: 1. There is no ready job, 2. There are only LO critical ready jobs, 3. There are only HI critical ready jobs, 4. There are both LO and HI critical ready jobs.

For cases 1, 2 and 3, CBEDF scheduling algorithm dispatches any ready jobs because considering criticality of jobs is meaningless for the cases. For case 4, CBEDF scheduling algorithm checks whether current slack is a free slack or not. If so (remaining or empty slack), then a LO critical job is dispatched to the current slack. Otherwise, a HI critical job is dispatched.

In CBEDF, Park modified the $Load_{LO}(I)$ to $Load_{MIX}(I)$, He pointed out that if $Load_{MIX}(I) \leq 1 \wedge Load_{HI}(I) \leq 1$, I would be CBEDF schedulable, However, it is not always true, we can see the following Example 2.

$$
Load_{MIX}(I) = \max_{0 \leq t1 \leq t3} \frac{\displaystyle\sum_{J_i:t1 \leq A_i \leq D'_i \leq t3} C_i(LO)}{t3 - t1}
$$

$D_i' = D_i + C_i(LO) - C_i(HI)$.

Example 2: Instance I_2 comprise HI job J_7, J_8, and LO job J_9, $_{10}$

   J7=(HI, 0, 5, 2, 2)

   J8=(HI, 0, 4, 1, 2)

   J9= (LO, 0, 3, 1, 1)

   J10= (LO, 3, 5, 1, 1)

$Load_{MIX}(I_2)$=0.8, $Load_{MIX}(I_2)$=1, in Park's opinion: I_2 would be CBEDF schedulable, We now try to construct the scheduling table , ES_{J7}=0, ES_{J8}=1, we execute I_2 in the order. As shown in Figure 3, we can see J_{10} miss the deadline, I_2 is not CBEDF schedulable. However, [2,3] is an remaining slack for $J_{10,}$ but it is not be used while J_{10} can't find enough slacks.

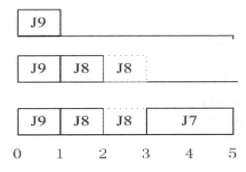

Fig. 3. CBEDF Algorithm

3   Offline Slack Shift Scheduling Algorithm

CBEDF is a Dynamic scheduling algorithm, ES is calculated according to the proposed formula, but the formula is not always true. Moreover, we can not consider the actual Situation of LO jobs when we assign HI jobs. Sometimes, LO jobs can not find enough slacks in their scheduling windows, but there may be enough slacks out of their scheduling windows. If we can shift these slacks into their scheduling windows, the schedulability for the instance will be obviously improved.

3.1   Description of OSS

In this section, we propose an offline scheduling algorithm that generate scheduling table before the execution of instance. Similar to CBEDF, our algorithm divides instance into two queues, one for HI jobs, and the other one for LO jobs, two queues are sorted according to their deadline. Then, we assign HI jobs into scheduling table in order, every time we assign a job into scheduling table when this job is schedulable, we let the job execute as late as possible. After all HI jobs are assigned, we assign LO jobs into scheduling table. If a lower priority job does not have enough slacks in the scheduling window, we will seek slacks out of its scheduling table and try to swap they into scheduling table if such swap do not destroy the higher priority jobs' schedulablility.

Algorithm: OSS
RUNQueue HI for HI jobs, LO for HI jobs
Table S as scheduling table
//Insert HI jobs

```
1:WHILE HI.HEAD!= NULL DO
2:   IF(IsSlack(Window(HI)))
3:     S.Insert(HI)
4:   ELSE IF IsESBefore(Window(HI))
5:    IF CanSwap(ES,W(HI))
6:      Swap(ES,W(HI))
7:      S.Insert(HI)
8:    END IF
9:   ELSE Return Failure
10: END IF
11:END WHILE
```

//Insert LO jobs

```
1:WHILE LO.HEAD!=NULL
2: If(IsSlack(Window(LO)))
3:       If(IsRS(Window(LO)))
4:         S.InsertRS(LO)
5:       END IF
6:       S..InsertES(LO)
7: ELSE If(IsRSBefore(W(LO)))
8:    IF CanSwap(RS,W(LO))
9:        SWAP（RS，W(LO)）
10:        S.InsertRS(LO)
11:    END IF
12: ELSE If(IsESBefore(W(LO)))
13:    IF CanSwap(ES,W(LO))
14:        SWAP（ES，W(LO)）
15:        S.InsertES(LO)
16:    END IF
17: ELSE IF(IsRSAfter(W(LO)))
18:    IF CanShift(RS,W(LO))
19:        Shift(RS,W(LO))
20:        S.InsertRS(LO)
21:    END IF
22:    ELSE RETRUN FAILURE
23: END IF
24: END WHILE
```

First Fit Principle. While assigning a job or swapping slacks into a scheduling window, there may be many feasible choices, choosing the best location is a NP-hard problem, so we use the first fit principle which can   reduce the time complexity greatly.

3.2   Calculate the Slack's Scope

In our algorithm, we assign the empty slack as early as possible, and we assign the remaining slack at the end of a HI job. However, the location of RS and ES are not fixed. We can shift these slacks according to the actual situation of the instance. In this paper, we redefined the empty slack and remaining slack. An empty slack means a unit of slack, for example, ES[k] denotes interval [k-1,k], and this interval is an ES for job J_i, $W(J_i)$ denote its scheduling window. $W(ES[k])$ denotes the scope of ES[k].

$$W(J_i) = [A_i, D_i]$$

$$W(ES[k]) = [k-1, \max_{ES[k] \in W(J_i)} D_i]$$

The location of RS is determined after the assignation of HI jobs, but we can shift it while assigning the LO jobs. like ES[k], RS[K] denotes interval [k-1,k], $W(RS[k])$ denotes the scope of RS[k].

$$W(RS[k]) = [A_i + C_i(LO), D_i] \mid RS[k] \in J_i$$

3.3   Schedulability Analysis of OSS

We now use OSS to schedule the Example 1 mentioned above.

Firstly, we assign HI job into the scheduling table, J_1's scheduling table is [0,2),we assign[1,2) to J_1, as J_3's scheduling table is [0,5],we assign[2,5] to J_3. The HI scheduling table is shown in Figure 4.

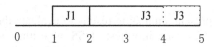

Fig. 4. The assignation of HI jobs

Secondly, we calculate the scope of ES and RS.

$W(ES[1])=[0,5]; W(RS[5])=[2,5]$

Finally, we assign LO job J_2 into the scheduling table. J_2's scheduling window [1,5] exists 1 units of slack, J_2 need 2 units of slacks to execute, we need to seek another unit of slack out of [1,5], we find ES[1]'s scope have intersection with $W(J_2)$, so we try to swap ES[1] to $W(J_2)$, as [1,2] can swap with ES[1], so we swap ES[1] to this position. Then we assign J_2 into the 2 units of slacks. The process is shown in figure 5.

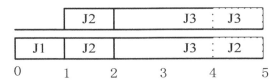

Fig. 5. Assignation of LO jobs

In section 2, Example 2 can't schedule using CBEDF, now, we try to use OSS to schedule it.

Firstly, we assign HI jobs into the scheduling table according to their priority, the HI scheduling table is shown in S_{HI} in Fig. 6.

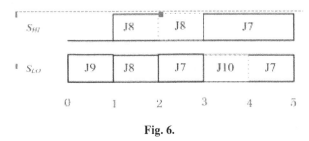

Fig. 6.

Secondly, we calculate the range of motion of slacks:

W(ES[1])=[0,5], W(RS[3])=[2,4]

Thirdly, we assign LO jobs into scheduling table. According to the scheduling table expressed in S_{LO} in Fig. 6, I is schedulable according to our method, so I is MC schedulable.

4   Performance Evaluation and Simulation

In this section, we will present simulation results to evaluate the performance of the proposed OSS method schedulability test. OSS algorithm was implemented in MATLAB, running on Lenovo Y460 computers with i3 CPUs at 2.27 GHz and 4 GB of RAM.

We evaluated the proposed OSS schedulability test with randomly generated instance, to generate an instance, the number of jobs is a parameter input by our main function \t, we use the random function "rand( )" to generate a job with keeping properties described in following formula.:

$$0 \leq A_i \leq A_i + C_i(LO) \leq Ai + C_i(HI) \leq D_i \leq 200$$

$$0 \leq C_i(LO) \leq C_i(HI) \leq 10$$

To determine the maximum number of jobs in an instance, we calculate the average of $Load_{LO}(I)$ and $Load_{HI}(I)$ with a randomly generated instance. The results are shown in Fig. 7.

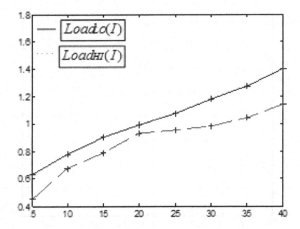

Fig. 7. The average load of instance with the increase of jobs

OSS was optimized from CBEDF, so we compared the schedulability of them in the same condition. Fig. 8 shows the percentage of instance that are schedulable by the two algorithm with the increase of the number of jobs in an instance, the schedulability of the 2 algorithms both dropped when the number of jobs increasing, when the number of jobs in an instance is 10, the two algorithms in the maximum gap.

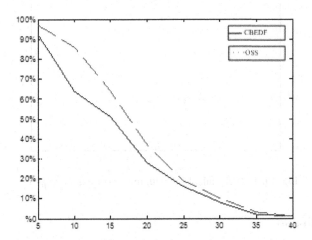

Fig. 8. The schedulablility of instance with the increase of jobs

Fig. 9 shows the results of the percentage of instance that are schedulable when $Load_{HI}(I) \leq 1$ and $Load_{LO}(I)$ from 0.5 to 1 change. Fig. 10 shows the results of the percentage of instance that are schedulable when $Load_{LO}(I) \leq 1$ and $Load_{HI}(I)$ from 0.5 to 1 change. According to Figure 10 and 11,we can see OSS have better schedulability from the results, .and the more $Load_{LO}(I)$ or $Load_{HI}(I)$ close to 1, the more obvious the difference between them

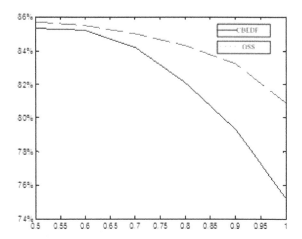

Fig. 9. The schedulablility of instance with the increase of $Load_{LO}(I)$

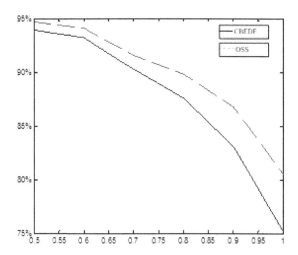

Fig. 10. The schedulablility with the increase of $Load_{HI}(I)$

5   Conclusion

With the increase of complexity and diversity, the certification of MC System has received more and more attention, we need to ensure the certification of system and ensure high utilization of platform resources at the same time. Our proposed algorithm improves the lack of flexibility of CBEDF and obviously enhances the schedulability of MC System. Our algorithm is easily extended to constructing scheduling table for periodic tasks, by representing the task system as the collection of independent jobs obtained by explicitly enumerating all the jobs that would be generated over the interval [0; P). In future, we will extend our algorithm to more general such as multicriticality and multicore system, we are challenging to extend it.

References

1. Mixed critical systems (2010), http://www.nitrd.gov/about/blog/whitepapers/20MixedCirticalitysystems.pdf
2. Baruah, S.K., Li, H., Stougie, L.: Towards the design of certifiable mixed-criticality systems. In: Caccamo, M. (ed.) IEEE Real-Time and Embedded Technology and Applications Symposium, pp. 13–22. IEEE Computer Society (2010)
3. de Niz, D., Lakshmanan, K., Rajkumar, R.: On the scheduling of mixed-criticality real-time task sets. In: Baker, T.P. (ed.) IEEE Real-Time Systems Symposium, pp. 291–300. IEEE Computer Society (2009)
4. Vestal, S.: Preemptive scheduling of multi-criticality systems with varying degrees of execution time assurance. In: Proc. Real-Time Systems Symposium, RTSS 2007, pp. 239–243. IEEE (2007)
5. Baruah, S., Fohler, G.: Certification-cognizant time-triggered scheduling of mixed-criticality systems. In: Proc. Real-Time Systems Symposium, RTSS 2011, pp. 3–12. IEEE (January 2011)
6. Park, T., Kim, S.: Dynamic scheduling algorithm and its schedulability analysis for certifiable dual-criticality systems. In: Proc. Intern. Conf. on Embedded Software, EMSOFT 2011, pp. 253–262. ACM (2011)
7. Mixed Critical Earliest Deadline First (2012), http://www.verimag.imag.fr/TR/TR-2012-22.pdf
8. Baruah, S.K., Li, H., Stougie, L.: Mixed-criticality scheduling: Improved resource-augmentation results. In: Philips, T. (ed.) Computers and Their Applications, ISCA, pp. 217–223 (2010)
9. Dorin, F., Richard, P., Richard, M., Goossens, J.: Schedulability and sensitivity analysis of multiple criticality tasks with fixed-priorities. Real-Time Systems 46, 305–331 (2010)
10. Baruah, S., Vestal, S.: Schedulability Analysis of Sporadic Tasks with Multiple Criticality Specifications. In: Proc. of ECRTS, pp. 147–155 (2008)
11. Audsley, N.C.: Optimal priority assignment and feasibility of static priority tasks with arbitrary start times. Tech. rep., The University of York, England (1991)
12. Kakshmanan, K., de Niz, D., Rajkumar, R.R., Moreno, G.: Resource allocation in distributed mixed-criticality cyber-physical systems. In: Proceedings of International Conference on Distributed Computing Systems, ICDCS (2010)
13. Li, H., Baruah, S.: An algorithm for scheduling certifiable mixed-criticality sporadic task systems. In: Proceedings of the Real-Time Systems Symposium (RTSS) (December 2010)

An Efficient Implementation of Entropic Lattice Boltzmann Method in a Hybrid CPU-GPU Computing Environment

Yu Ye[1,*], Peng Chi[2], and Yan Wang[1]

[1] Hunan University, College of Information Science and Engineering,
Changsha, 410082, China
[2] National Supercomputing Center of Changsha, Hunan University Office,
Changsha, 410082, China
`yeyu.hnu@gmail.com, lkl@hnu.edu.cn, bessie11@yeah.net`

Abstract. In the high performance computing market, CPU-GPU hybrid computing is gradually becoming the tendency. Entropic Lattice Boltzmann method(ELBM) parallelization, like many parallel algorithms in the field of rapid scientific and engineering computing, has given rise to much attention for applications of computational fluid dynamics. This paper presents an efficient implementation of ELBM for a D3Q19 lattice Boltzmann flow simulation in a hybrid CPU-GPU computing environment, which is consisted of AMD multi-core CPU with NVIDIA graphics processors unit (GPU). To overcome the GPU memory size limitation and communication overhead, we propose a set of techniques that can be used to develop efficient ELBM algorithms for the hybrid system. Considering that the respective contributions of CPU versus GPU and the lattice scale of application, the optimal load balancing model is built. These approaches result in an efficient implementation with balanced use of multi-core processor and a graphics processor based on software framework OpenMP and CUDA. Finally, we show that the comparison of performance results using both CPU and GPU with using either a CPU core or a GPU.

Keywords: Computational fluid dynamics, Entropic Lattice Boltzmann Method(ELBM), Hybrid computing, Parallelization, CUDA, OpenMP, GPU.

1   Introduction

In the field of scientific computing and engineering simulation, many new and complex computationally demanding problems with increased accuracy and enhanced numerical performance expect to solve. Graphics Processing Unit (GPU) as computational accelerator is a massively multi-threaded architecture and then is widely used for graphical, and general purpose computations, such as molecular dynamics simulations and computational fluid dynamics (CFD)[1]. In the early years,

---

* Corresponding author.

K. Li et al. (Eds.): ParCFD 2013, CCIS 405, pp. 136–148, 2014.

GPU programming was indirectly mapped computational tasks to graphic manipulations and used graphic libraries such as OpenGL and DirectX. That is General-purpose computing on graphics processing unit (GPGPU)[2], which is becoming popular due to its priorities of high, peak performance. Although this programming method is cumbersome, it was soon obvious that the GPUs' potential and capabilities could be utilized for accelerating these applications, especially since they have considerably lower cost than current supercomputers or workstation clusters. Moreover, GPU has been further used for the general purpose with the release of CUDA, which stands for Compute Unified Device Architecture by NVIDIA. In particular, the advent of the CUDA programming environment[3,4] has made it possible and convenience to use the computing power of NVIDIA GPU with a simple extension to the standard C language.   Despite GPU possesses the above advantages, its real performance is not necessarily higher than that of the current high-performance CPU, especially with recent trends towards multi-core and many-core. The reason of lower real performance of GPU can be illustrated from two aspects. Firstly, the communication overhead of memory transfer between CPU and GPU has a huge impact on raw GPU performance improvements. Secondly, GPU memory size and its usage restriction limit the maximum data size that can be computed by the data transfer from CPU to a GPU, thus further aggravating the memory bandwidth limitation. It is noteworthy that manually conducting proper load balancing under a hybrid CPU-GPU environment for arbitrary data sizes turn into a hot topic and also remain a difficult challenge.

The entropic Lattice Boltzmann method (ELBM) originated from lattice Boltzmann method (LBM), which is a mesoscopic numerical method that simulates macroscopic incompressible fluid dynamics based on discrete kinetic equations (Lattice Boltzmann Equation, LBE)[5]. ELBM takes into account that the stability of the LBM can be guaranteed by satisfying the second law of thermodynamics, that is to say Boltzmann H-theorem[6-9]. Comparisons between the LBM and ELBM mainly include that both the local equilibrium distribution function and the relaxation parameter should be restricted by H-theorem per lattice. More specifically, on one hand, the equilibrium state in the ELBM is not explicitly needed because of the collision operators can be computed based on knowledge of H function[10]. In order to ensure the implementation of H-theorem, one must first find the kinetic state after particles collision that does not increase entropy during the collision procedure, and finally this kinetic state returns a limit for the new state after the collision. On the other hand, the ELBM has to be solved the non-linear equation at each lattice site and every time step[11], this is extremely computationally expensive. Hence, the development of efficient parallel algorithms and optimized way to solve such problem has become an important research direction. For LBM parallelization, owing to its simple kernel structure and natural parallelism, LBM has been successfully implemented on multi-core CPU and GPU by many researchers from related fields for high performance computing in the past few years. As early as in 2003, Lie et al.[12] obtained first promising results of a LBM based flow solver on GPU, applying the OpenGL graphics API. The other implementations of LBM on a single GPU have been reported[13-17] with good speedup ratios relative to a single CPU core using stencils with different discrete distributions. In the case of LBM implementations for multi-GPU and heterogeneous CPU-GPU clusters, Wang et al.[18] performed simulations of lid-driven cavity flow on an HPC system named Tsubame comprising 170 NVIDIA Tesla S1070 boxes. Christian et al.[19] developed an approach for heterogeneous simulations on clusters equipped with varying node configurations, using WaLBerla framework. In terms of ELBM parallelization and optimization strategies, there are a few research works[20,21] in order to reduce the computational overhead, most of them are improved from the numerical calculation aspect. Considering the point of view of parallel computing capabilities, the research work of ELBM parallelization is relatively scarce.

In the present study, D3Q19-ELBM flow simulation is executed in hybrid CPU-GPU computing environment. We start with a brief description of ELBM in Section 2. Section 3 gives an overview of CPU-GPU synergetic computing and programming environment via the CUDA v4.2 framework, shared memory parallelization using OpenMP to improve the performance of hybrid CPU-GPU LBM simulations. Section 4 describes the detailed implementation of D3Q19 flow simulation for combining GPU and multi-core CPU in ELBM hybrid parallelization algorithm. In Section 5, some analyses and comparisons are made on the performance of the simulations, which are performed on a single CPU core, a singe GPU and hybrid CPU-GPU. Besides, the decomposition mode of computation and communication is presented and compared with the non-decomposition mode. Finally, Section 6 gives a few conclusions and directions for future research.

2   Entropic Lattice Boltzmann Method

Work pertaining to LBM had been applied to a large variety of applications before ELBM was proposed. As we all know, the LBM is aimed to model a physical system in terms of the dynamics of fictitious particles (or mass distribution functions) and the macroscopic quantities (such as mass density and momentum density) that can be obtained by evaluating the flow dynamic moments of the distribution function. Generally speaking, LBM can be split into collision and propagation steps, which are required to deal with the density distribution function. However, the non-positivity of the distribution function in this method causes numerical instablities[22][23]. To conquer this problem, Karlin etc. in some articles[6,8,9,24] put forward an improved scheme that named ELBM that satisfy the second principle of the thermodynamic by imposing the monotonicity and the minimality of the H function.

2.1   Main Points of ELBM

To obtain the ELBM, the velocity space and time must be discretized; then the evolution equation[25,26] reads (in lattice units, Δt means the time step)

$$f_i(x+e_i\delta t, t+\delta t) = f_i(x,t) + \alpha\beta[f_i^{eq}(x,t) - f_i(x,t)] \tag{1}$$

where $f_i(x,t) = f(x,u,t)\big|_{u=e_i}$, for $i = 0,1,...q-1$ are the density distribution functions at lattice site x at time t, corresponding to the q lattice speeds e_i. On the left-hand side of Eq.(1) represents the particle free-streaming, whereas the right-hand side includes the particle collisions via the effective relaxation frequency with α as defined by the solution of the following nonlinear equation Eq.(2) and β as defined by Eq.(3).

$$H(f) = H(f + \alpha(f^{eq} - f)) \ , f = \{f_i\}_{i=0}^{q-1} \ , f^{eq} = \{f_i^{eq}\}_{i=0}^{q-1} \tag{2}$$

$$\beta = c_s^2 \frac{\delta t}{2\upsilon + \delta t} \tag{3}$$

where $c_s = 1/\sqrt{3}$ is the speed of sound and υ is kinematic viscosity.

In addition, the local equilibrium function f_i^{eq} is defined as the extremum of the following discretized H function[26]:

$$H(f) = \sum_{i=0}^{q-1} f_i \ln(\frac{f_i}{w_i}) \tag{4}$$

here the w_i are the weights associated with each lattice direction in Eq.(4). In the case of isothermal, the explicit expression of the f_i^{eq} is the product of three times the one-dimensional solution and given by

$$f_i^{eq}(x,t) = \rho w_i \prod_{d=1}^{D} (2 - \sqrt{1 + 3u_d^2})(\frac{2u_d + \sqrt{1 + 3u_d^2}}{1 - u_d})^{v_{id}} \tag{5}$$

where d is the index of the spatial directions, ρ is fluid density and $u = \{u_d\}_{d=1}^{D}$ are flow velocity, with D physical dimensions and $v_{id} \in \{-1,0,1\}$. The above H function is calculated under the constraint of mass and momentum conservation , that is ,

$$\rho = \sum_{i=0}^{q-1} f_i = \sum_{i=0}^{q-1} f_i^{eq}, \quad \rho u = \sum_{i=0}^{q-1} c_i f_i = \sum_{i=0}^{q-1} c_i f_i^{eq} \tag{6}$$

It is worth mentioning that Eq.(2) can be solved by numerical methods, typically with the Newton-Raphson (NR) method. This operation needs to spend a lot of computational cost; therefore, the present work is aim to overcome this difficulty through the rapid development of hardware resources, such as multi-core CPU or GPU.

2.2   D3Q19 Discretization Model

Indeed, there exists some related concept already mentioned in the previous subsection. Among the above described many equation, e.g. Eq.(1), Eq.(2) and Eq.(5), $DdQq$ models for d spatial dimensions and q velocities have been widely adopted by most flow simulations. In the present study, we shall refer to the D3Q19 discretization model, i.e. 19 discrete velocities in three spatial dimensions. The particle velocity e_i may be defined as:

$$e_i = \begin{cases} (0,0,0), \ i = 0 \\ (\pm1,0,0)e, (0,\pm1,0)e, (0,0,\pm1)e, \ i = 1,...,6 \\ (\pm1,\pm1,0)e, (\pm1,0,\pm1)e, (0,\pm1,\pm1)e, \ i = 7,...,18 \end{cases}$$

here $e = \delta x / \delta t$ with δx, δt representing the lattice spacing and the time increment respectively. Meanwhile, the corresponding weighting factors are, $w_0 = 1/3$, $w_i = 1/18, i = 1,...,6$ and $w_i = 1/36, i = 7,...,18$. Fig.1 visually shows the D3Q19 model.

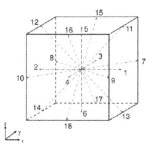

Fig. 1. Discrete velocity vectors for the D3Q19 model [18]

3   Overview of CPU-GPU Synergetic Computing and Programming Environment

In this section, we will overview of CPU-GPU synergetic computing and programming environment. For hybrid CPU-GPU computing hardware environment, our small high-performance computing workstation, which is consisted of AMD multi-core CPU with NVIDIA GPU linking through PCI Express X16, often appears in the area of scientific computing. As far as their roles are concerned, GPU is often viewed as the intensive computing core, while CPU collaborate with GPU to transfer data and control program. With respect to software programming environment, most application developers develop efficient programs based on OpenMP and CUDA. Specifically, intensive tasks will be allocated and executed on GPU using CUDA; other tasks adopt other process to control program and migrate data on CPU, besides extra computing tasks.

3.1   Multi-Core CPU Programming Using OpenMP

OpenMP[27][28] is an abbreviation for Open Multi-Processing, which is an application programming interface that supports multi-platform shared-memory parallel programming in C/C++ and Fortran, it uses a portable and scalable model that gives programmers a simple and flexible interface for developing parallel applications for platforms ranging from the standard desktop computer to the supercomputer[29]. OpenMP is designed for multi-processor/core, shared memory machines which may have the underlying architecture including Uniform Memory Access (UMA) and Non-Uniform Memory Access (NUMA).

OpenMP is composed of several core elements, involving the constructs for thread creation, workload distribution (work sharing), data environment management, thread synchronization, user-level runtime routines and environment variables. For the major components can be described as follows:

- OpenMP provides flexible but simple ways to annotate the program that specific parts can be run in parallel. It uses *#pragmas* when C/C++ language is chosen. For example, the pragma *omp parallel* is used to fork additional threads to carry out the work enclosed in the construct in parallel. However, the original thread will be denoted as *master thread* with thread ID 0.
- Work-sharing constructs can be used to divide a task among the threads so that each thread executes its allocated part of the code. Under normal circumstances, there are four annotation ways to work independently assigned to one or all of the threads, including *omp for* or *omp do, sections, single, master*.

Since some private variables are necessary to pass values between the sequential part and the parallel region (i.e. the code block executed in parallel), data environment management and thread synchronization are introduced as data sharing attribute clauses and synchronization clauses by appending them to the OpenMP directive, such as *shared, private, critical, atomic,* etc.

3.2   GPU Programming Using CUDA

Compute Unified Device Architecture (CUDA) as a general-purpose GPU computing technology developed by NVIDIA has been attracted much attention for more and more scientific and engineering researchers. CUDA capable GPU is composed of a large number of streaming multiprocessors (SM) with multiple processing cores (SP). Each SP has its own arithmetic units in order to undertake the computational operation. The single-instruction multiple data (SIMD) execution scheme is followed by all SPs within one SM, but the overall execution scheme may be described as single-instruction multiple thread (SIMT) due to all SMs are not globally synchronized.

Compared to the CPU memory architecture, CUDA computing devices on GPU show a complex memory hierarchy in Fig. 2(a) so as to achieve high performance. The total storage of GPU mainly contains a rather large off-chip device memory and a little scarce on-chip memory. An off-chip memory named global memory is shared for all SMs, which is responsible for interaction with the host/CPU. When the data is processed by the device GPU, it is first transferred from the host memory to the global memory via calling the command *cudaMemcpy()* with the parameter *cudaMemcpyHostToDevice*. Also, output data from the device required to be transported back to the host memory with the parameter *cudaMemcpyDeviceToHost*. Constant memory also provides interaction with the host, which is not allowed to be written but be read. In addition, texture memory is introduced to accelerate frequently performed operations[30]. An on-chip shared memory is visible for all the threads executed on a SM and on-chip registers are private to each thread. It has to be remarked that the data communication with on-chip registers and shared memory are much faster than that with off-chip global memory, and shared memories are as fast as registers while also allowing cooperation between threads of the same block. Regrettably, the sizes of shared memories and register are so small that specific attention is required not to exceed their limited capacities.

Programming in CUDA is easier than traditional GPU, because of it is an extension to C/C++ language. CUDA program can basically be divided into CPU code and one kernel. In fact, the kernel is a void returning function to be executed in several threads with private local variables on the GPU. Threads are grouped together as thread blocks which may have up to three dimensions using the command *dim3 threads(...)*, they can communicate through the very fast shared memory in the same block and through the device global memory in different blocks. Blocks are grouped into different dimensional grids using the command *dim3 grid(...)*, they are executed asynchronously, and there is no efficient dedicated mechanism to ensure global synchronization. However, global synchronization is achieved by performing multiple kernel launches. In brief, the general hybrid processing flow of CUDA and OpenMP programming and the basic steps are depicted in Fig. 2(b).

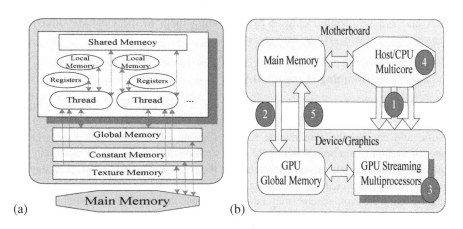

Fig. 2. Illustration of CUDA for (a) Memory hierarchy in GPU device and (b) Hybrid programming flow paradigm. ①CPU multi-threaded control GPU. ②CPU Data transfer to Global Memory. ③GPU parallel computing. ④CPU parallel computing. ⑤Result transfer to main memory.

4   Hybrid CPU-GPU Implementation of D3Q19 Model

As mentioned previously in Section.2, the ELBM implementation can be divided into three steps: *solution* relaxation parameter, which needs to satisfy the nonlinear equation Eq.(2). *Collision* in which the collision operator i.e. the right side of Eq.(1) is applied to the particle distribution, and *propagation* in which updated particle populations are propagated to the neighboring nodes as the left side of Eq.(1) according to *D3Q19* model. Thus, the ELBM implementation is summarized by the following pseudo-code:

1. **for each** time step t **do**
2.   **for each** lattice node x **do**
3.   reading velocity distribution $f_i(x,t)$
4.   **if** node x is on boundaries **then**
5.   applying boundary conditions to process
6.   **end if**
7.   computing density ρ and momentum ρu
8.   computing equilibrium distribution $f_i^{eq}(x,t)$
9.   computing relaxation parameter α via H-α solver
10.   computing updated distribution $f'_i(x,t)$
11.   computing updated equilibrium distribution $f_i'^{eq}(x,t)$
12.   propagating to neighboring nodes $x + \delta x$
13.   **end for**
14. **end for**

As we can learn from Fig.2(b) and the above implementation steps, the computing process of the individual particles may be both done on the GPU and CPU. For our parallel computation, domain partitioning method based on optimal load balancing allocation model firstly is used in the solution domain. In order to take full advantage of the GPU and CPU computing power respectively, data structure design and memory access model are also concerned with computing environment restrictions. In addition, in point of solving the relaxation parameter α, the Newton-Raphson iteration method does not work well due to the derivation of the function in Eq.(4) is too small and the load imbalance is occurred by the difference of iteration number on each grid point. We hereby use a combination of the bisection method and Newton-Raphson iteration method[31] for parallel computing in a hybrid CPU-GPU environment.

4.1   Model-Based Optimal Load Balancing

To derive the optimal load balancing model, we divide the entire ELBM computation into several sub steps, also including pre-processing stage, i.e. memory allocation and data migration. The execution time of these steps is represented with some model parameters, which denote primitive performance of underlying operations and hardware. For a given *D3Q19* model of size n^3 lattices and the distribution ratio r to a CPU, we seek the most appropriate value of r such that the model predicts gives the shortest execution time. As expressed at the beginning of this section, the computation time of propagation in association with collision run on GPU is marked as $T_{G\text{-}COL\text{-}PRO}$, $T_{C\text{-}COL\text{-}PRO}$ on multi-core CPU. Another crucial sub-step is the solving relaxation parameter whose time spent on GPU and CPU, $T_{G\text{-}PAR}$ and $T_{C\text{-}PAR}$ respectively. T_{CTG} denotes the data transmission time from CPU to GPU and the inverse process is denoted as T_{GTC}.

Thus, the hybrid CPU-GPU computing model for ELBM is as follows:

$$T = n^3 \cdot (1-r) \cdot (T_{CTG} + T_{GTC}) + \max\{ \frac{n^3 \cdot (1-r) \cdot (T_{G\text{-}COL\text{-}PRO} + T_{G\text{-}PAR})}{TD_C}, \frac{n^3 \cdot r \cdot (T_{C\text{-}COL\text{-}PRO} + T_{C\text{-}PAR})}{TD_G} \} \qquad (7)$$

In the above model, we assume that ELBM is done by using TD_C threads on multi-core CPU and TD_G threads on GPU. In fact, the second term on the right side of Eq.(7) is not so easy due to the difference of computing resources and the size of calculation scale. For the sake of simplicity, we have consciously ignored these factors.

4.2   Data Structure Design and Memory Access Model

There are two key aspects for achieving a good ELBM performance in a hybrid CPU-GPU computing environment. One of them is data structure design which can affect the speed of memory access. Array of Structure (AoS)[19] is chosen on multi-core CPU, which means that the particle distribution functions (PDFs) of each cell are stored adjacent in memory. Whereas, for the Structure-of-Arrays (SoA) layout used on GPU, the PDFs pointing in the same lattice direction are adjacent in global memory. As for global memory access, owing to the scattered loads that occur in this way can be efficiently coalesced by the memory sub-system, we can use less shared memory of the GPU. Another problem is the configuration of the execution grid since it may only have up to two dimensions. In our implementation, we choose to use a two-dimensional grid of size $n^3/2^q \times 2^{q\text{-}p}$ with one-dimensional blocks of size 2^p, here p and q are free parameters. The optimal values for p and q is determined by the size of lattices.

5   Performance Results

We demonstrate the hybrid CPU-GPU synergetic ELBM solver with the 3D lid driven cavity, which has been extensively studied and usually used as a benchmark solution to test the fluid flow. In Section 5.1, we introduce the experiment environment including basic information on the hardware structure and the relevant parameters of the simulation. Subsequently, we investigate the computation time of ELBM on a single core CPU, single GPU and hybrid CPU-GPU computing framework in Section 5.2. Additionally, the Million Lattice Updates Per Second(MLUPS) as another performance index is also discussed.

5.1   Experimental Environment

To evaluate the effectiveness of our proposed method, two experimental studies are employed to compare the entire ELBM computation time, that is to say, we show that the comparison of performance results using both CPU and GPU with using either a CPU core or a GPU. For both of the studies, we use a two AMD Opteron(TM) processor (2.2GHz), eight-core machine with 8GB main memory, and a Tesla C2050 GPU. The GPU is equipped with 448 stream processors running at 1.15GHz processor clock with 3GB of graphics memory. We use Linux kernel 2.6.38 with NVIDIA display driver version 256.53 and CUDA 4.2 and GCC version 4.4.5.

Our numerical simulations are performed for Reynolds number 1000 with different mesh grid sizes. Thereamong, the Reynolds number is defined as: $Re = LU_{max}/v$, here v is the viscosity, L is the cavity side. Only the U_{max} is changed to get fine grids. With the fluid viscosity $v = 0.0256$ and $Re = 1000$, 64, 128 and 256 lattices per side are need to imposed velocity $U_{max} = 0.4$, 0.2, 0.1 respectively.

5.2   Performance of ELBM with Hybrid CPU-GPU Computing

Table 1 compares the total computing time and MLUPS of each implementation for different experimental platforms, scaling the simulations to various domain grid sizes varying from 64^3 to 256^3 cells. The performance of ELBM achieved with hybrid CPU-GPU results between 4 and 6 times faster than ELBM-CPU, depending on the domain size and data distribution ratio. For single core CPU, we obtain the results over 1000 iterations. Nevertheless, the GPU and hybrid CPU-GPU results have been performed for 10000 iterations.

Table 1. Comparison of execution time(in seconds) and MULPS of ELBM implementation on single core CPU, single GPU and hybrid CPU-GPU

Mesh grid size	CPU		GPU			Hybrid CPU-GPU		
	Total time	MLUPS	Total time	MLUPS	Speedup	Total time	MLUPS	Speedup
64^3	219.2	1.20	58.6	44.73	3.74	49.1	53.39	4.46
128^3	1652.5	1.27	426.5	49.17	3.87	321.3	65.27	5.14
256^3	9586.6	1.75	2136.8	78.52	4.49	1682.5	99.72	5.70

To see how optimal choice of r affects the performance, we plot the speedup of the hybrid CPU-GPU implementation as a function of data distribution ratio r. Here, we fixed the mesh grid size n^3 to 128^3 and r varies from 1/512 to 6/512. The results are shown in Fig.3. The optimal value is $r = 4/512$ in this case.

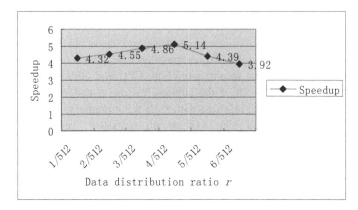

Fig. 3. Hybrid CPU-GPU computing speedup as a function of data distribution ratio r ($n^3=128^3$)

6   Conclusions and Future Work

In this contribution, we have presented the hybrid CPU-GPU computing environment of ELBM, based on mainstream parallel programming platform, i.e. CUDA and OpenMP. With the help of optimal load balancing model, the optimal data distribution ratios among CPU and GPU is chosen. Moreover, this approach not only takes advantage of GPU processing ability for intensive data and parallel data, but also exploits the computing power of CPU adequately. We have tested our hybrid CPU-GPU implementation with 3D lid driven cavity using two AMD Opteron(TM) processor (2.2GHz), eight-core machine with 8GB main memory and a Tesla C2050 GPU. The overall computing time improvements with the optimal load balancing model range from 16.2% to 82.4% compared to the CPU-only and GPU-only configurations.

Our future work includes the following. Firstly, we plan to research many GPUs and multi-core CPU both in hybrid architecture system of ELBM. Specifically, the performance of ELBM implementation with MPI parallelization on large heterogeneous cluster will be given much attention. Secondly, the accuracy of optimal load balancing model needs to further discussion and demonstration in detail. Finally, we will implement the simulation by multi-block entropic Lattice Boltzmann method based on GPU as well as hybrid CPU-GPU computing environment.

Acknowledgements. This work was partially funded by the Key Program of National Natural Science Foundation of China (Grant No. 61133005), and the Ph. D. Programs Foundation of Ministry of Education of China (20100161110019).

References

1. Kampolis, I.C., Trompoukis, X.S., Asouti, V.G., Giannakoglou, K.: CFD-based analysis and two-level aerodynamic optimization on graphics processing units. Computer Methods in Applied Mechanics and Engineering 199, 712–722 (2010)
2. GPGPU.org., http://gpgpu.org/

3. NVIDIA Corporation. NVIDIA CUDA Compute Unified Device Architecture Programming Guide, http://developer.nvidia.com/object/cuda.html
4. NVIDIA Cuda Toolkit 2.3 (2009), http://www.nvidia.com/object/cuda_get.html
5. Chen, S., Doolen, G.D.: Lattice Boltzmann method for fluid flows. Annual Review of Fluid Mechanics 30(1), 329–364 (1998)
6. Ansumali, S., Karlin, I.V.: Stabilization of the lattice Boltzmann method by the H theorem: A numerical test. Phys. Rev. E 62, 7999 (2000)
7. Boghosian, B.M., Yepez, J., Coveney, P.V., Wagner, A.J.: Entropic lattice boltzmann methods. Proc. R. Soc. London, Ser. A 457, 717 (2001)
8. Ansumali, S., Karlin, I.V.: Entropy function approach to the lattice boltzmann method. J. Stat. Phys. 107, 291–308 (2002)
9. Karlin, I.V., Gorban, A.N., Succi, S., Boffi: Maximum entropy principle for lattice kinetic equations. Phys. Rev. Lett. 81, 6–9 (1998)
10. Ansumali, S., Karlin, I.V.: Single relaxation time model for entropic lattice Boltzmann methods. Physical Review E 65, 056312 (2002)
11. Yong, W.-A., Luo, L.-S.: Nonexistence of H theorem for the athermal lattice Boltzmann models with polynomial equilibria. Physical Review E 67, 051105, 1–4 (2003)
12. Lie, W., Wei, X., Kaufmann, A.: Implementing lattice Boltzmann computation on graphics hardware. Vis. Comput. 19(7-8), 444–456 (2003)
13. Tanno, I., et al.: Simulation of turbulent flow by lattice Boltzmann method and conventional method on a GPU. Computers & Fluids (2012)
14. Tölke, J., Krafczyk, M.: TeraFLOP computing on a desktop PC with GPUs for 3D CFD. Int. J. Comput. Fluid Dynam. 22(7), 443–456 (2008)
15. Bernaschi, M., Fatica, M., Melchionna, S., et al.: A flexible high performance lattice Boltzmann GPU code for the simulations of fluid flows in complex geometries. Concurr. Comp-Pract. E 22, 1–14 (2010)
16. Kuznik, F., Obrecht, C., Rusaouen, G., et al.: LBM based flow simulation using GPU computing processor. Comput. Math. Appl. 59, 2380–2392 (2010)
17. Tölke, J.: Implementation of a lattice boltzmann kernel using the compute unified device architecture developed by nvidia. Computing and Visualization in Science 13(1), 29–39 (2010)
18. Xian, W., Takayuki, A.: Multi-GPU performance of incompressible flow computation by lattice Boltzmann method on GPU cluster. Parallel Computing 37, 521–535 (2011)
19. Feichtinger, C., et al.: A flexible Patch-based lattice Boltzmann parallelization approach for heterogeneous GPU–CPU clusters. Parallel Computing 37, 521–535 (2011)
20. Tosi, F., Ubertini, S., Succi, S., Karlin, I.: Optimization strategies for the entropic lattice boltzmann method. Journal of Scientific Computing 30(3), 369–387 (2007)
21. Yasuda, T., Satofuka, N.: An improved entropic lattice boltzmann model for parallel computation. Computers & Fluids (2011)
22. Higuera, F.J., Succi, S., Benzi, R.: Lattice gas dynamics with enhanced collisions. Europhys. Lett. 9, 345–349 (1989)
23. Succi, S.: The Lattice Boltzmann Equation for fluid dynamics and beyond. Claredon press, Oxford University Press (2001)
24. Karlin, I.V., Succi, S.: Equilibria for discrete kinetic equations. Phys. Rev. E 58, 4053 (1998)

148   Y. Ye, P. Chi, and Y. Wang

25. Ansumali, S., Karlin, I.V., Ottinger, H.C.: Minimal entropic kinetic models for hydrodynamics. EPL (Europhysics Letters) 63(6), 798 (2007)
26. Malaspinas, O., Deville, M., Chopard, B.: Towards a physical interpretation of the entropic lattice Boltzmann method. Phys. Rev. E 78(6), 066705 (2008)
27. Chandra, R., Menon, R., Dagum, L., Kohr, D., Maydan, D., McDonald, J.: Parallel Programming in OpenMP. Morgan Kaufmann (2001)
28. OpenMP (1997), http://openmp.org/
29. OpenMP 3.0 Status (2008),
   http://openmp.org/wp/2008/11/openmp-30-status/
30. Using Texture Memory in CUDA (2009),
   http://www.drdobbs.com/high-performance-computing/218100902
31. Geerdink, J.: Entropic and multiple relaxation time lattice Boltzmann methods compared for time harmonic flows (2008)

Parallelization of a DEM Code Based on CPU-GPU Heterogeneous Architecture

Xiaoqiang Yue[1], Hao Zhang[2], Congshu Luo[1], Shi Shu[3,*], and Chunsheng Feng[1]

[1] School of Mathematics and Computational Science, Xiangtan University,
411105, Hunan, China
[2] Heat and Mass Transfer Technological Center, Technical University of Catalonia,
08222, Terrassa, Spain
[3] Hunan Key Laboratory for Computation and Simulation in Science and Engineering,
Key Laboratory of Intelligent Computing and Information Processing of
Ministry of Education, Xiangtan University, 411105, Hunan, China
siukyoo@163.com, tourzhang@gmail.com, luocs105@126.com,
{shushi,spring}@xtu.edu.cn

Abstract. Particulate flows are commonly encountered in both engineering and environmental applications. The discrete element method (DEM) has attracted plentiful attentions since it can predict the whole motion of the particulate flow by monitoring every single particle. However the computational capability of the method relies strongly on the numerical scheme as well as the hardware environment. In this study, a parallelization of a DEM based code titled Trubal was implemented. Numerical simulations were carried out to show the benefits of this research. It is shown that the final parallel code gave a substantial acceleration on the Trubal. By simulating 6,000 particles using a NVIDIA Tesla C2050 card together with Intel Core-Dual 2.93 GHz CPU, an average speedup of 4.69 in computational time was obtained.

Keywords: Parallelization, Discrete element method, CPU-GPU heterogeneous architecture.

1 Introduction

Particulate flows are commonly encountered in both engineering and environmental applications. However due to the stochastic nature of the particles, until now the fundamental physical mechanism in these systems is generally not well understood. The researchers failed to formulate a general method for the reliable scale-up, design and control of processes of different types [1]. The adoption of numerical simulation can assist people in making decisions on trial conditions. Comparing with the actual experiments, it is a cheaper and more convenient option. At present, numerical modeling has been a powerful tool in developing new or optimizing existing engineering facilities. As a typical Lagrangian method, the discrete element method (DEM) [2] has attracted plentiful attentions of researchers from different fields. DEM can predict the whole motion of the particulate flow by monitoring every single particle.

---

* Corresponding author.

K. Li et al. (Eds.): ParCFD 2013, CCIS 405, pp. 149–159, 2014.
© Springer-Verlag Berlin Heidelberg 2014

Trubal is a software package based on DEM which is originally developed by Prof. Cundall [2]. Then Dr. Thornton from Aston University proposed some interaction laws [3-4] and introduced them into Trubal which considered more multi-physical factors. Sheng used Trubal to investigate the powder compaction processes [5-6]. Charley Wu and his colleagues have coupled Trubal with a computational fluid dynamics (CFD) solver to simulate complex particle-fluid interaction problems [7-10]. It should be stressed that the computational capability of DEM relies strongly on the numerical scheme as well as the hardware environment. The researches mentioned above are limited by the numbers of the particles since the serial characteristics of the original Trubal. Lately Trubal was parallelized by Kafui et al. from University of Birmingham using a single program multiple data strategy [11], and successfully applied the new code to three dimensional (3D) applications [12]. Another parallelization work of Trubal is from of Washington et al. who ported the parallel Trubal on the CM-5 architecture at the Pittsburgh supercomputing center [13]. Ghaboussi also made Trubal parallel using neural networks on the connection machine (CM-2) with 32,768 processors [14]. Otherwise, Maknickas et al. parallelized the DEMMAT code to simulate visco-elastic frictional granular media utilizing the spatial domain decomposition strategy, where a speedup around 11 has been obtained on 16 processors [15]. Darmana et al. parallelized an Euler-Lagrange model using mixed domain decomposition and a mirror domain technique. They applied their code to simulate dispersed gas-liquid two-phase flow and obtained a maximum speed-up up to 20 using 32 processors [16]. At the same time, the widely used commercial software like EDEM [17] and PFC3D [18] also exploit partial parallel functions to widen their applications to engineering problems. From the survey of references, it is found that the existing work is mainly on the MPI/OpenMP programming environment to eliminate bottlenecks for computational efficiency and memory capacity.

Graphics processing units (GPUs) have recently burst onto the scientific computing scene as a technology that has yielded substantial performance and energy-efficiency improvements. Some old supercomputers, such as JAGAUR (now known as TITAN) of the Oak Ridge National Laboratory, are being redesigned in order to incorporate GPUs and thereby achieve better performance. CPU-GPU heterogeneous architecture has become an important trend in the development of high performance computers with GPUs successfully used in supercomputers [19]. A GPU is a symmetric multi-core processor that can be accessed and controlled by CPU. The Intel/AMD CPU accelerated by NVIDIA/AMD GPUs is probably the most commonly used heterogeneous high performance computing architecture at present. Under conditions often met in scientific computing, modern GPUs surpass CPUs in computational power, data throughput and computational efficiency per watt by almost one order of magnitude [20]. Shigeto et al. proposed a new algorithm for multi-thread parallel computation of DEM, and pointed out that their calculation speed ratio of the GPU to CPU was up to 3.4 using single-precision floating-point numbers [21]. However the superiority in speed of the GPU decreased as the number of calculated particles increased. Recently, Li et al. developed a DEM based software named GDEM, exploited certain GPU technologies to accelerate the continuous-based DEM and achieved an average 650 times speedup using a NVIDIA GTX VGA card to Intel Core-Dual 2.66 GHz CPU [21-22]. Ye et al. proposed a spatial subdivision algorithm to partition space into a uniform grid and sorted the particles base on their hash values, their results showed that the rendering speed of large-scale granular flow scene can still reach as high as 37.9 frames per second when the number of particles reaches 200,000 [23]. Radeke et al. proposed an approach of using massively parallel compute unified device architecture (CUDA) technique on GPUs for the implementation of the DEM algorithms which enables for simulations of more than two million particles per Giga Byte of memory [24]. Applications of GPU based-DEM are limited but more and more popular nowadays, and numerical simulations with actual-engineering-level numbers of particles are of especially high demand. We reconstructed the Trubal based on a CPU-GPU heterogeneous architecture, and attained an average speedup of 4.69 in simulating 6,000 particles of 200,000 time-steps from four classical moments.

The framework of the paper is organized as follows. We made a brief introduction of the theoretical and numerical issues of the DEM in Section 2. In Section 3, numerical simulations were conducted and a comparison was made among Trubal and the new solvers. Finally, relevant results were summarized and conclusions were given in Section 4.

2   Discrete Particle Modeling

2.1   Governing Equations

The basic idea behind DEM is to calculate the trajectory of every single element based on the Newton's second law. Meanwhile the collisions between the moving particles were considered and treated using interaction laws. The dynamic equations of the discrete element can be symbolically expressed as

$$\begin{cases} m\mathbf{a} = m\mathbf{g} + \mathbf{F}_c \\ I\dfrac{\partial^2 \boldsymbol{\theta}}{\partial t^2} = \boldsymbol{\tau}_c \end{cases} \tag{1}$$

where m and I are respectively the mass and the moment of inertia of the particle, $\mathbf{a}$ is the acceleration, $\boldsymbol{\theta}$ is the angular displacement, $\mathbf{g}$ is the acceleration of gravity if considered, $\mathbf{F}_c$ and $\boldsymbol{\tau}_c$ are the contact force and moment of force respectively generated by the direct collisions. Among the commonest interaction laws are 'Hard' contact, linear law and the nonlinear law which all based on classical contact mechanics. The calculation of the interaction force is not necessary in the 'Hard' contact models. The latter two are called 'Soft' contact, where a small overlap is allowed to represent the physical deformation of the contacting bodies which takes place at the interface. In Trubal as adopted in present work the normal force-displacement relationship of the particles are calculated based on the theory of Hertz [25].

For two particles of radius R_i, Young's modulus E_i and Poisson's ratios v_i ($i=1,2$), the normal force-displacement relationship read

$$F_n = \frac{4}{3}E^* R^{*1/2}\delta_n^{3/2} \tag{2}$$

where

$$\frac{1}{E^*} = \frac{1-v_1^2}{E_1} + \frac{1-v_2^2}{E_2} \tag{3}$$

and

$$\frac{1}{R^*} = \frac{1}{R_1} + \frac{1}{R_2} \tag{4}$$

The incremental tangential force arising from an incremental tangential displacement depends on the loading history as well as the normal force and is given by Mindlin and Deresiewicz [26]

$$\Delta T = 8G^* r_a \theta_k \Delta\delta_t + (-1)^k \mu\Delta F_n (1-\theta_k) \tag{5}$$

where

$$\frac{1}{G^*} = \frac{1-v_1^2}{G_1} + \frac{1-v_2^2}{G_2} \tag{6}$$

$r_a = (R^*\delta_n)^{1/2}$ is the radius of the contact area, $\Delta\delta_t$ is the relative tangential incremental surface displacement, μ is the coefficient of friction, k and θ_k changes with the loading history.

2.2   Numerical Strategy: Two Simulators under CPU

Trubal, written in Fortran 77 and C, can be broadly divided into three parts including setup phrase, solve phrase and post-processing phrase. Setup phrase aims at reading parameters, such as the number and material characteristics of particles and walls, bulk of physical domains and logical boxes dividing the whole domain, and generating what solve phrase requires, such as time-step and contact situations between particles and walls in each box. Solve phrase, the crucial component of numerical simulations, computes explicitly the linear and angular velocity, linear and angular displacement, composite force and resultant moment of each particle and wall at every moment. Post-processing phrase saves the computing results into files and displays their images to analyze the validity of the simulation. The entire calculation flow of Trubal is shown in Fig. 1.

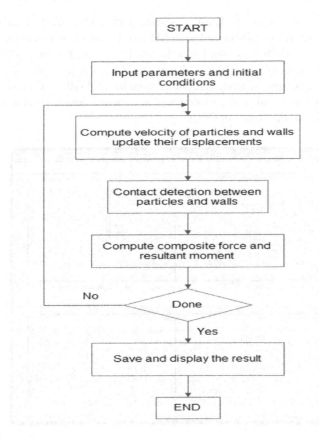

Fig. 1. Flowchart of simulators under CPU

The main storage structure in Trubal is a globally static array in single precision. It eases of programming, data-accessing and memory-saving, but it's prone to interrupt our simulation because we couldn't predict how much memory is sufficient during the entire process. The regular solution is to set up the maximum storage of the used machine. This simulator is denoted as Trubal-org-s in what follows.

In order to avoid the above shortcomings of the static storage structure, we dynamically spare the required local arrays according to the number of particles, walls or contacts. This can prevent a waste of memory and enhance the computational capability, i.e. we can simulate more particles than Trubal. In the following, we name this new simulator as Trubal-new-s.

2.3   GPU Computing and a Simulator under CPU-GPU

Based on NVIDIA Fermi GPU architecture, as shown in Fig. 2, Tesla C2050 GPUs deliver equivalent supercomputing performance at 1/10th the cost and 1/20th the power consumption comparing to the latest quad-core CPUs [27]. Tesla C2050 has 14 streaming multiprocessors (SMs), and each SM has 32 streaming processors (SPs) or CUDA cores. Each SM has its own L1 cache (64 KB), shared memory (48 KB) and register (32,768 available per block). They share L2 cache (768 KB), constant memory (64 KB), texture memory and global memory (3.0 GB, 2.625 GB with ECC on). The GPU memory and peak performances in float and double precisions are both about 10 times faster than those of CPUs.

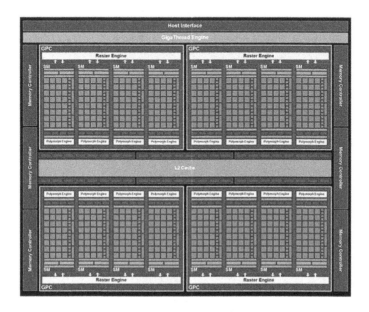

Fig. 2. NVIDIA Fermi GPU architecture

The CPU-GPU heterogeneous parallelism consists of two parts, CPU is responsible for computations unsuitable for data-parallelization, like complex logical transactions, GPU is in charge of large-scale intensive computations. It is a significant advantage to explore the potential performance and cost effective of computers, and compensate for the bottleneck of CPU utilizing powerful processing capability and high bandwidth of GPU.

As CUDA doesn't encapsulate the heterogeneous nature of the storage system, we can get the maximum throughput by optimizing the use of various types of memory, thereby boost up the overall performance, such as taking advantage of shared memory to reduce access latency by hanging threads temporarily, texture memory to randomly access, aiming at maximizing the frequency of GPU memory bandwidth. Fig. 3 shows the entire calculation flow under CPU-GPU heterogeneous architecture. We indicate this simulator as Trubal-new-p hereinafter.

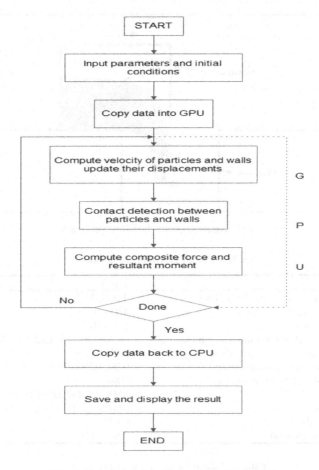

Fig. 3. Flowchart of simulator under CPU-GPU

3   Numerical Experiments

The die filling process, as sketched in Fig. 4, has wide applications ranging from pharmacy and metallurgy to food processing. Charley Wu et al. have successfully used Trubal to simulate the die filling process [7-10]. In this study, several numerical experiments are carried out to demonstrate the efficiencies of the above three simulators directed towards a class of die filling, whose parameters are shown in Table 1.

Table 2 lists the specifications of our testbed. For the sake of fairness, we compile the Trubal-org-s and Trubal-new-s with optimization options being "-O2 -IPA", "-arch=sm_20 -O2" for Trubal-new-p. Here, the specified thread hierarchy of "grid-block-thread" in CUDA is "1-13-512".

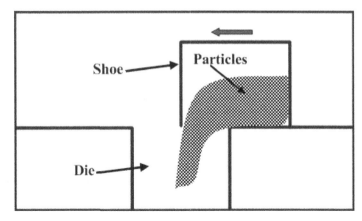

Fig. 4. Sketch map of a die filling process

Table 1. Parameters of our simulation

Parameter	Value
Number of light, heavy particles and walls	3,000, 3,000, 11
Density of light, heavy particles	400, 7,800
Diameter of particles	1.30×10^{-4}
(Young's modulus, Poisson's ratio) of particles, walls	$(8.70 \times 109, 0.30), (2.10 \times 1011, 0.29)$
Friction of particle-particle, particle-wall	0.30, 0.30
Damping coefficient of mass, stiffness	$0.00, 1.59 \times 10^{-2}$
Acceleration of gravity (downward)	9.80
Domain of die	$(0.002, 0.009) \times (0.020, 0.027)$
Domain of shoe	$(0.009, 0.021) \times (0.029, 0.043)$
Velocity of the shoe (left)	0.07
Time step of the simulation (s)	7.6283×10^{-9}

Table 2. Specifications of our test platform

CPU	GPU	Operating System	Host	Device
Intel(R) CPU E7500	Tesla C2050	Linux		
2.0 GB	3.0 GB			
2 Cores	448 CUDA Cores		gcc 4.4.5	nvcc 4.0
2.93 GHz	1.15 GHz	Fedora 13-2.6.34		

Fig. 5 lists the distributions of particles from Trubal-org-s, Trubal-new-s and Trubal-new-p on 0.0382 s, 0.0763 s, 0.0915 s, 0.114 s, 0.130 s, 0.168 s, 0.244 s and 0.305 s, which verify their validity as the distributions are all in accord with the actual physical processes.

The comparison among Trubal-org-s, Trubal-new-s and Trubal-new-p on simulations of 200,000 time-steps from four classical moments is shown in Table 3. These moments match along with when the shoe arrives at the die (0.0382 s), goes through the die (0.0763 s), starts to leave the die (0.130 s) and gets on for getting clear away from the die (0.305 s), respectively.

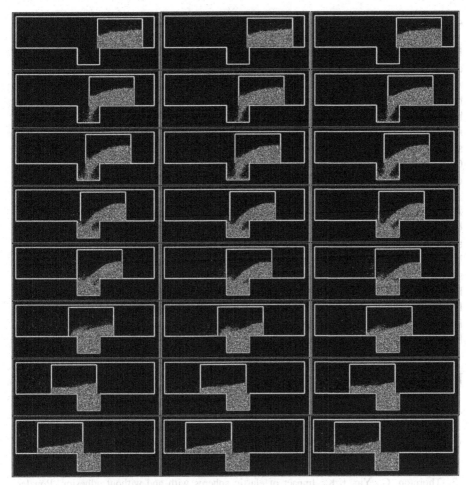

Fig. 5. Comparison on the distributions of particles (left, centered and right are from Trubal-org-s, Trubal-new-s and Trubal-new-p, respectively)

Table 3. Wall time and Ratio/Speedup of partial simulations of 6,000 particles

	Trubal-org-s	Trubal-new-s		Trubal-new-p	
	Wall time	Wall time	Ratio	Wall time	Speedup
0.0382 s	3,464.99 s	3,459.67 s	1.54‰	726.27 s	4.77
0.0763 s	2,878.35 s	2,871.09 s	2.53‰	612.83 s	4.70
0.1300 s	2,473.77 s	2,467.99 s	2.34‰	520.65 s	4.75
0.3050 s	3,333.51 s	3,316.78 s	5.04‰	731.40 s	4.56

As shown in Table 3, Trubal-new-s is a little bit faster than Trubal-org-s, and Trubal-new-p reaps an speedup of 4.77, 4.70, 4.75 and 4.56 in contrast with Trubal-org-s, on the average speedup of 4.69, where Ratio=-1+Trubal-org-s/Trubal-new-s and Speedup=Trubal-org-s/Trubal-new-p.

4   Conclusions

In this study, a parallelization of a serial discrete particle algorithm titled Trubal was carried out by following two steps: 1. Reconstruction of the static storage structure; 2. An essential parallelism on the relative newer code using shared memory without bank conflict and texture memory to maximize the frequency of GPU memory bandwidth based on a CPU-GPU heterogeneous architecture. Numerical simulation showed that the final parallel code gave a substantial acceleration on the Trubal. By simulating 6,000 particles using a NVIDIA Tesla C2050 card together with Intel Core-Dual 2.93 GHz CPU, an average speedup of 4.69 in computational time was obtained.

Acknowledgments. The authors are grateful to Prof. Yuanqiang Tan from Xiangtan University for providing the Trubal code, which is essentially helpful for the understanding of DEM. We also would like to thank Prof. Mingjun Li from Xiangtan University for his helpful comments and suggestions on the reconstruction of the data structure. Yue and Feng are partially supported by the National Natural Science Foundation of China (11201398), Specialized research Fund for the Doctoral Program of Higher Education (20124301110003) and Project of Scientific Research Fund of Hunan Provincial Education Department of China (12A138). Shu is partially supported by the National Natural Science Foundation of China (91130002, 11171281).

References

1. Zhu, H.P., Zhou, Z.Y., Hou, Q.F., Yu, A.B.: Linking discrete particle simulation to continuum process modelling for granular matter: Theory and application. Particuology 9, 342 (2011)
2. Cundall, P.A.: A computer model for simulating progressive large scale movement in block rock system. In: Symposium ISRM Proc., vol. 2, p. 129 (1971)
3. Thornton, C., Yin, K.K.: Impact of elastic spheres with and without adhesion. Powder Technology 65, 113 (1991)
4. Thornton, C., Ning, Z.: A theoretical model for the stick/bounce behavior of adhesive, elastic-plastic spheres. Powder Technology 99, 154 (1998)
5. Sheng, Y., Lawrence, C.J., Briscoe, B.J.: 3D DEM simulation of powder compaction. In: 3rd International Conference on Discrete Element Methods, Santa Fe, Mexico, p. 305 (2002)
6. Sheng, Y., Lawrence, C.J., Briscoe, B.J.: Numerical studies of uniaxial powder compaction process by 3D DEM. Engineering Computations 62, 304 (2010)
7. Wu, C.Y.: DEM simulations of die filling during pharmaceutical tabletting. Particuology 6, 412 (2008)
8. Wu, C.Y., Guo, Y.: Modelling of the flow of cohesive powders during pharmaceutical tabletting. Journal of Pharmacy and Pharmacology 62, 1450 (2010)
9. Guo, Y., Wu, C.Y., Kaifui, D.K., Thornton, C.: 3D DEM/CFD analysis of size-induced segregation during die filling. Powder Technology 206, 177 (2011)
10. Guo, Y., Wu, C.Y., Thornton, C.: The effects of air and particle density difference on segregation of powder mixtures during die filling. Chemical Engineering Science 66, 661 (2011)

11. Kaifui, D.K., Johnson, S., Thornton, C., Seville, J.P.K.: Parallelization of a Lagrangian-Eulerian DEM/CFD code for application to fluidised beds. Powder Technology 207, 270 (2011)
12. Guo, Y., Wu, C.Y.: Numerical modelling of suction filling using DEM/CFD. Chemical Engineering Science 73, 231 (2012)
13. Washington, D.W., Meegoda, J.N.: Micro-mechanical simulation of geotechnical problems using massively parallel computers. International Journal of Numerical and Analytical Mehods in Geomechanics 27, 1227 (2003)
14. Ghaboussi, J., Basole, M., Ranjithan, S.: Three dimensional discrete element analysis on massively parallel computers. In: 2nd International Conference on Discrete Element Methods. Massachusetts Institute of Technology, Cambridge (1993)
15. Maknickas, A., Kaceniauskas, A., Kaceniauskas, R., Balebicius, R., Dziugys, A.: Parallel DEM Software for simulation of granular media. Informatica 17, 207 (2006)
16. Darmana, D., Deen, N.G., Kuipers, J.A.M.: Parallelization of a Euler-Lagrange model using mixed domain decomposition and a mirror domain technique: Application to dispersed gas-liquid two-phase flow. Journal of Computational Physics 220, 216 (2006)
17. EDEM, http://www.dem-solutions.com/software/edem-software/
18. PFC, http://www.itasca.cn/index.jsp
19. Top 500 SuperComputer lists, http://www.top500.org/lists/2011/11
20. Feng, C.S., Shu, S., Xu, J., Zhang, C.S.: Numerical study of geometric multigrid methods on CPU-GPU heterogenous computers (2012) (preprint),
    http://arxiv.org/abs/1208.4247v2
21. CDEM, GDEM, http://www.sinoelite.cc/
22. Ma, Z.S., Feng, C., Liu, T.P., Li, S.H.: A GPU accelerated continuous-based discrete element method for elastodynamics analysis. Advanced Materials Research 320, 329 (2011)
23. Ye, J., Chen, J.X., Chen, X.Q., Tao, H.P.: Modeling and rendering of real-time large scale granular flow scene on GPU. In: Procedia Environmental Sciences, p. 1035 (2011)
24. Radeke, C.A., Glasser, B.J., Khinast, J.G.: Large-scale powder mixer simulations using massively parallel GPU architectures. Chemical Engineering Science 65, 6435 (2010)
25. Johnson, K.L.: Contact mechanics. Cambridge University Press, Cambridge (1985)
26. Mindlin, R.D., Deresiewicz, H.: Elastic spheres in contact under varying oblique forces. Journal of Applied Mechanics 20, 327 (1953)
27. NVIDIA Tesla C2050/C2070 GPU Computing Processor,
    http://www.nvidia.com/object/personal-supercomputing.html

GPU Parallelization of Unstructured/Hybrid Grid ALE Multi-Grid Solver for Moving Bodies

WenPeng Ma[*], ZhongHua Lu, and Jian Zhang

SuperComputing Center of CAS, Computer Network Information Center,
Chinese Academy of Science, Beijing,100190, China
{mawp,zhlu,zhangjian}@sccas.cn

Abstract. Graphics Processing Units(GPUs) are currently being used to accelerate Computational Fluid Dynamics codes and many GPU based CFD solvers have showed high computational performance potential of GPUs. In this study, we discuss the development of an universal compressible Navier-Stokes solver based on both unstructured and hybrid grids, and its implementation and optimization on GPUs for moving bodies problems. The GPU solver solves the fluid flow equations on an unstructured/hybrid grid in the Arbitary Lagrangian-Euler Euqation(ALE) formulation with grid movement. Geometrical Multi-Grid (GMG) algorithm is adopted for convergence acceleration and the detail implementation operations are introduced as well. Mesh deformation/moving module, which is used to update nodes of mesh to new positions as the interfaces of bodies move, is also parallelized on GPU to avoid extra data copy from CPU to GPU device. Since torsional spring based mesh deformation algorithm is stable but low efficiency at the same time, a Krylov subspace based method – BICGSTAB is implemented on GPU for mesh deformation module. Various validation cases are carried out to analyze the accuracy and efficiency of this solver.

Keywords: Graphics Processing Units(GPUs), unstructured/hybrid grid, mesh deformation, optimization, solver.

1   Introduction

Graphics Processing Units(GPUs) which were originally intended for gaming applications, are quickly becoming a key element of high performance computing owing to its ability to perform a large number of numerical operations by massive multi-threading concurrently. Many GPU based solvers [1], [2], [3] have already demonstrated huge potentiality of GPUs on both structured and unstructured stationary grids. The superiority of structured grid is that it is simple, fast to generate and easier to implement high order numerical schemes. However, unstructured grids technique is increasingly becoming popular because of its ability to discrete more complicated computational domain. Although multi-block approach can be adopted to

---

[*] Corresponding author.

K. Li et al. (Eds.): ParCFD 2013, CCIS 405, pp. 160–171, 2014.

fill a geometrically complex domain with structured grids, much more information such as data structure for each blocks and neighbor to neighbor interfaces, exchange of information between the blocks, data dependency at block interfaces should be taken care, which give rise to difficulties when performing parallel operations. Hybrid grids, mixed by structured and unstructured grid, inherits advantages of both structured and unstructured grid. Compared with structured grid, it is suitable for geometrically complex domain without loss in computational accuracy at solid wall.

In order to develop an universal compressible Navier-Stokes solver which supports both unstructured and hybrid grids, cell-vertex scheme with median-dual control volumes rather than cell-centred scheme   is preferred since data structure in CFD procedure retains   unchanging   as elements consists of grid changes. Flow variables are stored at the grid vertices, the control volumes are created by connecting the centroids of the surrounding elements, face-centroids and edge-midpoints. The multigrid methods, including geometrical multigrid (GMG) and algebraic multigrid (AMG) are both powerful acceleration techniques. However, the geometric multigrid is still more widely used in case of unstructured or hybrid grids. In this paper, geometrical multigrid method is adopted to accelerate Navier-Stokes equations and turbulence model equations. As compared to the structured grids, the construction of the coarse grid, which is also called multigrid generation, is much more involved in case of unstructured grids. And there are three main methods for the generation of coarse grids: nonnested-grids approach, topological methods and agglomeration of control volumes. Agglomeration multigrid method [5], very efficient for unstructured grids, is implemented as a pre-step before computational iterations on CPU. The method generates a coarse grid by fusing the control volumes of the finer grid with their neighbours. The resulting coarse grids consist of successively larger, irregularly shaped polyhedral cells. Because of its cell-vertex based control volumes feature, it can be easily applied to hybrid grids.

Many fluid flows problems involve geometries changing with time owing to boundaries movement or relative motion between multiple bodies during the simulation. For problems of this type, there are two popular approaches in use. The chimera/overset method [6], which has been used with both structured [7] and unstructured [8] meshes, consists of supplying each component of moving body with its own mesh. Although the method results in a robust and fast computational procedure, experience is often needed to ensure adequate numerical resolution through the entire simulation. The usage of a single, consistent mesh which is adapted in time to account for the changing geometry is an alternative approach to solve moving bodies problems. For many problems, it is sufficient to employ mesh deformation approaches to satisfy the changes of geometry. In such approaches, the connectivity remains unchanged between time steps but the elements are deformed to conform to the new geometrical shape. Approaches such as spring analogy [9], torsional spring [10], [11] analogy, Delaunay graph mapping [12] are belong to the later tenique. The approach employed in this paper is spring like algorithm in which the edges of the mesh behave like springs connecting the nodes. A GPU based parallelization is performed in present paper based on the analysis of the computational efficiency bottleneck of the spring like mesh deformation approaches in our previous work [13].

Both the speed and the accuracy which are regard as the two main factors to gauge the performance of any flow solver are demonstrated in this paper. And the speed-up obtained on the GPU platform and the scalability on GPU platform are also discussed. This paper is organized as follows: In section 2, the GPU programming model is introduced at first; In section 3, the computational model for solving the compressible Navier-Stokes equations together with turbulence model equations under a moving or deforming grid is discussed in detail; In section 4, sample test cases are investigated to test the GPU performance and accuracy of the numerical method; And the last section is about conclusions and our future work.

2   GPU Programming Model

CUDA [14], NVIDIA's C/C++ language extension known as Compute Unified Device Architecture, enables one to write programs that can execute on the GPU platform using a Single Instruction Multiple Data programming(SIMD) paradigm. The CUDA programming strategy centers around the usage of streams and kernels. A stream is a collection of data similar to an array, and kernels are similar to standard programming language functions, except for manner in which these functions are invoked from the main program. Anyone who is familiar with C/C++ language can write kernels for each arithmetic expression, or warp of a set of expressions into one kernel. GPUs have kernels calls which operate on the specified number of threads similar to function calls in standard programming languages.

3   Problem Formulation

3.1   Compressible Navier-Stokes Equations

Written in time-dependent integral form for moving or deforming control volume Ω with a surface element dS, the Navier-Stokes equations read

$$\frac{\partial}{\partial t} \int_{\Omega} \vec{W} d\Omega + \oint_{\partial \Omega} (\vec{F}_c^M - \vec{F}_v) dS = 0$$

where the vectors

$$\vec{W} = \begin{bmatrix} \rho \\ \rho u \\ \rho v \\ \rho w \\ \rho E \end{bmatrix}, \ \vec{F}_c^M = \begin{bmatrix} \rho V_r \\ \rho u V_r + n_x p \\ \rho v V_r + n_y p \\ \rho w V_r + n_z p \\ \rho H V_r + V_t p \end{bmatrix}, \vec{F}_v = \begin{bmatrix} 0 \\ n_x \tau_{xx} + n_y \tau_{xy} + n_z \tau_{xz} \\ n_x \tau_{yx} + n_y \tau_{yy} + n_z \tau_{yz} \\ n_x \tau_{zx} + n_y \tau_{zy} + n_z \tau_{zz} \\ n_x \Theta_x + n_y \Theta_y + n_z \Theta_z \end{bmatrix}$$

represents conservative variables, convective fluxes on dynamic grids and viscous fluxes, respectively. In above vectors, ρ, u, v, w, E denote the density, the Cartesian velocity components and the total energy per unit mass, respectively, and

H stands for the total enthalpy and p for the static pressure, respectively. Furthermore, V_r represents the contravariant velocity relative to the motion of the grid, V_t is the contravariant velocity of the face of the control volume, n_i denote the components of the outward facing unit normal vector of the surface. The components of the viscous stress tensor τ_{ij} together with the work of viscous stresses and the heat conduction Θ_i have the following expressions:

$$\Theta_x = u\tau_{xx} + v\tau_{xy} + w\tau_{xz} + k\frac{\partial T}{\partial x} \qquad \tau_{xx} = \lambda(\frac{\partial u}{\partial x} + \frac{\partial v}{\partial y} + \frac{\partial w}{\partial z}) + 2\mu\frac{\partial u}{\partial x}$$

$$\Theta_y = u\tau_{yx} + v\tau_{yy} + w\tau_{yz} + k\frac{\partial T}{\partial y} \qquad \tau_{yy} = \lambda(\frac{\partial u}{\partial x} + \frac{\partial v}{\partial y} + \frac{\partial w}{\partial z}) + 2\mu\frac{\partial v}{\partial y}$$

$$\Theta_z = u\tau_{zx} + v\tau_{zy} + w\tau_{zz} + k\frac{\partial T}{\partial z} \qquad \tau_{zz} = \lambda(\frac{\partial u}{\partial x} + \frac{\partial v}{\partial y} + \frac{\partial w}{\partial z}) + 2\mu\frac{\partial w}{\partial z}$$

$$\tau_{xy} = \tau_{yz} = \mu(\frac{\partial u}{\partial y} + \frac{\partial v}{\partial x})$$

$$\tau_{xz} = \tau_{zx} = \mu(\frac{\partial u}{\partial z} + \frac{\partial w}{\partial x})$$

$$\tau_{yz} = \tau_{zy} = \mu(\frac{\partial v}{\partial z} + \frac{\partial w}{\partial y})$$

in which λ represents the second viscosity coefficient, and μ denotes the dynamic viscosity coefficient.

3.2 Spalart-Allmaras One-Equation Turbulence Model

The Spalart-Allmaras one-equation turbulence model is implemented in present paper since it has several favourable numerical features. It is "local" which means that the equation at one point does not depend on the solution at other points. Therefore, it can be readily implemented on both unstructured and hybrid grids. It is also robust, converges fast to steady-state and requires only moderate grid resolution in the near-wall region. The Spalart-Allmaras turbulence model can be written in integral form as follows

$$\frac{\partial}{\partial t}\int_\Omega \tilde{v}d\Omega + \oint_{\partial\Omega}(F_{c,T} - F_{v,T})dS = \int_\Omega Q_T d\Omega$$

where Ω represents the control volume, $\partial\Omega$ its surface, and dS is a surface element of Ω. The convective flux is defined as

$$F_{c,T} = \tilde{v}V$$

with V being the contravariant velocity. The viscous flux is given by

$$F_{v,T} = n_x \tau_{xx}^T + n_y \tau_{yy}^T + n_z \tau_{zz}^T$$

where n_x, n_y, and n_z are the components of the unit normal vector. The normal viscous stresses reads

$$\tau_{xx}^T = \frac{1}{\sigma}(v_L + \tilde{v})\frac{\partial \tilde{v}}{\partial x}, \quad \tau_{yy}^T = \frac{1}{\sigma}(v_L + \tilde{v})\frac{\partial \tilde{v}}{\partial y}, \quad \tau_{zz}^T = \frac{1}{\sigma}(v_L + \tilde{v})\frac{\partial \tilde{v}}{\partial z}$$

Finally, the source term is expressed as

$$Q_T = C_{b1}(1 - f_{t2})\tilde{S}\tilde{v} + \frac{C_{b2}}{\sigma}\left[(\frac{\partial \tilde{v}}{\partial x})^2 + (\frac{\partial \tilde{v}}{\partial y})^2 + (\frac{\partial \tilde{v}}{\partial z})^2\right] -$$

$$\left[C_{w1}f_w - \frac{C_{b1}}{k^2}f_{t2}\right](\frac{\tilde{v}}{d})^2 + f_{t1}\|\Delta \tilde{v}\|_2^2$$

The components of the source term and the model constant are introduced in [15].

3.3   Geometric Conservation Law

It is reported by Thomas and Lombard that besides the conservation of mass, momentum and energy, the Geometric Conservation Law (GCL) must be satisfied in order to avoid errors induced by a deformation of the control volumes. The integral form of GCL can be written as

$$\frac{\partial}{\partial t}\int_\Omega d\Omega - \oint_{\partial\Omega} V_t dS = 0$$

By performing second order time discretization operation on time term of above equation, control volume in n+1 time state can be expressed as

$$\Omega^{n+1} = \frac{4}{3}\Omega^n - \frac{1}{3}\Omega^{n-1} + \frac{2}{3}\Delta t\sum_{m=1}^{N_f}(V_t)_m \Delta S_m$$

3.4   Basic Numerical Schemes

In this paper, both Navier-Stokes equations and Spalart-Allmaras turbulence model equation are discretized using a finite volume method with a standard edge-based structure on a dual grid with control volume constructed using a median-dual, vertex-based scheme as shown in Fig. 1.

Fig. 1. Control volume of median-dual scheme (in 2D) for unstructued grid and hybrid grid

The discretization methods for Navier-Stokes equations and Spalart-Allmaras turbulence mode equation employed in present paper are summarized as follows:

For Navier-Stokes equations,

(1). The convective fluxes is discretized using the flux-difference splitting (FDS) scheme of Roe, which is classified among upwind schemes.

(2). The viscous fluxes is discretized using central schemes, in which flow quantities are simply averaged at the control volume surface. And the average of gradients approach is implemented to evaluate the first derivatives (gradients) of the velocity components and of temperature.

(3). 3 stages Runge-Kutta multistage scheme is adopted to discretized governing equations in time.

The methods employed on Spalart-Allmaras turbulence model equation are same as that on Navier-Stokes. In addition, the quantities in source term of turbulence equation are evaluated by average values of cell-vertics connected by one edge. For unsteady cases, dual time stepping strategy is used to achieve high-order accuracy in time. In this method, the unsteady problem is transformed into a steady problem at each physical time step which can then be solved using all of the well known convergence acceleration for steady problems.

3.5   Computational Flow Chart

The solver we developed with whole computational steps is demonstrated clearly as computational flow chart in Fig.2.

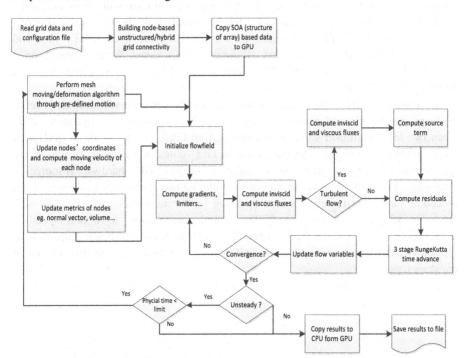

Fig. 2. Computational flow chart of ALE flow solver with mesh deformation

4   Validation Cases

4.1   Transonic Flow Past RAE2822 Airfoil

To validate the accuracy of solution based on GPU solver that has been presented, RAE2822 transonic flow case is implemented since the RAE2822 airfoil is a supercritical airfoil commonly used for the validation of turbulence models. The transonic flow past a RAE2822 airfoil at Mach number M=0.729, and angle of attack alpha=2.31 is considered using hybrid grid with quadrilaterals in the region adjacent to the airfoil surface and triangles in the remaining portion of the computational domain as described in Fig. 3. The Reynolds number is 6.5 million based on a unit chord length. One, two level geometrical multigrid technique is employed respectively to demonstrate the acceleration effects of multigrid. Fig. 4 shows the pressure coefficient on the airfoil surface in comparison with the experiment data. Fig. 5. shows the Mach contours surrounding the airfoil after convergence has been obtained. Convergence histories obtained by different level of multigrid are shown in Fig. 6.

To assess the performance of the GPU, several tests were conducted on different grids. The corresponding serial code is compiled with a higher compiler optimization level –O3 and also a zero optimization level –O0 to enable a fair comparison with the GPU code. The reason that we compare the GPU code to the lowest level optimization is that, at times the higher level optimization results in incorrect results. Table 1 list the GPU/CPU performance for one iteration of the flow solver on two different grids. The wall clock times for one iteration are averaged by first 100 iterations. It should be noted that all serial C/C++ codes were executed on a 2.67GHz Intel(R) Xeon(R) X5650 CPU core and all GPU kernels were executed on a Tesla C2075 GPU card.

It is shown in Table1. that over 10x speed-up can be obtained with respect to serial –O3 optimized code and nearly 32x speed-up with respect to zero optimized code when two level multigrid solver was employed on Grid1. Larger scale of grid gives higher speed-ups owing to the utilization of GPU cores at the most. However, the speed-up would not go higher when the saturated usage of GPU hardware resources is obtained. Furthermore, it is meaningful to point out that the whole steady simulation procedure can be extremely speeded up using GPU based multigrid solver through Fig.6, in which no more than 2700 iterations were used to obtain specified convergence criterion since flux computations account for a significant proportion of wall clock time during one iteration and GPU has a very strong acceleration for that at the same time.

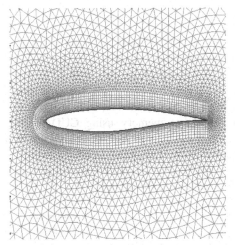

Fig. 3. Hybrid grid around RAE2822 airfoil

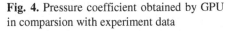

Fig. 4. Pressure coefficient obtained by GPU in comparsion with experiment data

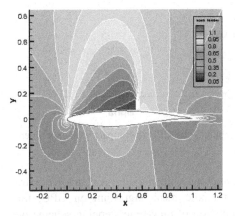

Fig. 5. Mach counters around RAE2822 airfoil

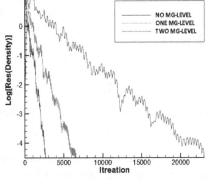

Fig. 6. Convergence histories comparation between different levels used in multigrid scheme

Table 1. GPU/CPU performance on two different grids

13937nodes(hybrid grid)	0 MG-Level	1MG-Level	2MG-Level
CPU-O0	485ms	789ms	915ms
CPU-O3	198ms	320ms	371ms
GPU	19.70ms	26.59ms	28.93ms

87149nodes(hybrid grid)	0 MG-Level	1MG-Level	2MG-Level
CPU-O0	3346ms	5377ms	6239ms
CPU-O3	1366ms	2179ms	2530ms
GPU	105.68ms	128.60ms	137.87ms

4.2   Unsteady Pitching NACA0012 Case

Unsteady calculations were performed for the NACA0012 airfoil pitching harmonically about the quarter chord with an amplitude of $\alpha = 2.51$ deg and a reduced frequency based on semichord of $k = 0.0814$ at $M_\infty = 0.755$ and $\alpha_0 = 0.016$ deg to validate Euler solvers, dynamic mesh algorithm, and dual-time stepping scheme on GPU platform. The steady state was obtained on CPU at first and then the steady results were copied to GPU global memory using CUDA API functions to prepare for subsequent computation. Unstructured grids of triangles were used to discretize computational domain around NACA0012 airfoil. In this case, three cycles of motion were computed to obtain a periodic solution and comparisons were done between GPU results and experiment data, which are shown in Fig. 7.

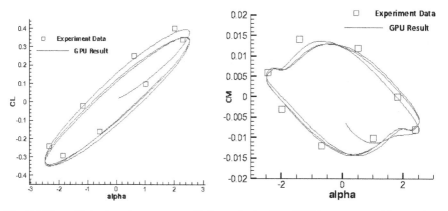

Fig. 7. Lift coefficients and moment coefficients obtained by GPU in compare with experiment data

Unlike steady simulations, unsteady simulations with moving grid involve extra problems such as the implementation of dynamic mesh algorithm on GPU, the technique of update mesh, and the implementation of dual-time stepping scheme on GPU platform. Our GPU implementation of torsional spring algorithm was based on the analysis in our previous work [13]. Mesh deformation problems is finally transformed to the problem of solving sparse linear equations [10]. Hence the backbone of the GPU implementation of dynamic mesh algorithm relies on developing efficient iterative linear solvers. The BiCGSTAB [4] iterative algorithm is parallelized using several GPU kernels such as sparse matrix multiply vector, matrix operations, and reduction in present paper. It is necessary to point out that communication is needed between CPU and GPU before the execution of gpu_bicgstab kernel since different linear equations are needed to be solved and new matrix and vector should be generated per physical time step. However, the time cost on communication between CPU and GPU can be hided using asynchronous operations because of our foreknowledge of mesh motion during unsteady simulation.

SPMV(sparse matrix multiply vector), regarded as an usual technique in unstructured grid applications, can be considered to handle mesh update and dual-time stepping details. GPU performance for BICGSTAB solver on different number of grids is demonstrated in Table 2.

Table 2. GPU performance for BICGSTAB solver on different number of grids

Number of nodes	Scale of sparse matrix 2*(nodesNum-boundaryNodes)	Speed up
21329	40614×40614	13.7x
34946	67974×67974	16.8x
44232	86386×86386	21.3x
76166	149814×149814	32.2x
93495	184272×184272	40.5x

4.3   Three Dimensional Case

The performance of the 3D GPU implementation is accessed on the inviscid flows developed around the DLR F6 aircraft, with $M_\infty = 0.8, \alpha_\infty = 0°$. The Mach number contours of the numerically predicted flow field and lift, drag coefficient convergence history are shown in Fig.8 and 9, respectively. About 18x speed-up in comparison with –O3 optimized serial CPU code was obtained using one level multigrid scheme and redundant flux computation with re-numbering technique, in which each node's neighbors are sorting in index of the node array to guarantee that the quantities of each node's neighbor are not so far from its own when a warp is dispatched to access global memory.   Higher speed-up was obtained on Fermi based than GTX series GPU since the access of global memory on Fermi based GPU is not as rigid as that of GTX series.

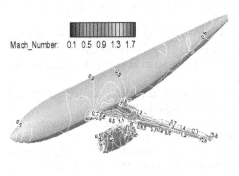

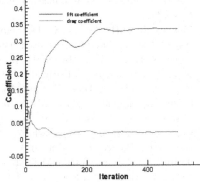

Fig. 8. Mach number contours around DLR F6 aircraft

Fig. 9. Convergence history of lift and drag coefficient

5   Conclusions and Future Work

A GPU based unstructured/hybrid ALE multigrid solver is presented in this paper. All calculations can be performed on GPU platform. It is shown that an average speed up of 10x-20x corresponding to the serial −O3 optimized code on one processor could be obtained from this solver. Currently, the solver is limited to explicit time integration, which takes longer times for convergence especially for larger grids. And this solver only supports two dimensional deforming meshes. An implicit based time integration algorithm using Krylov subspace methods such as GMRES/BICGSTAB, which is already adopted in dynamic mesh module, will be considered to add to this solver. Three dimensional deforming meshes algorithm using spring like technique, in which more parameters is needed to consider to prevent tetrahedron grids from collapsing , is under consideration. Furthermore, efforts are underway to implement and multi-GPU version.

Acknowledgments. This work is supported by National Nature Science Foundation of China(No. 91130019) and National High Technology Research and Development Program of China(863 Program No. 2012AA01A304).

References

1. Hagen, T.R., Lie, K.-A., Natvig, J.R.: Solving the Euler Equations on Graphics Processing Units. In: Alexandrov, V.N., van Albada, G.D., Sloot, P.M.A., Dongarra, J. (eds.) ICCS 2006. LNCS, vol. 3994, pp. 220–227. Springer, Heidelberg (2006)
2. Elsen, E., LeGresley, P., Darve, E.: Large Calculation of the Flow over a Hypersonic Vehicle using a GPU. J. Comput. Phys. 227(24), 10148–10161 (2008)
3. Brandvik, T., Pullan, G.: Acceleration of a 3D Euler Solver using Commodity Graphics Hardware. In: AIAA Paper 2008, 0607 (2008)
4. Van der Vorst, H.A.: Bi-CGSTAB: A Fast and Smoothly Converging Variant of Bi CG For the Solution of Nonsymmetric Linear Systems. SIAM J. Sci. Stat. Comput. 23, 631–644 (1992)
5. Lallemand, M.H., Steve, H., Dervieux, A.: Unstructured Multigridding by Volume Agglomeration: Current Status. Computers and Fluids 21, 397–433 (1992)
6. Steger, J., Dougherty, F., Benek, J.: Advances in grid generation, vol. 5. American Society of Mechanical Engineers, Fairfield (1983)
7. Roger, S., Suhs, N., Dietz, W.: PEGASUS5: an automated preprocessor for overset-grid computational fluid dynamics. AIAA J 41(6), 1037–1045 (2003)
8. Nakahashi, K., Togashi, F., Sharov, D.: An intergrid-boundary definition method for overset unstructured grid approach. AIAA J. 38(11), 2077–2084 (2000)
9. Hassan, O., Probert, E.J., Morgan, K., Weatherill, N.P.: Unsteady flow simulation using unstructured meshes. Comput Methods Appl. Mech. Eng. 189, 1247–1275 (2000)
10. Farhat, C., Degand, C., Koobus, B., Lesoinne, M.: Torsional springs for two-dimensional dynamic unstructured fluid meshws. Comput. Methods Appl. Mech. Eng. 163, 231–245 (1998)

11. Degand, C., Farhat, C.: A three-dimensional torsional spring analogy method for unstructured dynamic meshes. Comp. Struct. 80, 305–316 (2002)
12. Liu, X., Qin, N., Xia, H.: Fast dynamic grid deformation based on Delaunay graph mapping. Journal of Computational Physics 211, 405–423 (2006)
13. Ma, W., Lu, Z., Hu, X.: Parallel solutions for node connectivity based mesh moving methods on different parallel architectures. Applied Mechanics and Materials 220-223, 2330–2337 (2012)
14. NVIDIA (2012),
    https://developer.nvidia.com/cuda-toolkit-42-archive
15. Blazek, J.: Computational fluid dynamics: principles and applications. Elsevier, Oxford (2001)

The Analysis of Pile Cap Hydrodynamic Added Mass Considering the Chamfer

Kehua You, Kai Wei, and Wancheng Yuan[*]

State Key Laboratory for Disaster Reduction in Civil Engineering,
Tongji University, Shanghai 200092, China
yuan@tongji.edu.cn

Abstract. The dynamic analysis model of cap considering structure-water interaction is built up, based on potential fluid theory. A double-layer water mesh generation method is suggested to simplify the modeling process. The influences of different parameters of the rectangular cap and the one with complicated chamfer on the hydrodynamic effect are investigated using the proposed methods, including the cap vibration frequency, the geometrical size, the chamfer and the submersion depth of the cap. The study indicated that the cap vibration frequency has little effect on the hydrodynamic effect; the increase of the ratio of the length to the width or the thickness will increase the hydrodynamic effect; The form and size of cap chamfer both have significant influences on the hydrodynamic effect, and ignoring the existence of the chamfer will amplify this effect; the hydrodynamic effect will increase with the increase of the submersion depth of the cap, while keeping in constant after the depth exceeds a certain value.

Keywords: deep-water bridge, elevated pile foundation, potential fluid theory, hydrodynamic effect, pile cap.

1   Introduction

The elevated pile foundation, one kind of important structure of the deep-water foundation, is widely used in the long-span bridge crossing the river and sea in China. This kind of foundation mainly consists of a group of long piles extending to the soil below water surface and the pile cap partially or totally submerged in the water, contributing to an increased influence of the seismic hydrodynamic effect on the structure [1]. At the same time, the complicated geometry boundary of the pile cap greatly increases the complication of the fluid-structure interaction of the deep-water group pile foundation. In recent years, lots of researches on hydrodynamic effect of the pile cap have been done. LAN Yamei [12] studied the hydrodynamic characteristic of the inclined group pile cap subjected to irregular wave and regular wave, using the experimental tank of the State Key Laboratory of Ocean Engineering of Shanghai Jiao Tong University considering the wind, the wave and the flow. SONG Bo [3] put forward the simplified calculation method of hydrodynamic force for circular elevated pile caps based on Morison hydrodynamic theory. In order to

K. Li et al. (Eds.): ParCFD 2013, CCIS 405, pp. 172–184, 2014.
© Springer-Verlag Berlin Heidelberg 2014

validate the accuracy and reliability of this simplified method, the underwater shaking table model test prototyping the south tower foundation of the Third Nanjing Changjiang River Bridge was carried out. The comparison between the result of model test and theoretical calculation subjected to the dynamic load with water or without water indicated that the simplified method result has good satisfactory coincidence with test result under the low frequency harmonic wave, but as for the high frequency harmonic wave, the former is smaller than the latter over 10%. WANG Junjie and LAI Wei [4-5] developed the theoretical solutions of the added mass and damping matrixes for the truncated cylinder by idealizing the cap of group-pile foundation as a truncated cylinder submerged in the water, and proposed the approximate methods to obtain the added mass and damping matrixes for the truncated prism with arbitrary section by modifying the ones for truncated cylinder.

However, most of the above analytic methods for the cap added mass focus on circular pile caps, which cannot be applied to the rectangular cap and the one with complicated chamfers showed in Fig.1. The method in references [4] and [5] is just an empirical equation fitted by a small amount of test data, which cannot consider the influence of the actual section commonly used in engineering, such as the section with chamfer.

In recent years, the numerical methods based on finite element and boundary element theory [6] become the effective to stimulate the complicated dynamic fluid-structure interaction. The proposition of the analysis method for the fluid-structure interaction based on the potential fluid theory makes the accurate numerical analysis for the dynamic response of the elevated pile caps foundation-water coupling system come true [7]. Based on the potential-based fluid formulation, WEI Kai [8] proposed the simplified finite analysis model of the pile foundation considering the hydrodynamic effect to calculate the cap added mass, and validated this method through the group piles foundation basin modal test. The method can consider the geometries and vibration periods of the cap.

This paper endeavors to study the influences of the vibration frequency, the cap geometry and the submersion depth of the cap on the cap hydrodynamic effect based on the method proposed in literature [8]. And before this, reasonable and effective mesh generation method is studied.

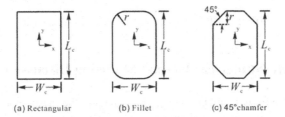

(a) Rectangular   (b) Fillet   (c) 45°chamfer

Fig. 1. The common geometric section of the cap

2   The Method to Calculate the Added Mass

According to literature [8], the model, showed in Fig.2, considering the pile cap-water interaction was built to calculate the cap hydrodynamic added mass based on potential fluid element using the program of ADINA. The pile cap was modeled using 3D solid finite elements considering its actual shape, while the pile was modeled using a virtual beam as long as the actual pile. And the vibration characteristics of the pile cap could be stimulated by the reasonably setting the stiffness of the virtual beam. The surrounding water was simulated using 3D potential-based fluid elements (PBFE), fluid-structure interaction was accounted for through special elements at the water-cap interfaces. The infinity water boundary was simulated by taking the water width twice as the water depth [7]. The modal analysis of the no water system and the system considering the water-structure interaction was carried out to calculate the period T_{nw} of the cap without water and the period T_w of the cap with water. Then the hydrodynamic added mass m_a of the cap could be calculated using Eq. (1)

$$m_a = m_c \left(\left(\frac{T_{nw}}{T_w} \right)^2 - 1 \right) \tag{1}$$

where m_c is the mass of the pile cap.

Through the above method, the pile cap-water interaction problem could be solved independently considering both the actual vibration of the pile cap and the cap geometry but avoiding the coupling between the pile cap and the pile

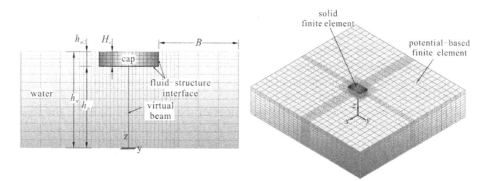

Fig. 2. Analysis model for the added mass of the cap

3   Complete Numerical Method Modeling Discussion

As to the complete finite element numerical simulation, the mesh generation has great influence on the convergence and stability of the numerical simulation results. The uppermost difference between the water-structure coupled system and single media system is that there is fluid-solid interface in the water-structure coupled system; and the different mesh size on both sides of the interface has obvious influence on the result [9]. The previous research shown that the numerical simulation result had satisfactory convergence when the ratio of the water mesh size l_w to the structure mesh size l_s on the sides of the interface is close to or less than 1.0 [7]. The big amount of water element nodes due to the same water mesh size will severely affect the efficiency of calculation. In order to solve this problem, this paper proposed the double-layer water mesh generation method. The water surrounding the structure was divided into two layers, the inner layer with dense mesh and the outer layer with sparse mesh.

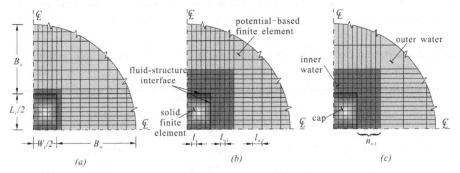

Fig. 3. The mesh generation of double-layer water

The model to calculate the hydrodynamic added mass of the rectangular pile cap was established using the method in section 2. The length, width, and height of the pile cap were taken as 15m, 10m and 3.5m respectively. The reasonable mesh way of the double-layer water mesh generation method was studied by comparing the different result when changing the range of inner water and the ratio of the outer water mesh size l_{w2} to the inner water mesh size l_{w1}.

The ratio of the inner water mesh size l_{w1} to the structure mesh size l_s was taken as 1.0 as described in literature [7]. The ratio l_{w2} / l_{w1} of the outer water mesh size to the inner water mesh size was assumed to be 2. The range of the inner water was changed by changing the number n_{w1} of the inner water mesh, shown in Fig. 3(a) and (b). The results of modal analysis in different inner water ranges are presented in Table 1.

Table 1. The influence of the inner water range on the cap frequency

Number of inner water mesh n_{w1}	First lateral mode（Hz）	Second lateral mode（Hz）	Torsional mode（Hz）
1	0.630614	0.813827	4.91467
2	0.630598	0.813813	4.9145
3	0.630596	0.813811	4.91448
4	0.630596	0.813811	4.91448
5	0.630596	0.813811	4.91448

Based on the above result, the number of inner water mesh was taken as 5, the ratio l_{w2} / l_{w1} was changed, shown as Fig.3 (b) and (c). The results of modal analysis in different ratio l_{w2} / l_{w1} are presented in Table 2.

Table 1 and Table 2 show that the stability of the result of modal analysis is related to the range of inner water and the ratio of the outer water mesh size to the inner water mesh size. When the number of the inner water mesh is larger than 3, the structure frequency tends to be constant. With the decrease of l_{w2}/l_{w1}, the frequency of the structure tends to be constant, and the calculation accuracy increases, but the efficiency of calculation severely decreases. So this paper suggests the ratio l_{w2}/l_{w1} to be taken as 4-6 in modal analysis to balance the accuracy and the efficiency of computation.

Table 2. The influence of the dimension ratio of the outer water mesh to the inner water mesh on the accuracy and efficiency of modal analyses

$l_{w2}/$ l_{w1}	Running time (s)	First lateral mode (Hz)	Second lateral mode (Hz)	Torsional mode (Hz)	Nodes number
2	1225	0.630596	0.813811	4.91448	287637
3	393	0.630596	0.813811	4.91448	171061
4	178	0.630596	0.813812	4.91448	124101
5	131	0.630597	0.813813	4.91448	103453
6	110	0.630598	0.813814	4.91448	93837
7	74	0.630602	0.813819	4.91449	76021
8	74	0.630602	0.813819	4.91449	76021
9	57	0.630607	0.813824	4.9445	67821
10	57	0.630607	0.813824	4.9145	67821

4   Parametric Study of the Pile Cap Hydrodynamic Effect

The influences of the frequency of the pile cap, the pile cap geometry and the submersion depth of the cap on the hydrodynamic effect were discussed using the complete numerical method in section 2 and the double-layer water mesh generation method in section 3. The caps shown in Fig.1 were modeled. The water surrounding the cap was divided into two layers, and the number of the inner water mesh is 5, with the ratio l_{w2}/l_{w1} taken as 5.

4.1   Frequency

To investigate the influence of the frequency on hydrodynamic effect, the frequency of the pile cap was changed by changing the stiffness of the virtual beam. The frequency changes from 0.1Hz to 12Hz according to frequency response characteristics of ground wave and common foundation. The rectangular pile cap shown in Fig.1 (a) was studied as a case study. Assuming the pile cap was just completely submerged in water and the water depth H_w was 23.5m, the hydrodynamic added mass m_a and the hydrodynamic added mass coefficient C_a were used to measure the hydrodynamic effect. The hydrodynamic added mass m_a was obtained from Eq. (1). The hydrodynamic added mass coefficient C_a was defined by Eq. (2)

$$C_a = m_a / \rho_w V_c \qquad (2)$$

where m_a is the hydrodynamic added mass, $\rho_w V_c$ is the water mass displaced by the cap, ρ_w is water density of 1000 kg/m^3, V_c is the submersion volume of the cap.

Fig.4 shows that the hydrodynamic added mass m_a and the hydrodynamic added mass coefficient C_a increase with the increase of frequency, but as for the variation range, both m_a and C_a increase less than 1%. The results imply that frequency has little influence on the hydrodynamic effect, so in the following analysis, the frequency of the pile cap in no water condition is assumed as 1Hz unless stated.

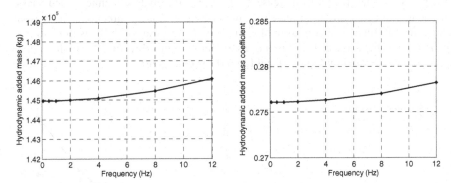

Fig. 4. The relationship between the hydrodynamic added mass m_a, coefficient C_a with the frequency

4.2   The Geometry of Pile Cap

The Ratio of Length to Width. Assuming the pile cap was just completely submerged in water, the width W_c, thickness H_c of the pile cap and the water depth H_w were equal to 10m, 3.5m and 23.5m respectively. The influences of the ratio L_c / W_c of the length to width of the pile cap on the hydrodynamic effect were investigated, the length L_c was taken as 2.5, 5, 7.5, 10, 12, 15, 20m successively as to change the value of L_c / W_c. To compare with the method presented in section 2, the simplified method proposed in reference [5] was used to obtain the hydrodynamic added mass m_a and the hydrodynamic added mass coefficient C_a. In reference [5], the rectangular pile cap was equivalent to a cylinder one, where the diameter of the cylinder one equaled to the length of the rectangular one's edge perpendicular to vibration direction. Then the added mass m_a^r of the rectangular pile cap was obtained by multiplying the added mass m_a^c of the cylinder one with the shape modified coefficient K_c

$$K_c = 0.94732 + \frac{2.59648}{1 + \left(\dfrac{D/B}{0.09516}\right)^{0.54638}}, \qquad 0.1 \le D/B \le 10 \qquad (3)$$

This paper used the complete numerical method presented in section 2 to calculate the added mass of the equivalent cylinder pile cap.

The hydrodynamic added mass m_a and the hydrodynamic added mass coefficient C_a obtained by the above two method along x, y direction are drawn in Fig.5 & 6 as a function of L_c / W_c.

Fig.5 indicates that no matter which method is used, the hydrodynamic added mass m_a increase with the increase of L_c / W_c. For the model in this paper, the increase of L_c / W_c causes the increase of the submersion volume of the pile cap, and then causes the increase of m_a.

Fig.6 shows that with the increase of L_c / W_c, the hydrodynamic added mass coefficient C_a along x direction increases, but decreases along y direction. The reason causing the difference is that in term of the upstream face, the width W_c as to vibration in y direction is the same as the length L_c as to vibration in x direction. So in this sight, the discipline indicated by Fig.6 (a) and Fig.6 (b) is consistent.

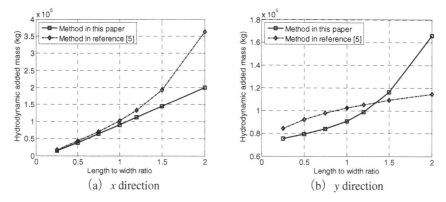

(a) x direction   (b) y direction

Fig. 5. The relationship between the hydrodynamic added mass m_a and the ratio of the length to the width

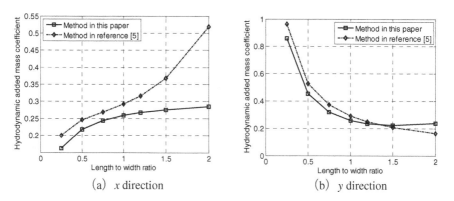

(a) x direction   (b) y direction

Fig. 6. The relationship between the hydrodynamic added mass coefficient C_a with the ratio of the length to the width

Comparing the result obtained from the numerical method in this paper and the method in reference [5], illustrated in Fig.5 and Fig.6, the following conclusion can be drawn: when L_c / W_c is less than 1.5, similar discipline can be seen along both x direction and y direction, while the result obtained from the later method is slightly higher than that obtained from the former one. When L_c / W_c is larger than 1.5, along x direction, the hydrodynamic added mass m_a and coefficient C_a obtained from the method in reference [5] are obviously larger than the value obtained from the numerical method in this paper, but along y direction, the former are smaller than the latter. And this tendency becomes more obvious with the increase of L_c / W_c. That is because that when L_c / W_c is large, in x direction, the method proposed in reference [5] amplifies the submersion volume in spite of the consideration of shape modified coefficient K_c as the rectangular pile cap was equivalent to the cylinder one according to the longer edge, but on the contrary, the enter water volume is diminished in y direction as the rectangular pile cap was equivalent to the cylinder one according to the shorter edge.

The Chamfer. For the lack of the theory analysis method and insufficiency of the method proposed in reference [5] on solving the hydrodynamic problem of the pile cap with chamfer, the influences of the form of chamfer, shown as Fig.1, and chamfer size on hydrodynamic effect were study in detail. In term of the chamfer form, two kinds of chamfers, fillet and $45°$ chamfer, were considered. As for chamfer size, the radius of the fillet and the edge length of $45°$ chamfer were taken as representation. Assuming the pile cap was just completely submerged in water, the length L_c, width W_c, thickness H_c of the pile cap and the water depth H_w were equal to 15m, 10m, 3.5m and 23.5m respectively. The chamfer size was taken as 0, 1, 2, 3, 4, 5m successively considering two kinds of chamfers mentioned above.

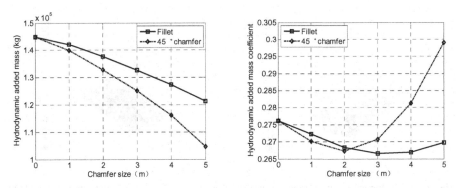

Fig. 7. The relationship between the hydrodynamic added mass m_a, coefficient C_a with the chamfer size

Fig.7 implies that with the increase of the chamfer size, the hydrodynamic added mass m_a decreases no matter which kind of chamfer form was used. And the hydrodynamic added mass m_a of $45°$ chamfer pile cap decreases faster than that of the fillet one, it is because the reduction of pile cap volume caused by $45°$ chamfer is greater than that caused by the fillet with the same chamfer size. Decrease of 20%-30% of the hydrodynamic added mass m_a can be reached after the chamfer is considered, so previous method neglecting the chamfer will amplify the hydrodynamic effect of the pile.

As for the hydrodynamic added mass coefficient C_a, with the increase of the chamfer size, C_a decreases first then increases no matter which kind of chamfer form was used, and comparing to the fillet pile cap, the fluctuation of the $45°$ chamfer one is greater. When the chamfer size is less than 2m, the decrease of C_a of the $45°$ chamfer pile cap is faster than that of the fillet one, but when the chamfer size is larger than 2m, C_a of the $45°$ chamfer pile cap increases fast and even exceeds that of the rectangular one.

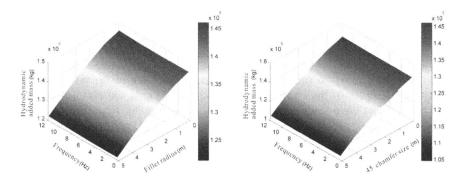

Fig. 8. The influence of the frequency and the the chamfer size on the hydrodynamic added mass m_a

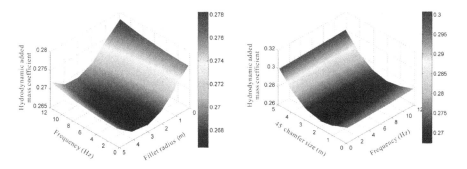

Fig. 9. The influence of the frequency and the the chamfer size on the hydrodynamic added mass coefficient C_a

The boundary condition of pile cap becomes complicated after the consideration of the chamfer, so in order to validate the universal applicability of the result obtained by assuming the frequency of the pile cap to be 1 Hz, the hydrodynamic added mass m_a and coefficient C_a were analyzed using two-parameter sensitivity analysis method, taking the change of the frequency and the chamfer size into account at the same time.

The following conclusion can be drawn from Fig.8 and Fig.9: the same discipline that with the increase of the chamfer size, the hydrodynamic added mass m_a decreases and the coefficient C_a decreases first then increases can be obtain when the frequency increases. So the above result is universal applied and the conclusion in section 4.1 that frequency has little influence on the hydrodynamic effect is proved again.

Thickness. Assuming the pile cap was just completely submerged in water, the length L_c, width W_c of the pile cap and the water depth H_w were equal to 15m, 10m and 23.5m respectively, the influences of the thickness H_c of the pile cap on hydrodynamic effect were studied. The rectangular pile cap and the fillet one with radio of 1.0 2.0, 3.0, 4.0 and 5.0m were taken into account. The thickness H_c of the pile cap was taken as 2.5, 3.5, 4.5, 5.5, 6.5m successively. Two-parameter sensitivity analysis method was used considering both the thickness and the chamfer size.

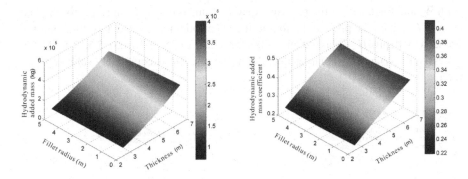

Fig. 10. The influence of the thickness H_c and the the chamfer size r on the hydrodynamic added mass and coefficient in x direction

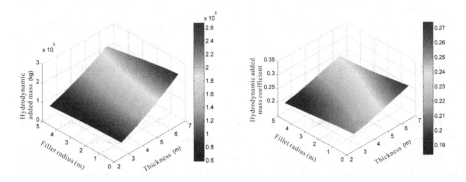

Fig. 11. The influence of the thickness H_c and the the chamfer size r on the hydrodynamic added mass and coefficient in y direction

Fig.10 & 11 shows that there is approximate linear relationship between the hydrodynamic effect and the thickness of the pile cap, with the increase of the thickness, both the hydrodynamic added mass m_a and coefficient C_a increase due to the increase of the submersion volume of the pile cap. And it can be clearly found that the influence of the thickness of the pile cap on hydrodynamic effect is obviously greater than the influence of the chamfer.

4.3   The Submersion Depth of Pile Cap

In term of the position of the pile cap relative to water surface, the following three kinds of situation are common in practical project due to the change of water level: partially submerged in water, just submerged in water, completely submerged in water. According to reference [10], the theoretical solution of both radiation and diffraction theory of the pile cap is relative to the submersion depth H_{w2} (the distance between the water surface and the pile cap bottom, shown in Fig.2). So the influences of the submersion depth on the hydrodynamic effect were studied in this section.

Assuming the pile cap was just completely submerged in water, the length L_c, width W_c and thickness of the pile cap equal to 15m, 10m and 3.5m respectively. The distance H_{w1} from the pile cap bottom to the water bottom was taken as 20m, and the submersion depth H_{w2} was taken as 0.875, 1.75, 2.625, 3.5, 4.5, 5.5, 7.5, 11.5m successively. When H_{w2} is larger than 3.5m, the pile cap is completely submerged in water.

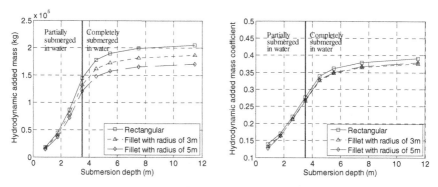

Fig. 12. The relationship between the hydrodynamic added mass m_a, coefficient C_a with H_{w2} in x direction

The following conclusion can be drawn from Fig.12. When the pile cap is partially submerged in the water ($H_{w2} \leqslant 3.5$m), with the increase of the submersion depth H_{w2}, the hydrodynamic added mass m_a and the coefficient C_a increases rapidly, while when the pile cap is completely submerged in the water, the speed of the increase slows down and the hydrodynamic added mass m_a and the coefficient C_a tend to be constant. In other word, the hydrodynamic effect will increase with the increase of the submersion depth of the cap, but keep in constant after the depth exceeds a certain value.

5   Conclusion

Based on the complete numerical method and the advantage of ADINA on simulating fluid-structure interaction, the influences of different parameters of the rectangular cap and the cap with complicated chamfer on the hydrodynamic effect were studied, including the cap vibration frequency, the geometrical size, the chamfer and the submersion depth of the cap. The double-layer water mesh generation method was proposed in model analysis, the influence of this method on the accuracy and efficiency of modal analyses was studied. Through the above research, the following conclusion can be drawn:

(1)   The double-layer water mesh generation method with reasonable mesh way could improve the computational efficiency without affecting the calculation accuracy in modal analysis

(2)   The frequency has limited affection on hydrodynamic effect which could be almost neglected. The hydrodynamic effect is mainly affected by the pile cap geometries: with the increase of the dimension perpendicular to vibration direction, the hydrodynamic added mass and coefficient of pile cap will increase; the increase of the pile cap thickness will cause the increase of the hydrodynamic added mass and coefficient; the chamfer of the pile cap has great influence on the hydrodynamic effect, with the increase of the chamfer size, the hydrodynamic added mass will decrease, in other word, neglecting the effect of the chamfer will amply the hydrodynamic effect. And the form of the chamfer is also great impact factor; Moreover, the submersion depth has great influence on the hydrodynamic effect. When the pile cap is partially submerged in the water, with the increase of the submersion depth, the hydrodynamic added mass and the coefficient increases rapidly, while when the pile cap is completely submerged in the water, the hydrodynamic effect slowly increases with the increase of the submersion depth of the cap, but keep in constant after the depth exceeds a certain value.

(3)   The method in this paper and the method proposed in reference [5] have a satisfactory agreement with each other for the pile cap with small ratio of the length to width, while for the cap with large ratio of the length to width, the method proposed in reference [5] will amplify the hydrodynamic effect in the vibration direction perpendicular to the longer edge and diminish the hydrodynamic effect in the vibration direction perpendicular to the shorter edge.

Acknowledgments. This research is supported by Kwang-Hua Fund for College of Civil Engineering, Tongji University and The National Science Foundation of China, Grant No.51278376 and No.90915011.

References

1. Wei, K., Yuan, W., Bouaanani, N.: Experimental and Numerical Assessment of the Three-Dimensional Modal Dynamic Response of Bridge Pile Foundations Submerged in Water. Journal of Bridge Engineering (2012) (previewed online)

2. Lan, Y.-M., Liu, H., et al.: Experimental studies on hydrodynamic loads on piles and slab of Donghai Bridge. Part II: Hydrodynamic forces on pile array and slab in wave-current combinations. Journal of Hydrodynamics, Ser. A 20(3), 332–339 (2005)
3. Song, B., Li, Y.: Simplified calculation method of hydrodynamic force for elevated pile caps. Journal of University of Science and Technology Beijing 33(4), 509–514 (2011)
4. Lai, W.: Dynamic interaction between deep-water bridges and water during earthquakes and wave. Tongji University, Civil Engineering College, Shanghai (2004)
5. Wang, J., Lai, W., Hu, S.: Seismic Hydrodynamic Effects on Group-pile Foundations with Caps Merged in Water. Journal of Tongji University (Natural Science) 39(5), 650–655 (2011)
6. Miquel, B., Bouaanani, N.: Practical dynamic analysis of structures laterally vibrating in contact with water. Computers & Structures 89(23-24), 2195–2210 (2011)
7. Wei, K., Wu, Y., Yuan, W.C., et al.: Numerical dynamic analysis for water-pile group bridge foundation interacted system. Engineering Mechanics 28(suppl. I), 195 (2010)
8. Wei, K., Yuan, W.: A Numerical-Analytical Mixed Method of Hydrodynamic Effect for Deep-Water Elevated Pile Cap Foundation under Earthquake. Journal of Tongji University (Natural Science) 41(3), 336–967 (2012)
9. Olson, L.G., Bathe, K.J.: An infinite element for analysis of transient fluid-structure interactions. Engineering Computations 2(4), 319–329 (1985)
10. Bhatta, D.D., Rahman, M.: On scattering and radiation problem for a cylinder in water of finite depth. International Journal of Engineering Science 41(9), 931–967 (2003)

Numerical Simulations for DLR-F6 Wing/Body/Nacelle/Pylon with Enhanced Implicit Hole Cutting Method

Jia Xu, Qiuhong Liu, and Jinsheng Cai*

Northwestern Ploytchnical University, 127 Youyi Xilu, Xi'an Shaanxi 710072, P.R. China
caijsh@nwpu.edu.cn

Abstract. Original implicit hole cutting method to solve the generation of overlapping grids connectivity is enhanced by three methodologies: the cell quality criterion is only based on the wall distance; an alternating digital tree algorithm is used to improve efficient on cell search; all cells inside body are identified and blanked for post-processing. A hierarchical overset grid system with layers of grids of varying resolution is developed to further improve the accurateness and automation of enhanced implicit hole cutting method. Numerical simulations for DLR-F6 wing/body/nacelle/pylon configuration were performed on overlapping grids by an in-house CFD solver called Exstream. Numerical results show: All the aerodynamic forces matched well with those of CFL3D and ANSYS CFX, and it demonstrates the accuracy and efficiency of enhanced implicit hole cutting method and Exstream solver. Correspond to experimental data, computed lift values follow a nearly linear trend as angle of attack varies from -3.0 to 1.5.

Keywords: Computational Fluid Dynamics, flow simulation, overlapping grid, implicit hole cutting method, wing/body/nacelle/pylon configuration.

1   Introduction

When such flows around complex configurations are simulated by Computational Fluid Dynamics (CFD), mesh generation becomes a challenge task to many researchers. It is well known that structured and Cartesian grid method can not be represented well in complex configurations, and structured/unstructured mixed grid method costs more memory and computed time compared with other methods. The overlapping grid is a good solution to deal with complex flow because it allows multi-block grids to overlap with each other. However, the generation of overlapping grids connectivity is an expensive and daunting task.

Lee and Baeder [1, 2] presented Implicit Hole Cutting (IHC) algorithm which is only a cell selection process based on the criterion of cell size when comparing the grid overlapping regions and the hole cutting around bodies is a byproduct of this

---

* Corresponding author.

K. Li et al. (Eds.): ParCFD 2013, CCIS 405, pp. 185–194, 2014.

operation. The advantages of this algorithm are those it ensures that the finer mesh will be used to enable best flow resolution and it is very simple to implement. However, some cells inside bodies, which are not blanked in this method, make influences on post-process. Cai [3] proposed a grid assembly strategy to improve IHC method and the effectiveness of mixed method was demonstrated with several aerodynamic test cases. Based on original IHC method, Landmann and Montagnac [4] developed a simple stencil walk for the donor search and a parallel load balancing to perform efficiently unsteady moving body simulations.

In this paper, enhanced IHC method based on a hierarchical overset grid strategy will be used to investigate viscous flows around DLR-F6 geometry. DLR-F6 geometry was performed in the 2nd AIAA CFD Drag Prediction Workshop [5] (DPW-2) and composed of wing, body, nacelle and pylon. Numerical simulation was completed on overlapping grids by an in-house CFD solver called Exstream. From the above, this paper is structured as follows: Firstly, IHC method with three enhancements and a hierarchical overset grid strategy can be presented and explained; Then, the Exstream solver is introduced; Finally, viscous flows around DLR-F6 geometry will be simulated and discussed.

2   Numerical Method

2.1   Enhanced Implicit Hole Cutting Method

Original implicit hole cutting (IHC) method was first proposed by Lee and Baeder. In contrast to the traditional Chimera method, the IHC method loops through every cell in the grid system when comparing the grid overlapping regions. The 'best' grid cell is selected by quality criterion and donor cell is sought for every cell at one time loop. These works replaces of original two steps: declarations of cell status and donor cell search. If multiple donor cells are found in cell-section process, the one with best quality is kept as the optimum donor cell. If no donor cell is found or the processed cell is the 'best' cell compared with all others, the processed cell remains as a calculated cell.

Apparently, original IHC method doesn't need to blank hole cells and special overlapping boundary which is supposed to be identified on traditional Chimera method, so this method can bring more automated and efficient for an assembly of overlapping structured grids in theory. Because of the non-blanked cells, the post-processing is problematic. Anther drawback of original IHC method is that appropriate algorithm is not used to accurate cell process. As a result, three improvements are presented for complex aircraft configures in this paper:

- A cell quality criterion which calculates grid density for cell-selection is only based on the wall distance of grid cell, and it leads up to reduce the occurrence of *orphan cells* which have invalid interpolation (shown in Fig. 1);

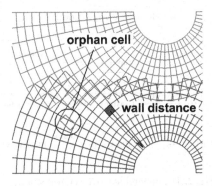

Fig. 1. Orphan cell and wall distance shown after hole cutting

- An alternating digital tree (ADT) algorithm [6] is used for IHC method in order to improve efficient on cell search. If every cell intersection is investigated, the solution of this problem should become very expensive. By building ADT data structure, many of cell intersections can be quickly discarded;
- A drawback of original IHC method is problematic post-processing, because blanking information, which is not identified in originally IHC method, is required for display of flowfield. As a result, some cells inside body are identified and blanked for post-processing.

2.2   A Hierarchical Overset Grid Strategy

A hierarchical overset grid strategy which was combined with IHC method has been used for complex geometrics to raise efficiency to generate overset grid connectivity. Three concepts for the hierarchical overset grid strategy are introduced: block, cluster, and layer in ascending order. Blocks are the basic elements in this strategy and a block is a structured cubical grid in three dimensions; a cluster is matched multi-block grid which consists of one or more blocks with matched boundaries between neighboring blocks; A cluster is usually generated for one component of aircraft geometrics, such as wing, fuselage, or horizontal tail. To obtain an overall grid system that offers high grid densities in the near field around bodies but coarsens gradually towards the far field, several layers of grids, each consisting of one or more overset clusters, are used. It ensures that The entire grid system assure that the 'higher' overlapping layer is embedded in the 'lower', and every grid point in a 'higher' layer must fall within the domain of a lower level layer. Figure 2 illustrates the hierarchical overset grid strategy.

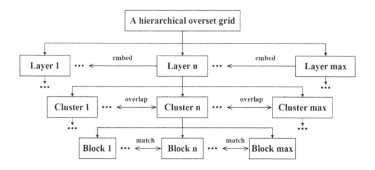

Fig. 2. The hierarchical overset grid strategy

2.3   Exstream Flow Solver

Exstream is a parallel multi-block structured overlapping grids flow solver and developed for aerodynamics analysis. Exstream solves the three-dimensional compressible Reynolds-averaged Navier–Stokes equations which are written in integral form:

$$\int_{\Omega} \frac{\partial \mathbf{W}}{\partial t} dV + \oint_{\partial\Omega} \mathbf{F} \cdot \mathbf{n} dS = 0 \tag{1}$$

Where V is an arbitrary control volume with closed boundary surface S and $\mathbf{n}$ is the unit normal vector in outward direction. The vector of the state variables is defined as

$$\mathbf{W} = (\rho, \rho u, \rho v, \rho w, \rho E)^T \tag{2}$$

Where ρ is density, u, v and w are three Cartesian velocity components, E is total energy of the flow, and e is internal energy. The flux tensor $\mathbf{F}$ consists of a convective (inviscid) part and a diffusive (viscous and thermal) part. The governing Eq. (1) is discretized separately in space and time. The convective (inviscid) form of the governing Eq. (1) is computed by AUSMDV schemes [7] for space discretization. AUSMDV is one of AUSM-family schemes, and this scheme has favorable properties: high-resolution for contact discontinuities, conservation of enthalpy for steady flows and numerical efficiency. a diffusive (viscous and thermal) form of the Eq. (1) is discretized by second-order central scheme. In conclusion, Eq. (1) holds for each cell in the solution domain and is approximated in cell (i, j, k) as

$$\frac{d}{dt}(\mathbf{W}_{i,j,k} \cdot V_{i,j,k}) + R(\mathbf{W}_{i,j,k}) = 0 \tag{3}$$

Compared with Eq. (1), Eq. (3) suppose that Ω is a cell (i, j, k) and consider $\mathbf{W}_{i,j,k}$, located in the cell center, as an approximation to the average flow variables $\mathbf{W}$ in this cell. In Eq. (3), $R(\mathbf{W}_{i,j,k})$ is the net flux leaving and entering the cell and $V_{i,j,k}$ are the cell volumes. Implicit LU-SGS scheme [8, 9] based on lower-upper factorization and symmetric Gauss-Seidel relaxation is used to integrate the discrete Eq. (3). Local time stepping is used to advance the flow solution at the local maximum speed and implicit residual smoothing is applied to increase the stability range. The coefficient of laminar viscosity is obtained by Sutherland's formula. The turbulent eddy viscosity is calculated by Menter's shear stress transport (SST) two-equation model [10]. Menter's SST model combines the k-ω and k-ε models in a way that would allow them to be used in the regions where they achieve the best advantage.

Meanwhile, Exstream solver is parallelized by Message Passing Interface (MPI) to reduce the computational time for large-scale steady and unsteady calculations. The different blocks are automatically distributed over a number of processors available on a parallel computer or a network of commodity machines based on the block size by a load-balancing algorithm. For chimera part of this solver, all grid cells including *interpolated* and *calculated cells* can be calculated to simulate viscous flow. Flow information of *calculated cell* will be updated to ensure that flow variables W are latest, and flow data on *interpolated cell* have to be interpolated after each of iterations is finished. The commonly interpolation method is a trilinear method based on the relative position of the interpolated cell midpoint in the respective dual-grid donor cell. The converged solution of the coarse grid computation is transferred to the next finer grid level using a trilinear interpolation procedure. The process of this solution on a coarse grid as the initial condition for the next finer grid is called mesh-sequencing (MS). Fully turbulent viscous flow computations can be performed on all levels of grids, but it is not very meaningful for turbulent computation on the coarse grid. Hence, we use Euler computations on the coarse grid, followed by laminar computations on the medium grid, and finally turbulent computations on the fine grid.

3   Results

3.1   DLR-F6 Geometry Descriptions

The international Drag Prediction Workshop (DPW) series were initiated by a working group of AIAA Applied Aerodynamics Technical Committee members focusing on realistic aerodynamic configurations. The DLR-F6 model has been used as the test case in the 2nd AIAA CFD Drag Prediction Workshop (DPW-2). Two configurations of DLR-F6 model were available: one is wing/body, and the others is wing/body/nacelle/pylon. In this paper, we have used wing/body/nacelle/pylon configuration to test accuracy and efficiency of enhanced IHC method and Exstream solver. Figure 3 shows general DLR-F6 geometry with nacelle and pylon. More information related to DLR-F6 wing/body/nacelle/pylon configuration is described in Ref. [5].

3.2   Overset Grid Generation

The generation of a multi-block matched grid for DLR-F6 wing/body/nacelle/pylon configuration is not an easy job so that the use of overset grid is a natural. The multi-block overlapping grid has a C-O-H topology for wing and O-O-O topology for fuselage to get better grid quality. The nacelle and pylon have more complex

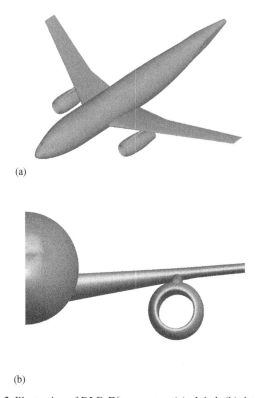

(a)

(b)

Fig. 3. Illustration of DLR-F6 geometry: (a) global; (b) detailed

topology. The standard practice of resolving the boundary layer down to a minimum of y+ = 1 is specified for the overlapping grid and the growth rate of the normal spacing through the boundary layer should not exceed 1.2. To effectively connect the related component grids, a collar grid was applied for the intersection region between wing and fuselage. In order to improve the computational efficiency, the half DLR-F6 model has been simulated and the total number of grid points used for the computations (excluding overlapped cells and the cells inside solid bodies) is 10,268,937.

By the hierarchical overset grid strategy as mention above, there are eight clusters and five layers for overlapping grids. The highest layer consists of two clusters which are collar and pylon. The second layer has three clusters: wing, fuselage and nacelle. The other three layers are background grids which cover the whole computed domain. Different finer Cartesian grids have been generated for background grids and provide a smooth transition between the different Cartesian grids. Enhanced IHC method has been used to create the connectivity of overlapping grids. Figure 4 and 5 show overlapping grids after hole cutting.

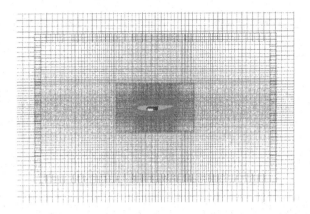

Fig. 4. Three layers overset grid for DLR-F6 wing/body/nacelle/pylon configuration

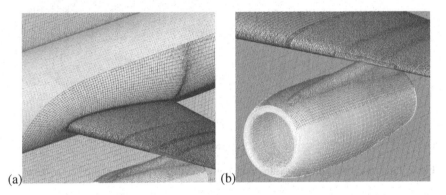

(a)   (b)

Fig. 5. Overset grid for (a) wing and fuselage; (b) pylon and nacelle

3.3   Results and Discussions

The aerodynamic conditions are the following: free stream Mach number is 0.75 and Reynolds number is 3×10^6 when angle of attack is at the design lift coefficient (C_L) of 0.5. To compute the fixed C_L condition, a C_L driver is required, which periodically adjusts the value of incidence angle to maintain the required lift value throughout grid convergence study. As mentioned earlier, AUSMDV, k-ω SST turbulence model and LU-SGS have been used for this simulation.

Figure 6(a) illustrates wing pressure distributions when the location (η) is 15.0% which is close to fuselage. In these plots, we can see computed results almost have a agreement with experimental data. DPW-2 participants were required to provide results on this case and CFL3D data presented in this paper were provided by NASA Langley Research Center (LaRC). When X/C is 0.4 on upper wing surface, shock point location computed by CFL3D is more close to experimental data compared with Exstream. Figure 6(b) compares pressures when the location (η) is 33.1% and depicts that shock is strong and well defined. As Fig.7 shown, the smooth transition of surface pressure (C_p) contour in the overlapping region indicates that the interpolation between the overlapping grids offers sufficient accuracy.

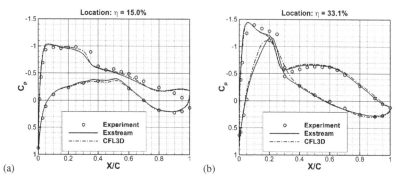

Fig. 6. Comparisons of pressure (C_p) distribution at the (a) location (η) of 15.0% and (b) location (η) of 33.1%

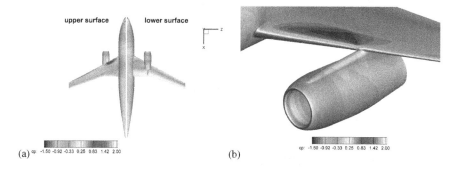

Fig. 7. Illustration of surface pressure (cp) contours on wall sufaces: (a) global; (b) detailed

A drag polar on the overlapping grid was also required by varying the incidence (-3.0, -2.0, -1.0, 0.0, 0.5, 1.0, and 1.5 deg) while holding the Mach and Reynolds number conditions fixed at the preceding values. Figure 8 and 9 include CFL3D and ANSYS CFX solutions. Computed and experimental lift data follows a nearly linear trend as angle of attack varies from -3.0 to 1.5. While incidenced angle is 0 deg, The result of Exstream is more close to experimental data and the same situation is also shown in Fig. 8.

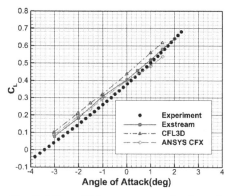

Fig. 8. Lift coefficients versus angle of attack

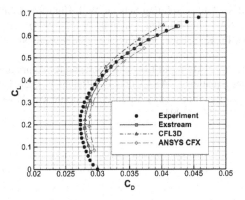

Fig. 9. Lift versus drag for DLR-F6

4   Summary

A hierarchical overset grid strategy and three improvements have been applied in this paper. In contrast to the original implicit holt cutting (IHC) method, a hierarchical overset grid strategy and new definition of cell quality criterion from enhanced IHC method could further improve accurateness on the overset grid connectivity problem. viscous flows around DLR-F6 wing/body/nacelle/pylon configuration has been simulated by an in-house CFD solver called Exstream. numerical results show: All the aerodynamic forces matched well with those of CFL3D and ANSYS CFX, and it demonstrates the accuracy and efficiency of Enhanced implicit hole cutting method and Exstream solver. Correspond to experimental lift data, computed lift values follow a nearly linear trend as angle of attack varies from -3.0 to 1.5.

References

1. Lee, Y.L., Baeder, J.D.: Implicit Hole Cutting - A New Approach to Overset Grid Connectivity. In: AIAA 16th Computational Fluid Dynamics Conference, Orlando, AIAA Paper 03-4128 (2003)
2. Lee, Y.L., Baeder, J.D.: High-order overset method for blade vortex interaction. In: AIAA 40th Aerospace Sciences Meeting, Reno, AIAA Paper 02-0559 (2002)
3. Cai, J.S., Tsai, M.H., Liu, F.: A parallel viscous flow solver on multi-block overset grids. Computers and Fluids 35, 1290–1301 (2006)
4. Landmann, B., Montagnac: A highly Automated Parallel Chimera method for Overset Grids based on the Implicit hole Cutting Technique. International Journal for Numerical Methods in Fluids 66, 778–804 (2010)
5. DPW website, http://aaac.larc.nasa.gov/tsab/ cfdlarc/aiaa-dpw/Workshop2/workshop2.html
6. Bonet, J., Peraire, J.: An Alternating Digital Tree (ADT) Algorithm for 3D Geometric Searching and Intersection Problems. International Journal for Numerical Methods in Engineering 31, 1–17 (1991)

7. Wada, Y., Liou, M.S.: A Flux Splitting Scheme With High-Resolution and Robustness for Discontinuities. NASA Technical Memorandum 106452 (1994)
8. Vos, J.B., Leyland, P., Kemenade, V.V., et al.: NSMB handbook version 5.0, Lausanne, pp. 36–38 (2003)
9. Yoon, S., Jameson, A.: A Multigrid LU-SSOR Scheme for Approximate Newton Iteration Applied to the Euler Equations. NASA Contractor Report 179524 (1986)
10. Menter, F.R.: Two-Equation Eddy-Viscosity Turbulence Models for Engineering Applications 32, 1598–1605 (1994)

Accelerating High-Order CFD Simulations for Multi-block Structured Grids on the TianHe-1A Supercomputer

Chuanfu Xu[1,*], Wei Cao[1], Lilun Zhang[1], Guangxue Wang[2], Yonggang Che[1], Yongxian Wang[1], and Wei Liu[1]

[1] School of Computer, National University of Defense Technology,
Changsha 410073, China
xuchuanfu@nudt.edu.cn
[2] State Key Laboratory of Aerodynamics,
China Aerodynamics Research and Development Center, Mianyang 621000, China

Abstract. In this paper, we present a MPI-CUDA implementation for our in-house CFD software HOSTA to accelerate large-scale high-order CFD simulations on the TianHe-1A supercomputer. HOSTA employs a fifth order weighted compact nonlinear scheme (WCNS-E5) for flux calculation and a Runge-Kutta method for time integration. In our GPU parallelization scheme, we use CUDA thrad blocks to efficiently exploit fine-grained parallelism within a 3D grid block, and CUDA multiple streams to exploit coarse-grained parallelism among multiple grid blocks. At the CUDA-device level, we decompose complex flux kernels to optimize the GPU performance . At the cluster level, we present a Scatter-Gather optimization to reduce the PEI-E data transfer times for 3D block boundary/singularity data, and we overlap MPI communication and GPU execution. We achieve a speedup of about 10 when comparing our GPU code on a Tesla M2050 with the serial code on a Xeon X5670, and our implementation scales well to 128 GPUs on TianHe-1A.

Keywords: GPU parallelization, high-order CFD, multi-block structured grids, GPU cluster.

1 Introduction

CFD(Computational Fluid Dynamics) solves Naiver-Stokes equations for the evolution of fluid flows and involves reasonably complex numerical algorithms which are used in computational science today. In the past several decades, low-order (e.g., second-order) schemes for CFD have been widely used in engineering applications. However, they are insufficient in capturing small disturbances in an

* This paper was supported by the National Science Foundation of China under Grant No.11272352, the National Basic Research Program of China under Grant No. 2009CB723803 and the Open Research Program of China State Key Laboratory of Aerodynamics.

K. Li et al. (Eds.): ParCFD 2013, CCIS 405, pp. 195–206, 2014.
© Springer-Verlag Berlin Heidelberg 2014

environment containing sharp gradients. To ensure high-resolution and fidelity, robust and high-order methods that can deal with complex flows in complex domains are therefore highly required. Over the past 20 to 30 years, there have been many studies in developing and applying various kinds of high-order and high accurate schemes for CFD. Among others, compact high-order finite difference schemes based on a compact stencil are very attractive for flows with multiscales (e.g., aeroacoustics and turbulence), due to their high formal order, good spectral resolution and flexibility. In former works, Deng et al. have developed several compact high-order finite difference schemes with inherent dissipation, e.g., the Dissipative Compact Schemes (DCS)[1] and the Weighted Compact Nonlinear Schemes (WCNS)[2]. In order to apply high-order finite difference schemes on complex multi-block grids, Deng et al. employ a Conservative Metric Method(CMM)[3] to calculate the grid derivatives, and a Characteristic-Based Interface Condition (CBIC)[4] to fulfill high-order multi-block computing. For the moment, we have developed a high-order CFD software, HOSTA(High-Order SimulaTor for Aerodynamics), using the high-order schemes with CMM and CBIC, for multi-block structural grids. HOSTA has been successfully applied to a wide range of flow simulations in many research and engineering projects so far, showing its flexibility and robustness[5]. Meanwhile, running high-order CFD applications like HOSTA for complex flows with large-scale grids requires more huge computing and storing resources than low-order ones. However, parallelizing and scaling high-order CFD applications on GPU-accelerated supercomputer like TianHe- 1A[12] is very challenging, because the physical models and numerical methods in them involves complex calculating and communicating procedures. Developers often need to manage different levels of parallelisms using different parallel programming models (e.g., NVIDIA's Compute Unified Device Architecture (CUDA) for GPUs and MPI or OpenMP for CPUs) for heterogeneous compute devices. Further, when performing complex high-order, multi-block grid CFD simulations, we need extensive implementation and optimization efforts to achieve high performance and efficiency.

Many publications have given the experiences of porting CFD codes to GPUs. In [6], Jacobsen et al. parallelized a CFD solver for incompressible flow. A speedup of 130 is achieved when comparing 128 GPUs with 8 CPU cores. Parallel tests are scaled up to 128 GPUs. In [7], they further demonstrated large eddy simulation of a turbulent channel flow on GPUs. Performance results are investigated using up to 256 GPUs. But they only simulated a lid-driven cavity problem using low-order schemes for both performance evaluation and validation. Due to the complexity, high-order CFD schemes for complex multi-block grids generally require extra implementation and optimization efforts on GPUs. Paper [8] implemented a high-order solver that can run on multi-GPUs for compressible turbulence using WENO(weighted essentially non-oscillatory) scheme. But the solver can only run on a single node platform containing 4 GPUs for CFD problems of very simple domains like 2D and 3D box. Results show that for the single-precision implementation, a speedup of 53 can be achieved by comparing 4 GPUs with a single CPU core. Paper [9] published the parallelization of the first high-order, compressible viscous flow solver for mixed unstructured grids by using MPI and CUDA. The Vincent-Castonguay-Jameson-Huynh method is used in the solver. A flow over SD7003 airfoil and a flow over sphere are simulated using up to 32 GPUs. Paper [10] reported a MPI-CUDA implementation to accelerate the solution of the level set equations for interface tracking using a HOUC(High-Order Upstream Central) scheme. But they only demonstrated performance results of 4 GPUs. Paper [11] described the implementation of an incompressible double-precision two-phase solver on GPU clusters using a fifth-order WENO scheme. The test problem is a rising bubble of air inside a tank of water with surface tension effects and parallel performance results are reported using up to 48 GPUs.

In this paper, with MPI+CUDA, we parallelize HOSTA using a fifth order weighted compact nonlinear scheme (WCNS-E5) on TianHe-1A. When parallelizing HOSTA on a single GPU, we exploit dual-level parallelism: fine-grained parallelism by using a CUDA thread to compute a cell within a grid block, and coarse-grained parallelism by using CUDA multiple streams to compute multiple blocks. At the CUDA-device level, we present kernel decomposition optimization to further enhance the GPU performance. For efficient simulations on large-scale GPUs, we present a Scatter-Gather optimization to reduce the PEI-E data transfer times for 3D block boundary/singularity data. We use non-blocking MPI, CUDA multiple streams and CUDA events to maximize the overlapping of kernel computation, intra-node data transfer and inter-node communication. The GPU-enabled HOSTA shows good strong and weak scalability on TianHe-1A. The work that we present here demonstrates a comprehensive effort to efficiently accelerate **high-order CFD simulations** on the **TianHe-1A supercomputer**.

2   Numerical Methods and HOSTA Implementation

In curvilinear coordinates the governing equations (Euler or Navier-Stokes) in strong conservative form are:

$$\frac{\partial \tilde{Q}}{\partial \tau} + \frac{\partial \tilde{F}}{\partial \xi} + \frac{\partial \tilde{G}}{\partial \eta} + \frac{\partial \tilde{H}}{\partial \zeta} = 0 \tag{1}$$

where $\tilde{F}$, $\tilde{G}$ and $\tilde{H}$ are the fluxes along the ξ, η and ζ direction respectively; $\tilde{Q}$ is the conservative variable.

We only consider the discretization of the inviscid flux derivative along the ξ direction. The discretization for the other inviscid fluxes can be computed in similar ways. The fifth order WCNS-E5 can be expressed as follows:

$$\frac{\partial \tilde{F}_i}{\partial \xi} = \frac{75}{64h}(\tilde{F}_{i+1/2} - \tilde{F}_{i-1/2}) - \frac{25}{384h}(\tilde{F}_{i+3/2} - \tilde{F}_{i-3/2}) + \frac{3}{640h}(\tilde{F}_{i+5/2} - \tilde{F}_{i-5/2}) \tag{2}$$

where h is the grid size, $\tilde{F}_{i\pm1/2} = \tilde{F}(U_{i\pm1/2})$ are the cell edge fluxes, and $\tilde{F}_{i+m} = \tilde{F}(U_{i+m})$ are the cell node fluxes. The cell-edge variables $(U_{i\pm1/2})$ are

```
Do nstep=nstepst,nsteped    !time-marching loop
  Do iter=1,nsubmax         !sub-iteration for unsteady flows
    Call boundary_conditions()       !boundary conditions
    Call Exchange_BC(PV)         !exchange primitive variables(PV) for boundaries
    Call Exchange_Singular(PV)    !exchange PV for singularities
    Call calc_spectral_radius()      !calculate delta of spectral radius
    Call calc_time_step()     !calculate delta of time step
    !begin of calculation of RHS
    Call calc_gradient()      !calculate gradient of PV (DPV)
    Call Exchange_BC(DPV)     !exchange DPVs for boundaries
    Call Exchange_Singular(DPV)     !exchange DPVs for singularities
    Call calc_viscous()      !calculate the viscous fluxes
    Call calc_inviscid()      !calculate the inviscid fluxes
    Call calc_source()      !calculate the source flux
    Call Exchange_BC(RHS)     !exchange RHSs for boundaries
    Call Exchange_Singular(RHS)      !exchange RHSs for singularities
    ! end of calculation of RHS
    Call sol_RK()      !Jacobi solver for delta of conservative variables(DQ)
    Call Exchange_BC(DQ)      !exchange DQs for boundaries
    Call Exchange_Singular(DQ)      !exchange DQs for singularities
    Call Update()      !update PV···
    Call Residual()      !calculate residual
  End do      !end of sub-iteration
End do      !end of time-marching
```

Fig. 1. The main pseudocode for the time-marching loop of HOSTA

```
Do nc=1,nblkcoms      !loop for local multiple blocks
  ! loop skeleton for calc_inviscid
  !I direction
  allocate temporary memory spaces for the nc-th blocks
  Do k=1,NK
  Do j=1,NJ
    determine boundary types for linear interpolation
    Call sub_intplt ()      !interpolate the cell-edge metrics
    determine boundary types for nonlinear interpolation
    Call sub_intnon()      !reconstruct the right/left-hand cell-edge primitives
    determine boundary types for derivative flux
    Do i=stn0,edn0
      Call sub_flux ()      !calculate the cell-node fluxes
    End do
    determine boundary types of cell-node fluxes
    Do i= ste0,ede0
      Call sub_fvs ()      !calculate the cell-edge fluxes (flux splitting)
    End do
    Call sub_scheme()      ! calculate the cell-node derivative fluxes
  End do      !end of Do j
  End do      !end of Do k
  deallocate temporary memory spaces for the nc-th blocks
  !J direction
  ...
  ! K direction
  ...
End do !end of Do nc
Do nc=1,nblkcoms      !loop for local multiple blocks
  ! loop skeleton for calc_spectral_radius
  preparation for the nc-th block
  Do k=0,NK+1
  Do j=0,NJ+1
  Do i=0,NI+1
    calculating spectral radius for cell (i,j,k) of the nc-th block
  End do      !end of Do i
  End do      !end of Do j
  End do      !end of Do k
End do !end of Do nc
```

Fig. 2. Two typical loop skeletons in HOSTA

interpolated, and the numerical flux $\tilde{F}_{i\pm1/2}$ can be evaluated by cell-edge variables:

$$\tilde{F}_{i\pm1/2} = \tilde{F}(U_{i\pm1/2}^L, U_{i\pm1/2}^R) \tag{3}$$

where $U_{i\pm1/2}^L$ and $U_{i\pm1/2}^R$ are the left-hand and right-hand cell-edge variables. For viscous flux, we also use a sixth order central difference scheme(see [2] for more details).

The third-order Runge-Kutta method used in this paper for the time integration can be expressed as follows:

$$\begin{aligned}
\tilde{Q}^{(0)} &= \tilde{Q}^{(n)}; \\
\tilde{Q}^{(1)} &= \tilde{Q}^{(0)} + \Delta t R(J^n, \tilde{Q}^{(0)}); \\
\tilde{Q}^{(2)} &= \tfrac{3}{4}\tilde{Q}^{(0)} + \tfrac{1}{4}\tilde{Q}^{(1)} + \tfrac{1}{4}\Delta t R(J^n, \tilde{Q}^{(1)}); \\
\tilde{Q}^{(3)} &= \tfrac{1}{3}\tilde{Q}^{(0)} + \tfrac{2}{3}\tilde{Q}^{(2)} + \tfrac{2}{3}\Delta t R(J^n, \tilde{Q}^{(2)}); \\
\tilde{Q}^{(n+1)} &= \tilde{Q}^{(3)};
\end{aligned} \tag{4}$$

HOSTA is a production-level in-house CFD software containing more than 25,000 lines of FORTRAN90 codes. Its main pseudo-code for the timing-marching loop is presented in Fig.1. The WCNS-E5 scheme is implemented when calculating the viscous (calc_viscous) flux, the inviscid flux (calc_inviscid). Due to the complex computational procedure of WCNS-E5, we decompose stencil computations in calc_viscous and calc_inviscid along the I, J and K directions when implementing HOSTA. Thus, data dependencies only exist in the corresponding direction and there are two typical loop skeletons in HOSTA as Fig.2 shows. In calc_inviscid, the loop skeleton is very complex. HOSTA calls several subroutines to calculate the cell-edge and cell-node flow variables for each direction. The bounds (e.g.,stn and edn) for the inner loop are determined by various boundary types. The complexity of the loop skeleton requires our extra implementation and optimization efforts when porting HOSTA to GPUs. The loop skeleton for calc_spectral_radius is relatively simple. Note that in each time step (or sub-iteration for unsteady flows), HOSTA performs four exchanges of high-order information among blocks to ensure the robustness of high-order schemes (see Fig.1). These information involves boundary (or ghost layer) data and singularity data, which is very common in finite difference schemes for complex multi-block structural grids.

3   Single GPU Parallelization and Optimization

On a single GPU, we present a dual-level parallelization: fine-grained data parallelism within a block and coarse-grained task parallelism among multiple blocks. For the fine-grained parallelism, we use two kinds of CUDA thread blocks (3D configuration or 2D configuration) according to data dependency among cells in a block. If there is no data dependency between cells (e.g., the procedure sol_RK() for the Runge-Kutta method), each GPU thread calculates a cell independently. The 3D domain decomposition for a block is illustrated in Fig.3: a grid block of size (NI,NJ,NK) is logically decomposed to some subblocks of size (x_blk, y_blk, z_blk) , each *subblock* is computed by a GPU thread block of the same size, and those thread blocks compose a GPU grid of size($\lceil NI/x\_blk \rceil$,$\lceil NJ/y\_blk \rceil$, $\lceil NK/z\_blk \rceil$), where $\lceil x \rceil$ is the minimum integer that is larger than x. Each cell (i, j, k) is calculated by a CUDA thread (idx, idy, idz), where

$$idx = threadIdx.x + blockDim.x * (blockIdx.x) + 1$$
$$idy = threadIdx.y + blockDim.y * (blockIdx.y) + 1$$
$$idz = threadIdx.z + blockDim.z * (blockIdx.z) + 1$$

Since CUDA has no global synchronization, we use a 2D configuration or 2D decomposition for this case, i.e., we use one GPU thread to compute all the cells on a direction. For example, in the I direction, the 2D thread block is configured as $(1, y\_blk, z\_blk)$ and the size of GPU grid is $(1, \lceil NJ/y\_blk \rceil, \lceil NK/z\_blk \rceil)$.

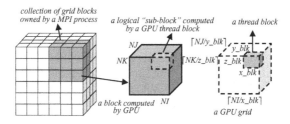

Fig. 3. De-composite 3D domain of a grid and map it to CUDA

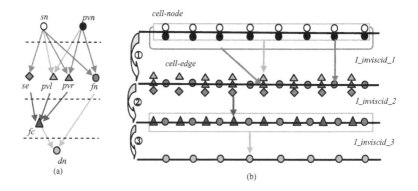

Fig. 4. Data dependency in I-direction inviscid flux calculation (a) and kernel decomposition (b)

Alternatively, we can decompose a large 2D kernel to several small kernels and use a 3D kernel configuration. Fig.4(a) shows a schematic about data dependency in the computing of inviscid flux for one direction. The two input cell-node variables are the grid derivative *sn* and the primitives *pvn*. Firstly, the cell-edge grid derivative se is computed by linear interpolation of *sn*; the left-value *pvl* and right-value *pvr* for cell-edge primitives are computed by nonlinear interpolation of *sn* and *pvn*; the derivative of cell-node flux is also computed according to *sn* and *pvn*. Then, the derivative of cell-edge flux *fc* can be computed based on *se*, *pvl* and *pvr*. And finally, the delta of inviscid flux for a cell-node *dn* can be computed based on *fc* and *fn*. By carefully investigating the data dependency, the 2D kernel for the inviscid flux of I direction is decomposed into three 3D kernels as Fig.4(b) shows: *I_inviscid_1* is used to compute *se*, *pvl*, *pvr* and *fn*; *I_inviscid_2* is used to compute *fc*; *I_inviscid_3* is used to compute *dn*.

We implement the coarse-grained parallelism based on multiple CUDA streams. Because there is no data dependency among grid blocks between exchanges of boundary/singularity data, we bind each block to a CUDA stream and issue all the streams simultaneously to the GPU. As Fig.5 shows, all the operations for block *i* such as computation, host to device (H2D) data copy and device to host (D2H) data copy are associated with stream *i*. The multi-stream implementation can fully exploit the potential power of modern GPU architecture. For example, when a stream is accessing global memory, the kernel engine can schedule and execute warps from other streams to hide memory access latency. More importantly, the kernel execution and PCI-E data transfer of different streams can be substantially overlapped, especially for GPUs with separate copy engines for H2D and D2H such as Tesla M2050 in TianHe-1A. Our multi-stream design is independent with the fine-grained GPU parallelization within a block. Furthermore, it can also be used to overlap the GPU computation, data transfer and MPI communication as Sect.4 describes.

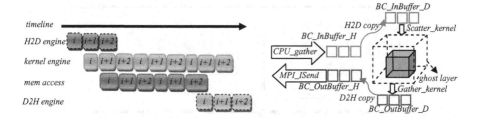

Fig. 5. Streaming 3 grid blocks using 3 CUDA streams

Fig. 6. Optimizing boundary data transfer for a 3D block

4   Scaling on TianHe-1A

Since a compute node (of TianHe-1A) contains only one GPU, we choose to use one MPI process on each node for large-scale simulations on multiple GPUs. Considering a 3D block with six boundaries (or ghost zones), the data for a single boundary is continuously stored in the device memory, while the data for different boundaries is not. Further, CUDA API for data transfer can only copy continuous data elements for a time. Thus, we use a Scatter-Gather optimization to minimize the times of data transfer for boundary/singularity data of a

3D grid block via PCI-E, as Fig.6 illustrated. Before performing D2H copy, we use a gather kernel (i.e., *Gather_kernel*) to collect all non-continuous data to a continuous device buffer *BC_OutBuffer_D*, and then the entire buffer is copied to host buffer *BC_OutBuffer_H*. Correspondingly, before performing H2D copy, we use a gather procedure (i.e., *CPU_gather*) on the CPU to pack all updated boundary data to a host buffer *BC_InBuffer_H*, and then the entire buffer is transferred to device buffer *BC_InBuffer_D*. Finally, we use a scatter kernel (i.e., *Scatter_kernel*) to distribute the data elements to each boundary.

Furthermore, we overlap the kernel execution, data transfer and MPI communication using CUDA multi-stream, non-blocking MPI and CUDA events. Fig.7 shows a schematic for the computation of the gradient of primitives, the inviscid and viscous fluxes. When the GPU finishes all the stream/block's operations for the gradient of primitives, a CUDA event with the same stream ID is recorded to represent data dependency between MPI communication and the boundary data computed by the stream. Before the host calls *MPI_Isend* to send the boundary data for a block, it must query the device to make sure that the event associated with the block/stream has been executed. As we can see, the data copy for block *i*, the non-blocking MPI send for block (*i-1*) and the computation of the gradient of primitives for block (*i+1*) are largely overlapped. When the GPU is executing the kernel or performing data copy, the CPU can also call *MPI_Irecv* to receive boundary data from blocks on other nodes(e.g., block(*i+1*), as illustrated by Fig.7). Note that *MPI_Waitall* must be called to ensure that *MPI_Irecv* has finished receiving data.

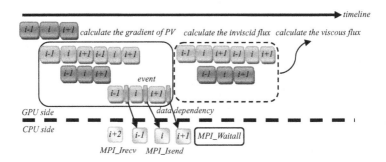

Fig. 7. A schematic for the overlapping of kernel execution, data transfer and MPI communication when computing the gradient of primitives, the inviscid and viscous fluxes

5   Performance Evaluation

Our GPU-enabled HOSTA uses a CUDA C and Fortran90 mixed implementation. We ported all the procedures (about 14000 lines of CUDA C codes) in the time-marching loop except the procedures for MPI communication (red codes in Fig.1). In our implementation, we often maximize the kernel's performance

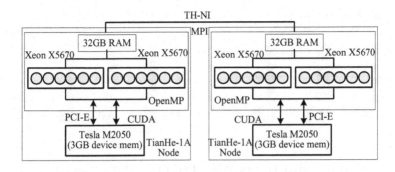

Fig. 8. Compute nodes and heterogeneous programming in TianHe-1A

when setting (x_blk, y_blk, z_blk) to $(16,4,4)$(i.e., the number of threads in a thread block is 256) and thus we choose it as the default setting.

We use the TianHe-1A supercomputer as our test platform. TianHe-1A is a GPU-accelerated massive parallel processing system developed by National University of Defense Technology (NUDT), China, and was ranked No.1 in the 36th Top500 list for HPC systems. Each node (see Fig.8) contains two Intel hexa-core Xeon X5670s sharing a 32GB main memory and one Nvidia Tesla M2050 with a 3GB global memory. Each GPU contains 14 Streaming Multiprocessors (SMs) and each SM has 32 CUDA Cores. The peak double-precision performance for the two X5670s is about 140 GFlops, which is about 27% of the M2050's 515 GFlops. However, the memory bandwidth for the two X5670s is about 64 GB/s, which is about 43% of the M2050's 148 GB/s. Since CFD is memory-bounded, the difference of memory bandwidth rather than the Flops is expected to be the dominant factor for the realistic performance difference between the CPUs and the GPU. Different nodes are connected by the self-developed fat-tree interconnection network *TH-NI*, with a latency of about $1.57\mu s$ and the bidirectional bandwidth of about 160 Gbps. We use MPICH2-GLEX for MPI communication. The CUDA version is 4.2, and the compilers for FORTRAN and C are icc11.1 and ifort 11.1. All the code is compiled with -O3 option.

In Fig.9, we present the speedup of a M2050 GPU over a single core of X5670 CPU, and the speedups of a M2050 GPU over a six-core X5670 CPU using 6 OpenMP threads and dual six-core X5670 CPUs using 12 OpenMP threads. The grid size is $128 \times 128 \times 128$, and the block number is varying from 2 to 8. We see that our GPU code can achieve a speedup of more than 10 over the serial CPU code. Note that the price of a M2050 is similar to the price of an X5670, and a speedup of about 2.2 when comparing a M2050 to a six-core X5670 is also comparable to the results of paper [11] as far as similar-priced comparison of CPU and GPU is concerned. A speedup of about 1.3 when comparing a M2050 to dual X5670s further validates GPU's cost-effectiveness. We observe slight performance degradation for both GPU and CPU when the block number is increased. This can be explained by the fact that multiple blocks will incur extra OpenMP and kernel overheads.

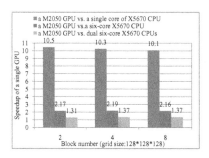

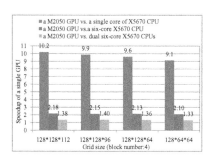

Fig. 9. Single GPU speedup for fixed grid size

Fig. 10. Single GPU speedup for different grid sizes

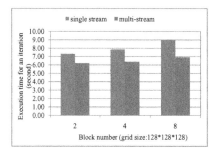

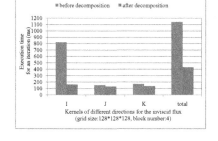

Fig. 11. Performance comparison for single stream and multi-stream implementation

Fig. 12. Performance comparison for before and after kernel decomposition

In Fig.11, we present performance results for different grid sizes with 4 blocks. We get better performance for larger problem sizes. This is because higher workloads can better overlap the computation and global memory access for GPUs. Fig.11 shows the results for multi-stream optimization. We see about 25% performance enhancement for a whole iteration. But our multi-stream implementation requires multiple blocks on a GPU to be associated with multiple streams and the extra GPU memory space to store the intermediate results for simultaneously executed blocks. Fig.12 shows the results when kernel decomposition is employed for the computation of the inviscid fluxes. We achieve about 75% performance improvement for the I direction, but for the J and K directions, the performance improvements are only about 15%. This is due to the decomposition in the I direction can ensure more GPU threads to access the global memory in a coalesced manner.

In Fig.13, we shows the strong scaling results with and without overlapping. We obtain the results without the overlapping by directly copying the whole grid block between GPU and CPU. We use the performance achieved on 16 GPUs as a baseline and the total grid size is fixed to $16 \times 128 \times 128 \times 128$. The GPU number is scaled from 16 to 128 and the block number per GPU is fixed to 4. We see that the overlapping of computation, data transfer and MPI communication

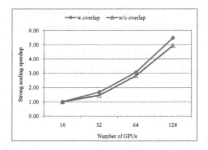
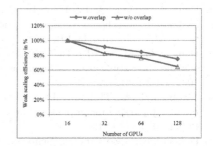

Fig. 13. Strong scaling speedup on TianHe-1A. The 16 GPU results are used as the baseline.

Fig. 14. Weak scaling efficiency on TianHe-1A. The 16 GPU results are used as the baseline.

plays an important role for good scalability. We observe a speedup of about 5.5 when scaling from 16 GPUs to 128 GPUs with overlapping, and a speedup of about 5.0 without overlapping, demonstrating a promising result for strong scalability test on large-scale GPU clusters. Fig.14 presents the weak scaling efficiency results with and without overlapping. The problem size for each GPU is fixed to $128 \times 128 \times 128$ with 4 blocks. Again we use the performance achieved on 16 GPUs as a baseline and the GPU number is increased from 16 to 128. We lose about 20% (from the perfect weak scaling efficiency of 100%) using our overlapping strategy and 128 GPUs, while the efficiency loss is up to 40% for the non-overlapping one.

6 Conclusion and Future Work

High-order CFD simulations require large amount of compute resources. However, the complexity of high-order CFD simulation for complex multi-block grids makes it very difficult to parallelize on modern large-scale GPU-accelerated HPC systems. In this work, we parallelize and optimize our in-house high-order CFD software HOSTA to accelerate large-scale CFD simulations on the TianHe-1A supercomputer. We conclude that TianHe-1A is a suitable platform to run HOSTA-like CFD softwares in terms of performance and scalability, although programming it takes many efforts. Furthermore, we plan to collaborate CPU and GPU to further accelerate large-scale CFD simulations.

References

1. Deng, X.G., Maekawa, H., Shen, Q.: A class of high-order dissipative compact schemes. AIAA Paper 96-1972 (1996)
2. Deng, X.G., Zhang, H.X.: Developing high-order weighted compact nonlinear schemes. J. Comput. Phys. 165, 22–44 (2000)
3. Deng, X.G., Mao, M.L., Tu, G.H., Liu, H.Y., Zhang, H.X.: Geometric conservation law and applications to high-order finite difference schemes with stationary grids. J. Comput. Phys. 230, 1100–1115 (2011)

4. Deng, X.G., Mao, M.L., Tu, G.H., et al.: Extending the fifth-order weighted compact nonlinear scheme to complex grids with characteristic-based interface conditions. AIAA Journal 48(12), 2840–2851 (2010)
5. Deng, X.G., Mao, M.L., Tu, G.H., et al.: High-order and high accurate CFD methods and their applications for complex grid problems. Commun. Comput. Phys. 11, 1081–1102 (2012)
6. Jacobsen, D.A., Thibault, J.C., Senocak, I.: An MPI-CUDA implementation for massively parallel incompressible flow computations on multi-GPU clusters. AIAA Paper 2010-522 (2010)
7. DeLeon, R., Jacobsen, D., Senocak, I.: Large-eddy simulations of turbulent incompressible flows on GPU Clusters. Computing in Science & Engine 15, 26–33 (2013)
8. Antoniou, A.S., Karantasis, K.I., Polychronopoulos, E.D.: Acceleration of a finite-difference WENO scheme for large-scale simulations on many-core architectures. AIAA paper 2010-0525 (2010)
9. Castonguay, P., Williams, D.M., Vincent, P.E., Lopez, M., Jameson, A.: On the development of a high-order, multi-GPU enabled, compressible viscous flow solver for mixed unstructured grids. AIAA paper 2011-3229 (2011)
10. Appleyard, J., Drikakis, D.: Higher-order CFD and interface tracking methods on highly-parallel MPI and GPU systems. Computers & Fluids 46, 101–105 (2011)
11. Zaspel, P., Griebel, M.: Solving incompressible two-phase flows on multi-GPU clusters. Comput & Fluids (2012)
12. Yang, X.J., Liao, X.K., Lu, K., et al.: The TianHe-1A supercomputer: its hardware and software. Journal of Computer Science and Technology 26, 344–351 (2011)

Large-Scale Parallelization Based on CPU and GPU Cluster for Cosmological Fluid Simulations

Chen Meng[1,2], Long Wang[1,*], Zongyan Cao[3,1], Long-long Feng[4], and Weishan Zhu[4]

[1] Supercomputing Center of Computer Network Information Center, Chinese Academy of Sciences, No.4 South 4th Street, ZhongGuanCun, Beijing 100190, China
[2] University of Chinese Academy of Sciences, No.19 YuQuan Road, ShiJingShan, Beijing 100049, China
[3] National Astronomical Observatories, Chinese Academy of Sciences, 20A Datun Road, Chaoyang District, Beijing 100012, China
[4] Purple Mountain Observatory, Chinese Academy of Sciences, 2 West Beijing Road, Nanjing 210008, China
{mengchen,wangl,zycao}@sccas.cn,
{fengll2000,wszhu1985}@gmail.com

Abstract. In this study, we present our parallel implementation for large-scale cosmological simulations of 3D supersonic fluids based on CPU and GPU clusters. Our developments are based on an OpenMP parallelized CPU code named WIGEON. It is shown that a speedup of 13~31 (depending on the specific GPU card) can be achieved compared to the sequential Fortran code by using the GPU as the accelerator. Further more, our results show that the pure MPI parallelization scales very well up to ten thousand CPU cores. In addition, a hybrid CPU/GPU parallelization scheme is introduced and a detailed analysis of the speedup and the scaling on the different number of CPU and GPU cards are presented (up to 256 GPU cards due to computing resource limitation). The efficiency of our scaling and high speedup relies on domain decomposition approach, optimization of the WENO algorithm and a series of techniques to optimize the CUDA implementation, especially in the memory access pattern. We believe this hybrid MPI+CUDA code can be an excellent candidate for 10 Peta-scale computing and beyond.

Keywords: Cosmological hydrodynamics, heterogeneous, WENO, GPU, large-scale cluster.

1   Introduction

The observed luminous objects in the universe have existed in the form of baryonic matter, a typical Navier-Stokes fluid. To account for the observational features, it would be necessary to incorporate a variety of computational hydrodynamics algorithms into cosmological simulations. WIGEON [1] is a hybrid cosmological hydrodynamic/N-body simulation software using high-order finite difference

---

* Corresponding author.

K. Li et al. (Eds.): ParCFD 2013, CCIS 405, pp. 207–220, 2014.

weighted essentially non-oscillatory (WENO) scheme to solve the computational fluid dynamic equations. The WENO scheme uses the idea of adaptive stencils in the reconstruction procedure based on the local smoothness of the numerical solution to automatically achieve high-order accuracy and non-oscillatory property near discontinuities. It is extremely robust and stable for solutions containing strong shock and complex solution structures [2-3].

Large-scale fluid computations based on CPU cluster have gained great success in the Tera-scale era [4-5]. From the list of the world's Top500 fastest supercomputers [6], the Peta-scale era has arrived with heterogeneous systems involving CPU cores and accelerators or co-processors (GPU, Xeon Phi, etc.). And GPU has gained significant performance for computational intensive tasks in recent years [7-8], so designing hybrid codes is increasingly important for applications, which can utilize the computing power of both CPU clusters and GPU clusters. In this paper, we present a heterogeneous parallel code for the large-scale 3D cosmological fluid dynamics in double precision on CPU/GPU cluster based on MPI and CUDA.

We started our work with a massively CPU parallelization based on MPI. WIGEON is solving hydrodynamic problems on a structured grid. The MPI-based parallelization uses domain decomposition assigning subdomains to different CPU cores, which are, then, calculated in parallel. However, several issues have to be taken into account: (1) The most efficient domain decomposition strategy for the best scalability is to be found. The 5th order WENO at least requires a five-point stencil for one point in the 3D domain in each dimension. When we decompose the computing domain, the nonlocal data of the stencil points are called as "ghost cells". The Euler equation solver solves a flow system with multi-iterations, each of which begins with a data exchange of ghost cells. This leads to a high amount of communication, since the points are a five-component vector and the ghost cells are relatively thick. (2) Improving the efficiency of the collective communication is critical to extreme-scale parallel computing. The global communication in WENO procedure will result in relatively bigger performance loss. So in this paper, we focused on designing an algorithm to extend the parallel scale to more than ten thousand CPU cores.

Then we though about porting the WENO computation (about 90% of total time) in the subdomain to local GPU for further speedup and scaling [9-12]. With the refinement of parallel granularity, the pure MPI parallelization code will meet the limitation because of the communications. So we made the WENO computation in the subdomain go through a second-level parallelization based on CUDA running on a shared memory system. In order to achieve a high speedup on the GPU, the following problems need to be solved: (1) There exist a lot of intermediate variables and frequent memory access in the WENO procedure derived from the adaptive-stencil calculation. However, memory access is the bottleneck compared with the computing power for GPUs. In other words, it is a memory-bound function; (2) The cache locality on CPU does not work on GPU and even produces negative effects. GPUs have their own "cache locality". So, we did a series of optimizations including making use of all levels of GPU on-chip memory, adjusting the data structure and the order of the instructions.

This article is organized as follows. In section 2, we introduce the algorithm of solving Euler equation based on the WENO scheme. Section 3 we outline the implementation and optimization details of MPI-parallelization on CPU cluster. In Section 4, we outline the implementation and optimization steps of GPU code on CPU/GPU cluster. In Section 5, we measure and analyze the performance of our implementation and in section 6 the results are summarized and a short outlook is given.

2   Numerical Algorithm

2.1   Governing Equation

We use Euler equation without any viscous and thermal conductivity terms for the compressible cosmological fluid as the governing equation. It can be written in the compact form of hyperbolic conservation laws:

$$\frac{\partial U}{\partial t} + \frac{\partial f(U)}{\partial X} + \frac{\partial g(U)}{\partial Y} + \frac{\partial h(U)}{\partial Z} = F(t, U) \tag{1}$$

where U and the fluxes $f(U)$, $g(U)$, and $h(U)$ are five-component column vectors:

$$U = \begin{pmatrix} \rho \\ \rho u \\ \rho v \\ \rho w \\ E \end{pmatrix} \quad f(U) = \begin{pmatrix} \rho u \\ \rho u^2 + P \\ \rho u v \\ \rho u w \\ u(E+P) \end{pmatrix} \quad g(U) = \begin{pmatrix} \rho v \\ \rho u v \\ \rho v^2 + P \\ \rho v w \\ v(E+P) \end{pmatrix} \quad h(U) = \begin{pmatrix} \rho w \\ \rho u w \\ \rho v w \\ \rho w^2 + P \\ w(E+P) \end{pmatrix} \tag{2}$$

t is the time and (X, Y, Z) are the coordinates. ρ is the density, $V = (u, v, w)$ is the velocity vector, P is comoving pressure, and E is the total energy including kinetic and internal energies:

$$E = \frac{P}{\gamma - 1} + \frac{1}{2}\rho(u^2 + v^2 + w^2)$$

γ is the ratio of the specific heats of the baryon. Here $\gamma = 5/3$. The "force" term $F(t, U)$ on the right-hand side includes the contributions from the gravitation.

2.2   WENO Scheme Algorithm

As a result of the high nonlinearity of gravitational clustering in the universe, there can occur shock waves in the cosmological flows. So the discretization of the fluxes for solving the governing equation is based on the 5th order WENO finite difference [13-14]. As an example, $\frac{\partial f(u)}{\partial x}$ is discussed, keeping the values for Y and Z constant:

$$\frac{\partial f(u)}{\partial x}\Big|x = x_j \approx \frac{1}{\Delta x}(\hat{f}_{j+1/2} - \hat{f}_{j-1/2})$$

here, $\hat{f}_{j+1/2}$ is the numerical flux; If $f'(u) \geq 0$, the 5th order finite difference WENO scheme has the flux given by:

$$\hat{f}_{j+1/2} = w_1 \hat{f}^{(1)}_{j+1/2} + w_2 \hat{f}^{(2)}_{j+1/2} + w_3 \hat{f}^{(3)}_{j+1/2}$$

where $\hat{f}^{(i)}_{j+1/2}$ are fluxes on three different stencils given by:

$$\hat{f}^{(1)}_{j+1/2} = \frac{1}{3} f(u_{j-2}) - \frac{7}{6} f(u_{j-1}) + \frac{11}{6} f(u_j),$$

$$\hat{f}^{(2)}_{j+1/2} = \frac{1}{6} f(u_{j-1}) + \frac{5}{6} f(u_j) + \frac{1}{3} f(u_{j+1}),$$

$$\hat{f}^{(3)}_{j+1/2} = \frac{1}{3} f(u_j) + \frac{5}{6} f(u_{j+1}) - \frac{1}{6} f(u_{j+2}),$$

The key for the success of WENO scheme relies on the design of the nonlinear weights w_i, which are given by:

$$w_i = \frac{\tilde{w}_i}{\sum_{k=1}^{3} \tilde{w}_k}, \quad \tilde{w}_k = \frac{\gamma_k}{(\varepsilon + \beta_k)^2},$$

where the linear weights γ_k are chosen to yield 5th order accuracy and are given by $\gamma_1 = \frac{1}{10}, \gamma_2 = \frac{3}{5}, \gamma_3 = \frac{3}{10}$. The smoothness indicators β_k are given by:

$$\beta_1 = \frac{13}{12}[f(u_{j-2}) - 2f(u_{j-1}) + f(u_j)]^2 + \frac{1}{4}[f(u_{j-2}) - 4f(u_{j-1}) + 3f(u_j)]^2,$$

$$\beta_2 = \frac{13}{12}[f(u_{j-1}) - 2f(u_j) + f(u_{j+1})]^2 + \frac{1}{4}[f(u_{j-1}) - f(u_{j+1})]^2,$$

$$\beta_3 = \frac{13}{12}[f(u_j) - 2f(u_{j+1}) + f(u_{j+2})]^2 + \frac{1}{4}[3f(u_j) - 4f(u_{j+1}) + f(u_{j+2})]^2,$$

Finally, ε is a parameter to keep the denominator from becoming 0 and is usually taken as $\varepsilon = 10^{-6}$.

We then indicate the scheme in our case, which is more complex situation without the property $f'(u) \geq 0$. In this paper, we use the Lax-Friedrichs flux splitting:

$$f(u) = f^+(u) + f^-(u),$$
$$\alpha = \max_u |f'(u)|$$
$$f^+(u) = \frac{1}{2}(f(u) + \alpha u), \frac{df^+(u)}{du} \geq 0,$$
$$f^-(u) = \frac{1}{2}(f(u) - \alpha u), \frac{df^-(u)}{du} \leq 0$$

Then, we apply the above procedure to $f^+(u)$ and a mirror image procedure to $f^-(u)$. For systems of hyperbolic conservation laws, the nonlinear part (the determination of the β_k and w_i) of the WENO procedure is carried out in local characteristic fields. Thus, we would first define an average $u_{j+1/2} = [\bar{\rho}, \bar{u}, \bar{v}, \bar{w}, \bar{p}]^T$ of u_j and u_{j+1} by using Roe average:

$$\bar{\rho} = \sqrt{\rho_j \rho_{j+1}},$$

$$\bar{V} = \frac{\bar{V}_j \sqrt{\rho_j} + \bar{V}_{j+1} \sqrt{\rho_{j+1}}}{\sqrt{\rho_j} + \sqrt{\rho_{j+1}}}, \qquad \bar{p} = \frac{P_j \sqrt{\rho_j} + P_{j+1} \sqrt{\rho_{j+1}}}{\sqrt{\rho_j} + \sqrt{\rho_{j+1}}}$$

to compute the left and right eigenvectors of $f'(u_{j+1/2})$:

$$R_{j+1/2}^{-1} f'(u_{j+1/2}) R_{j+1/2} = \Lambda_{j+1/2}$$

One then projects all the quantities needed for evaluating the numerical flux $\hat{f}(u_{j+1/2})$ on the local characteristic space by left multiplying them with $R_{j+1/2}^{-1}$ and then re-project back to original physical space by right multiplying with $R_{j+1/2}$.

2.3   Time Discretization

To solve the Euler equation, time accuracy is as important as spatial accuracy. We used the 3th order nonlinearly stable Runge-Kutta time discretization [15] with a time step restriction proportional to that for the forward Euler step to be stable. This proportion coefficient is termed as CFL (Courant-Friedrichs-Levy) coefficient of the high-order Runge-Kutta method.

3   Parallel Scheme Based on MPI

The Euler solver for simulating fluids in WIGEON solves a system with the iterative method based on the structured grid. It begins with the parameter settings and grid-value initializing. Then the program goes into the multi-iterations.

3.1   Domain Decomposition

Though decomposition along three dimensions (cubic decomposition) brings in a more complex communication mode than one- [16] or two-dimensional decomposition, the amount of the ghost cells generated by cubic decomposition (Fig. 1) is the smallest when the subdomain is in the same size. And the finest parallel granularity of one- or two-dimensional decomposition is restricted by the side-lengths while that of cubic decomposition is more flexible. In a word, cubic decomposition method has the best scalability.

So we chose cubic decomposition method to divide our computing domain (a 3D grid data) and distributed these subdomains and their ghost cells among the processors using MPI. Fig. 1 shows that in one subdomain there are six-block ghost cells that need to be exchanged in every iterative step because they are all updated by the six neighbor processes instead of local process. MPI allows users to submit a custom datatype for the

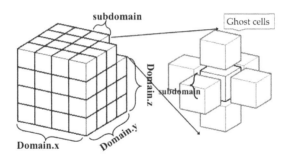

Fig. 1. Domain decomposition on CPU-cluster

data in discontinuous memory for communication. The communication mode should be six steps: (1) process (x, y, z) sends the custom-type updated local cells to process (x+1, y, z) and at the same time receives the left side ghost cells from process (x-1, y, z) using MPI API "sendrecv"; (2) process (x, y, z) sends cells to process (x-1, y, z) and receives the right side ghost cells from process (x+1, y, z); The same two steps are respectively performed in the other two spatial directions y and z.

3.2   Modification in WENO Flux Splitting

To ensure upwinding in WENO procedure for the stability in the non-smooth regions, we should use a flux splitting at first. Global Lax-Friedrichs flux splitting brings in global communications, which will result in significant performance loss in a massively parallelization. So we choose to use local Lax-Friedrichs flux splitting. In 5th order WENO scheme, we only used the maximum of 5-point values around, which means we need extra ghost cells to do the splitting for the original ghost cells. Though the number of ghost-cell layers grows to 10 from 5 and the amount of end-to-end communication increases, it is still worthy that we successfully remove the global communications for the massively parallelization. And the experiments showed the dissipation and dispersion errors of the local one are acceptable.

4   Parallel Scheme Based on CUDA

The challenge for the GPU programming is not simply getting good performance on the GPU, but also in coordinating the scheduling of computation on the CPU and the GPU processor and the transfer of data between CPU and GPU memory [17]. In our implementation, the unit of the heterogeneous cluster is a CPU process attached to a GPU device. In a subdomain assigned to a MPI process, the GPU processes the WENO computation, which is the time-consuming part in the whole cosmological simulation and the CPU handles the left part including the communications between processes and other light computations. The CPU transfers the data in memory to The GPU. Then the MPI process on the CPU and threads on the GPU will execute asynchronously until the next data-copying operation (Fig. 2).

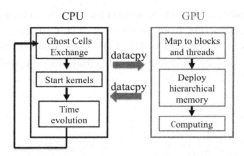

Fig. 2. CPU and GPU co-processing

4.1   Mapping Strategy on GPU

The data of the subdomain assigned to a specific MPI process are transferred to its local GPU memory. There a second-level decomposition is based on CUDA. We split the WENO procedure into three sub-procedures: WENO_fx, WENO_gy and WENO_hz, which are calculating $\frac{\partial f(U)}{\partial X}$, $\frac{\partial g(U)}{\partial Y}$ and $\frac{\partial h(U)}{\partial Z}$ respectively. We launched three kernels for them and used different mapping strategy for optimizing memory access and reusing variables. For kernel WENO_fx, the Y-Z plane of the local cubic grid is partitioned into sub-plane that can be processed independently in parallel by 2D blocks. Each of these threads in one block then processes all calculations along X-axis. The strategy for other two kernels is similar but along the different axes. This mapping strategy is actually a 2D decomposition. We have discussed the best scalability of 3D decomposition in MPI parallelization, which can also ensure more threads launched in CUDA parallelization. However, since the independence requirement of blocks in CUDA allows thread blocks to be scheduled in any order across cores, we should extra ghost cells for each block. It results a big loss on performance for a subdomain of its size that the ghost cells in blocks bring in the redundant computations and memory access.

4.2   Optimization Technologies

Since the WENO computation is memory-bound [18], the improvement of memory throughout is the primary optimization step.

First of all, we need to emphasize that one point in the cubic domain is a five-component vector (showed in Fig. 3 in the left part), which are density, 3D-velocity and energy for a 3D N-S fluid only without any viscous terms. For the serial Fortran code, the domain is stored as a 3D array of vector structure, such that five variables of a point are in the continuous memory. This is favorable to CPU cache locality. However, the "cache locality" on a GPU is different. When a warp (32 threads in consecutive index) executes an instruction that accesses global memory, it coalesces the memory accesses within the warp several transactions. If the distribution of the memory addresses across the threads is continuous as their index, the number of transactions will be one or two depending on the word size. Otherwise, the number of transactions will be more and 32 in the worst case, which is equal to serial access. So we changed the data structure from an array of vector structure (AOS) to a vector structure of array (SOA, parallel array) (Fig. 3) in which all values of each variable in the points are in the consecutive addresses. This transposition work has been done on the GPU.

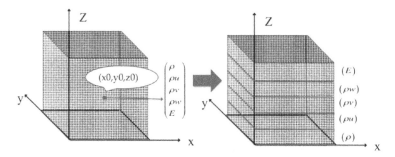

Fig. 3. AOS To SOA

After the transposition work, the addressing in WENO_fx, X-axis directional computing, is still uncoalescing. The simple way to find that is the memory accessed by one thread in WENO_fx is continuous. So in order to improve memory throughout further, we need to consider utilizing the memory hierarchy of GPU. We used texture memory for read-only mesh data that are processed before the three main kernels begin in each iteration step. We can see it as a kind of special caching mechanism with 2D or 3D coalescing.

Global memory is the main memory on a GPU and the access latency is the longest while on-chip memory has much higher bandwidth and much lower latency. Shared memory is a limited resource for stream multiprocessors (SM). When we used it in the one of three main kernels, it severely reduced the number of active threads, which directly brings up bad performance, since the latency in a large number of memory accesses need to be overlapped by many active threads. So we split the kernels appropriately and used shared memory in these kernels, which are read/write functions and have a problem in memory coalescing.

5   Testing and Analysis

We have conducted experiments using different experimental platform. The experimental platform for multi-CPU tests is Tianhe-1A. We used 1366 nodes, one of which is supplied with a six-core Intel Xeon X5670 CPU with 12 threads. The experimental platform for mono-GPU tests consists of one NVIDIA Tesla C2050 with Fermi architecture using CUDA 4.0, one NVIDIA Tesla C2075 with Fermi architecture using CUDA 4.2, one NVIDIA Tesla K20m with Kepler architecture using CUDA 5.0. The GPU is connected with a quad-core AMD Phenom(tm) 9850 CPU by PCI-express2.0. The experimental platform for multi-CPU/GPU is Mole-8.5. We used

43 nodes, one of which is supplied with two quad-core Intel Xeon E5520 CPUs and 6 Tesla C2050 GPUs. In our test, each MPI process is bound to one CPU core attached to a single GPU card. We counted one CPU core plus one GPU as one CPU/GPU computing unit.

5.1 Testing Case

Galactic winds are large-scale outflows driven by the feedback from intensive star formation and they are thought to play an important role in the formation and evolution of dwarf galaxies. We used WIGEON to simulate the galactic-wind dynamics and investigate the fate of enriched gas in dwarf starburst galaxies. The numerical results highlight the strong influence of geometry structure of dwarf galaxies on their formation and evolution.

5.2 Results and Analysis

5.2.1 Performance on CPU Cluster

We concentrate on the Euler solver as depicted in Fig. 2. Fig. 4 shows us the scaling of one step time for Euler solver. We see that it is close to linear scaling when the number of CPU cores increases from 2048 to 16384. When the number of cores reaches 16384, the subdomain on each process is smallest and is in the scale of 128×128×256. We could predict that our code can scale well on more CPU cores if we have, since we can increase the ratio of computation and communication to make even better scalability by computing larger domain and enlarging the size of subdomain within the memory capacity.

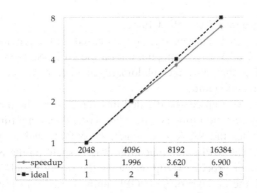

Fig. 4. Strong scaling for the domain of 4096^3 on CPU cluster

5.2.2 Performance on Single GPU

WENO computation is the hotspot of Euler solver. We ported this part on GPU to make use of its impressive computing power. However, because of the feature of the algorithm of WENO scheme and the different memory access pattern between CPU and GPU, we should do a series of optimizations. Fig. 5 shows the speedups after we performed each of the key optimizing steps on Tesla C2075. We can measure the effect of each optimizing step by the speedup gap. Clearly, the transposition from AOS to SOA for global memory coalescing made the most significant contribution.

We also tested our GPU code of WENO computation speedups on other two different GPU cards. The speedups on C2050, C2075 and K20m are respectively ×13, ×19 and ×31. We can see the performance of C2057 is 1.5 times that of C2050 and the performance of K20m is 1.6 times that of C2075. Except for double precision peak GFLOPS and memory bandwidth [19], "Register spilling" is one of the most main causes. "Register spilling" will appear when the number of one thread used registers exceeds the maximum number.   The CUDA Profiler [20] showed our code had generated thousands of bytes "register spilling" on C2050 and C2075 while zero bytes on K20m.

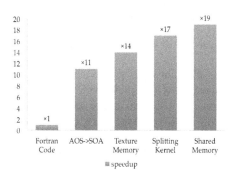

Fig. 5. Speedup after key steps to optimize WENO computation code on Tesla C2075. The size of the subdomain is 128^3.

5.2.3   Performance on CPU/GPU Cluster

The development of our heterogeneous code is based on the previous MPI code. On each process, we ported WENO computation on the GPU. So there is one CPU core plus one GPU card in charge of one subdomain calculation. We call the unit of CPU and GPU as one CPU/GPU unit.

The total time of one step can be divided into three parts: the numerical operation time, the MPI communication time and the CPU-GPU data-copy time. The numerical operation time includes the WENO computation on GPU and Runge-Kutta scheme performed on CPU. The MPI communication time is spent on the exchange of ghost cells between neighbor processes. Fig. 6 shows the time of each part and the time reducing trend with the number of CPU/GPU units increase. In Fig. 7, we show the strong scaling of each part showed in Fig. 6. We see that the numerical operations scale well while MPI communication and CPU-GPU data-copy stop scaling when the number of units exceeds 64. This is mainly because the total scale of computing domain is not big enough. When we use 256 GPU cards, each MPI process only handle subdomain with scale of 64×32×64. As the ratio of computation and communication decrease, the scaling of numerical operation will be worse and the MPI communication time and CPU-GPU data-copy time will even increase. Fortunately, in the real cosmological simulation, the total size of domain is much bigger than our test, so we can increase the subdomain size under the memory limit of one GPU card and keep the scalability very well.

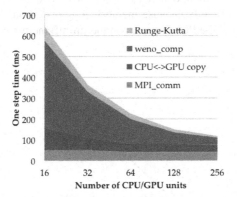

Fig. 6. One-step time of the Euler solver and the time contributions of each part using different numbers of CPU/GPU units for the domain of 512×256×256

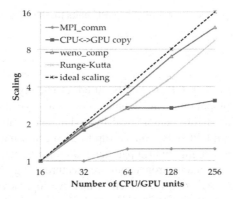

Fig. 7. The strong scaling to the number of CPU/GPU units of each part for the domain of 512×256×256

Then we tested the weak scaling with the fixed-size subdomain of 128^3 to verify that it scales well that we use more GPU cards to computing the cosmological simulation in a larger scale. Fig. 8 shows the weak scaling of one step on the scale of 128^3 per CPU/GPU unit. The computation of 128^3 subdomain calls for 300M memory in one CPU process while 800M in one GPU card, which is caused by the non-reuse of the memory on GPU because of the zero protection against multithreaded race conditions. Though bigger size of subdomain is better, one CPU/GPU unit can only accommodate 128×256×256 double-precision domain data and other related variables at most because of the memory capacity of GPU Tesla C2050. This limit on subdomain size influences the weak scaling. Another reason for the decreasing of parallel efficiency is the resource contention between different CPU/GPU units in one node. In our experimental platform for multi-CPU/GPU test, there are only 43 nodes. So when the number of units exceeds 43, more than one GPU card will be used on some nodes. For example, all 6 GPUs that have attached to the same node will be used when the number of units reaches 256. The run time increases when the number of GPU cards used in one node increases. This is mainly because memory copy operations and MPI inside one node cause contention of the PCI Express and the InfiniBand network.

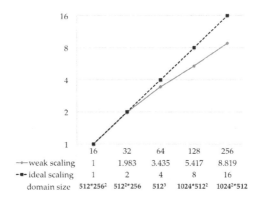

Fig. 8. The weak scaling to the number of CPU/GPU units for the subdomain of 128^3 per unit

6   Conclusion

We have demonstrated that GPUs can be used efficiently for high-order finite difference WENO computation in double precision (speedup ×13~×31), and Large-scale parallelization for cosmological hydrodynamic simulations on the CPU cluster (up to 16384) and CPU/GPU cluster (up to 256) can achieve good scalability. Our work proposes a new highly hybrid parallel code for the cosmological simulation software WIGEON based on a heterogeneous architecture using MPI and CUDA. Our tests simulated the large-scale outflow driven by massive supernova explosions, which is currently referred as galactic wind. This is a typical supersonic fluid phenomena and of importance to understand the kinetic feedback effect in galaxy formation and evolution. In practice, implementing such computations on CPU cluster or GPU cluster has demonstrated a paradigm for the state-of-art technologies in application to cosmological hydrodynamic simulations.

In our MPI-based large parallelization on CPU cluster, the good scalability relies on the approach of cubic domain decomposition and the modification about the algorithm of high-order finite difference WENO computation that is aimed at maximizing the independence of each process.

The MPI/CUDA based code can be scaled to a large number of CPU/GPU computing units, though its scalability is worse than the original MPI-based code. This is mainly caused by the memory of GPU, which can at most accommodate 128×256×256 double precision vector data and related variables. After we take the CPU-GPU data-copy time and the MPI communication time into account, we see that the ratio of computation and communication is much lower than MPI-based code. It is important to further improve the scalability in the future. One way to do that is to port more computations to the GPU like Runge-Kutta operation, which increases the amount of computation and remove some intermediate results copying operations between CPU and GPU. Another way is to improve the speedup of the GPU code. We see there is a big gap in speedups between different GPU cards. We should notice that our test is running on mole-8.5 GPU cluster in which there are 6 GPU cards within one node, but for the most GPU clusters in other supercomputing center (Tianhe-1A, Bluewater and Titan etc.), there is one or two GPU cards within one node. So the multi-GPU issues will be released. And as GPU architecture is changing very fast and the performance of memory access is improved every once in a while, we can achieve higher speedup on GPUs with new architecture without the memory issues like "register spilling".

Acknowledgments. We would like to thank Liang Wang, Weile Jia and David for helping us with the professional knowledge about cosmological hydrodynamics and some advices on optimizations on GPU. The work of the first 3 authors is supported by NSF of China 61202054, 91230115; Knowledge Innovation Program of CAS CNIC_ZR_201202; 863 Program 2012AA01A309.

References

1. Feng, L.-L., Shu, C.-W., Zhang, M.: A hybrid cosmological hydrodynamic/N-body code based on a weighted essentially non-oscillatory scheme. The Astrophysical Journal (September 2004)
2. Anderson Jr., J.D.: Fundamentals of Aerodynamics, 3rd edn. (January 2001)
3. Robert, W.F., Alan, T.M.: Introduction To Fluid Mechanics, 4th edn.
4. Juan-Chen, H., Herng, L., Tsang-Jen, H., Tse-Yang, H.: Parallel preconditioned WENO scheme for three-dimensional flow simulation of NREL Phase VI Rotor. Computers & Fluids, 276-282 (2011)
5. Laurent, T., Andres, E.T., Thomas, B.G., Gilmar, M.: A massively parallel hybrid scheme for direct numerical simulation of turbulent viscoelastic channel flow. Computers & Fluids, 134–142 (2011)
6. http://www.top500.org/
7. Kestener, P., Château, F., Teyssier, R.: Accelerating euler equations numerical solver on graphics processing units. In: Hsu, C.-H., Yang, L.T., Park, J.H., Yeo, S.-S. (eds.) ICA3PP 2010, Part I. LNCS, vol. 6082, pp. 281–288. Springer, Heidelberg (2010)
8. Tölke, J., Krafczyk, M.: TeraFLOP computing on a desktop PC with GPUs for 3D CFD. International Journal of Computational Fluid Dynamics, 443–456 (2008)
9. Athanasios, S.A., Konstantinos, I.K., Eleftherios, D.P., John, A.E.: Acceleration of a Finite-Difference WENO Scheme for Large-Scale Simulations on Many-Core Architectures. The American Institute of Aeronautics and Astronautics (2010)
10. Appleyard, J., Drikakis, D.: Higher-order CFD and interface tracking methods on highly-Parallel MPI and GPU systems. Computers & Fluids, 101–105 (2011)
11. Michael, G., Peter, Z.: A multi-GPU accelerated solver for the three-dimensional two-phase incompressible Navier-Stokes equations. Computer Science-Research and Development, 65–73 (2010)

12. Paulius, M.: 3D finite difference computation on GPUs using CUDA. Architectual Support for Programming Languages and Operating Systems, 79–84 (2009)
13. Jiang, G.S., Shu, C.W.: Efficient Implementation of Weighted ENO Schemes. J. Computational Physics, 202–208 (1996)
14. Balsara, D.S., Shu, C.W.: Monotonicity Preserving Weighted Essentially Non-oscillatory Schemes with Increasingly High Order of Accuracy. J. Computational Physics, 405–452 (2000)
15. Chi-Wang, S.: Total Variation Diminishing Time Discretizations. Siam Journal on Scientific and Statistical Computing (1988)
16. Dana, A.J., Julien, C.T., Inanc, S.: An MPI-CUDA Implementation for Massively Parallel Incompressible Flow Computaions on multi-CPU clusters. The American Institute of Aeronautics and Astronautics (2010)
17. John, L.H., David, A.P.: Computer Architecture: A Quantitative Approach, 5th edn.
18. Paulius, M.: Analysis-Driven Optimization. In: SC 2010. ACM (2010)
19. NVIDIA's Next Generation CUDA Compute Architecture: Kepler GK110 (v1.0, 2012)
20. Compute Command Line Profiler User Guide. DU-05982-001_v03 (November 2011)

Large Eddy Simulation of a Rectangular Lobed Mixer

Qiancheng Wang, Jing Lei, Junhong Feng, and Zhenguo Wang

Science & Technology on Scramjet Laboratory,
National University of Defense Technology, 410073 Hunan changsha, China
wqc1235@163.com

Abstract. Lobed mixer is an efficient mixing enhancing device. Extensive experimental and computational works have been done to investigate the mechanism of mixing enhancing and vortex dynamics downstream of the lobed trailing edge. It is generally believed that the normal vortices and the shed streamwise vortices contribute a lot to the mixing enhancement. In present investigation, an incompressible Large Eddy Simulation is performed in a high performance computational system. Three computational cases with different length of mixing duct and amount of grids are compared to verify the reliability of the simulation. Results revealed that the lobed mixer is able to reach rapid mixing in short distance. The large scale streamwise vortices formed at the trailing edge break up into small scale streamwise vortices during the process of lower stream and upper stream penetrating into each other when convect downstream. The spanwise vorticity is found to generate and develop similar to that in the plate mixing layer.

Keywords: large eddy simulation, lobed mixer, streamwise vorticity, mixing enhancement, spanwise vorticity.

1 Introduction

Mixing enhancing technology related to lobed mixer has been investigated for several decades since 1960s. Early researches were mainly focus on general performance of the mixer. Extensive studies on mixing enhancing mechanism of the lobed mixer started from 1980s. Results reveal that three factors contribute most to the mixing promotion, which are the increased mixing interfacial area, large scale streamwise vortices shed from the lobed trailing edge and the normal vortices induced by the Kelvin-Helmholz instability [1-3]. By studying a daisy-shaped orifice jet and employing proper orthogonal decomposition (POD) analysis, Hassan [4] point out that in addition to the main role of the streamwise vortices in entrainment, the role of the K-H vortex is also undeniable. A series of significant works conducted by Hu et al [6-8] clearly shows the streamwise and K-H structures downstream of the lobed trailing edge as well as breakdown of the vortices. It is believed that the interaction of the streamwise and normal vortices plays a significant role in breakdown of the large scale vortices into small scale vortices. The interaction of these two kinds of vortex is a complex process. Both of the vortex rings are distorted by each other [9]. The present research is an attempt to reveal the breakdown process of the streamwise vorticity downstream of the rectangular lobed mixer through LES.

K. Li et al. (Eds.): ParCFD 2013, CCIS 405, pp. 221–231, 2014.

2   Computational Scheme

2.1   Computational Method

The calculation presented here is a three dimensional LES for incompressible flows employing dynamic smagorinsky Subgrid model. The Navier-Stokes equations are filtered using a top-hat filter with filter width Δ_1 , thus the governing equation can be written as

$$\frac{\partial \overline{u}}{\partial x} = 0 \quad . \tag{1}$$

$$\frac{\partial \overline{u}_i}{\partial t} + \frac{\partial \overline{u}_i \, \overline{u}_j}{\partial x_i} = -\frac{1}{\rho}\frac{\partial \overline{p}}{\partial x_i} + \nu \frac{\partial^2 \overline{u}_i}{\partial x_j \partial x_j} + \frac{\partial \overline{\tau}_{ij}}{\partial x_j} \quad . \tag{2}$$

where eddy viscosity ν is assumed constant and subgrid stress tensor $\overline{\tau}_{ij}$ is obtained from

$$\tau_{ij} - \frac{1}{3}\tau_{kk}\delta_{ij} = 2\nu_t \overline{S}_{ij} = 2C_D \Delta_1^2 \left| \overline{S} \right| \overline{S}_{ij} \quad . \tag{3}$$

where ν_t is the subgrid eddy-viscosity, δ_{ij} is Kronecker delta, $\overline{S}_{ij}$ is the viscous stress tensor, $\overline{S}_{ij}$ and $\left| \overline{S} \right|$ is defined by

$$\overline{S}_{ij} = \frac{1}{2}(\frac{\partial \overline{u}_i}{\partial x_j} + \frac{\partial \overline{u}_i}{\partial x_i}) \quad . \tag{4}$$

$$\left| \overline{S} \right| = (2\overline{S}_{ij}\overline{S}_{ij})^{1/2} \quad . \tag{5}$$

C_D is obtained through the dynamic procedure of performing the test filter operation with filter width Δ_2 twice the filter width Δ_1 . Here, the test filter operation on f is written as $\tilde{f}$.
Thus

$$C_D = \frac{\left\langle M_{ij}L_{ij} \right\rangle}{\left\langle M_{ij}M_{ij} \right\rangle} \quad . \tag{6}$$

with

$$M_{ij} = 2\left[\Delta_2^2 \left| \tilde{S} \right| \tilde{S}_{ij} - \Delta_1^2 \widetilde{\left| \overline{S} \right| \overline{S}_{ij}} \right] \quad . \tag{7}$$

$$L_{ij} = \tilde{\overline{u}}_i \, \tilde{\overline{u}}_j - \widetilde{\overline{u}_i \, \overline{u}_j} \quad . \tag{8}$$

Velocity of the upper and lower stream set to be 4.143m/s and 10.357m/s respectively. The temperature and pressure of the outlet are assumed to be the atmosphere of 101,325 Pa and 300 K.

Simulation was performed in HP Blade System. It is a high performance computational rig consists of 51 computational nodes, and each node contains 12 CPUs. In present simulation, ten computational nodes, which are equal to 120 CPUs, are utilized.

2.2   Computational Geometry and Grid

Fig. 1 shows the computational geometry of the rectangular lobed mixer with wave length $l = 60mm$ and lobe height $h = 60mm$. To evaluate and isolate the effect of the outlet condition on the near field downstream of the trailing edge, two LES cases with different length of mixing duct are simulated here, which are denoted by A and B, as shown in table 1. Additionally, to verify independence of the grid, case C with larger amount of grid nodes of 3.48 million is performed.

Profiles of streamwise velocity obtained from the three cases in different transverse planes are showed in Figure 2. It can be found that difference in the results acquired from the three computational cases is not significant. Thus, it is reasonable to conclude that case C with 1000mm mixing duct and 3.48 million grid nodes is acceptable.

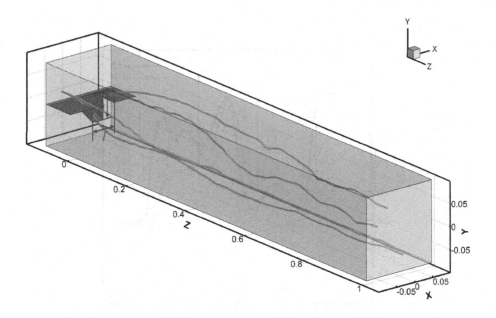

Fig. 1. Computational geometry of the lobed mixer

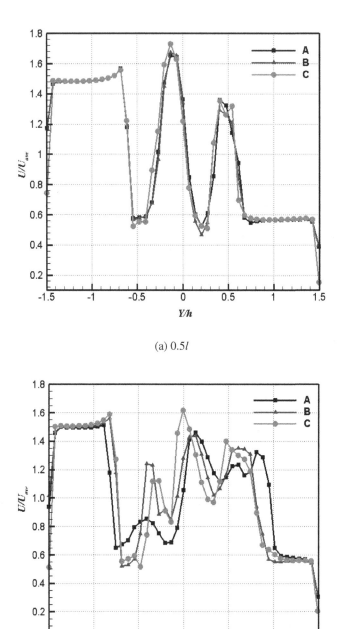

(a) 0.5*l*

(b) 1.5*l*

Fig. 2. Profiles of streamwise velocity in transverse plane at different streamwise positions

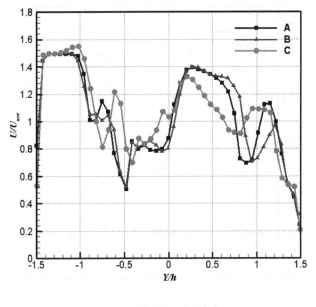

(c) 3.0 *l*

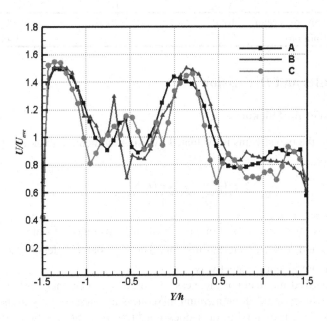

(d) 6.0*l*

Fig. 2. (*Continued.*)

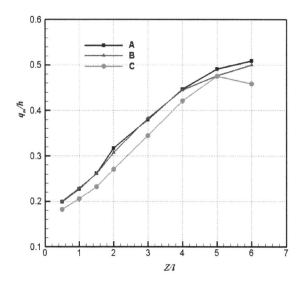

Fig. 3. Variation of normalized momentum thickness for three computational cases

Table 1. Three LES cases

Case	A	B	C
Length of mixing duct (mm)	1000	2000	1000
Size of grid (million)	2.15	2.85	3.48

3   Results and Discussion

3.1   Momentum Thickness

Mixedness of the two streams is evaluated by using momentum thickness [5] which is defined as

$$q_m = \int_{-\infty}^{+\infty} \frac{(U_1 - u) \times (u - U_2)}{(U_1 - U_2)^2} \times dy \ .$$
(9)

where u is the mean streamwise velocity averaged from $x = -45mm$ to $x = +45mm$, and Y is the lateral direction. The U_1 and U_2 denote the velocity of the upper and lower inlet respectively.

The normalized momentum thickness for three computational cases is showed in Figure 3. As can be noticed, momentum mixedness increases rapidly in the near field. Difference in length of mixing duct does not bring evident variation in mixedness, which demonstrates in another aspect that the selected length of mixing duct of 1000mm has no obvious influence on the flow field in six wave lengths downstream of the trailing edge. Case C with large amount of grid shows slightly lower momentum thickness, whereas the variation is not substantial.

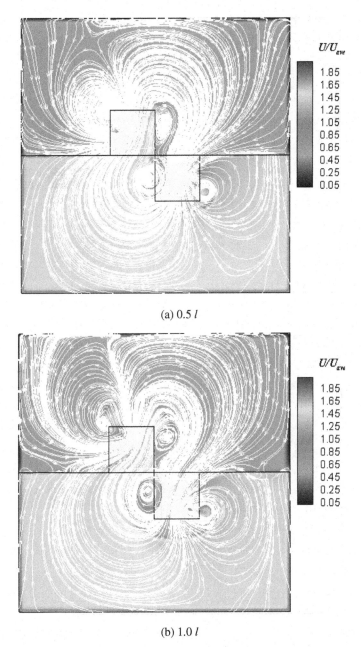

(a) 0.5 *l*

(b) 1.0 *l*

Fig. 4. Distribution of normalized streamwise velocity in transverse planes at four different streamwise positions

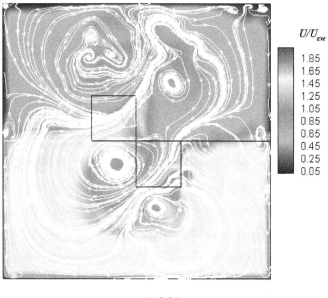

(c) 3.0 *l*

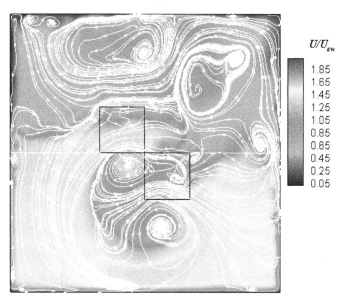

(d) 6.0 *l*

Fig. 4. (*Continued.*)

3.2   Streamwise Vortices

Distribution of normalized streamwise vorticity in transverse planes at different streamwise positions is showed in figure 4. At one wave length downstream of the trailing edge as shown in figure 4(a), it is noticeable that there exist four streamwise vortex cores in the transverse plane which are distributed in regions near the side wall. While further downstream to the position of six lobe wave length, more but smaller streamwise vortex cores are presented in the transverse plane. It is reasonable to deduce that the initial large scale streamwise vortices break up into smaller vortices during mixing process.

3.3   Spanwise Vorticity

In Fig. 5, iso-surfaces of normalized spanwise vorticity of 0.25 at different time with interval of 0.001s are presented. The normalized spanwise vorticity is calculated as

$$\omega_x = \left| \frac{l}{U_{ave}} \left(\frac{\partial w}{\partial y} - \frac{\partial v}{\partial z} \right) \right| . \qquad (10)$$

where l is the wave length of the lobe, U_{ave} is the average of the lower and upper inlet velocity.

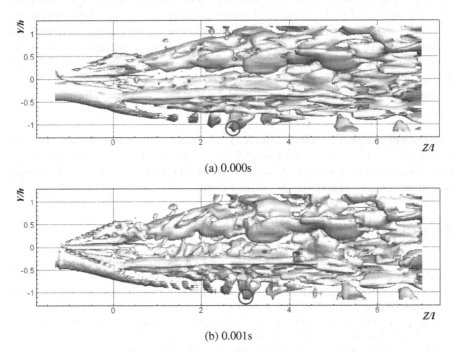

(a) 0.000s

(b) 0.001s

Fig. 5. Variation of spanwise vorticity with time interval of 0.001s

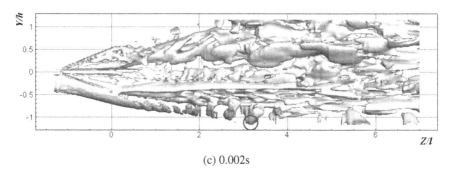

(c) 0.002s

Fig. 6. (*Continued.*)

It can be seen from the figure that the spanwise vortex rings shed at the trough region of the mixer and grow gradually when convect downstream, which are similar to that exist in plate mixing layer.

4   Conclusions

LES calculation of a rectangular lobed mixer was conducted based on the HP Blade System. Comparison of three computational cases with different length of mixing duct and amount of grids showed that results given by case C with 1000mm mixing duct and 3.48 million grids are reliable. Mixedness evaluated by momentum thickness demonstrates that the lobed mixer is beneficial to achieving rapid mixing. The break-up and diffusing process of the large scale streamwise vortices formed at the lobed trailing edge into small scale vortices when convect downstream is clearly presented. Spanwise vorticity is found to generate and develop similar to that in the plate mixing layer.

Acknowledgement. The authors gratefully acknowledge the financial supports of the National Natural Science Foundation of China (Grant No. 11002158), the Equipment Development Foundation (Grant No. 9140A28030112KG01084) and the University Scientific Research Plan (Grant No. JC12-01-06).

References

1. Paterson, R.W.: Turbofan mixer nozzle flow field-a benchmark experimental study. Journal of Engineering for Gas Turbines and Power 106, 672–698 (1984)
2. Skebe, S., Paterson, R., Barber, T.: Experimental investigation of three-dimensional forced mixer lobe flow fields. AIAA paper 88-3783 (1988)
3. McCormick, D.C., Bennett, J.C.: Vortical and turbulent structure of a lobed mixer free shear layer. AIAA Journal 32(9), 1852–1859 (1994)
4. Hassan, M.E., Meslem, A.: Time-resolved stereoscopic particle image velocimetry investigation of the entrainment in the near field of circular and daisy-shaped orifice jets. Physics of Fluids 22(3), 035107 (2010)

5. Mao, R., Yu, S.C.M., Zhou, T., Chua, L.P.: On the vorticity characteristic of lobe-force mixer at different configurations. Exp. Fluids. 46, 1049–1066 (2009)
6. Hu, H., Saga, T., Kobayashi, T., Taniguchi, N.: Simultaneous measurements of all three components of velocity and vorticity vectors in a lobed jet flow by means of dual-plane stereoscopic. Physics of Fluids 14(7), 2128–2138 (2002)
7. Hu, H., Saga, T., Kobayashi, T., et al.: Research on the vortical and turbulent structures in the lobed jet flow using laser induced fluorescence and particle image velocimetry techniques. Meas. Sci. Technol. 11, 698–711 (2000)
8. Hu, H., Saga, T., Kobayashi, T., et al.: A study on a lobed jet mixing flow by using stereoscopic particle image velocimetry technique. Physics of Fluids 13(11), 3425–3441 (2001)
9. Toyoda, K., Hiramoto, R.: Manopulation of vortex rings for flow control. Fluid Dynamics Research 41, 051402 (2009)

The Application of Preconditioned AUSM+ in Viscous Flow at Low Speeds

Feng Yu,Wu Meng, Qin Jiang, Li Tao, and Huang Hongyan

Harbin Institute of Technology, No.92, Xidazhi Street, Harbin and 150001, China

Abstract. The convection heat transfer of hydrocarbon fuel under super-critical pressure has a great influence to regenerative cooling technology of scramjet. Some initial work has been completed aiming as supercritical convection heat transfer process of hydrocarbon fuel in the cooling channel. Base on the preconditioned AUSM+ (advection upwind splitting method+) combining Weiss-Smith preconditioned method, two dimension flow and heat transfer program is developed. In this paper, the developing process of program is discussed in detail. For the governing equation with preconditioned time derivatives, the modified method to AUSM+ scheme is described. Base on the current two dimension model, finally, the future work aiming as supercritical convection heat transfer process of hydrocarbon fuel is proposed.

Keywords: Preconditioned, AUSM+, Heat transfer.

1   Introduction

The air taking from air inlets only has been unable to satisfy cooling requirements of flight with high efficiency and high Mach number. Therefore, hydrocarbon fuel brought by engine and served as propellant has been another ideal coolant [1]. In the fuel-air heat exchanger the hot compressive air transfer heat to the fuel whose temperature is cooler, thus, the air is able to cool engine parts more effectively. Meanwhile, the rise of fuel temperature is benefit to improvement of combustion efficiency [2]. However, in the scramjet, inflow air is unable to cool the combustor wall for the high temperature of air. Then, the cooling capacity of hydrocarbon fuel is more and more important [3]. Generally, In the process of cooling, in order to avoid heat transfer deterioration caused by boiling, hydrocarbon fuel is under super-critical pressure in the heat transfer process inside parallel channel [4]. Because of violent changes of physical property nearby critical point, the heat transfer process of hydrocarbon fuel is very complicated and it has a great influence to the cooling process [5].

In the past, among the researches to heat transfer of supercritical fluid, lots of experiments and numerical simulations aim to carbon dioxide [6-8] and water [9-12] mainly. But the researches aiming to hydrocarbon fuel is relatively less, especially the numerical researches which use the computing method of real fluid physical property. Comparing with experiment researches, multidimensional numerical simulation is able to reappear process of convection heat transfer in detail,

K. Li et al. (Eds.): ParCFD 2013, CCIS 405, pp. 232–239, 2014.
© Springer-Verlag Berlin Heidelberg 2014

therefore, with developing of scramjet technology, the research to convection heat transfer characteristic using numerical simulation has became more and more important method.

In this paper, some initial works have been completed aiming as supercritical convection heat transfer process of hydrocarbon fuel in the cooling channel. In the initial works, a two dimension flow and heat transfer model applying to unstructured grid using finite volume method is established. The governing equation is preconditioned using the method proposed by Weiss-Smith, and then, the preconditioned governing equation is dispersed using preconditioned AUSM+. The discrete equation is solved using three order Runge-Kutta method. Base on the current two dimension model, finally, the future work aiming as supercritical convection heat transfer process of hydrocarbon fuel is proposed.

2   Formulation of Model

Governing equations used in this paper are described as follows:

$$\frac{\partial Q}{\partial t}+\frac{\partial}{\partial x}(E-E_v)+\frac{\partial}{\partial y}(F-F_v)=0 \tag{1}$$

$$Q=\begin{bmatrix}\rho\\ \rho u\\ \rho v\\ \rho e\end{bmatrix}\quad E=\begin{bmatrix}\rho u\\ \rho u^2+p\\ \rho uv\\ (\rho e+P)u\end{bmatrix}\quad F=\begin{bmatrix}\rho v\\ \rho uv\\ \rho v^2+p\\ (\rho e+P)v\end{bmatrix} \tag{2}$$

$$E_v=\begin{bmatrix}0\\ \tau_{xx}\\ \tau_{xy}\\ k\dfrac{\partial T}{\partial x}+u\tau_{xx}+v\tau_{xy}\end{bmatrix}\quad F_v=\begin{bmatrix}0\\ \tau_{xy}\\ \tau_{yy}\\ k\dfrac{\partial T}{\partial y}+u\tau_{xy}+v\tau_{yy}\end{bmatrix} \tag{3}$$

2.1   Preconditioning

For a low speed and compressible problem studied in this paper, the governing equations need to precondition to eliminate difference among eigenvalues in the low speed calculation and to make the discrete equations easily converge [13]. In the present study, base on the preconditioning matrix proposed by Weiss-Smith, the primitive variables is the variables to be solved. The 2D, preconditioned N-S system can be written as follows:

$$\Gamma\frac{\partial W}{\partial t}+\frac{\partial}{\partial x}(E-E_v)+\frac{\partial}{\partial y}(F-F_v)=0 \tag{4}$$

where

$$\Gamma=\begin{bmatrix} \Phi & 0 & 0 & -\rho/T \\ u\Phi & \rho & 0 & -\rho u/T \\ v\Phi & 0 & \rho & -\rho v/T \\ H\Phi & \rho u & \rho v & \rho[C_p-(H/T)] \end{bmatrix}$$

$$\Phi=\Theta+(1/RT)$$

$$\Theta=\left(1/U_{ref}^2\right)-(1/a^2)$$

$$U_{ref}=\min[c,\max(|V|,\varepsilon c)]$$

Where, U_{ref} is reference velocity, $|V|$ is the local velocity magnitude, c is local sound speed, and ε is a small number ($\sim 10^{-5}$).

2.2   Spatial Discretization

The physical domain is subdivided into cells. Using finite volume scheme, the preconditioned governing equations are dispersed. Then, equations are applied to each cell, which represent a control volume, and the integral flow field information is got by solve the discrete equation associating with each control volume. So the discrete method is:

$$\Gamma\frac{\partial W'}{\partial t}+\frac{1}{V}\iint(E-E_v)n_x dS+\frac{1}{V}\iint(F-F_v)n_y dS=0 \tag{5}$$

Where, $\vec{n}=n_x\vec{i}+n_y\vec{j}$, $\vec{n}$ is normal vector of interface, and

$$W'=\frac{1}{V}\iiint W dV$$

So the Eq.[5] is written to spatial discrete form as follows:

$$\Gamma\frac{\partial W'}{\partial t}+\frac{1}{V}\sum_i^3[(E-E_v)_i n_{ix}+(F-F_v)_i n_{iy}]S_i=0 \tag{6}$$

Where, the vector W' is the cell average value, S is interface area of cell, and the substitution, i, is ith interface of cell.

2.3   Reconstruction

Base on the methods of MUSCL, the physical quantities of interface center is gat by interpolating used gradient of physical quantities in the grid center. In this paper, second order reconfiguration is conduct using primitive variables $\tilde{W} = [p, u, v, T]$ [14]:

$$\tilde{W}_f = \tilde{W}_c + \Phi \cdot \nabla \tilde{W} \cdot d\vec{r} \tag{7}$$

$$\nabla w = \frac{\sum_i^3 w_i S_i \vec{n}_i}{V}$$

Where, w represents the element of $\tilde{W}$. In order to make the calculation more stability, it needs Limiting in the reconfiguration process. In this paper, the Second Order Limiting proposed by Barth and Jespersen is:

$$\Phi \begin{cases} \min(1, \dfrac{\delta w_i^{\max}}{w_{ij} - w_i}), & if \quad w_{ij} - w_i > 0 \\[4mm] \min(1, \dfrac{\delta w_i^{\min}}{w_{ij} - w_i}) & if \quad w_{ij} - w_i < 0 \\[4mm] 1 & if \quad w_{ij} - w_i = 0 \end{cases} \tag{8}$$

Where,. $\delta w_i^{\max}$ ($\delta w_i^{\max} = \max(w - w_i)$ and $\delta w_i^{\min}$ ($\delta w_i^{\min} = \min(w - w_i)$) are the largest negative and positive difference between the neighbors cell and control cell.

2.4   Flux Difference Splitting

Base on the AUSM+, the convective term can split as follows:

$$F = (\rho u)_{1/2} \begin{bmatrix} 1 \\ u \\ v \\ h \end{bmatrix}_{L/R} + \begin{bmatrix} p_{1/2} \\ \\ \\ \\ \end{bmatrix} \tag{9}$$

Where, subscript 1/2 respects interface between two cells and L/R respects the left cell and right cell respectively. When flux > 0, the variables of vector $\begin{bmatrix} 1 & u & v & h \end{bmatrix}^T$ takes the values of left cell, when flux < 0, taking the values of left cell.

Preconditioned governing equations system are different from original governing equations, so the AUSM+ need to be modified to operate effectively at very low speed when we calculate the interface flux. According to [15], the preconditioned sound speed $a'_{1/2}$ is given by:

$$a'_{1/2} = f_{1/2} a_{1/2}$$

where

$$f_{1/2} = \frac{\sqrt{\left(1 - M^2_{ref1/2}\right)^2 M^2_{1/2} + 4M^2_{ref1/2}}}{1 + M^2_{ref1/2}}$$

Where, $M^2_{ref} = U^2_{ref}/a^2$. Then $M^2_{ref1/2}$ and $M^2_{1/2}$ are algebraic average value between left and right cell. Then we can get the preconditioned Mach number:

$$\tilde{M}_{L/R} = \frac{M_{L/R}}{f_{1/2}}$$

$$\overline{M}_L = 0.5\left[\left(1 + M^2_{ref1/2}\right)\tilde{M}_L + \left(1 - M^2_{ref1/2}\right)\tilde{M}_R\right]$$

and

$$\overline{M}_R = 0.5\left[\left(1 + M^2_{ref1/2}\right)\tilde{M}_R + \left(1 - M^2_{ref1/2}\right)\tilde{M}_L\right]$$

Compared with computational process without preconditioned, the Mach number splitting function and pressure splitting function have no changes in the following calculation. So, the splitting calculation method of pressure and flux at the interface are:

$$P_{1/2} = P^+_{(5)}(\overline{M}_L)P_L + P^-_{(5)}(\overline{M}_R)P_R \tag{10}$$

$$(\rho u)_{1/2} = (\rho u)_{1/2AUSM+} + a'_{1/2}(\frac{1}{M^2_{ref}} - 1) \cdot \begin{bmatrix} M^+_{(4)}(\overline{M}_L) - M^+_{(1)}(\overline{M}_L) \\ M^-_{(4)}(\overline{M}_R) + M^-_{(1)}(\overline{M}_R) \end{bmatrix}$$

$$\cdot [P_L - P_R]/\left[\frac{P_L}{\rho_L} + \frac{P_R}{\rho_R}\right] \tag{11}$$

Where, $(\rho u)_{1/2AUSM+}$ is calculated using the local Mach number.

2.5   Time-Stepping Scheme

In this paper, the turbulence is modeled by sst and the governing equations are dispersed using finite volume method base on unstructured mesh. An explicit multistage time-stepping scheme, three order Runge-Kutta scheme, is used to solve the discrete equation. The solution procedure is given by:

$$\Gamma \frac{d\tilde{W}}{dt} + \frac{1}{V} RHS = 0 \tag{12}$$

Where

$$RHS = \sum_{i=1}^{3} \left(E - E_v \right)_i n_x S_i + \sum_{i=1}^{3} \left(F - F_v \right)_i n_y S_i$$

The Eq.[12] is rewritten as follows:

$$\frac{d\tilde{W}}{dt} = -\frac{1}{V} \Gamma^{-1} RHS$$

$$RHS^* = -\frac{1}{V} \Gamma^{-1} RHS$$

The preconditioning three order Runge-Kutta scheme is represented as follows:

$$\tilde{W}^{(0)} = \tilde{W}^n$$

$$\tilde{W}^{(1)} = \tilde{W}^{(0)} + \Delta t \Gamma^{-1} RHS^* (\tilde{W}^{(0)})$$

$$\tilde{W}^{(2)} = \alpha_1 \tilde{W}^{(0)} + \alpha_2 \tilde{W}^{(1)} + \alpha_2 \Delta t \Gamma^{-1} RHS^* (\tilde{W}^{(0)})$$

$$\tilde{W}^{(3)} = \alpha_3 \tilde{W}^{(0)} + \alpha_4 \tilde{W}^{(1)} + \alpha_4 \Delta t \Gamma^{-1} RHS^* (\tilde{W}^{(0)})$$

$$\tilde{W}^{(n+1)} = \tilde{W}^{(3)}$$

$$\alpha_1 = \frac{3}{4}, \quad \alpha_2 = \frac{1}{4}, \quad \alpha_3 = \frac{1}{3}, \quad \alpha_4 = \frac{2}{3}$$

2.6   Boundary Conditions

For the Preconditioned governing equations system, the preconditioning method has an influence on the boundary [16], so the boundary conditions have some changes accordingly. For the far field boundary on the low speed condition, the simplify boundary condition [17] is used. The simplify boundary condition is given by:

inflow : $(\rho_i)_b = (\rho_i)_\infty$; $u_b = u_\infty$; $v_b = v_\infty$; $P_b = P_e$

outflow : $(\rho_i)_b = (\rho_i)_e$; $u_b = u_e$; $v_b = v_e$; $P_b = P_\infty$

where the subscript, ∞ and e, represent inflow parameter and parameter of internal cell. However, when $\sqrt{u^2 + v^2} / c \geq 0.3$, the compressible nonreflecting boundary condition is used.

3   Conclusion

In this paper, a two dimensional heat convection model is built. In order to extend it to low speed and incompressible condition, the time-derivative term of model pre-multiply with a preconditioning matrix. For the preconditioned governing equations system, the eigenvalues of Jacobian matrix have changed, therefore, AUSM+ scheme and boundary condition need to be modified to operate effectively at very low speed. Base on current two dimensional heat convection model, a further improvement is conducted in the future work to extend it to heat convection process of hydrocarbon fuel on the supercritical pressure:

1) The relation among P, V, T, is described using P-R equation. The derivatives of pressure to temperature and pressure to volume are derived using P-R equation. Then isobaric specific heat capacity is calculated using the follow equations. Viscosity is calculated using the empirical methods proposed by Brule and Starling and thermal conductivity is calculated using method proposed by Chung [18].

2) Base on the preconditioning matrix, applying to real fluid, proposed by Edwards and Franklin, a modification is conducted to the preconditioning part of current model, extending it to heat convection process of hydrocarbon fuel on the supercritical pressure.

References

1. Glickstein, M.R., Spadaccini, L.J.: Applications of Endothermic Reaction Technology to the High Speed Civil Transport. NASA no. 19980046572
2. Bruening, G. B., Chang, W. S.: Cooled Cooling Air Systems for Turbine Thermal Management. ASME Paper No. 99-GT-14 (1999)
3. Huang, H., Spadaccini, L.J., Sobel, D.R.: Fuel-cooled thermal managementfor advanced aeroengines. J. Eng. Gas Turb. Power-Trans. ASME 126, 284–293 (2004)
4. Powell, O.A., Edwards, J.T., Norris, R.B., et al.: Development of Hydrocarbon-Fuel Scramjet Engines: The Hypersonic Technology (Hytech) Program. Journal of Propulsion and Power 17, 1170–1176
5. Wang, Y., Hua, Y., Meng, H.: Numerical Studies of Supercritical Turbulent Convective Heat Transfer of Cryogenic-Propellant Methane. Journal of Thermophysics and Heat Transfer 24, 490–500 (2004, 2010)
6. Huai, X.L., Koyama, S., Zhao, T.S.: An experimental study of flow and heat transfer of supercritical carbon dioxide in multi-port mini channels under cooling conditions. Chemical Engineering Science 60, 3337–3345 (2005)
7. Li, H., Anderson, M., Corradini, M.: Supercritical Carbon Dioxide Heat Transfer in Horizontal Semicircular Channels. Journal of Heat Transfer, 081802-1–081802-10 (2012)
8. Pioro, I.L., Khartabi, H.F., Duffey, R.B.: Heat Transfer to Supercritical Fluids Flowing in Channels-Empirical Correlations (Survey). Nuclear Engineering and Design, 69–91 (2003)
9. Licht, J., Anderson, M., Corradini, M.: Heat Transfer to Water at Supercritical Pressures in a Circular and Square Annular Flow Geometry. International Journal of Heat and Fluid Flow, 102–115 (2007)

10. Wang, H., Bi, Q., Yang, Z., et al.: Experimental and numerical study on the enhanced effect of spiral spacer to heat transfer of supercritical pressure water in vertical annular channels. Applied Thermal Engineering 48, 436–445 (2012)
11. Cheng, X., Kuang, B., Yang, Y.H.: Numerical analysis of heat transfer in supercritical water cooled flow channels. Nucl. Eng. Des. 237, 240–252 (2007)
12. Gajapathy, R., Velusamy, K., Selvaraj, P., et al.: CFD investigation of helical wirewrapped 7-pin fuel bundle and the challenges in modeling full scale 217 pin bundle. Nucl. Eng. Des. 237, 2332–2342 (2007)
13. Weiss, J.M., Smith, W.A.: Preconditioning Applied to Variable and Constant Density Flows. AIAA Journal 33, 2050–2056 (1995)
14. Michalak, K., Ollivier-Gooch, C.: Limiters for Unstructured Higher-Order Accurate Solutions of the Euler Equations. In: 46th AIAA Aerospace Science Meeting and Exhibit, Reno, Nevada. AIAA 2008-776, pp. 1–14 (2008)
15. Edwards, J.R., Liou, M.-S.: Low-Diffusion Flux-Splitting Method for Flows at All Speeds. AIAA Journal 36, 1610–1617 (1998)
16. Lia, S.Y., Wang, C.Y.: Boundary Condition for Solving Flowfields at Low Mach Number by Preconditioning. Journal of National University of defense Technology 23, 52–56
17. Turkel, E., Vatsa, V.N., Radespiel, R.: Preconditioning Methods for Low-Speed Flows. In: AIAA-96-2460-CP, pp. 650–660
18. Poling, B.E., Prausnitz, J.M., O'connell, J.P.: The Properties of Gases and Liquids. McGraw-Hill Professional, USA

A High-Order Weighted Essentially Non-Oscillatory Schemes for Solving Euler Equations on Unstructured Meshes

Li Tao, Feng Yu, Zhu Kaidi, and Huang Hongyan

No. 92, Xidazhi Street, 150001, Harbin, China

Abstract. High-order accurate Weighted Essentially Non-oscillatory (WENO) Schemes have recently been developed for finite volume methods in unstructured meshes with the developing of Mesh generation method. In this paper, the finite volume method is adopted for solving Euler equation, and the weighted least squares method is used to construct a fourth-order accuracy WENO scheme. A relatively stable method to construct stencils is presented, and a mathematical model used to solve linear weights is established. In order to obtain the non-negative linear weights, the compatibility conditions is considered as equality constraints, and non-negative conditions is considered as inequality constraints. Then, we can obtain the target function by least-square adjustment theory. Therefore, the process of solving linear weights is transformed into process of solving the optimal solution. Finally, for verifying the stability and high resolution of the schemes, two typical numerical examples are given.

Keywords: unstructured mesh, WENO, least-square reconstruction, linear weight.

1 Introduction

The high order finite volume Weighted Essentially Non-oscillatory (WENO) scheme is proposed by Liu Xu-dong, Osher and Chan [1]. This scheme bases on the ENO scheme. In the reconstruction procedure, the idea of adaptive stencils is used by both schemes, therefore, they are able to achieve high-order accuracy and non oscillatory property near discontinuities. ENO uses just one out of many candidate stencils when doing the reconstruction; while WENO uses a convex combination of all the candidate stencils, each being assigned a nonlinear weight which depends on the local smoothness of the numerical solution based on that stencil. WENO schemes are developed by Jiang and Shu[2]. They make the WENO schemes have better stability and better accuracy. In recent years, with development of unstructured grid generation methods, the WENO schemes are promoted to unstructured grid and several types of WENO scheme[3-12] with higher order accuracy by finite volume method is obtained on the unstructured grid. A kind of WENO scheme in the unstructured grid is constructed by Friedrich[3]. But this discrete scheme is able to achieve the same

K. Li et al. (Eds.): ParCFD 2013, CCIS 405, pp. 240–251, 2014.
© Springer-Verlag Berlin Heidelberg 2014

accuracy to ENO scheme for the same stencils. A kind of discrete scheme, which use the same stencils to ENO and is able to achieve higher accuracy, in the unstructured grid is proposed by Shu[4]. The key point for this kind of WENO discrete scheme is obtainment of high order reconstruction polynomial by linear combination of low order reconstruction polynomial. Linear weights, which are coefficients of this linear combination, are decided by geometric dimensioning and order of reconstruction polynomial. Moreover, the linear weights need to be positive [13], otherwise the discrete scheme is unable to stabilize.

Now there are two main ways to deal with negative linear weights. Shu[4] used an efficient method of selecting stencils, and obtained non-negative linear weights by regrouping of stencils. This method will produce negative weights, which will have some impact on the stability of the scheme, when the fourth-order schemes was adopted .Jing Shi [13]gives a splitting method to deal with the negative linear weight to keep the stability of the scheme .

In this paper, we adopt finite volume method for solving Euler equation, and use the weighted least squares method to construct a fourth-order accuracy WENO scheme. A relatively stable method of constructing stencils is presented, and a mathematical model for solving linear weights is established .In order to obtain the non-negative linear weights, the compatibility conditions is considered as equality constraints, and non-negative conditions is considered as inequality constraints, then we obtain the target function by least-square adjustment theory, so the process of solving linear weights is transformed into process of solving the optimal solution. Although this method will cause a loss of accuracy, it can achieve optimal approximation of high order accuracy solution.

2   Finite Volume Formulation

2.1   Governing Equations

The time dependent Euler equations in integral form are given by

$$\frac{\partial U}{\partial t} + \frac{\partial F}{\partial x} + \frac{\partial G}{\partial y} = 0 \tag{1}$$

where U is the vector of conserved variables, F and G represents the inviscid flux.

$$U = \begin{bmatrix} \rho \\ \rho u \\ \rho v \\ e \end{bmatrix}, \quad F = \begin{bmatrix} \rho u \\ \rho u^2 + p \\ \rho uv \\ (e+p)u \end{bmatrix}, \quad G = \begin{bmatrix} \rho v \\ \rho vu \\ \rho v^2 + p \\ (e+p)v \end{bmatrix}$$

2.2   Finite Volume Method

The finite volume discretization of the integral (1) at the control unit i is given by

$$\frac{\partial}{\partial t}\int_{\Omega_i} U dV + \int_{\Omega_i}\left(\frac{\partial F}{\partial x}+\frac{\partial G}{\partial y}\right) dV = 0 \qquad (2)$$

$$\int_{\Omega_i}(\frac{\partial F}{\partial x}+\frac{\partial G}{\partial y})dV = \int_{\Gamma_i}(F,G)\bullet n dA = \sum_{k=1}^{3}(\sum_{j=1}^{g}\omega_{kj}(F,G)_{kj}\bullet n_k) \qquad (3)$$

Ω_i is the triangular element, Γ_i is its edge, ω_{kj} is the weight coefficient of the Gaussian integration, g is the number of Gaussian integration points .we should use the high-order Gaussian integrals for the high-order schemes .In this paper, we arrange two Gaussian integration points(G1 ,G2)for every edge, their weights are both 0.5.

$$G_1 = cP_1+(1-c)P_2 \qquad\qquad G_2 = cP_2+(1-c)P_1 \qquad\qquad c = \frac{1}{2}+\frac{\sqrt{3}}{6}$$

The discrete format is given by

$$\frac{\partial \overline{U}_i}{\partial t} = -\frac{1}{\Delta V_i}\sum_{k=1}^{3}(\sum_{j=1}^{gs}\omega_{kj}(F,G)_{kj}\bullet n_k)$$

$\overline{U}_i$ is the average U of the cell i at the time t .

$$\overline{U}_i = \frac{1}{\Delta V_i}\int_{\Omega_i} U_i dV \qquad (4)$$

The flux of Gaussian integration points in equation (3) is solved by Steger-Warming scheme[14]..

2.3   Time Discretization

A three stage TVD Runge Kutta scheme is given by[15]

$$\overline{U}_i^{(0)} = \overline{U}_i^{n}$$

$$\overline{U}_i^{(1)} = \overline{U}_i^{(0)} + \Delta t R\left(\overline{U}_i^{(0)}\right)$$

$$\overline{U}_i^{(2)} = \frac{3}{4}\overline{U}_i^{(0)} + \frac{1}{4}\overline{U}_i^{(1)} + \frac{1}{4}\Delta t R\left(\overline{U}_i^{(1)}\right)$$

$$\overline{U}_i^{n+1} = \frac{1}{3}\overline{U}_i^{(0)} + \frac{2}{3}\overline{U}_i^{(2)} + \frac{2}{3}\Delta t R\left(\overline{U}_i^{(2)}\right)$$

2.4   High-Order Reconstruction Polynomial

The reconstruction polynomial is obtained by Taylor expansion.

$$U_i^R(x-x_i,y-y_i)=U|_i+\frac{\partial U}{\partial x}|_i(x-x_i)+\frac{\partial U}{\partial y}|_i(y-y_i)$$

$$+\frac{\partial^2 U}{\partial x^2}|_i\frac{(x-x_i)^2}{2}+\frac{\partial^2 U}{\partial x\partial y}|_i(x-x_i)(y-y_i)+\frac{\partial^2 U}{\partial y^2}|_i\frac{(y-y_i)^2}{2}+\cdots$$

The integral of this polynomial at the control unit i is given by

$$\overline{U}_i=\frac{1}{\Delta V_i}\int_{\Omega_i}U_i\,dV=U|_i+\frac{\partial U}{\partial x}|_i\,\overline{x}_i+\frac{\partial U}{\partial y}|_i\,\overline{y}_i$$

$$+\frac{\partial^2 U}{\partial x^2}|_i\frac{\overline{x_i}^2}{2}+\frac{\partial^2 U}{\partial x\partial y}|_i\,\overline{xy_i}+\frac{\partial^2 U}{\partial y^2}|_i\frac{\overline{y_i}^2}{2}+\cdots$$

Where $\overline{x^n y_i^m}\equiv\dfrac{1}{\Delta V_i}\displaystyle\int_{\Omega_i}(x-x_i)^n(y-y_i)^m dV$

The volume integral here is computed by the Hammer integration formula, whose accuracy corresponds to the accuracy of reconstruction. In this paper, the weighted least squares method is used for solving coefficients of reconstruction polynomial.

$$\Delta U=SdU\ ,\quad \Delta U=\begin{bmatrix}U_1-U_i\\U_2-U_i\\ \cdots\\ \cdots\\U_n-U_i\end{bmatrix},\quad S=\begin{bmatrix}\overline{x}|_1 & \overline{y}|_1 & \frac{\overline{x_i}^2}{2}|_1 & \overline{xy}|_1 & \frac{\overline{y_i}^2}{2}|_1\\ & & \cdots & & \\ & & \cdots & & \\ \overline{x}|_n & \overline{y}|_n & \frac{\overline{x_i}^2}{2}|_n & \overline{xy}|_n & \frac{\overline{y_i}^2}{2}|_n\end{bmatrix}$$

Where $\overline{x^n y_i^m}\Big|_j=\dfrac{1}{\Delta V_j}\displaystyle\int_{\Omega_j}(x-x_i)^n(y-y_i)^m dV$

$$dU=\left[\frac{\partial U}{\partial x}|_i\ \ \frac{\partial U}{\partial y}|_i\ \ \frac{\partial^2 U}{\partial x^2}|_i\ \ \frac{\partial^2 U}{\partial x\partial y}|_i\ \ \frac{\partial^2 U}{\partial y^2}|_i\right]^T$$

W= diag(w1, . . . ,wn) is the diagonal weight matrix, the expressions for weights used here is $w_{k,k}=1/\overline{r_k}$, $\overline{r_k}=\sqrt{\overline{x_i}|_k^2+\overline{y_i}|_k^2}/d_0$, d_0 is the maximum radius of the interpolation stencil.

The coefficients are calculated by solving weighted normal equations, which are shown as follows.

$$S^T WSdU=S^T W\,\Delta U$$

According to the matrix algorithms,

$$dU=(S^T WS)^{-1}S^T W\,\Delta U$$

We can now obtain the reconstruction polynomial.

$$U_i\big|_{g_j} = U_i + S\big|_{g_j}(S^TWS)^{-1}S^TW\Delta U \tag{5}$$

And $\quad S\big|_{g_j} = \left[x_{g_j} - x_i \quad y_{g_j} - y_i \quad \dfrac{(x_{g_j} - x_i)^2}{2} \quad (x_{g_j} - x_i)(y_{g_j} - y_i) \quad \dfrac{(y_{g_j} - y_i)^2}{2} \right]$

2.5   Reconstruction Stencils

A key step of the WENO scheme is choosing the reasonable reconstruction stencils, whose number must be as small as possible in order to ensure the computing speed, and the arrangement must be rational in order to ensure the stability of the scheme.

The cell number is shown in Fig.1, the stencils of third-order scheme are shown as follows.

$$p_1\{\Delta_0,\Delta_1,\Delta_2\}, \quad p_2\{\Delta_0,\Delta_2,\Delta_3\}, \quad p_3\{\Delta_0,\Delta_1,\Delta_3\}, \quad p_4\{\Delta_0,\Delta_4,\Delta_5\},$$

$$p_5\{\Delta_0,\Delta_6,\Delta_7\}, \quad p_6\{\Delta_0,\Delta_8,\Delta_9\}.$$

The stencils of fourth-order scheme are shown as follows,

$$p_1\{\Delta_0,\Delta_1,\Delta_2,\Delta_4,\Delta_5,\Delta_6,\Delta_7\}, \quad p_2\{\Delta_0,\Delta_2,\Delta_3,\Delta_6,\Delta_7,\Delta_8,\Delta_9\}$$

$$p_3\{\Delta_0,\Delta_1,\Delta_3,\Delta_4,\Delta_5,\Delta_8,\Delta_9\}, \quad p_4\{\Delta_0,\Delta_4,\Delta_5,\Delta_{16},\Delta_{17},\Delta_{18}\},$$

$$p_5\{\Delta_0,\Delta_6,\Delta_7,\Delta_{13},\Delta_{14},\Delta_{15}\}, \quad p_6\{\Delta_0,\Delta_8,\Delta_9,\Delta_{10},\Delta_{11},\Delta_{12}\}.$$

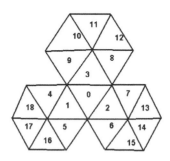

Fig. 1. Cells of reconstruction stencils

For the boundary cell, because it is unable to constitute integrated stencil, the method reducing accuracy is used. For three back stencils (p4,p5,p6) ,whose cell number may be less than 5, the method is selecting cell from neighboring stencils. The distribution of first three ones among third-order and fourth-order reconstruction stencils is uniform and tight and they have a great influence to the stability of schemes. The distribution of three ones of back among third-order and fourth-order reconstruction stencils is disperse and they are able to ensure that the discontinuity cannot exist simultaneously and linear weights are rather small under the inverse distance weights condition with small influence to the stability of the scheme . For the selection method of fourth-order reconstruction stencils, although the total cell number is more than stencils provided by [4] refs and the computing cost has been increased, Stability has been improved.

2.6   Calculation of Linear Weights

Third-order reconstruction polynomial is given by

$$\Delta U_{R_k}{}^3 = a_{k_1}\Delta U_{k_1} + a_{k_2}\Delta U_{k_2} + \cdots + a_{k_{e-1}}\Delta U_{k_{e-1}} + a_{k_e}\Delta U_{k_e}$$

Fourth-order reconstruction is

$$\Delta U_R{}^4 = b_1\Delta U_1 + b_2\Delta U_2 + \cdots + b_{n-1}\Delta U_{n-1} + b_n\Delta U_n$$

satisfies

$$\Delta U_R{}^4 = \sum_{k=1}^{m}\lambda_k\Delta U_{R_k}{}^3 \tag{6}$$

Where e represents mesh cell number in stencil K, n represents total number of cells relating to all the reconstruction stencil. m represents total number of stencils. λ_k represents linear weights of the stencil K. a_{k_j} is the third-order reconstruction coefficient of Kth stencils of l cell and b_l is the fourth-order reconstruction coefficient of l cell, then equation (6) can lead several equations ,which are given by,

$$\sum_{k=1}^{nn}\lambda_k a_{k_j} = b_l$$

Through compatibility we know:

$$\lambda_1 + \lambda_2 + \lambda_3 + \lambda_4 + \lambda_5 + \lambda_6 = 1$$

With stencils shown in Fig.1, the equations of linear weights is constructed.

$$AX = B, \quad X = [\lambda_1\ \lambda_2\ \lambda_3\ \lambda_4\ \lambda_5\ \lambda_6]^T \quad B = [1\ b_1\ b_2\ b_3\ \ldots\ldots\ b_{18}]^T$$

$$A = \begin{bmatrix} 1 & 1 & 1 & 1 & 1 & 1 \\ a_{11} & a_{31} & a_{41} & 0 & 0 & 0 \\ a_{12} & a_{21} & 0 & 0 & a_{51} & 0 \\ 0 & a_{22} & a_{32} & 0 & 0 & a_{61} \\ & & \cdots & & & \\ & & \cdots & & & \\ 0 & 0 & 0 & a_{46} & 0 & 0 \end{bmatrix}$$

Because only optimal solution exist in this equation, inverse distance weight coefficient is used to ensure the closer it leave cell 0, the higher computational accuracy is. This method is able to improve accuracy, and a very great weight value is used in the first line of weights functions matrix to ensure the weights obtained finally satisfy compatibility condition.

W is a diagonal matrix. When k=1, $w_{k,k} = 10000$, When k>1, $w_{k,k} = 1/\overline{r_{k-1}}$,

$\overline{r_{k-1}} = \sqrt{\overline{x_i}|_{k-1}^2 + \overline{y_i}|_{k-1}^2}/d_0$, d_0 is the same as above. Therefore we are able to get:

$$WAX = WB$$

It is satisfied that the Unknown variables of this overdetermined linear equations are greater than 0 or equal to 0. Above equations is turned into optimization problems with non-negative constraints:

$$\min\left\{(WAX - WB)^T (WAX - WB) : X \geq 0\right\}$$

The target function is:

$$F(X) = (WAX - WB)^T (WAX - WB) = \frac{1}{2} X^T (2(WA)^T WA) X +$$

$$(-2(WA)^T WB)^T X + (WB)^T WB$$

It is a quadratic programming problem, which is solved to get the non-negative linear weight. For the compatibility condition, in addition to using very great weight value, it is able to be achieved by using inequality constraints.

2.7   Smooth Factor and Nonlinear Weight

Smooth factor is expressed as follows:

$$S = \sum_{1 \leq |\alpha| \leq k} \int_{\Omega} \Delta V^{|\alpha|-1} (D^{\alpha} p(x, y))^2 dxdy$$

D is differential operator; $|\alpha|$ is the order of differential; $p(x, y)$ is the kth-order reconstruction polynomial. When $\alpha = (1, 2)$:

$$D^3 p(x, y) = \partial p^3 (x, y) / \partial x \partial y^2$$

The nonlinear weight ω is:

$$\omega_j = \frac{\overline{\omega_j}}{\sum_i \overline{\omega_i}} \quad \overline{\omega_i} = \frac{\lambda_i}{(\varepsilon + S_i)^2}$$

The range of ε is between 10^2 and 10^{-6}, ε has a influence to the dissipation of scheme. The greater the value of ε is, the smaller the dissipation is. Then the reconstruction polynomial can be written as follows:

$$U = U_i + \sum_{k=1}^{m} \omega_k \Delta U_{R_k}{}^3$$

3   Results and Discussion

3.1   Forward Step Problem

We solve the Euler equations at Mach 3 in a wind tunnel with a step. The wind tunnel is 3 length long and 1 length in breadth. The step is 0.2 length and placed in the 0.6 length distant from the inlet. Initially, the tunnel is full of the ideal gas, and $\gamma = 4$, $\rho = 1.4$, $p = 1.0$. In the x direction, $u = 3$ and in the y direction, $v = 0$. The left inflow is supersonic velocity boundary condition and right outflow is extrapolation boundary condition. Symmetry boundary is applied in the up boundary and the wall of tunnel. The mesh number is 28542. As shown in the Fig 2 to Fig 4 is the contour picture for the density at time t=4.0 with 30 contours from 0.32 to 6.15. Applying the Barth and Jespersen limiter, second order is obtained in the Fig2. Comparing with Fig 2 to Fig 4, four order scheme and three order scheme have more sensitivity than second scheme to shocks. For the bow shock and reflected shock, the shock width calculated is less than other order schemes, and the calculation result with second scheme is worst. Therefore, the four order scheme has the best ability in the three order schemes to capture shock wave.

3.2   Double Mach Reflection

This problem describes that a incident strong shock wave with mach 10 on the slope, which forms 30°with plane, interact with wall to form shock reflection. Calculation region is [0, 3]×[0, 1], and mesh number is 66318. Initial condition and boundary condition can be seen in the [12]. As shown in the Fig 5 to Fig 7 is the contour picture for the density at time t=0.2 with 30 contours from 1.5 to 21.5.

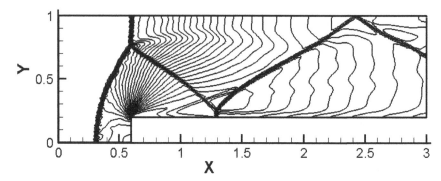

Fig. 2. Density: 2rd order

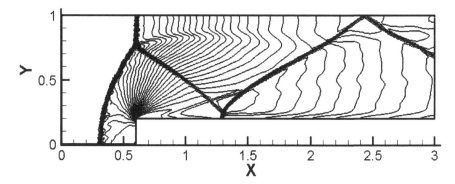

Fig. 3. Density: 3rd order

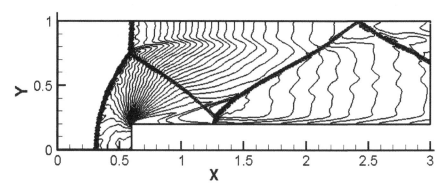

Fig. 4. Density: 4th order

We can see that the fourth-order scheme has the higher sensitivity to the shock. It can be seen that the format of the high-precision has stronger ability to capture the shock.

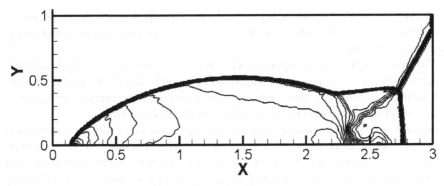

Fig. 5. Density: 2th order

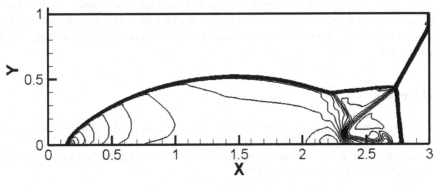

Fig. 6. Density: 3th order

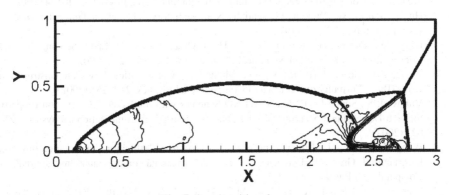

Fig. 7. Density: 4th order

4   Conclusions

Based on low-level reconstruction polynomial, we construct a more accurate WENO scheme, The coefficients of the reconstruction polynomial, which is calculated only once in the calculation process, only has the relationship with the grid. High accuracy of the volume integral is only used in the construction process of the reconstructed polynomial, so increasing the accuracy of the volume integral has no effect on the cost of computation.

The choice of the stencils plays a very big role in the process of successfully constructing a stable format, in this paper, the three main stencils are used to improve the accuracy and stability, three auxiliary stencils are used to increase the degree of dispersion of the stencils to ensure the effectiveness of the WENO.

In order to obtain the non-negative linear weights, the compatibility conditions is considered as equality constraints, and non-negative conditions is considered as inequality constraints ,then we obtain the target function by least-square adjustment theory, so the process of solving linear weights is transformed into process of solving the optimal solution.

We can see that the fourth-order scheme has the higher sensitivity to the shock through numerical experiments. Although the method of calculating linear weights will cause a loss of accuracy, it can achieve optimal approximation of high order accuracy solution.

References

1. Liuxd, Osher So, Chant.: Weighted essentially, non-oscillatory schemes. Journal of Computational Physics, 200–212 (1994)
2. Jiang, G., Shu, C.W.: Efficient Implementation of Weighted ENO Schemes. Journal of Computational Physics, 126–202 (1996)
3. Friedrichs, O.: Weighted: Essentially Non-oscillatory Schemes for the Interpolation of Mean Values on Unstructured Grids. Journal of Computational Physics, 144–194 (1998)
4. Hu, C., Shu, C.-W.: Weighted Essentially Non-oscillatory Schemes on Triangular Meshes. J. Comput. Phys., 97–127 (1999)
5. Levy, D., Puppo, G., Russo, G.: A Third Order Central WENO Scheme for 2D Conservation Laws. Applied Numerical Mathematics 33, 415–421 (2000)
6. Wang, Z.J.: Spectral (finite) Volume Method for Conservation Laws on Unstructured Grids (Basic Formulation). Journal of Computational Physics, 210–251 (2002)
7. Vukovicl, S., Sopta, L.: ENO and WENO Schemes with the Exact Conservation Property for One-Dimensional Shallow Water Equations. Journal of Computational Physics, 593–621 (2002)
8. Wang, Z.J., Zhang, L., Liu, Y.: Spectral (finite) Volume Method for Conservation Laws on Unstructured Grids II. Extension to Two Dimensional Euler Equations. Journal of Computational Physics, 665–697 (2002)
9. Peer, A.A.I., Gopaul, A., Dauhoo, M.Z., et al.: A New Fourth-order Non-oscillatory Central Scheme for Hyperbolic Conservation Laws. Journal of Computational Physics 179, 593–621 (2008)
10. Titarev, V.A., Toro, E.F.: Finite-volume WENO Schemes for Three-Dimensional Conservation Laws. Journal of Computational Physics 201, 238–260 (2004)

11. Qiu, J., Shu, C.-W.: On the Construction, Comparison, and Local Characteristic Decomposition for High-Order Central WENO Schemes. Journal of Computational Physics 219, 715–732 (2002)
12. Johnsen, E., Colonius, T.: Implementation of WENO Schemes in Compressible Multicomponent Flow Problems. Journal of Computational Physics 219, 715–732 (2006)
13. Shi, J., Hu, C.: A Technique of Treating Negative Weights in WENO Schemes. Journal of Computational Physics, 108–127 (2002)
14. Blazek, J.: Computational Fluid Dynamics Principles and Applications. Kidington, Oxford OX5 IGB, UK
15. Gottlieb, S., Shu, C.-W.: Total Variation Diminishing Runge-Kutta Schemes. Math of Computation, 73–85 (1998)

Unified Computational Aeroacoustic Integral Methods for Noise Radiation and Scattering with Noncompact Bodies

Fang Wang[*], Qiuhong Liu, and Jinsheng Cai

Northwestern Polytechnical University, School of Aeronaustics,
127 Youyi Xilu, Shaanxi, Xi'an, 710072, China
fangw1211@163.com, {liuqh,caijs}@nwpu.edu.cn

Abstract. In order to overcome high requirement for computation resources of high order method, and considering the scattering effects from noncompact bodies, an unified computational aeroacoustic method of noise radiation and scattering is presented, combining with the scattering noise calculation and radiated noise from compressible flow computation. In this paper, the pulsation of flow field variables are divided into hydrodynamic component and acoustic component, then the integral solution for scattered noise and far field noise is obtained based on Lighthill's acoustic analogy theory and wave equation of Green's function. According to this method, numerical calculation is developed in two steps. The boundary scattered pressure distribution is firstly obtained by solving the unified integral equation with the observing points located on the integral boundary, then the far field pressure of arbitrary point is computed when the observing point is located in the far field. Verification work is developed in connection with numerical calculation of two and three dimensional circular cylinder and two dimensional NACA0012 airfoil. The aeroacoustic result agree well with experimental data and numerical result of FW-H equation in combination with incompressible flow calculation. It indicates that this unified integral method calculates scattering effect exactly, and improves computation efficiency simultaneously.

Keywords: Aeroacoustic noise, noncompact, radiation and scattering, integral equation, compressible flow.

1   Introduction

At present, the large commercial aircraft is in the period of rapid development, aircraft noise become increasingly serious with the augment of commercial transport, relevant provisions and rules about acceptable level of noise are published abroad. The aircraft noise is mainly aerodynamic noise which is validly reduced by improving design of aircraft shape, and numerical prediction of aerodynamic noise is one of basic methods to study noise generation mechanism. Compared to experimental

---

[*] Corresponding author.

K. Li et al. (Eds.): ParCFD 2013, CCIS 405, pp. 252–264, 2014.
© Springer-Verlag Berlin Heidelberg 2014

method, numerical simulation method is a quantitative analysis way to collect physical information, and the noise is directly computed in combination with simple physical model. Otherwise, the demands of extensive engineering applications bring computational aeroacoustics (CAA) into sharp focus of the need for verifying noise prediction method, so that reduction aircraft noise and environmental pollution are probably realizable. Recently, Hybrid computational aeroacoustics (HCAA) is always used to develop noise calculation.

Based on Lighthill's [1,2] theory, Curle [3] proposed a computational method considered boundary influence, then Ffowcs and Hawking [4] presented FW-H equation which become an valid tool to compute noise produced by arbitrarily moving objects. Revell [5] developed a series of experiments to predict cylinder noise, Orselli [6] adopted FW-H equation into noise prediction of two dimensional and three dimensional cylinder with $D=0.019$, Re=90000. However, scattering noise of acoustic feedback effects near the body is not captured by an incompressible code or a compressible code with general order schemes, noncompact noise is not directly calculated with traditional HCAA but have to combine with high-order schemes in fluid computation. Meanwhile, high-order schemes bring huge amount of work especially for complex flow, the computational resources limit and low time efficiency make HCAA unsuitable for practical applications. To overcome above difficulties, two kinds of numerical methods are presented to consider scattering noise of noncompact bodies [7~14], tailored Green function and boundary integral equation with acoustic fluctuation. Hu and Jones [8~10] presented scattered Green functions with primary functions, which satisfy relevant boundary conditions. Takaishi [11] come up with integral solution of Green function in frequency domain, the cylinder noise was directly computed with vortex theory on condition of acquired numerical scattered Green function. On the other hand, Schram [12] divided pressure pulsation into hydrodynamic component and acoustic component, then the integral equation was used to develop noise prediction of internal flow. Mao [13] have improved pulsation decomposition from Schram's research work, and the corrected method was applied to simulate aerodynamic noise of two dimensional cylinder and NACA0012 airfoil. Moreover, Khalighi [14] proposed aeroacoustic method for arbitrarily shaped bodies by complex flow at low Mach number, the laminar noise and turbulent noise were validated for cylinder model. Although noise prediction method of Schram and Khalighi were appropriate for noncompact bodies, these methods were developed under the assumption of flow incompressibility.

In this paper, an unified method for radiated noise and scattered noise with noncompact bodies is proposed to reduce numerical simulation work of high-order computation, and considering the influence of compressible effects simultaneously. Under the hypothesis of applications with general order method in fluid computation, the pulsation of flow field variables are divided into hydrodynamic component mainly obtained by fluid computation and acoustic component mainly induced by noise propagation. The body surface is chosen as integral boundary, acoustic component on body surface is firstly captured, then the far field noise is calculated by solving integral equation.

2   Integral Computational Method of Noncompact Bodies

Based on compressible Navier-Strokes(N-S) equation, Lighthill's wave equation[1,2] is given as

$$\frac{\partial^2 \rho}{\partial t^2} - c_0^2 \nabla^2 \rho = \frac{\partial^2 T_{ij}}{\partial x_i \partial x_j} . \tag{1}$$

where $p' = p - p_0$, $\rho' = \rho - \rho_0$ are respectively the density pulsation and pressure pulsation.

Combined with free Green function g in time domain, acoustic solution is expressed as

$$C(\mathbf{x})c_0^2 \rho'(\mathbf{x},t) = \int_{-\infty}^{\infty} \int_V T_{ij} \frac{\partial^2 g}{\partial y_i \partial y_j} d\mathbf{y} \, d\tau$$
$$- \int_{-\infty}^{\infty} \int_S p' n_i \frac{\partial g}{\partial y_i} ds d\tau + \int_{-\infty}^{\infty} \int_S \rho_0 v_n \frac{\partial g}{\partial \tau} ds d\tau \tag{2}$$

when general order schemes are used to develop fluid computation, the fluctuations of noise propagation is not captured. The pulsation decomposition is proposed under completion of compressible calculation, and the fluid variables are given as

$$\begin{aligned} p &= p_0 + p_h + p_a \\ \boldsymbol{u} &= \boldsymbol{u_0} + \boldsymbol{u_h} + \boldsymbol{u_a} \\ \rho &= \rho_0 + \rho_h + \rho_a \end{aligned} . \tag{3}$$

Where subscript h and subscript a represent hydrodynamic component mainly induced by fluid flow and acoustic component mainly induced by noise propagation, respectively. Otherwise, the influence of fluid viscosity is always neglected as illustrated in reference [15], and the noise propagation satisfy linear relation, $p_a = c_0^2 \rho_a$. Therefore, the integral solution is written as

$$C(\mathbf{z})p_a(\mathbf{x},t) = -C(\mathbf{z})c_0^2 \rho_h(\mathbf{x},t) +$$
$$\int_{-\infty}^{\infty} \int_{V \backslash \{\mathbf{z}\}} T_{ij}' \frac{\partial^2 g}{\partial y_i \partial y_j} d\mathbf{y} \, d\tau - \int_{-\infty}^{\infty} \int_{S \backslash \{\mathbf{z}\}} p_h \frac{\partial g}{\partial y_i} n_i ds d\tau - . \tag{4}$$
$$\int_{-\infty}^{\infty} \int_{S \backslash \{\mathbf{z}\}} p_a \frac{\partial g}{\partial y_i} n_i ds d\tau + \int_{-\infty}^{\infty} \int_{S \backslash \{\mathbf{z}\}} \rho_0 u_i \frac{\partial g}{\partial \tau} n_i ds d\tau$$

the stress tensor T_{ij}' and the solid angle function $C(\mathbf{z})$ are written in the following forms

$$T_{ij}' = \rho u_i u_j + (p_h - c_0^2 \rho_h) \delta_{ij} . \tag{5}$$

$$C(\mathbf{z}) = 1 - \frac{1}{4\pi} \int_{S\setminus\{z\}} \frac{\partial}{\partial n} (\frac{1}{|\mathbf{z} - \mathbf{y}|}) ds \ . \tag{6}$$

For smooth integral boundary, $C(\mathbf{z}) = 1/2$, and n_i represents normal vector of integral boundary which directs into body surface from fluid field, u_i is the moving velocity of solid body surface. Eq (4)~(6) is the unified noise radiation and scattering integral equation of noncompact bodies. Due to the complexity of retarded time algorithm in time domain, the frequency computation is developed to study noise propagation. The integral equation of stationary objects in frequency domain is simplified as

$$Cp_a(\mathbf{z}, \omega) = -Cc_0^2 \rho_h (\mathbf{z}, \omega) + \tag{7}$$

$$\int_{V\setminus\{z\}} T_{ij}' \frac{\partial^2 G}{\partial y_i \partial y_j} dy - \int_{S\setminus\{z\}} p_h \frac{\partial G}{\partial y_i} n_i ds - \int_{S\setminus\{z\}} p_a \frac{\partial G}{\partial y_i} n_i ds \ .$$

Where G is the free space Green function in frequency domain, ω is the circular frequency.

The terms on the right hand side of Eq (7) are discussed as below, the first term is equal to 0 in far field, expressing the influence of flow compressibility; the second term and the third term are radiated source terms, representing volume sources and boundary sources generated by fluctuated fluid stresses and hydrodynamic forces on the body surface respectively; the last term describes scattered effect of noncompact bodies, these three terms are accordingly denoted by Pq, Pd and Ps. Above all, the scattered sources on integral boundary are firstly obtained with fluid information of compressible calculation, then the noise of far field observers are exactly solved connecting with scattered sources, including noncompact scattered noise especially recognizable for large size objects.

3   Noncompact Bodies Numerical Examples and Validations

3.1   Sound Generated by Turbulent Flow over Two Dimensional Cylinder

Turbulence vortex shedding phenomenon of circular cylinder and flow induced noise problem is a concern for hydrodynamics and aeroacoustics recently. The prime objective of present numerical simulation is to investigate scattered noise of noncompact bodies. The cylinder diameter is D=0.019m, the mean velocity is U=68.3m/s, corresponding Reynolds number is Re=9×10^4, the time step is chosen as Δt =2×10^{-5} s. As shown in Fig 1, the computational area extends from -15D to 45D in the horizontal direction, and -15D to 15D in the vertical direction for two dimensional cylinder.

The $k - \omega$ *SST* turbulence model is used to solve two dimensional unsteady compressible N-S equation, computational area is meshed with structured grids. In order to compute the near-wall flow field exactly and improve quality of numerical simulation, the spatial mesh resolution of Y^+ is approximately equal to 1, computational mesh is given as Fig. 1.

Fig. 2 shows time history of lift and drag coefficient acting on the cylinder surface. Meanwhile, The turbulent flow over two dimensional cylinder is different from the three dimensional cylinder which is influenced by spanwise flow, the shedding vortex is steady for two dimensional flow whereas the three dimension is irregular. Numerical results of URANS model indicate that the two dimensional flow is perfectly periodic, the cycle of Cl is twice time step of Cd over a vortex shedding period, and Cd 's pulsation is far less than pulsation of Cl, the maximum noise is pointed at vertical direction at vortex shedding frequency. Otherwise, it is observed that the vortex shedding cycle is $T \approx 56\Delta t$, and the vortex shedding frequency is correspondingly obtained, f_0=892.85 Hz. For three dimensional cylinder, the vortex

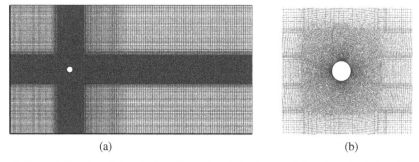

(a)   (b)

Fig. 1. Computational mesh for the two dimensional simulation: (a) total mesh, (b) local mesh

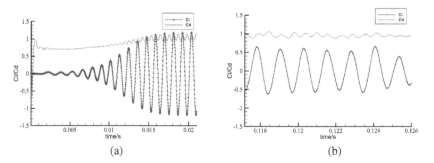

(a)   (b)

Fig. 2. Time history of lift and drag coefficients: (a) two dimensional flow, (b) three dimensional flow

Table 1. Numerical result of St, C_l', $\bar{C}_d$ with different turbulence model

	St	C_l'	$\bar{C}_d$
Experimental data[5]	0.180-0.191 Norberg	0.45-0.60 Norberg	1.0-1.4 Canwell
$k - \omega\, SST\ transition$[6]	0.235	0.823	1.09
$k - \omega\, SST$[6]	0.247	0.762	0.944
Two dimension	0.248	0.846	1.05
Three dimension	0.228	0.461	0.927

shedding frequency is slight lower, f_0=819.60Hz. Table 1 shows the obtained results of two dimensional(URANS) and the three dimensional(DES) numerical results compared with relevant experimental data. As Table 1 shows, aerodynamic force of two dimensional model is much higher than experimental data whereas three dimensional model is much closer to experimental data.

Fig. 3 shows the vortex shedding in a period when fluid flow reaches a steady case , the vortex sheds from cylinder upside and Cl reaches the minimum whereas the vortex sheds from cylinder downside and Cl reaches the maximum. The vortex shedding induces the production of aerodynamic forces, and the later the vortex sheds from cylinder, the less the fluctuation of forces and mean drag is. According to the unified method for noise radiation and scattering, the computation of scattered sources on cylinder surface is the first step of aerodynamic noise calculation, the acoustic computation grid of scattered source is chosen the same as fluid computational mesh. In comparison with Revell's experimental data, the observers are located on a circle with radius R=128D to investigate acoustic noise distribution in the far field. The acoustic results are measured in the form of Sound Pressure Level (SPL) in the decibel scale(dB)， the SPL is defined as

$$SPL = 20 \log_{10}(p_a/p_{ref}).$$ (8)

where *Pref* denotes a reference pressure, it is used a value of 20μ Pa in air. The time step of source sampling is identical with the time step of fluid computation. With N specimens chosen along time direction, the frequency resolution is given as

$$df = \frac{1}{N\Delta t}.$$ (9)

According to Eq (9), the frequency resolution is $df = 74.40Hz$ when choosing 672 specimens along time direction. The purpose of this paper is to verify the correctness of the present method, and the contribution of Pq ,Pd and Ps to total noise at the medium and high frequencies is another key point to study, then calculation of Pq is contained in the following research. At first, Fig 4 shows the SPL directivity at

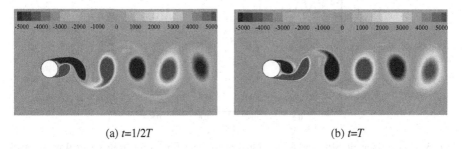

(a) t=1/2T (b) t=T

Fig. 3. Two dimensional instantaneous vorticity

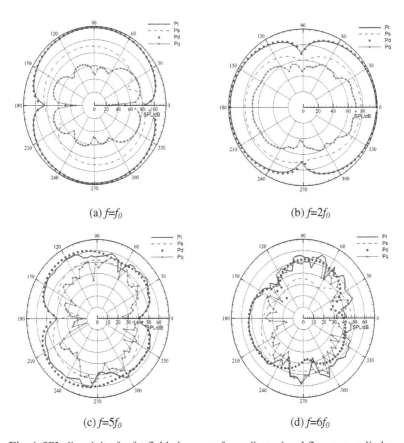

(a) $f=f_0$ (b) $f=2f_0$

(c) $f=5f_0$ (d) $f=6f_0$

Fig. 4. SPL directivity for far field observer of two dimensional flow over cylinder

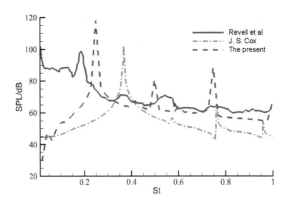

Fig. 5. Comparison of SPL variation with observer positioned 90°from mean flow for two dimensional cylinder

different frequency, where Pt is the total noise. According to the numerical result, the maximum radiation directions are along vertical direction and horizontal direction at vortex shedding frequency and the first harmonic frequency, which agree well with numerical result of Hu's [8] tailored Green function and Takaishi's [11] scattered Green function. For the present cylinder model, acoustic noise is mainly due to Pd, the effect of Ps is almost negligible particularly at low frequency. Because acoustic wavelength is greatly larger compared with cylinder diameter, and sound wave directly propagates in the physical space, so that scattered effect is slightly weak. However, wavelength becomes shorter with increased frequency, and the acoustic scattered effect is gradually strengthened, as shown in Fig. 4 (c) and Fig. 4 (d). It is observed that Ps increases with frequency compared to Pd, and Pq increases simultaneously. Secondly, the variation of acoustic field is another investigated aspect. Fig. 5 displays SPL variation with increased frequency, the present result is compared with Revell's experimental data and two dimensional result of Cox [16]. Numerical results indicate that SPL is continuously decreased with frequency but slightly increased at harmonic frequency, and radiating effect reduces by a large margin but scattering effect relatively increases. Therefore, the scattered effect due to noncompact bodies is not neglectful, the present method is valid to develop aerodynamic noise of noncompact bodies.

3.2   Sound Field of Three Dimensional Circular Cylinder

Refer to above research, Fig. 5 shows that the two dimensional computational result is slightly larger compared with experimental data, this conclusion agrees well with Orselli's two dimensional cylinder model. In order to verify the correctness of the present method, three dimensional cylinder with span length $L=4D$ is considered. The middle cross section along spanwise direction is selected as source area, fluid information over 70 vortex shedding cycles were stored to develop noise calculation. In the square zone with 2 meter side length, 1760 observers are placed to investigate pressure distribution at low frequencies. Fig. 6 shows pressure contours at $f=f_0$ and

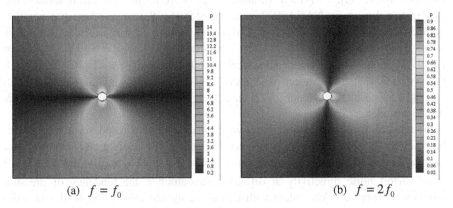

(a) $f = f_0$ (b) $f = 2f_0$

Fig. 6. Contours of total pressure for three dimensional cylinder

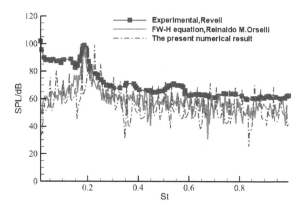

Fig. 7. Comparison of SPL variation with vortex shedding frequency for three dimensional cylinder, observer positioned 90°from mean flow

$f=2f_0$, and numerical results indicate that the pressure amplitude is continuously reduced during noise propagation under the same frequency. Furthermore, in order to verify the reliability of the present method, Fig. 7 shows comparison of SPL variation with increased frequency for numerical simulations and experimental data, it demonstrates that the present method is in coincidence with both Oreslli's [6] three dimensional simulation obtained from FW-H equation and Revell's [5] experimental results.

3.3   NACA0012 Airfoil Noise

NACA0012 airfoil at low Mach number is chosen as another research object, the chord length of two dimensional model is l=0.6096m and blunt treatment is used at the trailing edge. The incident attack angle is 6^0 with Ma=0.205, the Reynolds number is corresponding obtained, Re=2.87×10^6. The computational area is a rectangular zone with $x \in [-10.5l, 30l]$, $y \in [-12l, 12l]$, and 336 grids are located on airfoil surface, the computational mesh for NACA0012 is displayed in Fig. 8, structured mesh generation method is used here, and the leading edge and trailing edge are refined as well as airfoil wake section to capture vortex structure sophisticated. The DES turbulent model is applied to develop numerical simulation with $\Delta t = 1 \times 10^{-4} s$. Fig. 8 demonstrates that the present calculated pressure coefficient agree well with experimental result of Gregory [17] and Fleig's [18] numerical result with LES turbulent model.

In order to inspect pressure directivity, observers are located on a circle with diameter D=100l and the circle center is coincidence with leading edge center. Fluid information of 1024 time steps are stored with $df = 9.77Hz$ due to Eq (9). Fig 9 shows airfoil noise directivity at different wavenumber, the tendency of pressure variation is completely consistent with Howe's analytical model. Fig 10 displays the SPL variation tendency of Pt, Pd and Ps with increased frequency. Numerical results

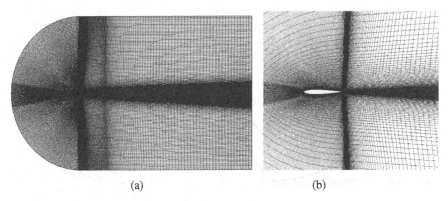

Fig. 8. Computational mesh for two dimensional NACA0012: (a) total mesh, (b) local mesh

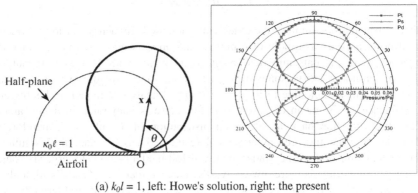

(a) $k_0 l = 1$, left: Howe's solution, right: the present

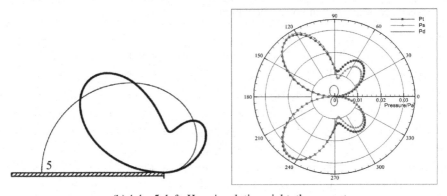

(b) $k_0 l = 5$, left: Howe's solution, right: the present

Fig. 9. SPL directivity of NACA0012 airfoil noise at different wavenumber with different frequency

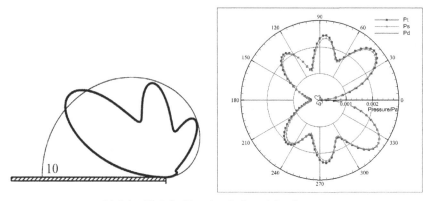

(c) $k_0l = 10$, left: Howe's solution, right: the present

Fig. 9. (*Continued.*)

indicate that the lobe number increases with increased frequency. At low frequency, airfoil noise appears as dipole distribution, and appears as petal shaped at medium frequency. The present numerical result is identical with Howe's [7] analytical solution, but there exists some difference about lobe structure, which is mainly induced by attack angle due to Roger's [19] airfoil analytical model. In his research, the influence of the mean direction to airfoil noise is elaborated in detail, and the mean flow direction have an effect on distribution of airfoil noise, therefore the difference between the present numerical result and Howe's analytical solution is acceptable. Compared with cylinder model, airfoil model belongs to large size object, noise scattering effect is more obviously. It's observed that *Pt*, *Pd* and *Ps* all gradually reduce with increased frequency. However, noise of scattered integral term(*Ps*) is the main part which is much greater than *Pd*, these result deeply verified that scattered noise is a necessary part in noise calculation.

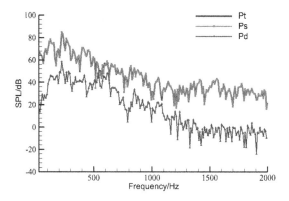

Fig. 10. SPL variation with increased frequency of NACA0012 airfoil

4   Conclusions

Scattered noise becomes a remarkable problem in the field of engineering application, but sound waves produce feedback signals near boundary zone which are not captured by traditional CAA and HCAA. This paper presents an unified computational aeroacoustic method of radiation and scattering noise, this integral method is used to calculate noncompact noise with general order compressible calculation. Based on two-order methods, two dimensional cylinder, three dimensional cylinder and NACA0012 airfoil are studied. The numerical results indicate that:

(1) At low frequency, acoustic wavelength is greatly longer compared with cylinder diameter so that the cylinder model is approximate as compact body, then scattered noise is almost negligible, but scattered noise gradually increases with amplified frequency. It demonstrates that the numerical result of the present method is identical with result of Curle's solution and FW-H equation at low frequency, scattered noise and volume term noise slightly increase with frequency.

(2) Scattering effect is closely related with object sizes, and scattered noise is obviously intense for large size but weak for small size. For example, the radiated noise of NACA0012 is relatively tiny compared with the scattered noise, which is the main part of airfoil noise but the negligible part for chosen cylinder model at low frequency.

(3) In this paper, two-order schemes are adopted to develop compressible calculation, it's assumed that the fluid variables consist of the mean flow component, the hydrodynamic component mainly produced by fluid flow and acoustic component mainly induced by noise propagation, then an unified computational method of noncompact bodies is presented to calculate radiation noise and scattered noise. This method has an advantage over high-order schemes in improving time efficiency, and simulates scattered noise of noncompact bodies exactly.

Acknowledgments. The work is supported by National Natural Science Foundation of China, NO. 11002116 and Basic Research Foundation of Northwestern Polytechnical University , NO.GCKY1006.

References

1. Lighthill, M.J.: On sound generated aerodynamically. I. Proc. R. Soc. Lond. A. 211, 564–587 (1952)
2. Lighthill, M.J.: On sound generated aerodynamically. II. Proc. R. Soc. Lond. A. 222, 1–32 (1954)
3. Curle, N.: The influence of solid boundaries on aerodynamic sound. Proc. R. Soc. Lond. A. 213, 505–514 (1969)
4. Ffowcs Williams, J.E., Hawking, D.L.: Sound generation by turbulence and surfaces in arbitrary motion. Phil. Trans. R. Soc. A. 264, 321–342 (1969)
5. Revell, J.D., Prydz, R.A., Hays, A.P.: Experimental study of airframe noise vs. drag relationship for circular cylinders. Final report NASA contrast NASI-14403 (1977)

6. Orselli, R.M., Meneghini, J.R., Saltara, F.: Two and three dimensional simulation of sound generated by flow around a circular cylinder. In: 15th AIAA/CEAS Aeroacoustics Conference, pp. 3270, 1–20. AIAA Press, Florida (2009)
7. Howe, M.S.: Edge-source acoustic Green's function for an airfoil chord, with application to trailing-edge noise. Q. Jl Mech. Appl. Maths 54, 139–155 (2001)
8. Hu, F.Q., Hussaini, Y.H., Manthey, J.L.: Low-dissipation and low-dispersion Runge-Kutta schemes for computational acoustics. J. Comput. Phy. 124, 177–191 (1996)
9. Hu, F.Q., Guo, Y.P., Jones, A.D.: On the computation and application of exact green's function in acoustic analogy. In: 11th AIAA Aeroacoustics Conference, pp. 2986,1–18. AIAA Press, California (2005)
10. Jones, A.D., Hu, F.Q.: A three-dimensional time-domain boundary element method for the computation of exact green's function in acoustic analogy. In: 13th AIAA/CEAS Aeroacoustics, pp. 3479, 1–18. AIAA Press, Rome (2007)
11. Takaishi, T., Miyazawa, M., Kato, C.: A computational method of evaluating noncompact sound based on vortex sound theory. J. Acoust. Soc. Am. 121, 1353–1361 (2007)
12. Schram, C.: A boundary element extension of Curle's analogy for non-compact geometries at low-Mach numbers. J. Sound Vib. 322, 264–281 (2009)
13. Mao, Y.J., Qi, D.T., Gu, Y.Y.: Prediction of hydrodynamic noise scattered by the non-compact circular cylinder. In: ASME 3rd Joint US-European Fluids Engineering Summer Meeting, Montreal, pp. 1235–1247 (2010)
14. Khalighi, Y.: Prediction of sound generated by complex flows at low mach numbers. AIAA Journal 48, 306–316 (2010)
15. Morfey, C.L.: The role of viscosity in aerodynamic sound generation. Acoustics 2, 225–240 (2003)
16. Cox, J.S.: Computation of vortex shedding and radiated sound for a circular cylinder: subcritical to transcritical reynolds numbers. Theoret. Comput. Fluid Dynamics 12, 233–253 (1998)
17. Ministry of defence (Procurement executive): areonautical research council reports and memoranda, No. 3726 (1973)
18. Fleig, O., Arakawa, C.: Large-eddy simulation of tip vortex flow at high reynolds number. In: 42nd AIAA Aerospace Science Meeting and Exhibit, pp. 261, 1–11. AIAA Press, Reno (2004)
19. Roger, M., Moreau, S.: Back-scattering correction and further extension of Amiet's trailing-edge noise model Part I: theory. J. Sound Vib. 286, 477–506 (2005)

Flow Characteristics of Gas-Liquid Phase in New Type of Umbrella Plate Scrubber

Li Shanhong[1,2,*], Guo Guanqing[1,2], Li Caiting[1,2], and Tangqi[1,2]

[1] College of Environmental Science and Engineering,
Hunan University, Changsha 410082, China
[2] Key Laboratory of Environmental Biology and Pollution Control (Hunan University),
Ministry of Education, Changsha 410082, China

Abstract. A new type of umbrella plate scrubber was invented to purify the harmful pollutants. The two-phase flow of the new device was studied through simulation approach between dust gas and water droplets. The continuous gas phase was modeled in an Eulerian framework, while the dispersed liquid phase, tracked with a Lagrangian approach. With inlet velocity 14.42 m/s, liquid-gas ratio 0.2 L/m3 and the Discrete Phase Model(DPM), the hydrodynamics peculiarity of this device was displayed with the velocity profile, pressure field and droplets trajectories. The results show that gas velocity in the export section is uniform, and the total pressure drop of the scrubber is about 1000 Pa with spray. In addition, the dewatering performance of the scrubber is relatively well. DPM model is successful in predicting the two phase flow in the spray tower.

Keywords: umbrella plate, scrubber, numerical simulation, two phase flow, hydrodynamics peculiarity, pressure drop.

1   Introduction

Air pollution caused by particles and SO_2 in flue gas from industrial boilers is a global issue and thus receives increasing attention over the recent years. Especially in China, the serious pollution has made huge damage to human health and economic development [1-4]. Several SO_2 emission control technologies, such as dry, semi-dry and wet flue gas desulphurization, have been presented and discussed in different publications [5-10]. The wet flue gas desulphurization (WFGD) is widely used in power plants for air pollution control and share over 90% of installed desulphurization capacities in the world nowadays. Different purification devices, such as the spray tower, bubbling tower, and grid packed tower, were used to improve desulphurization efficiency, and the spray towers are the most frequently installed scrubber types for limestone WFGD plants and cover the major part of the market today [11-17].

The new type of umbrella plate scrubber was invented on the basis of the traditional spray tower, and its performance has been discussed through experiments and CFD simulation [18-19]. However, its dewatering performance was always unsatisfactory. In order to improve its dewatering performance, the height of demisting segment was

---

* Corresponding author.

K. Li et al. (Eds.): ParCFD 2013, CCIS 405, pp. 265–275, 2014.

increased by 300 mm together with the installation angle of the demister blades was adjusted to 25°. Therefore, this work is to perform a CFD simulation and experimental study on the improved umbrella plate scrubber.

2   Experiments

The schematic diagram of the experimental set-up is shown in Fig.1. Therein, the upper and lower umbrella plates are laid out reversely. Absorbing liquid forms membrane as it flows down from the upper umbrella plates. The plate surfaces increase gradually and obtain the maximum, which is beneficial to the further contacting with droplets and dust gas. And then, the droplets flows along the opposite umbrella plate and shed form orifice at the bottom layer plate. Meanwhile, gas with dust enters the scrubber from inlet tube, up-flows along the lower umbrella plates and front collides with the absorbing liquid. The dust gas is scrubbed through further contacting with the liquid membrane, and then dewatered by demister, where, the gas flow entrained with droplets is forced to whirl and the droplets are knocked on the wall because of the centrifugal force. Finally, the purified gas is released to the atmosphere by the exhaust fan. The scrubbed liquid returns to the circulating water tanker. The waste is cleared up periodically. Dust gas is purified through inertial collision, intercepts of the umbrella plates, wet, absorption of the absorbing liquid and the adsorption among the particles.

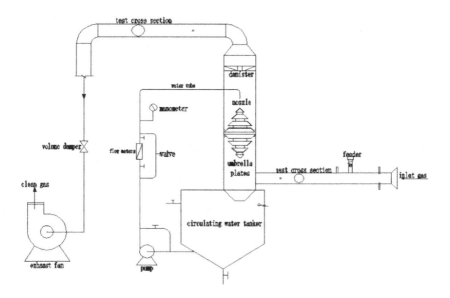

Fig. 1. Schematic diagram of experimental set-up

Note: The height of demisting segment (over the demister) has been increased by 300mm.

3   Numerical Simulations

3.1   Geometrical Models for the Scrubber

Fig.2 shows the computational domain of the original model. It consists of a simplified rectangular tank with a diameter of 400 mm and height of 100 mm. The diameter of inlet section is 100 mm as same as the outlet section, but different in length, which is 400 mm and 800 mm, respectively. The height of tower is 1550 mm with the diameter of 200 mm. Meshing was performed with GAMBIT2.3.6. Size function was also used to reach mesh size. The mesh consists of 252995 hexahedral and hybrid cells. The schematic diagram of the demister is shown in Fig.3. A total of 12 blades are placed with the elevation angle of 25°in the demister.

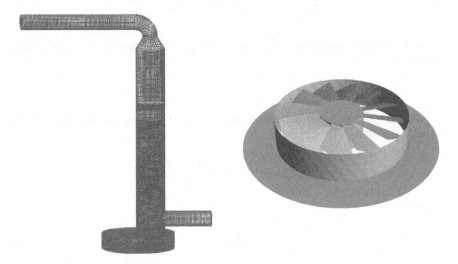

Fig. 2. Computational domain and grid representation   **Fig. 3.** Schematic diagram of the demister

3.2   Mathematical Models

3.2.1   Model Equation

Based on the mass, momentum and energy conservation principle, in this paper, the inlet gas was assumed as the continuous phase and the spray liquid as the particle phase. Meanwhile, the FLUENT was used to investigate the gas-liquid two-phase flow with an Euler-Lagrange approach. Existence and movement of the droplets affected the air flow, and, in turn, air flow was bound to impact the droplet trajectory. Therefore, the calculation of droplets and air flow must be coupled with each other in order to describe their movement accurately [20-21]. Euler equation of gas field and Lagrange equation of the liquid was coupled by mass, momentum and energy exchange of the interface [22]. Accordingly, the general control equation was list as follows:

$$\frac{\partial(\rho\Phi)}{\partial t}+\frac{\partial(\rho u_i\Phi)}{\partial x_i}=\frac{\partial}{\partial x_i}\left(\Gamma_\Phi\frac{\partial\Phi}{\partial x_j}\right)+S_\Phi+S_{\rho\Phi} \tag{1}$$

Standard k-ε turbulence model is applied in the calculation. k and ε are obtained from the following transport-equations:

$$\rho\frac{\partial k}{\partial t}+\rho\frac{\partial(ku_i)}{\partial x_i}=\frac{\partial}{\partial x_j}[(\mu+\frac{\mu_t}{\sigma_k})\frac{\partial k}{\partial x_j}]+G_\varepsilon-\rho\varepsilon \tag{2}$$

$$\rho\frac{\partial\varepsilon}{\partial t}+\rho\frac{\partial(\varepsilon u_i)}{\partial x_i}=\frac{\partial}{\partial x_j}[(\mu+\frac{\mu_t}{\sigma_\varepsilon})\frac{\partial\varepsilon}{\partial x_j}]+C_{1\varepsilon}\frac{\varepsilon}{k}G_k-\rho C_{2\varepsilon} \tag{3}$$

G_k represents the generation of turbulence kinetic energy due to the mean velocity gradients:

$$G_k=\mu_t(\frac{\partial u_i}{\partial x_j}+\frac{\partial u_j}{\partial x_i})\frac{\partial u_i}{\partial x_j} \tag{4}$$

DPM was used to track particles trajectories and it could be described as the following-equation.

$$\frac{du_p}{dt}=F_D(u-u_p)+\frac{g_x(\rho_p-\rho)}{\rho_P}+F_x \tag{5}$$

With

$$F_D=\frac{18\mu}{d_p^2\rho_p C_D} \tag{6}$$

$$C_D=1+\frac{2\lambda}{d_p}\left(1.257+0.4e^{-(1.1d_p/2\lambda)}\right) \tag{7}$$

In addition, other role forces on the particles including pressure gradient force, rotation force, thermophoretic force, Brown proliferation ability, Saffman lift and so on. Here, we only take the gravity into consideration.

3.2.2   Boundary Conditions

A "velocity inlet" boundary condition was applied at the scrubber inlet, and "pressure outlet" condition at the outlet. Meanwhile, the closed wall surfaces were treated as standard wall function and non-slip conditions are imposed on the walls. The particles were supposed to obey the Rosin- Rammler distribution. The spray liquid was injected from a solid cone and its properties were listed in table 1.

Table 1. Particle diameter distribution and spry parameters

Diameter distribution	Rosin-Rammler
Minimum diameter	0.2mm
Maximum diameter	5mm
Mean diameter	2.5mm
Spread parameter	3
Spray type	Solid-cone
Angle	120
Velocity	18m/s
Radius	1cm
Flow rate	0.0226kg/s

4   Results and Discussion

4.1   The Velocity Distribution

The velocity of the gas phase is strongly modified by the existence of the spray liquid, as illustrated in Fig.4. The gas phase velocity is about 4m/s in the spray region. After passing through the demister, the gas flow velocity eventually reaches 15m/s in outlet section. Meanwhile, there are some vortex in the entrance and exit of the scrubber because of 90 ° deflection. We can see that there is a low velocity region in the middle of the area above the demister, which is mainly caused by the whirl movement of the gas flow. From Fig.5 it can be observed that the turbulence is more intense around the umbrella cover and the gas phase velocity is significantly small at external edge of umbrella cover due to the impact of the spray liquid. The strong turbulence near the umbrella cover increases the accessibility of each phase, which contributes to enhance cohesion and purification efficiency. From Fig.6 it is noticeable that gas flow entrained with droplets whirl upon movement when passing the demister, where the droplets were knocked on the wall because of the centrifugal force, then flow down along wall surface.

4.2   Gas Pressure Field

As shown in Fig.7, the pressure drop is mainly generated nearby the umbrella plates and the demister owing to their unique structures. The pressure drop at the two regions reaches 300 Pa and 500 Pa respectively. The fluid flow is forced to hit the umbrella and demist blade. The dissipated energy and kinetic energy of the fluid are transformed because of the wall resistance, leading to a local high pressure drop zone. The gas pressure changes in wide extension due to the increased airflow turbulence intensity. Countercurrent spray liquid resists the airflow, and hence leads to significant changes of airflow, followed by the increase of gas pressure drop.

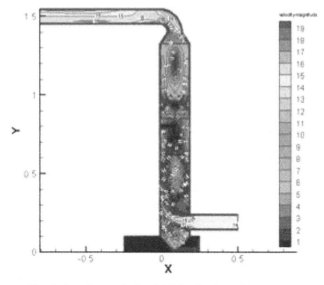

Fig. 4. Gas phase velocity field distribution with spray

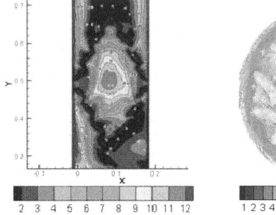

Fig. 5. Gas phase velocity distribution around umbrella cover

Fig. 6. Gas phase velocity vector above demister

4.3   Liquid Droplets Trajectory

Fig.8 illustrates the droplets trajectory tracking results. Droplets uniformly distributed in the tower. This ensured full contact of the gas-liquid two-phase. Majority of the droplets fall off to the circulating water tanker after scrubbing flue gas, along with smaller droplet particles which are forced to move upward until through the demister. Meantime, there is a still considerable part of the droplets downward along the wall

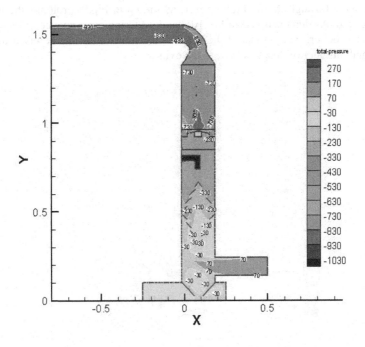

Fig. 7. Gas phase pressure distribution with spray

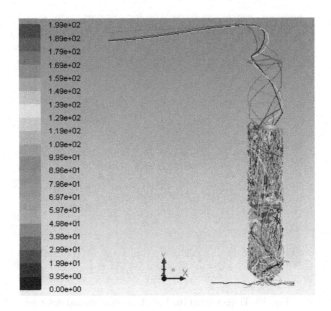

Fig. 8. Trajectory of the liquid droplets

272   S. LI et al.

surface. The downward movement of droplets forms multiple umbrella curtains when they flowing through the umbrella cover, as shown in Fig.9, prolongs the gas-liquid contact time. As demonstrated in Fig.10, the dewatering performance of the improved scrubber is better, where most of the droplets are removed in the demister and only a very small number of droplets flow to the exits.

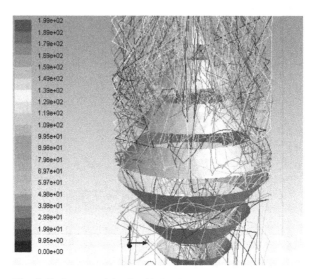

Fig. 9. Trajectory of the liquid droplets around umbrella cover

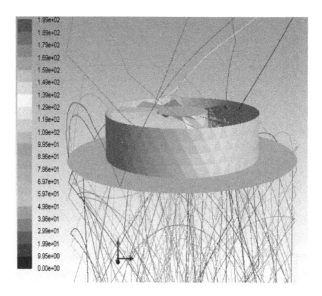

Fig. 10. Trajectory of the liquid droplets around demister

5   Conclusions

Numerical simulations of the improved scrubber were conducted on gas-liquid two-phase flow and the results demonstrated that the DPM model is successful in predicting the two phase flow in the spray tower. The results show that the gas-liquid two-phase flow is fully mixed in the tower and the demister plays an inessential role in dewatering. The number of droplets significantly reduces owing to the increased height of demisting segment and the adjustment of blades' installation angle, which means that the dewatering performance of the scrubber has been greatly improved. The air flow forms strong turbulent flow in the spray zone due to the impact of the umbrella plates and the spray liquid, and then it became more stable through the demister. The pressure drop of the scrubber is mainly caused by countercurrent spray liquid, with the help of unique structures of the umbrella plates and the demister. Based on the results, optimal design of the equipment set-up can be realized. CFD simulation allows considerable low cost and time savings when used as a research tool instead of building a physical laboratory device. Furthermore, it can deliver detailed and visualizable data which are hard to obtain via experiments.

Acknowledgements. The authors gratefully acknowledge the financial support of the National Natural Science Foundation of China (51108168),China Post doctoral Science Foundation (2011M501271), as well as Science and Technology Department of Project in Hunan Province(2012RS4001).

Nomenclature

x cartesian coordinates
t   time (s)
P pressure (Pa)
u   fluid velocity (m/s)
d_p particle diameter (μm)
g   gravity acceleration (m/s^2)
C_D drag coefficient
C dust concentration (g/m^3)
k turbulent kinetic energy (m^2/s^2)
G   Mass fraction
$c_1, c_2, \delta_k, \delta_\varepsilon$, constant, respectively, $c_1 = 1.44$, $c_2 = 1.92$, $\delta_k = 1.0$, $\delta_\varepsilon = 1.3$

Greek letters

ρ flow density (kg/m^3)
Φ variable
μ flow viscosity (Pa.s)
ε dissipation rate (m^2/s^3)
S source term. (kg/m.s^3)
Γ diffusion coefficient

Subscripts

i, j, k   constant, respectively, i, j, k=1, 2, 3

p   particle phase

g   gas phase

References

[1] Zhao, Y., Wang, S., Duan, L., Lei, Y., Cao, P., Hao, J.: Primary air pollutant emissions of coal-fired power plants in China: Current status and future prediction. Atmospheric Environment 42(36), 8442–8452 (2008)

[2] Matus, K., Nam, K.-M., Selin, N.E.: Health damage from air pollution in China. Global Environment Change 22(1), 55–66 (2012)

[3] Kampa, M., Castanas, E.: Human health effects of air pollution. Environmental Pollution 151(2), 362–367 (2008)

[4] Altindag, H., Yusuf, G., Nevin, S.: Sulfur capture for fluidized-bed combustion of high-sulful content lignites. Applied Energy 79(4), 403–424 (2004)

[5] Gao, H., Li, C., Zeng, G., Zhang, W., Shi, L., Li, S., Zeng, Y., Fan, X., Wen, Q., Shu, X.: Flue gas desulphurization based on limestone-gypsum with a novel wet-type PCF device. Separation and Purification Technology 76, 253–260 (2011)

[6] Sarkar, S., Meikap, B.C., Chatterjee, S.G.: Modeling of removal of sulfur dioxide from flue gases in a horizontal cocurrent gas–liquid scrubber. Chemical Engineering Journal 131, 263–271 (2007)

[7] Zheng, Y., Kiil, S.-R., Johnsson, J.E.: Experimental investigation of a pilot-scale jet bubbling reactor for wet flue gas desulphurization. Chemical Engineering Science 58, 4695–4703 (2003)

[8] F.F. Hill, J. Zank.: Flue gas desulphurization by spray dry absorption. Chemical Engineering and Processing, 3945–3952 (2000)

[9] Görkem, B., Öguz, H.: Development of an active sorbent from fly ash for dry desulphurization of simulated flue gas in a fluidized-bed reactor. Chemical Engineering Journal 119, 147–152 (2006)

[10] Gómez, A., Fueyo, N., Tomás, A.: Detailed modelling of a flue-gas desulfurisation plant. Computers & Chemical Engineering 31(11), 1419–1431 (2007)

[11] Lancia, A., Musmarrrra, D., Pepe, F.: SO_2 absorption in a bubbling reactor using limestone suspensions. Chemical Engineering Science 49(24), 4523–4532 (1994)

[12] Kid, S., Michelsen, M.L., Johansen, K.D.: Experimental investigation and modeling of a wet flue gas desulfurization pilot plant. Industrial Engineering Chemistry Research 37(7), 2792–2806 (1998)

[13] Jorge, I., Genice, G.: Abatement costs of SO_2-control options in the Mexican electric-power sector. Applied Energy 85(2-3), 80–94 (2008)

[14] Maroccoa, L., Inzolib, F.: Multiphase Euler–Lagrange CFD simulation applied to Wet Flue Gas Desulphurisation technology. International Journal of Multiphase Flow 35(2), 185–194 (2009)

[15] Marocco, L.: Modeling of the fluid dynamics and SO_2 absorption in a gas-liquid reactor. Chemical Engineering Journal 162(1), 217–226 (2010)

[16] Sun, Z., Wang, S., Zhou, Q.: Experimental study on desulfulization efficiency and gas-liquid mass transfer in a new liquid-screen desulfurization system. Applied Energy 87(6), 1505–1512 (2010)

[17] Hrastel, I., Gerbec, M., Stergarsek, A.: Technology Optimization of Wet Flue Gas Desulfurization Process. Chemical Engineering and Technology 30(2), 220–233 (2007)

[18] Li, S., Li, C., Zeng, G.: Simulation and experimental validation studies on a new type umbrella plate scrubber. Separation and Purification Technology 62(2), 323–329 (2008)

[19] Li, S., Li, C., Zeng, G.: CFD simulation on performance of new type umbrella plate scrubber. Transactions of Nonferrous Metals Society of China 18(2), 488–492 (2008)

[20] Launder, B.E., Spalding, D.B.: The numerical computation of turbulent flows. Computer Methods in Applied Mechanics and Engineering 3(2), 269–289 (1974)

[21] Schmidt, B., Stichlmair, J.: Two-phase flow and mass transfer in scrubbers. Chemical Engineering and Technology 14(3), 162–166 (1991)

[22] Versteeg, H.K., Malalasekera, W.: An Introduction to Computational Fluid Dynamics: the finite volume method. British Library Cataloguing in publication data, London (1995)

Three-Dimensional Aeroacoustic Numerical Simulation of Flow Induced Noise of Mufflers

Yan Yang[1,*] and Hongling Sun[2]

[1] LHD, Institute of Mechanics, Chinese Academy of Sciences,
No. 15 Beisihuanxi Road, Beijing 100190, P.R. China
yangy@ustc.edu
[2] Key Laboratory of Noise and Vibration Research, Institute of Acoustics,
Chinese Academy of Sciences, No. 21 Beisihuanxi Road, Beijing 100190, P.R. China
hlsun@mail.ioa.ac.cn

Abstract. Mufflers are widely applied in industrial flow duct systems or internal combustion engines, to reduce the amount of noise carried by the upstream flow. Although the flow in the duct of the muffler is commonly unsteady, complex and turbulent, which generates noise by itself. The flow noise should be considered for design and optimization of the muffler. By means of a three-dimensional numerical simulation integrated CFD (computational fluid dynamics) and CAA (computational aeroacoustics), the paper investigated two typical mufflers. The first one has an expanded chamber in the duct, and the second one has the same chamber but whilst has a perforated wall between the duct and the chamber. The nonlinear acoustic solver is implemented to model noise generation and transmission from an initial statistically-steady turbulent flow, which provided by RANS (Reynolds-averaged Navier-Stokes) simulation, and to simulate the noise in near field. The radiated far-field noise of the mufflers was predicted by FW-H (Ffowcs Williams-Hawking) acoustic analogy. The mechanisms of the vortex and sound generation were revealed, and results indicate that the perforated tube muffler has much lower flow induced noise level. The solver of the numerical simulation has been parallelized with MPI, and run on a HPC cluster, due to the large computation cost.

Keywords: computational fluid dynamics (CFD), computational aeroacoustics (CAA), flow induced noise, muffler.

1 Introduction

Mufflers (or silencers) are commonly used as silencing elements in HVAC ducts, automotive exhaust systems or other internal fluid machineries, to attenuate the noise emitted by upstream sound sources. The acoustic attenuation mechanisms in the absence of flow medium have been quite well understood. However, flow in the duct and chamber of muffler is commonly unsteady, complex and turbulent, which generates noise by itself. The flow induced noise should be carefully

---

* Corresponding author.

K. Li et al. (Eds.): ParCFD 2013, CCIS 405, pp. 276–286, 2014.

considered for design and optimization of the muffler, especially at high speed [1–6].

With development of computational fluid dynamics (CFD) and computational aeroacoustics (CAA), numerical simulation should be able to applied to predict the flow excited noise. The methods of CAA can be classified in two basic approaches, the first one is directional approach, also called as directional noise computation (DNC) and the second is hybrid approach [7, 8]. Because the acoustic perturbation is much smaller than the flow dynamic quantities, the directional noise computation often costs a lot and the numerical error should overwhelm the acoustic quantities. In order to accurately simulate sound in the flow with acceptable computational amount, hybrid approach is commonly adopted, that is of two-step, i) acoustic source computation and ii) sound propagation computation, where different methods are used in corresponding domains and integrated through data transmission. The first step should be accomplished by directional computational fluid dynamic simulation, through RANS/LES/DNS approach, where the flow perturbation and acoustic source are computed or modeled. The second step, in general, consists of sound computation in near field and far field, of which the former is to solve the partial derivative equation of acoustic perturbation and the later is to solve the acoustic analogy equation or other similar equations. In present work, the numerical method is based on the NLAS (nonlinear acoustic solver) approach, derived by Batten et al [9, 10]. NLAS provides a more sophisticated sub-grid treatment that allows the extraction of acoustic sources from the temporal variation within the (modeled) sub-grid structures. The main advantage of this approach is that the noise in the near field can be simulated with less computation cost comparing to the directional noise computation approaches with traditional LES, hybrid RANS/LES, because the grid requirements is relaxed in the near-wall region. Furthermore, it has the important advantage of being able to account for both for broadband, turbulence-related noise and discrete tones arising from coherent structures or resonance, which can not be neglected in present study on the flow noise issues of mufflers.

Two typical kinds of mufflers were studied in this paper, one of which is constructed by a expanded chamber in the duct, and another with a perforated wall between the chamber and the duct. With the qualitative and quantitative comparison with experimental measurement shows that the simulation has credible results. The results helps to understand the mechanisms and control of the flow induced noise in the typical mufflers, which is great useful for the muffler design.

2 Numerical Methods

In present work, the hybrid approach of CAA, NLAS was implemented. The strategy can be described as the four steps as below. Firstly, the CFD simulation is performed to obtain the averaged flow field, with a conventional RANS method. Followed that, the noise source fluctuations are generated by the synthetic reconstruction of turbulence. Then, the acoustic perturbation equations, called nonlinear disturbance equation (NLDE), are solved though the NLAS.

Finally, the far-field sound pressure is computed by the FW-H acoustic analogy. Following subsections present the details of the methods.

In order to compute the broad-band sound noise, because of the large computational cost, the parallel computation is implemented in the RANS step, and in the NLAS step. The domain partition was done with the tool package of metis [11].

2.1   Noise Source Computation

Firstly, the standard RANS with k-ϵ model is chosen to model the turbulence in the study. The governing equations of the viscous compressible Navier-Stokes equations of perfect gas are given with index notation as:

$$\frac{\partial Q}{\partial t} + \frac{\partial F_i}{\partial x_i} - \frac{\partial G_i}{\partial x_i} = \dot{S} , \tag{1}$$

where Q is the dependent variable vector; F_i is the inviscid flux vector; G_i is the viscous flux vector; and $\dot{S}$ is the source term vector, equal to zero here. They are given as:

$$Q = \begin{pmatrix} \rho \\ \rho u_j \\ e \end{pmatrix}, F_i = \begin{pmatrix} \rho u_i \\ \rho u_i u_j + p\delta_{ij} \\ u_i(e + p) \end{pmatrix}, G_i = \begin{pmatrix} 0 \\ \tau_{ij} \\ -\theta_i + u_k \tau_{ki} \end{pmatrix},$$

where ρ is the density, e is the total energy, p is the pressure, u_i is the velocity, θ_i is the heat flux, and τ_{ij} is the viscous stress tensor. With linear turbulence models, the dynamic viscosity coefficient μ in the constitutive relationship becomes to $\mu + \mu_t$ and the thermal conductivity k becomes to $k + k_t$.

The two-equation nonlinear (cubic) k-ϵ model is used to obtain Reynolds stresses from the modeled eddy viscosity (μ_t) and the available mean-strain tensor. The model equations are written as:

$$\frac{\partial}{\partial t}(\bar{\rho}\tilde{k}) + \frac{\partial}{\partial x_i}(\bar{\rho}\tilde{u}_i\tilde{k}) = \frac{\partial}{\partial x_i}\left[\left(\mu + \frac{\mu_t}{\sigma_k}\right)\frac{\partial \tilde{k}}{\partial x_j}\right] + P_k - \bar{\rho}\tilde{\epsilon} , \tag{2}$$

$$\frac{\partial}{\partial t}(\bar{\rho}\tilde{\epsilon}) + \frac{\partial}{\partial x_i}(\bar{\rho}\tilde{u}_i\tilde{\epsilon}) = \frac{\partial}{\partial x_i}\left[\left(\mu + \frac{\mu_t}{\sigma_\epsilon}\right)\frac{\partial \tilde{\epsilon}}{\partial x_j}\right] + (C_{\epsilon 1}P_k - C_{\epsilon 1}\bar{\rho}\tilde{\epsilon} + E)T_t^{-1} . \tag{3}$$

Because the flow in the mufflers is entirely low-speed ($M = 0.03$), the preconditioning approach [12] is adopted to overcome the numerical issues encountered by the standard algorithm of compressible flow equations.

Secondly, the synthetic reconstruction of turbulence is used to generate the a full-spectrum noise source from the set of RANS turbulence statistics. This step is important for use with acoustic wave propagation equations solver, either numerical or analytic methods. Details of the synthetic method adopted in the study can be found in [10].

2.2 Noise Propagation Computation

The hybrid CAA approach NLAS, was developed by Batten et al [9, 10], advanced from the derivation of Morris et al [13]. The governing equations are referred to as nonlinear disturbance equations (NLDE), derived from the origninal Navier-Stokes equations (1), by rearranging for fluctuation and mean quantities, written as:

$$\frac{\partial Q'}{\partial t} + \frac{\partial F_i'}{\partial x_i} - \frac{\partial G_i'}{\partial x_i} = -\frac{\partial \overline{Q}}{\partial t} - \frac{\partial \overline{F}_i}{\partial x_i} + \frac{\partial \overline{G}_i}{\partial x_i} , \tag{4}$$

where

$$\overline{Q} = \begin{pmatrix} \overline{\rho} \\ \overline{\rho u_j} \\ \overline{e} \end{pmatrix}, \ \overline{F}_i = \begin{pmatrix} \overline{\rho u_i} \\ \overline{\rho u_i u_j} + \overline{p}\delta_{ij} \\ \overline{u}(\overline{e}+\overline{p}) \end{pmatrix}, \ \overline{G}_i = \begin{pmatrix} 0 \\ \overline{\tau}_{ij} \\ -\overline{\theta}_i + \overline{u}_k\overline{\tau}_{ki} \end{pmatrix},$$

$$Q' = \begin{pmatrix} \rho' \\ \overline{\rho}u_j' + \rho'u_j' \\ e' \end{pmatrix}, \ G_i' = \begin{pmatrix} 0 \\ \tau_{ij}' \\ -\theta_i' + u_k'\overline{\tau}_{ki} + \overline{u}_k\tau_{ki}' \end{pmatrix},$$

$$F_i' = \begin{pmatrix} \overline{\rho}u_i' + \rho'\overline{u}_i \\ \rho'\overline{u}_i\overline{u}_j + \overline{\rho u_i}u_j' + \overline{\rho u_i'}\overline{u}_j + p'\delta_{ij} \\ u_i' + \overline{u}_i(e'+p') \end{pmatrix} + \begin{pmatrix} \rho'u_i' \\ \overline{\rho}u_i'u_j' + \rho'u_i'\overline{u}_j + \rho'\overline{u}_iu_j' + \rho'u_i'u_j' \\ u_i'(e'+p') \end{pmatrix}.$$

Neglecting density fluctuations and taking time averages leads to:

$$\overline{LHS} = \overline{RHS} = \frac{\partial R_i}{\partial x_i} ,$$

where

$$R_i = \begin{pmatrix} 0 \\ \overline{\rho u_i'u_j'} \\ c_p\overline{\rho T'u_i'} + \overline{\rho u_i'u_k'\overline{u}_k} + \frac{1}{2}\overline{\rho u_k'u_k'u_i'} + \overline{u_k'\tau_{ki}} \end{pmatrix}.$$

In above equations, the mean-flow quantities are obtained from the separate solution of the RANS equations (1), and the unknown perturbation quantities are obtained from the time-dependent nonlinear disturbance equations (4). The key step in NLAS is to obtain the unknown perturbation terms in R_i, from the RANS. Once the mean levels and sub-grid sources established at the initial time, by the synthetic reconstruction of turbulence mentioned above, time-dependent computations can then be made to determine the transmitted perturbations about this mean using the above set of disturbance equations (4).

The far-field sound can be computed at the specific observer points using FW-H (Ffowcs Williams-Hawking) acoustic analogy [14], before that, the time-dependent surface data was computed and saved in each NLAS step. In the present study, the sound surface is specified as the whole outlet surface, to compute the radiation to far-field, since the outlet is the only surface where the flow induced noise radiated through. While the sound pressure $p'(t)$ in time domain obtained from FW-H method, the sound pressure level should be given with FFT tools.

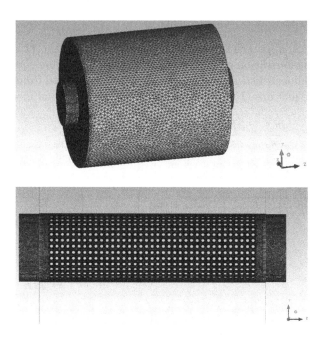

Fig. 1. The grids of (a) muffler-A , exterior view, without perforated wall, (b) muffler-B, interior view to show the perforated wall.

2.3 Physical Model and Boundary Conditions

The two kinds of mufflers is referred to muffler-A, an expanded chamber without a perforated wall, and muffler-B, with the perforated wall along the duct, which are of the common forms of an acoustic filter. The diameter of the ends of both mufflers is 100 mm, and the total length is 400 mm; the chamber is with diameter of 300 mm and length of 350 mm. As to muffler-B, the diameter of the holes of the perforated wall is 5 mm, and the porosity ratio of the wall is 25%. The tetrahedral/pyramid/prism mixed-type unstructured grids were generated. The grids around all of the walls were densified, especially around the holes, because the holes is relatively very small. The models' grids are showed in Fig. 1. The number of total elements of muffler-A is 779784, and that of muffler-B is 10400946, noted that the later is much larger than the former. The flow speed though the muffler is 10 m/s. For muffler-A, cases of flow speed 5 m/s and 8 m/s were also simulated.

The standard atmosphere air state, i.e. pressure 101325 Pa and temperature 298.5 K, was set as the free-stream condition, which was specified at outlet. The inlet turbulent degree is set as 0.01. The non-slip, adiabatic condition were set at solid wall.

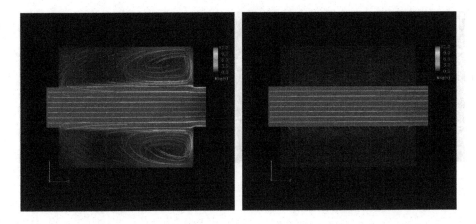

Fig. 2. Streamlines in the middle cross section ($x = 0$ plane) in the mufflers, shaded with the velocity magnitude, (a) muffler-A, (b) muffler-B. Note that the seeds to compute the streamlines is at $z = 0, \pm 0.05, \pm 0.10, \pm 0.15,$ and $- 0.20$.

3   Results and Discussions

In order to distinguish the differences between muffler-A and muffler-B, results are given below with comparisons between them.

3.1   Mean Flow Physics

The mean flow is computed by RANS. The mean flow fields of velocity and pressure are showed in Fig. 2 and Fig. 3, respectively.

In fact, muffler-A is identical to a cavity in a duct, such flow has been studied by many previous works. With respect to muffler-A, the flow from the inlet encounters a backward facing step at first, and a forward facing step before the end of the duct. The flow structures change a lot, that the crosswise flow and refluence happen, influenced by the expanded chamber, or cavity, comparing to the basic pipe flow, which is referred to Poiseuille's flow. On the other hand, to muffler-B, because of the existence of the perforated wall, the influence of the chamber is reduced quite a lot, the flow in the duct remain almost the same as the basic Poiseuille's flow. Fig. 2 reveals these characteristics. It can be seen that flow in the flow field has a discontinuity across the perforated wall in muffler-B, in Fig. 2 and Fig. 3.

Moreover, the velocity profile, Fig. 4, shows this characteristic difference more clearly. Note that, free shear layer dominates the flow around the steps in muffler-A, and the shear layers is quite thick. Furthermore, in the expanded section there exists refluence and large vortex structures, like the flow in a cavity. However, as to muffler-B, the boundary layer dominate the flow around the perforated wall. It looks like that flow in the chamber and flow in the main duct are separated by the perforated wall, that is, fluid in the chamber retains quiescence almost and the flow in the main duct seems to have no change.

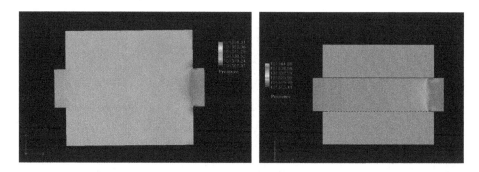

Fig. 3. The mean pressure field in the mufflers (a) muffler-A, (b) muffler-B

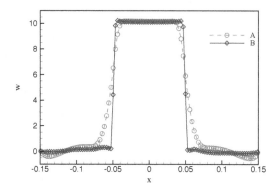

Fig. 4. The velocity profile at the middle cross section ($z = 0$) of muffler-A and muffler-B

3.2   Sound Field at Near-Field

The near-field sound field are shown in Fig. 5 represented by the quantity of acoustic pressure, which is defined as $p' = p(t) - \bar{p}$, where the transient pressure $p(t)$ is computed by NLAS, and $\bar{p}$ is obtained via RANS. It can be observed that, flow in muffler-A, mainly along the down stream of the backward step, generate remarkable fluctuation. Otherwise, in muffler-B, the magnitude of the pressure fluctuations is much smaller, and there is few visible fluctuated regions.

The noise source mechanism of muffler-A can be considered as the result of the shear layer, where vortexes shed from the backward facing step periodically. Moreover, the shear layer and vortexes impinge into the down corner of the expanded chamber in the down stream. Although, such large and strong vortex shedding does not happen in muffler-B because of the existence of the perforated wall, while small eddies can be observed around the perforated wall, holes and the corner region neighbor to the outlet.

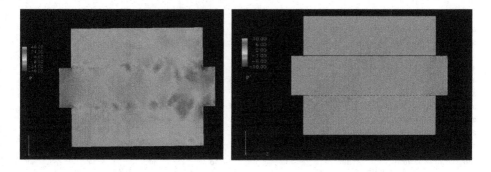

Fig. 5. The acoustic pressure field in the mufflers (a) muffler-A (b) muffler-B

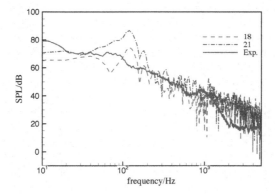

Fig. 6. Sound pressure level spectrum of the pressure fluctuation at the near-field observer point (*Exp.*) in muffler-B, comparing with the simulation results of the observer points (*18* and *21*) close to the measuring point, close to the outlet in the axis

With respect to the muffler with perforated wall, muffler-B, the measurement has been done by the authors. Therefore, results were compared to experimental measured, as presented by Fig. 6, where the 18 and 21 represent the observer points located in the axis, close to the outlet in the simulation, near the experimentally measured observer point. It can be considered that the level and spectrum shape results from the simulation are in well agreement with reality.

3.3   Noise Radiation at Far-Field

The far-field radiation was computed at observer points at a semi-circle about the center of outlet, in order to compute the directivity of the sound radiation from the outlet. The radius of the semi-circle is 1 m, and the points were arranged with equal circumferential interval of 15 degree. The sound pressure level spectrum is showed by Fig. 7, where *SPL* represents sound pressure level. It can be seen

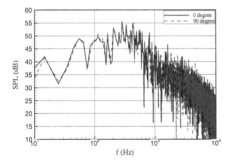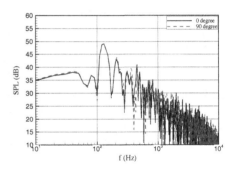

Fig. 7. The sound pressure level spectrum of far-field noise (a) muffler-A, (b) muffler-B, where '0 degree' indicates axial (+z) direction, and '90 degree' indicates the radial (+y) direction

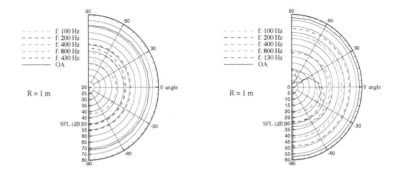

Fig. 8. The directivity of far-field noise, in the specified frequencies and the over-all (OA) value, (a) muffler-A, (b) muffler-B

that, the spectrum of z direction and of y direction coincide mostly. However, the sound pressure level of muffler-A is remarkably larger than that of muffler-B, in most frequency bands.

The far-field noise directivity is shown in Fig. 8. According to Fig. 8, the noise radiated from the mufflers can be regarded as spherical, for the noise level appears equal in almost all directions, except in some single frequencies. Thus, the sound power of the noise radiated from the outlet can be regarded as the sum of the sound power integrated on the unit semi-sphere ($R = 1$ m), so the sound power level may be calculated as $L_w = SPL + 10\lg(2\pi R^2) = SPL + 8.0$ (dB).

Varying the flow speed, the sound pressure level varies. Table. 1 shows results of these cases, with total sound pressure level and sound power level listed. With increase of the flow speed, the noise level increases. The sound power level of muffler-A with flow speed of 10 m/s is 79.6 dB, 14 dB larger than that of

Table 1. The sound power level and sound pressure level of the mufflers

muffler- flow speed (m/s)	A 5	A 8	A 10	B 10
SPL (dB)	59.6	67.9	71.7	57.7
L_w (dB)	67.6	75.9	79.6	65.7

muffler-B with the same flow speed, which is qualitatively correct. Because the experiment is difficult, no quantitive data of noise induced purely by flow has been obtained by the authors.

4   Conclusions

The flow-induced noise of two kinds of the typical mufflers were investigated, by means of numerical simulation, with a sophisticated approach of computational aeroacoustics. The method has advantages in high accuracy and low computation cost in acoustic simulation. Results show good agreement with the practical measurement in quality and quantity. Several conclusions on the mechanisms and characteristics of the flow physics and flow induced noise of mufflers may be drawn as below.

- The main noise generation mechanism of the mufflers is the shear layer and vortex shedding behind the first cavity corner of the expanded chamber.
- The muffler with the perforated wall produces much smaller flow induced noise than that without the wall in the expanded chamber, in that perforated wall reduces the affection of the chamber and suppress flow fluctuation.
- The radiation from the muffler outlet of the flow induced noise presents spheric directivity, for both mufflers.

Acknowledgments. This work was supported by NSFC (No. 11272325) , Knowledge Innovation of Chinese Academy of Sciences (KJCX2-EW-L02-1) and the Knowledge Innovation Program of Institute of Acoustics, Chinese Academy of Sciences, which are gratefully acknowledged by the authors.

References

1. Munjal, M., Krishnan, S., Reddy, M.: Flow-Acoustic Performance of Perforated Element Mufflers with Application to Design. Noise Control Eng. J. 40, 159–167 (1993)
2. Broatch, A., Margot, X., Gil, A., Denia, F.: A CFD Approach to the Computation of the Acoustic Response of Exhaust Mufflers. J. Comput. Acoust. 13, 301–316 (2005)
3. Chen, J., Shi, X.: CFD Numerical Simulation of Exhaust Muffler. In: 2011 Seventh International Conference on Computational Intelligence and Security (CIS), pp. 1438–1441. IEEE (2011)

4. Parsani, M., Ghorbaniasl, G., Lacor, C.: Validation and Application of an High-Order Spectral Difference Method for Flow Induced Noise Simulation. J. Comput. Acoust. 19, 241–268 (2011)
5. Montenegro, G., Onorati, A., Della Torre, A.: The Prediction of Silencer Acoustical Performances by 1d, 1d-3d and Quasi-3d Non-Linear Approaches. Comput. Fluids 71, 208–223 (2012)
6. Lee, J.W., Jang, G.: Topology Design of Reactive Mufflers for Enhancing Their Acoustic Attenuation Performance and Flow Characteristics Simultaneously. Int. J. Numer. Meth. Eng. 91, 552–570 (2012)
7. Tam, C.K.W.: Computational Aeroacoustics - Issues and Methods. AIAA J. 33, 1788–1796 (1995)
8. Wagner, C., Hüttl, T., Sagaut, P. (eds.): Large Eddy Simulation for Acoustics. Cambridge University Press (2007)
9. Batten, P., Goldberg, U., Chakravarthy, S.: Reconstructed Sub-Grid Methods for Acoustics Predictions at All Reynolds Numbers. AIAA-2002-2511 (2002)
10. Batten, P., Ribaldone, E., Casella, M., Chakravarthy, S.: Towards a Generalized Non-Linear Acoustics Solver. AIAA-2004-3001 (2004)
11. Karypis, G.: METIS - Family of Multilevel Partitioning Algorithms (2008), http://glaros.dtc.umn.edu/gkhome/views/metis
12. Weiss, J.M., Smith, W.A.: Preconditioning Applied to Variable and Constant Density Flows. AIAA J. 33, 2050–2057 (1995)
13. Morris, P.J., Long, L.N., Bangalore, A., Wang, Q.: A Parallel Three-Dimensional Computational Aeroacoustics Method Using Nonlinear Disturbance Equations. J. Comput. Phys. 133, 56–74 (1997)
14. Ffowcs Williams, J.E., Hawkings, D.L.: Sound Generation by Turbulence and Surfaces in Arbitrary Motion. Philos. T. Roy. Soc. A 264, 321–342 (1969)

Dynamic Slack Reclamation with EDL Scheduling for Periodic Multimode Real-Time Task*

Huan Hu and Renfa Li

Key Laboratory for Embedded and Network Computing of Hunan Province,
Changsha 410086, China
hn_huhuan@163.com

Abstract. The multiframe task has been considered in dynamic real-time scheduling, its different execution mode optional feature can handle the resource waste caused by pessimistic estimation of the execution requirement. But in runtime, the selection of an instance execution mode with more execution requirement may cause a deadline miss. In this paper, we propose a slack reclamation mechanism of configuring an appropriate execution mode under deadline guarantee. This mechanism is composed of offline phase and online phase. In offline, the initial execution mode of task instances is selected and the static slack is calculated. In online, on the basis of EDL scheduling list, mode upgrade list and actual execution requirement of the instance, the slack is assigned to the instance with the highest value of the r/R in *Slack available zone*. Our simulation shows that this scheme can obtain a better result of the accured reward when the task's BCET is greater than 40% of its WCET.

Keywords: real-time, multiframe, slack reclamation, reward.

1   Introduction

In real-time system, the reward-based scheduling is always referred to the dynamic real-time scheduling [1] and its corresponding task model. The dynamic real-time scheduling is more flexible than traditional static scheduling, and it has certain response ability to the actual execution requirement of the task. In the framework of this scheduling, some task models have been introduced. The imprecise computation model [2] is a common technique, in which each task is composed of a mandatory part and an optional part. The former ensures the basic requirement, and the latter is executed selectively to improve the task execution result, the more time optional part executes, the better quality of the result (the higher the reward) is. The IRIS[3] model allows task to get increasing reward with increasing service, a task executes for as long as the scheduler allows it to. The technique based on these task models make use of the task model characteristics, efficiently utilize the slack to make most critical task schedulable and the total value maximum. In addition to the imprecise computation

---

* This work was supported in part by the NSFC (Grant No.61202102, 61173036), Department of Science & Technology of Hunan Province, China (Grant No. 2011GK3131), and Department of Education of Hunan Province(Grant No.CX2011B137).

K. Li et al. (Eds.): ParCFD 2013, CCIS 405, pp. 287–300, 2014.

and IRIS model, Mok and Chen proposed a multiframe task model[4], presented a task instance sequence with different execution time which reduced the constraint of the periodic task model with only one execution mode proposed by Liu and Layland [5]. This model has not yet been considered in dynamic real-time scheduling framework in previous work. Applying multiframe task model to dynamic real-time scheduling system, we focus on how to utilize the slack based on the features of this task model efficiently.

Most of the prior work on the slack reclamation are based on their respective task model. [6] proposed an IRIS real-time composite task model, which was composed by a set of different reward assigned dependent component task. If there had not enough time to schedule all the component tasks of the composite task, those component tasks having the least impact on the total reward of the composite task would not be scheduled. This policy just clipped the less reward component task when the system is overloaded, without considering how to utilize the remainder slack to contribute a better execution result efficiently. [7] proposed a 'design-to-time' task model, which is generated based on mandatory and available optional parts of the imprecise computation model. If there is some unused capacity, the 'design-to-time' task will be allocated by the feedback scheduling when its dispatch period arrives, the situation of low resource utilization will be eased up. Whereas there is a problem that the variation of the actual schedulability boundary (ASB) will result in deadline miss of the task. In [8] an Incremental Server (INCA) is proposed based on algorithm AP(k), when there are some slacks in schedule, the INCA invokes AP(k) and computes the set of optional parts chosen for execution. But as the complexity of the algorithm AP(k) is rather high, in general, the value of the k is set $k \leq 2$, it means that just only two tasks can execute their option parts at most when some slacks exist.

In this paper, we propose a new slack reclamation scheme for multiframe task model in dynamic real-time scheduling. The multiframe in this paper is no longer a static instance sequence with different execution time. We define that each task has different optional execution mode with corresponding reward value and can be configured any one of these modes, which is called multimode real-time task. With respect to the task instance execution mode choice, [9] proposed an efficient method to prevent the explosive growth of state combination in a time interval. On this basis, we will set reward value as a pruning condition, and give the instance initial execute mode selection in a hyper-period.

Our research mainly focuses on the problem of using the unused slack by the multimode model features efficiently. The rest of this paper is organized as follows: Section 2 defines the task model and provides a motivational example for this work. Our proposed mechanism will be presented in Section 3. Simulations used to evaluate the performance of our proposed mechanism are shown in Section 4. Section 5 gives a conclusion.

Nomenclature

Timer: the instant of instance has been completed

R: instance mode upgrade additional resources requirement

r: instance reward increment by the mode upgrade

r/R: r ratio to R

2   Task Model and Motivational Example

2.1   Task Model

In the system, each periodic task τ_i with m_i execution modes is characterized by the following tuple: $\{\omega_i, E_i, D_i, P_i\}$ for $i = 1, \cdots, n$. ω_i is the reward sequence, presented as $\omega_i = \{\omega_{i,1}, \omega_{i,2}, \cdots, \omega_{i,m_i}\}$, each kind mode is assigned to a certain reward value, a mode has larger reward value and more execution requirement if it has a higher mode grade. And $E_i = \{E_{i,1}, E_{i,2}, \cdots, E_{i,m_i}\}$, E_i is execution requirement sequence, with each execution mode has corresponding execution requirement. D_i denotes relative deadline, and P_i represents period. We assume that $P_i = D_i$ in this model. Supposing that all task first initial time is time 0, and when all the task instances select their lowest grade mode, the task sets are EDF schedulable, namely, $\sum_{i=1}^{n} E_{i,1} / P_i \leq 1$ [10]. The scheduling goal is that the multimode task set can be scheduled in the hyper-period, and the total accrued reward value of all task instances, $\sum_{i=1}^{n} \sum_{1}^{N_i} \sum_{j=1}^{m_i} s_{i,j} \cdot \omega_{i,j}$ is maximized. $s_{i,j} \in (0,1)$ represents the jth model of a task is selected or not, N_i denotes task τ_i instance number in a hyper-period. The notation f_{i,φ_i^k} is used to represent the kth instance of task τ_i in a hyper-period, where $\varphi_i^k \in (1, \cdots, m_i)$ represents the mode selection of the f_{i,φ_i^k}.

2.2   Motivational Example

As shown in Fig. 1, there are two periodic multimode tasks, one has 1 mode when the other has 2. In a hyper-period, the task τ_1 has 4 instances, and τ_2 has 3 instances. It's supposed that the feasible instance mode selection has been obtained, all the instances of the task τ_1 and τ_2 are respectively configured mode 1 initially. The task set composed by these two tasks is scheduled by two scheduling schemes, EDF [5] and EDL [11] which regard the deadline as priority. EDF schedules periodic task as soon as possible, whereas EDL schedules periodic task as late as possible. As shown in Fig.1, static EDF and EDL method all have one unit time slack, but the slack distributions of them are different. Supposing that the *actual execution time* AET of the task τ_1 in the mode 1 has only one unit time, then f_{2,φ_2^1} can be upgraded to mode 2, namely $\varphi_2^1 = 2$, after the completion of f_{1,φ_1^1}, EDL scheduling can produce a better

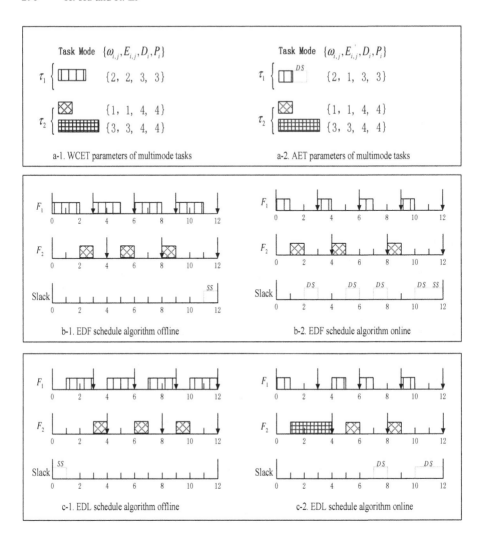

Fig. 1. Compare slack utilization between EDF and EDL

result, the reason is that the task instance utilizes static slack SS and dynamic slack DS more efficiently, when f_{1,φ_1^1} shifts forward, SS is transferred to f_{2,φ_2^1}, meanwhile, the remaining one unit time DS of f_{1,φ_1^1} also is used by f_{2,φ_2^1}, which contributes the f_{2,φ_2^1} upgrade to mode 2.

From the above motivational example, we are considering how to utilize slack efficiently, which have a strong impact on the value of accured reward. However, the EDL scheduling is not an optimal scheme when different reward values are assigned to the task instances. It is not optimal that the instance's slacks are simply transferred to next instance in the scheduling list for the objective function we have defined.

3   Slack Reclamation

3.1   Offline Phase

Supposing that we have already obtained the instances' execution mode selection, which satisfies the accured reward optima. In order to have a more convenient formulation, the notation J_i is used to present the ith instance in EDL scheduling list.

With respect to calculation of SS_i for each instance J_i in EDL scheduling list, a method proposed in [12] can be applied. We assume that the static slack SS_i belongs to instance J_i, and these static slacks will be reallocated in online phase, combining the dynamic slack DS_i.

3.2   Online Phase

The online phase of the mechanism should be built on the offline phase, which has two essential elements: the instance with configured execution mode and the static slack with distribution message and size information.

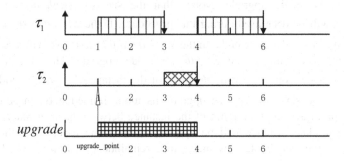

Fig. 2. Upgrade point setting example

3.2.1   Establish Upgrade List

As the scheduling point of instance is determined by the EDL scheduling algorithm, we can set these points as the reference of the upgrade point, and establish a upgrade list for instance in EDL scheduling list. The thought is same to Zero-slack instant in [13]. An example is shown in Fig. 2.

3.2.2   Slack Reclamation Scheme

Based on the mode upgrade list presented above, the procedure of the slack reclamation process becomes very simple. Noting that the case in Fig. 1(c-2) just transfers slacks one instance by another in EDL scheduling list. In this procedure, once the successive instance can use this slack to upgrade mode, the slack is assigned to this instance. Such an approach may cause less valuable instance to occupy too much resources. So a rational scheme is proposed in this section.

Available slack: the slack can be utilized by instance

Slack available zone: the zone of slack that can be utilized by any instance when the slack shifts back along the sequence of the instance in EDL scheduling list

What we concern the most is when any instance has the opportunity to upgrade mode. The instances in the range of the slack's *Slack available zone* will be considered, it means that the slack can assign to a different instance with different reward contribution. The process of this scheme is: the completion instant of instance J_i is denoted as Timer. For the interval between the Timer and the scheduling point of the successive instance J_{i+1} in EDL scheduling list, [Timer, Timer+ $DS_i + SS_{i+1}$], we will determine whether upgrade point of J_{i+1} is in this interval or not. If it is, the '$DS_i + SS_{i+1}$' is set as *Available slack* of the instance J_{i+1}. This *Available slack* will be transferred one instance by another in *Slack available zone*, which can be considered as the source slack for successive instances. During the procedure of the transferring, the *Available slack* for the subsequent instance will be calculated, if the instance *Available slack* plus its static slack can contribute its mode upgrade. We will calculate the instance additional resources requirement(R), reward increment(r) and reward increment ratio to the extra resources requirement(r/R), incurred by the mode upgrade. Notice that the size of *Available slack* of the instance J_{i+1} will be decreased during this procedure. If the *Available slack* becomes zero, the *Slack available zone* ends. In the *Slack available zone*, we will search for the candidate instance with the largest r/R for mode upgrade. Then the R value of candidate instance from the *Available slack* of the instance J_{i+1} will be added to the candidate's static slack rather than upgrade its mode immediately. In addition, the scheduling point and upgrade point of the instance between head of *Slack available zone* and candidate instance will be updated at the same time. After the slack is assigned to the candidate instance, the remainder *Available slack* of the instance J_{i+1} still satisfies its requirement of mode upgrade. This case should be considered. So the pseudo-code is as follows:

```
when completion of one instance J_i
if any upgrade point of J_i in the [Timer,Timer+ DS_i + SS_{i+1} ]
   calculate the  Available slack of J_{i+1}
  while not end of  Slack available zone
     calculate instance's  R, r, r/R
    mark J_candidate with largest  r/R
  endwhile
  if  J_candidate  •  J_{i+1}
    update J_candidate static slack, adding J_candidate 's  R
```

update scheduling point of $J_{i+1} \sim J_{candidate-1}$, shifting

forward $J_{candidate}$'s R

update upgrade point of $J_{i+1} \sim J_{candidate-1}$

endif

if any upgrade point of J_{i+1} in the [Timer, Timer+ $DS_i + SS_{i+1}$]

       update J_{i+1} mode

endif

endif

update scheduling point of J_{i+1}, start to execute J_{i+1}

We will illustrate with an example how the above scheme to reclaim the slack with selection. The task set is shown in Fig. 3, the task τ_1 has 2 optional modes and 3 optional modes are assigned to task τ_2, τ_3. We will take a fragment of the scheduling to show the mechanism of the scheme. The step 'Initial' in Fig. 4 is the initial state of the EDL scheduling list(the initial mode is shown in Table 1), when the instance f_{2,φ_2^1} has completed, the Timer is 10.2, there is a slack interval in[10.2, 18], obviously, the upgrade point of the instance f_{1,φ_1^2} in this interval, so we will invoke the process of selection(step 1 in Fig. 4). The *Slack available zone* is [10.2, 31], and the calculation results of the selection is shown in Table 2. The instance f_{1,φ_1^2} has the highest r/R, so this slack is assigned to f_{1,φ_1^2}, then upgrade f_{1,φ_1^2} (Step 2 in Fig. 4), and update its new scheduling point(Step 3in Fig. 4). The next stage is to execute f_{1,φ_1^2},

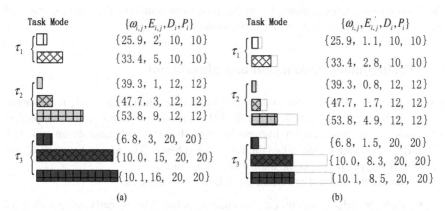

Fig. 3. Task set for illustration (a)WCET parameters of tasks, (b)AET parameters of tasks

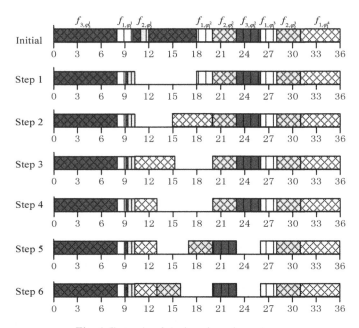

Fig. 4. Example of slack reclamation scheme

the interval[13,18], then we will start the process of selection again (step 4 in Fig. 4). The *Slack available zone* is [13, 31], the calculation results of the selection is shown in Table 3, because of the instance f_{1,φ_1^3} has the highest r/R, the f_{1,φ_1^3}'s R from f_{2,φ_2^2}'s *Available slack* will be assigned to f_{1,φ_1^3}, the instance f_{2,φ_2^2} and f_{3,φ_3^2} shift forward f_{1,φ_1^3}'s R 3 units time(step5 in Fig. 4), the scheduling point of f_{2,φ_2^2} will be updated(step 6 in Fig. 4), and then the execution of the successive instance will be manipulated in the same manner. From the above illustration of the example, we can obtain a better results from the scheme with selection strategy.

4   Performance Evaluation and Simulation

In this paper, we will conduct our experiment to evaluate the slack reclamation scheme. At first , the task sets depicted in [14] are modified in order to be compatible to the task characteristic in our framework. And then we will generate an task sets randomly, as to evaluate the adaptability of our scheme. The accured reward of the task set in the hyper-period is the main evaluation criteria.

We compare the accured reward of the following techniques:

● EDF_NoSelect: where the instance is scheduled as early as possible in offline phase. And the slack is transferred one instance by another with no selection.

Table 1. Instances' initial mode configured

φ_i^k	φ_3^1	φ_1^1	φ_2^1	φ_1^2	φ_2^2	φ_3^2	φ_1^3	φ_2^3	φ_1^4
Initial mode	2	1	1	1	2	1	1	2	2
E_{i,φ_i^k}	15	2	1	2	3	3	2	3	5

Table 2. When Timer = 10.2

	f_{1,φ_1^2}	f_{2,φ_2^2}	f_{3,φ_3^2}	f_{1,φ_1^3}	f_{2,φ_2^3}	f_{1,φ_1^4}
Available slack	7.8	7.8	3	3	3	1
R	3	6	0	3	0	0
r	7.5	6.1	0	7.5	0	0
r/R	2.5	1.0	0	2.5	0	0

Table 3. When Timer = 13

	f_{2,φ_2^2}	f_{3,φ_3^2}	f_{1,φ_1^3}	f_{2,φ_2^2}	f_{1,φ_1^4}	f_{2,φ_2^4}
Available slack	7	3	3	3	1	0
R	6	0	3	0	0	0
r	6.1	0	7.5	0	0	0
r/R	1.0	0	2.5	0	0	0

- EDL_NoSelect: where the instance is scheduled as late as possible in offline phase. And the slack is transferred one instance by another with no selection.
- EDL_Select: where the instance is scheduled as late as possible in offline phase. And the slack is assigned to instance with selection.

4.1   Special Task Set

The task sets in [14] are the imprecise computation model, and their execution requirement includes a mandatory and an optional part, $E_i = m_i + o_i$. It is supposed that the execution requirement of the lowest grade mode is m_i (in [14]), and the higher grade mode execution requirement is the sum of m_i and a random value which is less than o_i. Then the reward value assignment is same to the original task sets, which consider exponential, logarithmic, and linear reward function respectively. The task sets parameters have been modified as shown in TABLE 4. m_i (in this paper) denotes the mode number of the task τ_i and the E_i is the execution requirement sequence,

Table 4. Task set for experiment

ID	1	2	3	4	5	6	7	8	9	10	11
P_i	20	30	40	60	60	80	90	120	240	270	2160
m_i	3	3	2	2	1	2	3	2	3	3	3
E_i	{2, 5, 10}	{5, 15, 18}	{2, 5}	{1, 2}	{2 }	{5, 12}	{7, 12, 18}	{8, 15}	{15, 30, 38}	{40, 52, 60}	{180, 240, 300}

where $\sum_{i=1}^{11} E_{i,1}/P_i = 0.8676 < 1$, which satisfies the constraint condition in our task model. The notation $E_{i,j}$, $j \in [1, m_i]$, is considered as the *worst case execute time* (WCET) of the instance which is configured in mode j. To obtain the AET of the instance, we generate varying AET by varying the *best case execution time* (BCET) of a task as a percentage of its WCET. The execution time is generated by a Gaussian distribution with mean, μ = (WCET+BCET)/2 and a standard deviation, δ^2 = 0.1. The AET of the tasks is limited in the range of [BCET, WCET], and the BCET is varied from 10% to 100% in steps of 10%. Experiments are performed on task sets with different reward function assignment as depicted in [14], and we repeat 100 times experiment on the task sets with the same reward function assignment. For every reward function assignment, the experiment is repeated 100 times. The average accured reward of the task sets in a hyper-period is our result, which is shown in Fig.5.

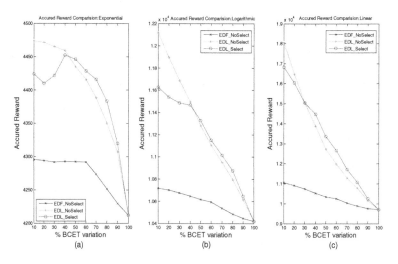

Fig. 5. Comparison of accured reward of the special task sets with different reward functions (a) exponential,(b)logarithmic,(c)linear

Fig. 5 shows the accured reward in hyper-period of the same task sets with different reward function. The results show that EDL scheduling can obtain more opportunities for instance mode upgrade and acquire more reward value. The reason is that the static slack of EDF scheduling cannot be utilized efficiently, and the dynamic slack of the instance adjacent to the static slack also is wasted. When BCET is equal to 10% of the WCET, all the instances have more chances for mode upgrade, EDL scheduling can utilize both the static and dynamic slack, so the differences are obvious. Whereas, with the BCET increasing, the number of Available slacks also decreases asymptotically. Finally, when the BCET is identical to WCET, the accured reward of three schemes is identical. In order to evaluate the performance difference between EDL_Select and EDL_NoSelect schemes, the accured reward under EDL_Select will be better than the one under the EDL_NoSelect scheme, when the BCET is larger than 40% of the WCET. When BCET is equal to 10 percent of the WCET, the number of slacks increases, the scheme with selection characteristic will incur that only the instance Available slack is assigned to can upgrade mode, but under no selection characteristic scheme, both the Available slack original owner (instance) and assigned instance can upgrade their modes. So EDL_Select will have a bad result. In the case of the exponential reward function, the reward differences between different modes of the same task are very small, so the excessive selection will aggravate this difference shown in Fig. 5(a).

4.2   Random Task Set

In our simulation process, we consider a random task set, each containing up to 20 generated tasks. Tasks are assigned a random period, WCET, and mode number in the range [10, 125], $[1, P_i]$ and [2,4]respectively. And the task set must satisfy the constraint of minimum utilization $\sum_{i=1}^{n} E_{i,1}/P_i \leq 1$, which is the admission control of the task set. The reward assignment of the task set can be any of the reward function:exponential, logarithmic, or linear. The AET of the task generated is same to description in part A, the AET varied by the task's BCET. Experiments were performed on task set with varying processor minimum utilization as the task set admission control. Except of the accured reward in the hyper-period of the task set, the idle remainder of the resource will also be considered. And the task set are scheduling under three different schemes.

The task sets in the Fig. 5-7 are with the constraint of the minimum utilization less than 0.4,0.6 and 0.8. Fig. 5(a)-7(a) are the accured reward comparison and Fig. 5(b)-7(b) are the idle remainder comparison with different minimum utilization constraint. Fig. 5(b)-7(b) show that the task sets can efficiently utilize the resource under the EDL_NoSelect and EDL_Select schemes. Whereas the task sets under EDF_NoSelect scheme, the resource wast is relatively serious. When the BCET identical to the WCET, the idle remainder are identical from different schemes, the value is the number of the total static slack.

298   H. Hu and R. Li

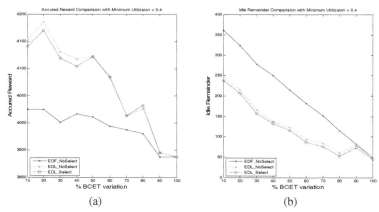

(a)　(b)

Fig. 6. Comparison of accured reward and idle remainder of the random task sets with minimum utilization < 0.4

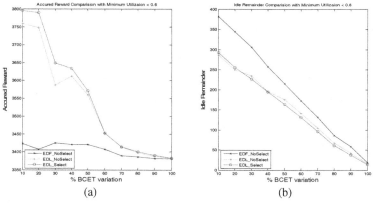

(a)　(b)

Fig. 7. Comparison of accured reward and idle remainder of the random task sets with minimum utilization < 0.6

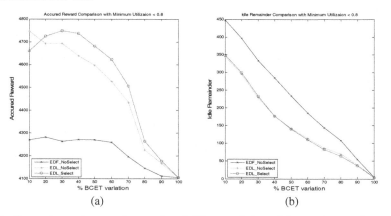

(a)　(b)

Fig. 8. Comparison of accured reward and idle remainder of the random task sets with minimum utilization < 0.8

From the Fig. 5(a)-7(a) showing, when the minimum utilization < 0.4, the accured reward under EDL_Select is not best all the time, because the opportunities of the mode upgrade for instances become more, an addictive selection operation will decrease these opportunities. Compare the different minimum utilization constraint performance, the higher constraint, the better performance from the scheme with selection, the reason is that there are relative limit opportunities for mode upgrade, so the scheme with selection features will be more effective to reclaim slacks.

5   Conclusion

In this paper, we propose a multimode task model for periodic task, which is applied to the dynamic real-time scheduling system. On the basis of the selectivity of the task execution mode and the variation of the actual execution requirement, we propose a slack allocation and reclamation scheme with the goal of maximizing the accured reward of the task set. This scheme avoids resources wasting of the EDF scheduling with slack postposition and the random behavior of the EDL scheduling which transfers slack to next instance without any selection. The results of our experiments show that our method can obtain a better result of the accured reward when the task's BCET is larger than 40% of its WCET.

References

1. Lu, C.Y.: Feedback control real-time scheduling, Phd thesis, School of Engineering and Applied Science, Virginia University (2001)
2. Lin, K.-J., Natarajan, S., Liu, J.W.S.: Imprecise result: Utilizing Partial Computations in Real-Time systems, In: 8th IEEE Symposium on Real-Time Systems, pp. 210–217 (1987)
3. Dey, J.K., Kurose, J.F., Towsley, D., Krishna, C.M., Girkar, M.: Efficient On-Line Processor Scheduling for a Class of IRIS (Increasing Reward with Increasing Service) Real-Time Tasks. In: Proc. of ACM SIGMETRICS Conf. Measurement and Modeling of Computer Systems, pp. 217–228 (1993)
4. Mok, A.K., Chen, D.: A multiframe model for real-time tasks. IEEE Trans. Software. Eng. 23(10), 635–645 (1997)
5. Liu, C.L., Layland, J.W.: Scheduling algorithms for multiprogramming in a hard-real-time environment. Journal of the ACM 20(1), 46–61 (1973)
6. Cam, H.: An on-line scheduling policy for IRIS real-time composite tasks. The Journal of Systems and Software 52, 25–32 (2000)
7. Feiler, P.H., Walker, J.J.: Adaptive feedback scheduling of incremental and design-to-time tasks. In: Proceedings of the 23rd International Conference on Software Engineering, pp. 318–326 (2001)
8. Mejia-Alvarez, P., Melhem, R., Mosse, D.: An incremental approach to scheduling during overloads in real-time systems. In: Proceedings of the IEEE Real-Time Systems Symposium (2000)
9. Moyo, N.T., Nicollet, E., Lafaye, F., Moy, C.: On schedulability analysis of non-cyclic generalized multiframe tasks. In: ECRTS, pp. 271–278 (2010)

10. Liu, J.W.: Real-Time Systems. Prentice Hall, Upper Saddle River (2000)
11. Chetto, H., Chetto, M.: Some result of the Earliest Deadline Scheduling Algorithm. IEEE Trans. on Soft. Eng. 15(10), 1261–1269 (1989)
12. Park, T., Kim, S.: Dynamic scheduling algorithm and its schedulability analysis for certifiable dual-criticality systems. In: 11th International Conference on Embedded Software, pp. 253–262. ACM (2011)
13. Niz, D., Lakshmanan, K., Rajkumar, R.: On the scheduling of mixed-criticality realtime task sets. In: Proceedings of the Real-Time Systems Symposium, pp. 291–300. IEEE Computer Society Press (2009)
14. Aydin, H., Melhem, R., Mossé, D., Alvarez, P.M.: Optimal Reward-Based Scheduling for Periodic Real-Time Tasks. IEEE Transactions on Computers 50(2), 111–130 (2001)

Modeling of the Pressure Variation during the Inflation Process of Unsteady Time-Pressure Dispensing

Yu Ji[1], Jiankui Chen[1,2,*], Haichen Qin[1], and Yaogen Wu[3]

[1] State Key Laboratory of Digital Manufacturing Equipment and Technology, Huazhong University of Science and Technology, Wuhan, 430074, P.R. China
[2] Dongguan- Huazhong University of Science and Technology Manufacturing Engineering Institute, Dongguan, 523808, P.R. China
[3] FSPG HI-TECH CO., LTD., Foshan, 528000, P.R. China

Abstract. Time-pressure dispensing has been widely applied in IC packaging industry as a core technology. In such a process, the fluid is forced out of the syringe by the pressurized air and the model of the pressure in the syringe is difficult to develop because of the compressibility of the air. This paper presents the development of a model describing how the volume average pressure in the syringe varies by defining the unsteady time-pressure dispensing inflation process as a thermal insulation process for container of fixed volume. Additionally, a finite element simulation is performed to test the model by using FLUENT. The results show that the analytical solution and the simulation results match well. We also find that the face average pressure of a certain cross section varies greatly in the process, which implies the pressure in the syringe fluctuates very much.

Keywords: unsteady, thermal insulation, inflation process, pressure model, simulation.

1   Introduction

Fluid dispensing is a process by which fluid is transferred to substrates in a controlled way so that the chips can be fixed, protected and the electric connected. Fluid dispensing is regarded as one of the core technologies in the electronic packaging process and has been widely applied to advanced integrated circuit packing process (AICE) and surface mount technology (SMT). Time-pressure dispensing, rotary screw dispensing, positive displacement piston dispensing and jet dispensing are the four most important kinds of fluid dispensing, among the above-mentioned four kinds, time-pressure dispensing is still the one that has been most widely used in microelectronic packaging because of its low cost, easy maintenance and wide applicability.[1, 2] In a time-pressure dispensing system, the air pressure is adjusted by pressure regulation device and when the solenoid valve is opened, the air enters into the syringe through the tube and then the fluid is forced through and out of the needle, forming points or lines on the substrate. The typical time-pressure system is

---

* Corresponding author.

K. Li et al. (Eds.): ParCFD 2013, CCIS 405, pp. 301–310, 2014.
© Springer-Verlag Berlin Heidelberg 2014

showed in Fig.1, and the part in the dotted box is what we mainly discuss in this paper.

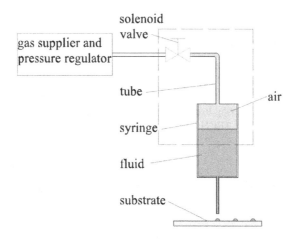

Fig. 1. The schematic of the time-pressure dispensing system

Time-pressure dispensing can be classified into two types according to whether the pressure in the syringe is stable or not: steady time-pressure dispensing and unsteady time-pressure dispensing. In an unsteady time-pressure dispensing, the pressure in the syringe is still increasing and haven't reached a stable status, i.e., the solenoid valve opens not long enough for the pressure in the syringe to become stable. In such a process, the volume of the fluid drop and the consistency of the volume are two most important indexes to evaluate the performance of the process. The volume of the fluid would be affected by time, pressure, the characteristic of fluid, temperature and the size of needle, however, time and pressure are of most importance. Other indexes unchanged, the volume of the fluid would increase with the passing of time or the increase of pressure. The development of a model describing the volume average pressure in the syringe is of significant value due to the increasing demand for more precise dispensing control. Using a first-order system, Chen X.B. set up a model of the time-pressure dispensing and gave a detailed analysis of the volume and the form of the fluid after experiments [3-6]. Zhao Y.X. developed a effective model to describe the whole dispensing system by taking into account of nonlinear flow passing through the valve, attenuation and time delay in the pneumatic lines, syringe chamber dynamics and fluid flow dynamics [7]. Chen C.P. developed a non-Newtonian fluid flow rate model by using a similar first-order system to represent the pneumatic system [8, 9]. However, an analytical model is needed to find out what parameters exactly are affecting the pressure in the syringe, so that the process can be controlled more precisely.

This paper presents the modeling of the inflation process of the unsteady time-pressure dispensing. By analyzing the process and treating it as a thermal insulation process for container of fixed volume, a model is developed to describe how the volume average pressure in the syringe varies with the passing of time. Furthermore, simulation has been performed to validate the model and the results are compared with that of the model.

2   Modeling and Simulation

2.1   Modeling of the Pressure in the Syringe

Usually, in an unsteady time-pressure dispensing system, the pressure regulating valve is pre-adjusted to set the pressure at a stable value, and then solenoid valve is used to control the duration that the air pressure acts on the fluid. The pressure in the syringe hasn't reached a stable status here and we try to develop a physical model of the pressure through analyzing the inflation process.

Since the duration of the inflation process is only tens of millisecond, we can assume that there is no heat exchange between the air in the syringe and the outside, and we can also assume that the drawdown of the liquid level in one dispensing cycle could be ignored because the weight of the fluid extruded in one dispensing cycle is just a few microliters. Based on these assumptions, an unsteady time-pressure dispensing inflation process could be treated as a thermal insulation process for a container of fixed volume.

According to the First Law of Thermodynamics, the energy equation can be expressed as

$$dq + dw = de \ . \tag{1}$$

Where dq is an incremental amount of heat added to the system by the surroundings, de is the change of internal energy, dw denotes the work done on the system by the surroundings.

The ideal gas equation of state

$$m = pV \ / \ RT \ . \tag{2}$$

The continuity equation

$$q_m = \rho uA = C \ . \tag{3}$$

The momentum equation

$$F = m \frac{du}{dt} \ . \tag{4}$$

Since the process is thermal insulation process for container of fixed volume, we have $dq = 0$, $dw = 0$, and with equations above, one has[10]:

When $p_2 / p_1 \leq b$, the inflation time it needed for the pressure in the syringe to rise from p_{20} to p_2 can be calculated as

$$t = 1.4603 \frac{V}{ks\sqrt{RT_1}} (\frac{p_2}{p_1} - \frac{p_{20}}{p_1}) \ . \tag{5}$$

$$p_2 = p_{20} + \frac{ks\sqrt{RT_1}}{V} \frac{p_1 t}{1.4603} \tag{6}$$

When $1 \geq p_2 / p_1 > b$, the mass flow rate can be expressed as

$$q_m = q_m^* \sqrt{1 - (\frac{p_2 / p_1 - b}{1 - b})^2} \qquad 1 \geq p_2 / p_1 > b \ . \tag{7}$$

The inflation time it needed for the pressure in the syringe to rise from P_{20} to P_2 can be calculated as

$$t = 1.4603 \frac{V(1-b)}{ks\sqrt{RT_1}} [\sin^{-1}(\frac{p_2 / p_1 - b}{1 - b}) - \sin^{-1}(\frac{p_{20} / p_1 - b}{1 - b})] \ . \tag{8}$$

$$p_2 = p_1 \{(1-b)\sin[\frac{ks\sqrt{RT_1}}{1.4603V(1-b)} t + \sin^{-1}(\frac{p_{20} / p_1 - b}{1 - b})] + b\} \tag{9}$$

We can identify how the pressure varies in the process with (6) and (9).

2.2   Simulation

We use FLUENT to perform the simulation to validate the model that has been developed. Fig.2 (a) shows the the simplified model for the inflation process, the air flows through the air inlet, the tube and into the syringe, and the pressure in the syringe increases accordingly. Fig.2 (b) shows the model we set up in ICEMCFD, half of the section along the axis is drew, 'in', 'wall', 'axis' are showed, too. Table 1 shows the boundary conditions set in FLUENT and Table 2 shows the parameters. The transient solver of FLUENT is used for simulating the process, time step is set to be 0.001s and there are 50 time steps in all.

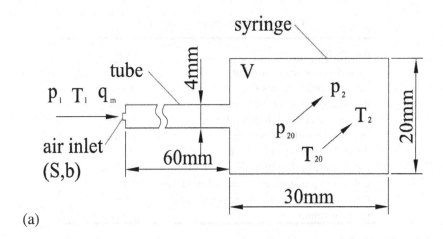

(a)

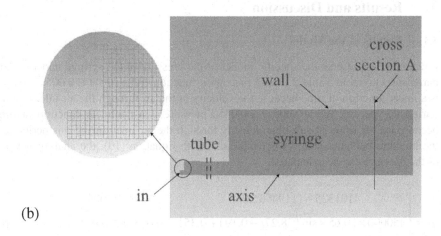

(b)

Fig. 2. (a) The schematic of the inflation process (b) The model drew in ICEMCFD

Table 1. The boundary conditions in the simulation

Zone name	type
in	pressure-inlet
axis	axis
wall	wall
fluid	interior

Table 2. The parameters of the model

parameters	values
the environmental temperature	300K
the environmental pressure	101325Pa
the inner diameter of the syringe	20mm
the altitude of the syringe left for air	30mm
the inner diameter of the tube	4mm
the initial pressure in the syringe	101325Pa
the pressure of the inflow air	450000Pa
the critical pressure ratio of the solenoid valve	0.35
the net sectional area of the solenoid valve	$0.9mm^2$
the total volume	$10178.8\ mm^3$

3   Results and Discussion

3.1   Results of the Model

Equation (10) presents the specific model of the pressure in the syringe under certain parameters given in Table 2. It is a piecewise function. When $0 \leq t \leq 0.005$, pressure is a linear function of time because the velocity of the air through the air inlet is sonic during this period. When $0.005 < t \leq 0.045$, pressure is a nonlinear function of time because the air flows at subsonic velocity through the air inlet during this period and the pressure becomes stable when $0.045 < t$. With Equation (10), the analytical value of the pressure can be calculated.

$$p = \begin{cases} 101325 + 11194936.03t & 0 \leq t \leq 0.005 \\ 450000 \times \left(0.65 \times \sin\left(38.27t - 0.19 \right) + 0.35 \right) & 0.005 < t \leq 0.045 \\ 450000 & 0.045 < t \end{cases} \quad . \tag{10}$$

3.2   Results of the Simulation

From the simulation, we can get the data shown in Table 3. It mainly records the value of two kinds of pressure: PA is the volume average pressure in the syringe which is described by the model developed in this paper. PB is the face average pressure of cross section A(Fig. 2 (b)). These data are obtained from FLUENT. The distribution of pressure in the syringe at different times is shown in Fig. 3, which suggests that the distribution of pressure changes from time to time so that the value of the pressure of a same cross section of the syringe varies greatly.

Table 3. The volume average pressure in the syringe P_A and the face average pressure of cross section A in the syringe P_B of every time step

t(s)	P_A(Pa)	P_B (Pa)	t(s)	P_A(Pa)	P_B (Pa)
0	101325	101325	0.026	372415.03	411721.72
0.001	115912.77	332303.34	0.027	384556.44	431446.97
0.002	122773.09	207327.86	0.028	395639.58	427478.63
0.003	134561.62	103017.28	0.029	405100.48	419011.66
0.004	145484.89	222723.52	0.03	407990.77	394662.41
0.005	156469.95	312964.78	0.031	419996.03	439467.31
0.006	166866.42	295559.81	0.032	422415.03	439653
0.007	171921.82	314145.69	0.033	424556.44	442936.03
0.008	182136.4	164486.31	0.034	425639.58	442298.94
0.009	193751.59	211924.66	0.035	425100.48	439947.66
0.01	199753.61	98220.625	0.036	440118.77	439636.69
0.011	212853.18	218608.47	0.037	440131.64	440797.47
0.012	222754.32	278377.56	0.038	439476.95	439436.34
0.013	237296.19	306619.03	0.039	438614.72	437420.78
0.014	250080.16	358331.31	0.04	438229.43	437396.75
0.015	259665.66	309570.31	0.041	438059.15	438168.38
0.016	265860.02	390720.69	0.042	437581.44	437056.03
0.017	277414.31	396223.25	0.043	437135.6	435536.69
0.018	294272.61	227434.5	0.044	437163.61	435938.84
0.019	301110.88	226780.16	0.045	437502.59	437239.78
0.02	311048.26	311429.03	0.046	437598.44	437084.6
0.021	318630.98	292691.91	0.047	437613.73	436369.69
0.022	331091.11	320553.78	0.048	438015.6	437120.63
0.023	342082.65	329439.09	0.049	438630.39	438458.75
0.024	351468.52	413368.84	0.05	438971.41	438671.97
0.025	360649.51	401529.66			

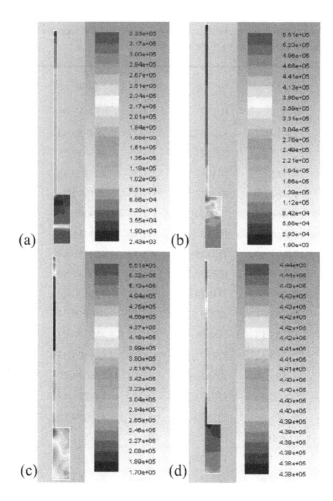

Fig. 3. The pressure contour of the syringe at different time: (a) t=0.001s, (b) t=0.01s, (c) t=0.03s, (d) t=0.05s

3.3   Discussion

Fig.4 (a) presents the comparison of the analytical results and the results of the simulation. It shows that the model that has been developed in this paper described the average pressure in the syringe well. The pressure rise rate does not match the model perfectly because of the uneven distribution of the pressure. In this situation, the pressure near the inlet may be very low and it makes the inflation at that moment still sonic. Because the analytical model doesn't take pressure loss into account, the stable pressure is less than 450000Pa. Fig.4 (b) shows that the average pressure of the certain cross session of the syringe varies a lot in the inflation process and this phenomenon tells us that there is no regularity in the fluctuation of the pressure in the syringe in this process.

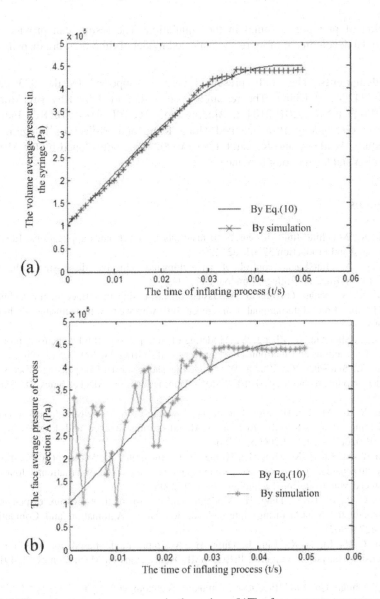

Fig. 4. (a)The volume average pressure in the syringe (b)The face average pressure of certain cross session of the syringe

4   Conclusion

This paper develops a model describing the variation of the volume average pressure by treating the inflation process as a thermal insulation process for container of fixed volume. The model has been validated by FEM simulation and the uneven distribution of pressure is found in the simulation. The results can provide some insight to the development of more sophisticated model of time-pressure dispensing.

Acknowledgments. The study presented here is supported by the 973 project (2009CB724204) of China. The research is also supported by Key Breakthrough Project (Project No. : 20100104-4, Bidding No. : TC10BH07-4) of Key Field for Bidding in Guangdong Province and Hong Kong and Project of Integration of Manufacture, Academy and Research (2010A090200012) developed by the Ministry of Education and Guangdong Province.

References

1. Bush, R.: Matching fluid dispensers to materials for electronics applications. Electronic Packaging and Production 37, 61–62 (1997)
2. Razban, A.: Intelligent control of an automated adhesive dispensing cell. Ph.D. dissertation. Imperial College, London, UK (1993)
3. Chen, X., Schoenau, G., Zhang, W.: Issues on dispensing in surface mount technology (SMT). In: Proc. International Conference on Advanced Manufacturing Technology (1999)
4. Chen, X., Shoenau, G., Zhang, W.: Modeling of time-pressure fluid dispensing processes. IEEE Transactions on Electronics Packaging Manufacturing 23, 300–305 (2000)
5. Chen, X., Schoenau, G., Zhang, W.: Modeling and control of dispensing processes for surface mount technology. IEEE/ASME Transactions on Mechatronics 10, 326–334 (2005)
6. Chen, X., Li, M., Ke, H.: Modeling of the flow rate in the dispensing-based process for fabricating tissue scaffolds. Journal of Manufacturing Science and Engineering 130, 020601.020601-024503.020605 (2008)
7. Zhao, Y.-X., Li, H.-X., Ding, H., Xiong, Y.-L.: Integrated modelling of a time-pressure fluid dispensing system for electronics manufacturing. The International Journal of Advanced Manufacturing Technology 26, 1–9 (2005)
8. Chen, C.-P., Li, H.-X., Ding, H.: Modeling and control of time-pressure dispensing for semiconductor manufacturing. International Journal of Automation and Computing 4, 422–427 (2007)
9. Chen, C.-P., Li, H.-X., Liu, J., Ding, H.: A simple model-based approach for fluid dispensing analysis and control. IEEE/ASME Transactions on Mechatronics 12, 491–503 (2007)
10. SMC (China) Co. Ltd.: Practical Pneumatic Technology(现代实用气动技术). China Machine Press, P.R. China (2004)

Performance Analysis and Optimization of PalaBos on Petascale Sunway BlueLight MPP Supercomputer

Min Tian[1,2], Weidong Gu[1,2], Jingshan Pan[2], and Meng Guo[1]

[1] Shandong Provincial Key Laboratory of Computer Network,
Shandong Computer Science Center, No19 Keyuan Road, Jinan, P.R. China
[2] National Supercomputer Center in Jinan, Jinan High-tech. Development Zone,
1768 Xinluo Ave., Jinan, P.R. China
{tianm,guwd,panjsh,guomeng}@sdas.org

Abstract. We present some results concerning computational performances of the open source CFD software PalaBos, in terms of scalability and efficiency, on the petascale Sunway BlueLight MPP system. Based on the numerical simulated program of 3D cavity lid driven flow, the optimization methods in I/O, communication, memory access, etc, are applied in debugging and optimization of the parallel MPI program. Experimental results of large scalar parallel computing of 3D cavity lid driven flow show that, the parallel strategy and optimization methods are correct and efficient. The parallel implementation scheme is very useful and can shorten the computing time explicitly.

Keywords: Palabos, petascale computing, 3D cavity lid driven flow, parallel I/O.

1 Introduction

As the importance of High Performance Computing (HPC) in Computational Fluid Dynamics (CFD) is increasing, industries are more and more interested in its applications. However, the cost of license of commercial CFD codes is proportional to the number of cores used and thus running large simulations in parallel on multi-core systems maybe economically prohibitive unless open source software like Palabos is used [1,2].

By studying computational performance requirement of industrial interest, we found that the performance capabilities of high-end computational resources have increased rapidly over recent years [3]. In particular, the introduction of petascale systems has brought with it massive increases in the number of processing units, where it is now common to have many tens of thousands of cores available for users' codes[4,5]. This development raises a number of significant challenges for the parallel performance of CFD applications.

As a software tool for classical CFD, particle-based models and complex physical interaction, Palabos offers a powerful environment for fluid flow simulations based on the lattice Boltzmann method (LBM) [6-8]. Thanks to its explicit formulation and exact advection operator, the lattice Boltzmann scheme involves only a very limited

K. Li et al. (Eds.): ParCFD 2013, CCIS 405, pp. 311–320, 2014.

amount of floating points operations per computational node. Furthermore, the lattice Boltzmann method is particularly well suited for computations on a parallel architecture, even with a slow interconnection network.

Recently, new parallelization and optimization techniques have been introduced to Palabos in order to address these challenges at several different stages of the calculation [9-12]. The introduction of LBM method and the hardware architecture are described in Section 2. In Section 3 we introduce the optimization methods in I/O, communication, memory access, etc. In Section 4, the impacts on scalability and performance of these new features have been analyzed on a range of prototype petascale system.

2   Method and Implementation

2.1   The Lattice Boltzmann Method

The lattice Boltzmann method is a numerical technique for the simulation of fluid dynamics, and in particular the numerical solution of the incompressible, time-dependent Navier-Stokes equation [13,14]. Its strength is however based on the ability to easily represent complex physical phenomena, ranging from multiphase flows to chemical interactions between the fluid and the borders. Indeed, the method finds its origin in a molecular description of a fluid and can directly incorporate physical terms stemming from knowledge of the interaction between molecules. For this reason, it is an invaluable tool in fundamental research, as it keeps the cycle between the elaboration of a theory and the formulation of a corresponding numerical model short.

Compared to other CFD approaches, lattice Boltzmann might at first sight seem quite resource consuming: the discrete probability distribution functions described by the model require more memory for their storage than the hydrodynamic variables used by a classical solver of the Navier-Stokes equation (nine real valued quantities per node against three for 2D incompressible solvers).

This is however never a real issue, especially on modern computers, and it is greatly compensated by an outstanding computational efficiency [15]. Thanks to its explicit formulation and exact advection operator, the lattice Boltzmann scheme involves only a very limited amount of floating points operations per computational node. Furthermore, thanks to the locality of its algorithm, the lattice Boltzmann method is particularly well suited for computations on various parallel architectures, even on those with slow interconnection networks.

The lattice Boltzmann method is a very successful tool for modeling fluids in science and engineering [16]. Compared to traditional Navier Stokes solvers, the method allows an easy implementation of complex boundary conditions and due to the high degree of locality of the algorithm—is well suited for the implementation on parallel supercomputers.

2.2   3D Lid-Driven Cavity Flow

The lid-driven cavity problem has long been used a test or validation case for new codes or new solution methods [17]. Lid-driven cavity flows are not only technologically important, but also they are of great scientific interest. These flows display many kinds of fluid mechanical phenomena, including corner eddies, Taylor-Gortler-like (TGL) vortices, transition, turbulence and so on. Simple geometrical settings and easily posed boundary conditions have made cavity flows become popular test cases for computational schemes.

As a classic benchmark, the 2D lid-driven cavity flows have been extensively studied with numerical methods. However, the pioneering experimental work of Koseff & Street and coworkers in the early 1980s clearly showed that cavity flows were inherently 3D in nature [18, 19]. With the increase of computing capability in recent years, the 3D lid-driven cavity problems have matured as a standard Re-dependent benchmark. This problem has been solved as both a laminar flow and a turbulent flow, and many different numerical techniques have been used to compute these solutions. Since this case has been solved many times, there is a great deal of data to compare with [20].

2.3   Hardware Architecture

Sunway BlueLight MPP Supercomputer is the first publicly announced PFLOPS supercomputer using ShenWei processors solely developed by the People's Republic of China. It ranked #2 in the 2011 China HPC Top100, #14 on the November 2011 TOP500 list, and #39 on the November 2011 Green500 List. The machine was installed at National Supercomputing Jinan Center in September 2011 and was developed by National Parallel Computer Engineering Technology Research Center and supported by Technology Department 863 project.

The water-cooled 9-rack system has 8704 ShenWei SW1600 processors (For the Top100 run 8575 CPUs were used, at 975 MHz each) organized as 34 super nodes (each consisting of 256 compute nodes), 150 TB main memory, 2 PB external storage, peak performance of 1.07016 PFLOPS, sustained performance of 795.9 TFLOPS, LINPACK efficiency 74.37%, and total power consumption 1074 kW. Operating at 1.1 GHz, ShenWei SW1600 achieves 140 GFLOPS floating point performance from its 16 cores RISC architecture.

3   Debugging and Optimization Techniques

Several advances have been made to Palabos that have improved significantly the petascale performance of the code. These optimizations have focused on the I/O, communication, memory access, etc.

3.1   Parallel I/O

The development of efficient methods for reading data from disk and writing data to disk has become increasingly important for codes that use high-end computing resources. This issue is particularly relevant for Palabos, as the large-scale simulations that the code undertakes often require the input of huge datasets from disk and the output of large amounts of results files. For example, a dataset comprised of 1 billion cells requires around 70G Bytes of storage. Moreover, the outputs are usually required at frequent intervals in order to model a system that changes with time.

Parallel I/O strategies have been introduced to the code in order to address the I/O bottleneck associated with runs on large numbers of cores. Both serial and parallel I/O implementations are designed to use a common interface. The parallel I/O is fully implemented for reading of preprocessor and partitioned output and restart files.

Generally, the common function for file output in Palabos is *saveBinaryBlock*, which needs to be distributed in different data collection on the compute nodes to the master node, and file operations shall be conducted by the master node.

Since the Sunway BlueLight MPP Supercomputer is equipped with a parallel file system and parallel I/O is supported, we use *parallelIO:: save* and *load* to save and load the data file. That is,

- In the main program, ensure *parallelIO* to be *true*:
  global::IOpolicy().activateParallelIO(true);
- The following two functions are used for outputting and loading respectively:

parallelIO::save(lattice, "lattice"); parallelIO::load("lattice", lattice);

By doing so, file operations speed will be accelerated so greatly that more than 2 hours of work, can be reduced to 1 minute or so.

3.2   Cache Optimization

The solution of the lattice Boltzmann equation model is a long time of iteration step process, which needs thousands or even millions of steps generally. Considering the stability of the machine, it is a very important and necessary measure to "Writing" breakpoint data to ensure the continuity of iterations. Due to writing files is a costly operation in the underlying operating system, typically it is proposed to write less as far as possible or at a time write as much as possible in the operating system.

3.3   Compiler Optimization

Different from compiler directives of GCC compiler, the ShenWei SW1600 processor on Sunway BlueLight MPP Supercomputer has its own compiler directives. To obtain the optimal performance, we have taken the following measures in *Makefile*:

- Set the optimization flags on: *optimize = true*
- Set the MPI_parallel mode on: *MPIparallel=true*

- Set the SW1600 compiler to use: *serialCC=swCC*
- Set the SW1600 compiler to use with MPI parallelism: *parallelCXX=mpiswCC*
- Set the optimization compiler flags: *optimFlags=-O3 -OPT:Ofast*
- ......

4   Performance Tests and Results

In this section our performance and scalability tests were performed for parallel simulation of 3D lid-driven cubic cavity flows on Sunway BlueLight MPP Supercomputer.

4.1   Benchmark Test

In the diagonally lid-driven 3D cavity flow, the top-lid is driven with constant velocity in a direction parallel to one of the two diagonals. This benchmark is challenging because of the velocity discontinuities on corner nodes.

In this benchmark test, we set the velocity in lattice units u=0.01, the Reynolds number Re=1, the lattice resolution N=400, the relaxation frequency omega=0.08, the extent of the system lx=1, ly=1, lz=1; the grid spacing deltaX dx=0.0025 and the time step deltaT dt=2.5e-05.

Fig. 1. Illustration of the velocity field for uz

In Fig.1 and Fig.2 we show illustrations of the velocity field for uz and uNrom.

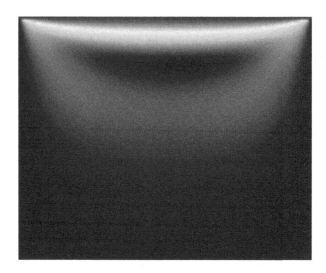

Fig. 2. Illustration of the velocity field for uNorm

4.2   The Speed of Execution

In the following we select different number of cores on Sunway BlueLight MPP Supercomputer to compare the values of iterations and mega site updates per second, the results are shown in Table 1.

The speed of execution of the application is measured in "mega site updates per second", Msu for short. Large number of Msu means high performance, while small number of Msu means low performance.

Table 1. Comparison of Iterations and Mega site updates per second with different number of cores

Number of Cores	Iterations	Mega site updates per second
1024	4764	442.135
512	2382	264.062
256	1191	144.646
128	596	78.2313
64	298	43.5745
32	149	23.1192
16	74	12.0334

Fig.3 and Fig.4 graphically illustrate the change of 3D lid-driven cubic cavity flows on Sunway BlueLight MPP Supercomputer with our optimization strategy.

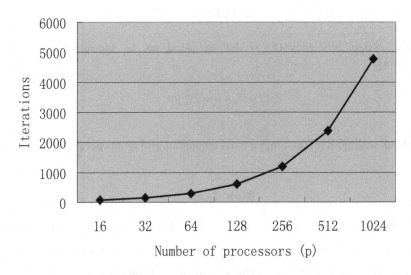

Fig. 3. Illustration of different number of processors for iterations

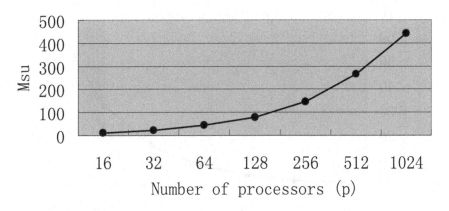

Fig. 4. Illustration of different number of processors for Msus

4.3   Performance Analysis

The standard definition of the speedup factor or strong scalability (which assumes a fixed problem size), $S(p)$, where p is the number of processors, was used to asses the parallel performance.

$S(p)$ is defined as the ratio of a execution time using s processors system (T_s) to an execution time using a multi processor system with p processors (T_p):

$$S(p)= T_s/T_p. \tag{1}$$

The system efficiency (E) is defined based on the speedup factor from the following:

$$E= Ts/(T_p\times p)= S(p)/p. \tag{2}$$

Weak scaling, $W(p)$, assumes a fixed amount of grid points per processor is defined as:

$$W(p)= T_p/T_s. \tag{3}$$

Here we take $s=16$, $p=16, 32, 64,$, 1024. The obtained results are presented in Fig. 5 and Fig. 6, which show speedup ratios of 3D lid-driven cubic cavity flows on Sunway BlueLight MPP Supercomputer with different processors.

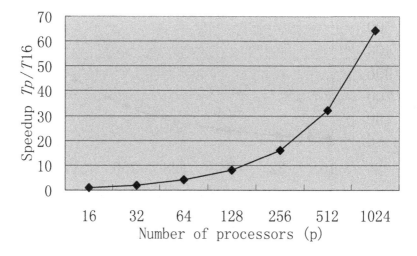

Fig. 5. Performance comparison for different number of processors

It is worth to note that increasing number of cores does not always result in better performance. This is because the Palabos tries to divide the grid fairly between the available cores. When the ratio grid size to processor slower greatly, the performance start decreasing.

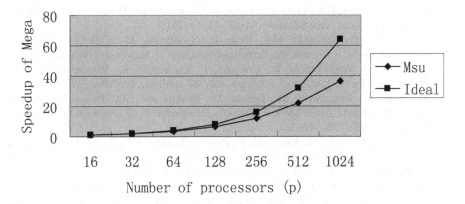

Fig. 6. Performance comparison for Mega with different number of processors

5   Conclusion

Palabos is highly portable, powerful, scalable CFD software for its all mentioned models and ingredients are parallelized with MPI for shared-memory and distributed-memory platforms. Several optimization strategies in I/O, communication, memory access, etc, are supposed for debugging and optimization of the parallel MPI program in this paper. Based on the large scalar parallel numerical computing of 3D cavity lid driven flow, experimental results show that, our parallel strategy and optimization methods have greatly shorten the computing time of the parallel implementation scheme.

Acknowledgements. This work has been financially supported by the National Key Technology Research and Development Program of the Ministry of Science and Technology of China (Grant No. 2012BAH09B03) and the National Science and Technology Major Project of Jinan, China (Grant No. 201208282).

References

1. Geller, S., Krafczyk, M., Tolke, J., Turek, S., Hron, J.: Benchmark computations based on lattice-Boltzmann, finite element and finite volume methods for laminar flows. Computer & Fluids 35, 888–897 (2006)
2. Palabos - CFD complex physics, http://www.palabos.org/
3. Stahl, B., Bastien, C., Jonas, L.: Measurements of wall shear stress with the lattice Boltzmann method and staircase approximation of boundaries. Computers and Fluids 39(9), 1625–1633 (2010)
4. Degruyter, W., Burgisser, A., Bachmann, O., Malaspinas, O.: Synchrotron X-ray microtomography and lattice Boltzmann simulations of gas flow through volcanic pumices. Geosphere 6(5), 470–481 (2010)

5. Blazewicz, M., Kurowski, K., Ludwiczak, B., Napierala, K.: High performance computing on new accelerated hardware architectures. Computational Methods in Science and Technology Special Issue SEMI-ANNUAL. 71–79 (2010)
6. Piotrowski, Z.P., Kurowski, M.J., Rosa, B., Ziemianski, M.Z.: EULAG Model for Multiscale Flows – Towards the Petascale Generation of Mesoscale Numerical Weather Prediction. In: Wyrzykowski, R., Dongarra, J., Karczewski, K., Wasniewski, J. (eds.) PPAM 2009, Part II. LNCS, vol. 6068, pp. 380–387. Springer, Heidelberg (2010)
7. Kurowski, K., Kulczewski, M., Dobski, M.: Parallel and GPU Based Strategies for Selected CFD and Climate Modeling Models. Information Technologies in Environmental Engineering 3(8), 735–747 (2011)
8. Kopta, P., Kulczewski, M., Kurowski, K., Piontek, T., Gepner, P., Puchalski, M., Komasa, J.: Parallel application benchmarks and performance evaluation of the Intel Xeon 7500 family processors. Procedia Computer Science 4, 372–381 (2011)
9. White, A.T., Chong, C.K.: Rotational invariance in the three-dimensional lattice Boltzmann method is dependent on the choice of lattice. Journal of Computational Physics 230(16), 6367–6378 (2011)
10. Parmigiani, A.: Lattice Boltzmann Calculations of Reactive Multiphase Flows in Porous Media. Universite de Geneve (2011)
11. Parmigiani, A., Huber, C., Bachmann, O., Bastien, C.: Porescale mass and reactant transport in multiphase porous media flows. Journal of Fluid Mechanics 686, 40–76 (2011)
12. Duda, A., Koza, Z., Matyka, M.: Hydraulic tortuosity in arbitrary porous media flow. Phys. Rev. E. 84(3), 36319 (2011)
13. Xu, H., Malaspinas, O., Sagaut, P.: Sensitivity analysis and determination of free relaxation parameters for the weakly-compressible MRT - LBM schemes. Journal of Computational Physics 231(21), 7335–7367 (2012)
14. Domitner, J., Holzl, C., Kharicha, A., Wu, M., Ludwig, A., Kohler, M., Ratke, L.: 3D simulation of interdendritic flow through a Al-18wt-Cu structure captured with X-ray microtomography. IOP Conference Series: Materials Science and Engineering 27(1), 12–16 (2012)
15. Lagrava, D., Malaspinas, O., Latt, J., Chopard, B.: Advances in multi-domain lattice Boltzmann grid refinement. Journal of Computational Physics 231(14), 4808–4822 (2012)
16. Palabos LBM Wiki, http://wiki.palabos.org/
17. Malaspinas, O., Sagaud, P.: Consistent subgrid scale modelling for lattice Boltzmann method. Journal of Fluid Mechanics 700, 514–542 (2012)
18. Bielecki, J., Bozek, S., Dutkiewicz, E., Hajduk, R., Jarzyna, J., Lekki, J., Pieprzyca, T., Stachura, Z., Szklarz, Z., Kwiatek, W.M.: Preliminary Investigations of Elemental Content, Microporosity, and Specific Surface Area of Porous Rocks Using PIXE and X-ray Microtomography Techniques. Acta Physica Polonica A 121(2), 474–476 (2012)
19. Wittmann, M., Zeiser, T., Hager, G., Wellein, G.: Comparison of different propagation steps for lattice Boltzmann methods. Computers, Mathematics with Applications 65(6), 924–935 (2012)
20. Malaspinas, O., Sagaud, P.: Consistent subgrid scale modelling for lattice Boltzmann method. Journal of Fluid Mechanics 700, 514–542 (2012)

Recursive Kernighan-Lin Algorithm (RKL) Scheme for Cooperative Road-Side Units in Vehicular Networks

Yao Weihong, Yang Yuehui, and Tan Guozhen

Dalian University of Technology, Department of Computer Science and Technology,
Linggong Road 2, 116024 Dalian, China
{weihongy,gztan}@dlut.edu.cn, hdxs061728@163.com

Abstract. In Vehicular networks, Vehicle-to-roadside (V2R) communications can support a wide range of applications for enhancing transportation efficiency. Through analyzing the difference between the non-cooperative V2R communication and the cooperative V2R communication, we propose a novel scheme called Recursive Kernighan-Lin algorithm (RKL) scheme that rapidly partitions the backbone network into several disjoint cooperative systems (sub-networks). On one hand, the proposed scheme can improve the diversity of information circulating in the network and exploit the data exchange capabilities of the underlying pair-wise V2V content-sharing network with the cooperative V2R communication in the same cooperative systems. On the other hand, the proposed scheme can decrease the cooperative V2R communication costs with the non-cooperative V2R communication among different cooperative systems. Finally, simulation results show how the proposed RKL algorithm improves the performance between 23.3% and 35.5% (in terms of the average payoff per roadside unit) compared to the non-cooperative scheme.

Keywords: vehicular networks, non-cooperative V2R Communication, cooperative V2R communication, the backbone network, KL algorithm.

1 Introduction

Vehicular networks have been envisioned to provide increased convenience and efficiency to drivers, with numerous applications ranging from traffic safety, traffic efficiency to entertainment [1, 2], especially after the advent of IEEE 802.11p and IEEE 1609 standards [3]. Current research trends in vehicular networks have focused on developing applications that can be categorized into two main classes. The first is to improve the safety level on the roads while the second relates to commercial and entertainment services, where the goal is to improve passenger comfort and traffic efficiency. Examples falling in the second category are systems that provide traffic and weather information, gas station or restaurant location, price information, Internet access or music and movie downloads [4]. In order to support different applications, both vehicle-to-roadside (V2R) communications and vehicle-to-vehicle (V2V) communications need to be supported in vehicular networks [5,6]. In V2V communications, on Board Units (OBUs) are mounted

K. Li et al. (Eds.): ParCFD 2013, CCIS 405, pp. 321–331, 2014.

on vehicles to provide wireless communication capability for vehicles. In V2R communications, Roadside Units (RSUs) are installed at interchanges, intersections and other locations to provide wireless interfaces for vehicles within their radio coverage. Meanwhile RSUs are connected with each other by wired links or wireless networks. The network connecting RSUs is denoted as the backbone network.

Existing work has already explored various aspects of V2R and V2V communications. For instance, the authors in [7], study the performance of the IEEE 1609 WAVE and IEEE 802.11p trial standards for vehicular communications. In [8], the authors consider that RSUs are placed at traffic junctions, major highways, and near restaurants, gas stations and various hot spots. It also assumed that RSUs are connected via the internet and that the distance between two consecutive RSUs is between 2 to 3 kilometers. Multiple antenna techniques are proposed in [9] for enhancing the performance of V2R communications. In [10], the authors propose a non-cooperative Bit Torrent-based approach for data distribution between the RSUs and the OBUs of the vehicles as well as a Nash bargaining solution for V2V data exchange. Further, the use of V2V communications and cooperation among sensor-equipped vehicles is studied in [11] for proactive urban data monitoring. The authors in [12] propose a coalitional game theoretic scheme for Vehicle-to-Roadside (V2R) communication in which, by cooperation, the RSUs coordinate different classes of data being transmitted through V2R communication and improve the diversity of information circulating in the network.

In this paper, based on the cooperative protocol in [12], we propose a novel scheme called Recursive Kernighan-Lin algorithm (RKL) scheme that rapidly partitions the backbone network (all RSUs are connected over some wired links or wireless networks.) into several disjoint cooperative systems (sub-networks). On one hand, the cooperative V2R communication is implemented in the same cooperative system to improve the diversity of information circulating in the network as well as exploit the data exchange capabilities of the underlying pair-wise V2V network. On the other hand, in order to control the size of cooperative system for decreasing the cooperation costs, we implement the non-cooperation V2R communication among different cooperative systems.

The rest of this paper is organized as follows. Section 2 presents the non-cooperative V2R communication and the cooperative V2R communication. Section 3 describes the cooperative system model. In section 4, we partition the backbone network with the proposed scheme. Section 5 presents the simulation results. Finally, the conclusions are drawn in Section 6.

2   The Non-cooperative V2R Communication and the Cooperative V2R Communication

Due to the limited communication range of the RSU and the speed of traveling vehicles, a vehicle can keep a short period at a RSU and download a limited number of chunks or packets, e.g., related to a single class of data . In this paper, we consider that each RSU selects only one class of data to transmit, at a time, to the vehicles in a given direction. In the considered network, we assume the presence of a pair-wise V2V content-sharing scheme [1] whereby V2V communication occurs between pairs of vehicles that can meet and exchange their data.

2.1 The Non-cooperative V2R Communication

In a non-cooperative V2R communication scenario, as is often the case, the RSUs cannot estimate the fraction of vehicles that can potentially meet and share content, nor the amount of vehicles moving in their direction, so the RSUs are not aware of the underlying pair-wise V2V content-sharing network. Therefore, in a non-cooperative scenario, it is beneficial for any RSU to transmit the chunks of data c_1 with highest priority for all the vehicles passing by this RSU. In Fig.1, we can see that there is only one class of data in the networks.

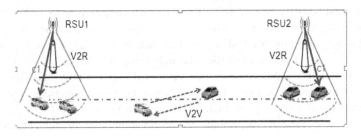

Fig. 1. The non-cooperative V2R communication

2.2 The Cooperative V2R Communication

In the cooperative V2R communication scenario, based on the cooperative protocol, the RSUs can communicate over the backbone network, so they are aware of the underlying pair-wise V2V content-sharing network. As shown in Fig.2, through the communication between RSU1 and RSU2, the RSU1 transmits data c_1 with the highest priority, while the RSU2 selects data c_2 with the second highest priority to transmit. When these vehicles traveling from RSU1 to RSU2 meet those vehicles traveling from RSU2 to RSU1, they can engage in pair-wise V2V content-sharing network and get more data. From Fig.2, we can see two classes of data in the network.

Therefore, the cooperative V2R communication improves the diversity of the data circulating in the network as well as exploits the data exchange capabilities of underlying pair-wise V2V content-sharing. Further, from the vehicles' perspective, all the vehicles moving between the two RSUs will be able to obtain more diverse classes of data without the need for passing by multiple RSUs.

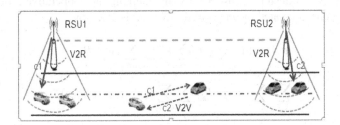

Fig. 2. The cooperative V2R communication

In this paper, we take advantage of the cooperative V2R communication to improve the efficiency of data transmission in the networks. What's more, considering the inherent costs that need to be paid by the RSUs when acting cooperatively in the meantime, we partition the backbone network into a number of small disjoint cooperative systems to control the size of each cooperative system for decreasing the cooperation cost.

3   The Cooperative System Model

As is discussed in [12], we consider a backbone network consisting of N RSUs, and let N denote the set of all RSUs. The set $C = \{c_1, ..., c_L\}$ represents the classes of data that can be distributed by any RSU $i \in N$. For each class of data c_i, a corresponding priority is $0 \le w_{c_i} \le 1$ which quantifies the importance of this data for the network, and $w_{c_1} > w_{c_2} > ... > w_{c_L}$. We consider that each RSU selects only one class of data from C to transmit, at a time, to the vehicles in given directions. Further, we let K_{ij} denote the set of vehicles moving from any RSU $i \in N$ towards RSU $j \in N, i \ne j$, and $|K_{ij}|$ represents the average number of vehicles belonging to K_{ij}. When a vehicle k passes by an RSU $i \in N$, it connects to this RSU a period of time and downloads an average of $P_{k,i}$ chunks of data. In the network, given an entity which takes care of collecting payments on behalf of the RSUs, after passing by its first RSU and prior to meeting its next RSU (or exiting the network), every vehicle k is charged by the entity. The fee charged is proportional to the total amount of data that this vehicle carries at that time. This amount of money is then distributed by the entity to the RSU(s) that transmitted the data obtained by vehicle k.

Consequently, in the non-cooperative scenario, the non-cooperative revenue generated by any RSU $i \in N$ can be given by

$$. \quad v(\{i\}) = \beta \cdot \sum_{j \in N, j \ne i} \sum_{k \in K_{ij}} (w_{c_1} \cdot P_{k,i}) \tag{1}$$

Where β is the price charged by the entity for one unit of effective data.

In the cooperative scenario, for any cooperative system $S \subset N$, $|S|$ is the number of all RSUs in S. Note that, for the vehicles moving from RSU $i \in S$ to any RSU $j \in N \setminus S$ outside the S, RSU $i \in S$ will always select the class of data c_1 with the highest priority to transmit. Consequently, by adopting the cooperative protocol [12], the total revenue generated by any coalition $S \subset N$ is given by

$$u(S) = \max_{B_S \in \mathbf{B}_S} (\beta \sum_{i \in S} (\sum_{\substack{j \in N \setminus S \\ j \ne i}} \sum_{k \in K_{ij}} (w_{c_1} \cdot P_{k,i}) +$$

$$\sum_{\substack{j \in S \\ j \ne i}} \sum_{k \in K_{ij} \setminus M_i} (w_{b_i} \cdot P_{k,i}) \sum_{\substack{j \in S \\ j \ne i}} \sum_{k \in M_i} ((w_{b_i} + w_{b_j}) \cdot P_{k,i}))) \tag{2}$$

Where $b_i \in C$ represents the class of data selected by an RSU $i \in S$, is the set $B_S = \{b_1, ..., b_{|S|}\}$ containing classes of data selected by all RSU $\in S$ and $\mathbf{B}_S$ represents the set of all such set B_S for cooperative system S. Further, we denote M_{ij} as the set of vehicles travelling from RSU$i \in N$ toward RSU$j \in N, i \neq j$ which meet those vehicles travelling from RSU j toward RSU i, and $|M_{ij}|$ as the number of vehicles in M_{ij}. Based on the model in [13], $|M_{ij}| = m_{ij} = \delta^{d_{ij}} \cdot \min(|K_{ij}|, |K_{ji}|)$, where δ is the fraction of vehicles that can meet when the distance d_{ij} between RSU i and RSU j is 1km away.

Although the cooperative V2R communication can improve the functionality of networks and achieve additional revenue for RSUs, these gains can be lessened by inherent costs that need to be paid by the RSUs when acting cooperatively. To describe the cost, we consider a cost function that varies linearly with the links in the cooperative system [14].

$$c(S) = \begin{cases} \alpha * (|S| - 1) & |S| \geq 1 \\ 0 & otherwise \end{cases} \tag{3}$$

Where α represents a pricing factor for cost function.

Finally, the revenue that the cooperative system S can receive is given by

$$v(S) = u(S) - c(S) \tag{4}$$

Thus, through an individually rational egalitarian rule, we distribute the revenue of S to any RSU$i \in S$.

$$\phi_i(S) = \frac{1}{|S|}(v(S) - \sum_{j \in S} v(\{j\})) + v(\{i\}) \tag{5}$$

4   Recursive Kernighan-Lin Algorithm(RKL) Scheme

Due to the disadvantages of cooperative systems, i.e., some inherent costs for cooperative V2R communication, it is necessary to control the size of each cooperative system for decreasing the cooperative costs. In this paper, we propose an improved scheme based on Kernighan-Lin algorithm [15] that called RKL scheme. In this scheme, the backbone network is partitioned into a number of small cooperative systems $N = \{S_1, ..., S_m\}, S_i \cap S_j \neq \phi, i \neq j$. In the cooperative system, we take advantage of the cooperative V2R communication for improving the diversity of information circulating in the network as well as exploiting the data exchange capabilities of the underlying pair-wise V2V networks. Meanwhile, in order to decrease the negative effects of the cooperative V2R communication, we implement the non-cooperative V2R communication among some different cooperative systems. Then, the efficiency of data transmission in vehicular networks will be increased. Following, we present the RKL scheme based on the system model in section 3.

4.1   The Undirected Graph Abstracted from the Backbone Network

Given an undirected graph $G = (V, E)$, it represents the whole backbone network. Define $V = \{v_1, ..., v_N\}$, and the value of v_i is the revenue received by RSU $i \in N$, i.e. $v_i = \phi_i$. Let E represent the set of $|M_{ij}|$. The value of edge e_{ij} is the number of vehicles travelling from RSU $i \in N$ toward RSU $j \in N, i \neq j$ which meet those vehicles travelling from RSU j toward RSU i, i.e., $e_{ij} = e_{ji} = |M_{ij}| = |M_{ji}|$, and $e_{ij} = 0$ when $i = j$.

4.2   Recursive Kernighan-Lin Algorithm

Through analysing the cooperative V2R communication scenario, the probability of implementing cooperative V2R communication between RSUi and RSUj is closely associated with the value of $|M_{ij}|$. In other words, the bigger the value $|M_{ij}|$, the greater chance of cooperative V2R communication has. Conversely, the chance of cooperative V2R communication reduces with the decreasing value of $|M_{ij}|$.

At first, we improve KL algorithm that can obtain a two-way partition with minimum average edge-cost, i.e., the average cost of edge between two zones is the smallest.

Define1. Let A, B be any arbitrary 2-way partition, $A \subseteq V, B \subseteq V, |A| = |B|$. Let us define for each $a \in A$, an external cost E_a by

$$E_a = \sum_{v \in B} e_{av} ,\qquad(6)$$

With $num(E_a)$ the number of edges $e_{av}, v \in B$, and an internal cost I_a by

$$I_a = \sum_{v \in A} e_{av} ,\qquad(7)$$

With $num(I_a)$ the number of edges $e_{av}, v \in A$ Similarly, we define $E_b, I_b, num(E_b)$, $num(I_b)$ for each $b \in B$. Meanwhile, let Z be the total cost of all edges connecting A with B,

$$Z = \sum_{v \in A \wedge v' \in B} e_{vv'} ,\qquad(8)$$

and $num(Z)$ the number of edges $e_{vv'}, v \in A \wedge v' \in B$. Finally, let

$$D_v = E_v - I_v ,\qquad(9)$$

for all $v \in A \cup B$ which is the difference between external and internal costs and

$$num(D_v) = num(E_v) - num(I_v) ,\qquad(10)$$

which is the difference between the number of external edges and the number of external edges.

Define 2(average gain of edges): Consider any $a \in A, b \in B$. If a and b are exchanged, the average gain of each edge connecting A and B (i.e., the average reduction in cost) is

$$g_{ab} = (Z / num(Z)) - ((Z - D_a - D_b + 2 \cdot e_{ab}) / (num(Z) - num(D_a) - num(D_b) + 2)) . (11)$$

According to Kernighan-Lin Algorithm, the parameter decides whether exchange two related members a and b or not is changed for g_{ab}. As a result, through the improved Kernighan-Lin Algorithm, a two-way partition with minimum average edge-cost is obtained.

Secondly, based on the improved algorithm presented above, we propose the Recursive Kernighan-Lin Algorithm. In the proposed Recursive Kernighan-Lin Algorithm, there are two phases: parting phase and merging phase. In the parting phase, in the undirected graph G, the set $S_0 = V$ is partitioned into two partition S_1 and S_2 with minimum average edge-cut, so that two members in S_1 and S_2 respectively have the least chance of cooperative V2R communication. Sequentially, S_1 is partitioned into S_3 and S_4, S_2 into S_5 and S_6, ..., until $S_{(n/2)-1}$ into S_{n-1} and S_n. Consequently, set V is partitioned into a number of disjoint set with only one member. In the merging phase, we calculate the revenues of $S_{(n/2)-1}$, S_{n-1} and S_n, i.e., $v(S_n)$, $v(S_{n-1})$ and $v(S_{(n/2)-1})$. If the revenue of $S_{(n/2)-1}$ is smaller than the sum revenues of S_{n-1} and S_n, i.e. $v(S_{(n/2)-1}) < v(S_{n-1}) + v(S_n)$, we store the partition $S_{(n/2)-1} \rightarrow \{S_{n-1}, S_n\}$; on the contrary, we cancel this partition. In the next, we calculate and compare the revenues of $S_{(n/2)-2}$, S_{n-3} and S_{n-2}, then store or cancel the partition $S_{(n/2)-2} \rightarrow \{S_{n-3}, S_2\}$ depending on the previous result. Repeat until store or cancel the partition $S_0 \rightarrow \{S_1, S_2\}$. The detailed description of the proposed RKL Algorithm is shown in Fig 3.

```
1:   The initial partition is Π_initial = {S_0}, store Π_initial;  S_0 = V;  S = S_0;
       compute v(S);
2:   If |S| = 1, return v(S);
3:   If |S| > 1, partition S into S_a and S_b, |S_a| = |S_b|, S_a ∩ S_b = ∅, S_a ∪ S_b = S;
4:   repeat
5:       compute D_v and num(D_v) for all v ∈ S, compute Z and num(Z) for
           all edges connecting S_a and S_b;
6:       For i = 1 to |S| / 2 do;
7:           Find a pair of unlocked vertices v_ai ∈ S_a and v_bi ∈ S_b, such that g_i (11) is maximal;
8:           Lock v_ai and v_bi, store the gain g_i, update the D_v, num(D_v) for all unlocked v ∈ S,
               Z and num(Z) for all edges connecting S_a and S_b;
9:       End for;
10:      Find k such that G_k = Σ_{i=1}^{i=k} g_i is maximized;
11:      If G_k > 0 then
12:          Move v_a1, ..., v_ak from S_a to S_b and move v_b1, ..., v_bk from S_b to S_a;
13:      Unlocked all v ∈ S;
14:   Until G_k ≤ 0;
15:   Store the partition S → {S_a, S_b}, compute v(S_a) and v(S_b), set S = S_a,
       go to line2; set S = S_b, go to line2;
16:   If v(S) > v(S_a) + v(S_b), cancel the partition S → {S_a, S_b}, return v(S);
       conversely, return v(S_a) + v(S_b).
```

Fig. 3. Detailed description of the proposed Recursive Kernighan-Lin Algorithm

4.3   Cooperative V2R communication

In *4.2*, we get the final optimized partition $\prod_{final} = \{S_1,...,S_m\}$. Those cooperative systems operate with the cooperative protocol. In order to adapt to any changes that have occurred in the environment, we repeat the proposed algorithm every period of time t . This period of time is determined depending on how rapidly the environment is changing, e.g., for rapidly changing environments t is chosen to have a small value while for static environments it can have a large value.

5   Simulation Results

According to the simulation in [12], we implement the simulation on VC++6.0. We set up the network for simulations as following: consider a backbone network consisted of some RSUs which are randomly deployed in a $3km\times 3km$ square area. For the sake of simplicity, the total number of vehicles initiating from any RSU $i\in N$ in the direction of any other RSU $j\in N, i\neq j$ is considered equal at all directions, i.e., $\left|K_{ij}\right| = \left|K_i\right| \forall j\in N$, $i\neq j$, and $0 < \left|K_i\right| \leq 25$. The average number of chunks of data downloaded by any vehicle k from any RSU $i\in N$ is set to $P_{k,i} = 10 \forall i, k$. There are three classes of data in the network $C = \{c_1, c_2, c_3\}$, with $w_{c_1} = 0.9$, $w_{c_2} = 0.8$ and $w_{c3} = 0.5$. The price factor for the cost function and the price per effective data unit are set to $\alpha = 100$ and $\beta = 1$ respectively, while the fraction of vehicles that can meet between two RSUs is set to $\delta = 0.8$ when the distant of the RSUs is 1km away. In this section, all of the statistical results presented are averaged over the random positions of the RSUs as well as the random traffic pattern.

Fig.3 shows the average payoff achieved per RSU as the number of RSUs in the network increases. In this figure, we compare the performance of the proposed Recursive Kernighan-Lin Algorithm to that of the non-cooperative case. Fig.3 shows that, as the number of RSUs N increases, both of the performances of the proposed Recursive Kernighan-Lin Algorithm scheme and the non-cooperative scheme increase. For the non-cooperative scheme, the increase in the performance of the non-cooperative scheme with the network size is only due to the additional data traffic yielded by the additional RSUs. Comparing with the non-cooperative scheme, the increase in the performance of the proposed Recursive Kernighan-Lin Algorithm scheme with the network size N is also a result of the increased possibility of finding better cooperating partners as the network grows. For the network sizes, a performance advantage compared to the non-cooperative case is maintained by the proposed Recursive Kernighan-Lin Algorithm scheme. This advantage ranges between 23.3% and 35.5% of improvement compared to the average non-cooperative payoff with the number of RSUs from 2 to 15.

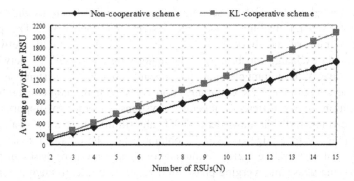

Fig. 4. Average payoff per RSU achieved as the number of RSUs in the network increases

In Fig.4, we show the average payoff achieved per RSU for a network with N =7 RSUs and $\alpha = 10$, as the parameter δ varies. As δ increases, the performance of the proposed Recursive Kernighan-Lin Algorithm scheme increases, while that of the non-cooperative scheme remains constant at all δ. In the non-cooperative scheme, because the RSUs are unaware of the underlying V2V communications network, the performance of the non-cooperative approach is not affected by the variations in δ. On the contrary, for the proposed Recursive Kernighan-Lin Algorithm case, as δ increases, it becomes more beneficial for the RSUs to exploit the pair-wise V2V communications network, so, the performance of average payoff per RSU increases with δ. It can be seen in Figure4, at $\delta = 0$, there is practically no possibility that pair-wise V2V communication takes place, and hence, the performance of the proposed Recursive Kernighan-Lin Algorithm scheme is the same to that of a non-cooperative approach. But, as δ increases, the advantage of the proposed scheme increases and at $\delta = 1$ it reaches up to around 35.8% of improvement relative to the non-cooperative case.

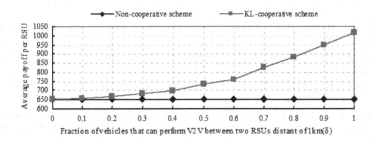

Fig. 5. Average payoff per RSU achieved as value of δ increases

6   Conclusion

In this paper, we have presented advantages and disadvantages of the cooperative V2R communication compared to the non-cooperative V2R communication. Based on the cooperative protocol, we propose a novel scheme called Recursive

Kernighan-Lin algorithm (RKL) scheme that can rapidly partitions the backbone network into several disjoint cooperative systems (sub-networks). The proposed scheme can improve the diversity of information circulating in the network and exploit the data exchange capabilities of the underlying pair-wise V2V network with the cooperative V2R communication in the same cooperative system, as well as decrease the cooperative V2R communication costs with the non-cooperative V2R communication among different cooperative systems. In order to support the RKL scheme, we bring forth the new ideas on KL algorithm, where a two-way partition with minimum average edge-cost can be obtained, i.e., the obtained zones with the least chance of cooperative V2R communication. There are two phases in the RKL scheme: parting phase and merging phase. In the parting phase, through the improved KL algorithm, we partition the backbone network into a number of small disjoint cooperative systems recursively until any cooperative systems contains only one member. In the merging phase, we calculate and compare the revenues of cooperative systems successively to decide whether to store or cancel the related partition. Further, by repeating the proposed RKL algorithm periodically, the RKL scheme can adapt to environmental changes such as a change in the vehicle traffic. Finally, simulation results show how the proposed RKL algorithm improves the performance between 23.3% and 35.5% (in terms of the average payoff per roadside unit) compared to the non-cooperative scheme.

Acknowledgements. This work was supported in part by the National High Technology Research and Development 863 Program of China under Grant no. 2012AA111902, the National Key Technology R&D Program of China under Grant No. 2011BAK02B02, the National Natural Science Foundation of China under Grant No. 60873256, and the Fundamental Research Funds for the Central Universities under Grant No. DUT12JS01.

References

1. Olariu, S., Weigle, M.C.: Vehicular networks: from theory to practice. Chapman & Hall/CRC (2009)
2. Hartenstein, H., Laberteaux, K.P.: A tutorial survey on vehicular ad hoc networks. IEEE Communications Magazine 46(6), 164–171 (2008)
3. Uzcategui, R., Acosta-Marum, G.: WAVE: a tutorial. IEEE Communications Magazine 47(5), 126–133 (2009)
4. Mershad, K., Artail, H.: Using RSUs as delegates for pervasive access to services in vehicle ad hoc networks. In: 17th IEEE International Conference on ICT, pp. 790–797 (2010)
5. Chang, C.J., Cheng, R.G., Shih, H.T., Chen, Y.S.: Maximum freedom last scheduling algorithm for downlinks of DSRC networks. IEEE Transactions on Intelligent Transportation Systems 8(2), 223–232 (2007)
6. Peng, Y., Abichar, Z., Chang, J.M.: Roadside-aided routing (RAR) in vehicular networks. In: IEEE International Conference on Communications, pp. 3602–3607 (2006)
7. Grafling, S., Mahonen, P., Riihijarvi, J.: Performance evaluation of IEEE 1609 WAVE and IEEE 802.11 p for vehicular communications. In: Second IEEE International Conference on Ubiquitous and Future Networks (ICUFN), pp. 344–348 (2010)

8. Mohandas, B.K., Nayak, A., Naik, K., Goel, N.: ABSRP-A Service Discovery Approach for Vehicular Ad Hoc Networks. In: Asia-Pacific Services Computing Conference, pp. 1590–1594 (2008)
9. Matthaiou, M., Laurenson, D.I., Wang, C.X.: Capacity study of vehicle-to-roadside MIMO channels with a line-of-sight component. In: Wireless Communications and Networking Conference, pp. 775–779 (2008)
10. Shrestha, B., Niyato, D., Han, Z., Hossain, E.: Wireless access in vehicular environments using BitTorrent and bargaining. In: IEEE Global Telecommunications Conference, pp. 1–5 (2008)
11. Lee, U., Magistretti, E., Gerla, M., Bellavista, P., Corradi, A.: Dissemination and harvesting of urban data using vehicular sensing platforms. IEEE Transactions on Vehicular Technology, 882–901 (2009)
12. Saad, W., Han, Z., Hjørungnes, A., Niyato, D., Hossain, E.: Coalition formation games for distributed cooperation among roadside units in vehicular networks. IEEE Journal on Selected Areas in Communications 29(1), 48–60 (2010)
13. Jackson, M.O.: A survey of network formation models: Stability and efficiency. Group Formation in Economics: Networks, Clubs and Coalitions 11–57 (2005)
14. Li, Y., Ying, K., Cheng, P., Yu, H., Luo, H.: Cooperative data dissemination in cellular-VANET heterogeneous wireless networks. In: 4th International High Speed Intelligent Communication Forum (HSIC), pp. 1–4 (2012)
15. Kernighan, B.W., LiN, S.: An efficient heuristic procedure for partitioning graphs. The Bell System Technical Journal 2(49), 291–307 (1970)

Drag Reduction of a Truck Using Append Devices and Optimization

Xiaolong Yang and Zihui Ma

State Key Laboratory of Advanced Design and Manufacturing for Vehicle Body,
Hunan University, Changsha, Hunan 4120082, China
xyangusc@163.com, vmazihui@gmail.com

Abstract. To reduce the aerodynamic drag of a truck, two different passive drag reduction methods are investigated to a real truck. First, a simulation model of the truck is built. The external flow field of the truck is studied in details using CFD method. Then a fairwater is added on the top of truck's head. The effects of different shrink angles of the fairwater on the flow flied and the aerodynamic drag are studied. It is found that the fairwaters can effective decrease the total drag. Then different sizes of cylinders are attached to the top and bottom edges of the tail. A detailed analysis of the flow field and the effect on drag are carried out. At last, these two methods are both applied to the truck and the value of the effective parameters is optimized. A maximum percentage of the drag reduction upped to 24.8% can be obtained.

Keywords: Aerodynamic drag, Drag reduction, External flow field, Truck, CFD.

1 Introduction

The energy saving and emission reduction are two world wild problems. For automobile industry, many new technologies are proposed to reduce the aerodynamic drag to saving the energy. However the aerodynamic drag of the truck has been maintained at a high level due to commercial consideration[1]. Reduction of aerodynamic drag of heavy-duty trucks can significantly save fuel costs. For example, reduction of aerodynamic drag by 30% can result in fuel cost savings in billions of dollars every year[2]. The aerodynamic characteristics of large trucks have become more and more important in recent vehicle designs[3]. The aerodynamic optimization of both the tractor and semitrailer units has achieved an average reduction in drag coefficient of 20% that gives an 8% fuel saving[4]. Mohamed-Kassim and Filippone shows that the fuel reductions by using selected drag-reducing devices individually on a large truck range from less than1% to almost 9% of the fuel cost on an annual mileage of 80,000 miles[5]. To reduce the fuel consumptions of the truck, it's necessary to look at the main energy requests of a long distance truck at 80km/h highway travel. According to [6], about 45% are losses in the rolling resistance and 40% of the energy is needed to overcome the aerodynamic drag. So it's clear that the aerodynamic drag play a key role at high speed. Effective drag reduction methods can improve the operation economy of vehicle[7, 8].

K. Li et al. (Eds.): ParCFD 2013, CCIS 405, pp. 332–343, 2014.

The methods for aerodynamic drag reduction can be divided into two categories: active drag reduction and passive drag reduction[1, 8-10]. Active drag reduction is actually to control the airflow around the truck by some special type of additional devices. On the other hand, passive drag reduction is mainly to optimize the body shape and structure of the lorry itself, or to add additional devices to steer the airflow thus reducing the aerodynamic drag. For those two strategies, the passive drag reduction is used wildly because the devices of the active drag reduction are complicated and expansive. It has shown that the passive drag reduction methods, such as a small cylinder located behind the bluff body and small tabs attached to the upper and lower trailing edges of a bluff body[11, 12], can reduce the air resistance effectively and in return reduce the fuel consumption. There are some other passive drag reduction methods proposed by different people. Selenbas[13] et al. optimized the cabin geometry and its various parts (that include the side deflectors, the mirrors and the sun visor) for drag reduction. Hsu and Davis studied the effect of an add-on humps and curved boat-tail flaps on drag[14]. Zhang[15] et al. present the method that fixing on the aft-body with different angle of declination and shape of the wing. Yang[16] et al. have taken side skirts of varying length, underbody skirts, a full gap seal, and tapered rear panels. Lin JC[17] and Modi VJ[18] et al. present some passive flow control technologies and boundary-layer flow-separation control by passive methods. In this paper two passive drag reduction methods are applied to a real truck model and their effects on drag are investigated. The paper is organized as following: first a real truck model is built and the computation method is introduced, then the effects of two drag reducing devices are studied. An optimization is proposed and the result before and after the optimization is compared. Finally some conclusion is given.

2   The Original Truck Model and Computation Setup

A real truck is used as the study case here and a 3-D CAD model is created by 1:1 scale, as shown in Fig. 1. This truck is a typical light truck in china and has large sales each year. Usually the actually external configuration of the truck is complicated because there are many small devices and cables etc. According to experience, those small parts has little effect on the flow field, while will increase the computation cost greatly. So a simplified model is used instead, which keeps the most main characteristics of the truck as shown in Fig. 1.

The grid and computation domain are shown in Fig. 2. Considering computation cost and accuracy, a mixed triangle and rectangle grid is adopted here. The total mesh is about 1623261. Assuming the length, height and width of the truck is a, b, c respectively, the length before the truck is set to $3a$,after the van is $6a$,the height of the domain is $6b$,and the width of the domain is $6c$ and symmetric[19].

To saving time, a set of traditional RANS simulations are carried out. And the SST k - ω turbulence model is used to close the N-S equations. The typical boundary conditions for the truck outflow field mainly include inlet, outlet and wall boundaries. The parameters set are listed in table 1.

Fig. 1. D model of the truck   **Fig. 2.** Sketch of computation mesh

Table 1. Boundary conditions

Inlet Boundary	Velocity Inlet; U=-80Km/h,V=0,W=0
	ρ =1.18415Kg/m^3;
	Turbulence Intensity=0.023;Turbulence Length Scale=0.5
Outlet Boundary	Pressure Outlet; Relative Pressure P=0Pa;
	Turbulence Intensity=0.023;Turbulence Length Scale=0.5
Wall	No-slip Boundary

3   Computed Results and Analysis of Original Truck

From Fig.3 and Fig.5, we can see that there is a large area of the positive pressure in the front of the truck, and the pressure value is very high in this area. This is due to the airflow is resisted when it hits the truck from a distance ahead. Its velocity (magnitude) will decrease rapidly; thereby the blocking phenomenon happens, as shown in Fig.6. In the windward side (that is, the airflow stagnation point), the pressure is the biggest. The fluid near the stagnation point flow around after being extruded to the windward side, so the pressure gradient is very high, as shown in Fig.4. Also, for Fig.3, the front of the wheels and the head of the boxcar have obvious positive pressure area. When the airflow goes through the upper of the head, the air velocity increases rapidly due to the air separation in turn which lead to pressure decrease rapidly. The pressure converts positive pressure to negative pressure. And the airflow continues to flow along the front edge, and then hits the boxcar. Finally the air flows along the boxcar. There are parts of the negative pressure in the rear of boxcar area. Form a pressure difference with the positive pressure zone in up and down of the tail, resulting in a lot of vortex, as shown in Fig.6. The complex vortex area makes the rear surface be in negative pressure state. This is a drawing force that acts opposite the moving direction of the truck. The calculation shows that the drag coefficient is 0.658.

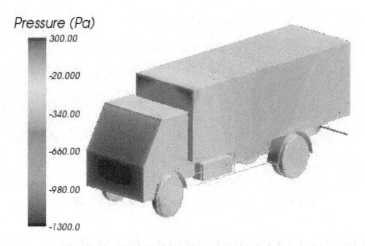

Fig. 3. Pressure distribution on the surface of the truck

Fig. 4. Pressure curve on top surface of the truck along X-Z plane

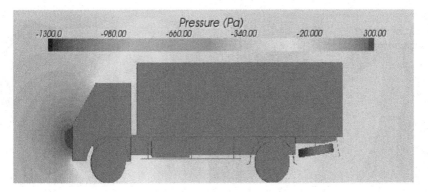

Fig. 5. Pressure distribution on X-Z plane of 1/2 width

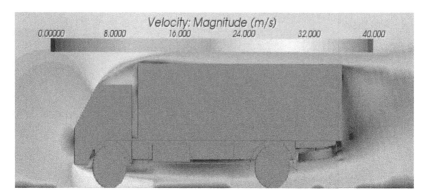

Fig. 6. Velocity distribution on X-Z plane of 1/2 width

4   Studies of Two Passive Drag Reduction Methods

Above results show that there are large separation areas near the back of the trailer and the gap between the head and trailer. Separation and large vortex structure have great influence on the drag of truck. In order to improve the aerodynamics characteristics of truck, the large separation must be controlled.

Using the above truck as the basic model, we present two drag reduction methods below (In Fig.7and Fig.8). And their effects on the external flow field and thus the aerodynamics drag are investigated In Fig.7 a fairwater is installed in the head of truck. Analyses are focus on drag reduction effects using different shrink angles. The shrink angle is changed on both sides of the nose of the fairwater from 0° to 45 °, 5 ° each time.

Then removing the fairwater and adding cylinders on the edges of top and bottom of the tail, as shown in Fig.8. Change the diameter of the cylinders from 20mm to 200mm, each time 20mm.The influences on flow structure and drag reduction are studies using different diameter of the cylinders.

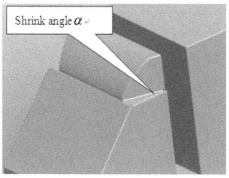
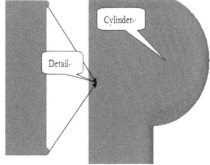

Fig. 7. Fairwater and its shrink angle   **Fig. 8.** Cylinders in the rear of the boxcar

4.1   The Effect of Fairwater

From the graph of Fig.9, we can see that the drag coefficient decreased oscillating with the shrink angle increased. The drag coefficient reaches its minimum value when the shrink angle is 25° and it is reduced almost 22.8% compared to the original mode. Further increases the shrink angle, the drag coefficient is increased instead. Because the windward area would increase that produced the resistance directly and the fairwater would not guide the airflow availably so that the structure of vortex of the gap happened to change. Fig.10 shows velocity vector distribution on X-Y plane of the gap between trailer and tractor, 3m above the floor. From Fig.10 we can see the changes of vortex shape under the changes of the shrink angle. When the shrink angle is 5°,there are two large vortices respectively on the both side of the central plane. Those vortices are produced by flow separation and the pressure of separation area is very low which make the viscous pressure resistance. With the shrink angle increased to 25°,the area of vortices decreased and the flow field structure improved. When the shrink angle make a further increased to 45°, the flow field of the gap begin deteriorate and some small vortices will be found. The vortices dissipate the energy and the zone of negative pressure formed again and become bigger. So being a certain shrink angle ($\alpha = 25°$) that guides the backward airflow efficiently and makes the drag reduction greater.

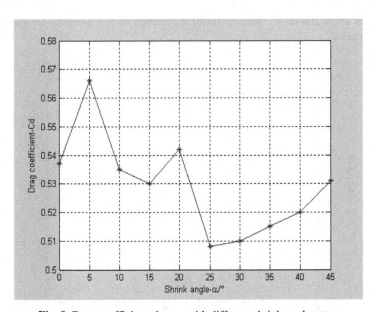

Fig. 9. Drag coefficient change with different shrink angle α

338   X. Yang and Z. Ma

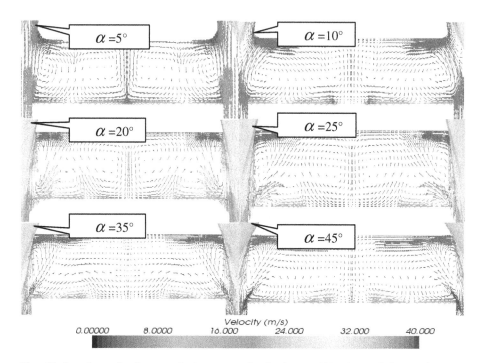

Fig. 10. 3m above the floor, velocity vector distribution on *X-Y* plane of the gap between trailer and tractor

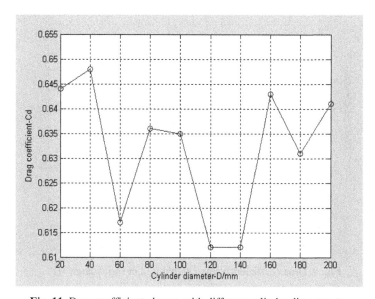

Fig. 11. Drag coefficient change with different cylinder diameter *D*

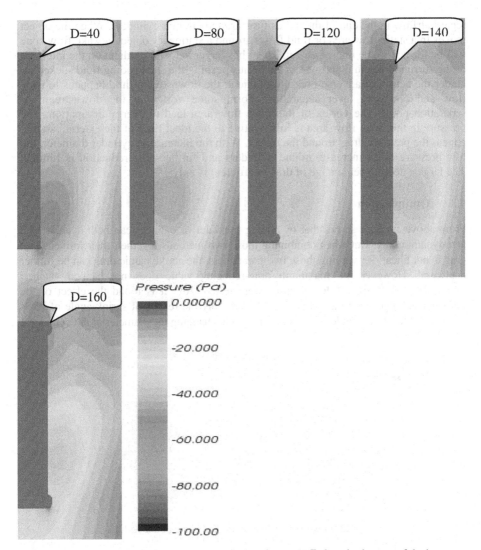

Fig. 12. In 1/2 width of the truck, pressure distribution on X-Z plane in the rear of the boxcar

4.2   The Effect of Attached Cylinders

From the graph of Fig.11, we can see that the drag coefficient decreased oscillating with the diameter of cylinders increased. The resistance coefficient reaches minimum when the cylinder diameter are 120mm and 140mm, and attains the largest decline percentage of drag coefficient which is 7.0%. In Fig.12 from the diameter of 40mm to 80mm, there are obvious low pressure areas in the rear which are produced by flow separation. When the diameter are 120mm and 140mm, the low pressure areas decrease in the rear which make the drag resistance reduced. With the diameter increase to 160mm the low pressure areas make a further decrease in the rear, but the separation area can be found obviously and largely closed to the cylinders. We can regard airflow in the end of the tail as flow around circular cylinders. When the object moves in a static flow area or fluid flows around a stationary object, a wake flow zone will be formed in the rear of object. There has larger velocity gradient on the interface of the surrounding fluid and wake flow. Thus pushing the surrounding fluid sucked in. Under the action of adverse pressure gradient, the downstream fluid happens to back flow and boundary layer separation. Form some vortex in the downstream of separation point. The vortex of the wake flow area lead to energy dissipation. The pressure in the wake flow area is low relative to the ideal fluid of the external. so that appear the pressure drag around the object. With the increase of cylinder diameter, the low pressure areas increase around cylinders and further drag reduction is limited. The largest decline percentage of drag coefficient is only 7%.

4.3   Optimization

From above study, it shows that by adding fairwater or cylinder can both decrease the aerodynamic drag. But when combining those two methods together, their influence on drag is not linear. By varying those two parameters, the aerodynamic drag can be further decreased. However the maximum drag-reducing value does not happen at their individual best cases. A lot of cases were tested. And it is found the effect of the fairwater is bigger than the cylinder's. So here only the results of shrink angle of 25°is shown, i.e. the shrink angle is kept constant while changing the diameter of the cylinders.

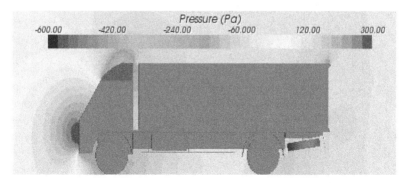

Fig. 13. Pressure distribution on *X-Z* plane of 1/2 width

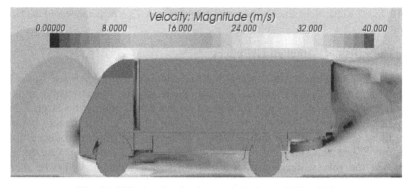

Fig. 14. Velocity distribution on *X-Z* plane of 1/2 width

Fig. 15. Streamline on the head and velocity vector distribution on *X-Y* plane of the gap between trailer and tractor, and in 1/2 width of the truck, pressure distribution on *X-Z* plane in the rear of the boxcar

The results show that when the diameter of cylinder is 120mm combined with the shrink angle of 25°, it can make a further drag reduction which is 0.495. As the resistance coefficient of the basic truck model is 0.658, in this case, the decline percentage of drag coefficient is 24.8%.

From Fig.13 and Fig.14, we can see that the pressure and velocity distribution on *X-Z* plane of 1/2 width in this case. The flow separation of larger area mainly appeared on the top of the fairwater, the bottom of the headstock and the rear of the boxcar.Fig.15 gives the streamline on the head and velocity vector distribution on *X-Y* plane of the gap between trailer and tractor, and in 1/2 width of the truck pressure distribution on *X-Z* plane in the rear of the boxcar. The fairwater with shrink angle of 25°guides the airflow backward efficiently and the cylinder of 120mm diameter can improve the tail vortex structure to some extent. Working together the two kinds of drag reduction mechanism, in the end, it makes a further drag reduction 24.8%.

5   Conclusion

Two drag reduction methods are discussed in this paper, which are fairwater mounted on top of head of the truck and cylinders installed in the rear of the boxcar. Simulation results show that the additional device of the fairwater can have good drag reduction effect, and the shrink angle exist an optimal value. When shrink angle is 25 °, the drag coefficient has the largest decline, upped to 22.8%. However, installed cylinders have limited effect on the drag coefficient reduction. When the cylinder diameter is 120 mm and 140 mm, drag coefficient has the largest decline, the value only comes to 7.0%. In the end, we combine the fairwater and cylinder together. Keeping the shrink angle of 25°,and changing the diameter of the cylinders. It is found that when the diameter is 120mm the drag coefficient can have a further reduction 24.8%. It shows that a proper shrink angle will help guide the airflow over the top and have the minimal drag coefficient; a proper cylinder diameter will contribute to mend the structure of the vortex in the rear of the boxcar. Finally, the combination of both effectively can make a difference further. On the whole the proper additional devices can have drag coefficient reduction significantly and reasonable passive drag reduction schemes are very effectively.

Acknowledgments. This research is supported by the Science Fund of State Key Laboratory of Advanced Design and Manufacturing for Vehicle Body No. 31075013 and Young Teacher Support Project of Hunan University.

References

1. Yang, X.L., Tang, J.X.: The Effects of Truck Structure Parameters on the Aerodynamic Drag and Optimization. Applied Mechanics and Materials 224, 138–141 (2012)
2. Lakshman, M., Aung, K.: Drag reduction through changes in cabin geometry and trailer gap of heavy-duty trucks. In: Proceedings of the ASME Heat Transfer/Fluids Engineering Summer Conference 2004, HT/FED 2004, July 11-15, pp. 769–774. American Society of Mechanical Engineers, Charlotte (2004)
3. Kim, M.-H.: Prediction of 3-dimensional turbulent flows around corner vane of a heavy-duty truck cab. International Journal of Vehicle Design 31, 86–95 (2002)
4. Mauro, C., Davide, L.: An optimized tractor-semitrailer solution for improved fuel efficiency. In: 32nd FISITA World Automotive Congress 2008, September 14-19, pp. 50–61. Springer Automotive Media, Munich (2008)
5. Mohamed-Kassim, Z., Filippone, A.: Fuel savings on a heavy vehicle via aerodynamic drag reduction. Transportation Research Part D: Transport and Environment 15, 275–284 (2010)
6. Kopp, S.: Heavy vehicle aerodynamics often undervalued, but nevertheless the future? Nutzfahrzeugaerodynamik - Oft Unterschatzt und doch die Zukunft? VDI Berichte, 47–59 (2009)
7. Pointer, D., Sofu, T., Chang, J., Weber, D.: Applicability of commercial CFD tools for assessment of heavy vehicle aerodynamic characteristics. In: The Aerodynamics of Heavy Vehicles II: Trucks, Buses, and Trains, August 26-31, 2007, pp. 349–361. Springer, Lake Tahoe (2009)
8. Bellman, M., Agarwal, R., Naber, J., Lee, C.: Reducing energy consumption of ground vehicles by active flow control. In: ASME 2010 4th International Conference on Energy Sustainability, ES 2010, May 17-22, pp. 785–793. American Society of Mechanical Engineers, Phoenix (2010)
9. Shtendel, T., Seifert, A.: Bluff body aerodynamic drag reduction by active flow control. In: 52nd Israel Annual Conference on Aerospace Sciences, February 29-March 1, pp. 621–682. Technion Israel Institute of Technology, Tel-Aviv (2012)
10. Seifert, A., Stalnov, O., Sperber, D., Arwatz, G., Palei, V., David, S., et al.: Large trucks drag reduction using active flow control. In: The Aerodynamics of Heavy Vehicles II: Trucks, Buses, and Trains, August 26-31, 2007, pp. 115–133. Springer, Lake Tahoe (2009)
11. Thiria, B., Cadot, O., Beaudoin, J.F.: Passive drag control of a blunt trailing edge cylinder. Journal of Fluids and Structures 25, 766–776 (2009)

12. Park, H., Lee, D., Jeon, W.-P., Hahn, S., Kim, J., Kim, J., et al.: Drag reduction in flow over a two-dimensional bluff body with a blunt trailing edge using a new passive device. J. Fluid Mech. 563, 389–414 (2006)

13. Selenbas, B., Gunes, H., Gocmen, K., Bahceci, U., Bayram, B.: An aerodynamic design and optimization of a heavy truck for drag reduction. In: ASME 2010 10th Biennial Conference on Engineering Systems Design and Analysis, ESDA2010, July 12–14, pp. 121–129. American Society of Mechanical Engineers, Istanbul (2010)

14. Hsu, F.-H., Davis, R.L.: Drag reduction of Tractor-trailers using optimized add-on devices. Journal of Fluids Engineering, Transactions of the ASME 132 (2010)

15. Li, S., Zhang, J., Ming, L., Liu, X., Jiang, L.: Rear add-on device for drag reduction of van body truck. In: 2011 International Conference on Advanced Design and Manufacturing Engineering, ADME 2011, September 16-18, pp. 1139–1142. Trans Tech Publications, Guangzhou (2011)

16. Hu, X.-J., Yang, B., Guo, P., Wang, J.-Y., Yang, Y., An, Y.: Aerodynamic drag reduction of van based on underbody skirt. Jilin Daxue Xuebao (Gongxueban)/Journal of Jilin University (Engineering and Technology Edition) 41, 108–113 (2011)

17. Lin, J.C.: Review of research on low-profile vortex generators to control boundary-layer separation. Progress in Aerospace Sciences 38, 389–420 (2002)

18. Modi, V.J., Ying, B., Yokomizo, T.: On the drag reduction of trucks through the application of fences and momentum injection. In: Proceedings of the 6th International Pacific Conference on Automotive Engingeering, October 28-November 1, pp. 1035–1051. Korea Soc. of Automotive Engineers, Inc., Seoul (1991)

19. Yang, X.-L., Lin, T.-P.: DES and RANS of vehicle external flow field. Hunan Daxue Xuebao/Journal of Hunan University Natural Sciences 38, 29–34 (2011)

Delayed-VLES Model for the Simulation of Turbulent Flows

Yang Zhang[*], Junqiang Bai, and Chen Wang

School of Aeronautics, Northwestern Polytechnical University, Xi`an, 710072, P.R. China
iamvip2@163.com

Abstract. Speziale's VLES is one of the hybrid RANS/LES methods according to previous researches. VLES method used a unified modelled stress equation that was adjusted by resolution control function. Due to the nature of compromising grid space information, VLES can conveniently lead to a modelled stress dissipation beneath the boundary layer by computing from coarse grid to fine grid. The present study proposes a delayed-VLES (DVLES) method which can improve the modelled stress dissipation phenomenon. The advantage of the DVLES is that the RANS simulation can be preserved in near-wall region by using a damping function. This new methodology is assembled with Menter's SST model. Applications are conducted for the turbulent flat plate and turbulent flow past a NACA0021 airfoil at 60° incidence. The corresponding results are compared with VLES and URANS. It is demonstrated that the DVLES is favorably robust with the grid refinement.

Keywords: RANS, VLES, Hybrid RANS/LES, Turbulent Flows Simulation.

1   Introduction

With the development of computational capability, human beings have received remarkable achievements in natural science. People can predict the time when earthquakes will happen and reveal the most micro structure of molecule, but when confronting with the turbulent problems, we have just make less process compared with the other aspects of natural science. Although the turbulent theorists and practitioners have deduced lots of theories and shown many sophisticated structures, people still cannot find a validate formula to express the natural turbulence when taking account of the computing cost. Industrial and engineering turbulent simulations are dominated by Reynolds-Averaged Navier-Stokes (RANS) approaches, the other two methods are Large Eddy Simulation (LES) and Direct Numerical Simulation (DNS). It is well known that RANS is the most favorable method in industrial simulation with many turbulence models in order to adapt the variation of Reynolds number. Meanwhile, RANS can also feedback a receptive precision and efficiency to users. In aeronautic industry, RANS based Computation Fluid Dynamics (CFD) has become the most important tool for aircrafts design and simulation. It has saved huge

---

[*] Corresponding author.

K. Li et al. (Eds.): ParCFD 2013, CCIS 405, pp. 344–353, 2014.

costs of simulation from wind tunnel experiments. In the last decade, the environment and energy issues have forced human being to face the power saving technologies after the explosive growth of vehicles. Especially in aeronautic transportation, the airlines send urgent signals for low drag aircrafts. The first motivation to solve this problem is precisely simulating the drag in the different flow conditions. However, the RANS method can only give a good result in stable flow field. When facing the separated flow, the RANS could merely render a poor accuracy because of the averaged operation suppresses the fluctuations of turbulence, most of these fluctuations are closely coupled with time especially in separated regions, which determines the flows characters . Using DNS can be the most immediate tool, but it solves scales of flow fluctuations which means an extremely fine grid to be prepared and fairly fine time-steps to capture the micro structures of flow. Hence it could only be conducted in the laboratories for rather small scale problems. As for the present LES approaches, they model the dissipation regions of turbulence energy spectra while still require rather fine grid near the wall for the local Reynolds number approaches to zero in the vicinity of the wall.

The hybrid RANS/LES method offers us a framework to combine both advantages of RANS and LES, RANS is used in the near-wall region to model scales of turbulence inside the boundary layer in order to reduce the fine grid requirement. For the flow field outside the boundary layer, the LES is employed to capture micro behaviors of flow structures. Among the hybrid RANS/LES methods, Very Large Eddy Simulation (VLES) was proposed by Speziale [1] which was the earliest VLES under such framework. VLES offered us a turbulence simulation model characterized with a single equation and multiple properties. Under the idealistic grid scope, VLES can render a result with similar precision against DNS. The VLES also can give us a very approving results close to Detached Eddy Simulation (DES) or LES. VLES introduces the grid scale in the resolution control function as employed in DES method. For fine grid, the alternation between RANS and LES can take place inside the boundary layer, and produce a premature separation in boundary layer which is a grid induced unphysical phenomenon in the flowfield. Other hybrid methods, such as Limited Numerical Scales (LNS) approach by Batten et al. [2], DES approach by Spalart [3] have similar ideas and suffers with this grid induced unphysical defect. The present study is to propose a common solution to alleviate such computing flaw through adjusting the VLES resolution control function.

2   Mathematical Formulation

Speziale's VLES method is also called Flow Simulation Methodology (FSM), which increases the turbulence production and reduces turbulence dissipation. The VLES operates directly on modelled stress equation and gives a smooth shift from RANS to LES region. The modelled stress equation is

$$\tau_{ij}^{mod} = X_r \tau_{ij}^{RANS} \tag{1}$$

in which the resolution control function is defined the form

$$X_r = \left[1.0 - \exp(\frac{-\beta\Delta}{L_k}) \right]^n \tag{2}$$

where $\beta = 0.002$, $n = 4/3$ are modelling parameters, Δ is the grid size and set to the longest edge or the cubic root of the local grid cell volume, L_k is the *Kolmogorov length scale* that is defined as $L_k = v^{0.75}/\varepsilon^{0.25}$ where v and ε are respectively the kinematic viscosity and the turbulence dissipation rate. When $\Delta/L_k \to \infty$, the τ_{ij}^{mod} equals τ_{ij}^{RANS} because $X_r \to 1$, on the side, the $\tau_{ij}^{mod} \to 0$. This behavior shows the two extreme values of VLES are corresponding to the RANS and the DNS values.

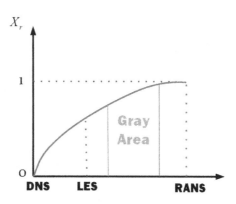

Fig. 1. Resolution control function

However, Menter described there would be a grey area when the grid is refined and Δ becomes smaller, the modelled stress τ_{ij}^{mod} will obviously decrease. [4]. From Equation (Eq.) 2 and Figure (Fig.) 1, we can easily deduce that the grey area exists in the VLES result.

The method proposed in this paper was to retain RANS beneath the boundary layer. In the Menter's $k-\omega$ SST model [5], one parameter F_1 represent the internal and external positions about the boundary layer. The F_1 is given by

$$F_1 = \tanh(\Phi_1^4) \tag{3}$$

$$\Phi_1 = \min\left[\max\left(\frac{\sqrt{k}}{0.09\omega d}, \frac{500\mu}{\rho d^2 \omega} \right), \frac{4\rho k}{\sigma_{\omega,2} D_\omega^+ d^2} \right] \tag{4}$$

$$D_\omega^+ = \max\left[2\rho \frac{1}{\sigma_{\omega,2}} \frac{1}{\omega} \frac{\partial k}{\partial x_j} \frac{\partial \omega}{\partial x_j}, 10^{-10} \right] \tag{5}$$

where k is the turbulence kinetic energy, ω is the specific dissipation rate, d is the distance from the wall, ρ is density, μ is laminar viscosity coefficient and $\sigma_{\omega,2}$ is a constant.

F_1 keeps 1 and damps to 0 from inside to the outside of the boundary layer. Define X_r as

$$X_r = \left[1.0 - \exp(\frac{-\beta\Delta}{L_k}) + F_1 \exp(\frac{-\beta\Delta}{L_k}) \right]^n \qquad (6)$$

which forced $X_r = 1$ when $F_1 = 1$ indicates the position is in boundary layer. This is called a delayed behavior compared to the original VLES. The DVLES model is coupled with Menter's $k-\omega$ SST model by tuning ε to ω using equation $\varepsilon = 0.09k\omega$ in which k and ω are respectively the turbulent kinetic energy and specific turbulent dissipation rate.

3   Numerical Techniques

The time-dependent conservation law form of RANS equations are solved by an in-house code TeAM (Technology based on Aeronautical Multidiscipline) that was developed by BaiJunqiang team in Northwestern Polytechnical University of China since 2003. Steady or unsteady flows are solved by using implicit time advancement. The Euler fluxes are implemented by upwind-biased differencing. The shear stress and heat transfer terms are carried out by central differencing. For accelerating the convergence, a multiple-grid method is used. Lots of turbulence models are constructed in TeAM, such as Spalart-Allmaras [6], Menter's $k-\omega$ SST, SA-DES, and SST-DES [7], etc.

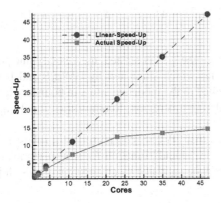

Fig. 2. Speed-Up as a function of number of cores

Message Passing Interface (MPI) library [8] is used to accelerate the unsteady simulation process. Figure 1 shows the computation speed-up factor as a function of number of CPU cores using the code TeAM with a grid scale of 0.1 million nodes. The data was generated on a Linux Cluster consisting of 192 CPUs of 3.06G Intel Xeno X5675.

4   Results of Turbulent Flat-Plate

The test case is a fully turbulent flat plate with Ma = 0.2 and Re =3,000,000 which was studied using RANS and the Splading Theory. It is selected to express the feasibility of RANS, VLES and DVLES models to simulate near-wall turbulence. The computational domain is $\pi \times 2\pi \times 1$ (unit: m). Two different grids were used, i.e. grid1 ($49 \times 29 \times 57$) and grid2 ($49 \times 29 \times 113$). The grids were clustered near the wall and the first node is under the location with $y^+ = 1$.

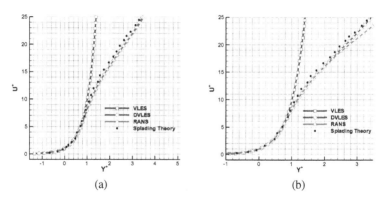

(a)   (b)

Fig. 3. Comparisons of velocity in different grid sizes for flat plate flow case (a): grid2, (b): grid1

Fig. 2 shows that when the grid is refined, the velocity line got by VLES raises up very quickly but the ones which simulated by DVLES and RANS are better. This phenomena can be ascribed to the modelled stress in boundary layer is underestimated because of VLES invaded in this region. Return to Eq. 2 and Eq. 3, above conclusion can be immediately got.

This test case implies that DVLES can preserved a robust RANS behavior inside boundary layer due to the "shield" function F_1. The performance of unstable flows simulation of DVLES will be validated by an airfoil at deep stall in next test case.

5   Results of NACA0021 at 60° Incidence

There must be a severely separated region behind an airfoil in deep stall in large angle of attack which is also a typical test case for hybrid RANS/LES. Swalwell et al. [9]

carried out an experiment of a NACA0021 airfoil at 60° angle of attack. Shur et al. [10] have used this test case for the first real 3D application of DES.

The present study used this case for comparing the precision of unsteady flow simulation by URANS, VLES and DVLES. Table 1 is the flow condition used by calculation.

Table 1. Flow condition used by calculation

Ma	0.1
Reynolds Number	270000
Chord Length	1m
Angle of Attack	60°
Turbulent Intensity	0.6%

Two sizes of grid are used in order to compare the impact of grid. The coarse grid is scaled with 3000000 nodes and the fine one with 6000000 nodes. The physical time step is non-dimensionalized by 0.001 second with freestream velocity and chord length.

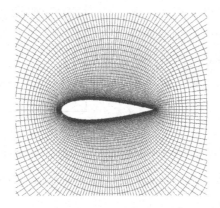

Fig. 4. Slice of fine grid at Y = 0.5m

A time-averaged process is needed by the averaged result for time-dependent flow. The total number of unsteady time-steps was 8000. Based on the values found by analyzing the lift and drag history, note that:

1. The URANS predicted lift coefficient Cl and drag coefficient Cd values of 1.1913 and 1.8459 on coarse grid, while, 1.1392 and 1.8160 on fine grid, respectively.
2. The VLES predicted Cl and Cd values of 0.9364 and 1.1859 on coarse grid, while, 0.7715 and 1.1859 on fine grid, respectively.
3. The DVLES predicted Cl of 0.8539 and Cd of 1.2514 on coarse grid, while, 0.7849 and 1.2049 on fine grid.

VLES and DVLES closely matched the experimental Cl and Cd values, which demonstrated that DVLES can give the same precision with VLES in the simulations of time-dependent flows.

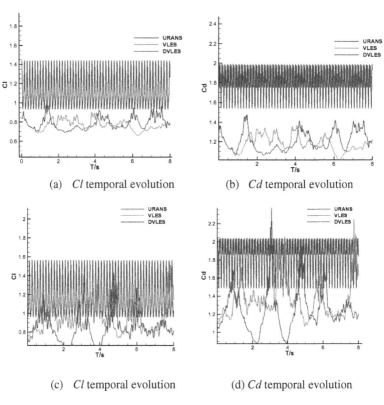

(a) Cl temporal evolution   (b) Cd temporal evolution

(c) Cl temporal evolution   (d) Cd temporal evolution

Fig. 5. NACA0021 lift and drag histories for three-dimensional simulations. ((a)(b): fine grid; (c)(d): coarse grid)

Table 2. Cl and Cd comparisons

	Cl	Cd
URANS_Coarse	1.1913	1.8459
URANS_Fine	1.1392	1.8160
VLES_Coarse	0.9364	1.3677
VLES_Fine	0.7715	1.1859
DVLES_Coarse	0.8539	1.2514
DVLES_Fine	0.7849	1.2049
Expt.	0.931	1.517

As expected, the URANS process produced a trim fluctuation both in the *Cl* or *Cd* convergence histories. It is known that the URANS resolved the dominant fluctuation as a single frequency was captured. On the contrary, VLES and DVLES presented very irregular peak values than URANS, because the resolution control function reduced the Reynolds stress and released much small scales of fluctuations. These fluctuations influence the dominant frequency and changed the peak values.

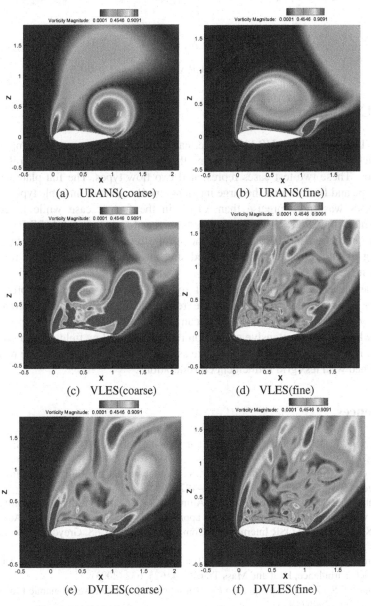

Fig. 6. NACA0021 instantaneous voracity contours at Y=0.5m.

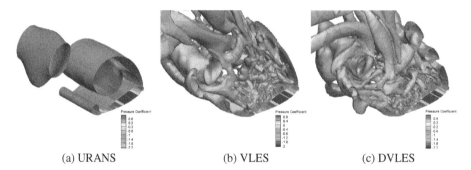

(a) URANS   (b) VLES   (c) DVLES

Fig. 7. Q contour of URANS, VLES and DVLES

6   Conclusion

The DVLES, VLES and URANS numerical simulation processes were implemented
to predict the flat-plate flow behavior and the flow past a NACA0021 airfoil with 60°
incidence. These two test cases represented two flow types. The flat plate case is of
stable type and flow around the large incident airfoil case is of unstable type.

URANS was more precise than VLES in the former case while failed to be
competent in the latter. URANS predicted a higher local stress while VLES rendered
a lower prediction. DVLES retained the local stress in a proper level by using a
damping function that kept the modelled stress to equal τ_{ij}^{RANS} in order to restrict the
U^+ raising rate.

In the unsteady test case, the result by DVLES was much more precise than
URANS. This can be attributed to the resolution control function switch out of
boundary layer in VLES. The DVLES can offer a result with the same precision as
VLES when there are intensive separation regions in the flow field. It also seems that
DVLES is not as sensitive to the grid size as VLES, which implies that the results can
be obtained with less grid refinement considerations.

References

1. Speziale, C.G.: Turbulence modeling for time-dependent RANS and VLES: a review.
   AIAA J. 36, 173–184 (1998)
2. Batten, P., Goldberg, U., Chakravarthy, S.: Interfacing statistical turbulence closures with
   large eddy simulation. AIAA J. 42, 485–492 (2004)
3. Spalart, P.R., Jou, W.-H., Strelets, M., Allmaras, S.R.: Comments on the feasibility of LES
   for wings, and on hybrid RANS/LES approach. In: Liu, C., Liu, Z. (eds.) Advances in
   LES/DNS, First AFOSR International Conference on DNS/LES. Greyden Press, Louisiana
   Tech. University (1997)
4. Menter, F.R., Kuntz, M., Langtry, R.: Ten Years of Experience with the SST Turbulence
   Model. Turbulence, Heat and Mass Transfer 4, 625–632 (2003)
5. Menter, F.R.: Zonal Two-equation k-ω Turbulence Models for Aerodynamic Flows. AIAA
   Paper 1993-2906 (1993)

6. Spalart, P.R., Allmaras, S.R.: A One-Equation Turbulence Model for Aerodynamic Flows. AIAA Paper 1992-0439 (1992)
7. Strelets, M.: Detached Eddy Simulation of Massively Separated Flows. AIAA Paper 2001-0879 (2001)
8. Groop, W., Lusk, E., Skjellum, A.: MPI: A Message-Passing Interface Standard. Scientific and Engineering Computation Series. The MIT Press, Cambridge (1994)
9. Swalwell, K.E.: The Effect of Turbulence on Stall of Horizontal Axis Wind Turbines. Ph.D. Thesis. Monash University (October 2005)
10. Shur, M., Spalart, P.R., Strelets, M., Travin, A.: Detached-eddy simulation of an airfoil at high angle of attack. In: Rodi, W., Laurence, D. (eds.) 4th Int. Symp. on Engineering Turbulence Modelling and Measurements, Corsica, May 24-26, pp. 669–678 (1999)

Parallel Direct Simulation Monte Carlo Using Graphics Processing Unit with CUDA

Jie Liang[*]

Hunan University, College of Information Science and Engineering, Changsha,
410082, China
liangjie1988@hnu.edu.cn

Abstract. The direct simulation Monte Carlo is a particle-based computational method for rarefied gas flows. It is a method to solve numerically Boltzmann equation with satisfied result. However, there exist two issues to be solved in DSMC simulation, including complex grids processing and large calculated amount. Therefore, finding available computing resources is crucial to optimize and accelerate computation of DSMC. In this paper we investigate data-parallel techniques on graphics processing unit (GPU) to calculate DSMC simulation of dynamic collision grids. We have evaluated and verified the statistical and theoretical accuracy of our implementation.

Keywords: Graphics processing unit, direct simulation Monte Carlo (DSMC), dynamic grid, parallel computing.

1 Introduction

The direct simulation Monte Carlo(DSMC) method is the most powerful and widely used to simulate rarefied gas flows. In the regime of gas dynamics, the continuum assumption is used to conduct gas. However, the effects of gas particles become significant when the density of gas is very low, undermining the assumption hypothesis. Under the circumstances, the method of rarefied gas dynamics need to be adopted for the correct results.

While the Boltzmann equation, which may be more appropriate for low-density flows, is extremely difficult to solve numerically due to the difficulty of correctly and efficiently modeling the integral collision term. To circumvent the difficulty of a direct solution of the Boltzmann equation, an alternative technique known as Direct Simulation Monte Carlo(DSMC) was proposed by Bird [1-3]. Compared with the traditional method, DSMC simplifies the simulation model. The results acquired by DSMC method is equivalent to that of the Boltzmann equation when the number of particles is large. DSMC now may be regarded as a numerical method for solving the problem of rarefied gas. Areas of study in which DSMC is used also include aerospace engineering, and vacuum science and engineering, materials processing, and nanotechnology.

---

[*] Corresponding author.

K. Li et al. (Eds.): ParCFD 2013, CCIS 405, pp. 354–362, 2014.
© Springer-Verlag Berlin Heidelberg 2014

The computation of DSMC is expensive with the demand of computing speed and storage capacity of computing devices, etc. The traditional single processor is impossible for satisfactory performance, the general wisdom for accelerating the DSMC computation is to parallelize the code using the message passing interface (MPI) protocol running on clusters with large numbers of processors[4-7]. Research of DSMC parallel programming technology and parallel programming tool software has significant theoretical significance and practical value. Some researchers around the world have run DSMC procedures on various architectures of parallel processing, achieving good results[8-13].

Recently, state-of-the-art GPUs (Graphical Processing Unit) have gradually outrun CPUs approximately 10 times in terms of non-graphic computation due to its high performance of floating-point arithmetic operation, wide memory bandwidth and enhanced programmability. It is said that GPU is especially designed for the task of intensively computation and a high degree of parallelism. With the release of CUDA(Compute Unified Device Architecture) by NVIDIA[14,15], GPU can issue and map computation task as a data-parallel computing device.

Thus, in this paper we intend to study the parallel DSMC of dynamic collisions grids run on the GPU with single instructions multiple data (SIMD) architecture. The paper is organized as follows. In section 2, the basic DSMC algorithm is described. Key features of the CUDA programming model are presented in section 3. In section 4, we introduce the details of implementation of DSMC on GPU including task decomposition method and kernels. The results of implementations are evaluated and compared with the corresponding other algorithm in section 5. Section 6 concludes the paper with a prospect to future research work.

2   DSMC Methodology

From the microcosmic angle, DSMC method provides a particle-based alternative for obtaining realistic numerical solutions in the flows simulation based on the kinetic theory. It is a stochastic numerical method of solving the nonlinear kinetic Boltzmann equation[2], where an important assumption in the DSMC formulation is that the gas is dilute. DSMC accomplishes this through a Monte Carlo integration of the formula for the bimolecular collision rate, as well as a Monte Carlo integration of collision dynamics[2].

In the DSMC simulation, each simulated molecule may represent millions upon millions of actual molecules. The movement and collisions behavior of a large number of simulated molecules within the flow field are decoupled over a time step. In the movement phase, the collision of molecules will not happen. Once the calculation of movement of all the molecules is finished, the execution of collisions start. If the molecules collide with the physical boundaries during the movement phase, the implementation of collisions with boundaries happen first, then execution of movement and intermolecular collisions.

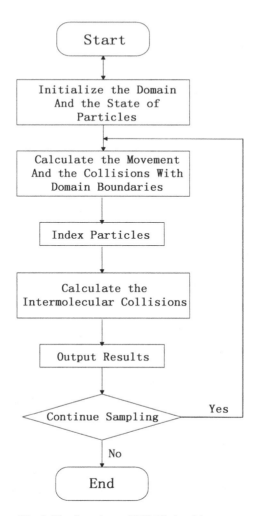

Fig. 1. The flowchart of DSMC algorithm

During the computation of DSMC, the computational domain around the examined model is divided into sufficiently small cells, including structured and unstructured grid of cells. These cells are regarded as computational units to process the intermolecular collisions and information statistics. The motion trajectory of simulated molecules and the state parameters of simulated molecules is tracked and recorded in DSMC simulation, obtaining the parameters of macro gas state with statistics.

From the flow chart of DSMC simulation (see fig.1), the main computation focus on three components: the movement, collisions with boundaries and intermolecular collisions. At the beginning of simulation, the state of the particles and the domain is initialized. Then the particles moved through a time step Δt, while the collisions with domain boundaries are executed. In the movement phase, the particles positions are updated based on the velocity of each individual molecule and the size of the time step. After collisions with boundary and movement, the particles are divided into the respective domain cells and indexed by the cell for the computation of intermolecular collisions. We adopt Bird's method for computing intermolecular collisions in a stochastic manner[2]. Once the collision portion of the simulation is finished, properties can be sampled in each cell, and the process is repeated until desired results is obtained.

From Fig.1 it can be seen that, the distribution of molecules is constantly changing in the process of movement, which leads to unbalance of the number of molecules in different collision meshes. The parallel efficiency of the DSMC method will be affected using the method of static grid generation. Given this, ref. [16] presents a DSMC of dynamic collision grids. The partition of collision grids and molecular index adopt the kd-tree algorithm. The detail of the algorithm can be seen in ref. [16]. The main thoughts of dynamic collision grids DSMC: during the implementation of every intermolecular collision, dynamically constructing and indexing grids according to the molecular distribution and then going through all the dynamic grids for collisions computation. DSMC of dynamic collision grids can ensure relative balance of the number of molecules of each collision mesh. This paper adopts the DSMC of dynamic grid mentioned in ref. [16] and parallelizes it on the GPU.

3   GPU and CUDA^{TM}

With increasing demand for advanced graphics, high-performance graphics systems have been flourished in the commodity market. And the Computer Unified Device Architecture (CUDA) is nowadays the contributing technology for GPGPU, which is used to issue and manage computations on the GPU as a data-parallel computing device without the need of mapping them to a graphic API [17]. Fig.2 demonstrates the architecture of CUDA hardware. On the GPU chip under the earlier Tesla architecture, there are video memory (global memory) and a set of streaming multiprocessors (SM). Each SM contains eight scalar processors (SP), a set of registers, a shared memory, a read-only constant cache and a read-only texture cache. An on-chip shared memory is visible for all the threads executed on a SM, providing with non-addressable registers and some addressable shared memory for inter-SP communication. An off-chip memory (global memory) is shared for all SMs.

In the CUDA programming model, GPU are treated as a set of SIMD multiprocessors. SPs within each SM follows a SIMD (Single Instruction Multiple Data) execution architecture while SM adopts the scheme of SIMT (Single Instruction Multiple Threads) to map each thread on one SP, although SMs are not globally synchronized. The use of SIMD processing units reduces power consumption and increases the number of floating point arithmetic units per unit area relative to conventional MIMD (multiple-instruction multiple-data) architecture.

A CUDA program principally consists of CPU code (hostcode) and (at least) one kernel (devicecode). The kernel is run on GPU. The CUDA map computation tasks to a large number of threads, which can be executed in parallel and dynamic scheduled by hardware. CUDA introduces the concept of thread, block, and grid to manage them, due to the large amount of the threads (maximum 65536*65536*512). Threads are grouped in different blocks. Blocks are assembled into a one or two-dimensional execution grids. The kernel is organized in the form of grid.

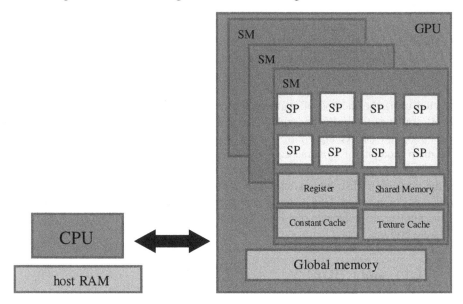

Fig. 2. The architecture of CUDA hardware

4   General Parallelization Scheme

In the DSMC simulation of dynamic collision grids, the main calculation can be divided into the following several parts: molecular movement, collisions with the domain boundaries, construction of dynamic grids and intermolecular collisions. The most expensive part of the total time is collision of molecules, and the calculation of remaining parts is not particular huge. However, in order to reduce the communication costs between CPU and GPU with GPU programming model, we set up corresponding kernels to run the whole DSMC simulation on the GPU. The algorithm described in Fig.3 demonstrates how a parallel DSMC of dynamic grids adopted GPU programming model works. First of all, the GPU kernel function is declared by global qualifier. Allocating memory on both host and the device is implemented. The initialization is accomplished on CPU. The related data are copied from host memory to device memory. When invoking a CUDA kernel, we use the "dim3" declaration to announce the number of blocks in a grid and the number of threads in a block. The relevant calculations will begin on GPU.

Host program implemented on CPU
(1) Initialize the status of simulation particles including initial configuration and velocity;
(2) Copy particles' information from the CPU host memory to GPU device memory and launch the kernel;

> *Kernels program implemented on GPU*
> For all time steps do
> **(3) Molecular movement and collision with the domain boundaries;**
> > (4) If particle escapes its calculation domain, do
> > **Update the particles' information;**
> > End if;
> > **(5) Construction of dynamic collision grids;**
> > **(6) Collision of molecules;**
> > (7) **Sampling**
> > End for

(8) Read back results to CPU and output results of each time step;
(9) Statistics of macroscopic information;

Fig. 3. CUDA-based DSMC simulation kernels

In the particle movement phase, the motion of each individual particle is independent of the remaining particles. Each particle is tracked by a thread. Assumed that there are NS number of molecules in the simulation system, each thread is assigned $NS/N_{thread} + 1$ particles, where N_{thread} is the number of thread employed by the GPU. This theme ensures sufficiently uniform computational loading of each thread. In the course of tracking the particles, the collisions with the boundaries is calculated simultaneously in a similar manner. During particles moving and collisions, particles will move randomly in the calculation domain, and some of the particles run away from the domain and continue to move. The migration across the domain boundary is called molecule transfer. In order to identify the motion of migratory particles in the domain of boundaries, molecular residence time Δst [18] is defined to calculate molecular migration and determine molecules whether depart the calculation domain. And then the statistics of the total number of molecules is carried on. Before generation of collision grids, the particles's information will be updated.

Achieving the parallelization of the kd-tree algorithm of DSMC of the dynamic collisions grids is difficult to run on GPU due to iterative structure of the kd-tree algorithm. In the processes of dynamic grids division, each thread handle a molecule. The processes include: determining which mesh each molecule belongs to, judging whether the mesh is full according to the threshold value presented in the kd-tree algorithm and creating a new mesh if the molecules do not belong to any mesh, and then assigning per molecule to its belonging mesh node. With the dynamic collision mesh, the Bird's method can be used to calculate molecular collision number [2,19] when the number of molecules within the node follow Possion distribution. Bird's method was derived according to physical considerations for the simulation of particle collisions [20], which allows multiple intermolecular collisions within each time step. In the molecules collisions phase, the number of collision pairs are generated for each grid node. The binary collisions are implemented in a loop. In this kernel, each thread is assigned to a single collision grid. During the above entire processes of DSMC run on the GPU, there is no communication with the CPU host. However, some statistical data and global information should be sampled and then read back to CPU memory at the end of the simulation. We use a kernel for sampling collision data and grid statistic.

In the process of the whole DSMC simulation, we adopt atomic operations to avoid conflict of read and write for global synchronization, resulting in a slight performance degradation. At last, the memories on the host and the device will be released. The whole simulation processes of DSMC is finished.

5   Results

The confirmation and efficiency of the developed algorithm was analyzed by an example of MEMS micro channel processing. Micro channel flow Kn number is Kn=0.046, the horizontal-to-vertical proportion is AR=5, the wall and flow temperature are $T_W = T_\infty = 300K$, the inflow velocity is $u_\infty = 140 \frac{m}{s}$, and nitrogen is used as a test gas. During the calculation, the import and export use boundary conditions of macroscopic fluid flow flux; Molecular collisions with the upper and lower wall adopt the diffuse reflection model and the reflecting molecular speed satisfy the Maxwell speed distribution.

Under the environment of the same inlet condition and wall boundaries condition, the results of pressure drop are calculated and they are in good agreement with the computational result of ref. [21]. It can be seen in fig. 4 that the calculation results of our parallel DSMC program accord with the results of serial program, the biggest relative error is less than 2%.

It can be seen from figure, the pressure across the channel experience linear decline except inlet with a slight increase influenced by the entrance effect, and each pressure point of transverse is evenly distributed. This rule is also confirmed by ref. [21,22].

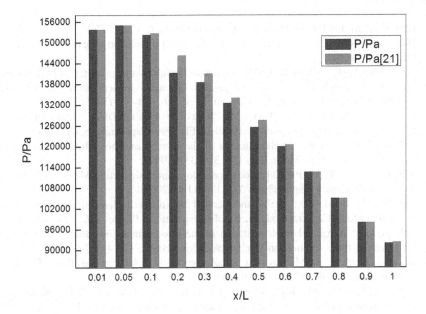

Fig. 4. The changes of pressure and comparision with that of literature [21]

6   Conclusions

In this paper, we have proposed a parallel CUDA-based DSMC simulation algorithm with the theory of dynamic grids division method. From the results of the simulation, the correctness of the algorithm is verified. In the following work, we will evaluate its computational performance and expand the scale of simulation using multi-GPU programming model or the GPU+CPU heterogeneous parallel computing architecture.

In addition, because the dynamic grids division method has tight coupling which is not appropriate for parallelization run on GPU, we adopted atomic operations for global synchronization, resulting in a slight performance degradation. Therefore, we will adopt the other optimized algorithms of grids division for further improving computational performance. And some assessment and evaluation of the new algorithms will be done, and a comprehensive comparison among various grids division methods will be made, such as static grids division, dynamic grids division.

Acknowledgements. This research was partially funded by the Key Program of National Natural Science Foundation of China (61133005) and the National Science Foundation of China (61070057 and 90715029), the PhD Programs Foundation of the Ministry of Education of China (201001611 10019), the Key Project Supported by the Development Foundation, Hunan University "985" Project, and the Program for New Century Excellent Talents in University (NCET-08-0177).

References

1. Bird, G.A.: Molecular Gas Dynamics. Clarendon Press, Oxford (1976)
2. Bird, G.A.: Molecular Gas Dynamics and the direct simulation of gas flow. Clarendon Press, Oxford (1994)
3. Bird, G.A.: Application of the DSMC method to the full shuttle geometry. A IAA-90-1692
4. Dietrich, S., Boyd, I.D.: Scalar and parallel optimized implementation of the direct simulation Monte Carlo method. J. Comput. Phys. 126, 328–342 (1996)
5. Ivanov, M., Markelov, G., Taylor, S., Watts, J.: Parallel DSMC strategies for 3D computations. In: Proceedings of the Parallel CFD 1996, Capri, Italy, p. 485 (1997)
6. LeBeau, G.J.: A parallel implementation of the direct simulation Monte Carlo method. Comput. Methods Appl. Mech. Eng. 174, 319–337 (1999)
7. Wu, J.-S., Lian, Y.-Y.: Parallel three-dimensional direct simulation Monte Carlo method and its applications. Comput. Fluids 32, 1133–1160 (2003)
8. Dietrich, S., Boyd, I.D.: Scalar and parallel optimized implementation of the direct simulation Monte Carlo method. Journal of Computational Physics 126, 328–342 (1996)
9. Lebeau, G.J.: A parallel implementation of the direct simulation Monte Carlo method. Computer Methods Application Mechanical Engineering 174, 319–337 (1999)
10. Macrossan, M.N.: DSMC: A fast simulation method for rarefied flow. Journal of Computational Physics 173, 600–619 (2001)
11. Nance, R.P., Wilmoth, R.G., Moon, B., et al.: Parallel Monte Carlo simulation of three-dimensional flow over a flat plate. Journal of Thermophysics and Heat Transfer 9(3), 471–477 (1995)
12. Thomas, R.F., John, A.L.: Implementation of the direct simulation Monte Carlo method for an exhaust plume flow field in a parallel computing environment. Computers & Fluids 18(2), 217–227 (1990)
13. Wilmoth, R.G.: Direct simulation Monte Carlo analysis of rarefied flows on parallel processors. Journal of Thermophysics and Heat Transfer 5(3), 292–300 (1991)
14. NVIDIA CUDA Homepage,
   http://developer.nvidia.com/object/cuda.html
15. nVIDIA, NVIDIA CUDA Computer Unified Device Architecture programming Guide Version 2.0, nVIDIA (2008)
16. Chen, Y., Liu, H., Li, M.: Dynamic collision grid DSMC and parallel. Computer Applications and Software 26(10), 260–262 (2009)
17. NVIDIA CUDA Compute Unified Device Architecture Programming Guide (V1.1) (November 2007), http://developer.download.nvidia.com/
   compute/cuda/1_1/NVIDIA_CUDA_Programming_Guide_1.1.pdf
18. Fu, Y., Hua, R., Kang, J.-C.: Migration Dependency Analysis of DSMC Parallel Simulation. Microelectronics & Computer 24(5), 175–183 (2007)
19. Bird, G.A.: Sophisticated DSMC [R/OL],
   http://www.gab.com.au/Resources/DSMC07notes.pdf
20. Gladkov, D., Tapia, J.-J., Alberts, S., D'Souza, R.M.: Graphics Processing Unit Based on Direct Simulation Monte Carlo. Simulation: Transactions of the Society for Modeling and Simulation International 88(6), 680–693 (2012)
21. Mavriplis, C., Ahn, J.C., Goulard, R.: Heat Tansfer and Flow fields in Short Microchannels Using Direct Simulation Monte Carlo. J. Thermophysics and Heat Tansfer 11(4), 489–496 (1997)
22. Sun, H.W., Faghri, M.: Effects of Rarefaction and Compressibility of Gaseous Flow in Microchannel Using DSMC. Numerical Heat Transfer, Part A 38, 153–168 (2000)

Internal Leakage Fault Feature Extraction
of Hydraulic Cylinder Using Wavelet Packet Energy

Xiuxu Zhao[1,2], Zhemin Hu[1,2], Rui Li[1,2], Chuanli Zhou[1,2], and Jihai Jiang[1,2]

[1] School of Mechatronics Engineering, Wuhan University of Technology,
Wuhan 430070, China
[2] School of Mechatronics Engineering, Harbin Institute of Technology,
Harbin 150001, China
zhaoxiuxu@whut.edu.cn, huzhemin87@gmail.com,
lirui540047296@163.com, 996108333@qq.com, jjhlxw@hit.edu.cn

Abstract. The leakage of hydraulic cylinder is usually caused by wear or damage of the seal, and it must be detected as early as possible to avoid worse breakdowns of system that may lead to the loss of production. In addition, the leakage is difficult to be diagnosed because it is concealed. In this paper, inlet and outlet pressure signals and position signal of piston rod of hydraulic cylinder have been collected from a special designed test-bed, which simulates different internal leakage levels of hydraulic cylinder. Fault features are extracted by wavelet packet analysis. The result shows that there are five features in total can be used to distinguish levels of the internal leakage obviously.

Keywords: Hydraulic cylinder, Internal leakage, Wavelet packet analysis, Feature Extraction.

1   Introduction

Hydraulic systems are widely applied, especially in power, control and execution system of construction machinery. Hydraulic cylinder is the actuator in hydraulic system, and its status affects system performance. Its working load is usually changing; the vibration and working speed are also unstable, especially in some special conditions, such as the transient conversion and the inertial impaction, leading to the failure of hydraulic cylinder and accounting for a large proportion of the maintenance of construction machinery. Most of leakage is caused by the seal failure, resulting in crawling of hydraulic cylinder, lack of thrust, fall of speed or instability of system, critically affecting the working of system. In addition, leakage is difficult to be diagnosed because it is concealed. Therefore, it is significant to research the leakage failure mechanism of hydraulic cylinder and detect it early to take appropriate actions timely.

In recent years, diagnosis of leakage of hydraulic cylinder gets more and more attention because their widely application in engineering equipment by many scholars. Du proposed the leakage fault diagnosis method based on the wavelet multi-scale edge detection.

K. Li et al. (Eds.): ParCFD 2013, CCIS 405, pp. 363–375, 2014.

The features of the pressure transient signals can be extracted by detecting the maxima in the appropriate scale of wavelet transform. In this way, it provides a quantitative basis for internal leakage fault diagnosis of the hydraulic cylinder [1]. Yang studied the leakage and found it can be detected accurately by the pressure rise time [2]. Tang applied wavelet transform and BP neural network into the diagnosis of hydraulic cylinder leakage [3]. Nonlinear self-adaptive robust observer was used by P. Garimella in modelling for the electric hydraulic cylinder system. The impact of unmolded dynamic factors could be reduced by robust filtering and the uncertainty of the range of model variables could be reduced by the controllable online self-adaptive parameters. The method was suitable for diagnosing the initial fault of hydraulic cylinder speed sensor failure, oil pollution and pressure shortage [4]. L.An, N.Sepehri applied the extended Kalman filter and serial test method to diagnose the leakage of fault hydraulic cylinder quantitatively [5]. Maria Werlefors applied the nonlinear observation model established by static feedback to diagnose the leakage successfully by measuring the piston position and piston speed [6]. By using the Unscented Kalman Filter, M.Sepasi monitored the operation of hydraulic systems online. The method can quickly and accurately diagnose the hydraulic cylinder internal and external leakage, the dynamic friction load and transient load changes of the hydraulic cylinder. Wavelet analysis showed clear advantage in processing faults signal of hydraulic pump and motor [7]. Amin Yazdanpanah Goharrizi established a wavelet transform-based approach to detect internal leakage in hydraulic actuators caused by seal damage or wear. But the proposed scheme requires a baseline (threshold) value, predetermined first by analyzing the pressure signal of a healthy actuator [8].

The main reason of hydraulic cylinder leakage is the damage of seal in practice, which is a gradual failure. The gradually process can be described as a potential failure mode that the system performance declines with the fault development. If the features of leakage can be extracted, the leakage can be diagnosed timely, to avoid worse breakdowns of system and prevent more loss of production. Therefore, this paper focuses on the application of wavelet packet analysis to reveal the connection between the external fault symptoms and the internal fault mode, and find out the features which can describe this relationship through a theoretical basis for diagnosing and predicting hydraulic cylinder leakage.

2   Review of Wavelet Analysis

Wavelet analysis is a time-frequency analysis method which can be applied to handle the non-stationary signals effectively. It can focus on details of the signal for automatically adaptation to the requirements of time-frequency signal. Similar to the Fourier transform, which decomposes the signal into different frequency with sine waves, wavelet analysis decomposes the signal into superposition of a series of wavelets function [10].

2.1   Wavelet Transform

Wavelet transform is classified as Continuous Wavelet Transform (CWT) and discrete wavelet transform (DWT). The CWT is a convolution of the input data sequence with a set of functions generated by the mother wavelet ψ (t).

$$CWT(a,b) = \frac{1}{\sqrt{a}} \int_{-\infty}^{+\infty} x(t)\psi\left(\frac{t-b}{a}\right) dt \tag{1}$$

Where ψ(t) is the mother wavelet that can be scaled and shifted, b ∈ R , a ∈ R+, and a ≠ 0, a is scale factor and b is shift factor.

In most applications, the signal is dispersed by a scale factor of 2^m and by a shift factor of $2^m n$. Then equation (1) can be defined as:

$$CWT(a,b) = \frac{1}{\sqrt{a}} \int_{-\infty}^{+\infty} x(t)\psi\left(\frac{t-b}{a}\right) dt \tag{2}$$

Where m and n are integers.

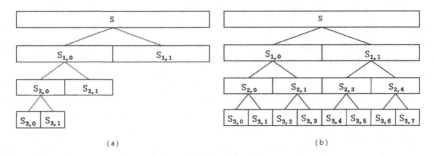

(a)   (b)

Fig. 1. Discrete wavelet transform (a) Wavelet decomposition (b) Wavelet pocket decomposition

Fast wavelet transform is commonly used in practical calculation of the discrete wavelet transform. In order to get the approximation signal, the original signal S is decomposed according to its frequency. As shown in Fig.1 (a), S3,0 is the approximation signal of original signal S.

2.2   Wavelet Packet Analysis

In application, the distinguishing ability of high frequency band signal is expected to be improved. Wavelet Packet Analysis is introduced to solve this problem [11]. It provides an elaborate method which divides the original signal into multi-layers in the full band frequency. It inherits the advantage of time-frequency localization from wavelet transform, while it continues a further decomposition for the high-frequency band. Thus, it has more comprehensive application. Fig. 1(b) shows the frequency division of the signal by wavelet packet.

The original signals S is decomposed into layers, and $S_{i,j}$ is used to represent the jth band reconstructed signal. The original signal s can be expressed as:

$$S = S_{i,0} + S_{i,1} + \cdots + S_{i,j} \tag{3}$$

2.3   Wavelet Packet Energy

For a further analysis of the signal, the energy value of detail signal of Wavelet Packet Decomposition is presented. Define the energy of $S_{i,j}$ as $E_{i,j}$:

$$E_{i,j} = \int \left| S_{i,j}(t) \right|^2 dt = \sum_{k=1}^{n} \left| x_{j,k} \right|^2 \tag{4}$$

Where $x_{i,k}$ is the amplitude of kth discrete points of the detail signal $S_{i,j}$. Construct feature vectors based on energy. Feature vector T is constructed as follows.

$$T = [E_{i,0}, E_{i,1}, \cdots, E_{i,j}] \tag{5}$$

When the energy is large, $E_{i,j}$ is usually a large value, causing some inconvenience in the analysis, then normalize the above feature vector as follows.

$$E = \sum_{j=0}^{2^i-1} E_{i,j} \tag{6}$$

$$T' = [E_{i,0}/E, E_{i,1}/E, \cdots, E_{i,j}/E] \tag{7}$$

Where vector T' is the normalized feature vector.

2.4   Wavelet Energy Entropy

The Wavelet Energy Entropy is defined as a measure of the degree of order/disorder of the signal, so it can provide useful information about the underlying dynamical process associated with the signal [12]. For a random signal, if it is generated by a completely unordered process, the amplitude and energy in each frequency band are approximately the same. Namely, the probability distribution of the signal is close to the disorder and the entropy is close to the theoretical maximum.

Define:

$$p_j = \frac{E_{i,j}}{E} \tag{8}$$

$$\sum_{j=0}^{2^i-1} p_j = 1 \qquad (9)$$

Then calculate corresponding wavelet energy entropy as:

$$W_{WE} = -\sum_{j=0}^{2^i-1} p_j \log p_j \qquad (10)$$

They should also be separated from the surrounding text by one line space.

2.5 Wavelet Packet Energy Variance

Similar to using "Entropy" to describe the distribution of wavelet packet energy, the "variance" is adopted to indicate the probability distribution of the wavelet packet energy value quantitatively in this paper. The wavelet packet energy variance is defined as:

$$s^2_{WE} = \frac{1}{2^i-1}\sum_{j=0}^{2^i-1}\left(E_j - E_{mean}\right)^2 \qquad (11)$$

Where s^2 is the variance, E_i is the energy values of ith band, E_{mean} is the average value of energy.

3 Experimental Study on Hydraulic Cylinder Leakage

With the reference to the test requirements in GB/T15622-2005 [13], the experimental principle of hydraulic cylinder internal and external leakage is shown in Fig.2.

The hydraulic cylinder internal leakage can be simulated by inserting the orifice 13 between the two chambers of the cylinder. The system pressure can be changed by adjusting the opening pressure of the relief valve 8, and the system flow can be changed by adjusting the input frequency of the variable frequency motor 4. For the load part, the load force can be changed by adjusting the opening pressure of the relief valve 23 and 27. Thus, not only the system pressure, flow and load can be regulated, but also the size of orifice can be selected in this experimental system, so the leakage of the hydraulic cylinder can be simulated under different conditions. In system, an industrial inverter 5 is used to adjust the rotating speed of the variable frequency motor 4.

The size of the load cylinder and the experimental hydraulic cylinder are the same; the stroke is 330mm and the diameter of the piston rod is 45mm. The maximum system pressure is 10MPa, and the maximum flow rate is 50L/min. Two AK-4 type pressure sensors collect the pressure signal of the hydraulic cylinder chamber with and without rod respectively, and SGC-5 type line grating sensor collects the position signal of the hydraulic cylinder piston rod with sampling frequency of 1 kHz.

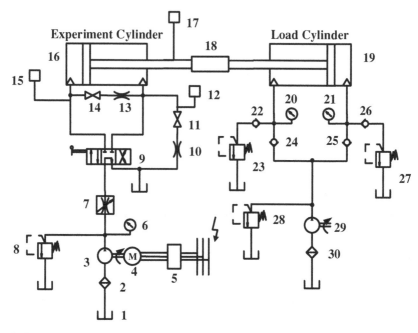

Fig. 2. Experiment Principle of hydraulic cylinder leakage. In the figure, 1-Tank; 2,30-Filter; 3,29-Hydraulic pump; 4-Variable frequency motor; 5- industrial inverter; 6,20,21-Pressure gauge; 7-Flow control valve; 8,23,27,28-Relief valve; 9-Manually operated directional valve; 10,13-Orifice; 11,14-Ball valve; 12,15-Pressure sensor; 16-Experiment cylinder; 17-Position sensor; 18-Connector; 19-Load cylinder; 22,24,25,26-Check valve

In order to reflect the actual condition of hydraulic cylinder leakage, a variable orifice is applied to simulate different size of leakage in the experiment, which is shown in Table 1.

Table 1. Different Orifice size

Number	1	2	3	4	5	6
Orifice Diameter (mm)	0.25	0.3	0.35	0.4	0.45	0.5
Orifice Length (mm)	3	3	3	3	3	4
Leakage (L/min)	0.0786	0.1629	0.3018	0.5148	0.8246	0.9426
Proportion in total flow (%)	0.4091	0.8483	1.5716	2.6810	4.2945	4.9091

During the process of piston rod stretching and retracting, the changes of pressure and piston position over time with no leakage and different levels of leakage are recorded by the pressure sensor and the position sensor.

4 Feature Extraction of Hydraulic Cylinder Leakage

4.1 Data Collected

The position and pressure signals of no-leakage and seven sizes of different leakage are collected in above test-bed. The time domain waveforms of the collected data are shown in Figure 3.

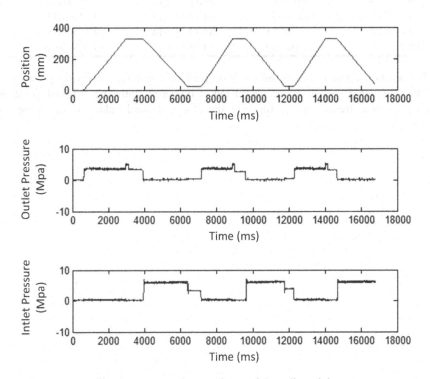

Fig. 3. Time domain waveforms of the collected data

Compared with the external leakage, the internal leakage is more harmful while it is more difficult to be detected. Therefore, this paper concentrates on the study of the internal leakage. Matlab wavelet analysis tools are applied to analyze the position signals of piston rod and the pressure signals of inlet and outlet of hydraulic cylinder. Daubechies 8 wavelet has been chosen as the basic function.

4.2 Piston Rod Stretching Speed

In this study, the inlet pressure signals of 7 different sizes of leakage are decomposed by 4-layers wavelet packet. The inverter is adjusted at 20Hz, calculating the rotating speed of pump is 1200 rpm. The load pressure is set at 5MPa and the sampling frequency is 1000Hz. Frequency ranges of detail signals are shown in Table 2.

Table 2. Frequency ranges of the detail signals

Signal/Energy	Frequency range /Hz	Signal/ Energy	Frequency range /Hz
S4,0 / E4,0	0~62.5	S4,8 / E4,8	500~562.5
S4,1 / E4,1	62.5~125	S4,9 / E4,9	562.5~625
S4,2 / E4,2	125~187.5	S4,10 / E4,10	625~687.5
S4,3 / E4,3	187.5~250	S4,11 / E4,11	687.5~750
S4,4 / E4,4	250~312.5	S4,12 / E4,12	750~812.5
S4,5 / E4,5	312.5~375	S4,13 / E4,13	812.5~875
S4,6 / E4,6	375~437.5	S4,14 / E4,14	875~937.5
S4,7 / E4,7	437.5~500	S4,15 / E4,15	937.5~1000

The position signal of the piston rod is decomposed by 4-layers wavelet packet and the low-frequency signal is reconstructed. Compared with the original position signals, the low frequency $S_{4,0}$ removes the effect of fluid pulsation and noise, as shown in Fig.4.

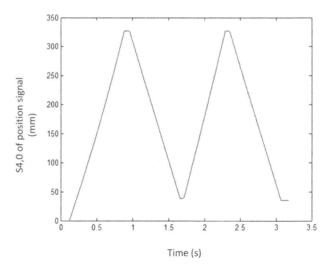

Fig. 4. Low frequency component S4,0 of position signal

Then calculate the velocity of piston rod as a feature by least-squares fitting method, which is shown in Table 3.

Table 3. Leakage- Piston rod stretching speed

No.	Orifice diameter (mm)	Piston rod stretching speed (mm/s)
1	0.00	141.19
2	0.25	130.82
3	0.30	129.97
4	0.35	124.79
5	0.40	124.25
6	0.45	120.87
7	0.50	113.87

From Table 3, it can be found that piston rod stretching speed falls with the increase of leakage, so it is set as fault feature D_1.

4.3   Pressure Rising Speed

Pressure signal is decomposed by 4-layers wavelet packet, and then reconstruct low-frequency signal $S_{4,0}$, which is shown in Fig.5.

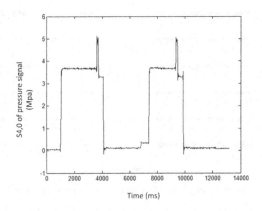

Fig. 5. Low frequency component S4,0 of pressure signal

Use the least square linear fitting to calculate pressure rising speed v with S. The result is listed in Table 4, which shows the piston rod pressure rising speed falls with the degree increase of the leakage, and set it as fault feature P_1.

Table 4. Leakage-Pressure rising speed

No.	Orifice diameter (mm)	Leakage (L/min)	Pressure rising speed v (MPa/s)
1	0.00	0	103.809
2	0.25	0.079	95.590
3	0.30	0.163	74.184
4	0.35	0.302	66.286
5	0.40	0.515	42.151
6	0.45	0.825	41.459
7	0.50	0.943	38.953

4.4   Wavelet Packet Energy of Pressure Signal

From Table 4, it can be found that pressure rising speed falls and hydraulic energy loss increases with the increase of leakage. Therefore, we try to reveal the trend by features of each frequency.

Pressure signal energy is mainly concentrated in the $S_{4,0}/E_{4,0}$, which can be processed as amplitude modulation signal, and the frequency of pressure fluctuation signal is $f_z = 90Hz$. So $S_{4,0}/E_{4,0}$ is disregarded when analyzing energy features by wavelet packet.

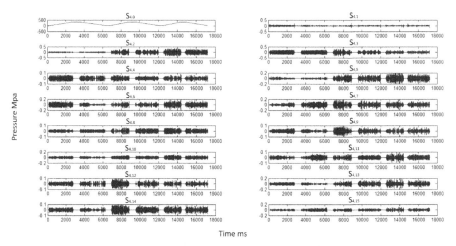

Fig. 6. Wavelet packet decomposition of pressure signals

As shown in Figure 6, Db8 wavelet packet is applied to decompose the pressure signal. Firstly, normalize the frequency energy of $S_{4,1}$ to $S_{4,15}$, and then combine the wavelet packet energy value of various leakage. The result is shown in Fig.7 by using the bar chart.

From Fig.7, it can be found that energy values of $S_{4,1}$ decline with the increase of leakage. Meanwhile, the energy value at f_z and the power generated by the hydraulic oil on the piston rod are decreasing, and the stretching speed of piston rod falls due to the increase of the leakage. Therefore, the energy value of $S_{4,1}$ signal can be set as fault feature $P2$.

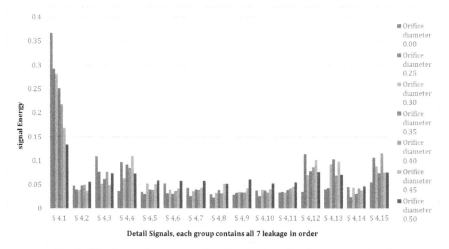

Fig. 7. Wavelet packet energy value distribution of outlet pressure signal

4.5   Wavelet Packet Energy Entropy of Pressure Signal

In order to analyze the influence of oil motion caused by the internal leakage, wavelet packet energy entropy is calculated listed in Table 5. The state of the fluid in the pipeline changes with the increase of the leakage. The distribution of energy value tends to be homogeneous and peakless, showing oil pulse is more disordered. This change can be reflected by the larger wavelet packet energy entropy of pressure signal. The experiment verifies theoretical inference is correct. Accordingly, wavelet packet energy entropy can be set as fault feature *P3*.

Table 5. Wavelet packet energy entropy

No.	Orifice diameter (mm)	Wavelet packet energy entropy
1	0.00	2.2823
2	0.25	2.3477
3	0.30	2.4454
4	0.35	2.4764
5	0.40	2.5170
6	0.45	2.5815
7	0.50	2.6707

4.6   Wavelet Packet Energy Variance of Pressure Signal

Similar to wavelet packet energy entropy, this study uses variance to describe the distribution of energy value of detail signal of wavelet packet decomposition of the pressure signal quantitatively.

Table 6. Wavelet packet energy variance

No.	Orifice diameter (mm)	Wavelet packet energy variance
1	0.00	0.006795
2	0.25	0.004576
3	0.30	0.003627
4	0.35	0.002914
5	0.40	0.002209
6	0.45	0.001324
7	0.50	0.000392

It can be found from Table 6 that the variance of wavelet packet energy value reduces with the increase of the leakage, and the energy value in each frequency band tends to average. It's a further proof that the fluid in the pipeline and tanks flows in more disordered state with the increase of the leakage, and distribute of energy of each frequency is more uniform. Accordingly, wavelet packet energy variance can be set as fault vector *P4*.

4.7   Sensitivity Analysis of Features

In order to make the features extracted from the hydraulic cylinder leakage be more practical, it is necessary to analyze the sensitivity of them. In this study, the sensitivity of results of above features is analyzed:

$$s^2_{PY} = \frac{1}{N} \sum_{i=1}^{N} \left(p_i - p_{mean} \right)^2 \tag{12}$$

Where p_i is value of feature, p_{mean} is the average value of the features, N is the amount of faults, and it is 7 in this study.

Table 7. Sensitivity of fault features

	Extracted Fault Features	Sensitivity (Normalized)
P1	Pressure rising speed	0.0028557
P2	Wavelet energy value of S4,1	0.0018453
P3	Wavelet packet energy entropy	0.0000503
P4	Wavelet packet energy variance	0.0082169
D1	Piston rod stretching speed	0.0000811

Table 7 is the sort table of the sensitivity of fault features. It can be found that the sensitivity of wavelet packet energy variance of pressure signal is the largest, and the pressure rising speed takes the second place.

5   Conclusion

By using the wavelet analysis, the position signal of piston rod is decomposed into four layers in different leakage conditions and the low frequency signal is reconstructed. The analysis reveals piston rod stretching speed tends to decrease with the increase of leakage. The same way is used to decompose the pressure signal, reconstruct low-frequency signal and collect pressure rising speed, which tends to decline with the increase of leakage. The piston rod stretching speed and pressure rising rate are the external symptom of hydraulic cylinder leakage. It can be found that the energy value of the second layer of the detail frequency signals of fluid pulsation decreases with the increasing leakage in the detail signals energy distribution. This result proves that the energy loss and hydraulic cylinder efficiency falling are caused by the leakage. In order to describe the energy distribution within hydraulic cylinder in different leakage conditions quantitatively, the wavelet packet energy entropy and wavelet packet energy variance are adopted to reveal the motion of the fluid. Five fault features are obtained to describe the hydraulic cylinder leakage quantitatively, and their sensitivity to the leakage are also analyzed. The study provides a theoretical basis for the diagnosis and early prediction of the hydraulic cylinder leakage.

Acknowledgment. This research is supported by Ministry of Education of China & Guangdong Prov. Corporation Research Project (2010B090400548).

References

1. Du, W.: The Inner Leakage Fault Diagnosis of the Hydraulic Cylinder Based on the Wavelet Multi-scale Edge Detection. Journal of Chinese Hydraulics & Pneumatics 3, 52–53 (2003)
2. Yang, L.: Research of Hydraulic Jack Leakage Diagnosis Base on Wavelet/AMEsim. Dissertation of Jilin University (2007)
3. Tang, H., Wu, Y., Ma, C., Gao, M.: Leakage Fault Diagnosis of Hydraulic Chamber using Wavelet Energy Feature. Journal of Computer Engineering and Applications 5, 221–223 (2012)
4. Garimella, P., Yao, B.: Model Based Fault Detection of an Electro-Hydraulic Cylinder. In: Proceedings of 2005 American Control Conference Press, pp. 484–488 (2005)
5. An, L., Sepehri, N.: Hydraulic actuator leakage quantification Scheme using extended Kalman filter and sequential test method. In: Proceedings of 2006 American Control Conference (2006)
6. Werlefors, M., Medvedev, A.: Observer-based Leakage Detection in Hydraulic Systems with Position and Velocity Feedback. In: Proceedings of 2006 American Control Conference, pp. 948–953 (2008)
7. Sepasi, M., Sassani, F.: On-line Fault Diagnosis of Hydraulic Systems Using Unscented Kalman Filter. International Journal of Control, Automation, and Systems 8, 149–156 (2010)
8. Yazdanpanah, G.A., Nariman, S.: A Wavelet-Based Approach to Internal Seal Damage Diagnosis in Hydraulic Actuators. IEEE Transactions on Industrial Electronics 57(5), 1755–1763 (2010)
9. Mark, A.: Introduction to Fourier analysis and wavelets. China Machine Press (2003)
10. Yen, G.G., Lin, K.C.: Wavelet packet feature extraction for vibration monitoring. IEEE Transactions on Industrial Electronics 47(3), 650–667 (2000)
11. Rosso, O.A., Blanco, S., Yordanova, J., et al.: Waveletentropy: a new tool for analysis of short duration brain electrical singals. Journal of Neuroscience Methods 105, 65–75 (2001)
12. General Administration of Quality Supervision, Inspection and Quarantine, GB/T 15622-2005: Hydraulic fluid power. Test method for the cylinders (July 11, 2005)

A Modified Energy Saving Scheduling Algorithm on Heterogeneous Systems

An Shen[1,*] and Yuming Xu[2]

[1] College of Information Science and Engineering,
Hunan University, Chang Sha, 400082, China
[2] Department of Computer Science, Hengyang Normal University,
Heng Yang, 421008, China
yongchurui@126.com

Abstract. Efficient application scheduling with low energy consumption is critical for achieving high performance in heterogeneous computing system (HCS). One of the classical approaches is the combination of heuristics and Dynamic Voltage Scaling (DVS). We propose a new schedule scheme which concentrates on the energy consumption of supply voltage's varying and a modified algorithm which analyses the extra energy cost by voltage switches and the energy saving by working at a lower level to get a better energy performance of the whole system. The performance comparison study shows that the proposed algorithm outperforms the existing scheduling algorithms.

Keywords: Heterogeneous computing, scheduling algorithm, DVS, DPM, energy saving.

1 Introduction

HCS [1-2] is an interesting computing platform due to the fact that a single parallel architecture may not be adequate for exploiting all of a programs available parallelism [2]. A popular representation of a parallel application is the *Directed Acyclic Graph* (DAG) in which the nodes represent application tasks and the directed arcs or edges represent inter-task dependencies, such as task's precedence [7]. The task scheduling problem in general is NP-complete [3-11]. The main objective of the scheduling is that the scheduling length and the energy consumption are minimized satisfying all precedence constraints [8]. To reduce processor power consumption, many hard-ware techniques have been proposed, such as *Dynamic Power Management* (DPM) [4] and *Dynamic Voltage Scaling* (DVS) [5]. In this paper we propose a new energy saving

---

* This research was partially funded by the Key Program of National Natural Science Foundation of China (Grant No. 61133005) , the National Science Foundation of China (Grant Nos. 61070057, 90715029), the Support Program of National Key Technology of China (Grant No. 2012BAH09B02), A Project Supported by Scientific Research Fund of Hunan Provincial Education Department (12A062) and A Project Supported by the Science and Technology Research Foundation of Hunan Province (Grant No. 2013GK3082).

K. Li et al. (Eds.): ParCFD 2013, CCIS 405, pp. 376–382, 2014.
© Springer-Verlag Berlin Heidelberg 2014

optimal algorithm. It takes the energy consumed by the voltage's varying into consideration, and chooses the best voltage level to save the energy. We give comparison results of a large number of random generated graphs [6].

The remainder of this paper is organized as follows. In Sect. 2, we introduce the energy saving schedule scheme. In Sect. 3, we outline the proposed schedule scheme and algorithm. In Sect. 4, results and analysis of the software simulation which was conducted to validate the algorithm has been given. Finally, conclusions and suggestions for future work have been presented in Sect. 5.

2   Related Work

In this chapter we will introduce the energy aware schedule scheme that already existed.

2.1   Energy Aware Schedule Scheme 1

In this scheme, every processor always works at the highest voltage level, and last to the moment that the application finishes its execution. Fig.1(a) gives the detail of a task working in this scheme. The energy cost can be computed as follows:

$$Energy_{Scheme\_1} = num_{proc} \cdot makespan \cdot Power_{level\_0}. \tag{1}$$

Where:

num_{proc} is the number of processors in HCS,

$makespan$ is the schedule length,

$Power_{level\_0}$ is the power when the processor working at level 0, the highest voltage level.

2.2   Energy Aware Schedule Scheme 2

In this scheme, DPM [4] was used to reduce the energy consumption when a processor didn't really have task to execute by turning itself to level idle. But the processor is still working at level 0 when it copes with the task's execution. Fig.1(b) gives the detail of a task working in this scheme. The energy cost can be computed as follows:

$$Energy_{Scheme\_2} = \sum_{q=1}^{num_{proc}} (T_{work} \cdot Power_{level\_0} + T_{idle} \cdot Power_{level\_idle}). \tag{2}$$

Where:

T_{work} is the total time that the processor working at level 0,

T_{idle} is the total time that the processor working at level idle,

$Power_{level\_idle}$ is the power when the processor working at level idle.

2.3   Energy Aware Schedule Scheme 3

In this scheme, DVS [5] was used to reduce the energy consumption by finding the available slack time slot of a task and adjusting the working voltage to the available minimum voltage level. Fig.1(c) gives the detail of a task working in this scheme. The energy cost can be computed as follows:

$$Energy_{Scheme\_3} = \sum_{q=1}^{numproc} (T_{work} \cdot Power_{level\_work} + T_{idle} \cdot Power_{level\_idle}). \tag{3}$$

Where:

$Power_{level\_work}$ is the power of a processor to execute a task after the DVS step.

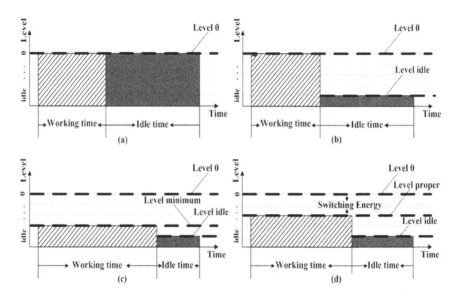

Fig. 1. Detail of schedule scheme. (a) schedule scheme 1, (b) schedule scheme 2, (c) schedule scheme 3 and (4) the proposed schedule scheme.

3   The Proposed Schedule Scheme and Algorithm

In the proposed scheme, the energy consumption of voltage switching was added to the energy equation. So we will adjust the working voltage to a proper level to minimize the energy consumption instead of the minimum voltage level used in schedule scheme 3. Fig.1(d) gives the detail of a task working in this scheme. For a large voltage changing (from Voltage$_{VDD1}$ to Voltage$_{VDD2}$), the energy consumed during this transition is:

$$Energy_{Tran} = K \cdot |Voltage_{VDD2}{}^2 - Voltage_{VDD1}{}^2|. \tag{4}$$

Where:

K is a variable related to the efficiency of the DC-DC converter.

The energy cost can be computed as follows:

$$Energy = \sum_{q=1}^{numproc} (T_{work} \cdot Power_{level\_work} + T_{idle} \cdot Power_{level\_idle}) + Energy_{Tran}. \quad (5)$$

The proposed algorithm will use the proposed schedule scheme and the detail was shown in Fig.2.

---

1. Use one of the basic algorithm to get the basic schedule result for the DAG.

2. set v_k = the first task in the schedule result.

3. while v_k is not the last task in the schedule result **do**

4.   if v_k has children **then**

5.   for each child, subtract the communication cost from the actual start time, then choose the minimum one as the available slack time.

6.   within the available slack time, use the proposed schedule scheme to compute energy consumption for each available working voltage level, then choose the level at which the energy consumption is minimum as the best voltage level.

7.   change the working voltage of v_k, and modify the schedule result.

8.   endif

9. endwhile

Fig. 2. Detail of the proposed schedule algorithm

4   Experimental Results and Performance Comparison

In this section, we choose HEFT [8], CPOP [8], HCPFD [9], and HLD [10] as our basic algorithm to present the comparative evaluation of our algorithm. Before the experiments, we introduce the input parameters used in our test. There are three parameters (CCR, K used for Energy$_{Tran}$ and the number of VL) used for the performance comparison, and we will take a single experiment for each parameter to analyses how it affect the result by setting this parameter to the value we gives, while the other information needed is stable.

4.1   CCR

CCR is the ratio of the average communication to average computation cost. The available CCR values in our research are 0.2, 0.5, 1.0, 2.0, and 5.0. Fig.3 gives the result of the experiment. For each basic algorithm shown in Fig.3, we will see that energy saving performance in our schedule scheme is always the best, while sometimes is the same as schedule scheme 3. With the increasing of CCR, the energy saving performance for all schedule schemes became better.

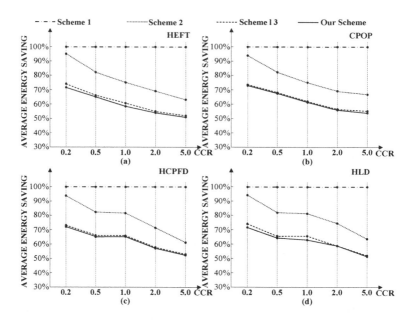

Fig. 3. Average energy saving vs. CCR. (a) HEFT Algorithm (b) CPOP Algorithm (c) HCPFD Algorithm (d) HLD Algorithm.

4.2 K

K is a variable related to the efficiency of the DC-DC converter. The available K values in our research are 5, 10, 15, 30, and 60, Fig.4 gives the result of the experiment. For each basic algorithm shown in Fig.4, with the increasing of K, the energy saving performance for all schedule schemes became worse. But at the same time, the different of energy saving performance between schedule scheme 3 and our schedule scheme became bigger. Another important fact was that the energy saving percentage of schedule scheme 2 was smaller than 0 when K was big enough.

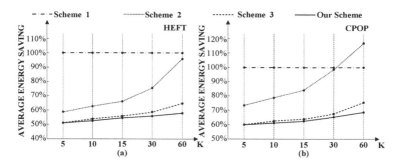

Fig. 4. Average energy saving vs. K. (a) HEFT Algorithm (b) CPOP Algorithm (c) HCPFD Algorithm (d) HLD Algorithm.

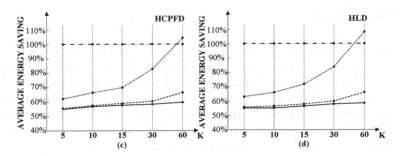

Fig. 4. (*Continued.*)

4.3   The Number of VL

In order to prove the outstanding performance of our schedule scheme and algorithm, we use different numbers of VL value to take the experiment. The available numbers of VL value in our research are 5, 10, 15, and 20. We set CCR as 5 and set K as 60. Fig.5 gives the result of the experiment. For each basic algorithm shown in Fig.5, we can see that the line of schedule scheme 2 is strait since it only uses the VL_{idle}. With the increasing of the number of VL, the energy saving performance of schedule scheme 3 became worse slowly since the minimum level became smaller at the same time. But in contract to schedule scheme 3, the energy saving performance of our schedule became better slowly since the algorithm can find more suitable voltage level to save the energy.

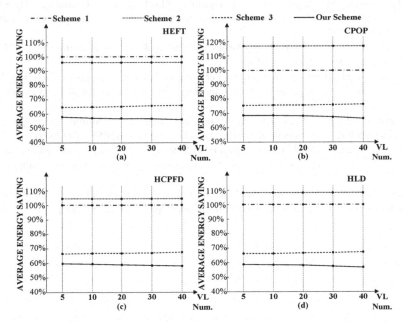

Fig. 5. Average energy saving vs. num of VL. (a) HEFT Algorithm (b) CPOP Algorithm (c) HCPFD Algorithm (d) HLD Algorithm.

5   Conclusions

In this paper, we propose a schedule scheme and an algorithm that concentrates on the energy consumption of supply voltage's varying. Based on the experiments using a large set of randomly generated application graphs with various characteristics, we can see that the increasing of CCR and the number of VL, and the decreasing of K will lead to better performance. The most important note is that the proposed algorithm outperformed the other algorithms. In the future, we will continue to use this algorithm to schedule the jobs contained in a task.

References

1. Webster, J.G.: Heterogeneous distributed computing. Encyclopedia of Electrical and Electronics Engineering 8, 679–690 (1999)
2. Feitelson, D., Rudolph, L., Schwiegelshohm, U., Sevcik, K., Wong, P.: Theory and practice in parallel job scheduling. In: JSSPP, pp. 1–34 (1997)
3. Kwok, Y., Ahmed, I.: Benchmarking the task graph scheduling algorithms. In: Proc. IPPS/SPDP, pp. 531–537 (1998)
4. Benini, L., Bogliolo, A., De Micheli, G.: A Survey of Design Techniques for System-Level Dynamic Power Management. IEEE Transactions on Very Large Scale Integration (VLSI) Systems 8, 229–316 (2000)
5. Thomas, D., Burd, R.W.: Brodersen: Design Issues for Dynamic Voltage Scaling. In: Low Power Electronics and Design, ISLPED, pp. 9–14 (2000)
6. Maheswaran, M., Siegel, H.J.: A Dynamic Matching and Scheduling Algorithm for Heterogeneous Computing System. In: Proc. Heterogeneous Computing Workshop, pp. 57–69 (1998)
7. Casanova, H.: Network modeling issues for grid application scheduling. Int. J. Found. Comput. Sci. 16, 145–162 (2005)
8. Topcuoglu, H., Hariri, S., Wu, M.-Y.: Performance-Effective and Low Complexity Task Scheduling for Heterogeneous Computing. IEEE Transactions on Parallel and Distributed Systems 13, 260–274 (2002)
9. Hagras, T., Janecek, J.: A high performance, low complexity algorithm for compile-time task scheduling in heterogeneous systems. Parallel Comput. 31, 653–670 (2005)
10. Bansal, S., Kumar, P., Singh, K.: Dealing with heterogeneity through limited duplication for scheduling precedence constrained task graphs. J. Parallel Distrib. Comput. 65, 479–491 (2005)
11. Radulescu, A., van Gemund, A.: Fast and effective task scheduling in heterogeneous systems. In: 9th Heterogeneous Computing Workshop, pp. 229–238 (2000)

Immersed Boundary-Lattice Boltzmann Method for Biological and Biomedical Flows

Wen-Hong Zu[1], Ju-Hua Zhang[1], Duan-Duan Chen[1], Yuan-Qing Xu[1,*],
Qiang Wei[1], and Fang-Bao Tian[2,*]

[1] School of Life Science, Beijing Institute of Technology, Beijing 100081, P.R. China
bitxyq@bit.edu.cn
[2] Department of Mechanical Engineering, Vanderbilt University,
2301 Vanderbilt Place, Nashville, Tennessee 37235-1592, USA
fangbao.tian@vanderbilt.edu

Abstract. In this paper, we describe an immersed boundary (IB)–lattice Boltzmann (LB) method for computing the fluid–structure interaction (FSI) encountered in biological and biomedical flows, such as fish swimming, red blood cell (RBC) dynamics and cell manipulating in micro scope. The approach combines a single relax time LB method for viscous incompressible flow and a delta function IB method for coupling the flexible boundary with the fluid. The IB method handles the effect of the moving boundary by spreading the stress exerted by the boundary on the fluid onto the collocated grid points near the boundary. For the boundary of FSI, the Lagrangian force is calculated by the standard second-order finite difference method, while the Lagrangian force of prescribed boundary is determined by a feedback scheme. The FSI solver has been validated and verified against previous studies. The details of this method and its applications in both fundamental study of biophysics of fish swimming, RBC behavior in micro flow and cell capturing in a micro architecture will be introduced.

Keywords: Immersed boundary method, Lattice Boltzmann method, Fluid–structure interaction, Fish swimming, Red blood cell.

1 Introduction

Many biological and biomedical systems involve moving boundaries and fluid–structure interaction at the tissue and organ levels. For example, the fish fins are elastic and may experience significant deformation while swimming in flow; the red blood cell (RBC) will deform when being carried by the blood through a microvessel; and the primary cilium in the kidney lumen will bend in response to the shear flow. Despite the wide application and significant improvement in the numerical simulation, there is still a lack of the robust numerical method for modeling such problems.

---

* Corresponding author.

K. Li et al. (Eds.): ParCFD 2013, CCIS 405, pp. 383–392, 2014.
© Springer-Verlag Berlin Heidelberg 2014

In these problems, the solid bodies may be geometrically complex, and sometimes experience large-displacement deformations. In the traditional numerical methods, such as ALE and space-time FEM [18,13], a mesh should be generated to provide adequate local resolution and in the meantime to minimize the number of total grid points. In addition, the mesh is deformed following the motion of the structure every time step. It will be reconstructed and/or regenerated if the deformation of the boundary is large. This treatment has high-order accuracy near the boundary. However, it is computationally very expensive. Moreover, the irregular boundary makes the mesh generation a challenging task and large deformation can lead to deterioration of the grid quality. In contrast, the methods based on a non-body-conformal Cartesian grid such as the IB–LB method are much simpler when handling the irregular geometries and motions of the immersed solid bodies.

The IB method developed first by Peskin [8] employs a fixed Cartesian grid and continuous forcing approach. In this method, an artificial force is distributed as a body-force term onto the volumetric mesh in the vicinity of the moving boundary in order to account for the effect of the boundary. A robust method for fluid-flow simulations is the LB method. Instead of discretizing the momentum equation, the LB method is an approach based on the particle kinetics. The method has achieved great success in the past decades and has proven to be an efficient solver for fluid flows. To combine the advantage of the IB method for its simple boundary treatment and that of the LB method for its fast flow simulation, hybrid methods coupling these two approaches have been developed recently [17,16,14,21,20,19]. Among the various IB methods, Peskin's diffuse-boundary approach is particularly suitable for this combination, since in this approach all the grid points within the computational domain are treated with a unified equation.

In this paper, we will first describe an IB–LB method for computing the FSI encountered in biological and biomedical flows. Then the validation and verification cases will be provided. Finally, the applications of IB–LB method in fundamental study of fish swimming, RBC behavior in micro flow and cell capturing in a micro architecture will be introduced to demonstrate the efficiency of this method in modeling this type of problem.

2   Governing Equations

The flow considered here is governed by the incompressible Navier–Stokes equations,

$$\rho\left(\frac{\partial \mathbf{u}}{\partial t} + \mathbf{u}\cdot\nabla\mathbf{u}\right) = -\nabla p + \mu\nabla^2\mathbf{u} + \mathbf{f}, \quad \nabla\cdot\mathbf{u} = 0, \tag{1}$$

where ρ is the fluid density, μ is the viscosity, $\mathbf{u}$ is the fluid velocity, p is the pressure, and $\mathbf{f}$ is is the momentum forcing applied to enforce the no-slip and no-penetration boundary conditions along the IB.

In this paper, we mainly focus on the thin shell structures (plates) which are used to model the RBCs and fish fins. The readers are referred to Refs. [11,10,9]

for the FSI of general structure. The governing equation for dynamics of the two-dimensional plate is [5,17,16,3,14,20,15]

$$m_s \frac{\partial^2 \mathbf{X}}{\partial t^2} - \frac{\partial}{\partial s}\left[T(s)\frac{\partial \mathbf{X}}{\partial s}\right] + E_b \frac{\partial^4 \mathbf{X}}{\partial s^4} = \mathbf{F}_f, \tag{2}$$

where m_s is the linear density, $\mathbf{X}$ is the position vector of a point on the plate, s is the arc length along the plate, $T(s) = E_s(|\frac{\partial \mathbf{X}}{\partial s}| - 1)$ is the in-plane tension, and $\mathbf{F}_f$ is the fluid force per unit length. Here E_s and E_b are the stretching and bending coefficients of the plate, respectively. The three-dimensional plate is governed by [7,12,4]

$$m_p \frac{\partial^2 \mathbf{X}}{\partial t^2} + \sum_{i,j=1}^{2}\left[-\frac{\partial}{\partial s_i}\left(\sigma_{ij}\frac{\partial \mathbf{X}}{\partial s_j}\right) + \frac{\partial^2}{\partial s_i \partial s_j}\left(\gamma_{ij}\frac{\partial^2 \mathbf{X}}{\partial s_i \partial s_j}\right)\right] = \mathbf{F}_f, \tag{3}$$

where m_p is the surface density of the plate, $\sigma_{ij} = \psi_{ij}(1 - \delta_{ij}/T_{ij})$ with $T_{ij} = (\partial \mathbf{X}/\partial s_i \cdot \partial \mathbf{X}/\partial s_j)^{1/2}$ being the stretching and shearing effects and ψ_{ij} being the stretching and shearing coefficients, and γ_{ij} is the bending and twisting coefficients. Additional terms may be involved when the initial configuration of the structure is considered. For example, a bending force was introduced to maintain the standard biconcave disk shape of the two-dimensional RBC in our previous work [20].

3   Numerical Method

3.1   LB Method

In the present work, a LBGK LB method is used to simulate the fluid dynamics. In this method, the kinematics of the fluid is governed by the discrete lattice Boltzmann equation of a single relaxation time model,

$$g_i(\mathbf{x} + \mathbf{e}_i \Delta t, t + \Delta t) - g_i(\mathbf{x}, t) = -\frac{1}{\tau}[g_i(\mathbf{x}, \mathbf{t}) - g_i^{eq}(\mathbf{x}, \mathbf{t})] + \Delta t G_i, \tag{4}$$

where $g_i(\mathbf{x}, t)$ is the distribution function for particles with velocity $\mathbf{e}_i$ at position $\mathbf{x}$ and time t, Δt is the size of the time step, $g_i^{eq}(\mathbf{x}, \mathbf{t})$ is the equilibrium distribution function, τ represents the relaxation time, and G_i is the body force term. In Eq. (4), g_i^{eq} and G_i are determined by

$$g_i^{eq} = \omega_i \rho \left[1 + \frac{\mathbf{e}_i \cdot \mathbf{u}}{c_s^2} + \frac{\mathbf{uu} : (\mathbf{e}_i \mathbf{e}_i - c_s^2 \mathbf{I})}{2c_s^4}\right], \tag{5}$$

$$G_i = \left(1 - \frac{1}{2\tau}\right)\omega_i \left[\frac{\mathbf{e}_i - \mathbf{u}}{c_s^2} + \frac{\mathbf{e}_i \cdot \mathbf{u}}{c_s^4}\mathbf{e}_i\right] \cdot \mathbf{f}, \tag{6}$$

where ω_i are the weighing factors, $\mathbf{u}$ is the velocity of the fluid, c_s is the speed of sound defined by $c_s = \Delta x/\sqrt{3}\Delta t$, and $\mathbf{f}$ is the body force acting on the fluid.

(a)   (b)

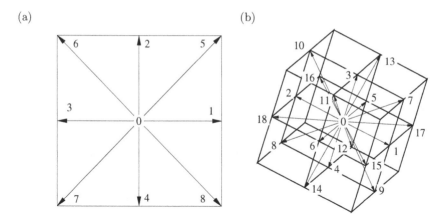

Fig. 1. Lattice Boltzmann models: (a) Nine base vectors representing 9 possible velocity directions in the D2Q9 lattice model; (b) Nineteen base vectors representing 19 possible velocity directions in the D3Q19 lattice model.

The relaxation time is related to the kinematic viscosity in the Navier–Stokes equations in terms of $\nu = (\tau - 0.5)c_s^2\Delta t$.

In the two-dimensional nine-speed (D2Q9) model, as shown in Fig. 1(a), the nine possible particle velocities are given by

$$\mathbf{e}_0 = (0, \quad 0),$$

$$\mathbf{e}_i = \left(\cos\frac{\pi(i-1)}{2}, \quad \sin\frac{\pi(i-1)}{2}\right)\frac{\Delta x}{\Delta t}, \qquad \text{for } i = 1 \text{ to } 4,$$

$$\mathbf{e}_i = \left(\cos\frac{\pi(i-9/2)}{2}, \quad \sin\frac{\pi(i-9/2)}{2}\right)\frac{\sqrt{2}\Delta x}{\Delta t}, \qquad \text{for } i = 5 \text{ to } 8,$$

where Δx is the lattice spacing. The weight factors are given by $w_0 = 4/9$, $w_i = 1/9$ for $i = 1$ to 4 and $w_i = 1/36$ for $i = 5$ to 8. In the three-dimensional nineteen-speed (D3Q19) model shown in Fig. 1(b), the particle velocities are defined by

$$\mathbf{e}_0 = (0, \quad 0, \quad 0),$$

$$\mathbf{e}_i = (\pm 1, 0, 0)\frac{\Delta x}{\Delta t}, (0, \pm 1, 0)\frac{\Delta x}{\Delta t}, (0, 0, \pm 1)\frac{\Delta x}{\Delta t}, \qquad \text{for } i = 1 \text{ to } 6,$$

$$\mathbf{e}_i = (\pm 1, \pm 1, 0)\frac{\Delta x}{\Delta t}, (\pm 1, 0, \pm 1)\frac{\Delta x}{\Delta t}, (0, \pm 1, \pm 1)\frac{\Delta x}{\Delta t}, \qquad \text{for } i = 7 \text{ to } 18.$$

The weight factors of D3Q19 model take the values of $w_0 = 1/3$, $w_i = 1/18$ for $i = 1$ to 6 and $w_i = 1/36$ for $i = 7$ to 18. The values of $\mathbf{e}_i$ ensure that within one time step, a fluid particle moves to one of the neighboring nodes as shown in Fig. 1, or stays at its current location.

Once the particle density distribution is known, the fluid density, velocity and pressure are then computed from $\rho = \sum_i g_i$, $\rho\mathbf{u} = \sum_i \mathbf{e}_i g_i + \mathbf{f}\Delta t/2$, $p = \rho c_s^2$. For small characteristic velocities, or small Mach numbers $|\mathbf{u}|/c_s$, the equations presented above are equivalent to the Navier–Stokes equations. It should be pointed out that LB method has proven to be highly efficient for high performance computing.

3.2   IB Method

In this method, the no-slip and no-penetration boundary conditions on the flexible boundary is achieved by adding a force $\mathbf{f}_{ib}$ to the fluid body force, which can be written as,

$$\mathbf{f}_{ib}(\mathbf{x},t) = \int \mathbf{F}(s,t)\delta_D(\mathbf{x} - \mathbf{X}(s,t))ds, \qquad (7)$$

where $\mathbf{F}(s,t)$ is the Lagrangian force density on the fluid by the elastic boundary, $\delta_D(\mathbf{x} - \mathbf{X}(\mathbf{s},t))$ is the Dirac δ function. It is known that at the interface, the hydrodynamic force acting on the solid and the Lagrangian force on the fluid by flexible boundary must be equal and opposite, i.e., $\mathbf{F}(s,t) = -\mathbf{F}_f$. Consequently, for the elastic thin shell, the Lagrangian force can be directly calculated by discretizing Eqs. (2) and (3). In this paper, the standard second-order finite difference method is used. For the time discretization of the inertial force, one might try to evaluate it by applying an explicit time difference. However, this method is only numerically stable when the boundary mass is very small. Alternatively, the penalty IB-LB method is an efficient treatment of the inertial term. For the boundaries of prescribed motion, the feedback forcing scheme is employed to determine the Lagrangian force, $\mathbf{F} = \alpha(\mathbf{X} - \mathbf{x}_{ib}) + \beta(\mathbf{U} - \mathbf{u}_{ib})$, where $\mathbf{u}_{ib}$ is the interpolated velocity based flow field, $\mathbf{x}_{ib}$ is the position integrated by using $\mathbf{u}_{ib}$, α and β are positive constants.

4   Validation and Verification

In this section, the numerical method will be validated and verified against the previous studies. The two-dimensional simulation is validated by a biconcave RBC in a Poiseuille flow and a RBC near the bifurcation of a microvessel, which are shown in Figs. 2(a) and (b), respectively. The numerical results and experimental observations from different sources are shown in the figure for comparison. From the results shown in Figs. 2(a) and (b), it is found that the present results are in good agreement with those in the previous simulations [22,2] and experiment [1].

To validation the three–dimensional solver, we perform a 3D fish with dorsal, pelvic and tail fins, and a three-dimensional red blood cell in a stenosed vessel, which are shown in Figs. 3(a) and (b). The motion of the integrated fish is $Y(s,t) = A(s)\sin(\kappa(s - ct))$ where A is the local amplitude, κ is the wave number, c is the phase velocity, and $s = (x - x_0)/L$ with x_0 being the head position and L being the model length. In the simulations, $A(s) = C_0 + C_1 s + C_2 s^2$ and the parameters, C_0, C_1 and C_3 are determined by $A(0) = 0.04$, $A(0.2) = 0.02$

(a)   (b)

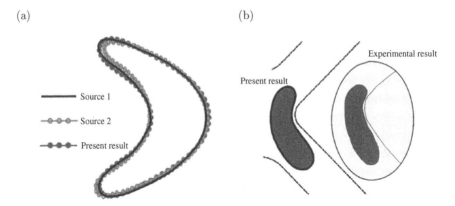

Fig. 2. Validation of the two-dimensional red blood cell moving in a microvessel: (a) a biconcave RBC in a Poiseuille flow, and (b) a RBC near the bifurcation of a microvessel. For comparison, the numerical results from source 1 [22] and source 2 [2] are shown in (a), and the experimental observation [1] is shown in (b).

(a)   (b)

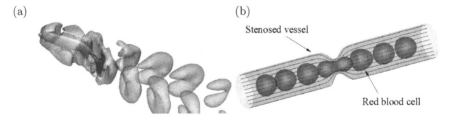

Fig. 3. Validation of the three-dimensional solver: (a) a 3D integrated fish, and (b) a three-dimensional red blood cell moving in a stenosed vessel.

and $A(1) = 0.2$. The other parameters are: $Re = 200$, $\kappa = 1.0$, and $c = 2.0$. From Fig. 3(a), it is found that a structure of two-row vortex rings is observed, which is consistent with the observation in nature locomotion. Fig. 3(b) shows a series of RBC configurations during it is moving through the stenosed vessel. The red blood cell is initially located at the center of the vessel and is released at $t = 0$. It moves by following the fluid flow with slight deformation before encountering the stenosis. When moving through the stenosed part, it is compressed due to the lubrication force without contacting directly with the walls of the vessel. Finally, it is relaxed and recovers its original shape in a short time after passing the stenosed part. These observations are consistent with those reported in Refs. [6,19].

5   A Cell Capturing Scheme in Microfluidic Device

In recent years, the technique of microfluidic chip has been receiving a considerable attention for the merits of high integration, automation, portability and small sample requirement. The corresponding cell manipulation modes including cell sorting, cell separation and cell capturing are the basic steps to perform a cell experiment on the chip, among which the cell capturing is a typical and fundamental process to keep the cells in a selector. In this section, a special cell capturing structure named C-shape sieve is designed to capture the passing cells by considering the deformability and the size of the cells. The IB–LB method described in Section 3 is applied to analyze the cell capturing abilities by systematically varying three important governing parameters, the width of the chamber inlet and outlet, the radius of the C-shape sieve and the radius of the sieve post.

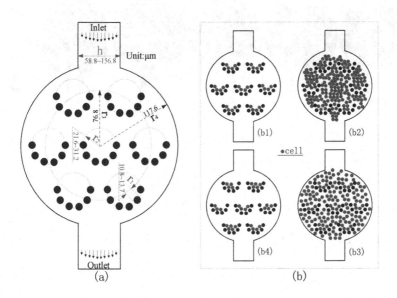

Fig. 4. The scheme of microfluidic design and cell capturing principle: (a) a spherical chamber with seven C-shape sieves and (b) four steps of continuous cell capturing in a micro chamber with C-shape sieves. In (b), b1–b4 represent loading, culturing, trypsinizing, and flushing of RBC, respectively.

Fig. 4 shows a spherical chamber with seven C-shape sieves and four typical steps in continuous cell capturing and culturing. The width of sieve pores between two neighboring posts can be controlled by r_1 or r_2. Therefore, when cells are drifted into the chamber with the flow, some of them will probably float to the interior of the sieve and be trapped. r_3 and r_4 are fixed while h, r_1 and r_2 can be adjusted to get an optimized design. The four steps in cell capturing are loading, culturing, trypsinizing, and flushing steps. In the simulation model, the density of fluid is $1.00 g/cm^3$, the viscosities of the fluid and the cytoplasm are both set as $1.2cp$. The non-dimensional unit, i.e. $dx = dy = 1$, is adopted for this calculation model, and the computational domain is divided into many lattices with the side length representing $2.4\mu m$ in the physical dimension, the cell is $12\mu m$ in diameter. The bounce-back principle is used to achieve the stationary boundary condition of solid walls. The pressure is set to be $20Pa$ at the inlet and $0Pa$ at the outlet. The Reynolds number is about 0.1 in the simulation. In the cell membrane mechanics model, the bending rigidity K_b is set as $1.0 \times 10^{-11} N \cdot m$ (the non-dimensional K_b is 0.1). The tension stiffness K_s is given as $2.0 \times 10^{-11} N \cdot m$ (the non-dimensional K_s is 0.2).

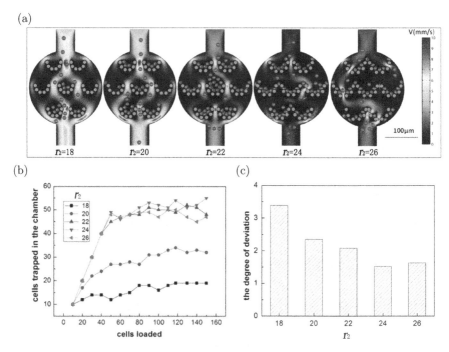

Fig. 5. The results for different sieve sizes at $r_1 = 4.5$: (a) RBC distributions and flow fields with $18 \leq r_2 \leq 26$, (b) the cells trapped in chamber, and (c) the degree of deviation.

The micro sieve structure will affect the flow field, and consequently affect the degree of uniformity of the location of the cells in each micro sieve which is made up of micro posts. The diameters of the sieve and the micro post are r_2 and r_1, respectively. The sieves are designed to form several low velocity regions and trap the cells from the fluid by providing a passage for the fluid only. A trapped cell will block the near sieve pore, and the resistance of the fluid will increase if the unobstructed pore of the sieves decreases. Consequently, the sequent cells are prevented from entering these sieves. It is convenient to adjust the relative position of the posts meanwhile change the size of sieve pore by increasing or decreasing r_2. As shown in Fig. 5(a), the simulation results suggest that the intercepting efficiency and the degree of distribution uniformity increase with r_2

at $r_1 = 4.5$. The intercepting efficiency and the distribution uniformity are not good when $r_2 = 18$. When r_2 is increased, more cells are drifted into the sieves as more fluid goes through sieves. Consequently, the distribution uniformity and capture efficiency is improved, as shown in Fig. 5(b). The width of the apertures increase as r_2 increase, the cells will either be stuck on the micro column surface or slip away. In addition, the velocity gradient inside the sieve area is smaller for larger r_2, as shown in Fig. 5(a), and the distribution uniformity increase with r_2, as shown in Fig. 5(c).

We also consider the effects of the width of the chamber inlet and outlet and the pillar diameter on the cell capturing efficiency. It is found that the cell capturing efficiency can be improved by increasing the ratio of r_2 to r_1 and varying the width h. The details of the flow field and the mechanisms will be discussed in the future studies.

6 Conclusions

We have introduced an IB-LB computational approach for simulating the fluid–structure interaction problems involved in biological and biomedical flows. The method features an IB method, which is used for handling the effect of the moving boundaries, and a LB method for computing fluid motions. We have performed the validation study and have demonstrated its application of the method in a cell capturing scheme in microfluidic device. In the future, this method will be further applied to the problems of this type to investigate the underlying biophysics of the flexible and complex boundaries, such as aquatic animal swimming, aerial animal flight, RBC flow, and phonation.

Acknowledgements. This work is supported by the National Natural Science Foundation of China (No.81301291) and the Fund for Basic Research (No.3160012211305) of Beijing Institute of Technology.

References

1. Barber, J.O., Alberding, J.P., Restrepo, J.M., Secomb, T.W.: Simulated two-dimensional red blood cell motion, deformation, and partitioning in microvessel bifurcations. Ann. Biomed. Eng. 36, 1690–1698 (2008)
2. Hosseini, S.M., Feng, J.J.: A particle-based model for simulating erythrocyte deformation and transport through capillaries. Chem. Eng. Sci. 64, 4488–4497 (2009)
3. Huang, W.X., Chang, C.B., Sung, H.J.: An improved penalty immersed boundary method for fluid–flexible body interaction. J. Comput. Phys. 230, 5061–5079 (2011)
4. Huang, W.X., Chang, C.B., Sung, H.J.: Three-dimensional simulation of elastic capsules in shear flow by the penalty immersed boundary method. J. Comput. Phys. 231, 3340–3364 (2012)
5. Huang, W.X., Shin, S.J., Sung, H.J.: Simulation of flexible filaments in a uniform flow by the immersed boundary method. J. Comput. Phys. 226, 2206–2228 (2007)
6. Huang, W.X., Sung, H.J.: An immersed boundary method for fluid–flexible structure interaction. Comput. Meth. Appl. Mech. Eng. 198, 2650–2661 (2009)

7. Huang, W.X., Sung, H.J.: Three-dimensional simulation of a flapping flag in a uniform flow. J. Fluid Mech. 653, 301–336 (2010)
8. Peskin, C.S.: Flow patterns around heart valves: a digital computer method for solving the equations of motion. PhD thesis, Yeshiva University (1972)
9. Tian, F.B., Chang, S., Luo, H., Rousseau, B.: A 3d numerical simulation of wave propagation on the vocal fold surface. In: Proceedings of the 10th International Conference on Advances in Quantitative Laryngology, Voice and Speech Research, Cincinnati, Ohio, p. 94921483 (2013)
10. Tian, F.B., Dai, H., Luo, H., Doyle, J.F., Rousseau, B.: Computational fluid–structure interaction for biological and biomedical flows. In: Proceedings of the ASME 2013 Fluids Engineering Division Summer Meeting, Incline Village, Nevada, p. 16408 (2013)
11. Tian, F.B., Dai, H., Luo, H., Doyle, J.F., Rousseau, B.: Fluid–structure interaction involving large deformations: 3D simulations and applications to biological systems. J. Comput. Phys. (under review, 2013)
12. Tian, F.B., Lu, X.Y., Luo, H.: Onset of instability of a flag in uniform flow. Theor. Appl. Mech. Lett. 2, 022005 (2012)
13. Tian, F.B., Lu, X.Y., Luo, H.: Propulsive performance of a body with a traveling wave surface. Phys. Rev. E 86, 016304 (2012)
14. Tian, F.B., Luo, H., Lu, X.Y.: Coupling modes of three filaments in side-by-side arrangement. Phys. Fluids 23, 111903 (2011)
15. Tian, F.B., Luo, H., Song, J., Lu, X.Y.: Force production and asymmetric deformation of a flexible flapping wing in forward flight. J. Fluids Struct. 36, 149–161 (2013)
16. Tian, F.B., Luo, H., Zhu, L., Liao, J.C., Lu, X.Y.: An immersed boundary-lattice Boltzmann method for elastic boundaries with mass. J. Comput. Phys. 230, 7266–7283 (2011)
17. Tian, F.B., Luo, H., Zhu, L., Lu, X.Y.: Interaction between a flexible filament and a downstream rigid body. Phys. Rev. E 82, 026301 (2010)
18. Wang, S.Y., Tian, F.B., Jia, L.B., Lu, X.Y., Yin, X.Z.: The secondary vortex street in the wake of two tandem circular cylinders at low Reynolds number. Phys. Rev. E 81, 036305 (2010)
19. Xu, Y.Q., Tang, X.Y., Tian, F.B., Peng, Y.H., Xu, Y., Zeng, Y.J.: IB–LBM simulation of the haemocyte dynamics in a stenotic capillary. Comput. Method Biomec. (in press, 2013), doi:10.1080/10255842.2012.729581
20. Xu, Y.Q., Tian, F.B., Deng, Y.L.: An efficient red blood cell model in the frame of IB–LBM and its application. Int. J. Biomath. 6, 1250061 (2013)
21. Xu, Y.Q., Tian, F.B., Li, H.J., Deng, Y.L.: Red blood cell partitioning and blood flux redistribution in microvascular bifurcation. Theor. Appl. Mech. Lett. 2, 024001 (2012)
22. Ye, T., Li, H., Lam, K.Y.: Modeling and simulation of microfluid effects on deformation behavior of a red blood cell in a capillary. Microvas. Resc. 80, 453–463 (2010)

Effect of Shape Parameterization
on Aerodynamic Shape Optimization
with SPSA Algorithm

Zheng Wang, Shengjiao Yu, and Tiegang Liu*

LMIB and School of Mathematics and Systems Science,
Beihang University, Beijing 100191, P.R. China
wzbuaa@smss.buaa.edu.cn, liutg@buaa.edu.cn

Abstract. In this paper several parameterization methods are investigated for two-dimensional airfoils, and applied to aerodynamic shape design optimization problems such as constrained airfoil design. The simultaneous perturbation stochastic approximation (SPSA) method is adopted to estimate the gradients of objective functions that are computed during each design iteration using a finite volume computational fluid dynamics technique for solving compressible Euler equations. The computational results for shape design show that the Hicks-Henne shape functions and NACA orthonormal shape functions perform better than other methods such as Wagner, and B-Spline representation methods, while the B-Spline method can easily adjust the movement by control points.

Keywords: Shape Parameterization, SPSA Algorithm, Aerodynamic Shape Optimization.

1   Introduction

During the recent years airfoil and wing design methodologies have made large steps forward in rapid improvement of aerodynamic performance[1]. These improvements include increasing the ratio of lift over drag, or increasing lift at higer flight speed with drag kept low, etc. As we know, in design process the shape should be parameterized, and then the gradient of the objective should be obtained to give the optimal direction. So the mathematical representation of airfoil shape is one of the challenging topics for all optimization approaches, which provide a wide variety of possible shapes for evaluation. Generally speaking, the parameterization methods should have the capability to represent a wide range of geometries with less number of design variables. There are plenty of methods for airfoil parameterization. However, most are not suitable for airfoil design in transonic airfoil shape optimization[2].

In this paper, we consider the effect of several popular airfoil parameterization applied to 2-D airfoil design with SPSA algorithm[3][4][5][6]. The optimization

---

* Corresponding author.

K. Li et al. (Eds.): ParCFD 2013, CCIS 405, pp. 393–402, 2014.
© Springer-Verlag Berlin Heidelberg 2014

is performed at transonic flow conditions with the numerical solution of Euler equations. The objective is to minimize the drag coefficient(C_d) with the lift coefficient(C_l) and volume of the shape(Vol) unchanged. The parameterization techniques to be discussed in this work include the polynomials and splines [7][13], the NACA orthonomial functions [8], Hicks-Henne bump functions [9] and Wagner shape functions[10][11].

The simultaneous perturbation stochastic approximation (SPSA) method is adopted to perform the optimal process. SPSA is effective for the optimization problem of complex system which is difficult or impossible to directly obtain the gradient of the objective function except the measurements of objective function. SPSA relies on two measurements of the objective function to estimate the gradient efficiently.

Finally, the comparison of different parameterization methods based on SPSA optimal method will be described and some numerical results will be shown with some suggestions. The rest of the paper proceeds as follows. Firstly, we describe the parameterization methods employed in this paper, and introduce the procedure of SPSA algorithm; secondly, we carry out some numerical examples, and the conclusions are drawn at last.

2   Parameterization Techniques

2.1   B-Spline Method

In the B-Spline parameterization method, the x and y coordinates of the shape could be written as:

$$x(t) = \sum_{i=1}^{n+1} X_i N_{i,k}(t), \quad y(t) = \sum_{i=1}^{n+1} Y_i N_{i,k}(t), \ n \geq k - 1. \tag{1}$$

Here x and y are the Cartesian coordinates of the shape, $N_{i,k}$ is the i-th B-Spline basis function of order k. t is the parameter variable and (X_i, Y_i) are the coordinates of the B-Spline control points, and the B-Spline functions are obtained using Deboor's relation:

$$N_{i,k}(t) = \frac{t - t_i}{t_{i+k-1} - t_i} N_{i,k-1}(t) + \frac{t_{i+k} - t}{t_{i+k} - t_{i+1}} N_{i+1,k-1}(t), \tag{2}$$

where

$$N_{i,1}(t) = \begin{cases} 1, t_i < t \leq t_{i+1} \\ 0, otherwise \end{cases}, \tag{3}$$

t_i is the non-decreasing set of real numbers also called the knot sequence. As a result, the shape of the basis function only depends on the knot spacing since the basis functions are based on knot differences. Fig.1 shows two airfoils NACA0012 and RAE2822 parameterized using B-Spline curve of order 4 with control points.

Fig. 1. B-Spline approximation of NACA0012 (left) and RAE2822 (right) airfoils

2.2 NACA Orthonormal Basis

The NACA airfoil is a typical example for conventional airfoils, and could be expressed by the following four shape functions:

$$g_1(x) = \sqrt{x} - x, \tag{4}$$
$$g_2(x) = x(1 - x), \tag{5}$$
$$g_3(x) = x^2(1 - x), \tag{6}$$
$$g_4(x) = x^3(1 - x), \tag{7}$$

where x is on the closed unit interval $[0, 1]$. These four functions are referred to as the generators of the NACA 4-digit airfoils. The orthonormal set $\{f_i(x)\}$ of the above functions is given by the Gram-Schmidt orthonormalization process as follows. First, an orthogonal set $\{h_i(x)\}$ is obtained by normalization:

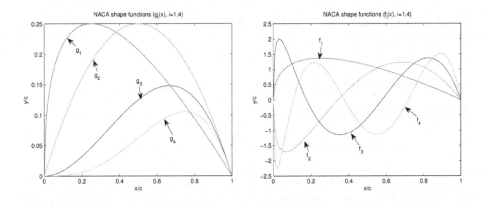

Fig. 2. NACA nonorthogonal and orthonormal basis functions

$$h_n(x) = g_n(x) - \sum_{i=1}^{n-1} a_{ni} h_i(x), \tag{8}$$

where $a_{ni} = \frac{(g_n, h_i)}{(h_i, h_i)}$, and $(g_n, h_i) = \int_0^1 g_n h_i dx$. Then, the orthonormal set $\{f_i(x)\}$ is obtained by the following relation:

$$f_i(x) = \frac{h_i(x)}{\|h_i\|}. \tag{9}$$

The NACA basis is shown in Fig. 2.

The mathematical formulation for the NACA basis is:

$$y_u = \sum_{n=1}^{4} a_n f_n(x), \quad y_l = \sum_{n=1}^{4} b_n f_n(x), \tag{10}$$

where a_n, b_n are design parameters to be solved by least square method. Fig. 3 shows the results of parameterization for NACA0012 and RAE2822 using NACA orthonormal basis functions. Obviously the curve fit the given points quite well.

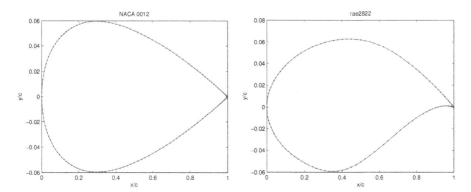

Fig. 3. Parameterization for NACA0012(left) and RAE2822(right) using NACA orthonormal basis functions

2.3   The Hicks-Henne Shape Function Method

The shape function are defined as

$$f_i(x) = \sin^4(\pi x^{m_i}), m_i = \frac{\ln(0.5)}{\ln(x_{M_i})}, \quad i = 1, \ldots, N, \tag{11}$$

where N stands for the number of basis functions one needs. For N=32, there are 16 Hicks-Henne shape functions for the upper surface and 16 for the lower surface, respectively. They are added to an initial shape to creat a new airfoil,

$$y = y_0 + \sum_{i=1}^{N} f_i(x). \tag{12}$$

The location of x_{M_i} could be chosen uniformly distributed or user defined. Obviously, the weight of these shape functions are design variables in the optimization and it's different from the above methods. Fig. 4(left) shows the Hicks-Henne Shape Functions.

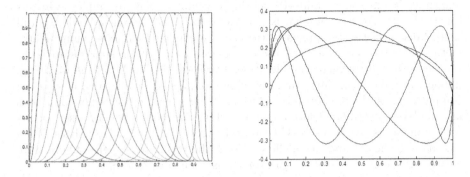

Fig. 4. A set of 16 Hicks-Henne Bump Functions(left) and 5 Wagner Bump functions(right)

2.4   The Wagner Function Method

This method is outlined in Ramamoorthy and Padmavathi [10], and the basis function is selected as

$$f_1(x) = (\theta + \sin\theta)/\pi - \sin^2(\theta/2), \quad f_k(x) = \sin(k\pi) + [sin(k-1)\theta]/\pi, \quad k > 1, \quad (13)$$

where $\theta = 2\sin^{-1}(\sqrt{x})$.

   Fig. 4(right) shows the 5 Wagner shape functions. These functions are also added to an initial shape to form a new airfoil, just like the way of Hicks-Henne functions in (12).

3   Flow Solver and SPSA Algorithm

We will consider the optimization based on Euler equations in this paper, the objective is obtained by solving Euler equations around an airfoil, which is

$$\frac{\partial}{\partial t} \int_\Omega W \, d\Omega + \oint_{\partial\Omega} F_c dS = 0 \qquad (14)$$

with

$$W = \begin{bmatrix} \rho \\ \rho u \\ \rho v \\ \rho E \end{bmatrix} \quad F_c = \begin{bmatrix} \rho V \\ \rho u V + n_x p \\ \rho v V + n_y p \\ \rho H V \end{bmatrix}$$

where

$$E = \frac{p}{\rho(\gamma - 1)} + \frac{1}{2}V^2, \quad H = E + \frac{p}{\rho}, \quad V = un_x + vn_y,$$

and $n = (n_x, n_y)$ denotes the unit normal vector at each cell boundary, W is conservative variables, F_c is vector of convective fluxes, V is the contravariant velocity, which is normal to the surface element dS, H is total enthalpy. The well known JST(Jameson-Schmidt-Turkel) finite volume scheme is employed in this solver[12]. The conservation law is semi-discretized and the second order spatial central discretization is applied to the flux, an explicit four-stage Runge-Kutta method is used to solve the semi-discretized equations until the steady state is obtained. Several convergence acceleration strategies, such as local time-stepping, implicit residual smoothing, and enthalpy damping are used to accelerate the computation of the steady-state solutions. Characteristic boundary conditions are employed at the far-field boundaries, while slip condition is imposed on the wall boundaries. A stuctured C-type grid is used for the CFD analysis. Then the drag coefficient and lift coefficient could be computed by the steady state variables. The constrained design problem is defined as follows.

Minimize

$$J(X) = C_d$$

subject to

$$E(W, X) = 0, \ g_1(X) = 1 - C_l/C_l^0 \le 0, \ g_2(X) = 1 - Vol/Vol^0 \le 0,$$

where $E(W, X)$ denotes the above flow equations (14), X is the vector of p−dimensional design variables, Vol is the airfoil profile volume, Vol^0 is the volume of the initial airfoil, and C_l^0 denotes the initial value of the lift coefficient. The drag reduction problem for Euler flow with constraints on the lift and the the volume are treated by penalty, the cost function is given by:

$$J(X) = \frac{C_d}{C_d^0} + \alpha \max\{0, 1 - \frac{C_l}{C_l^0}\} + \beta \max\{0, 1 - \frac{Vol}{Vol^0}\}, \tag{15}$$

where α and β are penalty factors, which are chosen as 10, 0.1 in this paper.

SPSA (Simultaneous Perturbation Stochastic Approximation) is a kind of stochastic optimization method, which has been applied to a number of difficult multivariate optimization problems. Details of the method can be found in Spall[4]. It is used to solve problems that the gradient of objective function are difficult to be computed in many diverse areas such as feedback control, simulation-based optimization, signal and image processing, etc.. The main idea of SPSA is to estimate the gradient by objective function values, the essential feature of SPSA is the underlying gradient approximation which requires only two measurements of the objective function to approximate the gradient regardless of the dimension of the optimization problem. This feature leads to the decrease of the computational cost, especially in the problems that have a lots of variables to be optimized. By simultaneous perturbation at each iteration, two function values and their difference can be computed, then multiply this value by a vector satisfying some given stochastic distribution, then we get the gradient. The advantage of this method is that twice objective function evaluation are used to generate gradient, while it needs $2p$ (p stands for the number of design variables) evaluations to compute gradient by an finite difference method. The iteration of the design variables in SPSA is

$$X_{k+1} = X_k - \alpha_k g(X_k) \tag{16}$$

where

$$g(X_k) = \frac{J(X_k + c_k \Delta_k) - J(X_k - c_k \Delta_k)}{2c_k} \begin{bmatrix} \Delta_{k1}^{-1} \\ \Delta_{k2}^{-1} \\ \vdots \\ \Delta_{kp}^{-1} \end{bmatrix}. \tag{17}$$

The term Δ_k represents the random perturbation vector generated by Monte Carlo approaches and the components of the perturbation are independently generated form a zero-mean probability distribution, the Bernoulli ± 1 distribution with probability of $\frac{1}{2}$ is used for each ± 1 in this paper. The parameter $c_k = \frac{c_0}{k^m}$ where c_0 is a small positive number and m is a coefficient which is $\frac{1}{6}$ in this study. The step size α_k can be set as a small constant . The cost function $J(X)$ is the objective value from the numerical solution of flow equations around the shape which is decided by the design variable X from the parameterization method. The choice of the parameters pertaining to the algorithm is crucial for the performance of the SPSA, some useful guidelines for choosing the parameters can be found in [5].

4   Results and Disscussion

Numerical experiments are carried out to investigate the efficiency of the parameterization method with the SPSA optimal algorithm. The optimization is carried out at a transonic Mach number of 0.726, and the angle of attack is 2.44 degrees. The RAE 2822 airfoil is considered as the initial airfoil. The initial C-type grid size is 193×33, and the grid of the new shape is deformed through the new parameters[14]. Computed results, pertaining to minimize the drag coefficient (C_d) airfoil design optimization problem using SPSA with the mentioned parameterization methods, are compared and shown in Table 1. From Table 1, we can say that Hicks-Henne parameterization method gave best results, while NACA basis functions gave satisfactory results. However, B-Spline and Wagner methods also reduced the drag coefficient, but not as much as other methods. The lift coefficient C_l and the volume of the shape Vol are compared in Table 2 and Table 3, respectively. As we can see, the lift coefficient C_l and the volume of the shape Vol changed little, which shows the success and effectiveness of the optimal method.

Table 1. Comparison of C_d under different parameterization

Method	Initial C_d	Opt. C_d	Reduced(%)
B-Spline	0.14160E-01	0.10773E-01	23.92%
NACA	0.14160E-01	0.64129E-02	54.71%
H-H	0.14160E-01	0.61115E-02	56.00%
Wagner	0.14160E-01	0.98748E-02	11.46%

Table 2. Comparison of C_l under different parameterization

Method	Initial C_l	Opt. C_l	Reduced(%)
B-Spline	0.93226E+00	0.92877E+00	-0.37%
NACA	0.93226E+00	0.93041E+00	-0.19%
H-H	0.93226E+00	0.92580E+00	-0.69%
Wagner	0.93226E+00	0.92878E+00	-0.075%

Table 3. Comparison of $Volume$ under different parameterization

Method	Initial Vol	Opt. Vol	Reduced(%)
B-Spline	0.77842E-01	0.77379E-01	-0.6%
NACA	0.77842E-01	0.77751E-01	-0.12%
H-H	0.77842E-01	0.77409E-01	-0.56%
Wagner	0.77842E-01	0.77416E-01	-0.548%

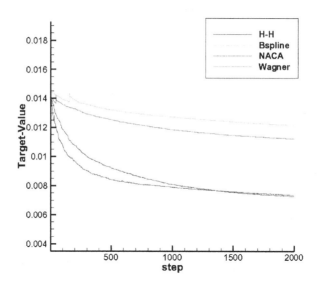

Fig. 5. Comparison of pressure contours under different parameterization

Fig. 5 shows the target values $J(x)$ of different parameterization methods in the iterations. The target values are decreasing to different extremal points. The reason for this phenomenon is probably that the non-linear optimization is a multi-extremum problem. Fig. 6 and Fig. 7 illustrate the pressure contours and pressure coefficients for the initial and optimal shapes, respectively, using different airfoil parameterization methods. The initial airfoil has a strong shock wave, which is the main flow feature in this case, however, this strong shock wave is weakened when applying the different parameterization methods. The shock is totally damped when the Hicks-Henne parameterization approach is applied,

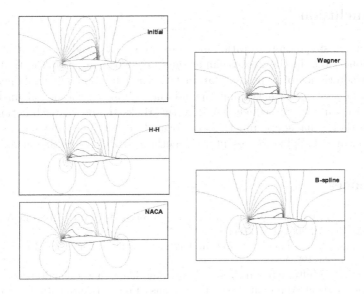

Fig. 6. Comparison of pressure contours under different parameterization

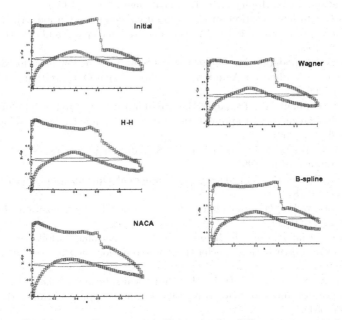

Fig. 7. Comparison of pressure coefficient under different parameterization

and it is similar for the NACA basis functions. The B-Spline and Wagner method gave moderate results, and we could see that the shock wave had been weaken from both Fig. 6 and Fig. 7.

5   Conclusion

Four common shape representation methods are investigated and compared with their applications in the aerodynamic shape design using SPSA optimization. The characteristics of a proper parameterization method are explained. The minimization of C_d with keeping C_l and the volume of the airfoil unchanged was carried out. It was concluded that the Hicks-Henne shape functions and NACA orthonormal shape functions performed better than other methods such as Wagner, and B-Spline representation methods under the SPSA optimization.

References

1. Jameson, A., Ou, K.: 50 years of transonic aircraft design. Progress in Aerospace Sciences 47(5), 308–318 (2011)
2. Sobieczky, H.: Parametric Airfoils and Wings. Notes on Numerical Fluid Mechanics 68, 71–88 (1998)
3. Spall, J.C.: Multiariate Stochastic Approximation Using a simultaneous Perturbation Gradient Approximation. IEEE Transactions on Automatic Control 37(3) (1992)
4. Spall, J.C.: An Overview of the Simultaneous Perturbation Method for Efficient Optimization. Johns Hopins APL Technical Digest 19(4) (1998)
5. Spall, J.C.: Implementation of the Simultaneous Perturbation Algorithm for Stochastic optimization. IEEE Transactions on aerospace and Electronic System 34(3) (1998)
6. Xing, X.Q., Damodaran, M.: Application of Simultaneous Perturbation Stochastic Apprximation Method for Aerodynamic Shape Design Optimization. AIAA Journal 43(2) (2005)
7. Lepine, J., Guibault, F., Trepanier, J.Y., Pepin, F.: Optimized Nonuniform Rational B-Spline geometrical Representation for Aerodynamic Design of Wings. AIAA Journal 39(11) (2001)
8. Chang, I.C., Torres, F.J.: Geometric Analysis of Wing Sections. NASA Technical Memorandum 110346 (1995)
9. Hicks, R., Henne, P.: Wing Design by Numerical Optimization. Journal of Aircraft 15(7) (1978)
10. Ramamoorthy, P., Padmavathi, K.: Airfoil Design by Optimization. Journal of Aircraft 14(2) (1977)
11. Xing, X.Q., Damodaran, M.: Inverse Design of Transonic Airfoils Using Parallel Simultaneous Perturbation Stochastic Approximation. Journal of Aircraft 42(2) (2005)
12. Jameson, A., Schmidt, W., Turkel, E.: Numerical solutions of the Euler equations by Finite volume methods using Runge-Kutta time-stepping schemes. AIAA Paper 81-1259 (1981)
13. Derksen, R.W., Rogalsky, T.: Bezier-PARSEC: An optimized aerofoil parameterization for design. Advances in Engineering Software 41(7-8SI), 923–930 (2010)
14. Luke, E., Collins, E., Blades, E.: A fast mesh deformation method using explicit interpolation. Journal of Computational Physics 231, 586–601 (2012)

Natural Frequency Ratio Effect on 2 DOF Flow Induced Vibration of Cylindrical Structures

Xiangxi Han[1], Chengbi Zhao[1,*], Youhong Tang[2,*], Xiaoming Chen[3], Wei Lin[1], and Karl Sammut[2]

[1] Department of Naval Architecture and Ocean Engineering,
School of Civil Engineering and Transportation, South China University of Technology,
Guangdong 510641, China
[2] Centre for Maritime Engineering, Control and Imaging, School of Computer Science,
Engineering and Mathematics, Flinders University, South Australia 5042, Australia
tccbzhao@scut.edu.cn, youhong.tang@flinders.edu.au
[3] China Ship Architecture Design & Research Institute Co., Ltd., Beijing 100024, China

Abstract. In this study, the vortex-induced vibration (VIV) of a circular cylinder at the low Reynolds number of 200 is simulated by a transient coupled fluid-structure interaction numerical model using the combination of FLUENT and ANSYS platforms. Considering VIV with low reduced damping parameters, the trend of the lift coefficient, the drag coefficient and the displacement of the cylinder are analyzed under different oscillating frequencies of the cylinder. The frequency ratio α is a very important parameter, which has been intensively investigated here. The typical nonlinear phenomena of locked-in, beat and phases switch can be captured successfully. The evolution of vortex shedding from the cylinder and the trajectory of the 2 DOF case with varied frequency ratio is also discussed.

Keywords: Fluid–structure interaction, Vortex-induced vibration, Workbench system coupling.

1 Introduction

The vortex-induced vibration (VIV) response of a cylindrical structure is of practical interest in many engineering fields (such as sub-sea pipelines, offshore risers, cables) and has led to the development of extensive fundamental studies in the recent decades. It is very important to research VIV for the design of a variety of engineering structures [1]. The VIV caused by the vortex shedding from the cylinder is a typical fluid-interaction problem. The periodic flow force, generated by the periodic vortex shefdding, affect the cylinder vibration, on the other hand, the oscillating cylinder will affect the fluid flow around cylinder, the fluid force and the vortex pattern, thus, a complex fluid-structure interaction forms. Most studies on VIV have been focused on one degree-of-freedom (1 DOF) vibration of a circular cylinder in the transverse direction of the flow (or cross-flow direction). Feng [2], Brika and Laneville [3], Anagnostopoulos [4], Kozakiewics *et al.* [5], and Khalak and Williamson [6] are only

---

* Corresponding author.

K. Li et al. (Eds.): ParCFD 2013, CCIS 405, pp. 403–417, 2014.

a few of them to mention. Sarpkaya [7], and Williamson and Govardhan [8] presented extensive reviews about transverse oscillation of a circular cylinder in steady flows.

However, the more practical case of VIV of a cylinder in two degree-of-freedom (2 DOF) has not been addressed as thoroughly as the 1 DOF VIV. Research on 2 DOF vibration of a circular cylinder in flow has been relatively rare. Jeon and Gharib [9] studied vortex wake behind a circular cylinder undergoing forced 1 DOF and 2 DOF vibrations. It was found that even small stream-wise component of motion inhibited the formation of 2P mode. Williamson and Jauvtis [10] studied the flow-induced 2 DOF vibration of a circular cylinder at low mass ratio and reported a new response branch, the 'super-upper' branch, which occurs when the mass ratios are reduced below $m* = 6$. The vibration in the 'super-upper' branch can have transverse amplitudes of 1.5 times the cylinder diameter. Dahl et al. [11] conducted 2 DOF tests on a rigid, smooth cylinder that was flexibly mounted in the cross-flow direction at Reynolds numbers ranging from 11,000 to 60,000. In their experiment, the in-line to transverse natural frequency ratios varied in the range from 1.0 to 1.9 and the mass ratios were less than 6.0. Their results showed that the maximum transverse amplitude exceeded 1.35 D, while the stream-wise response reached 0.6 D. A crescent-shaped orbital trajectory was observed in the largest amplitude response in which the power transfer between the 2 DOF motions reached a maximum.

In this work, we present the computational results for the VIV response of cylindrical structures, which are free to vibrate in 2 DOF with varying natural frequency ratios. The Reynolds number is fixed at a value of 200; therefore, laminar 2D flow is assumed to be a valid assumption in this investigation. The main objective of the present work is to systematically study the effect of the natural frequency ratio on 2 DOF vortex-induced responses in laminar flow regimes. The VIV response is characterized by the vortex shedding frequencies and amplitudes and the hydrodynamic forces. The vortex shedding modes are also scrutinized to reveal their effect on the unsteady wake patterns.

2   Governing Equations and Transient Dynamic Analysis

2.1   Governing Equations

The fluid flow is governed by the two-dimensional, incompressible, Navier–Stokes equations, which can be expressed with the primary variables in the Cartesian coordinate system as follows:

$$\nabla \cdot (\rho \vec{v}) = 0 \tag{1}$$

$$\frac{\partial}{\partial t}(\rho \vec{v}) + \nabla \cdot (\rho \vec{v}\vec{v}) = -\nabla p + \nabla \cdot (\tau) + \vec{F} \tag{2}$$

Where p is the static pressure, τ is the stress tensor (described below), and $\vec{F}$ are the external body forces, respectively.

The stress tensor τ is given by

$$\tau = \mu(\nabla \vec{v} + \nabla \vec{v}^T) \tag{3}$$

Where μ is the molecular viscosity, I is the unit tensor.

The motion of the cylinder can be described by the dimensionless equations:

$$\ddot{u}_x + 2\zeta f_n \dot{u}_x + f_n^2 u_x = F_d / m \qquad (4)$$

$$\ddot{u}_y + 2\zeta f_n \dot{u}_y + f_n^2 u_y = F_l / m \qquad (5)$$

Where u_x and u_y are the displacement of the cylinder in x and y direction, respectively; ζ is the damping factor of the spring-damper-mass system; f_n is the natural frequency of the cylinder; F_d and F_l are the drag and lift force of the cylinder respectively; m is the mass of the cylinder.

The drag coefficient and lift coefficient reflect the force on the cylinder, which are described as follows:

$$C_d = \frac{2F_d}{\rho U^2 D} \qquad (6)$$

$$C_l = \frac{2F_l}{\rho U^2 D} \qquad (7)$$

Where, U is the inlet stream-wise velocity and D is the diameter of cylinder.

2.2   Transient Dynamic Theory

Transient dynamic analysis (sometimes called time-history analysis) is a technique used to determine the dynamic response of a structure under the action of any general time-dependent loads. This type of analysis can be used to determine the time-varying displacements, strains, stresses and forces in a structure as it responds to any combination of static, transient and harmonic loads.

The basic equation of motion solved by a transient dynamic analysis is

$$(M)\{\ddot{u}\} + (C)\{\dot{u}\} + (K)\{u\} = \{F(t)\} \qquad (8)$$

Equations should be punctuated in the same way as ordinary text but with a small space before the end punctuation mark. Where, (M)=mass matrix , (C)=damping matrix , (K)=stiffness matrix , $\{\ddot{u}\}$=nodal acceleration vetor , $\{\dot{u}\}$=nodal velocity vetor , $\{u\}$=nodal displacement vetor , $\{F(t)\}$=load vector .

The newmark method is employed for the solution of Equation (8).

2.3   Fluid-structure Interaction

In the every time step of interaction process, firstly, Equations (1) and (2) are solved with the **Fluent** to get the forces on the cylinder; secondly, the response of the cylinder is obtained by taking the drag and lift force of the fluid on the cylinder as the right-hand side of Equations (4) and (5), which are solved using the newmark method;

Finally, the mesh is updated with the diffusion-based smoothing method based on the response of the cylinder. The interaction process is repeated in an iterative way so that the interactions between the fluid and the cylinder are accounted for properly.

2.4   Diffusion-Based Smoothing Method

For diffusion-based smoothing, the mesh motion is governed by the diffusion equation

$$\nabla \cdot (\gamma \nabla \vec{u}) = 0 \tag{9}$$

Where $\vec{u}$ is the mesh displacement velocity. The boundary conditions for Equation (9) are obtained from the user prescribed or computed (6 DOF) boundary motion. On deforming boundaries, the boundary conditions are such that the mesh motion is tangent to the boundary (i.e., the normal velocity component vanishes). The Laplace equation (Equation (9)) then describes how the prescribed boundary motion diffuses into the interior of the deforming mesh. The diffusion coefficient γ in Equation (9) can be used to control how the boundary motion affects the interior mesh motion. A constant coefficient means that the boundary motion diffuses uniformly throughout the mesh. With a non-uniform diffusion coefficient, mesh nodes in regions with high diffusivity tend to move together (i.e., with less relative motion).

For diffusivity based on boundary distance, the diffusion coefficient γ is equal to the following formula.

$$\gamma = \frac{1}{d^{\alpha}} \tag{10}$$

Using boundary-distance-based diffusion, Equation (10) allows us to control how the boundary motion diffuses into the interior of the domain as a function of boundary distance. Decreasing the diffusivity away from the moving boundary causes those regions to absorb more of the mesh motion, and better preserves the mesh quality near the moving boundary. This is particularly helpful for a moving boundary that has pronounced geometrical features (such as sharp corners) along with a prescribed motion that is predominantly rotational.

The diffusion coefficient γ is adjusted by the diffusion parameter α. A range of 0 to 2 has been shown to be of practical use. A value of 0 (the default value) specifies that $\gamma = 1$ and yields a uniform diffusion of the boundary motion throughout the mesh. Higher values of α preserve larger regions of the mesh near the moving boundary, and cause the regions away from the moving boundary to absorb more of the motion.

3   Computational Domain and Mesh

In this section, we describe the fluid-structure problem of unsteady 2D flow past a cylinder at Re = 200. The vortex-induced vibration of the cylinder with 2 DOF, both the lateral and stream-wise motion of the cylinder is allowed is shown in Fig. 1. The inflow velocity is specified as 0.02 m/s at the inflow boundary. The right boundary is assigned with an outflow boundary condition with normal gradients $\frac{\partial U}{\partial x}$ and $\frac{\partial v}{\partial x}$ set to zero. The upper and lower boundaries are assigned with symmetry boundary condition ($\frac{\partial U}{\partial y} = 0, v = 0$). The number 0.01 is selected for the dimensionless time step. The mesh consists of 41160 nodes and 20240 quadrilateral elements. There are 80 nodes on the surface of the cylinder. The mesh near the circular cylinder is shown in Fig. 2.

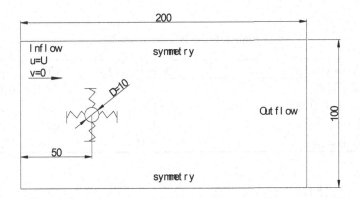

Fig. 1. Schematic of 2 DOF computational domain

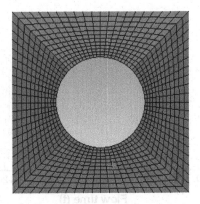

Fig. 2. Mesh near the circular cylinder

4   Validation Tests

We use the grid and time step determined in the previous section to solve one test case. That is a fixed circular cylinder in cross-flow at Re=200. Table 1 presents a comparison of our predictions for the flow past a fixed cylinder at Re = 200 with results found in the literature. The drag and lift coefficients and the Strouhal number have been obtained by analyzing their time history over an interval of 30 vortex shedding periods .The drag coefficient is the mean value of the in-line non-dimensionalized force and the lift coefficient is the maximum value of the non-dimensionalized transverse load. Our results are in good agreement with those previously published in the literature. Fig. 4 shows the time histories of the lift and drag coefficients. The frequency of the drag force is about twice that of the lift force. Fig. 5 shows a spectral analysis of the lift coefficient curve. Obviously, the natural frequency of vortex shedding $f_0 = 0.38$, which means that the St is equal to 0.19.

Table 1. Fixed cylinder at Re=200

Fixed cylinder	Average of Cd	Cl	St
Halse [12]	1.35	0.62	0.196
Liu et al. [13]	1.31	0.69	1.92
Li et al. [14]	1.34	0.69	1.92
Our results	1.315	0.68	0.19

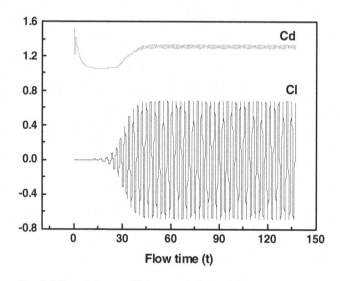

Fig. 3. Lift and drag coefficients variations of flow past a cylinder

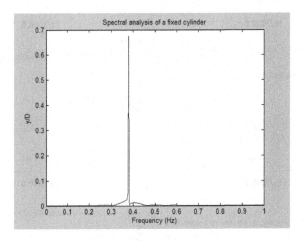

Fig. 4. Spectral analysis of a fixed cylinder

5 Vortex-Induced Vibration of Cylinder with Two Degree of Freedom

Flow-induced vibrations on an elastic structure are, in general, nonlinear. The vibration of the structure affects the fluid flow around the structure which, in turn, changes the induced forces on the structure and hence the structural response. In order to have a significant vortex-induced response, the frequency ratio $\alpha = f_n / f_0$ is chosen to vary from 0.5 to 2.0 with spacing of 0.1.

5.1 Force Time History and Cross-Flow and Stream-Wise Response

Fig. 5 shows time histories of the drag and lift force together with the cross-flow displacement of the cylinder. It should be noted that, at high values of $\alpha = f_n / f_0 = 2$, these time of histories are very similar to the show (Fig. 3) of a rigid cylinder. At lower values of $\alpha = f_n / f_0$, some interesting features can be observed. When the frequency ratio α varies from 0.5 to 0.7, the amplitude of lift coefficient of an elastic cylinder is smaller than that of a fixed cylinder and the lateral displacement of the cylinder becomes larger, but the amplitude of lift coefficient becomes smaller. Besides, resonance oscillation is present in the lift time history. When the frequency ratio is between 0.7 and 0.8, the amplitude of lift coefficient reaches its minimum value.

The phase between the lift force and the lateral displacement undergoes an interesting change from the "out of phase" to the "in-phase" mode, which is called the "phases switch" phenomena. When the frequency ratio is between 0.5 and 0.7, the lift force and the displacement is completely out of phase. The beat phenomena of lift coefficient and lateral displacement are appeared when the frequency ratio equals to 1.5. The drag force distinctly shows two major frequencies, the frequency of vortex and the natural frequency of the cylinder interact with each other.

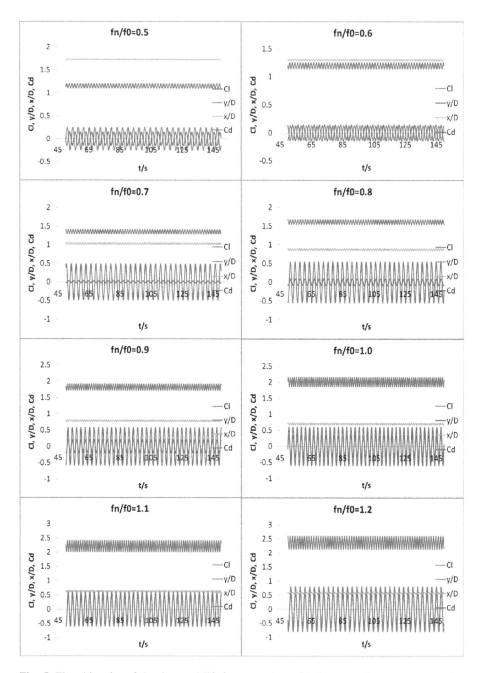

Fig. 5. Time histories of the drag and lift force together with the cross-flow and stream-wise displacement

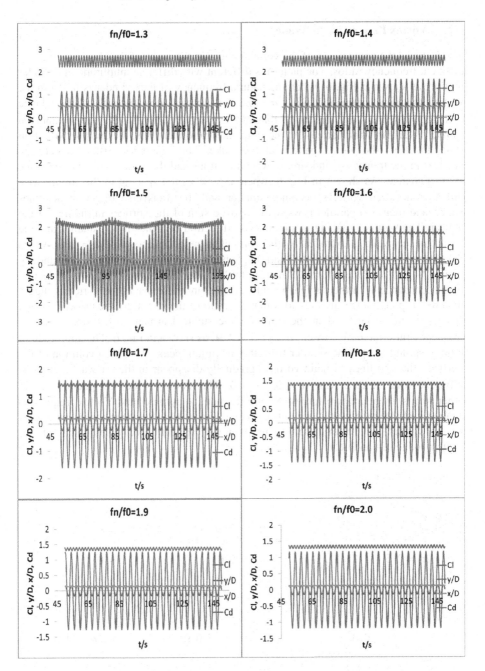

Fig. 5. (*Continued.*)

5.2   Vortex Pattern in the Wake

Fig. 6 shows the comparison of the vortex pattern in the wake of the elastic cylinder at different frequency ratios. The pattern is different with different amplitude of cylinder motion, as shown in Fig. 6. When the natural frequency of the cylinder is far from the vortex shedding frequency, i.e., $\alpha = 0.5, 2.0$, the vortex pattern of the elastic cylinder, which is very similar to that of the fixed cylinder, is 2S pattern and the standard Karman vortex street. As the frequency ratio increases, the cylinder vibration starts to affect the vortex pattern in the wake. The separation distances between vortices in the transverse and stream-wise directions and the width of the vortex wake start to change. As shown in Fig. 6, when $\alpha = 0.7$, the spacing in the stream-wise direction between vortices becomes smaller and the transverse direction becomes wider, and then two parallel rows with opposite sign of the vortices in the near wake appear. The vortices spacing in stream-wise direction becomes much smaller and the vortex in the wake is extruded by the vortices in neighborhoods at $\alpha = 0.9$. When the frequency ratio is between 0.7 and 0.8, "phases switch" phenomena occurs and the pattern begins to change form 2S pattern to 2P pattern correspond. The phenomenon is in accordance with the curve (Fig. 11). At the out-phase stage, the vortex is bigger than the in-phase stage. It is obvious that the ratio of the lateral to stream-wise vortex spacing is much larger than the limit for the stable Karman vortex street. As the frequency ratio increases, when $\alpha = 1.1 \sim 1.9$, as shown in Fig. 6. The amplitude of motion started to become smaller from the maximum peak. With the evolution of the vortices, the two lines of main vortices gradually disappear in the far wake, which is different from the case with $\alpha = 0.7 \sim 1.0$. That is due to the beat phenomena, in other words, there are two forces (Nature frequent of cylinder and Vortex frequency) against each other, but who are not dominant. From what has been discussed above, we know that the vortex-induced vibration will appear three phenomena: phases switch, locked-in and beat.

Fixed cylinder

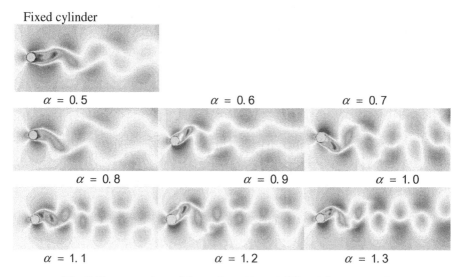

Fig. 6. The comparison of the vortex pattern at different frequency ratios

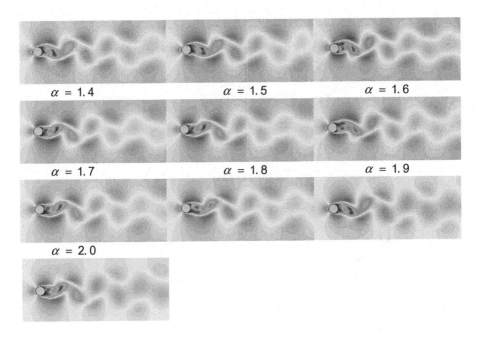

$\alpha = 1.4$ $\alpha = 1.5$ $\alpha = 1.6$

$\alpha = 1.7$ $\alpha = 1.8$ $\alpha = 1.9$

$\alpha = 2.0$

Fig. 6. (*Continued.*)

5.3   The Trajectory of the Cylinder at Different Natural Frequency Ratios

Fig. 7 shows the periodical trajectory of the elastic cylinder with different authors. Fig. 7(a) is numerical results reported by Blackburn and Karniadakis [15] and Yang *et al.* [16] and Pelletier and Etienne [17]. Fig. 7(b) is the present result. There is small discrepancy between them. In the present computations, we have verified that results are converged to them. These show that predictions from our method using the selected time steps and grid size are reliable.

Fig. 8 shows the trajectory of an elastic cylinder for two degree of freedom with varied frequency ratio. These plots clearly show that the oscillations are self-limiting and they all appear to have an "8" shape. It is seen that with the increment of frequency ratio, the equilibrium position of the vibration in the stream-wise direction becomes smaller, besides, the lateral amplitude increase firstly and then decrease. Note that the equilibrium position of the vibration in the stream-wise direction is not zero as the cylinder is subject to a mean drag force.

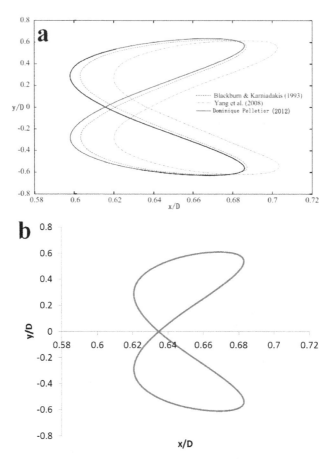

Fig. 7. Comparison of the periodical trajectory of an elastic cylinder at U*=5 and Re=200 with (a) previous results [15-17] and (b) present result

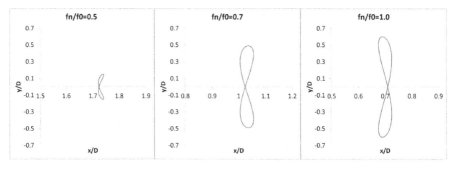

Fig. 8. The trajectory of an elastic cylinder for two degree of freedom

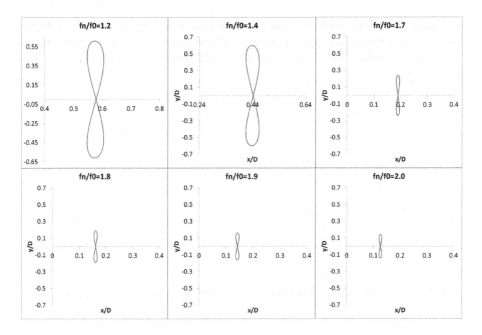

Fig. 8. (*Continued.*)

5.4   The Analysis of Two Degree Result

Fig. 9 shows the r.m.s lift coefficient and r.m.s transverse displacement for varied frequency ratio. When the frequency ratio is small (= 0.5), the r.m.s of lift coefficient of an elastic cylinder is large and the response of cylinder is weak. With the increase of frequency ratio, the r.m.s of lateral displacement of the cylinder becomes larger, but the amplitude of lift coefficient becomes smaller. When the frequency ratio is between 0.7 and 0.8, the r.m.s of the lift coefficient reaches its minimum value. After that, the r.m.s of the lift coefficient begins to increase, when the frequency ratio is between 1.4 and 1.5, the r.m.s of the lift coefficient reaches its maximum value, and then the frequency ratio $\alpha > 1.5$, the r.m.s of the lift coefficient begins to decrease. When the frequency ratio is between 1.1 and 1.4, the r.m.s transverse displacement reaches its maximum value. After that, the r.m.s of the transverse displacement begins to decrease.

Fig. 10 shows the mean drag coefficient and mean stream-wise displacement for varied frequency ratio. When the frequency ratio is small (= 0.5), the mean drag coefficient of an elastic cylinder is small and the mean stream-wise displacement of cylinder is large. With the increase of frequency ratio, the mean drag coefficient of the cylinder becomes larger, but the mean stream-wise displacement of cylinder becomes smaller. When the frequency ratio is between 1.3 and 1.4, the mean drag coefficient reaches its maximum value. After that, the mean drag coefficient begins to decrease.

Fig. 11 shows the phase difference between the lift force and the lateral displacement. When the frequency ratio is between 0.7 and 0.8, the amplitude of lift

416   X. Han et al.

coefficient reaches its minimum value and the main frequency is suddenly changed. The phase difference undergoes a suddenly change from the "out-of-phase" to the "in-phase" mode. The "phases-with" phenomenon appeared at about $\alpha = f_n / f_0 = 0.7$.

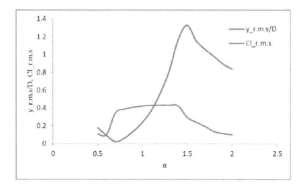

Fig. 9. The r.m.s lift coefficient and r.m.s transverse displacement for varied frequency ratio

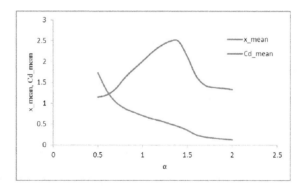

Fig. 10. The mean drag coefficient and mean stream-wise displacement for varied frequency ratio

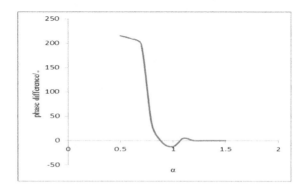

Fig. 11. The phase difference between the lift force and the lateral displacement

Acknowledgments. This work was supported by the National Natural Science Foundation of China (51009069) and the Fundamental Research Funds for the Central Universities - South China University of Technology, Ministry of Education of China (2012ZZ0097).

References

1. Anagnostopoulos, P., Bearman, P.W.: Response Characteristics of a Vortex-Excited Cylinder at Low Reynolds Number. J. Fluids Struct. 6, 39–50 (1992)
2. Feng, C.: The Measurement of Vortex-Induced Effects in Flow Past Stationary and Oscillation Circular and D-Section Cylinders. M.A.Sc. Thesis. British Columbia, Vancouver, B.C., Canada (1968)
3. Brika, D., Laneville, A.: Vortex-Induced Vibrations of a Long Flexible Circular Cylinder. J. Fluid Mech. 250, 481–508 (1993)
4. Anagnostopoulos, P.: Numerical Investigation of Response and Wake Characteristics of a Vortex Excited Cylinder in a Uniform Stream. J. Fluids Struct. 8, 367–390 (1994)
5. Brika, D., Laneville, A.: Wake Interference between Two Circular Cylinders. J. Wind Eng. Ind. Aerod. 72, 61–70 (1997)
6. Khalak, A., Williamson, C.H.K.: Dynamics of a Hydroelastic Cylinder with Very Low Mass and Damping. J. Fluids Struct. 10, 455–472 (1996)
7. Sarpkaya, T.: A Critical Review of the Intrinsic Nature of Vortex-induced Vibrations. J. Fluids Struct. 19, 389–447 (2004)
8. Williamson, C.H.K., Govardhan, R.: Vortex-induced Vibrations. Annu. Rev. Fluid Mech. 36, 413–455 (2004)
9. Jeon, D., Gharib, M.: On Circular Cylinders Undergoing Two-degree-of-freedom Forced Motions. J. Fluids Struct. 15, 533–541 (2001)
10. Jauvtis, N., Williamson, C.H.K.: The Effect of Two Degrees of Freedom on Vortex-induced Vibration at Low Mass and Damping. J. Fluid Mech. 509, 23–62 (2004)
11. Dahl, J.M., Hover, F.S., Triantafyllou, M.S.: Two-degree-of-freedom Vortex-induced Vibrations Using a Force Assisted Apparatus. J. Fluids Struct. 22, 807–818 (2006)
12. Halse, K.: On Vortex Shedding & Predictions of VIV of Circular Cylinders. Ph.D. Thesis. NTNU Trondheim (1997)
13. Liu, C., Zheng, X., Sung, C.H.: Preconditioned Multigrid Methods for Unsteady Incompressible Flows. J. Comput. Phys. 139, 35–57 (1998)
14. Li, T., Zhang, J., Zhang, W.: Nonlinear Characteristics of Vortex-induced Vibration at Low Reynolds Number. Commun. Nonlinear Sci. Numer. Simul. 16, 2753–2771 (2011)
15. Blackburn, H., Karniadakis, G.: Two- and Three-dimensional Simulations of Vortex-induced Vibration of a Circular Cylinder. In: Proceedings of the Third International Offshore and Polar Engineering Conference, Singapore, pp. 715–720 (1993)
16. Yang, J., Preidikman, S., Balaras, E.: A Strongly Coupled, Embedded Boundary Method for Fluid–structure Interactions of Elastically Mounted Rigid-bodies. J. Fluids Struct. 24, 167–182 (2008)
17. Etienne, S., Pelletier, D.: The Low Reynolds Number Limit of Vortex-induced Vibrations. J. Fluids Struct. 31, 18–29 (2012)

A Grid Reordering Technique for Hybrid Unstructured Flow Solver Based on OpenMP Parallel Environment

Meng Cheng, Gang Wang, and Haris Hameed Mian

National Key Laboratory of Science and Technology on Aerodynamic Design and Research
School of Aeronautics, Northwestern Polytechnical University, Xi'an 710072, P.R. China
wanggang@nwpu.edu.cn

Abstract. Grid reordering is an efficient way to obtain better implicit convergence acceleration in viscous flow simulation based on unstructured hybrid grids, whose data storage is usually random. To improve the matrix quality of the implicit LU-SGS time-stepping scheme and the compatibility of the numerical schemes and OpenMP parallel environment, a grid reordering method for unstructured hybrid grids is proposed. In this method, the structured grids in the viscous layer near-body surface are reordered along the normal direction (like columns) while the unstructured parts are reordered layer by layer in accordance with the neighboring relations. To investigate the performance of the current implementation, 2D and 3D turbulent flows around the RAE2822 airfoil, DLR-F6 wing-body configuration and an aerospace plane are simulated on unstructured hybrid grids. The numerical results show that the grid reordering method is an efficient strategy for improving the convergence rate and the overall efficiency of the flow solver.

Keywords: unstructured hybrid grids, grid reordering, LU-SGS scheme, CFD, parallel computation.

1 Introduction

With the fast development in the field of computational fluid dynamics (CFD), research topics of CFD area have become more and more complex. As a result, the computational requirement has increased so rapidly that even the existing computing technology is far from being able to meet this requirement. Parallel computing [1-3] has become an inevitable choice to perform these extensive numerical computations. The open multi-processing (OpenMP) [4-6] which based on the shared-memory platform and the massage-passing interfaces (MPI) [7, 8] based on massage-passing platform offers are the two key standards usually adopted for parallelization. For complex geometries, the rational demands of domain decomposition are always challenges for the MPI technology. But OpenMP doesn't have this problem.

At the same time, the complexity of the geometry gave birth to the development of the unstructured hybrid grids technology [9-11]. The use of hybrid grids combines the geometric flexibility offered by unstructured grids and the numerical accuracy of the

K. Li et al. (Eds.): ParCFD 2013, CCIS 405, pp. 418–428, 2014.
© Springer-Verlag Berlin Heidelberg 2014

structured grids. This meshing technique offers the potential of attaining a balance between mesh quality, efficiency, and flexibility. For unstructured hybrid grids, structured grids are used in the viscous boundary layers and unstructured grids are employed elsewhere [12].

The negative factor also exists. The data storage of unstructured grids is random, which has negative impacts on the convergence property of the computation. Dmitri et al. [13] propose a grid reordering method by improving the balance between lower and upper matrices of the lower-upper symmetric Gauss-Seidel (LU-SGS) implicit time-marching method [14]. Li, J.-J. et al. [15] propose to reorder the grids layer by layer according to the neighboring relations. Aiming at the characteristics of the computation in the OpenMP parallel environment based on unstructured hybrid grids, we propose a grid reordering method that improves the matrix quality of the implicit LU-SGS time-stepping scheme and the compatibility of the numerical schemes and the parallel environment based on OpenMP.

2   Numerical Methods

The computation is implemented in an in-house flow solver HUNS3D [16], developed for viscous flow based on unstructured hybrid grids.

2.1   Governing Equation

The integral form of non-dimensionlized three-dimensional unsteady Reynolds averaged Navier-Stokes (RANS) equations can be written as

$$\frac{\partial}{\partial t} \iiint_{\Omega} Q dV + \iint_{\partial \Omega} F(Q) \cdot n dS = \iint_{\partial \Omega} G(Q) \cdot n dS \qquad (1)$$

where Ω is the control volume; $\partial \Omega$ is the boundary of the control volume; Q is the conservative variable; $F(Q)$ is the inviscid flux; and the right side is the viscous term.

By using the cell-center finite volume method, the spatial discretization of Eq. (1) can be expressed as

$$\frac{dQ_i}{dt} = -\frac{1}{V_i}(R_i - R_i^V) \qquad (2)$$

where R_i is the inviscid flux and R_i^V is the viscous flux.

2.2   LU-SGS Scheme

The HUNS3D solver uses a LU-SGS implicit scheme for high reynolds number flow, which could be found in previous publication [17]. By using the LU-SGS scheme, the expression becomes

$$\Delta Q_i^* = D^{-1}\left[R_i^n - \sum_{j:j<i}\frac{1}{2}\left(\frac{\partial F(Q_j)}{\partial Q_j}\cdot n - \left|\lambda_{ij}\right|I\right)\Delta S \cdot \Delta Q_j^*\right], i = 1, 2, \cdots, N \qquad (3)$$

$$\Delta Q_i^n = \Delta Q_i^* - D^{-1}\sum_{j:j>i}\frac{1}{2}\left[\frac{\partial F(Q_j)}{\partial Q_j}\cdot n - \left|\lambda_{ij}\right|I\right]\Delta S \cdot \Delta Q_j^n, i = N, N-1, \cdots, 1 \qquad (4)$$

where j is the grid adjacent to grid i; λ_{ij} is the maxim eigenvalue of Jacobi matrix on the grid face; and D is the diagonal matrix expressed as:

$$D = \left(\frac{V_i}{\Delta t} + \sum_{all\ face}\frac{1}{2}\left|\lambda_{ij}\right|\Delta S\right)I \qquad (5)$$

3   Grid Reordering

As seen from Eq. (3) and Eq. (4) the LU-SGS scheme requires two sweeps: forward sweep through grid numbers from 1 to N and backward sweep. In case of forward sweep (lower), summation for grid i is over all surrounding grids whose number is less than i. Backward sweep (upper) is summation over surrounding grids whose number exceeds the current grid number. However, the lower/upper balance of the method highly depends on grid numbering. In other words, some grids might be surrounded by only those grids whose numbers are greater than current grid number. This leads to local degeneration from Gauss-Seidel iterations to Jacobi iterations [13]. In order to avoid the occurrence of the above unfavourable situation, we can improve the matrix quality by reordering the grids.

When computed on the HUNS3D solver in the parallel environment based on OpenMP, the grids are divided averagely into N domains according to the grids numbers and allocated to N processors. The convergence process is affected by the number of the grids at the interface between two domains. Reducing the number of grids at the interfaces is an effective way to accelerate the convergence.

In the boundary layers, the viscous dominated regions of high Reynolds number flows, the gradient of the flow parameters along the normal direction is far greater than the flow direction. The efficient computation of boundary layers requires structured or semi-structured grids of high aspect ratio to describe the flow. For the high aspect ratio grids, the fluxes on the grid face parallel to the flow direction play the decisive role to the residuals of the grid cell. So we should avoid making the grid face parallel to flow direction as the interface between parallel domains.

Based on the reasons above mentioned, we propose a grid reordering method for unstructured hybrid grids: The structured grids in the viscous layer near-body surface are reordered along the normal direction (like columns) while the unstructured parts are reordered layer by layer in accordance with the neighboring relations.

We define the group of grids on the surfaces as the first layer, the one adjacent to the first layer as the second layer, etc. The grid reordering method is as follows:

1. Pre-reordering of the grids in the first layer:

Number the grids around the surface one by one in circles for two-dimensional grids. For three-dimensional grids, take any grid as the start and number the grids outward in circles according to the adjacent relation until all the grids in the first layer are numbered.

2. Reorder the structured grids:

Number the grids along the normal direction (like columns) in the order formed in the first step until all the structured grids are numbered.

3. Reorder the unstructured grids:

Number the grids that have not numbered outward layer by layer until all the unstructured grids are numbered.

Take the two-dimensional local grids as shown in Fig. 1. (a) as an example. Number the grids clockwise (or anticlockwise) starting from grid A, the new order of the grids in the first layer is: A, B, C, D, E, F. Then start to number the structured grids along the normal direction like columns. For example, the grid adjacent to A in the upper layer is G. The grid adjacent to G in the upper layer is O, an unstructured grid. So the column based on A is finished and then return to grid B in the first layer and so on. The new order of the structured grids is: A, G, B, H, C, I, D, J, E, K, F, L. Finally, the unstructured grids are numbered layer by layer. The new order of the grids in the third and fourth layer is: O, Q, T, V, X, Z, N, P, R, S, U, W, Y, M. (The order of the grids in the third and fourth layer is related to the order of the grids in the lower layers not described here.)

The new grid numbers after reordering are presented in Fig. 1. (b):

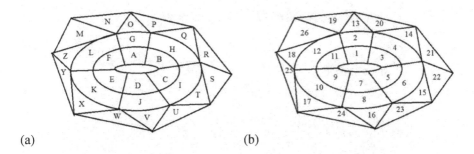

(a)   (b)

Fig. 1. (a) The grids before grid reordering and (b) The grids after grid reordering

4   Test Cases and Results

Three typical test cases are selected to illustrate the computational efficiency of the present grid reordering method. These test cases include the transonic viscous flow around RAE2822 airfoil, transonic viscous flow around DLR-F6 wing/body configuration and hypersonic viscous flow around the aerospace plane. It was observed that it cost less than a second to reorder a 2D mesh of 14 thousand grid cells and about 20 seconds to reorder a 3D mesh of 5.53 million grid cells. For the grid reordering increases the chance for cache hits as well, the single-step calculation time reduces a little. The computations were performed using INTEL COREi7 (four-cores 3.4GHz) and 16GB memory.

4.1   RAE2822 Airfoil

The RAE2822 is a supercritical aerofoil [18], which has become a standard testcase for turbulence modelling validation. The mesh consists of 5 632 structured-grid cells surrounding the airfoil surfaces and 7 788 unstructured-grid cells in other area. The free-stream conditions were as follows: $Ma = 0.734, Re=6.5\times10^6, \alpha=2.8°$.

The grids are divided into sixteen domains according to the task assignment principle of the parallel computation, as marked with different colors in Fig. 2 and Fig. 3.

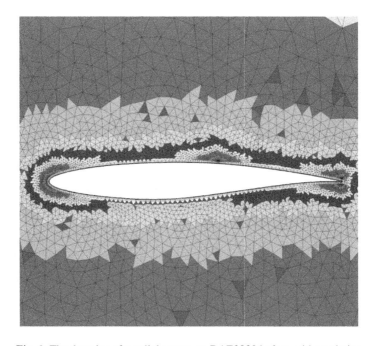

Fig. 2. The domains of parallel course on RAE2822 before grid reordering

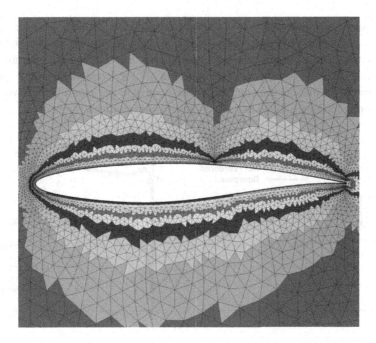

Fig. 3. The domains of parallel course on RAE2822 after grid reordering

As one can see in Fig. 2 and Fig. 3, there are less crosses between the different domains of parallel course after grid reordering. The partitions appear to be clearer than before.

Fig. 4 shows the local grids in the viscous layer near-body surface. Before grid reordering, the domains of parallel course appear to be layers because of the flow direction reordering method. After grid reordering, the domains appear to be columns because of the normal direction reordering method.

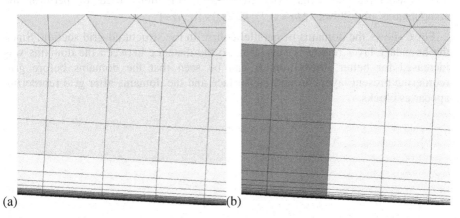

(a)   (b)

Fig. 4. (a) The grids in the viscous layer near-body surface of RAE2822 before grid reordering and (b) The grids in the viscous layer near-body surface of RAE2822 after grid reordering

The convergence histories of the maximal residual in terms of time iteration numbers are shown and compared in Fig. 5. (a). As shown in the figure, the convergence speed of the maximal residual after grid reordering is noticeably faster than before. Fig. 5. (b) shows a comparison of the computed surface pressure coefficients with the experimental data. The computed pressure distributions before and after reordering are found to be in good agreement with each other.

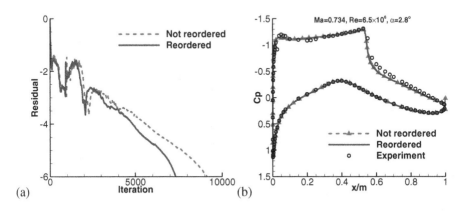

Fig. 5. (a) Convergence histories of the maximal residual in terms of iterations for transonic viscous flow past RAE2822 airfoil and (b) Comparison of computed surface pressure coefficients on RAE2822 airfoil with experimental data

4.2   DLR-F6 Wing-Body Configuration

The DLR-F6 wing-body configuration was measured in august 1990 in the ONERA S2MA wind tunnel. The mesh consists of 3 146 176 structured-grid cells and 2 385 963 unstructured-grid cells. The free-stream conditions used to perform the computations are follows: $Ma = 0.75, Re=3.0\times10^6, \alpha=1°$.

Fig. 6 shows the domains of parallel course in the structured-grid section. Since the boundary layer region is very thin, so the distance between the domains was increased for better illustration. It can be seen that the domains before grid reordering present layers around the surface and the domains after grid reordering appear as blocks.

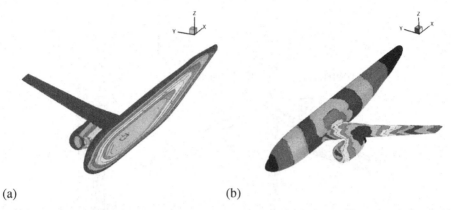

(a)   (b)

Fig. 6. (a) The domains of parallel course on DLR-F6 wing-body configuration before grid reordering and (b) The domains of parallel course on DLR-F6 wing-body configuration after grid reordering

Fig. 7. (a) shows the convergence histories of the maximal residual. We can see the convergence speed after grid reordering is faster. The pressure coefficients of the section at 23.9% wing span are shown in Fig. 7. (b). The computed pressure coefficients before and after reordering agree with each other pretty well.

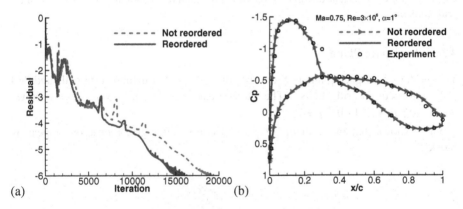

(a)   (b)

Fig. 7. (a) Convergence histories of the maximal residual in terms of iterations for transonic viscous flow past DLR-F6 wing-body configuration and (b) Comparison of computed surface pressure coefficients on DLR-F6 wing-body configuration with experimental data

The pressure distribution is shown in Fig. 8. The pressure distribution after grid reordering on the right side is the same with the pressure distribution before reordering on the left side.

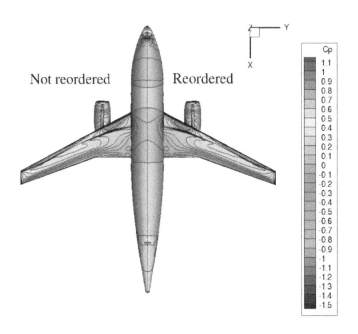

Fig. 8. Pressure coefficient distribution on DLR-F6 wing-body configuration before and after grid reordering

4.3   Aerospace Plane

The mesh of aerospace plane [19] consists of 1 064 814 structured-grid cells and 780 891 unstructured-grid cells. The free-stream conditions were as follows: $Ma = 8.02, Re=1.34\times10^7, \alpha=0$.

Fig. 9 shows that the domains of parallel course after grid reordering appear as blocks.

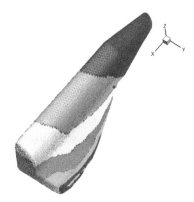

Fig. 9. The domains of parallel course on aerospace plane after grid reordering

The convergence histories of the maximal residual are shown in Fig. 10. (a). As one can see, the maximal residual before grid reordering stalled after 5,000 iterations. But the maximal residual after reordering continues to decline. This demonstrates that the convergence property has been improved. The pressure coefficients on symmetrical plane are shown in Fig. 10. (b). The computed pressure coefficients before and after reordering agree with experimental data pretty well.

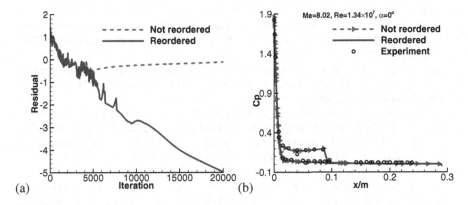

Fig. 10. (a) Convergence histories of the maximal residual in terms of iterations for hypersonic viscous flow past aerospace plane and (b) Comparison of computed surface pressure coefficients on symmetrical plane on aerospace plane with experimental data

5   Conclusions

In this paper we present a reordering technique for unstructured hybrid grids. It improves the convergence property of the computation by improving the matrix quality of the implicit LU-SGS time-stepping scheme and the compatibility of the numerical schemes and OpenMP parallel environment. The results using the method on cases of the RAE2822 airfoil, DLR-F6 wing-body configuration and an aerospace plane configuration show that the reordering strategy effectively improves the computational efficiency in the flow field based on the shared-memory parallel environment. It is very practical in numerical simulation of the viscous flow with unstructured hybrid grids.

Acknowledgements. The research was supported by NPU Foundation of Fundamental Research (NPU-FFR-JC201212) and Advanced Research Foundation of Commercial Aircraft Corporation of China (COMAC). The authors thankfully acknowledge these institutions.

References

1. Gropp, D., Kaushik, K., Keyes, E.: High-performance parallel implicit CFD. Parallel Computing 27, 337–362 (2001)
2. Moureau, V., Domingo, P., Vervisch, L.: Design of a massively parallel CFD code for complex geometries. Comptes Rendus Ecanique 339(2-3), 141–148 (2011)
3. Introduction to Parallel Computing, `https://computing.llnl.gov/tutorials/parallel_comp/`
4. Hoeflinger, J., Alavilli, P., Jackson, T., Kuhn, B.: Producing scalable performance with OpenMP: Experiments with two CFD applications. Parallel Computing 27(4), 391–413 (2001)
5. Bessonov, O.: OpenMP Parallelization of a CFD Code for Multicore Computers: Analysis and Comparison. In: Malyshkin, V. (ed.) PaCT 2011. LNCS, vol. 6873, pp. 13–22. Springer, Heidelberg (2011)
6. Introduction to OpenMP, `https://computing.llnl.gov/tutorials/openMP/`
7. Appleyard, J., Drikakis, D.: Higher-order CFD and interface tracking methods on highly-Parallel MPI and GPU systems. In: Computers & Fluids - 10th Institute-for-Computational-Fluid-Dynamics (ICFD) Conference, vol. 46(1), pp. 101–105 (2010)
8. Introduction to MPI, `https://computing.llnl.gov/tutorials/mpi/`
9. Nakahashi, K., Sharov, D., Kano, S., Kodera, M.: Applications of unstructured hybrid grid method to high-Reynolds number viscous flows. International Journal for Numerical Methods in Fluids 31(1), 97–111 (1999)
10. Wang, Y.-L., Murgie, S.: Hybrid mesh generation for viscous flow simulation. In: Proceedings of the 15th International Meshing Roundtable, pp. 109–126 (2006)
11. Wang, G., Ye, Z.-Y.: Generation of Three Dimensional Mixed and Unstructured Grids and its Application in Solving Navier-Stokes Equations. Acta Aeronautica Et Astronautica Sinica 24(5), 385–390 (2003) (in Chinese)
12. Moeljo, S., Scott, I., Donald, R., David, T.: Development of a 3-D zonal implicit procedure for hybrid structured-unstructured grids. In: 34th Aerospace Sciences Meeting and Exhibit. AIAA 10.2514/6.1996-167
13. Dmitri, S., Kazuhiro, N., Dmitri, S., Kazuhiro, N.: Reordering of 3-D hybrid unstructured grids for vectorized LU-SGS Navier-Stokes computations. 13th Computational Fluid Dynamics Conference. AIAA 10.2514/6.1997-2102
14. Yoon, S., Jameson, A.: An LU-SSOR scheme for the Euler and Navier-Stokes equations. AIAA Journal 26(9), 1025–1026 (1988)
15. Li, J.-J., Wang, G., Shi, A.-M., Yang, Y.-N.: Reordering of 3-D Unstructured Grids for Computing Efficiency Improvement. Aeronautical Computer Technique 35(3), 25–28 (2005) (in Chinese)
16. Wang, G., Ye, Z.-Y.: Element Type Unstructured Grid Generation and its Application to Viscous Flow Simulation. In: 24th International Congress of Aeronautical Sciences, Yokohama, Japan (2004)
17. Wang, G., Jiang, Y.-W., Ye, Z.-Y.: An Improved LU-SGS Implicit Scheme for High Reynolds Number Flow Computations on Hybrid Unstructured Mesh. Chinese Journal of Aeronautics 25, 33–41 (2012)
18. Cook, H., Mcdonald, A., Fireman, P.: Experimental data base for computers program assessment. AGARD-AR-138 (1979)
19. Li, S.X.: Hypersonic Flow over Typical Geometries. National Defense Industry Press, Beijing (2007) (in Chinese)

A Novel Method Based on Chemical Reaction Optimization for Pairwise Sequence Alignment

Danqing Huang[1,*] and Xiangyuan Zhu[2]

[1] Hunan University, College of Information Science and Engineering,
Changsha, 410082, China
[2] National Supercomputing Center of Changsha,
Hunan University Office, Changsha, 410082, China
blueberry7563@126.com

Abstract. The problem of pairwise sequence alignment is the fundamental and important problem in computational biology. The success of pairwise sequence alignment algorithm lies in its accuracy of the sequences being aligned in bioinformatics. For getting higher accuracy in an ideal period of time, we proposed a new method based on Chemical reaction optimization. Chemical reaction optimization (CRO) is a new metaheuristic algorithm, which inspired by the nature of chemical reactions. Be similar to genetic algorithm, CRO is a design framework and has gained excellent performance in solving many problems, for example, grid scheduling problem, quadratic assignment etc. In this paper, we firstly apply CRO to solve pairwise sequence alignment, modify the four operators to satisfy the requirement of sequence alignment. From the simulation results, the performance of proposed algorithm is better or equivalent but never worse than GA and ACO.

Keywords: CRO algorithm, Nucleic acid, DNA, Sequence alignment.

1 Introduction

Alignment of nucleotide or protein sequences is a fundamental problem in bioinformatics. In case of pairwise or multiple sequence alignment, the purpose is to find the maximum similarity between those sequences which is composed of nucleotides for DNA/RNA and amino acids for proteins, so as to infer biological structure, function and evolutionary relationship [1]. Pairwise sequence alignment is the foundation of multiple sequence alignment and database research, and also is one of the hot research subject in molecular biology. Pairwise sequence alignment intends to find a best alignment by inserting or deleting some char between two sequences. As so far, there are some algorithms to solving this problem. The well-known Needleman-Wunsch algorithm [2] and Smith-Waterman algorithm[3] is based on dynamic programming. We can get higher accuracy of alignment using the those algorithms, but need larger memory. Various heuristic approaches have been developed besides dynamic programming approaches to optimize computational

---

* Corresponding author.

K. Li et al. (Eds.): ParCFD 2013, CCIS 405, pp. 429–439, 2014.

ability such as T-Coffee [4] and BLAST [5], they are widely used for database searches, but those methods sacrifice the accuracy for faster speed. Sequence alignment has been proven to be NP-hard problem for some special cases and we usually approximate the best solution with some classical algorithm, such as genetic algorithm [6] [7] [8] [9] and ACO [7][10]. The traditional genetic algorithm has two shortages: the problem of falling into local minimum easily and the poor ability of local search. So researchers put forward improved genetic algorithm or other new method continuously.

According to the No-Free-Lunch theorem [11], the algorithm1 doesn't always outperform algorithm 2 for all problems, and specific algorithm is not always better than random algorithm. Based on the above consideration, we propose a new method based on chemical reaction optimization (CRO) framework [12] [13] to solve sequence alignment.

Similarity with genetic algorithm, CRO is a variable population-based metaheuristic that mimics the interactions of molecules driving towards the most stable state. The CRO has a good searching ability that shows excellent operation in intensification and diversification. There are two main innovative points of this study are listed as follows:

- CRO algorithm enjoys the advantages of both SA and GA, and we apply CRO algorithm to solve sequence alignment for the first time
- The CRO is a framework which allows deploying different operators to suit different problems. According to the characteristics of sequence alignment problem we improve the performance of the CRO by modifying some operations for the sequence alignment problem. We will extend this method to run in parallel in the near future work.

The framework of this paper is organized as follows. We formulate the related work about our problem in Section 2. Section 3 describes the proposed CRO-based pairwise sequence align algorithm. In Section 4 the simulation results compared with genetic algorithm is given. At last, in Section 5, we conclude this paper and suggest possible future work.

2   Related Work

2.1   Problem Formulation

The biological sequence generally divided into DNA sequences and protein sequences. For DNA sequences, the nucleotide alphabet is the four letter set {A, T, G, C} and protein sequences consist of the 20 letter set {A,C-T,K-N,P-T,VWY}. For simplicity the description of the problem, we consider only DNA sequence in this paper. This chapter mainly elaborates the mathematical model of pairwise sequence alignment.

There are two aligned sequences $S = \left(s_1 s_2 \cdots s_i \right)$ and $T = \left(t_1 t_2 \cdots t_j \right)$, and $|S|, |T|$ represents the length of sequence S, T respectively. $S[i]$, $T[j]$ represents the ith characters of sequence S and the jth characters of sequence T respectively

$(0, i \leq |S|, 0, j \leq |T|)$. S', T' are representative of the sequences which are inserted into gaps, and they were as arrays with the following properties:

- The length of sequence S' equals to the length of sequence T', namely $|S'| = |T'| = L$
- They constitute of elements from the set {A, T, G, C, —}, where A, T, G and C represented the four DNA nucleotides. The symbol "—" means that there is an inserted gap at the position in the alignment.

Let $S'[m]$, $T'[n]$ belongs to the sequence S' and T' respectively, the score for aligning $S'[m]$ and $T'[n]$ is $\sigma(S'[m], T'[n])$, which defined simple by:

$$\sigma(S'[m], T'[n]) = \begin{cases} 1, S'[m] = T'[n] \neq - \\ 0, S'[m] \neq T'[n], S'[m] \neq -, T'[n] \neq - \\ -1, S'[m] = - \text{ or } T'[n] = - \end{cases} \quad (1)$$

then the last score of the two aligned sequences is computed by

$$Score(S', T') = \sum_{n=1}^{L} \sigma(S'[m], T'[n]) \quad (2)$$

We regard the highest score as the score of the best alignment. Fig 1 presents a simple example of pairwise sequence alignment. According to the score function, we can get a score 2 before inserting gaps into sequences, and scoring 5 after insert gaps.

Sequence S, AGCACACA	Sequence S, AGCACAC–A
Sequence T, ACACACTA	Sequence T, A–CACACTA
(1-1) the aligned sequences	(1-2) after inserting gaps

Fig. 1. An example of alignment. Fig(1-1) shows the two aligned sequences, the score is 2, and the alignment after inserting gaps is shown in Fig (1-2), the score is 5.

2.2   Chemical Reaction Optimization

CRO is a chemical-reaction-inspired metaheuristic that mimics the interactions of molecules in a chemical reaction. The manipulated agents of the algorithm are molecules, each of which has a molecular structure ω, potential energy (*PE*), kinetic energy (*KE*), and some other optional attributes. The molecular structure ω and *PE* corresponds to a solution of given problem and its objective function value, respectively, then $PE_\omega = fitness(\omega)$ which is objective function. KE represents the tolerance of a molecular getting a worse solution than the existing one. In every collision, ω attempts to change to ω', and we will replace ω with ω' when $PE_{\omega'} \leq PE_\omega$ or $PE_{\omega'} \leq PE_\omega + KE_\omega$. With the law (conservation of energy), we output the molecular structure with the lowest *PE* as the best solution. The pseudocode of CRO is described in Algorithm 1.

Algorithm 1. The pseudocode of CRO framework

```
\\ Initialization
   Set parameter values to PopSize, KELossRate ,MoleColl,
buffer, InitialKE ,α and β
   Initialization molecules with size equal to PopSize
\\ Iteration
    For each molecules do
    assign a random solution to the molecular structure,
calculate the PE by object function f(ω)
    end for
    While the stopping criteria not met do
          generate t•[0 , 1]
    if t > MoleColl
      then randomly select one molecule Mω
      if Decomposition criterion met
        then Trigger Decomposition
      else Trigger On-wall Ineffective Collision
      end if
        else Randomly select two molecules Mω₁ and Mω₂
    if Synthesis criterion met
        then Trigger Synthesis
        else Trigger Intermolecular Ineffective Collision
    end if
    Year := 0;
    end if
    Check for any new minimum solution
    end while
\\ The final stage
   Output the overall minimum solution , its objective
function value and corresponding results
```

3   Algorithm Design

In this paper, we follow the framework of chemical reaction optimization algorithm described in [12] to solve pairwise sequence alignment. The core of our new method based CRO is to find the maximum matching value of two sequences. CRO algorithm consists of three stages: initialization, iterations and the final stage. In the initial stage, we assign values for parameters *PopSize, KELossRate, InitialKE, MoleColl,* $\alpha \in [KELossRate, 1]$ and β .While we produce molecules with size equal to *PopSize* by randomly inserting some gaps to aligned sequences in the way described in section3.1, and calculate the corresponding *PE* values of the molecules. In iteration process, there are four types of elementary reaction, namely, on-wall ineffective collision, decomposition, inter-molecular ineffective collision and synthesis, and we generate a random number t which is in the interval of [0,1] to decide there is a single molecular collision or inter-molecular collision. If t is smaller than *Molecol*l, it will be a unimolecular collision, otherwise, an inter-molecular collision will occur. The iteration continues until the stopping criterion is satisfied, we output the so far best solution in the final stage.

In our work, we can model a one dimensional array ω as a solution, which is composed of the two aligned sequence. A simple example described as Fig 2.

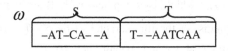

Fig. 2. An example of the definition of the molecular structure

3.1   Initialization

Similar to other population-based algorithms, CRO starts with a population of random solutions and search for optimal solutions through a random sequence of elementary reactions. In our work, the initial population *Pop* is generated by randomly inserting some gaps in the following ways.

- *Step 1*. We respectively compute the length L_1 and L_2 of the two aligned sequences. Let denote $L_{max} = max\{L_1, L_2\}$ as the max length between L_1 and L_2.
- *Step 2*. The maximum length of the inserted sequence was limited to $k = \lceil \alpha L_{max} \rceil$, where $\lceil x \rceil$ represents the smallest integer greater than or equal to x. α is generally set 1.2, which is a scaling factor allowed the alignment to be 20% longer than the longest sequence. Then, we produce a one-dimensional array ω with length $2k$.
- *Step 3*. A random permutation is produced form the set 1,2,3···, k.The first L_1 number of the permutation are sorted in ascending order. The new sorted permutation was chosen to be the positions for the symbols in sequence S_1.The remaining positions in sequence are filled with gaps. The initial sequence put into the first k number of array ω.But to sequence S_2, we chose the ($L_{max} - L_1$) number of the permutation are sorted in ascending order, and put the symbols at the corresponding positions in the same way. Fig.3 illustrates the process of initialization.

	sequence	length	permutation (1~k)	Positions	Sorted positions	Initial alignment
S1	ATCAA	(5)	352691748	35269	23569	–AT –CA– –A
S2	TAATCAA	(7)	967148532	9671425	1456789	T– –AATCAA
The initial structure: –AT–CA– –A T– –AATCAA						

Fig. 3. Initialization: The initial array ω is composed of the two initial sequences.

3.2   Fitness Function

Fitness function is defined as objective function, which is used to evaluate PE value of each molecular structure, namely $PE_\omega = fitness(\omega)$ in CRO. The molecular whether do iterate or not depend on its corresponding fitness value. Because we use this algorithm to solve pairwise sequence alignment, we firstly define a score function $Score(\omega)$, which is computed with Blast matrix and defined as Equation (3). ω_{si}, ω_{ti} stands for the ith character of the S, T part of ω. The match score is 5, and mismatch get -4, vacancy penalty get -10.

$$Score(\omega) = \sum_{i=1}^{L} score(w_{si}, w_{ti})$$

and,   (3)

$$score(w_{si}, w_{ti}) = \begin{cases} 5, w_{si} = w_{ti} \neq - \\ -4, w_{si} \neq w_{ti}, w_{si} \neq -, w_{ti} \neq - \\ -10, w_{si} \neq - \, or w_{ti} \neq - \\ 0, w_{si} = w_{ti} = - \end{cases}$$

In this algorithm, we define the *fitness function* as follow:

$$PE = fitness(\omega) = -Score(\omega)$$

the higher score of alignment, then the value of *PE* is smaller, the system is more stable. At last we output the molecular structure with the lowest *PE* as the best solution.

3.3   CRO Elementary Reaction Operators

A sequence of collisions among molecules will be occurred in a chemical reaction process. There is one molecule involved in on-wall ineffective collision and decomposition collision, while inter-molecular ineffective collision and synthesis represents the conditions that the two or more molecule collides with each other. After those reactions, we output the molecular structure with the lowest PE as the best solution.

3.3.1   On-wall Ineffective Collision
There is a molecule hits the wall of the container and then bounces back remaining in one single unit in this on-wall ineffective collision. In this collision, we will get a new solution ω' from the exiting one ω.

Because this collision is not so energetic, the new solution ω' should not be too different from the original one ω. So, in this paper we use *movespace* operator to obtain a new solution ω' form ω. Firstly randomly pick one gap symbol g_s in the sequence S, then research the first char c_s that is not a gap after that gap g_s. At last, we exchange g_s and the aforementioned char c_s. Fig.4 illustrates an example of this operator.

Fig. 4. An example of *movespace* operator

3.3.2   Decomposition

A decomposition describes the situation when a molecule ω hits the wall and decomposes into more molecule (suppose two ω_1', ω_2' in this work). As this collision is vigorous, the resultant molecular structure would be different from the original structure ω. In our work, we produce ω_1', ω_2' from ω by circular shifting. Firstly, we select a char p_1 that is not a gap from S randomly. Then, we research a gap g_1 which is the nearest gap from S in the neighborhood by the p_1. There are two cases in this operate:

- g_1 after p_1: we obtain S_1 of ω_1' by circular shifting to the right between g_1 and p_1, and T of ω is used for the T_1 of ω_1'

- g_1 before p_1: we obtain S_1 of ω_1' by circular shifting to the left between g_1 and p_1, and T of ω is used for the T_1 of ω_1'.

We also obtain ω_2' in the same way, select a char p_2 from T randomly, then research the g_2 and circular shifting to the left between g_2 and p_2. Fig.5 outlines this operator.

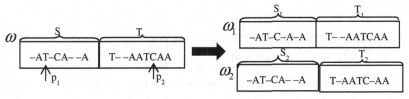

Fig. 5. An example of one molecule decomposition

3.3.3 Inter-molecular Ineffective Collision

This collision occurs when two molecules ω_1, ω_2 collide with each other and bounce away. There will produce two new solutions $\omega_1{}'$, $\omega_2{}'$ in the neighborhood of the given solutions. So, we apply the mechanism used for the on-wall ineffective collision to both ω_1、ω_2 separately. An example has been described in Fig.6.

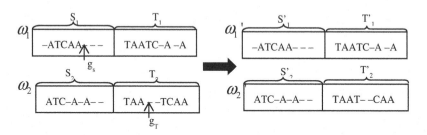

Fig. 6. An example of inter-molecule ineffective collision

3.3.4 Synthesis

In this collision, we try to integrate two solutions ω_1, ω_2 into a new solution ω' through permutating ω_1 and ω_2. In our work, we also firstly get a random number between 0 and 1, if the random number is greater than 0.5 then we choose the method a, else choose the method b. We can see a specific example in the Fig.7.

- method a: obtain ω' from the S_1 part of ω_1 and T_2 part of ω_2
- method b: get the ω' from the S_2 part of ω_1 and T_1 part of ω_2

String before synthesis:

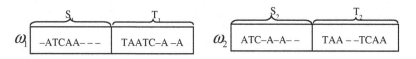

String after synthesis:

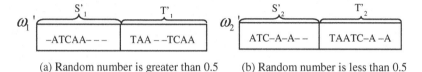

(a) Random number is greater than 0.5   (b) Random number is less than 0.5

Fig. 7. An example for two molecules synthesis

4   Simulation

In our paper, we will compare the performance of CRO with relevant pairwise sequence alignment method, such as NW algorithm and ACO. Due to CRO is based on stochastic algorithm, we obtain a satisfactory result through repeatedly running simulation. According to our extensive comparative evaluation research, the simulation results indicate that our method can be applied in sequence alignment and the performance of the method is accurate and fairly quick compared to some classic heuristic algorithm, such as classical ACO.

4.1   Parameter Setting

There are some initial parameters involved in the CRO algorithm: *PopSize*, *KELossRate*, *InitialKE*, *MoleColl*, $\alpha \in [KELossRate, 1]$ and β .Those parameter values of CRO are given in Table 1. We program this algorithm in C# language and run on personal computer with Pentium E6700 Dual-Core CPU at 3.20GHz.

Table 1. Parameter values of CRO

Parameter	Value
PopSize	1000
KElossRate	0.2
InitialKE	1000
MoleColl	0.2
α	500
β	5

4.2   Experiments and Results

We select DNA sequences (homo spaiens, pongo pygmaeus.) as the experimental data, which derived from Genome sequence Data Base (http://www.ncbi.nlm.nih.gov/).

- Case 1.The average length of the two segments of DNA sequences is 50.
  Sequence A (53):
    AGAGCTGAGGTGTCGAGAAACTTCCTACCGCCCGTTCGCACCTCGCTACTCCA
  Sequence B (47):
    GTCTGTGTGCTGGCCCATCACTTTGGCAAAGAATTCACCCCGCAAGT

In this case, we can see the best alignment with NW algorithm and our method in Table2.Seen from the above Table2, we get the number of matching char is 21 which equals to the number got by NW algorithm and the score is also -85. Thus it can be seen that our method can get the best alignment with NW algorithm in short sequences.

Table 2. The best alignment with NW algorithm and our method

NW algorithm

```
            1                                               40
Sequence A'  AGAGCTGAGGTGTCGAGAAACT–TCCTACCGCCCGTTCGC
Sequence B'  – GT– CTGTG – TGCTGGCCCATCACTTTGGCAAAGAATT–C
            41              54
Sequence A'  ACCTCGCTACTCCA
Sequence B'  ACCCCGCAAGT–––
```

Our method

```
            1                                               40
Sequence A'  AGAGCTGAGGTGTCGAGAAACTTCCTACCGCCCGT–TCGC
Sequence B'  GTCTGTGTGCTGGCC–CA–TCA– –CTTTGGCAAAGAATTC
            41              54
Sequence A'  ACCTCGCTACTCCA
Sequence B'  ACCCCGCAAGT–––
```

- Case 2. Compared with some classic heuristic algorithm, such as ACO and GA, is to test the performance of our method based on CRO. We have simulated two set date twenty times, and write down the highest score, the lowest score and the average score of each alignment. We have tabulated a summary of the simulated results in Table 3.

Table 3. The performance of our method, ACO and GA in pairwise sequence alignment

The length of sequences	Algorithm	The best score	The worst score	The average score
223,187	Our method	-515	-530	-522.5
	ACO	-515	-545	-530
	GA	-515	-545	-530
452,408	Our method	-955	-1018	-986.5
	ACO	-961	-1035	-998
	GA	-961	-1041	-1001

The series of experimental results demonstrate that the performance of method based on CRO is better or equivalent but never worse than GA and ACO in shorter sequences. In longer sequences alignment, the distance of average score with best score is relatively large, so the performance of short sequences alignment is better than the alignment of longer sequences.

5   Summary

According to the No-Free-Lunch theorem, we proposed a new method based on CRO method for pair sequence alignment. With the framework of CRO, we design some operators so as to generate some good solution that can satisfy alignment requirement.

With this method, we can obtain the same score of alignment with NW algorithm in short sequence, and the performance of this method is accurate and fairly quick as compared with some classic heuristic algorithms, while the ability of convergence needs to be strengthened. In the future work, the process can also be run in parallel, so as to improve the running speed. And we intend to combine CRO framework with other classical algorithm to boost the convergence speed.

Acknowledgements. Thanks to my supervisor and my classmates who give me some helpful comments, and the editors and the anonymous reviewers who put forward suggestions which have enhanced the quality of paper. This research was supported by the Science and Technology Research Foundation of Hunan Province (Grant No. 2013GK3082).

References

1. Krane, D.E., Raymer, M.L.: Introduction to bioinformatics. Tsinghua University Press, Beijing (2004)
2. Needleman, S.B., Wunson, C.D.: A General Method Applicable to the Search for Similarities in the Amino Acid Sequence of Two proteins. J. Mol. Biol. 48, 443–453 (1970)
3. Smith, T.F., Waterman, M.S.: Identification of Common Molecular Subsequences. J. Mol. Biol. 147, 195–197 (1981)
4. Ljpman, D.J., Pearson, W.R.: Rapid and sensitive protein similarity searches. Science 227, 1435–1441 (1981)
5. Altschul, S.F., Gish, W., Miller, W., Myer, E.W., et al.: Basic local alignment search tool. Journal of Molecular Biology 215, 403–410 (1990)
6. Gondro, C., Kinghorn, B.P.: A simple genetic algorithm for multiple sequence alignment. Genetic and Molecular Research 6, 964–982 (2007)
7. Jangam, S.R., Chakraborti, N.: A novel method for alignment of two nucleic acid sequences using ant colony optimization and genetic algorithms. Applied Soft Computing 7, 1121–1130 (2007)
8. Notredame, C., Higgins, G.D.: SAGA: sequence alignment by genetic algorithm. Nucleic Acids Res. 8, 1515–1524 (1996)
9. Notredame, C., O'Brien, E.A., Higgins, D.G.: Raga: RNA sequence alignment by genetic algorithm. Nucl. Acids Res. 22, 4570–4580 (1997)
10. Dorigo, M., Maniezzo, V., Colorni, A.: The ant system: optimization by a colony of cooperating agents. IEEE Trans. Systems Man Cybern., Part B 1, 29–41 (1996)
11. Wolpert, D.H., Macready, W.G.: No free lunch theorems for optimization. IEEE Trans. Evol. Comput. 3, 67 (1997)
12. Lam, A.Y.S., Li, V.O.K.: Chemical-Reaction-Inspired Metaheuristic for Optimization. IEEE Transactions on Evolutionary Computation 7, 381–399 (2010)
13. Lam, A.Y.S., Li, V.O.K.: Chemical Reaction Optimization: a tutorial. Memetic Computing 4, 3–17 (2012)
14. National Center for Biotechnology Information, http://www.ncbi.nlm.nih.gov
15. Bioinformatics tools for pairwise sequence alignment, http://www.ebi.ac.uk/Tools/psa/

Hydrodynamic Analysis of Floating Marine Structures Based on an IBM-VOF Two-Phase Flow Model

Nansheng Lin[1], Xiaoming Chen[2], Chengbi Zhao[1,*], Youhong Tang[3,*], and Wei Lin[1]

[1] Department of Naval Architecture and Ocean Engineering,
School of Civil Engineering and Transportation, South China University of Technology,
Guangdong 510641, China
tccbzhao@scut.edu.cn
[2] China Ship Architecture Design & Research Institute Co., Ltd., Beijing 100024, China
[3] Centre for Maritime Engineering, Control and Imaging, School of Computer Science,
Engineering and Mathematics, Flinders University, South Australia 5042, Australia
youhong.tang@flinders.edu.au

Abstract. In this study, we develop an immersed boundary method - volume of fluid (IBM-VOF) two-phase flow solver to simulate two-phase flow problem contains solid boundaries and free surface and use it to solve the typical problems for floating marine structures. In the solver, the IBM method is adapted to solve the problems of the moving marine structures and the VOF method for solving the problems of a free surface flow. The free surface at the fluid is considered as the mixed fluid of sea water and air in the solver. Base on this IBM-VOF two-phase flow model, hydrodynamic analysis of a floating marine structure with forced heave motion is done, and hydrodynamic force coefficients are computed. In this case, we firstly calculate the forces of the floating marine structure under different frequencies, and then we get added mass and added damping through fitting the data of the forces by the least square method. The results obtained from the present model are compared, which verified the reliability and accuracy of this numerical model.

Keywords: IBM-VOF two-phase flow model, Floating marine structure, Hydrodynamic force coefficients.

1   Introduction

In the field of marine and offshore engineering, it is very important to do hydrodynamic analysis for a floating marine structure. However, there are some difficulties to calculate hydrodynamic force coefficients such as the complete added mass and the complete add damping by potential theory and experiment in the viscous flow. With the development of computer technology and computational fluid dynamics (CFD) methods, many problems of hydrodynamic processes for floating marine structure in two phase flow can be solved by CFD directly. Due to more advantages of low cost, no effect of scale ratio, and easily modifying the conditions

---

* Corresponding authors.

K. Li et al. (Eds.): ParCFD 2013, CCIS 405, pp. 440–449, 2014.

and parameters of the experiment, CFD numerical simulation can offer optimization design of floating marine structure a better reference. Based on our group's study about immersed boundary method (IBM) [1], volume of fluid (VOF) [2] and the two-phase flow model [3], an IBM-VOF two-phase flow CFD method is proposed to simulate marine problems of viscous two-phase flow with free surface and solid immersed boundary in this study.

In the solver, the IBM method is adapted to solve the problems of the moving marine structures and the VOF method for solving the problems of a free surface flow. IBM was developed by Peskin [4] firstly and applied mostly based on Cartesian grid system. The basic principle of IBM is taking the messages of the submerged body's Lagrangian nodes on the boundary to Euler nodes in the flow field near the border by interpolation in the form of force. VOF was developed by Hirt and Nichols [5] firstly. Utilizing VOF to treat free surface, a fluid fraction variable F, with values between zero and one, is used to indicate the fraction of each computational cell that is filled with a fluid phase. PLIC (piecewise line interface calculation) method is an interface reconstruction algorithm for reconstructing the interface by a sloping segment. Once the interface has been reconstructed, variable F is updated by the motion of underlying fluid with Lagrangian propagation method. Meanwhile, in the simulation of the free surface problems which are based on one-phase flow models, the effects of air movement above the free surface are ignored and the density difference between gas and liquid is also neglected. This may result in missing information about the quantities, and become a source of errors of the numerical simulation. Thus, in order to avoid the difficulties mentioned above, it is preferable to construct a two-phase flow model coupling with the VOF method for solving the problems of a free surface flow.

In this study, we will simulate a floating marine structure with forced heave motion and compute its hydrodynamic force coefficients base on the IBM-VOF viscous two-phase flow model.

2 Numerical Model

2.1 Mathematical Formation

In this study, incompressible and immiscible fluids are considered. The aggregated-fluid approach is chosen for the two-phase model [6-9], meaning that the behavior of each fluid is described by an independent set of equations. For incompressible conditions, the governing equations are the mass conservation equation and the Navier-Stokes momentum conservation equation written as:

$$\frac{\partial u_j}{\partial x_j} = 0 \tag{1}$$

$$\frac{\partial u_i}{\partial t} + u_j \frac{\partial (u_i)}{\partial x_j} = -\frac{1}{\rho}\frac{\partial p}{\partial x_i} + \frac{1}{\rho}\frac{\partial \tau_{ij}}{\partial x_j} + f_i \tag{2}$$

where subscript $i = 1, 2$ denotes the 2D geometrical descriptions and Cartesian tensor notation is used. u_j, p and x_j are the velocities, pressure and spatial coordinates. f_i represents the external body force. τ_{ij} is the viscous term given by

$$\tau_{ij} = \mu(\frac{\partial u_i}{\partial x_j} + \frac{\partial u_j}{\partial x_i}) \tag{3}$$

ρ, μ are the density and viscosity appropriate for the phase occupying the particular spatial location at a given instance of time. For immiscible fluids, density and viscosity are constant along particle paths and they are adverted by fluid velocity; therefore, they satisfy

$$\frac{\partial \rho}{\partial t} + u_j \frac{\partial \rho}{\partial x_j} = 0 \tag{4}$$

$$\frac{\partial \mu}{\partial t} + u_j \frac{\partial \mu}{\partial x_j} = 0 \tag{5}$$

The staggered grid mesh is applied to discrete the control equations in this study, as is shown in Fig. 1 [2]. The velocity components and external forces are defined at cell faces while scalar quantities are evaluated at the cell centre.

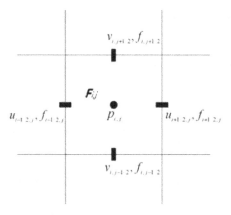

Fig. 1. The staggered grid mesh

2.2   The Treatment of Immersed Boundaries

In the model, the IBM method is adapted to solving the problems of the moving marine structures. With adding the force to the incompressible Navier-Stokes equations, the flow field can take the object into account. In our solver, the equation for the immersed boundary is constructed in this following [2]:

$$\vec{f} = \frac{\vec{u_b} - \vec{u}}{\Delta t} + \left(\vec{u} \cdot \nabla \vec{u}\right) - \mu \nabla_h^2 \vec{u} + \frac{Gp}{\rho} - \vec{g} \tag{6}$$

where u_b is the velocity of immersed boundary in the corresponding grid and u represents the velocity of the flow field within the grid.

2.3   Interface Treatment by Volume of Fluid Method

For the two-phase model, owing to the existence of steep gradients in density and viscosity around the free surface, excessive numerical diffusion is experienced when computing viscous flows by solving above equations. Therefore, the VOF method is used to capture the interface, which is no longer considered as a free-surface in the two-phase model; in contrast, in a one-phase model the incompressible Navier-Stokes equations are solved with a free-surface condition on the free boundary.

Defining the volume fraction of gas phase F as 0, liquid phase F as 1, the interface as $0 < F < 1$, the advection equation of the interface can be described as

$$\frac{\partial F}{\partial t} + u_j \frac{\partial F}{\partial x_j} = 0 \tag{7}$$

To determine the variable F in every cell at each time step, two core algorithms of VOF method, i.e. interface reconstruction and volume advection algorithms, are important to be selected carefully, which will significantly influence on the computational accuracy and efficiency.

In the present model, the second-order PLIC method of the VOF method is used to reconstruct the interface and to determine the VOF fluxes. The linear interface reconstruction is accomplished by knowing both the normal vector of the interface and the intercept of the interface-line on the meshes. The modified Youngs' least square method [10], which is second-order accurate, is employed to estimate the normal vector of the interface. In terms of free-surface advection algorithm, a Lagrangian advection method according to Gueyffier et al. [11] is used after the reconstruction of the interface in each cell at each time step. After implementing the above algorithms, the fluid fraction variable F can be updated to the next time step. The whole scheme is second-order accurate. Then the local density and viscosity can be calculated from the fluid fraction variable F. It is noted that the update process of VOF function is basically the update of density, therefore the transport of density with the interpolation of velocity may result in air bubble entrainment or droplets after the reconstruction of the interface. No special treatments are needed in this two-phase flow model when dealing with flow with broken free surfaces.

2.4   Analysis of Numerical Simulation Problem

The heave motion of marine engineering can be expressed as:

$$x_1 = x_{10} \sin \omega t \tag{8}$$

where x_{10} is the motion amplitude and ω is the frequency.

The suffered force of marine engineering can be expressed as [12]:

$$A_1 \ddot{x}_1 + B_1 \dot{x}_1 + F_1 = 0 \tag{9}$$

where subscript 1 denotes the heave motion. A_1, B_1 are the added mass and added damping. F_1 represents the hydrodynamic force.

The fluid's forces on the marine engineering can be obtained by integrating pressure along the wet surface. The value of the pressure p along the wet surface is composed by the dynamic pressure p_d and static pressure p_s, $p = p_d + p_s$ by integrating dynamic pressure p_d along the wet surface, we can get the hydrodynamic force of the marine structure in each direction.

Fitting the data of the hydrodynamic forces by the least square method, then we can get:

$$F_1 = F_{10} + F_{1A} \sin \omega t + F_{1B} \cos \omega t \tag{10}$$

Substituting Eq. (8) and Eq. (10) into Eq. (9), making the equation coefficient of both sides is equal, and then we can get the added mass and damping coefficients of each frequency:

$$A_1 = \frac{F_{1A}}{x_1 \omega^2} \qquad B_1 = -\frac{F_{1B}}{x_1 \omega} \tag{11}$$

Accordingly, when the marine engineering makes "pure heave" motion, we can get the added mass and damping coefficient about heave. The added mass and damping coefficient about six degrees can be obtained by this method.

3   Computational Model and Analysis

3.1   The Marine Engineering Model and Parameter Settings

The computational model and principal dimensions parameters for the marine engineering problem are showed in Fig. 2 and Table 1. We can see that the marine engineering model is a typical hull.

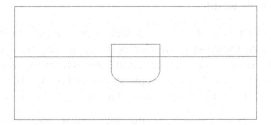

Fig. 2. The marine engineering hull model

Table 1. The parameters of model

Computational domin		The hull model size	
Length	2m	Height	0.3m
Width	0.9m	Width (B)	0.4m
Water Level	0.5m	Draught (D)	0.2m

According to Liao *et al.* [13], the flow field within the immersed boundaries has an impact on the results in the simulation of moving boundary. In order to minimize this effect, the solve constructs force source term on all solid nodes. In the present simulation, the corresponding meshing for computational domain and the hull model are as follows:

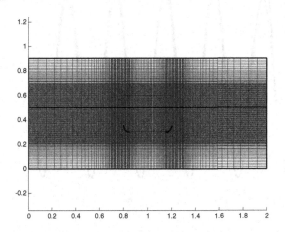

Fig. 3. The mesh of the marine structure (T=1S)

With reference to Fig. 3 we can see that the mesh of IBM method is different from some other CFD methods, such as the mesh of traditional body-fit mesh. In order to get correlation variables of the flow field around the marine structure accurately, the Cartesian grids around and within the marine structure should be encrypted. Since only the forced heave motion of the marine structure is considered in this paper, Non-uniform Cartesian grid is used, in which the vertical mesh is encrypted deeply while the level mesh is not, and the total mesh is 152×520 when the period is 1s.

3.2   Analysis of the Results

Base on the IBM-VOF two-phase flow model, hydrodynamic analysis of a floating marine structure with forced heave motion is done. In this case, we firstly calculate the forces and moments of the floating marine structure in the forced heave motion under different frequencies. As an example shown in Fig. 4, while the period of the marine structure is 1 s, the amplitude is 0.01 m, and the heave motion law of displacement is $x_1 = 0.01\sin(\frac{2\pi}{T}t)$ during the forced heave motion, the heave dynamic force-time curve of the floating marine structure is obtained by the IBM-VOF two-phase flow model. It can be seen that the present result agree with CFD RANS method and experimental results [12], reported by other researchers well.

After calculated the forces and moments of the floating marine structure in the forced heave motion under different frequencies, added mass and added damping of the moving floating marine structure under different frequencies is obtained through fitting the data of the forces and moments by the least square method according to Eq. 10. By fitting the data of above 1s period simulation case by the least square method, it show that the corresponding added mass and added damping are $A_1 = 68.3918$, $B_1 = 154.0461$, which is close to CFD RANS method's result [12].

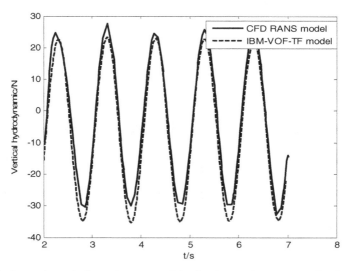

Fig. 4. The heave dynamic force-time curve of the floating marine structure (T=1S, A=0.01m)

By calculating the forces of the floating marine structure in the forced heave motion under different dimensionless factors($\omega\sqrt{B/2g} = 0.5$, 0.6, 0.8971, 1.0, 1.5), added mass and added damping of the moving floating marine structure under different periods are computed through fitting the data, which are shown as Figs. 5 and 6.

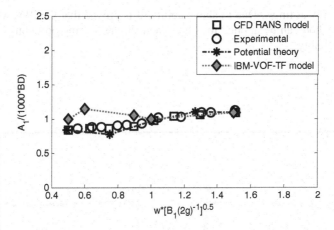

Fig. 5. Added mass in the forced heave motion

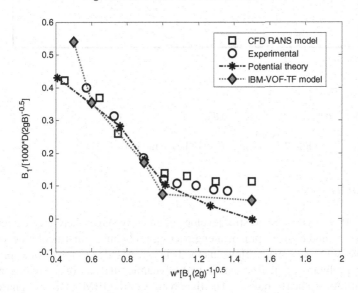

Fig. 6. Added damping in the forced heave motion

Obviously, from Fig. 5 and Fig. 6, it is proved that the hydrodynamic calculation results of the IBM-VOF two-phase flow method agree with the theoretical and experimental results reported by other researchers' well [12], which verified the reliability and accuracy of the numerical model.

In the simulation of floating marine structure with forced heave motion by the IBM-VOF two-phase flow method, more detail information about fluid can be observed, which help to study the rule of floating marine structure with forced heave motion in fluid. For example, the vortex field of heave motion of 1s period case are showed in Fig. 7. We can see that there are some vortexes around the hull in Fig. 7, which the theoretical method can't captured, which means that it is very important to consider nonlinear features and vortexes disturbance that will affect the final result of simulation deeply at times. Due to above ability, it is proved that the IBM-VOF two-phase flow method can be applied to solve practical engineering problems of marine flexibly and reliably.

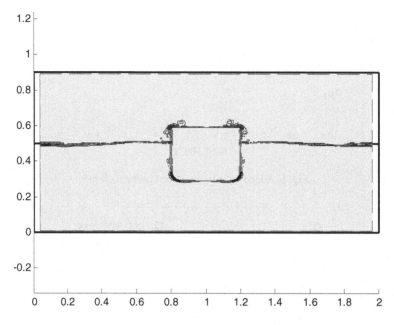

Fig. 7. The vortex field of heave motion ($T = 1\ S$)

4   Conclusion

Because the IBM-VOF method still develops at an early stage, there are scarcely any cases for the method to solve practical engineering problems of marine. In the study, a robust IBM-VOF two-phase flow method is proposed to solve one practical engineering problems of marine that is hydrodynamic analysis of a floating marine structure with forced heave motion. The final results of the IBM-VOF two-phase flow method are agreed with the theoretical and experimental results reported by other researchers' well, which verified the reliability and accuracy of the numerical model. Due to such applicability and flexibility of the IBM-VOF two-phase flow method, more practical engineering problems will be simulated in the future. It is believed that the IBM-VOF two-phase flow method can be a potential tool for solving practical engineering problems of marine after more improvement and practice.

Acknowledgments. This work was supported by the National Natural Science Foundation of China (51009069) and the Fundamental Research Funds for the Central Universities -South China University of Technology, Ministry of Education of China (2012ZZ0097).

References

1. Cheng, X.M., Zhao, C.B., Tang, Y.H., Zhang, C., Wang, H.M., Lin, W.: Immersed Boundary Method Using an Approximate Projection Methods on Non-staggered Grids. In: The 6th International Conference on Fluid Mechanics, Guangzhou China, June 30-July 3 (2011)
2. Zhang, W., Tang, Y.H., Zhao, C.B., Zhang, C.: A Two-phase Flow Model with VOF for Free Surface Flow Problems. Appl. Mech. Mater. 232, 279–283 (2012)
3. Chen, X.M., Zhang, C., Tang, Y.H., Zhao, C.B., Lin, W.: A Novel Immersed Boundary Method With an Approximate Projection on Non-staggered Grids to Solve Unsteady Fluid Flow with a Submerged Moving rigid Object. Proceedings of the Institution of Mechanical Engineers, Part M, Journal of Engineering for the Maritime Environment (accepted, 2013)
4. Peskin, C.S.: Flow Patterns Around Heart Valves: A Numerical Method. J. Comput. Phys. 10, 252–271 (1972)
5. Hirt, C.W., Nichols, B.D.: Volume of Fluid (VOF Method) For Dynamics of Free Boundaries. J. Comput. Phys. 39, 201–225 (1981)
6. Hu, C., Kashiwagi, M.: A CIP-based Method for Numerical Simulations of Violent Free Surface Flows. J. Mater. Sci. Technol. 9, 143–157 (2004)
7. Rudman, A.: A Volume-tracking Method for Incompressible Multifluid Flows with Large Density Variations. Int. J. Numer. Meth. Fl. 28, 357–378 (1998)
8. Tryggvason, G., Bunner, B., Esmaeeli, A., Juric, D., Al-Rawahi, N., Tauber, N., Han, J., Nas, S., Jan, Y.J.: A Front-tracking Method for the Computations of Multiphase Flow. J. Comput. Phys. 169, 708–759 (2001)
9. Yabe, T., Xiao, F., Utsumi, T.: The Constrained Interpolation Profile Method for Multiphase Analysis. J. Comput. Phys. 169, 556–593 (2001)
10. Rider, W.J., Kothe, D.B.: Reconstructing Volume Tracking. J. Comput. Phys. 141, 112–152 (1998)
11. Gueyffier, D., Nadim, A., Li, J., Scardovelli, R., Zaleski, S.: Volume of Fluid Interface Tracking with Smoothed Surface Stress Methods for Three-dimensional Flows. J. Comput. Phy. 152, 423–456 (1999)
12. Luo, M.L., Mao, X.F., Wang, X.X.: CFD Based Hydrodynamic Coefficients Calculation to Forced Motion of Two-demensional Section. Chinese J. Hydrodynamics 26, 509–515 (2011)
13. Liao, C.C., Chang, Y.W., Lin, C.A., McDonough, J.M.: Simulating Flows with Moving Boundary Using Immersed-boundary Method. Comput. Fluids 39, 152–167 (2010)

An Improved Fictitious Domain Method for Simulating Sedimenting Rigid Particle in a Viscous Fluid

Shifeng Wu[1,2,*] and Li Yuan[1]

[1] Institute of Computational Mathematics, Academy of Mathematics and Systems Science,
Chinese Academy of Sciences, Beijing 100080, China
[2] Department of Computer Sciences, Guangdong Polytechnic Normal University,
Guangzhou 510665, P.R. China
shifengwu@lsec.cc.ac.cn

Abstract. In this article, the dynamics of particle-particle collisions in a viscous fluid is numerically investigated. An improved fictitious domain–based computational method for a solid-fluid system is developed and a collision strategy for multiple particles is presented. In earlier methods, a repulsive force is applied to the particles when their separation is less than a critical value and depending on the magnitude of this repulsive force, collision of two or more particles may bounce unrealistically. In the present method, when the collision of two or more particles happens, a direct force is added to each particle through Discrete Element Method (DEM) for particle collision. At the same time, a direct-forcing domain method, which is development of the fictitious domain(FD) method, is applied for simulation of multi-particle fluid flows. It employs a discrete δ-function in the form of bi-function to transfer quantities between the Eulerian and Lagrangian nodes as in the immersed boundary method. This method avoids the need to use Lagrange multipliers for imposition of the rigid body motion. Results for motions of several particles in a viscous fluid are presented.

Keywords: Collision, Particulate flow, Numerical simulation, Fictitious domain method, Discrete Element Method, Lagrange multiplier.

1   Introduction

In order to accurately predict the behavior of particulate flows, a fundamental knowledge of the mechanism of particles collision is required. Classical lubrication theory predicts that the lubrication force becomes singular as the distance between two smooth spheres approaches zero and hence prevent smooth spheres from touching. In practice, no general numerical method can afford the computational cost of resolving the flow in the narrow gaps between closely-spaced particles and therefore some modeling is needed. In reality, the surface of particles has some roughness and the bumps make physical contact due to the discrete molecular nature of the fluid and/or attractive London-van der Waals forces. Thus further approach is prevented and solid–solid contact occurs [1].

---

* Corresponding author.

K. Li et al. (Eds.): ParCFD 2013, CCIS 405, pp. 450–459, 2014.
© Springer-Verlag Berlin Heidelberg 2014

Historically, the non-boundary-fitted (or Cartesian grid) method is a popular choice for popular for the solution of the fluid flow problems in a complex geometry or with moving boundaries. A variety of non-boundary-fitted approaches have been developed, and they can be roughly classified into two families [2,3]: the body-force based method (e.g., [4]) and the non-body-force based method (e.g., [2]). For the former, a body force (or momentum forcing) is introduced into the momentum equation. The fractional step scheme is often used in the body-force based method to simplify the computation in the following way: the Navier–Stokes equations are solved for the known body-force obtained at the previous fractional steps, with the boundary condition on the immersed boundary disregarded, and the boundary condition is used to determine the body-force at the subsequent fractional steps. There exist various body-force based methods in the literature that differ in the way that how the body-force calculated. Unlike the body-force based method, the non-body-force based method does not introduce a body-force, instead, the immersed interface method (IIM) accounts for the boundary condition by either transforming it into independent equations [5] or using it to modify the expressions of differential operators for the Eulerian nodes in the immediate vicinity of the boundary [6, 7]. One advantage of the non-body-force based method is that the jump boundary conditions on the surface can be more accurately handled. While its disadvantage is the increased complexity.

We are concerned with the simulation of particulate flows in the present study. In principle, all aforementioned methods can be applied to the particulate flows, however, the body-force based method has been predominantly used so far. A common feature for the body-force based method is that the hydrodynamic force on the particles can be calculated from the body-force and is not required to be explicitly computed. For the distributed-Lagrange-multiplier/fictitious-domain (DLM/FD) method proposed by Glowinski et al., the particle velocities and the body-force (Lagrange multiplier) are solved simultaneously with the implicit scheme, while for the immersed boundary method, they are obtained explicitly. The DLM/FD method has been successfully applied to a wide range of particulate flow problems. However, its calculation and iteratively determined of the particle velocity and body-force is a little more involved and expensive compared to the direct-forcing immersed boundary(IB) method. At the same time, the DLM/FD do not allow contact when two particles are closer. The aim of the present study is to present a simpler non-Lagrange-multiplier version of without sacrificing the accuracy by employing a discrete $\delta -$ function in the form of bi-function to transfer explicitly quantities between the Eulerian and Lagrangian nodes, as done as in the immersed boundary method. Also, we used a collision strategy of DEM, in which no repulsive force is applied to the particles rather, the contact force between particles is computed directly by using the DEM, both particles can be rigidified together. One advantage of this method over the IB method is that the particle velocity is not updated explicitly thus preventing numerical instabilities often encountered in IB method.

2   Numerical Method

2.1   Theoretical Formulation

The governing equations in the fluid domain for the particulate flow are

$$
\begin{aligned}
\rho_f \frac{d\boldsymbol{u}}{dt} &= \nabla \cdot \boldsymbol{\sigma} \quad \text{in} \quad \boldsymbol{\Omega}_f, \\
\nabla \cdot \boldsymbol{u} &= 0 \quad \text{in} \quad \boldsymbol{\Omega}_f, \\
\boldsymbol{u} &= \boldsymbol{U} + \boldsymbol{\omega} \times \boldsymbol{r} \quad \text{on} \ \partial P \\
\boldsymbol{u}\big|_{t=0} &= \boldsymbol{u}_0(\boldsymbol{x}) \quad \text{in} \quad \boldsymbol{\Omega}_f,
\end{aligned}
\tag{1}
$$

Where ρ_f is the fluid density, $\boldsymbol{u}$ the fluid velocity, and $\boldsymbol{\sigma}$ the fluid stress. $\boldsymbol{U}$ is the i-the particles velocity, and $\boldsymbol{\omega}$ is i-the particle angular velocity. The initial velocity $\boldsymbol{u}_0$ satisfies the continuity equation. Only the Newtonian fluid is considered in this study, thus $\boldsymbol{\sigma} = -p\boldsymbol{I} + 2\mu\boldsymbol{D}$, with p being the fluid pressure, μ the dynamic viscosity coefficient and $\boldsymbol{D}$ the rate-of-strain tensor.

The governing equations in the particle domain are

$$
\begin{aligned}
M \frac{d\boldsymbol{U}}{dt} &= \boldsymbol{F}^H + (1 - \frac{1}{\rho_r})M\boldsymbol{g} \\
\frac{d(\boldsymbol{J} \cdot \boldsymbol{\omega})}{dt} &= \boldsymbol{T}^H,
\end{aligned}
\tag{2}
$$

where M, J, U and $\boldsymbol{\omega}$ are the particle mass, moment of inertia tensor, translational velocity and angular velocity, respectively. $\boldsymbol{g}$ is the gravitational acceleration and ρ_r is the solid–fluid density ratio. $\boldsymbol{F}^H$ and $\boldsymbol{T}^H$ are the hydrodynamic force and torque on the particle, respectively, defined by

$$
\begin{aligned}
\boldsymbol{F}^H &= \int_{\partial P} \boldsymbol{n} \cdot \boldsymbol{\sigma} ds, \\
\boldsymbol{T}^H &= \int_{\partial P} \boldsymbol{r} \times (\boldsymbol{n} \cdot \boldsymbol{\sigma}) ds.
\end{aligned}
\tag{3}
$$

Where $\boldsymbol{n}$ is the unit outward normal on the particle surface and $\boldsymbol{r}$ is the position vector with respect to the particle mass center. Note that the gravity term is not considered in (1), which has no effect on the flow, but can produces a hydrostatic pressure and thereby a buoyance force on the particle. Since the buoyance force is not included in $\boldsymbol{F}^H$, we need to include it directly in (2).

As in the DLM/FD method, the interior of the particle is filled with the fluid and a pseudo body-force is introduced over the particle inner domain to enforce the fictitious fluid to satisfy the rigid-body motion constraint, namely, the following equations are introduced for the interior of the particle:

$$\rho_f \frac{du}{dt} = \nabla \cdot \sigma + \lambda \quad \text{in} \quad P(t),$$

$$u = U + \omega \times r \quad \text{in} \quad P(t).$$

$$(4)$$

The $(2) - \int_P (4) dx$, then F^H and σ terms are eliminated to get the governing equations . Then the governing equations can be non-dimensionlized by introducing the following scales: L_c for length, U_c for velocity, L_c / U_c for time, $\rho_f U_c^2$ for pressure p and $\rho_f U_c^2 / L_c$ for the pseudo body-force. For convenience, we write the dimensionless quantities in the same form as their dimensional counterparts, unless otherwise specified. The dimensionless equations for the incompressible fluid can be written as follows:

$$\frac{\partial u}{\partial t} + u \cdot \nabla u = \frac{\nabla \cdot \tau}{Re} - \nabla p + \lambda \quad \text{in} \quad \Omega,$$

$$\nabla \cdot u = 0 \quad \text{in} \quad \Omega,$$

$$u = U + \omega \times r \quad \text{in} \quad P,$$

$$(\rho_r - 1) V_p^* \left(\frac{dU}{dt} - Fr \frac{g}{g} \right) = - \int_P \lambda ds \quad \text{in} \quad P,$$

$$(\rho_r - 1) \frac{d(J^* \cdot \omega)}{dt} = \int_P r \times \lambda ds \quad \text{in} \quad P.$$

$$(5)$$

In the above equations, Re represents the Reynolds number defined by $Re = \rho_f U_c L_c / \mu$, Fr the Froude number defined by $Fr = gL_c / U_c^2$, V_p^* the dimensionless particle volume define by $V_p^* = M / \rho_s L_c^d$ and J^* the dimensionless moment of inertia tensor defined by $V_p^* = J / \rho_s L_c^{d+2}$, here ρ_s being the particle density and d being the dimensionality of the problem involved. Note that the pseudo body-force λ in (5) is defined in the solid domain $P(t)$.

2.2   Numerical Implementation

A finite-volume method using a staggered grid for incompressible flow is implemented. The SIMPLE algorithm is used to solve the fluid equations with modifications to account for the presence of particles. The Implicit Euler scheme is used for time discretization.

The discretize momentum equations for 2-D flows in the x and y directions

$$a_{i,J} u^*_{i,J} = \sum a_{nb} u^*_{nb} - \frac{p^*_{I,J} - p^*_{I-1,J}}{\delta x} \Delta V_u + b_{i,J} + \lambda^*_{xi,J} \tag{7}$$

$$a_{I,j} v^*_{I,j} = \sum a_{nb} v^*_{nb} - \frac{p^*_{I,J} - p^*_{I-1,J}}{\delta y} \Delta V_v + b_{I,j} + \lambda^*_{yI,j} \tag{8}$$

The pressure correction equations

$$a_{I,J} p'_{I,J} = a_{I-1,J} p'_{I-1,J} + a_{I+1,J} p'_{I+1,J} + a_{I,J-1} p'_{I,J-1} + a_{I,J+1} p'_{I,J+1} + b'_{I,J} \tag{9}$$

Correct the pressure, rigidity forces, and velocities

$$p_{I,J} = p^*_{I,J} + p'_{I,J} \tag{10}$$

$$u_{i,J} = u^*_{i,J} + d_{i,J}(p'_{I-1,J} - p'_{I,J}) \tag{11}$$

$$v_{I,j} = v^*_{I,j} + d_{I,j}(p'_{I,J-1} - p'_{I,J}) \tag{12}$$

Calculate U^{n+1}, ω^{n+1} and forces

$$\lambda = \lambda^* + \frac{U^{n+1} + \omega^{n+1} \times r - u^*}{\Delta t} \tag{13}$$

Then update $\lambda^* = \lambda$, $u^* = u$, $v^* = v$, $p^* = p$, until the equations (7)-(10) are convergence. Check the collision, if it is happened, DEM is used, otherwise update U^{n+1}, ω^{n+1} and the position of particle

$$\rho_r V_p \frac{U^{n+1}}{\Delta t} = (\rho_r - 1) V_p \left(\frac{U^n}{\Delta t} + Fr \frac{g}{g} \right) + \int_P \left(\frac{u^*}{\Delta t} - \lambda^n \right) dx \tag{14}$$

$$\rho_r \frac{(J^* \cdot \omega^{n+1})}{\Delta t} = (\rho_r - 1) \left[\frac{J^* \cdot \omega^n}{\Delta t} - \omega^n \times (J^* \cdot \omega^n) \right] + \int_P r \times \left(\frac{u^*}{\Delta t} - \lambda^n \right) dx \tag{15}$$

Finally, let $\lambda^{n+1} = \lambda^*$ and the fluid velocities u^{n+1} at the Eulerian nodes are determined

$$u^{n+1} = u^* + \Delta t (\lambda^{n+1} - \lambda^n) \tag{16}$$

3   Numerical Experiments

3.1   Sedimentation of a Circular Particle in Channel

Throughout the present study, the results are computed and presented in the dimensionless form, thus we need to define the characteristic velocity and length for each case. For low Reynolds numbers, there exists an analytical expression for the drag force on a circular particle settling in a channel at the velocity U:

$$F_d = 4\pi K \mu U \qquad (17)$$

where K is a constant related to the effect of the channel width on the drag force and can be expressed in terms of the ratio of the channel width to the particle diameter W* (i.e., W/D) [8]:

$$K = \frac{1}{\ln W^* - 0.9157 + 1.7244/(W^*)^2 - 1.7302/(W^*)^4 + 2.4056/(W^*)^6 - 4.5913/(W^*)^8}. \qquad (18)$$

By taking the characteristic velocity as U_c

$$U_c = \frac{D^2}{16 K \mu}(\rho_s - \rho_f)g, \qquad (19)$$

the dimensionless terminal settling velocity is expected to be unity. The characteristic length is the particle diameter. We take the Reynolds number Re and the density ratio ρ_r as the independent dimensionless control parameters, and then the Froude number Fr is not independent , but can be expressed in terms of Re and ρ_r as follows:

$$Fr = \frac{16K}{(\rho_r - 1)\,\mathrm{Re}} \qquad (20)$$

For the case of a relatively strong inertial effect, we take the characteristic velocity U_c as

$$U_c = \sqrt{\frac{D}{2}(\rho_r - 1)g}, \qquad (21)$$

so that one can conveniently obtain the standard drag coefficient from C_d from $C_d = 1/(U^*_T)^2$, here U^*_T being the computed dimensionless terminal settling velocity. Another advantage of this non-dimensionlization scheme is that U^*_T is always not far away from unity. The Froude number in this case becomes

$$Fr = \frac{2}{(\rho_r - 1)\pi} \qquad (22)$$

We will consider the sedimentation of a circular particle in a vertical channel at Re = 0.1 and 200, respectively. The characteristic velocity is defined by (19) for Re = 0.1 and by (21) for Re = 200. The particle is released at the center of the channel. Fig. 1-2 show the time developments of the settling velocities at Δt = 0.0005 for Re = 0.1,W/D = 4, and the results exhibit a satisfactory time-step independence. Using Δt = 0.0005, the simulation of the acceleration process from zero velocity to the steady-state velocity only requires less than 100 time steps.

From Fig.2 (a), we can see that the dimensionless terminal settling velocity is expected to be unity. This is well within the range of results that theoretical analysis gets (19). Total iterations' developments of SIMPLE of a circular particle in a vertical channel of are show in Fig.2. (b). This show that our method is stabilities. Fig.4. is result of the big Reynolds number situation. The result is also within the range of results that theoretical analysis gets (19)-(22). Because the Reynolds number is 200, the total iterations' developments of   SIMPLE is almost linear increase, which is not as same as the Fig.2.(b).

The results is shown in Fig.1-4. Generally, our results are well within the range of results that theoretical analysis gets (17)-(22). Also, our results are well within the range of results reported by other researchers[10]. This method avoids the need to simultaneously solve coupled Lagrange multipliers and flow velocity for imposition of the rigid body motion.

We also succeed to get the sedimentation of three circular particles in a two dimensional channel Fig.5-Fig.6.. When the collision of two or more particles happens, the DEM is use to solve this problem. The result is also within the range of results that theoretical analysis.

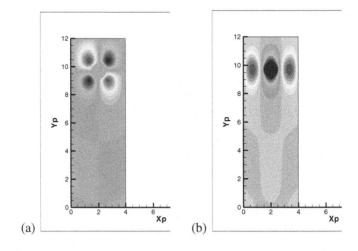

(a)   (b)

Fig. 1. Contour for the fluid velocity for $W/D = 4, Re = 0.1, r = 0.5, \Delta t = 0.0005, \rho_r = 1.2,$ $h = 1/64$ at $t = 0.02$ (a):x directions of the fluid velocity contour (b) :y directions of the fluid velocity contour

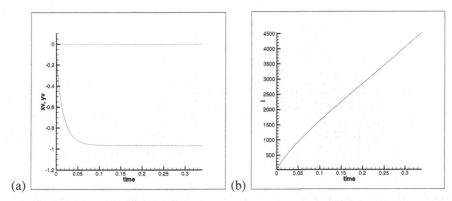

(a)   (b)

Fig. 2. Time developments of the settling velocities of a circular particle in a vertical channel (a) U_x and U_y of the particle (b) Number of total iterations, When $W/D = 4, \mathrm{Re} = 0.1,$ $r = 0.5, \Delta t = 0.0005, \rho_r = 1.2, h = 1/64.$

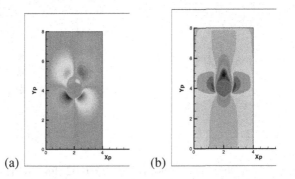

(a)   (b)

Fig. 3. Contour for the fluid velocity for at $t = 0.05$ (a) U_x :x directions of the fluid velocity contour (b) U_y :y directions of the fluid velocity contour, When $W/D = 4, \mathrm{Re} = 200,$ $\Delta t = 0.005, \rho_r = 1.1$

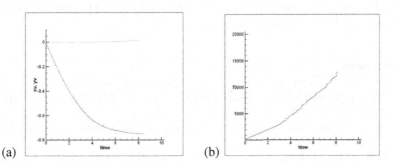

(a)   (b)

Fig. 4. Time developments of the settling velocities of a circular particle in a vertical channel (a) U_x and U_y of the particle (b) Number of total iterations, When $W/D = 4, \mathrm{Re} = 200,$ $\Delta t = 0.005, \rho_r = 1.1$

458   S. Wu and L. Yuan

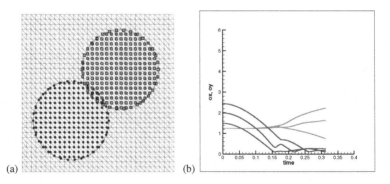

(a)   (b)

Fig. 5. (a)The situation of DEM's happened (b) Time developments of x- and y- position of three circular particle's center in a vertical channel for $W/D = 4, \text{Re} = 0.1, r = 0.5$, $\Delta t = 0.0005, \rho_r = 1.2$

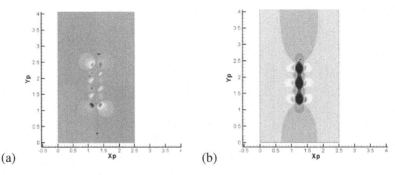

(a)   (b)

Fig. 6. Contour for the fluid velocity at $t = 0.02$ for $W/D = 4, \text{Re} = 0.1, r = 0.5$, $\Delta t = 0.0005, \rho_r = 1.2$, : (a) U_x :x directions of the fluid velocity contour (b) U_y :y directions of the fluid velocity contour, for three particles

Acknowledgments. The authors would like to acknowledge the support of National Natural Science Foundation of China (Grant Nos.:Y011.915T1), and thank the anonymous referees for helpful suggestions.

References

[1] Davis, R.H.: Elastohydrodynamic collisions of particles. PCH PhysicoChem. Hydrodyn. 9, 41–52 (1987)
[2] Mittal, R., Iaccarino, G.: Immersed boundary methods. Annu. Rev. Fluid Mech. 37, 239–261 (2005)
[3] Marella, S., Krishnan, S., Liu, H., Udaykumar, H.S.: Sharp interface Cartesian grid method I: an easily implemented technique for 3D moving boundary computations. J. Comput. Phys. 210, 1–31 (2005)
[4] Glowinski, R., Pan, T.-W., Périaux, J.: A fictitious domain method for Dirichlet problems and applications. Comp. Meth. Appl. Mech. Eng. 111, 283–303 (1994)

[5] Fadlun, E.A., Verzicco, R., Orlandi, P., Mohd-Yusof, J.: Combined immersed-boundary finite-difference methods for three-dimensional complex flow simulations. J. Comput. Phys. 161 (2000)

[6] Le, D.V., Khoo, B.C., Peraire, J.: An immersed interface method for viscous incompressible flows involving rigid and flexible boundaries. J. Comput. Phys. 220, 109–138 (2006)

[7] Xu, S., Wang, Z.J.: An immersed interface method for simulating the interaction of a fluid with moving boundaries. J. Comput. Phys. 216, 454–493 (2006)

[8] Happel, J., Brenner, H.: Low Reynolds Number Hydrodynamics. Prentice-Hall, New York (1965)

[9] Yu, Z.S., Shao, X.M.: A direct-forcing fictitious domain method for particulate flows. Journal of Computational Physics 227, 292–314 (2007)

[10] Ardekani, A.M., Dabiri, S., Rangel, R.H.: Collision of multi-particle and general shape objects in a viscous fluid. Journal of Computational Physics 227, 10094–10107 (2008)

[11] Glowinski, R., Pan, T.-W., Hesla, T.I., Joseph, D.D.: A distributed Lagrange multiplier/fictitious domain method for particulate flows. Int. J. Multiphase Flow 25, 755–794 (1999)

[12] Glowinski, R., Pan, T.-W., Hesla, T.I., Joseph, D.D., Periaux, J.: A fictitious domain approach to the direct numerical simulation of incompressible viscous flow past moving rigid bodies: application to particulate flow. J. Comput. Phys. 169, 363–426 (2001)

[13] Yu, Z., Shao, X., Wachs, A.: A fictitious domain method for particulate flows with heat transfer. J. Comput. Phys. 217, 424–452 (2006)

[14] Peskin, C.S.: Numerical analysis of blood flow in the heart. J. Comput. Phys. 25, 220–252 (1977)

[15] Lai, M.-C., Peskin, C.: An immersed boundary method with formal second-order accuracy and reduced numerical viscosity. J.C. Phys. 160, 705–719 (2000)

A Divide-and-Conquer Method for Multiple Sequence Alignment on Multi-core Computers

Xiangyuan Zhu

School of Computer Science,
Zhaoqing University, Zhaoqing 526061, China
hnzxy@hnu.edu.cn

Abstract. A parallel Divide-and-Conquer Alignment procedure (DCA) for multiple sequence alignment is presented. DCA improves alignment speed by using the Divide-and-Conquer paradigm, which is suitable for handling large-scale processing problems on multi-core computers. DCA works by dividing the large-scale alignment problem into smaller and more tractable sub-problems which can be solved by the existing algorithms. We assess the execution time and accuracy of our implementation of DCA on an 8-core computer using the classical benchmarks, BAliBASE, PREFAB, IRMBase and OXBENCH, and twenty-eight artificially generated test sets. DCA achieves up to 111-fold improvements in execution time with comparable accuracy.

Keywords: data parallelism, parallel algorithm, multi-core, multiple sequence alignment, biological sequences.

1 Introduction

Multiple sequence alignment (MSA) has become an essential tool in Computational Biology, including phylogenetic reconstruction, predicting the structure and functions for biomolecules, identification of conserved sequence motifs and homology modeling. Construction of a multiple sequence alignment aims at arranging residues with inferred common evolutionary origin in the same position for a set of sequences [1]. As increasing amounts of sequence data are being generated by high-throughput sequencing projects, alignment of large-scale biological sequences is computationally demanding.

Due to the computationally intensive operation and vast amount of available sequence data, there has been tremendous effort in the development of parallel MSA algorithms [2, 3]. However, most of these solutions are designed on clusters of workstations, networks, mesh-based multiprocessor architectures and clouds. On the other hand, accelerators using other hardware architectures such as Field-Programmable Gate Array (FPGA) [4], General Purpose Graphics Processing Unit (GPU) [5], Cell Broadband Engine (CBE) [6] and Network-on-Chip (NoC) [7] have been developed for sequence alignment. Despite the improvement in accuracy and speed, these architectures are both hard and expensive to harness for non-expert users.

K. Li et al. (Eds.): ParCFD 2013, CCIS 405, pp. 460–469, 2014.
© Springer-Verlag Berlin Heidelberg 2014

Divide-and-Conquer is a basic parallelism paradigm and has been pursued for many sequence analysis applications. In [2], Saeed et al. proposed a domain decomposition strategy to solve the large-scale MSA problem on multiprocessor platform. In [3], kim et al. introduced ClustalXeed, a GUI-based grid computation version for terabyte size multiple sequence alignment on both single PC and distributed cluster systems. In [8, 9], CDAM works on multi-core computers by clustering the input sequence sets into subsets, aligning the subsets dependently, and merging to form the final alignment solution.

It is generally acknowledged that computers with multiple processor cores using shared memory are now ubiquitous. Current laptop computers all have 2 or 4 cores, and desktop computers can easily have 4 or 8 cores, with many cores in high-end computers. In this paper, we investigate a parallel Divide-and-Conquer algorithm for aligning large-scale biological sequences on multi-core computer. We effectively exploit computing power provided by multi-core architectures and thus are able to align abundant sequences.

The rest of this paper is organized as follows. Section 2 introduces the presentation of our proposed algorithm. Section 3 is devoted to evaluate the performance of the algorithm. Finally, Section 4 outlines the main conclusions.

2 Divide-and-Conquer Alignment Algorithm

In this section, we present a parallel algorithm for aligning large-scale sequences, namely Divide-and-Conquer Alignment (DCA). The motivation of DCA is to divide the input large-scale set of sequences into subsets which are small enough for the existing MSA programs to handle. It means that we can construct a high-quality large multiple alignments with up to a tens of thousands sequences in minutes or at most a few hours, while other traditional MSA programs fail to handle because of the memory requirements or infeasible execution time. DCA has three computationa phases, i.e., dividing and distribution, alignment independently on processor cores, and concatenating to form the final alignment.

2.1 Equal Division

Given n sequences S_1, S_2, ... , S_n with different lengths $l_{(1)}$, $l_{(2)}$, ... , $l_{(n)}$. Let m be the number of processor cores. The goal of the equal division algorithm is to partition the n sequences into k disjoint subsets, where $k \geq m$. It is known that the execution time of MSA is effected by the number of sequences and the length of sequences [9]. Therefore, to achieve the load balance between the subsets, both the number of sequences and the length of sequences should be considered when designing the equal division algorithm. Algorithms 1 outlines the equal division algorithm. The n sequences are sorted by their lengths in non-increasing order, and then partition to k subsets equally.

Algorithm 1. Equal Division Algorithm

Input: A sequence set $S = \{S_i | 1 \leq i \leq n\}$ and an integer k, in which S_i has different
length $l_{(i)}$ for each i.
Output: A k-partition of $Q = \{Q_i | 1 \leq i \leq k\}$.
1. Sort $S_1, S_2, ..., S_x$ in non-increasing order of the sequence length so that $l(S_i) \geq$
   $l(S_{i+1})$ for $i = 1, \cdots, n - 1$.
2. Divide S into k subsets Q_i, where Q_i has $\lceil n/k \rceil$ sequences for $1 \leq i \leq k - 1$ and
   $n - (k - 1) \times \lceil n/k \rceil$ sequences for $i = k$.
3. Output Q.

2.2 Longest Sequence Length First Distribution

After dividing the input sequences, we design a Longest Sequence Length First
Distribution Algorithm to distribute the k subsets to m processor cores. To
achieve the load-balancing, we assign the subsets to available cores according to
the sequence lengths. Algorithm 2 shows the intuitive description of the Longest
Sequence Length First Distribution.

Algorithm 2. Longest Sequence Length First Algorithm

Input: A set $Q = \{Q_i | 1 \leq i \leq k\}$ and an integer m, in which $m \leq k$.
Output: A m-partition of $Q' = \{Q'_i | 1 \leq i \leq m\}$.
1. **for** $i \leftarrow 1$ to m **do**
2. $Q'_i \leftarrow \phi$;
3. **end for**
4. **for** $i \leftarrow 1$ to k **do**
5.   Insert Q_i into a set of currently smallest length of the first sequence in Q'.
6. **end for**
7. Output Q'.

2.3 Alignment

In theory, any existing MSA algorithm can be used to align the subsets on each
cores. We selected MUSCLE [10, 11], a effective MSA algorithm, to apply to the
alignment process of DCA. The reason we choose it is both its high citations
(over 5,500 for [10, 11] in the Web of Science) and high performance on alignment
accuracy and speed.

   Aligning the subsets on each core dependently, many local alignment solutions
are obtained. Since our goal is to get a global alignment of all the n sequences,
a procedure should be developed to glue the locally aligned profile sequences
into a global alignment. We applied the progressive profile-profile alignment
presented in [9] to glue the aligned clusters. The procedure is depicted in Figure
1, where C_{ij} denotes the subsets i ($1 \leq i \leq k$) processed on core j ($1 \leq j \leq m$).
Profile-profile alignments are processed progressively within cores firstly, and
then processed between cores until a global alignment achieved. The order of
profile-profile alignment is the index of subsets and cores.

We adopted the group-to-group alignments proposed in MAFFT [12] to merge the temporary alignment of each cores to get the final solution of the all n sequences. More details about group-to-group alignments of MAFFT can be found in [12].

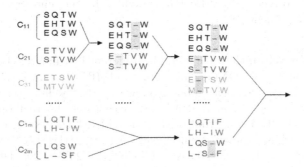

Fig. 1. Profile aligning progressively and combining sequence subsets

Combined with the ideas mentioned above, we designed the Divide-and-Conquer Algorithm. The details are shown in Algorithm 3.

Algorithm 3. Divide-and-Conquer Algorithm
___

Input: A sequence set $S = \{S_i | 1 \leq i \leq n\}$ and two integers k and m, in which S_i has different length $l_{(i)}$ for each i and $k \geq m$.

Output: A aligned sequence set $S' = \{S'_i | 1 \leq i \leq n\}$.

1. Sort $S_1, S_2, ..., S_x$ in non-increasing order of the sequence length so that $l(S_i) \geq l(S_{i+1})$ for $i = 1, \cdots, n - 1$.
2. Divide S into k subsets using Algorithm 1.
3. Distribute k subsets to m cores using Algorithm 2.
4. In parallel, align the subsets on each core using MUSCLE algorithm.
5. In parallel, concatenate the aligned subsets using group-to-group alignment proposed in MAFFT.
6. Output S'.

---

3 Performance Evaluation

We evaluate the performance of DCA on traditional benchmarks as well as generated sequence test sets in terms of accuracy and speed. The performance evaluation is carried out on an 8 Intel Xeon (E5506) cores computer, running at 2.13 GHz, with 8GB DRAM memory. The operating system is Windows 7.

3.1   Quality Assessment

Two accuracy measures were used to score the alignment, the quality score (Q), which is the number of correctly aligned residue pairs divided by the number of residue pairs in the reference alignment, and total column score (TC), which is the number of correctly aligned columns divided by the number of columns in the reference alignment [10].

Traditional Benchmarks. We used four different benchmarks: BAliBASE3.0 [13], PREFAB4.0 [10], OXBench1.3 [14] and IRMBASE2.0 [15] to assess the performance of DCA in comparison with other well-known MSA algorithms: MUSCLE3.8.31 [10], PicXAA [16] with three different options('-PF', '-PHMM', and '-SPHMM'), ProbCons1.12 [17], MAFFT6.708 [12] with four different options ('-linsi', '-ginsi', '-einsi', and '-fftnsi'), MUMMALS1.01 [18] with HMM_1_3_1 option, T-Coffee6.00 [19], CLUSTALW2.0.10 [20], DIALIGN-TX [15] and ProbAlign1.1 [21]. The scores for the sequential algorithms have been derived from [16] except MUSCLE3.8.31 tested by us.

The Q and TC scores are given in Table 1. In all the experiments for quality assessment using benchmarks, it can be seen that DCA has comparable performance to the MUSCLE system, especially on IRMBASE and OXBench. This is because DCA was implemented with MUSCLE system as the underlying MSA algorithm at each core. Compared with MUSCLE, DCA loses average quality by 3.69% on the four benchmarks. Therefore, the quality obtained is limited by the quality of the underlying alignment system.

Table 1. Performance on benchmarks

Method	BAliBASE3.0 Q/TC	IRMBASE2.0 Q/TC	PRREFAB4.0 Q	OXBench1.3 Q/TC
DCA	0.732/0.321	0.098/0.028	0.584	0.684/0.610
MUSCLE	0.819/0.478	0.114/0.038	0.650	0.699/0.631
T-Coffee	0.859/0.552	0.878/0.463	0.708	0.822/0.751
DIALIGN-TX	0.788/0.443	0.929/0.710	0.625	0.852/0.783
CLUSTALW	0.754/0.380	0.263/0.024	0.618	0.868/0.801
PicXAA-PF	0.879/0.593	0.890/0.501	0.713	0.888/0.831
PicXAA-PHMM	0.866/0.563	0.908/0.545	0.712	0.882/0.823
PicXAA-SPHMM	0.867/0.561	0.728/0.330	0.724	0.891/0.835
ProbAlign	0.876/0.588	0.817/0.367	0.719	0.888/0.832
ProbCons	0.864/0.560	0.853/0.425	0.716	0.883/0.825
MUMMALS	0.855/0.539	0.684/0.246	0.727	0.885/0.827
MAFFT-linsi	0.872/0.593	0.894/0.460	0.722	0.880/0.821
MAFFT-ginsi	0.866/0.567	0.845/0.402	0.717	0.879/0.820
MAFFT-einsi	0.871/0.590	0.918/0.482	0.720	0.881/0.822
MAFFT-fftnsi	0.841/0.531	0.828/0.385	0.688	0.869/0.806

Generated Sequence Test Sets. The benchmarks are all small sizes. To obtain the correlation between the underlying MSA system and the proposed strategy, we conducted experiments on twenty-eight generated sequence test sets, in which the number of sequences, the average length and distance of sequences varied from 1,000 to 8,000, 200 to 2,000 and 150 to 1,050 respectively. We compared DCA only with MUSCLE. The experiments were conducted with different datasets while keeping two of the parameters held constant[1], using different number (1-8) of cores.

Figures 2(a) and 2(b) depict performance in terms of Q and TC scores with increasing number of cores, while increasing the average length of sequences from 200 to 2,000. It can be seen that the increase in the number of cores to 8 has no effect on the Q and TC scores, which effectively verifies the validity of DCA. The Q and TC scores remaine 0.971 and 0.627 respectively for average length of 2,000.

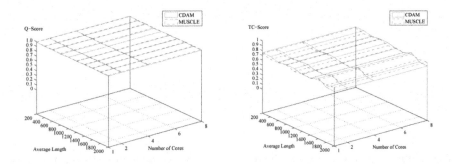

Fig. 2. Illustration of scores for different test set varied in average length (a) Q scores and (b) TC scores

Figures 3(a) and 3(b) show the Q and TC scores while increasing the average sequence distance from 150 to 1,050. As can be seen from these figures, the alignment accuracy in fact decreases with increasing average pairwise distance. The Q scores of DCA depicted in Figure 3(a) correlate well with the Q scores of the MUSCLE system. In Figure 3(b), DCA outperforms MUSCLE by 5.03% in the TC scores on average because of the effective progressive profile-profile alignment.

Finally, we assessed the accuracy while increasing the number of sequences from 1,000 to 8,000. Figures 4(a) and 4(b) show the Q and TC scores for DCA and MUSCLE. We can see that the quality of DCA strongly depends on the quality of the alignments obtained by the MUSCLE system. We only showed the quality for up to 8,000 sequences, because the sequential MUSCLE program failed to align larger datasets.

---

[1] Constants held for the experiments are: Length=200, Number of sequence=200 and Phylogenetic distance =150.

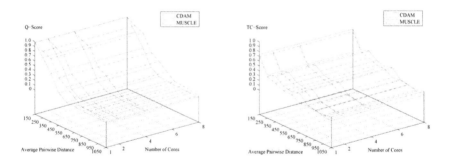

Fig. 3. Illustration of scores for different test set varied in average distance (a) Q scores and (b) TC scores

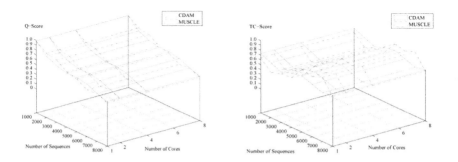

Fig. 4. Illustration of scores for different test set varied in number of sequences (a) Q scores and (b) TC scores

The average accuracy loss on the twenty-eight large-scale test sets and four benchmarks is 2.87%. We conclude that DCA can align large number of sequences while losing a reasonable biological accuracy.

3.2   Speedup Assessment

To determine the scalability of DCA in terms of speedup, we performed rigorous experiments on eight sets of sequences generated by Rose [22], in which the number of sequences varied from 1,000 to 8,000 while the average pairwise distance and length of sequences set to be 150 and 100 respectively. We defined *Speedup* $= \frac{T_{MUSCLE}}{T_p}$, where T_{MUSCLE} is the processing time of MUSCLE and T_p is the processing time of DCA using p cores.

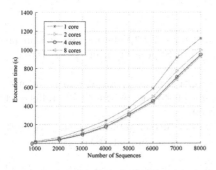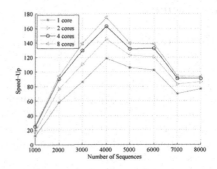

Fig. 5. (a) Execution time of DCA on different number of CPU-cores and (b) Speedup of DCA over MUSCLE for different number of CPU cores

In Figure 5(a), the execution time of DCA increases sharply with an increase number of sequences, while decreases with increasing the number of cores. Figure 5(b) depicts the speedup of MUSCLE by DCA. It is obvious that DCA exhibits super linear speedup on an 8-core computer for less than 4,000 sequences. When the number of sequences larger than 4,000, the speedup decreases but still more than 90 for 8 cores.

4   Conclusions

We have proposed DCA, a general Divide-and-Conquer method to speed up any multiple sequence alignment on modern multi-core computers. This parallel strategy allowed us to develop a highly scalable multiple alignment system. Using the four classical benchmarks which are BAliBASE, PREFAB, IRMBASE and OXBench and twenty-eight large-scale artificial datasets, DCA achieves average 111-fold improvements in execution time while losing 2.87% alignment accuracy on average. The exponential growth of biological sequence databases demands even more powerful high-performance solutions in the near future. Hence, it can be a good practice to use Divide-and-Conquer parallel strategy to generate alignments for large-scale sequences on multi-core computers.

Acknowledgments. This research is supported by the Key Program of National Natural Science Foundation of China (Grant No. 61133005), Hunan Provincial Natural Science Foundation of China (Grant No. 13JJ4038), the Science and Technology Project of Hunan Provincial Science and Technology Department, China (Grant No. 2012WK3053) and Hunan Provincial Innovation Foundation for Postgraduate, China(Grant NO. CX2012B143).

References

[1] Orobitg, M., Guirado, F., Notredame, C., Cores, F.: Exploiting parallelism on progressive alignment methods. The Journal of Supercomputing 58(2), 186–194 (2011)

[2] Saeed, F., Khokhar, A.: A domain decomposition strategy for alignment of multiple biological sequences on multiprocessor platforms. Journal of Parallel and Distributed Computing 69(7), 666–677 (2009)

[3] Kim, T., Joo, H.: ClustalXeed: A GUI-based grid computation version for high performance and terabyte size multiple sequence alignment. BMC Bioinformatics 11(1), 467 (2010)

[4] Lloyd, S., Snell, Q.O.: Accelerated large-scale multiple sequence alignment. BMC Bioinformatics 12(1), 1–10 (2011)

[5] Liu, W., Schmidt, B., Muller-Wittig, W.: CUDA-BLASTP: accelerating BLASTP on CUDA-enabled graphics hardware. IEEE/ACM Transactions on Computational Biology and Bioinformatics (TCBB) 8(6), 1678–1684 (2011)

[6] Wirawan, A., Kwoh, C.K., Schmidt, B.: Multi-threaded vectorized distance matrix computation on the CELL/BE and x86/SSE2 architectures. Bioinformatics 26(10), 1368–1369 (2010)

[7] Sarkar, S., Kulkarni, G.R., Pande, P.P., Kalyanaraman, A.: Network-on-Chip hardware accelerators for biological sequence alignment. IEEE Transactions on Computers 59(1), 29–41 (2010)

[8] Zhu, X., Li, K., Li, R.: A Data Parallel Strategy for Aligning Multiple Biological Sequences on Homogeneous Multiprocessor Platform. In: 2011 Sixth Annual Chinagrid Conference (ChinaGrid), pp. 188–195. IEEE (2011)

[9] Zhu, X., Li, K., Salah, A.: A data parallel strategy for aligning multiple biological sequences on multi-core computers. Computers in Biology and Medicine 43(4), 350–361 (2013)

[10] Edgar, R.: MUSCLE: a multiple sequence alignment method with reduced time and space complexity. BMC Bioinformatics 5(1), 113 (2004)

[11] Edgar, R.C.: MUSCLE: multiple sequence alignment with high accuracy and high throughput. Nucleic Acids Research 32(5), 1792–1797 (2004)

[12] Katoh, K., Frith, C.M.: Adding unaligned sequences into an existing alignment using MAFFT and LAST. Bioinformatics Applications Note 28(23), 3144–3146 (2012)

[13] Thompson, J.D., Koehl, P., Ripp, R., Poch, O.: BAliBASE 3.0: latest developments of the multiple sequence alignment benchmark. Proteins: Structure, Function, and Bioinformatics 61(1), 127–136 (2005)

[14] Raghava, G., Searle, S.M., Audley, P.C., Barber, J.D., Barton, G.J.: OXBench: a benchmark for evaluation of protein multiple sequence alignment accuracy. BMC Bioinformatics 4(1), 47 (2003)

[15] Subramanian, A.R., Kaufmann, M., Morgenstern, B., et al.: DIALIGN-TX: greedy and progressive approaches for segment-based multiple sequence alignment. Algorithms Mol. Biol. 3(6) (2008)

[16] Sahraeian, S.M.E., Yoon, B.J.: PicXAA: greedy probabilistic construction of maximum expected accuracy alignment of multiple sequences. Nucleic Acids Research 38(15), 4917–4928 (2010)

[17] Do, C.B., Mahabhashyam, M.S., Brudno, M., Batzoglou, S.: ProbCons: Probabilistic consistency-based multiple sequence alignment. Genome Research 15(2), 330–340 (2005)

[18] Pei, J., Grishin, N.V.: MUMMALS: multiple sequence alignment improved by using hidden Markov models with local structural information. Nucleic Acids Research 34(16), 4364–4374 (2006)

[19] Notredame, C., Higgins, D.G., Heringa, J., et al.: T-Coffee: A novel method for fast and accurate multiple sequence alignment. Journal of Molecular Biology 302(1), 205–218 (2000)

[20] Thompson, J.D., Higgins, D.G., Gibson, T.J.: CLUSTAL W: improving the sensitivity of progressive multiple sequence alignment through sequence weighting, position-specific gap penalties and weight matrix choice. Nucleic Acids Research 22(22), 4673–4680 (1994)

[21] Roshan, U., Livesay, D.R.: Probalign: multiple sequence alignment using partition function posterior probabilities. Bioinformatics 22(22), 2715–2721 (2006)

[22] Stoye, J., Evers, D., Meyer, F.: Rose: generating sequence families. Bioinformatics 14(2), 157–163 (1998)

Hybrid CPU/GPU Checkpoint for GPU-Based Heterogeneous Systems

Lin Shi[1,2], Hao Chen[2], and Ting Li[1]

[1] School of Computer Science and Enginerring,
Hunan University of Science and Technology, Xiang Tan, China
[2] School of Computer and Communication,
Hunan University, Chang Sha, China

Abstract. Fault tolerance has become a major concern in exascale computing, especially for the large scale CPU/GPU heterogeneous clusters. The performance/cost benefit of GPU based system is subject to their abilities to provide high reliability, availability, and serviceability. The traditional CPU-based checkpoint technologies have been deployed on the GPU platform but all of them treat the GPU as a second class controllable and shared entity. As existing GPU checkpoint/restart implementations do not support checkpointing the internal GPU status, the codes running on GPU (kernel) can not be checked/restored just like the CPU codes, all the checkpoint operation is done outside the kernel. In this paper, we propose a hybrid checkpoint technology, HKC (Hybrid Kernel Checkpoint). HKC combines the PTX stub inject technology and dynamic library hijack mechanism, to save/store the internal state of a GPU kernel. Our evaluation shows that HKC increases the system reliability of CPU/GPU hybrid system with a very reasonable cost, and show more resilience than other checkpoint scheme.

Keywords: checkpoint, GPU, CUDA, kernel.

1 Introduction

Over the past few years, the modern 3D graphics processing unit (GPU) has evolved from a fixed-function graphics pipeline to a programmable parallel processor with computing power exceeding that of multicore CPUs. Under the GPGPU concept, NVIDIA has developed a C language based programming model, Compute Unified Device Architecture (CUDA) [1], which provides greater programmability for high-performance graphics devices. GPU programming has been successfully exploited in recent years for resolving a broad range of computationally demanding and complex problems.

For the high performance computing (HPC), the exponential growth of GPU supercomputers in the Top500 list has prove the efficiency of large GPU clusters. Since 2000, a large number of large-scale GPU-based clusters merged as the fasted supercomputer in the world. For example, the first (Tianhe-1A), the third (Nebula), and the fourth (Tsubame2.0) fastest supercomputer in the top 500 list of November 2010 are all CPU/GPU heterogeneous systems.

K. Li et al. (Eds.): ParCFD 2013, CCIS 405, pp. 470–481, 2014.
© Springer-Verlag Berlin Heidelberg 2014

Although the GPGPU paradigm successfully provides significant computation throughput, the reliability of GPUs in error-intolerant applications is largely unproven. Traditionally the 100% accuracy is not necessary for GPU because the errors only affect a few pixels or a few frames and where performance is more important than accuracy. However, an error in a GPGPU application will crash down the whole program or produce an incorrect result. Since the purpose of GPGPU is to perform massive amounts of computation, the failure of a GPU could result in significant loss of application progress. The Fermi and Kepler GPUs of Nvidia already support the ECC (Error Correcting Code) in graphic memory to provide some kinds of fault tolerance, but the GPU is still vulnerable to control logic errors and multi-bit errors in memory. A test in the Tokyo Institute of Technology observed eight errors in a 72-hour run of a GPGPU testing program on 60 NVIDIA GeForce 8800GTS 512 [2]. Stanford University find that the two-thirds of tested GPUs on Folding@home exhibit a detectable, pattern-sensitive rate of soft error [3] .

The NVIDIA developed a new compute mode SIMT (single-instruction, multiple-thread) based on the SIMD (single-instruction, multiple-data). The feature of SIMT lead us to develop the HKC (Hybrid Kernel Checkpoint), a novel state store/recovery method for GPU code. HKC support to check a running kernel at any time, at any place, and recover from errors detected in a code region by partially recomputing the region. Meanwhile HKC is totally transparent to the programmer, no source code modification is needed to perform the checkpoint.

To the best of our knowledge, HKC is the first work on how to check/restore the kernel level state in a transparent way.

In summary, the main contributions of our work are:

- We introduce HKC, a hybrid-kernel-checkpoint method to recover from some given GPGPU faults efficiently by exploiting the SIMT characteristics of programs running on GPGPUs. HKC overcome some serious shortcoming of traditional method: the inefficiency from the full re-computation, the lack of flexibility in check interval and the intrusiveness arise from some compiler-aid method.
- We give a detail search on the key features of SIMT architecture and show the possible to checkpoint this new architecture in a transparent way.
- We describe an implementation of our framework on the CUDA platform for NVIDIA GPGPUs.
- We carry out detailed performance evaluation on the overhead of our framework. This evaluation shows that the HKC framework is practical and can deliver high performance for checking/restoring GPGPU applications in the CPU/GPU hybrid system.

While this work focuses on checkpoint on CPU/GPU heterogeneous systems, HKC is also applicable to any distributed systems equipped with the SIMT-style processors.

The rest of the paper is organized as follows: In Section 2, we provide some necessary background about this work. Section 3 discusses the design and implementation of HKC respectively. Next we evaluate HKC in Section 4 . In Section 6, we discuss related work. Finally, in Section 7 we present our conclusions.

2   Backgroud

2.1   CUDA

In 2007 NVIDIA propose the CUDA (Compute Unified Device Architecture) framework. CUDA is the first dedicate GPGPU interface on the GPU platform, which provide a C-like semantics to write the parallel code (kernel), and give programmer the ability to direct control the GPU. In recent years a large number of compute-intensive applications have been ported to CUDA platform, the power of CUDA and GPU has been proved in many cases. The device code running on the GPU is usually called a KERNEL according to the CUDA's terminology.

Runtime and Driver API of CUDA. There are two different kinds of CUDA API exist in the CUDA software stack. The low-level API system is called the CUDA driver API, the high-level, runtime API. The runtime API is easier to use, but the driver API gives programmer more control over low level details. They both provide the interface to allocate/withdraw the graphic memory objects, and launch the kernel.

3   Design and Implementation

The checkpoint-based GPU fault-tolerant technology will periodically save the current execution state of the GPU, and roll back the GPU state to a certain checkpoint when a failure happened. It comprise two phases: checking phase and restore phase.

Checking Phase. During the normal execution of GPU application, triggered by the user or system, the current GPU state is copied and stored in the persistent media, which is called a checkpoint file.

Restore Phase. When a fault occurs or application get unexpected results, the GPU rollback to a previous checkpoint, then continue to run from this state.

The key issue of checkpoint technology is how to define, check and restore the application state. The checkpoint image should be the complete unity combining the internal and external state of a program which support the its successful execution in the future. Typical states for Linux and Windows applications include registers, heap, stack, thread, address space, and signal, lock, file, socket, handler, I/O device, external connections etc. Relative to the applications running on the CPU, the internal state of code running on the GPU (Kernel) exhibit some different characters. The kernel state lies in the GPU and device memory against CPU and host memory, the address space of kernel is organized by the CUDA runtime against the operating system. Further, Kernel state can be divided into in-kernel state and out-of-kernel states, depending on the life cycle of objects.

For example, the global memory belongs to the out-of-kernel states because the object in global memory will persist during different kernel's execution unless an explicit API is called to delete them. The on-chip resource (register file,control unit,local memory, share memory) are in-kernel state because they are valid only when a kernel is running. A CUDA application may involve many kernels, each one of them involves different internal state when they are executing on the SMs.

In short, the out-of-kernel state is relatively simple, while the in-kernel state is more complex. In order to reduce the complexity of the GPU checkpoint, the existing CPU/GPU hybrid checkpoint mechanism [17, 23–26] focus only the simplified out-of-kernel state. Figure 1 shows the flow chart of OKC: When the CPU receives the checkpoint signal it does not immediately perform a checkpoint, but to determine the current state of the GPU. If there is no any running kernel and pending kernel in the queue, the checkpoint is performed. Otherwise OKC will wait until running or pending kernels all finished. If an error happened in the the kernel execution, the entire system is rolled back to the previous checkpoint.

As can be seen with reference to Figure 1 , OKC achieve both concision and effectiveness by keeping the check/restore mechanism out of the kernel. But there are many shortcomings with OKC as follows:

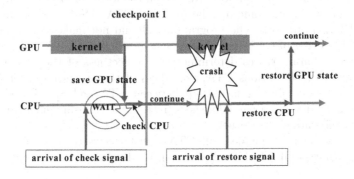

Fig. 1. The control flow of OKC

Non Real-Time Processing in Check Stage. OKC must wait until the kernel completed means there exists a delay between the arrival of check signal and actual check operation. The delay time depend the total execution time of running and pending kernels. For long-running kernel the check operation is postponed in a great extend. This has a negative impact on application require strong real time capacity. Whats more, in the GPU cluster, a large number of GPUs must be synchronized to the keep the consistency of global checkpoint. If some of them are running heavy kernel the overall OKC check time will be extended even lead to domino effect (A distributed system can not find the global consistent checkpoint, all task roll back to the initial state and lost all the effective computation).

Unbalance Interval Time of Check. Checkpoint technology needs to balance the relationship between the fault tolerance capability and inspection overhead. Only when the check event is distributed evenly during the execution of GPGPU applications, can the checkpoint technology achieve optimal tradeoff balance between performance and reliability. But the check interval of OKC is heavily depend on the workload of kernel. For example, although the administrator can set a reasonable check interval to one hour, the OKC has to stretched this interval to threes hours because of a long-running kernel. Theoretically the longer a KERNEL is running, the more frequently it should be checked since it is more vulnerable to errors, which OKC can not do.

Time-Consuming in Recovery Phase. In recovery phase OKC should recompute the entire kernel from the last checkpoint even only one transient fault is detected on the GPU. Each kernel need be re-started from scratch and thousands of threads in it are fully recalculated. The kernel represent the most intensive computation in GPGPU applications, the cost of such full-fledged recomputing may be unnecessarily high.

The shortcoming of OKC lead us to find a more flexile checkpoint mechanism. In CUDA framework a kernel is decomposed into many CTAs, which run independently from each other and occupy SMs in the forms of groups. The execute order of these groups, the binding relationship of CTA to SMs are not guaranteed by the CUDA framework. The programmer should not make any assumptions or rely on the order of CTAs or coupling schemes between CTA and SM.

The above characteristics determines the correctness of the kernel depend on the correctness of various CTA, regardless of the execution order between the CTA or the coupling relationship between CTA and SM. Based on this observation, we develop a partially check/restore mechanism which cares about the CTA-level state in the kernel.

When a kernel is suspended, all CTAs must freezed in one of the following three situation: finished (endCTA), on-the-fly (halfCTA), or unborn (beginCTA).

endCTA contains the threads have ended their job, the calculation results are reflected in the global memory

halfCTA: contains threads are running on the SMs. Notes in CUDA the threads in the same CTA may execute different instructions.

beginCTA: the threads in it do not start yet.

So a sophisticated check/restore scheme should save the internal state for the halfCTA and record which CTA is finished or unborn in the check phase. In the restore phase, the check/restore scheme make is sure to never re-execute the endCTA, and re-execute the halfCTA from the place it break and re-launch the beginCTA from the beginning. In some case the kernel is reenterable so it is ok to re-execute the endCTA but it is difficult to distinguish whether a kernel is reentrant or not. For performance reasons, the restore operation should not repeat the already completed calculation.

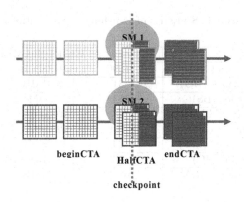

beginCTA   HalfCTA   endCTA

checkpoint

Fig. 2. Three kinds of CTA in a suspended kernel

The above analysis tell us the the CTA running the same kernel code must forked in the restore phase according to their execution state in the check phase. The restore code with different branches should be injected to the kernel which we called the *HKC stub*.

There are many ways to realize such a check/restore scheme, in our design of HKC, we put three main factors in minds:

Transparency. HKC should not force the programmer do anything outside the CUDA program model, which means, HKC need not any source code modification or introduce extra programming rules. In addition, we would like our techniques to easily extend to other SIMT/SIMD architecture, allowing people to use GPU checkpoint tools just like the traditional system-level CPU checkpoint tools.

Performance. The main advantage of GPGPU computation is the high performance, while the checkpoint is recognize as a high overhead fault tolerance technology. HKC should minimize these overhead, combine the strengths of high performance from CUDA and reliability from checkpoint.

Compatibility. We would like our HKC to easily combined to the already exist CPU-based checkpoint technology, to form a sophisticate CPU/GPU hybrid checkpoint system.

4 Evaluation

While the previous sections have presented detailed technical descriptions of the HKC, this section evaluates the efficiency of HKC using programs selected from official SDK examples: a set of general-purpose algorithms from various research area. The benchmarks range from simple data management to more complex WalshTransform computation and MonteCarlo simulation. Table 1 shows the statistical characteristics of these benchmarks, such as the quantity of API calls,

Table 1. Statistics of Benchmark Applications

	Number of APIs	GPU RAM	Data Volume
AlignedTypes (AT)	1990	94.00MB	611.00MB
BinomialOptions (BO)	31	0.01MB	0.01MB
BlackScholes (BS)	5143	61.03MB	76.29MB
ConvolutionSeparable (CS)	48	108.00MB	72.00MB
FastWalshTransform (FWT)	144	128.00MB	128.00MB
MersenneTwister (MT)	24	91.56MB	91.56MB
MonteCarlo (MC)	53	187.13MB	0.00MB
ScanLargeArray (SLA)	6890	7.64MB	11.44MB

the device memory size they consume and the data volume transferred from or to GPU device. As a comparison we re-implement the OKC mechanism developed in the [13].

The following testbed has been used for all benchmarks: A HP Proliant ML150G6 server equipped with one Intel E5504 processors with four cores and provided with 8 GBytes of memory. Furthermore, the graphics hardware was NVIDIA's GTX470 with 1.2GBytes graphic memory. As for software, the test machine ran the Fedora 13 Linux distribution with the 2.6.33.3 kernel, with the official NVIDIA driver version 169.19.26 for Linux and CUDA toolkits version 3.2.

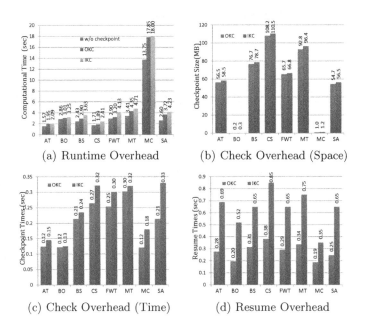

(a) Runtime Overhead   (b) Check Overhead (Space)

(c) Check Overhead (Time)   (d) Resume Overhead

4.1   Runtime Overhead

Even no check is performed, HKC mechanism will also introduce some overhead which come from the monitoring operations on CUDA library and the stub injection. Figure 3(a) depicts the execution time of each benchmark under three different configuration: without any checkpoint mechanism, with HKC and with OKC. As it shows, the maximum overhead of OKC is up to 42% (SA), minimum of 5% (BO), an average of 21%. The runtime overhead of HKC is up to 62% (SA), and average of 38%. The HKC runtime overhead is relatively high because the HKC initialization involves the establishment of a memory pool and the operation to inject the stub. OKC also need to keep track of the CUDA API, but they do not need to adjust the KERNEL code so gained some performance advantages. From another perspective, as the supplementation of OKC, HKC only add maximum of 29%, an average of 14% of the overhead at the base of OKC.

Although in eight samples the HKC runtime overhead can not be ignored, partly arise from the facts they involves relative short running kernel. Taking the constant initialization time into account, HKC is still practical to long-running applications. If HKC provide some options to switch on/off itself, so as to distinguish between critical and non-critical KERNEL, the runtime overhead of HKC will be further reduced.

4.2   Checking Overhead

The checking overhead include the time and space overhead introduced by the checkpoint operation. Figure 3(b) shows the average capacity of the checkpoint file. Since the check in HKC happened when the kernel is running the internal state is more complex then OKC, the space overhead of HKC is higher (9% on average) than OKC, the degree depends on the numbers of halfCTA, numbers of CTA and the usage of registers, shared memory. In the BO and MC test HKC increase the check contents to a extent of 40% and 17%, the reason is their state set are relatively smaller making the HKC overhead more obvious.

Time overhead from the checkpoint means the interval between the arrival of the checkpoint signal and the finish of the checkpoint snapshot, as shown in Figure 3(c). Relative to the space overhead, time overhead of the HKC achieve an average of 16% and a maximum of 35%. This is due to the fact HKC need to exploit the CUDA debugging API to obtain the internal state, each of this API involves one or more system calls.

On the basis of both Figure 3(b) and Figure 3(c), it is easy to find a strong positive relationship between space overhead and time overhead. This is because most of time overhead of checking is the write operation on checkpoint file.

4.3   Restore Overhead

The recovery is the process to rebuild the CUDA state on a GPU. Figure 3(d) measure the time for the recovery of each sample program. A main portion of the recovery operation is the reconstruction of the GPU state, and thus the size of the state set has direct impact on the recovery time. In addition to the factors of states, the endCTA still occupy the dispatch unit and instruction unit, the increase of endCTA also degrade the performance of HKC.

5   Discussion

The debug interface of CUDA is exploited in our HKC scheme which may cause some side effect. For example, according to the official document, leave the debug interface open will force the KERNEL running in synchronization mode. Some debug API require the detailed debug information which can be found only in the debug version of CUDA application. The requirement is unacceptable for commodity software, not to mention debug version generally shows awesome performance compared with the release version. We argued the debug interface is not native designed for the check/restore operation, a more sophisticate interface should be provided by the graphic vendor.

In this embodiment of HKC we choose to ignore the state in the halfCTA, it is not only because its complexity but also the lack of method to write the PC (Program Counter) in a warp. The CUDA debugger API provide the device state inspection interface *readPC* and *readVirtualPC*, but no corresponding device state alteration APIs.

6   Related Work

Checkpointing and rollback recovery (Checkpoint and Rollback Recovery) technology is commonly used in post-recovery techniques to fault-tolerant. Before the advent of the GPU checkpoint technology has been widely used in the CPU-based computing systems, such as CRAK [10] BLCR [11], ckpt [12]. Recent years many research concentrate on the GPU-oriented checkpoint mechanism.

CheCUDA [13] is the first GPU checkpoint mechanisms based on the BLCR. Since the BLCR itself does not support GPU device, CheCUDA had to remove the GPU context before starting BLCR, and restore the GPU state after BLCR finished.

As a first dedicate checkpoint for GPU, CheCUDA has some apparent drawback: Firstly the combination way with BLCR is not elegant enough because the context of GPU must be destroyed and rebuilt out of the BLCR. Secondly only two simplest SDK examples involves 20 CUDA APIs out of total 60 official APIs can not prove the effective of CheCUDA. The last but not less important, the performance of CheCUDA is not good enough, it cost more than ten times the normal execution in checking phase. NVCR [15] strengthen the CheCUDA in transparency and adaptability. The authors of CheCUDA put their idea on another GPGPU framwork: OPENCL [20] to form a new checkpoint scheme CheCL [14]. VCCP project [18] discussed the GPU checkpoint mechanism in theory and analyse its optimized CUDA asynchronous mechanism. The biggest problem is VCCP do not implement its mechanism at all (no implementation), the theoretical design can not be verified in practice. Tokyo Institute of Technology has some important progress in the distributed GPU cluster checkpoint technology. Based on the CPU/GPU hybrid Tsubame2.0 supercomputer, in [19]they integrated the BLCR, OpenMPI and GPU checkpoint mechanism, extended the single-node GPU checkpoint technology to multi-GPU field. [17] is the further improvement of distribute GPU checkpoint, the authors take a variety of techniques to optimize the initial design. First, it completely abandoned BLCR, put the checkpointing base on the Reed-Solomon encoding. Second, it dug the compute potential of idle nodes to accelerate the check operation. The third it make full use of the asynchronous mode of CUDA and diskless storage. It is worth noting that although the project shows impressive high efficiency, its GPU checkpoint program is still based on the interception and encapsulation of *cudaMemCpy* function, the check events occurred outside of the KERNEL, thus it still belongs a outside-kernel-checkpoint category.

7   Conclusion

In this paper we proposed HKC, an inside-kernel-checkpoint mechanism for CUDA applications. HKC allow the administrator to fully leverage the traditional check/restore technology to increase the reliability of GPUs. We explained how to access the kernel state by using the CUDA debugger interface, and how to suspend/resume a running kernel. Compare to the OKC, HKC is not limit to the check interval and exhibit high performance because of its partial recover nature. HKC need no any source code modification and is totally transparent to the programmer. Our evaluation showed that HKC for HPC applications is feasible and competitive with OKC.

The new methodology proposed in HKC is simple yet effective as it is particularly suited for an implementation of fault recovery techniques for GPGPU programs, by leveraging the tremendous computing power of GPGPUs and exploiting the SIMT characteristics of GPGPU programs.

Acknowledgment. We thank the anonymous reviewers for their helpful feedback. This research was supported in part by Hunan Provincial Natural Science Foundation of China under grant 13JJB006, the National Science Foundation of China under grants 61133005, 61070057 and 61272190.

References

1. CUDA: Compute Unified Device Architecture (accessed September 2012), http://www.nvidia.com/object/cuda_home_new.html
2. Maruyama, N., Nukada, A., Matsuoka, S.: A high-performance fault-tolerant software framework for memory on commodity GPUs. In: Proc. Int'l Symp. Parallel and Distributed Processing (IPDPS 2010), pp. 1–11 (April 2010)

3. Haque, I.S., Pande, V.S.: Hard Data on Soft Errors: A Large-Scale Assessment of Real-World Error Rates in GPGPU. In: 10th IEEE/ACM International Conference on Cluster, Cloud and Grid Computing (CCGrid), pp. 691–696 (2010)
4. NVIDIA CUDA debugger API Reference Manual, http://developer.nvidia.com/cuda/nvidia-gpu-computing-documentation
5. Allinea DDT, http://www.allinea.com/products/ddt
6. TotalView, http://www.roguewave.com/products/totalview.aspx
7. Shi, L., Chen, H., Sun, J.: vCUDA: GPU Accelerated High Performance Computing in Virtual Machines. In: Proc. Int'l Symp. Parallel and Distributed Processing (IPDPS 2009), pp. 1–11 (May 2009)
8. GPGPU: General Purpose Programming on GPUs, http://www.gpgpu.org/w/index.php/FAQ#WhatprogrammingAPIsexistforGPGPU.3F
9. Tian, Z.A., Liu, R.S., Liu, H.R., Zheng, C.X., Hou, Z.Y., Peng, P.: Molecular dynamics simulation for cooling rate dependence of solidification microstructures of silver. Journal of Non-Crystalline Solids 354, 3705–3712 (2009)
10. Zhong, H., Nieh, J.: CRAK: Linux Checkpoint/Restart As a KERNEL Module. Technical Report, Columbia University,2002
11. Duell, J.: The Design and Implementation of Berkeley Labs Linux Checkpoint/Restart. Paper LBNL-54941. Berkeley,2005
12. Litzkow, M., Tannenbaum, T.: J. Basney, et al. Checkpoint and Migration of UNIX Process in the Condor Distributed Processing System. Technical Report, 1346, University of Wisconsin Madison
13. Takizawa, H., Sato, K., Komatsu, K., et al.: CheCUDA: A Checkpoint/Restart Tool for CUDA Applications. In: Proc. of International Conference on Parallel and Distributed Computing Applications and Technologies, Higashi Hiroshima, pp. 408–413 (2009)
14. Takizawa, H., Koyama, K., Sato, K., et al.: CheCL: Transparent Checkpointing and Process Migration of OpenCL Applications. In: Proc. of International Parallel and Distributed Processing Symposium, Anchorage, pp. 864–876 (2011)
15. Nukada, A., Takizawa, H., Matsuoka, S.: NVCR: A Transparent Checkpoint-Restart Library for NVIDIA CUDA. In: Proc. of IPDPS Workshop, Alaska, pp. 104–113 (2011)
16. Li, T., Narayana, V.K., El-Araby, E., et al.: GPU Resource Sharing and Virtualization on High Performance Computing Systems. In: Proc. of International Conference on Parallel Processing, Taipei, pp. 733–742 (2011)
17. Bautista, L., Nukada, A., Maruyama, N., et al.: Low-overhead diskless checkpoint for hybrid computing systems. In: Proc. of High Performance Computing, Dona Paula, pp. 1–10 (2010)
18. Laosooksathit, S., Naksinehaboon, N., Leangsuksan, C., et al.: Lightweight Checkpoint Mechanism and Modeling in GPGPU Environment. In: Proc. of HPCVirt Workshop, Paris (2010)
19. Toan, N., Jitsumoto, H., Maruyama, N., et al.: MPI-CUDA Applications Checkpointing. In: Proc. of Summer United Workshops on Parallel, Distributed and Cooperative Processing. Technical Report, Kanazawa (2010)
20. OpenCL: Parallel Computing on the GPU and CPU. In Beyond Programmable Shading Course of SIGGRAPH 2008 (August 14, 2008)
21. Chen, H., Shi, L., Sun, J.: VMRPC: A High Efficiency and Light Weight RPC System for Virtual Machines. In: The 18th IEEE International Workshop on Quality of Service (IWQoS), Beijing, China (2010)

22. Mohr, A., Gleicher, M.: HijackGL: Reconstructing from Streams for Stylized Rendering. In: Proc. of International Symposium on Non-photorealistic Animation and Rendering, New York, p. 13 (2002)
23. Xu, X., Lin, Y., Tang, T., et al.: HiAL-Ckpt: A hierarchical application-level checkpointing for CPU-GPU hybrid systems. In: Proc. of International Conference on Computer Science and Education, Hefei, pp. 1895–1899 (2010)
24. Dimitrov, M., Mantor, M., Zhou, H.: Understanding software approaches for gpgpu reliability. In: Proc. of Workshop on General-Purpose Computation on Graphics Processing Units, Washington, pp. 94–104 (2009)
25. Sheaffer, J., Luebke, D., Skadron, K.: A Hardware Redundancy and Recovery Mechanism for Reliable Scientific Computation on Graphics Processors. In: Proc. of ACM SIGGRAPH/EUROGRAPHICS Symposium on Graphics Hardware, San Diego, pp. 55–64 (2007)
26. Maruyama, N., Nukada, A., Matsuoka, S.: A High-Performance Fault-Tolerant Software Framework for Memory on Commodity GPUs. In: Proc. of IEEE International Symposium on Parallel & Distributed Processing, Atlanta, pp. 1–12 (2010)

A Parallel Chemical Reaction Optimization for Multiple Choice Knapsack Problem

Tung Khac Truong[1], Ahmad Salah[2], Yuming Xu[3], and Shuangnan Fan[4,*]

[1] Faculty of Information Technology, Industrial University of Hochiminh City,
Hochiminh, Vietnam
[2] Department of Computer Science, Faculty of Computers and Informatics,
Zagazig University, Zagazig, Sharkia,44519, Egypt
[3] Department of Computer Science, Hengyang Normal University, Hengyang,
Hunan, 421008, China
[4] College of Computer, Hunan Science & Technology Economy Trade Vocation
College, Hengyang, Hunan, 421001, China
kjjmfsn@163.com

Abstract. This research proposed a new parallel algorithm based on chemical reaction optimization for multiple-choice knapsack problem (MCKP). In the proposed algorithm, master-slave parallel architecture is used and four problem-specific chemical reaction operators are suggested. The experimental results have proven the superior performance of the proposed algorithm compared to the basic chemical reaction optimization.

Keywords: paralleled artificial chemical reaction optimization, soft computing, knapsack problem.

1 Introduction

Given m classes $N_i = \{1, \ldots n_i\}$, $i = \{1, \ldots, m\}$ of items to pack in some knapsack of capacity W. Each item $j \in N_i$ has a cost c_{ij} and a size w_{ij}, and the problem is to choose one item from each class such that the total cost is minimized without having the total size to exceed W. The multiple-choice knapsack problem (MCKP) may thus be formulated as:

$$minimize \quad \sum_{i=1}^{m} \sum_{j=1}^{n_i} c_{ij} x_{ij} \tag{1}$$

$$subject\ to \quad \sum_{i=1}^{m} \sum_{j=1}^{n_i} w_{ij} x_{ij} \leq W, \tag{2}$$

$$\sum_{j=1}^{n_i} x_{ij} = 1, \quad \forall i \in \{1, 2, \ldots, m\}, \tag{3}$$

---

* Corresponding author.

K. Li et al. (Eds.): ParCFD 2013, CCIS 405, pp. 482–489, 2014.

$$x_{ij} \in \{0,1\}, \forall i = \{1, \ldots, m\}, j \in N_i. \tag{4}$$

All coefficients c_{ij}, w_{ij}, and W are positive numbers, and the classes $N_1, \ldots, N_m$ are mutually disjoint.

MCKP is known as an NP-hard (Non-deterministic Polynomial-time hard) problem [1]. The problem has a large range of applications: Capital Budgeting [2], Menu Planning [3], transportation programming [4], nonlinear knapsack problems [2], sales resource allocation [3], design of information systems [5], etc. The MCKP also appear by Lagrange relaxation of several integer programming problems [6].

Over the last four decades, researchers have proposed many approaches to solve MCKP. We can classify the methods for this problem into two classes namely, exact algorithms and approximate algorithms.

For exactly method, the branch-bound method is an enumeration approach, which reduces its search space by excluding impossible solutions. The branch-and-bound algorithm and its variants have been proposed in [7,2,3]. Dynamic programming algorithm are proposed in [8,9]. Two hybrid algorithms that combine dynamic programming and branch-and-bound are proposed in [10,9].

Since MCKP is an NP-hard problem. The exactly algorithms have complexity time in exponential functions. The heuristic algorithm has an advantage in finding approximate optimal in polynomial time. One of the well-known heuristic algorithm is GA [11]. Although, GA is pioneer in solving MCKP but it is still met a drawback that it get stack in local optima. The CRO, by outperforming many existing evolutionary algorithms, it has successfully solved many problems in recent years.

CRO has been successfully applied to the quadratic assignment problem [12], resource-constrained project scheduling problem [12], channel assignment problem in wireless mesh networks [13], 0-1 Knapsack problem [14] and to many other problems.

Recently, some parallel algorithms are developed to solve knapsack problem [15] [16] [17]. The parallel chemical reaction optimization (PCRO) is proposed to solve quadratic assignment problem [18]. Since the PCRO shown some advances in solving hard problem. We developed a parallel chemical reaction optimization for MCKP. In the proposed algorithm, the four elementary reactions adapt to MCKP are proposed.

The rest of the paper is organized in sections: Section 2 briefly gives the original framework of CRO. Section 3 presents a PCRO for MCKP problem. The simulation results are shown in Section 4. We conclude this paper and suggest potential future work in Section 5.

2   An Overview of Chemical Reaction Optimization

CRO [12] is a metaheristic inspired by the chemical reaction process. In CRO, one molecule (M) that has the molecular structure ω, potential energy (PE), Kinetic energy (KE), minimum structure ($minStruct$), hits number ($numHit$), number of hit that *minStruct* is obtained (*minHit*) and other characteristics represent a potential solution. It simulates four types of chemical reactions including on-wall ineffective collision, decomposition, inter-molecular ineffective collision and synthesis.

In the reaction process, the PE goes toward the minimal state, similar to objective function in optimization problems. *PE* is usually used as the fitness of the objective function.

CRO includes three phases: initial phase, iteration phase and final phase. The initial phase, assigning initial values for parameters *PopSize, KElossRate, InitialKE, MoleColl, α, β and buffer*. A initial population (*Pop*) including *PopSize* molecules is generated. For each iteration, depend on an provability parameter, one of the reactions is executed. The pseudocode of basic CRO is described in Algorithm 1 [12].

3   A PCRO for MCKP

3.1   PCRO structure

The PCRO's flow chart is shown in Fig. 1. The algorithm include three phases that are initial phase, parallel phase, and exchange phase and terminated phase. In the initial phase, the system parameters are loaded, the initial populations

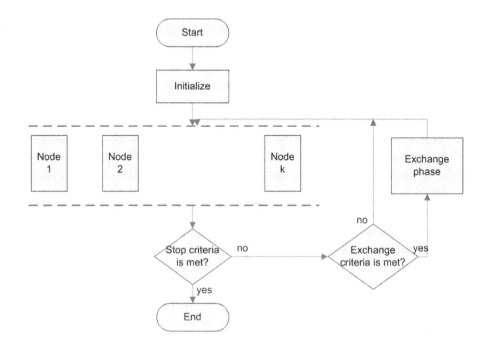

Fig. 1. PCRO's flow chart

Algorithm 1. CRO algorithm

---

1. **Input:** Problem-specific informations
2. Assign parameter values to *PopSize*, *KELossRate*, *MoleColl* and *InitialKE*
3. Let Pop be the set of molecules {1, 2,..., *PopSize*}
4. **for** each of the molecules **do**
5.   Assign a random solution to the molecular structure
6.   Calculate the *PE* by $f(\omega)$
7.   Assign the *KE* with *InitialKE*
8. **end for**
9. Let the central energy buffer be buffer and assign $buffer = 0$
10. **while** the stopping criteria not met **do**
11.   Get t randomly in interval [0, 1]
12.   **if** $t > MoleColl$ **then**
13.   Select a molecule M from Pop randomly
14.   **if** decomposition criterion met **then**
15. $(M_1', M_2', Success)$=decompose$(M, buffer)$
16.   **if** Success **then**
17.   Remove M from Pop
18.   Add M_1' and M_2' to Pop
19.   **end if**
20.   **else**
21.   ineff-coll-on-wall$(M, buffer)$
22.   **end if**
23.   **else**
24.   Select molecules M_1 and M_2 from Pop randomly
25.   **if** synthesis criterion met **then**
26. $(M', Success)$=synthesis(M_1, M_2)
27.   **if** Success **then**
28.   Remove M_1' and M_2' from Pop
29.   Add M' to Pop
30.   **end if**
31.   **else**
32.   inter-ineff-coll(M_1, M_2)
33.   **end if**
34.   **end if**
35.   Check for any new minimum solution
36. **end while**
37. **Output:** The overall minimum solution and its function value

---

are created. In the parallel phase, the chemical reaction algorithms are executed on computing nodes. After a certain number of loop, the global best molecule is broadcasted, and the worst molecules in each nodes are discarded.

3.2 Solution Representation

According to [19], similar to GA in represent an solution. An integer string is used to represent a solution. The y_i receives an integer in N_i, it represent $y_i \in N_i$ is chosen. The string length is m corresponding to a solution in MCKP.

The solution presentation is depict in Fig. 2. By defining an indicator variable, y_i is as follows:

$$y_i = j \quad if \quad x_{ij} = 1, \quad j \in N_i, \quad i = 1, 2, \ldots, m$$

Fig. 2. Solution presentation

3.3   Objective Function

To adopt to *PE*, it is set as follows:

$$PE = \sum_{i=1}^{m} \sum_{i=1}^{n_i} c_{ij} x_{ij} + g(x) \tag{5}$$

where $g(x)$ is penalty function as following:

$$g(k) = \begin{cases} 0 & if \ (2) \quad is \ hold \\ \Omega_0 + (\sum_{i=1}^{m} \sum_{i=1}^{n_i} w_{ij} x_{ij} - W) & if \ otherwise. \end{cases}$$

where Ω_0 is a given positive constant. The idea here is that, for violate solution will have a larger PE. It forces the algorithm search both sides of search space that is feasible and infeasible domains.

3.4   Elementary Operators

On-Wall Operator. This operator use for On-Wall Ineffective Collision reaction. One position i^{th} is randomly selected from $\{1, \ldots, m\}$, and value of y_i is replaced by a random number in $\{1, \ldots, n_i\}$.

Inter-molecular Ineffective Collision Operator. Two solutions ω_1' and ω_2' are obtained from two solutions ω_1 and ω_2. The two points crossover operator commonly used in GA is adopted.

Decomposition Operator. This process produces two solutions from one original solution. This operator effects diversification and makes the algorithm explorer the search space. The decomposition operator is designed inspiring from the "half-total-exchange" operator that is used to solve the channel assignment problem in [12].

Synthesis Operator. In this algorithm, the synthesis operator in [20] is used. The operator combines two molecules with solutions ω_1 and ω_2 into one molecule with solution ω'. For each ω' (i) is randomly selected from $\omega_1(i)$ or $\omega_2(i)$.

4   Experiment and Analysis

4.1   Data Test Set

One type of randomly generated data instances are considered, each instance tested with data-range $R = 1000$ for different number of classes m and sizes n_i:

Strongly correlated data instances (SC): In knapsack problem w_j is randomly generated in $[1, R]$ and $c_j = w_j + 10$. For each class i generate n_i items (w'_j, c'_j) as for knapsack problem, and order these by increasing weight. The data instance for MCKP is then $w_{ij} = \sum_{h=1}^{j} w'_h$ and $c_{ij} = \sum_{h=1}^{j} c'_h$, $j = 1, 2, \ldots, n_i$. Such instances have no dominated items, and form an upper convex set.

4.2   Experiment Results

The parameters are setting as follows: $KElossRate = 0.8, InitialKE = 1000, PopSize = 20, MoleColl = 0.2, buffer = 0, \alpha = 10000$ and $\beta = 10$.

The experiments are performed on 2.3 GHz AMD Opteron processor 6134, 8 GB Ram and 2 CPUs each contains 8 cores. The running OS is Windows XP. All the algorithms are written in Matlab R2011b and Java language, using JDK version 1.6.0 33. The figure 3 is an example of Multi-Core Multi-Threaded processor architecture.

To compare the the computation time of CRO and PCRO, we use the speedup value is given as follow:

$$Speedup_k = \frac{E[T_1]}{E[T_k]}$$

where k is the number of node in parallel model. $E[T_i]$, $i = 1, \ldots, k$ is the average computation time of PCRO.

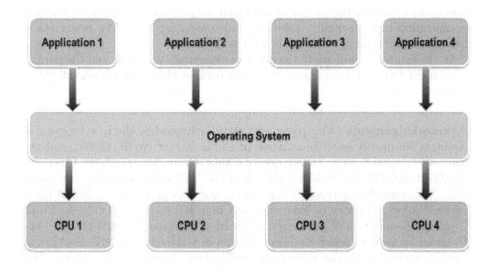

Fig. 3. Multi-Core Multi-Threaded processor architecture

The simulation results on strong correlated instances with ($m = 100, n = 100$) in Table 1 and ($m = 1000, n = 1000$) in Table 2, respectively. It shown that the PCRO not only speed up the time, but also increases the quality of solutions.

Table 1. Experimental results for strong correlated instance with $m = 100, n = 100$. The maximum number of function evaluations 200 000, the number of runs 25

#cores	Average fitness value	Average time(s)	Speed up
1	1024	46	N/A
2	1005	37	1.24
4	992	26	1.77
8	975	12	3.83

Table 2. Experimental results for strong correlated instance with m=1000, n=1000. The maximum number of function evaluations 200 000, the number of runs 25

#cores	Average fitness value	Average time(s)	Speed up
1	100122	48	N/A
2	100014	33	1.39
4	98750	24	1.92
8	97687	15	3.07

5   Conclusion

A parallel chemical reaction optimization algorithm is proposed to solve multiple-choice knapsack problem that is a well-known NP-hard problem. The simulation results showed that the proposed approach outperform the chemical reaction optimization in both quality solutions and computing time. The new method has shown potential in solving this hard problem.

In the future, we will study the effect of elementary reactions and the parameters in PCRO. The experiments on other parallel platforms are considered to study.

Acknowledgements. This paper was partially funded by the Key Program of National Natural Science Foundation of China (Grant No.61133005), and the National Natural Science Foundation of China (Grant Nos.90715029, 61070057, 60603053 and 61202109), Key Projects in the National Science & Technology Pillar Program the Cultivation Fund of the Key Scientific and Technical Innovation Project, Ministry of Education of China (Grant No.708066), the Ph.D. Programs Foundation of Ministry of Education of China (20100161110019) the Program for New Century Excellent Talents in University (NCET-08-0177), A Project Supported by the Science and Technology Research Foundation of Hunan Province (Grant No.2013GK3082), A Project supported by the Research Foundation of Education Bureau of Hunan Province,China(Grant No.11C0573).

References

1. Garey, M.R., Johnson, D.S.: Computers and Intractability: A Guide to the Theory of NP-Completeness. W.H. Freeman, America (1979)
2. Nauss, R.M.: The 0-1 knapsack problem with multiple choice constraints. European Journal of Operational Research 2(2), 125–131 (1978)
3. Sinha, P., Zoltners, A.A.: The multiple-choice knapsack problem. Operational Research 27(3), 503 (1979)
4. Zhong, T., Young, R.: Multiple choice knapsack problem: Example of planning choice in transportation. Evaluation and Program Planning 33(2), 128–137 (2010)
5. Yue, P.C., Wong, C.K.: Storage cost considerations in secondary index selection. International Journal of Parallel Programming 4, 307–327 (1975)
6. Fisher, M.L.: The lagrangian relaxation method for solving integer programming problems. Manage. Sci. 50(12 suppl.), 1861–1871 (2004)
7. Dyer, M., Kayal, N., Walker, J.: A branch and bound algorithm for solving the multiple-choice knapsack problem. Journal of Computational and Applied Mathematics 11(2), 231–249 (1984)
8. Dudzinski, K., Walukiewicz, S.: Exact methods for the knapsack problem and its generalizations. European Journal of Operational Research 28(1), 3–21 (1987)
9. Pisinger, D.: A minimal algorithm for the multiple-choice knapsack problem. European Journal of Operational Research 83(2), 394–410 (1995)
10. Dyer, M., Riha, W., Walker, J.: A hybrid dynamic programming/branch-and-bound algorithm for the multiple-choice knapsack problem. Journal of Computational and Applied Mathematics 58(1), 43–54 (1995)
11. Gen, M.R., Cheng, R., Sasaki, M., Jin, Y.: Multiple-choice knapsack problem using genetic algorithms. Integrated Technology Systems, Maui (1998)
12. Lam, A.Y.S., Li, V.O.K.: Chemical-reaction-inspired metaheuristic for optimization. IEEE Transactions on Evolutionary Computation 14(3), 381–399 (2010)
13. Pan, A.Y.S.B., Lam, Li, V.O.K.: Chemical reaction optimization: a tutorial - (invited paper). Memetic Computing, 3–17 (2012)
14. Truong, T.K., Li, K., Xu, Y.: Chemical reaction optimization with greedy strategy for the 0-1 knapsack problem. Applied Soft Computing 13(4), 1774–1780 (2013)
15. Goldman, A., Trystram, D.: An efficient parallel algorithm for solving the knapsack problem on the hypercube. In: Proceedings of 11th International Parallel Processing Symposium, pp. 608–615 (1997)
16. Taheri, J., Sharif, S., Penju, X., Zomaya, A.: Paralleled genetic algorithm for solving the knapsack problem in the cloud. In: 2012 Seventh International Conference on P2P, Parallel, Grid, Cloud and Internet Computing (3PGCIC), pp. 303–308 (2012)
17. Szeto, K.Y., Zhang, J.: Adaptive genetic algorithm and quasi-parallel genetic algorithm: application to knapsack problem. In: Lirkov, I., Margenov, S., Waśniewski, J. (eds.) LSSC 2005. LNCS, vol. 3743, pp. 189–196. Springer, Heidelberg (2006)
18. Xu, J., Lam, A.Y.S., Li, V.O.K.: Parallel chemical reaction optimization for the quadratic assignment problem. In: GEM 2010, pp. 125–131 (2010)
19. Gen, M., Cheng, R.: Genetic algorithms and engineering optimization. John Wiley and Sons, New York (2000)
20. Lam, A.Y.S., Li, V.O.K., Yu, J.J.Q.: Real-coded chemical reaction optimization. IEEE Transactions on Evolutionary Computation PP(99), 1 (2011)

Study of Mesh Generation for Complex Geometries

Dongliang Cui[1,2], Bowen Wang[1], and Meng Li[1,3]

[1] State Key Laboratory of Synthetical Automation for Process Industries,
Shenyang, 110819, China
[2] Liaoning Province Key Laboratory of Multidisciplinary Optimal Design
for Complex Equipment, Shenyang, 110819, China
[3] College of Science, Northeastern University, Shenyang 110819, China
bowenwang1234@gmail.com, cuidongliang@mail.neu.edu.cn

Abstract. As the crucial step of FEM, mesh generation has a great influence on the accuracy and efficiency of CAE results. Because products in engineering are of complex geometric models and they are always applied in sophisticated environment, the CAE analysis of them becomes more and more challenging, which in turn calls for more attention paid to the accuracy and efficiency of mesh generation. Based on the research of metric methods, this paper proposes an adaptive meshing approach from the view of engineering. ALPHA system developed by researchers in Northeastern University applies these technologies to mesh generation and product analysis. Experiment mesh generated by ALPHA system are presented and comparisons with ANSYS are made to attest the accuracy and efficiency of ALPHA system, results show that the method proposed in this paper is of great efficiency and quite applicable.

Keywords: Mesh generation, adaptive meshing, Delaunay, complex geometries.

1 Introduction

Mesh generation is of great importance for researches in multi-physics areas such as fluid dynamics, heat transfer and structural analysis. The quality of mesh generation has a great effect on the computation efficiency and analysis accuracy. With the development of science and technology, products are becoming more and more complex, which in turn makes the design and analysis processes more and more challenging. By such promotion, CAD and CAE technologies, especially the finite element methods (FEM), have marched great steps in the last decades based on the advancement of computer and software systems.

As the first step of CAE, mesh generation has attracted much attention from scientists and engineers. Typically a meeting name "International Meshing Roundtable" is held annually, which is firstly held by Sandia National Laboratories of USA in 1992. In addition, many papers about mesh generation are published by engineering and scientific journals such as "International journal for numerical methods in engineering" and "Computer aided geometric design". The increasing

K. Li et al. (Eds.): ParCFD 2013, CCIS 405, pp. 490–503, 2014.
© Springer-Verlag Berlin Heidelberg 2014

needs for analysis accuracy and efficiency make adaptive mesh generation a hot topic, and many groups have made great progress. Watson and Lawson started the research of the Delaunay technique in 1970s [1, 2], and many methods proposed are based on Delaunay technique. From the first time of presentation of Advanced-front technology (AFT) by Lohner and Pari in 1988[3], frontal method has become more and more widely used, and this method is adopted by ANSYS, ABAQUS and many other CAE software systems. An improved AFT method proposed by Song and Guan of Dalian University of Technology can suit the shape of the boundaries well [4]. During the application of these meshing methods, size control is most important for adaptive meshing. Recently the Riemannian metric is applied to measure the mesh size and shape for each point in research field [5, 6, 7, 8], and to some degree it can meet all the needs for mesh generation.

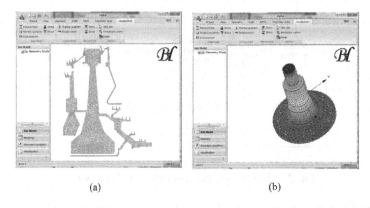

(a)   (b)

Fig. 1. Examples by ALPHA system, (a) is mesh result for turbine assembly (b) is displacement contour for automobile rear bridge

Our team from the State Key Laboratory of Synthetical Automation for Process Industries of Northeastern University pays more attention to the design and analysis of products all these days, and made obvious and great progress in CAD and CAE [9, 10]. With these technologies, a CAE system named "ALPHA" is developed. This software system can be applied to analyze thermal-structural coupling problems, and its capability has been validated in the design of components of aero-engine. Figure 1 gives two mesh examples generated ALPHA system. In this system, geometric data can be derived from B-Rep model (e.g. Parasolid) and triangular patches (with STL format), and isomeric geometric data can also be imported from ANSYS and other platforms [11]. This paper focuses on the adaptive mesh generation technologies based on B-Rep representation.

The remaining part of the paper is organized as follows: Section 2 demonstrates the mesh generation approach in ALPHA system. Meshing experiments and comparisons are presented in section 3. Finally, conclusions are made in Section 4.

2   Mesh Generation Approach in ALPHA System

To improve the accuracy of analysis, a good adaptive mesh generation method, which can suit the geometrical and physical characteristic of the entities well, should be applied. ALPHA system provides two mesh control methods: 1) the mesh size field can be defined by the geometric parameter such as global geometric size of the analysis domain and curvature of the curve; 2) Other size parameters of the boundary conditions can be introduced. The mesh generation architecture in ALPHA system is illustrated in figure 2.

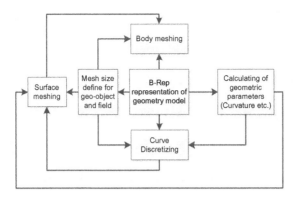

Fig. 2. Adaptive meshing approach in ALPHA system

The B-Rep representation and related calculation of the geometry models is the kernel of this architecture. By the accurate record of B-Rep, the first derivative, second derivative and curvature of any point on a curve or surface can be calculated easily. Moreover, the topological relationship of "point-line-surface-body-assembly components" can be derived. Therefore the hierarchy of mesh generation, "curve discretion → surface meshing → body meshing", is organized based on the B-Rep model, and the results of lower dimension form the input data of higher layers. In this way, the finite elements are created for any objects with any dimensions. Technologies used in each layer are described thoroughly as follows.

2.1   Riemannian Metric

A metric M in R^n is a $n \times n$ symmetric definite positive matrix. The eigenvector and eigenvalue matrices of the metric M are denoted as e and Λ respectively. So the metric M can be decomposed as Eq. (1):

$$M = e^T \Lambda e . \tag{1}$$

For R^2, such a metric is defined by Eq. (2,3,4):

$$M = \begin{bmatrix} a & b \\ b & c \end{bmatrix} \quad \text{with } a,c > 0 \text{,and} \quad ac - b^2 > 0. \tag{2}$$

$$e = [e_1, e_2] \quad \text{with } e_i \text{ being the eigenvectors of the } M. \tag{3}$$

$$\Lambda = \begin{bmatrix} \lambda_1 & 0 \\ 0 & \lambda_2 \end{bmatrix} = \begin{bmatrix} \dfrac{1}{h_1} & 0 \\ 0 & \dfrac{1}{h_2} \end{bmatrix}, \quad \lambda_i \text{ being the eigenvalues of } M. \tag{4}$$

According to the definition of M, the scalar product of two vectors in R^n is defined by Eq. (5):

$$(x, y)_M = (x, My) = x^T My. \tag{5}$$

Under this notion, Riemannian norm of vector x in R^n is defined by Eq. (6):

$$\|x\|_M = \sqrt{x^T Mx}. \tag{6}$$

In R^2, metric M could be measured by a unit ball, i.e., an ellipse, which is defined by Eq. (7):

$$\varepsilon_M = \left\{ P \middle| \sqrt{OP^T MOP} = 1 \right\}. \tag{7}$$

where O is the center of the ellipse, e_1, e_2 are main axes of the ellipse. h_i is the length of e_i, as shown in figure 3.

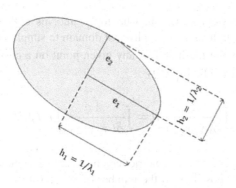

Fig. 3. Metric ellipse

2.2   Distance in Metric Space

Define Ω as the parametric space (u,v) of surface Σ, and A is a point in surface Σ. In Ω the point corresponding to A is described by Eq. (8):

$$\sigma(u,v) = \{x(u,v), y(u,v), z(u,v)\}. \tag{8}$$

PQ is a curve in the surface. Moreover, the curve PQ is presented by $r(t)$ in the parametric space t and the curve AB is the image of PQ in the space of Ω. By Eq. (6) the norm of $r'(t)$ is derived from Eq. (9):

$$(r'(t),r'(t)) = \overrightarrow{AB}^T \begin{pmatrix} \sigma_u(u,v) \\ \sigma_v(u,v) \end{pmatrix} \begin{pmatrix} \sigma_u(u,v) & \sigma_v(u,v) \end{pmatrix} \overrightarrow{AB}. \tag{9}$$

By donating $\vec{r_1} = \sigma_u(u,v)$ $\vec{r_2} = \sigma_v(u,v)$, Eq. (9) is transformed to Eq. (10):

$$(r'(t),r'(t)) = \overrightarrow{AB}^T \begin{pmatrix} \vec{r_1} \\ \vec{r_2} \end{pmatrix} \begin{pmatrix} \vec{r_1} & \vec{r_2} \end{pmatrix} \overrightarrow{AB} = \overrightarrow{AB}^T \begin{pmatrix} \vec{r_1}^2 & \vec{r_1 r_2} \\ \vec{r_1 r_2} & \vec{r_2}^2 \end{pmatrix} \overrightarrow{AB}. \tag{10}$$

Furthermore, by donating $M_1 = \begin{pmatrix} \vec{r_1}^2 & \vec{r_1 r_2} \\ \vec{r_1 r_2} & \vec{r_2}^2 \end{pmatrix}$, Eq. (10) becomes

$(r'(t),r'(t)) = \overrightarrow{AB}^T M_1 \overrightarrow{AB}$, Under this notion, the length of PQ in the metric space is:

$$d_M(P,Q) = l(P,Q) = \int_0^1 \|r'(t)\| dt = \int_0^1 \sqrt{\overrightarrow{AB}^T M_1 \overrightarrow{AB}} dt. \tag{11}$$

In the software system of Gmsh, Christophe and his colleagues set mesh size directly as the metric indicator in the physical domain to simplify the calculation [12]. Define $\delta(x,y,z)$ as the mesh size of any given point on a curve, the metric length of this curve is calculated by Eq. (12):

$$d_M = \int \frac{1}{\delta(x,y,z)} dl = \int_{t_1}^{t_2} \frac{1}{\delta(x,y,z)} |\partial_t r(t)| dt. \tag{12}$$

Adaptive meshing enforces the metric length of each discrete segment of the curve to be as close to 1 as possible, so the number of subdivisions is an integer no more than d_M. ALPHA system uses this method to enhance the speed of computation.

2.3   Curve Discretization

Curve discretization is normally considered as one-dimensional mesh generation, with the result seeds planted on each curve of a surface, and the important initial information is formatted in this way. The surface meshing following curve discretization must keep the segments by the seeds as the element edge. Obviously, the discrete effects will influence the success of the whole meshing and analysis.

From the information mentioned above, all boundary lines such as straight line, arc line, elliptic line, can de expressed by Eq. (13):

$$r(t) = (x(t), y(t), z(t))^T .$$ (13)

For any point on $r(t)$, tangent ,curvature and curvature radius are described by Eq. (14):

$$
\left\{
\begin{aligned}
&r'(t) = dr / dt \\
&r''(t) = d^2 r / d^2 t \\
&C_r(t) = \frac{\left| r'(t) \times r''(t) \right|}{\left| r'(t) \right|^3} \\
&R_r(t) = \frac{1}{C_r(t)} = \frac{\left| r'(t) \right|^3}{\left| r'(t) \times r''(t) \right|}
\end{aligned}
\right.
$$ (14)

In engineering environment, many factors should be taken into account in order to achieve discretization of good quality. As mentioned above, such factors are of two types:

- Type 1:   Geometric properties: size scope S_0, curvature C_r of curve and surface;

- Type 2: User-defined (or environment-based) properties: global mesh size S_v by roughly defined element node number, user-defined mesh size S_p of any geometry vertex, subdivision number N_l of any curve ,discretization number D_c of equivalence circle (default D_c is 8 in ABAQUS);

With the information above, the metric length and subdivision number can be calculated. The uniform discretization of the curve in metric space will produce an adaptive discretization in physical domain.

Next, the methods to get the parameters mentioned above will be described:

Size scope S_0 can be calculated from the bounding box:

$$S_0 = \sqrt{(\Delta x)^2 + (\Delta y)^2 + (\Delta z)^2} \text{ , with } \Delta x = \max(x) - \min(x) \text{ ,}$$
$$\Delta y = \max(y) - \min(y) \text{ , } \Delta z = \max(z) - \min(z) \tag{15}$$

Global mesh size by roughly defined element node number N_v is calculated from the volume of the bounding box:

$$S_v = \sqrt[3]{\frac{\Delta x * \Delta y * \Delta z}{N_v}} . \tag{16}$$

From the mesh size of two geometry vertex of a curve, the size of any point on it is calculated by linear interpolate operation:

$$S_{P_t} = (1-t)S_{P_0} + tS_{P_1} . \tag{17}$$

Where S_{P_0}, S_{P_1} are mesh sizes of beginning vertex P_0 and terminal vertex P_1.

The mesh size of any point from the curvature is calculated by Eq. (18):

$$S_{r_t} = \frac{2 * \pi * R_t(t)}{D_c} = \frac{2 * \pi}{C_r(t) * D_c} = \frac{2 * \pi * \left| r'(t) \right|^3}{\left| r'(t) \times r''(t) \right| * D_c} . \tag{18}$$

If the curvature of the surface (i.e. $C_f(t)$) at this point is greater then $C_f(t)$, then S_{r_t} will be:

$$S_{r_t} = \frac{2 * \pi}{C_f(t) * D_c} . \tag{19}$$

So the comprehensive mesh size for any point on a curve is a minimal value of several aspects:

$$S_t = \min(S_0, S_v, S_{P_t}, S_{r_t}) . \tag{20}$$

The discretization number of the curve is:

$$N = \max(\text{int}(l_M), N_l) . \tag{21}$$

Accordingly each seed on this curve have a distance d_i to the beginning vertex:

$$\left\{ d_i = \frac{d_M}{N} * i, i \in [1, N-1] \right\}. \tag{22}$$

The method to get these seeds is described as following: Firstly point set $\{P_m\}$ is interpolated on the curve with a prescribed accuracy, together with the metric distance $\{D_m\}$ and parametric $\{t_m\}$, from the information by Eq. (20), an metric interval $(D_m, D_{m+1}]$ can be found, during this interval, with linear interpolation operation Eq. (23) gives the method to get parameter t:

$$t = t_m + \frac{t_{m+1} - t_m}{D_{m+1} - D_m} * (d_i - D_m). \tag{23}$$

where t_m and t_{m+1} are values in parametric space, D_{m+1} and D_m are upper limit and lower limit of the interval.

2.4   Surface Meshing

Some researchers mesh the surface in 3D space directly, which has a low accuracy and efficiency. To get better discretization results, more and more attention is paid to the mesh generation in parametric space (UV space define in Eq. (8)), and many mature methods such as Delaunay and AFT can be applied to generate good mesh.

In ALPHA system, transfinite mapping, Delaunay technique and AFT can be used together for planar areas. Figure 4 is an example where these methods are used. The mapping method is used in the left area, the AFT method is used in the middle area, and the Delaunay method is used in the right area.

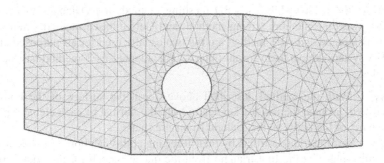

Fig. 4. A meshing example for planar areas by ALPHA system

With regard to surface, mapping method has a narrow life environment for its rigid demand of regularity of shape, AFT method must deal with special case of extreme point and comes to be an complex method, but it is a fast method and can generate elements with good quality. Therefore, ALPHA system used Delaunay and AFT methods to mesh the curve surface. The Delaunay method is described as follows:

- Step 1. Discretize the boundary of surface and record the points set $\{P_i\}$ and segments set $\{E_i\}$, get the UV coordinate of each point and calculate the UV bounding box of these points ;
- Step 2. Enlarge the scope of the bounding box (default 3 times to the original), get 4 vertexes $\{V_1, V_2, V_3, V_4\}$ of this rectangle area;
- Step 3. With the point set of $\{P_i\}$ and $\{V_1, V_2, V_3, V_4\}$, divide and conquer algorithm is used to form the initial triangulate mesh.
- Step 4. With the constraint of segments set $\{E_i\}$, edges are swapped to recover the boundaries.
- Step 5. Coloring algorithm is used to remove the elements out of the analysis domain.
- Step 6. Calculate the mesh size of each node in the metric field;
- Step 7. With the mesh size information, optimization is processed to get the initial Delaunay triangle;
- Step 8. Calculate the metric length of each element edge and sort these edges by this length, get the longest edge, if its length is longer than value α (default is 1.8), then insert nodes uniformly in metric space and calculate its surrounding cavity, connect the inserted nodes to the vertexes of the cavity to process this node. After that mesh quality is used to modulate the adjacent element.
- Step 9. Keep doing step 8 until all the metric length of all edge is less than α.

2.5   Body Meshing

Nowadays the most widely used 3D meshing methods are Delaunay method, AFT method, sweeping method, paving method, and Octree-based method, among which Delaunay method and AFT method are the two usually used for all-purposed analysis. ALPHA system adopts them for all objects. The adopted AFT method has the follow strategies:

- Step 1. With the method described above, mesh the surface of the body to be analyzed, arrange the result triangles to keep the normal of each element points to the inner of the body, so the triangle fronts are shaped ;
- Step 2. Sort the triangle fronts by their inserting ability, and process these triangles as following: Get the first triangle from the queue, search for the nodes around it by a defined distance to form points set $\{P_i\}$, calculate the idealized node P by the coordinates of the triangle together with its mesh size, push P to set $\{P_i\}$, search for a node from these points to find a node which is compatible with other triangles and has a better quality, then a tetrahedron is produced. Finally, insert the new faces of the tetrahedron into the triangle fronts by its inserting ability.
- Step 3. Optimize the tetrahedrons of the results and output the finite elements.

The inserting priority in step 3 can be expressed by several parameters. After comparison, ALPHA system chooses the indicator described by Guan, Z.Q. who uses the area and quality of the triangle front to estimate the priority [4].

3   Experiments and Comparison Analysis

Quality is most important for all mesh methods; there are many method to judge the mesh quality. In this article Quality of 2D problems is defined by the ratio between the radius of the largest inscribed circle and the smallest circumscribed circle:

$$p = \frac{2 * r_2}{R_2}. \tag{24}$$

For 3D problems, Quality is defined by the ratio between the radius of the largest inscribed sphere and the smallest circumscribed sphere:

$$p = \frac{3 * r_3}{R_3}. \tag{25}$$

3.1   One-Dimensional Meshing Experiments

In figure 5, a surface is bounded with a long B-Spline curve and a short straight line, and there are two geometry points on this boundary. Different mesh sizes are defined for these points and different discretization are resulted. In figure 5(a), large mesh sizes of the points are defined, and in figure 5(b), small mesh sizes are defined. As it can be seen, the larger the curvature is, the more seeds are planted on the curve.

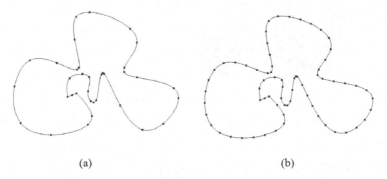

(a)   (b)

Fig. 5. Curve discretization with different mesh size, (a) is result with big mesh size and (b) is result with small mesh size

3.2   Two-Dimensional Meshing Experiments

To show the meshing ability for planar area, two complex areas are triangulated. Figure 6(a) shows a mesh result by AFT method; Figure 6(b) shows a mesh result of

Bowyer-Watson Delaunay method. And it can be seen obviously that more and smaller triangles are generated for mouth where fine geometry is located. Figure 6(c) presents a mesh result for a turbine disc. The mesh sizes are well controlled for these three examples.

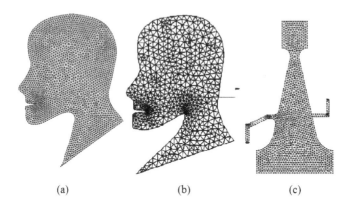

(a)   (b)   (c)

Fig. 6. Triangulation for planar area, (a) is mesh of a portrait by AFT method, (b) is mesh by Delaunay method, (c) is mesh of a turbine disc by AFT method

Figure 7 presents the meshing of a curve surface. Figure 7(a) is a B-Spline surface governed by two B-Spline curves of two bodies: a vertical B-Spline curve of left body and a horizon B-Spline curve of the right body. Figure 7(b) shows the initial Delaunay triangles in parametric space. Figure 7(c) is the ultimate meshing result of the same space, and figure 7(d) is the meshing result in 3D domain.

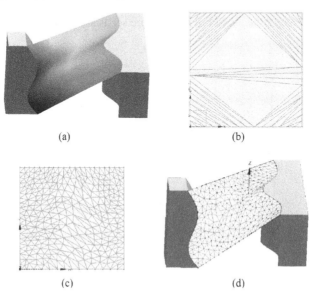

(a)   (b)

(c)   (d)

Fig. 7. Delaunay meshing of a B-Spline Surface, (a) is a surface model design with UG,(b) is initial mesh in metric space,(c) is final mesh in metric space ,and(d) is mesh of curve surface

Obviously in Fig.7(c) the element shape of middle part in vertical is long and narrow because it is a metric space, but from Fig.7(d) It can be seen each element is of good shape in 3D domain.

3.3   Tri-dimensional Meshing Experiments

A 3D nameplate with logo "NEU" in figure 8 is meshed with tetrahedrons. Figure 8(a) is an overall view of the meshing result while figure 8(b) is the detail view for the region between letter "E" and "U" where more geometry details locate.

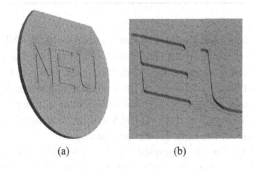

(a)   (b)

Fig. 8. Tetrahedron result of a 3D nameplate with logo "NEU", (a) is an overall view of the result, (b) is zoom in between "E" and "U"

ALPHA system and ANSYS are used respectively to mesh a part of automobile rear bridge. Figure 9(a) is an "X_T" model designed with UG, while figure 9(b) is the mesh result by ALPHA system, figure 9(c) is the displacement resolved by ALPHA.

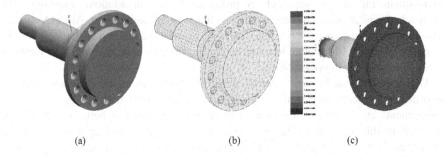

(a)   (b)   (c)

Fig. 9. Tetrahedron result of a part of automobile ,(a) is the geometry model , (b) is the mesh generated by ALPHA system, (c) is the displacement which is analyzed by ALPHA system

3.4   Comparisons between ANSYS and ALPHA System

Finally, ANSYS is used to confirm the quality and validity of ALPHA system. The examples mentioned above are meshed by ANSYS and the statistical parameters of them are described in table 1. the method used in ALPHA is AFT,and in ANSYS is FREE. The fourth column is the number of element whose quality is less than 0.2.

Table 1. Comparison of mesh parameter between ALPHA system and ANSYS

Examples	Node Number		Element Number		$p < 0.2$		Minimum p		Average p	
	ALPHA	ANSYS	ALPHA	ANSYS	ALPHA	ANSYS	ALPHA	ANSYS	ALPHA	ANSYS
Fig.6 (a)	2320	8317	4417	16161	0	0	0.5100	0.5403	0.9790	0.9793
Fig.6 (c)	1319	1329	2361	2380	0	0	0.5362	0.5298	0.9870	0.9838
Fig.7	317	311	558	545	0	0	0.5208	0.5013	0.9138	0.9014
Fig.8	1905	1866	5218	5000	96	168	0.0273	0.0219	0.6472	0.5237
Fig.9	2918	2743	11266	9888	9	9	0.1153	0.1025	0.7437	0.7372

In table 1, figure 6 (a) and figure 6 (c) are meshed with PLANE2 by ANSYS too. For the convenience of comparison, mid-nodes of the results are eliminated and not presented in the table. For figure 6 (a), ANSYS cannot generate mesh with the same mesh size because of shape problems. With a smaller mesh size, results of the same quality can be obtained using ANSYS, but its element number is about 4 times as many as that of results obtained from ALPHA system. For figure 6 (c), the results of two systems are almost of the same results and quality.

For figure 7, mesh result is generated by ANSYS with SHELL63 too. It can be seen that ALPHA system can get results with the same quality using the same mesh size. For figure 8 and figure 9, the results of ALPHA system are of better quality.

4   Conclusion

Mesh generation is of great importance for FEM. Based on the simplifying of Riemannian metric, an approach is proposed to obtain adaptive meshing. The approach together with the underlying technology is adopted in ALPHA system which aims to improve the analysis capability and computation efficiency for the complex products. More attention will be paid to the parallelization of these methods to accelerate the mesh operation.

The size field can be well controlled with Riemannian metric. The speed of the algorithm has been improved greatly by using the simplified size parameter δ. Experiments and comparison presented in section 3 proves that better results can be obtained in this way. With the open interface of the proposed approach, isomeric mesh data from ANSYS and other platforms can be imported, so engineers can make full use of the analysis capability of ALPHA system.

The mesh generation approach has been applied to analyzing and solving thermal-structural coupling problems on component of aero-engine. Experiments show that the adaptive mesh generation technologies are helpful to the analysis, and ALPHA system is of great efficiency and quite applicable.

After appropriate adaptations, ALPHA system is expected to be more and more widely used in mesh generation in both research and engineering.

References

1. Watson, D.F.: Computing the n-dimensional Delaunay Tesselation with applications to Voronoi polytopes. Computer Journal 24, 167–172 (1981)
2. Lawson, C.L.: Properties of n-dimensional triangulations. Computer Aided Geometric Design 3, 231–246 (1986)
3. Lohner, R., Parikh, P.: Generation of three dimensional unstructured grids by the advancing front method. Int. J. Num. Math. Fluids 8, 1135–1149 (1988)
4. Shan, J.-L., Guan, Z.-Q., Song, C.: A Reliable and Effective Tetrahedral Meshing Algorithm. Chinese Journal of Computers 30, 1989–1997 (2007) (in Chinese)
5. Frey, P.J., George, P.L.: Mesh Generation Application to Finite Elements, 2nd edn. ISTE&Wiley Ltd., London (2008)
6. Lo, S.H.: Finite Element Mesh Generation and Adaptive Meshing. Structural Engineering and Materials 4, 219–242 (2002)
7. Alauzet, F.: Size gradation control of anisotropic meshes. Finite Elements in Analysis and Design 46, 181–202 (2010)
8. Romain, A., Kaan, K., Eric, M., et al.: Singularities in Parametric Meshing. In: Proceedings of 21st International Meshing Roundtable, pp. 225–241. Springer press, San Jose (2012)
9. Wang, C.: Mesh Generation and Visualization technologies For Scientific Computing. Science Press, Beijing (2011) (in Chinese)
10. Wang, C., Cui, D.L., Qu, R.X., et al.: Finite Element Method and Its Application for Thermal and Structural Analysis. Science Press, Beijing (2012) (in Chinese)
11. Wang, C., Cui, D.L., Yan, Z.Y., et al.: Finite element triangle mesh generation in planar area. Computer Integrated Manufacturing Systems 17, 256–260 (2011) (in Chinese)
12. Christophe, G., Jean-Francois, R.: GMsh-A 3-D finite element mesh generator with built-in pre-and post-processing facilities. International Journal for Numerical Methods in Engineering 79, 1309–1331 (2009)

Numerical Study on Interaction of Ramp-Induced Oblique Detonation Wave with a Boundary Layer

Yu Liu, Xu Han, Zhiyong Lin, and Jin Zhou

Science and Technology on Scramjet Laboratory,
National University of Defense Technology, Hunan Changsha 410073, China
{Jin Zhou,yuesefuliu}@yahoo.com.cn

Abstract. A two dimensional numerical simulation based on finite-volume method is performed to investigate the ramp-induced oblique detonation wave(ODW)'s interaction with a boundary layer, giving some details of this phenomenon. A comparison among cases which include inviscid-model ODW, viscous-model ODW and inert shock wave, all induced by a ramp, well shows the effect of boundary layer on the ODW, as well as the difference between ODW-boundary-layer interaction and shock-wave-boundary-layer interaction. The separation region of the boundary layer ahead of the ramp induced by the ODW is much larger than by the corresponding shock wave. Furthermore, as the separation region extends upstream, the effective angle of the ramp decreases for the ODW. As a result, the ramp cannot hold the ODW just at its tip. Instead, the ODW now stands at the rear of the ramp, likely to be a self-sustained detonation rather than an overdriven one.

Keywords: oblique detonation, boundary layer, interaction.

1   Introduction

The ODW has been paid more and more attention recent years because of its potential utilization for future hypersonic propulsion and flight. The concept of oblique detonation wave engine has been proposed as an alternative of hypersonic propulsive system in addition to traditional scramjet engine[1]. A series of extensive numerical studies have been conducted for the ODW in past decades, most of which considering high Mach number flow over a wedge, with an inviscid model or a laminar model[2-9]. These studies covered many aspects of ODW, such as the initiation process of ODW, the unstable and oscillating nature and the fine structure of the ODW. This is a prevailing processing method and generally can obtain acceptable results. However, the inviscid model or laminar model ceases to be valid in some special cases such as shock-induced combustion with a boundary layer separation bubble existing. Since the detonation can be seen as a special shock-induced combustion phenomenon, in which a shock is closely coupled by the reaction zone, viscorcity must be considered when there is a boundary layer separation caused by a detonation. Choi[10] et al investigated the combustion induced by shock-wave boundary-layer interaction in premixed gas. They identified two combustion regime: a steady boundary-layer flame

K. Li et al. (Eds.): ParCFD 2013, CCIS 405, pp. 504–513, 2014.
© Springer-Verlag Berlin Heidelberg 2014

held by the separation bubble at the shock impinging point and an unstable oblique detonation wave that propagates forward. The behavior with respect to the fluid dynamic length scale may be attributed to the different values of the Damköhler number defined as a ratio of flow residence time to the chemical induction time. If the flow residence time is sufficiently long to accommodate the complete combustion, the detonative explosion is possible, and the oblique detonation may be observed. If not, the combustion is restricted as boundary-layer flame or oblique shock-induced combustion.

Basically, the detonation-boundary-layer interaction(DBLI) should be similar to shock-wave-boundary-layer interaction(SBLI) because of the shock nature of detonation. However, as there couples chemical reaction within the problem, the DBLI is supposed to be more complicated than SBLI. Furthermore, since the detonation's propagation is sensitive to flow field parameters, the DBLI may have certain influence on the propagating nature of the detonation. A large quantity of studies focusing on SBLI have determined its basic physical insights[11-16], such as boundary layer separation due to adverse pressure gradient exerted by the shock wave, and the mechanism of formation of separation shock and reattachment shock, and the inherent unsteadiness of SBLI. In contrast to SBLI, there are almost no investigation with respect to DBLI, no matter experiments or numerical simulation. As the DBLI will inevitably emerge in an oblique detonation wave engine and most probably have great influence on the performance of the engine, this paper aims to give some details of the DBLI through a numerical method considering viscosity and turbulence by studying a supersonic premixed flow over a ramp.

2   Computational Modeling

2.1   Governing Equations

To simulate the flow field, the basic governing reacting Navier-Stokes equations are employed as follows[17]:

$$\frac{\partial \mathbf{Q}}{\partial t} + \frac{\partial(\mathbf{E} - \mathbf{E}_v)}{\partial x} + \frac{\partial(\mathbf{F} - \mathbf{F}_v)}{\partial y} + \frac{\partial(\mathbf{G} - \mathbf{G}_v)}{\partial z} = \mathbf{H}$$

where

$$\mathbf{Q} = \begin{bmatrix} \rho \\ \rho u \\ \rho v \\ \rho w \\ \rho e \\ \rho Y_i \end{bmatrix} \quad \mathbf{E} = \begin{bmatrix} \rho u \\ \rho uu + p \\ \rho uv \\ \rho uw \\ u(\rho e + p) \\ \rho u Y_i \end{bmatrix} \quad \mathbf{F} = \begin{bmatrix} \rho v \\ \rho vv + p \\ \rho uv \\ \rho vw \\ v(\rho e + p) \\ \rho v Y_i \end{bmatrix} \quad \mathbf{G} = \begin{bmatrix} \rho w \\ \rho wu \\ \rho ww + p \\ \rho uw \\ w(\rho e + p) \\ \rho w Y_i \end{bmatrix}$$

$$E_v = \begin{bmatrix} 0 \\ \tau_{xx} \\ \tau_{xy} \\ \tau_{xz} \\ u\tau_{xx} + v\tau_{xy} + w\tau_{xz} - q_x \\ \rho_i D_{imi} \, \partial Y_i / \partial x \end{bmatrix} \quad F_v = \begin{bmatrix} 0 \\ \tau_{yx} \\ \tau_{yy} \\ \tau_{yz} \\ u\tau_{xy} + v\tau_{yy} + w\tau_{yz} - q_y \\ \rho_i D_{im} \, \partial Y_i / \partial y \end{bmatrix} \quad G_v = \begin{bmatrix} 0 \\ \tau_{zx} \\ \tau_{zy} \\ \tau_{zz} \\ u\tau_{zy} + v\tau_{zy} + w\tau_{zz} - q_z \\ \rho_i D_{im} \, \partial Y_i / \partial z \end{bmatrix} \quad H = \begin{bmatrix} 0 \\ 0 \\ 0 \\ 0 \\ 0 \\ \omega_i \end{bmatrix}$$

Q is the conservation solution vector, E, F and G are the convective flux vectors, E_v, F_v and G_v are the viscous flux vectors, H is the reaction source term. The simulation in this paper is two dimensional, thus, the Z direction is deleted in the governing equations in the simulation. ρ, p, e is the density, pressure, energy, respectively. τ_{xx}, τ_{xy}, τ_{xz}, etc, are the stress of different directions, q is the transferred heat, D is the mass diffusion coefficient, Y_i is the mass fraction of species i, and ω_i is the production rate of species i.

2.2   Chemical Reactions and Turbulence Model

The detailed H_2/air chemical reaction mechanism containing 9 species and 21 steps developed by Connaire[18] is selected in the simulation, and the SST(shear stress transport) $k - \omega$ turbulence model[19] is used because this model is found to be very suitable for adverse pressure gradient flows.

2.3   Computational Method and Domain

The discretization of governing equations is based on the finite-volume method. The convective fluxes are formulated by Roe's flux-difference splitting approach. Second-order upwind dicretization is employed for pressure, momentum and energy equations. The viscous fluxes are discretized by central difference scheme. The time marching is through second-order implicit method.

The computational domain is shown in Fig.1. The domain is a 300×300mm region, with a ramp of 30-degree angle at the location of x=200mm. The choice of the height of the domain is very important, because if the domain is not high enough, the ODW would impinge on the up wall, and in some cases a mach reflection of ODW may occur and as a result, a local overdriven detonation forms at the right place of Mach stem. Thus, the ODW would propagate upstream very easily and not stabilize near the ramp, as illustrated in Fig.2. Due to reasons above, this paper chooses a domain high enough to avoid impingement of the ODW on the up wall. The length of the ramp surface is 60mm.The parameters of oncoming flow contains: Mach number $Ma = 4$, total temperature $T_0 = 2100K$, static pressure $P = 11KPa$, and the equivalence ratio of the H_2/air premixed flow is 0.5. The grid of the domain is 600×800, with the $y^+ = 3.12$ at the wall. The computational domain is divided into 16 individual zones to perform paralleled numerical simulation.

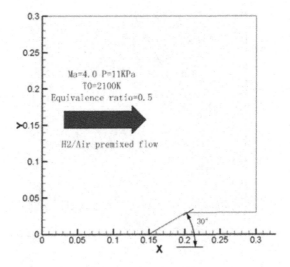

Fig. 1. computational domain and oncoming flow parameters

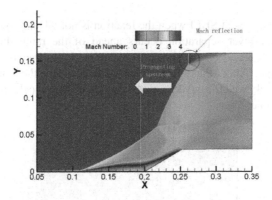

Fig. 2. The Mach reflection of the ODW when the ODW impinges on the up wall (for simplicity, a slip-condition is applied to the up wall)

3   Results and Discussion

Before the DBLI is simulated, the configuration of ODW in an inviscid model where there is no boundary layer at the bottom wall , as well as the SBLI in a viscous model, should be re-determined in order to be compared to the case of the DBLI.

The basic configuration of inviscid ODW over a ramp is illustrated in Fig.3, which is a "numerical schilieren" indicating $d\rho/dy$. With current oncoming flow parameters, the ODW assumes an abrupt manner following an induction shock wave. A transverse shock wave and a slip line are also clearly presented in the figure. This is the typical configuration of the inviscid ODW over a ramp or a wedge.

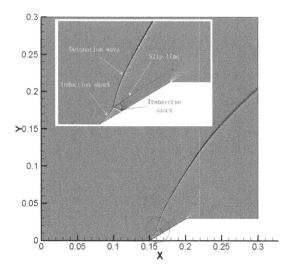

Fig. 3. Contours of $d\rho / dy$ of inviscid ODW

Fig.4 shows the typical SBLI when the reaction is not taken into account. It is seen that the boundary layer separation occurs ahead of the ramp due to the adverse pressure gradient exerted by the shock wave and a shear layer is formed above the separation region. After the shear layer reattaches to the ramp, it transmits reattachment shock which converge with the separation shock, producing another shock and a slip line.

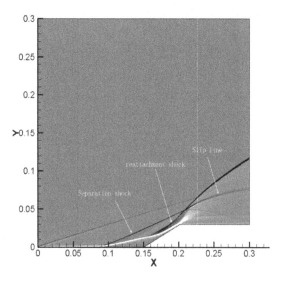

Fig. 4. Contours of $d\rho / dy$ of SBLI

The SBLI is a viscous case with no reaction term in the governing equations. The DBLI is simulated after the SBLI case, with reaction "turned on". Fig.5(a) and Fig.5(b) show the numerical schlieren of ODW's initiation stage and near-steady stage, respectively. Fig.6 shows the corresponding pressure distribution of the bottom wall at different moments. It is seen that after the reaction is turned on, the ODW is first initiated near the top of the ramp, and the pressure on the ramp surface experiences an abrupt jump. Subsequently, the ODW moves downstream and the pressure at the top of the ramp gradually drops down. Meanwhile, the separation region of the boundary layer gradually extends upstream. Now define the separation length of the boundary layer as the distance from the separation point to the bottom vertex of the ramp, then, from Fig.6(a) it can be seen that at the $0\,\mu s$, the separation length D_s=62mm, while in Fig.6(b) the final separation length increases to 117mm, almost 2 times the SBLI separation length.

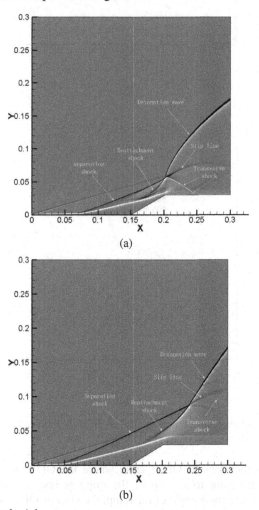

(a)

(b)

Fig. 5. Contours of $d\rho / dy$ of (a)ODW's initiation stage and (b)near-steady stage of DBLI

510   Y. Liu et al.

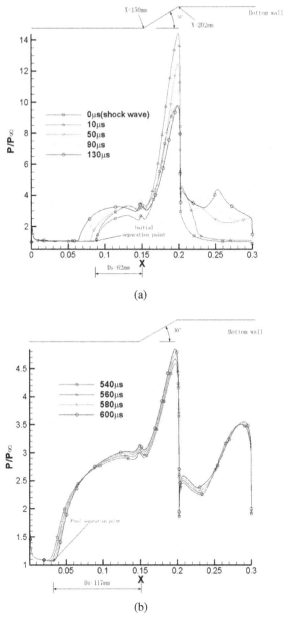

Fig. 6. Pressure distribution of the bottom wall at different moments of (a)ODW's initiation stage and (b)near-steady stage of DBLI

Different from the inviscid ODW case, where the ODW is overdriven and the induction shock attaching to the tip of the ramp is just the oblique shock wave corresponding to a defection angle of the ramp, the viscous ODW stands at the rear of the ramp, and the induction shock now consists of a separation shock and a reattachment shock. This is because the separation region of the boundary layer covers over the ramp, decreasing the effective angle of the ramp. That is to say, what the approaching flow will first encounter now is not the ramp, but the separation region, which now serves as a new ramp of smaller angle. In Fig.5(b), it can be seen that the separation angle is about 15 degree, much smaller than the original ramp angle of 30 degree. Thus, the weaker separation shock cannot initiate the ODW until it converges with the reattachment shock to produce another stronger shock. On the other hand, the current effective-angle-decreased ramp now cannot support the ODW, leading to a downstream movement of the ODW. Finally, the ODW stands at the rear of the ramp and becomes a self-sustained detonation wave, as illustrated in Fig.7.

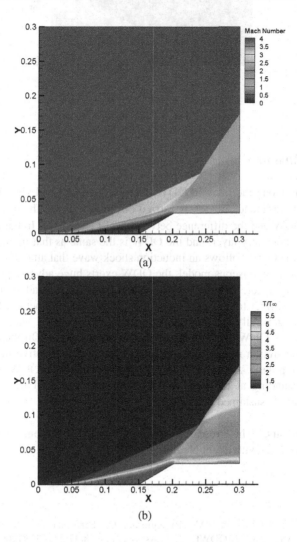

Fig. 7. Contours of (a) Mach number, (b) temperature, (c) pressure of near-steady stage of DBLI

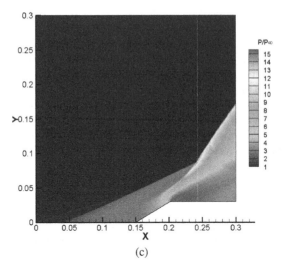

(c)

Fig. 7. (*continued*)

4   Conclusions

A comparison among the inviscid ODW, the viscous SBLI and viscous DBLI, based on SST $k - \omega$ turbulence model, is carried out to investigate the effect of boundary layer on the ODW and the difference between SBLI and DBLI. In the inviscid model, there exists no boundary layer, and the ODW is the same as that induced by a wedge, that is to say, the ODW follows an induction shock wave that attaches to the tip of the ramp. Whereas in the viscous model, the ODW exerts huge adverse pressure gradient on the boundary layer, inducing wide separation region ahead of the ramp. This phenomenon is similar to the shock-wave-boundary-layer interaction. However, since a detonation is generally stronger than a corresponding shock wave, the separation region induced by ODW is much larger than by shock wave. On the other hand, the existence of separation region leads to a decrease of the effective ramp angle. This makes the ramp less supportive for the ODW. Thus, the ODW tends to move downstream, standing at the rear of the ramp and weakened from an overdriven detonation to a self-sustained detonation.

Acknowledgments. This research is supported by National Nature Science Foundation of China with Grant Number 91016012.

References

1. Valorani, M., Di Giacinto, M., Buongiorno, C.: Performance prediction for oblique detonation wave engines(ODWE). Acta Astronautica 48(4), 211–228 (2001)
2. Fusina, G.: Numerical investigation of oblique detonation waves for shcramjet combustor. University of Toronto, Toronto (2003)

3. Miltiadis: A numerical study of wedge-induced detonations. Combustion and Flame 120, 526–538 (2000)
4. Pimentel, Azevedo, Figueira da Silva, et al.: Numerical study of wedge supported oblique shock wave-oblique detonation wave transitions. J. of the Braz. Soc, Mechanical Sciences XXIV, 149–157 (2002)
5. Choi, J.Y., Kim, D.W., In-Seuck, J., et al.: Cell-like structure of unstable oblique detonation wave from high-resolution numerical simulation. Proceedings of the Combustion Institute 31(2), 2473–2480 (2007)
6. Dudebout, R., Sislian, J.P., Oppitz, R.: Numerical simulation of hypersonic shock-induced combustion ramjets. Journal of Propulsion and Power 14(6), 869–879 (1998)
7. Xu, H., Jin, Z., Zhiyong, L., Shijie, L.: Initiation mechanism investigation of saltation and smoothness oblique detonation waves. Journal of Aerospace Power 27(12), 2674–2680 (2012)
8. Gui, M., Fan, B.: Wavelet Structure of Wedge-induced Oblique Detonation Waves. Combust. Sci. Technol 184, 1456–1470 (2012)
9. Teng, H., Jiang, Z.: On the transition pattern of the oblique detonation structure. J. Fluid Mech. 713, 659–669 (2012)
10. Choi, J.Y., In-Seuck, J., Youngbin, Y.: Scaling effect of the combustion induced by shock-wave boundary-layer interaction in premixed gas. In: Twenty-Seventh Sympostum(International) on Combustion/The Combustion Institute, pp. 2181–2188 (1998)
11. Kerimberkov, R.M., Ruban, A.I., Walker, I.D.A.: Hypersonic boundary layer separation on a cold wall. Journal of Fluid Mechanics (89), 535–552 (1978)
12. Hassaini, M.V., Baldwin, B.S., MacCormack, R.W.: Asymptotic features of shock wave boundary layer interaction. AIAA Journal 8(18), 1014–1016 (1980)
13. Lee, S., Loth, E., Wang, C.: LES of Supersonic Turbulent Boundary Layers with μVG's. AIAA 2007-3916 (2007)
14. Anderson, B.H., Tinapple, J., Surber, L.: Optimal Control of Shock Wave Turbulent Boundary Layer Interactions Using Micro-Array Actuation. AIAA 2006-3197 (2006)
15. Hirt, S., Anderson, B.: Application of Micro-ramp Flow Control Devices to an Oblique Shock Interaction. AIAA (2008)
16. Babinsky, H., Li, Y., Ford, C.W.P.: Microramp Control of Supersonic Oblique Shock-Wave/Boundary-Layer Interactions. AIAA JOURNAL 47(3), 668–675 (2009)
17. Anderson, J.D.: Computational Fluid Dynamics: The Basis with Applications. Mcgraw-Hill (1994)
18. Connaire, M.O., Curran, H.J., Simmie, J.M., Pitz, W.J., et al.: A comprehensive modeling study of hydrogen oxidation. International Journal of Chemical Kinetics 36(11), 603–622 (2004)
19. Menter, F.R.: Two-Equation Eddy-Viscorsity Turbulence Models for Engineering Applications. AIAA Journal 32(8), 1598–1605 (1994)

Parallelization of the Local Mesh Refinement on Multi-Core CPU

Hang Chen[1], Yu Ye[1], and Ren Lin[2]

[1] Hunan University, College of Information Science and
Engineering, Changsha, 410082, China
1052351671@qq.com, yeyu.hnu@gmail.com
[2] Hunan City University, College of Mathematics and Computational
Science, Yiyang, 413002, China
linren0739@126.com

Abstract. This contribution presents the characteristics of three methods of the lattice Boltzmann local mesh refinement algorithms: Filippova-Hänel (FH), Lin-Lai (LL) and Dupuis-chopard (DC). Thus large-scale flow features can be resolved efficiently at a relatively low cost. At a later time, the parallel algorithms are presented. As a demonstration, the lid-driven cavity flow is selected for study in the C++ project using OpenMP. The results show that the DC method has the better accuracy and efficiency.

Keywords: the local mesh refinement, FH, LL, DC, OpenMP.

1 Introduction

The Lattice Boltzmann Method (LBM) is a mesoscopic method between microscopic and macroscopic, it has the comprehensive advantage in dealing with the multi-phase flow, interfacial flow phenomena, and flow through porous media, and so on[1]. The main idea of this approach is to model the physical reality at a mesoscopic level: the generic features of microscopic processes can be expressed through simple rules, from which the desired macroscopic behavior emerges as a collective effect of the interactions between many elementary components. So it has been capable of arousing and holding the attention in the computational physics and engineering communities.

Historically, the LBM is directly inherited from its predecessor, the lattice gas automata (LGA) method [2-3].Consequently, LBM is also described as a physical model of fluid motion. Although LBM has been proven to be very promising, it also has some questions. For example, the usual LBM adopt the regular grids (uniform lattices). If the grids are coarse, the simulation is inaccuracy; If the lattices are fine, the model is accuracy, however, the efficiency is poor. And also some fine lattices have no use for the certain fields in the flow. Then two scholars, Filippova and Hänel from Germany, proposed the local mesh refinement method in the lattice Boltzmann Equation (LBE) [4-5]. Then more progress has been made by some researchers. The LL and DC method were put forward then. In this paper, we describe the three

K. Li et al. (Eds.): ParCFD 2013, CCIS 405, pp. 514–521, 2014.
© Springer-Verlag Berlin Heidelberg 2014

methods of local mesh refinement: FH, LL and DC in detail. We demonstrate the advantage of the DC method and parallel its acceleration method.

This paper is organized as follows. Section 2 briefly reviews the three methods of the local mesh refinement and the D2Q9 architecture. In Section 3 we present the proposed parallelization concept using OpenMP and describe the parallelization algorithm of the DC method. The results are shown and discussed in Section 4. Finally, we present some concluding remarks and future works in the Section 5.

2   Background

2.1   Lattice Boltzmann Equation(LBE)

LBE is a conservation equation stimulating the dynamics of particle distribution functions in phase space [6-8]. And the velocity distribution functions between particle transport and collisions:

$$\frac{\partial f}{\partial t} + \vec{\xi} \cdot \nabla_{\vec{x}} f + \vec{a} \nabla_{\vec{\xi}} f = \Omega(f) \tag{1}$$

Where $\vec{f} = f(\vec{x}, \vec{\xi}, t)$ is defined in the space with position $\vec{x}$ and velocity $\vec{\xi}$ at the time t; $\Omega(f)$ means the collision operator. In numerical LBE, the continuous transient phase space is replaced by a discrete space with spacing $\vec{x}$ for the positions, a set of m vectors $\vec{\xi}$ for the velocities and spacing δt for time.

Usually, a collision model (J(f)) should satisfy the fundamental characteristics of the $\Omega(f)$:

(1) Meet the conservation of mass, momentum, and energy;
(2) Reflect the system tendency to equilibrium state;

The Bhatnagar-Gross-Krook (BGK) is the simplest and most famous model based on this theory [9].

$$J_{BGK(f)} = \frac{1}{\tau}[f^{eq} - f] \tag{2}$$

where f^{eq} is the equilibrium distribution function (the Maxwell-Boltzmann distribution function), τ is the relaxation time.

The LBE with the single relaxation time approximation is computed by the following sequence :

(1) collision step: $f_i'(\vec{x}, t) = f_i(\vec{x}, t) + \Omega_i(f(\vec{x}, t))$ (3)

(2) Streaming step: $f_i(\vec{x} + \vec{c_i} \delta t, t + \delta t) = f_i'(\vec{x}, t)$ (4)

Where ' denotes the post-collision state of the distribution. And [10-12]

$$\Omega_i(f(\vec{x},t)) = -\frac{1}{\tau}[f_i(\vec{x},t) - f_i^{eq}(\vec{x},t)] \tag{5}$$

Where $\tau = {t_c}\big/{\delta_t}$.

2.2   The Local Mesh Refinement

In order to save the simulation coast and get the better simulation results, several studies addressing the grid refinement have appeared in the literature. In the method of the local mesh refinement, at first, we define a coarse lattice everywhere, and then define a fine grid where extra accuracy is needed. In the present grid refinement computation, the transfer of the information between the coarse and the fine requires an accurate match in the time level. Then One consequently needs an algorithm to connect coarse and fine lattices. The following we present the three methods of the local mesh refinement.

(1) Filippova-Hänell(FH) algorithm

This scheme proposes the following relations between the fields of fine and the coarse lattices.

$$f_i^{out,c} = f_i^{eq,f} + (f_i^{out,f} - f_i^{eq,f})\frac{n(\tau_c - 1)}{\tau_f - 1},$$

$$f_i^{out,f} = \tilde{f}_i^{eq,c} + (\tilde{f}_i^{out,c} - \tilde{f}_i^{eq,c})\frac{\tau_f - 1}{n(\tau_c - 1)} \tag{6}$$

Where $\tilde{f}_i$ denotes the spatially and temporally interpolated value of the coarse grid fields. The indices c and f indicate quantities belonging to the coarse or the fine lattice, respectively. Finally n is the ration between the coarse and the fine lattice spacing.

The FH method adopts bidirectional couple and have better precision. But it may be instability, especially when $\tau \approx 1$.

(2) Lin-Lai(LL) algorithm

This approach   proposes a simpler algorithm without considering a rescaling of the $\tilde{f}_i$. It argues that the fields $\tilde{f}_i$ are interchangeable after streaming step, which is inaccurate.

(3) Dupuis-chopard(DC) algorithm

The method offers an accurate scheme that does not neglect the nonequilibrium parts of the $\tilde{f}_i$. In addition, it is simpler than FH algorithm and has no singularity for $\tau = 1$.

In the local mesh refinement, we can use the different refinement grids in the different fields and can use the Multi-level refinement. But the following we just introduce the two-level refinement.

In order to have the same molecular velocities and viscosity on different lattices, we must guarantee the following equations.

$$\delta_t^f = \frac{1}{n}\delta_t^c$$

$$\tau_f = \frac{1}{2} + n(\tau_c - \frac{1}{2}) \tag{7}$$

And fields are transformed by the following relations:

$$f_i^{in,c} = f_i^{eq} + (f_i^{in,f} - f_i^{eq})\frac{n\tau_c}{\tau_f}$$

$$f_i^{in,f} = \tilde{f}_i^{eq} + (\tilde{f}_i^{in,c} - \tilde{f}_i^{eq})\frac{\tau_f}{n\tau_c} \tag{8}$$

In summary, this approach rescales the income fields, which has the advantage of being more general than the FH method and is more accurate than the LL algorithm.

2.3   Nine-Bit Incompressible Lattice BGK Model

The DnQb model (n: space dimension; b: disperse velocity) is typical in the BGK. The nine-bit square model, which is often referred to as the D2Q9 (Figure 1) has been successfully used for simulating 2-D flows. For the D2Q9 model, we use e_α to denote the discrete velocity set and we use ω_i to denote the weighting factor.

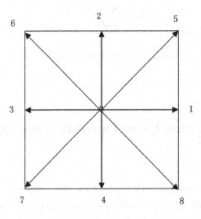

Fig. 1. D2Q9 Model

$$e_\alpha = \begin{cases} (0,0), \alpha = 0 \\ c(\cos\theta_\alpha, \sin\theta_\alpha), \alpha = 1,3,5,7 \\ \sqrt{2}c(\cos\theta_\alpha, \sin\theta_\alpha), \alpha = 2,4,6,8 \end{cases} \tag{9}$$

$$\omega_i = \begin{cases} \dfrac{4}{9}, \alpha = 0 \\ \dfrac{1}{9}, \alpha = 1,2,3,4 \\ \dfrac{1}{36}, \alpha = 5,6,7,8 \end{cases} \tag{10}$$

Where $c = \dfrac{\delta x}{\delta t}$, δx and δt are the lattice spacing and the time step size.
The equilibrium for the D2Q9 model is in the form of [13]

$$f_i^{(eq)} = \omega_i \rho [1 + \frac{c_i \cdot u}{c_s^2} + \frac{(c_i \cdot u)^2}{2c_s^2} - \frac{u^2}{2c_s^2}] \tag{11}$$

here $c_s = \dfrac{c}{\sqrt{3}}$.

To the D2Q9 model, the discrete velocity space, the density and momentum fluxes can be evaluated as

$$\rho = \sum_{i=0}^{8} f_i^{(eq)} \tag{12}$$

$$\rho u = \sum_{i=0}^{8} c_i f_i^{(eq)} \tag{13}$$

And the equation of the state is that of an ideal gas,

$$p = \rho c_s^2 \tag{14}$$

3   Parallel Algorithm Using OpenMP Environment

3.1   OpenMP

OpenMP (Open Multi-Processing) represents the important step of providing a software standard for these shared-memory multiprocessors[14]. Applications that rely on the power of more than a single processor are numerous.

OpenMP is not a new computer language. It works in conjunction with either standard Fortran or C/C++. It is comprised of a set of complier directives that describe the parallelism in the source code. Furthermore, C and C++ OpenMP implementations provide a standard include file, called omp.h, that provides the OpenMP type definitions and library function prototypes. This file should therefore be included by all C and C++ OpenMP programs.

However, the language extensions in OpenMP lead to the following possibly critical issues: control structures for expressing parallelism, data environment constructs for communicating between threads, and synchronization constructs for coordinating the execute on multiple threads.

Many typical programs in scientific and engineering application domains spend most of their time executing loops, in particular, do loops in Fortran and for loops in C. OpenMP provides the parallel do directive for specifying that a loop be executed in parallel.

Based on the features of the OpenMP, the LBM is very easy to be implemented in parallel. Then the parallel algorithm will be presented in subsequent.

3.2   Parallel Algorithm

As we know, the DC method has the better performance than the FH and LL method. An even more difficult programming problem arises when parallelization is considered on a dynamical grid. We now describe a useful utilization of the grid refinement techniques: the acceleration of the flow settlement[15]. And this algorithm can be presented as the following.

(1) Allocate memory space for the coarse lattice.

(2) Initialize the coarse one with the equilibrium distribution functions.

(3) Repeat collision-propagation steps until the stopping criterion is reached.

(4) Allocate memory space for the fine lattice; Initialize the density distributions using data from the coarse one; Spatially interpolate the missing density distributions; Repeat the collision-propagation steps on fine lattice until the stopping criterion is reached.

When it comes to the parallel algorithm, outside of the parallel loops, a single master thread executes the program serially. Upon encountering a parallel loop, the master thread creates a team of parallel threads consisting of the master along with zero or more additional slave threads. This team of threads executes the parallel loop together. In this way can we save more time in the simulation.

4   Experiments and Results

In order to validate the proposed parallel approach we consider the classical 2D benchmark problem lid driven cavity using two-grid system, which is shown in Fig.2.

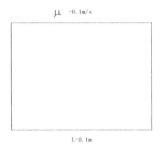

Fig. 2. Lid driven cavity

As shown in Fig.3, simulation of the lid driven cavity flow at a Reynolds number 1000 are carried on the two-level refinement: the coarse grids(128*128) for the whole domain and the fine grids(255*137) at the lower half of the domain.

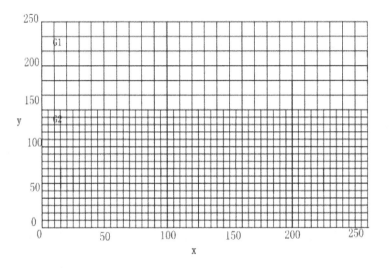

Fig. 3. Two-level grid refinement

The result is as follows:

Table 1. Computing times

Size	1000*1000
Threads	Improvement(based on single thread)
2	47%
3	61%
4	70%

From the results, we can see that the simulation time coast is becoming less along with increasing threads.

5   Conclusions

This paper introduces the theory of the LBM and LBE. And it demonstrates the local mesh refinement: FH, LL and DC. We present the three methods of the local mesh refinement in detail. Even though the FH model is accurate, a singularity   may be presented when $\tau = 1$. And the LL model is inaccurate as it considers the fields as interchangeable. In summary, the DC model offers an accurate scheme that does   not neglect the nonequilibrium and has no singularity.

At last, the parallelization of the DC is presented. The results show that the parallel method can reduce the simulation coast. But the OpenMP also has some disadvantage. Its acceleration ration cannot be increased more. In this field, the MPI has the more advantage. In the future it will be promising.

References

1. 郭照立，郑楚光.格子Boltzmann方法的原理与应用.北京：科学出版社 (2008)
2. Frish, U., Hasslacher, B., Pomeau, Y.: Lattice-gas automata for the Naviere-Stokes equation. Phys. Rev. Lett. 56, 1505 (1986)
3. Kandhai, D., Soll, W., Chen, S., Hoekstra, A., Sloot, P.: Finite-Difference Lattice -BGK method on nested grids. Computer Physics Communications 129, 100–109 (2000)
4. Filippova, Hänel: Grid refinement for lattice-BGK models. Journal of Computational Physics 147, 219–228 (1998)
5. Lin, C.L., Lai, Y.G.: Lattice Boltzmann method on composite grids. Physical Review E 62(pt. A), 2219–2225 (2000)
6. Sukop, M.C., Thorne, D.T.: Lattice Boltzmann Modeling. Springer (2006)
7. Chopard, B., Droz, M.: Cellular Automata Modeling of Physical Systems. Cambridge University Press (1998)
8. Hanel, D.: Molekulare Gas dynamic. Springer (2004)
9. Chen, Y., OHashi, H.: Lattice-BGK methods for simulating incompressible fluid flow. Int. L. Mod. Phys. C8, 793–803 (1997)
10. Chen, S., Chen, H., Martinez, D.O., Matthaeus, W.H.: Lattice Boltzmann model for simulation of magnetohydrodynamics. Phys. Rev. Lett. 67, 3776–3779 (1991)
11. Koelman, J.: A simple lattice Boltzmann scheme for Naviere-Stockes fluid flow. Europhys. Lett. 15, 603–607 (1991)
12. Qian, Y.: Lattice BGK models for Naviere-Stokes equation. Europhys. Lett. 17, 479–484 (1992)
13. Yu, D., Mei, R., Shyy, W.: A multi-block lattice Boltzmann method for viscous fluid flows. Int. J. Numer. Meth. Fluids 39, 99–120 (2002)
14. Chandra, R., Menon, R., Dagum, L., Kohr, D., Maydan, D.: Parallel Programming in OpenMP. Morgan Kaufmann (2001)
15. Dupuis, A., Chopard, B.: Theory and applications of an alternative lattices Boltzmann grid refinement algorithm. Phys. Rev. E67, 066707 (2003)

Optimized Roles Set Algorithm in Distributed Parallel Computing System

Wenkang Wu and Zhuo Tang

Key Laboratory for Embedded and Network Computing of Hunan Province, Changsha, Hunan, 410082, China
walker_young@163.com, hust_tz@126.com, lirenfa@vip.sina.com

Abstract. With the rapid development of computer technology, distributed computing and parallel computing have made great progress. Distributed parallel computing system is a combination of distributed computing and parallel computing, which can provide fast solutions to information sharing and subtasks in high-speed network environment. In this paper, we propose a new access control model-Distributed Parallel Computing Role Based Access Control (DPCRBAC) Model on the basis of the traditional RBAC model. We propose a new roles set assignment algorithm-Optimized Roles Set (ORS) algorithm. According to the results of simulation, the proposed algorithm ORS can effectively improve the efficiency roles and is effective in reducing role conflicts in the process of role assignment, and ensure the safety and reliability of the distributed parallel computing system .

Keywords: Distributed parallel computing, RBAC, ORS;security constraint.

1   Introduction

With the rapid development of computer technology, distributed computing and parallel computing have made great progress. Distributed computing refers that different computer platforms are connected through a computer network to achieve information sharing and communication, while parallel computing means that multiple processors concurrently perform multiple subtasks to solve complex computational problems quickly. Distributed parallel computing system is a combination of distributed computing and parallel computing, which can provide fast solutions to information sharing and subtasks in high-speed network environment[1].

In distributed parallel computing environment, resources and management are distributed on different nodes, and users get access to them by being authorized. However, it's easy to cause security risks, especially when multiple subtasks are processed currently, which will produce more complex security problems. Therefore, access control for distributed parallel computing system resources should comply with the principle of consistency of security constraints, namely the least privilege principle and separation of duty principle.

In this paper, we propose a new access control model-Distributed Parallel Computing Role Based Access Control (DPCRBAC) Model on the basis of the traditional RBAC model, which can meet the task requests of workflow in distributed

K. Li et al. (Eds.): ParCFD 2013, CCIS 405, pp. 522–531, 2014.

parallel computing environment. The model includes basic components, complex role hierarchy and security constraints, we also give full consideration to resource management and task requests in distributed parallel computing environment. Since resources, task requests, and security policies are located on the different nodes, an efficient and safe roles assignment search algorithm is needed to meet the conformance requirements of multi-task requests and security constraints. We propose a new roles set assignment algorithm-Optimized Roles Set(ORS)algorithm. According to the results of simulation, we conclude that the proposed algorithm ORS can effectively improve the efficiency roles assignment in distributed parallel computing environment, and ensure the safety of distributed parallel computing system.

The paper is organized as follows: In Section 2, we introduce the related work. In Section 3, we introduce the DPCRBAC model and ORS algorithm in DPCRBAC model. In Section 4 we present the simulation of ORS algorithm and MUR algorithm and make a comparison of the results. The conclusion of the paper is given in Section5.

2 Related Work

In distributed parallel computing service, different resources, users and security policies are distributed at different nodes. Traditional access control models include Discretionary Access Control (DAC) and Mandatory Access Control (MAC). The DAC model [2] allows the subject to assign the permission of its owned resources to other entities designated by the subject, Since the DAC model access control permissions can be transmitted, it brings security risk to the distributed parallel computing system. MAC model [3] is similar to Bell.LaPadula model which is a multi-level security model. Since all access management is highly centralized, it can not meet the flexible authorization requirements in distributed parallel computing system .

Role Based Access Control (RBAC) has been widely studied and applied in the field of information security. RBAC model was proposed by Sandhu et al. [4] in 1996, which includes four conceptualization RBAC model framework:basic model-RBAC 0, role hierarchy model-RBAC 1, role constraints model-RBAC 2, and the composite model-RBAC 3. The framework for RBAC model develops a modular structure to meet the needs of different levels. On the basis of RBAC, NIST (National Institute of Standards and Technology) [5] proposed a standardized NIST RBAC model in 2004, so as to promote the further study of the various types of the extended RBAC models.

With the rapid development of distributed parallel computing, a single security policy is facing a growing number of security risks, so a combination of multiple security policies should be proposed to meet the security needs of the dynamic and complex workflow. Security constraints can provide effective security policies for complex distributed parallel computing environment to ensure the consistency of these security constraints in the workflow environment [6].

Unlike traditional access control model, Task-Based Authorization Control(TBAC) [8], which is task-oriented, introduces the combination of permissions and task management, life cycle management and workflow task management. TBAC can effectively improve the real-time access control security in the workflow management. However, this model doesn't consider the security constraints in distributed and parallel computing environment, which ensure the workflow system to run safety.

In order to solve the problem of the large-scale subjects and objects in distributed system, Kapadia et al. [9] proposed the IRBAC model in 2000, which supports a flexible dynamic role conversion to establish the relationship among different roles hierarchies, but roles conversion may violate the security constraints of the roles.

RBAC model builds relationship among roles, users and permissions, but does not take the temporal factors into consideration. Bertino et al. proposed the Temporal RBAC (TRBAC) [10] model, which supports the the periodic role activation, but don't consider the role hierarchy and security constraints.

Joshi et al. proposed a Generalized Temporal Role Based Access Control(GTRBAC) Model [11], which supports a wider range of temporal constraints, such as duration constraints, periodic constraints and other forms of active constraints. GTRBAC Model also supports inheritance-only hierarchy (I-hierarchy), activation-only hierarchy (A-hierarchy) and inheritance-activation hierarchy (IA-hierarchy). However, this model is limited to the interoperability between two subsystems, which can not meet the multi-tasks requests and the dynamic changes of the security constraints in distributed parallel computing environment.

LiuYang, TangZhuo et al. propose the Minimizing Uniquely Roles (MUR) algorithm which is a new roles query algorithm in cloud computing environment [12][15]. The MUR algorithm simplifies the task requests in distributed system as the combination of roles which are assigned to execute the tasks and get minimizing uniquely roles which satisfy these requests. MUR algorithm has great advantages over Uniquely Activable Set (UAS) algorithm [13], for it effectively improve the efficiency of the roles assignment, and can meet the needs of cloud computing service. However, CACRBAC Model [16] does not take into account the consistency of role security constraints, thus can not guarantee that the roles assigned to the tasks will not violate prerequisite constraints, mutually exclusive constraints and other security constraints.

Based on the deficiencies of UAS algorithm and MUR algorithms, we propose ORS algorithm, which can meet task requests and effectively improve the search efficiency. What's more, ORS algorithm is effective in reducing role conflicts in the process of role assignment, and ensure the safety and reliability of the distributed parallel computing system .

3   DPCRBAC Model

The DPRBAC model is based on the RBAC96 model proposed by Sandhu et al. [4] and has the following components:

U,R,P, and S (users, roles, permissions and sessions respectively),
$PA \subseteq P \times R$, a many-to-many permission to role assignment mapping,
$UA \subseteq U \times R$, a many-to-many user to role assignment mapping,
user: $S \rightarrow U$,a function mapping each session S_i to the single user user   and
roles: $S \rightarrow 2^R$, a function mapping each session S_i to a set of roles and session S_i has
the permissions.

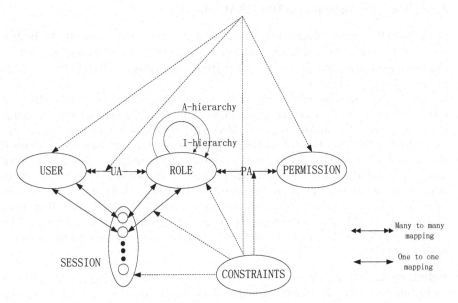

Fig. 1. DPCRBAC Model diagram

3.1   DPCRBAC Role Hierarchy

Role hierarchy is an important feature of the DPCRBAC model. The proposed
DPCRBAC model supports three types of roles hierarchy : I-hierarchy, A-hierarchy
and IA-hierarchy, so this composite level structure is well adapted to the fine-grained
access control requirements in distributed and parallel computing environment. We
define the role hierarchy in the following rules: $RH \subseteq R \times R$, which is a partial order
on the set of roles, R is the set of roles carried by a subtask.

3.2   DPCRBAC Security Constraints

In DPCRBAC model tasks are constituted by a plurality of subtasks, and each subtask
can be simplified as roles set. In DPCRBAC model, we consider two important
security constraints [7]:

(1) Mutually Exclusive (MER)constraints: the same user can only be assigned to at
most one role in the mutually exclusive set of roles, MER constraints support the
separation of duties principle. For instance, $MER(r_i, r_j)$ $(i \neq j)$ means that the role ri
and rj are mutually exclusive roles.

(2) Prerequisite constraints: the same user has a specific role, and need to take one or more other roles. For example, $PRE(r_2 \cap r_3, r_1)$ means that the same user is a member of role r_1, he should also have to be a member of role r_2 and r_3. In particular, the role hierarchy can be presented by using prerequisite constraints. For instance, $PRE\ (r_2, r_1)$ means that role r_1 is senior to r_2.

3.3   The ORS Algorithm in DPCRBAC Model

In the workflow environment, the execution of the tasks will eventually be broken down into a number of authorized service sets. A task can be decomposed into a plurality of subtasks, and we will formalize the task requests as: $TRQ=(TRQ\ (1), TRQ\ (2), \ldots, TRQ\ (n))$ $(n \in R^*)$.

For the workflow system user's task request $TRQ(i)$, we can assign different combinations of roles to meet the requirement. With the problem how to find a unique roles set to meet the subtask requests, UAS [13] algorithm generates a hybrid role hierarchy tree by using Depth First Search (DFS) algorithm, and then brokes down it into several separate sub-trees, and then assign a group of unique roles set to meet the appropriate authorizations. Yangliu, Tang Zhuo et al. propose UAS algorithm to improve the efficiency of role assignment [12]. However, MUR algorithm does not take into account security constraints consistency problem which may come from PRE constraints, MER constraints and other security constraints in distributed parallel computing systems.The proposed ORS algorithm can provide an effective solution to these problems.

Definition 1. ORS:we define $RHT = (S, T, C)$ as a role hierarchy tree, where S represents the set of roles in RHT, T is the relationship of the RHT nodes, C is a group of role based security constraints. $ORS(RHT)=\{S_1,S_2,...,S_n\}(n \in R^*)$, where S_i is the optimized roles set.

Algorithm 1   ORS_Generation (ORS_PRE, ORS_MER)
Input: ORS_PRE -- the optimized role set satisfied with PRE constraints
     ORS_MER -- the optimized role set satisfied with MER constraints
Output: ORS-- The optimized roles set satisfied with task requests $TRQ(i)$, PRE constraints and MER constraints
1   Initialize $ORS=\varnothing$
2     $ORS \leftarrow ORS\_PRE \cap ORS\_MER$ //return the optimized role
//set satisfied with PRE constraints and MER constraints
3   **return** ORS

Algorithm 2   S_Generation $(RHT,TRQ(i))$
Input: RHT --a composite role hierarchy tree, $RHT=\{ SBT_1, SBT_2, ..., SBT_n\}$, all the sub-tree SBT_i are generated by RHT
$TRQ(i)$--a group of task requests,$TRQ=(TRQ\ (1), TRQ\ (2), \ldots, TRQ\ (n))$.
Output: S--a role set which is generated by RHT and satisfied with task requests
1   Initialize $S=\varnothing$
2   Initialize $RHT=\varnothing$

3	**While** $S \neq \varnothing$ **DO**
4	**RHT**← DFS//Start DFS Research under the composite role hierarchy tree
5	Decompose *RHT* into several sub-trees SBT_i
6	**foreach** SBT_i in *RHT*
7	$S \leftarrow r \in SBT_i$
8	**return** S

Algorithm 3   ORS_PRE(PRE,S)
Input: r_i -- a role with PRE constraints
       PRE --the *PRE* constraints of role r_i
       S--a role set which is generated by RHT and satisfied with task requests
Output: *ORS_PRE* -- the optimized role set satisfied with PRE constraints

1	Initialize $PRE\_R_{i=}\varnothing$
2	**foreach** $r_i (i \in n)$ in S
3	**if** $r_j \subseteq PRE(cond, r_i)(i \neq j)$
4	PRE_R_i ← r_j //add prerequisite condition role set of r_i into PRE_R_i
5	$i++$
6	**foreach** $r_i (i \in n)$ in S
7	**if** $S \bigcap PRE\_R_i \neq \varnothing$ //when there are roles intersection between PRE_R_i and S
8	ORS_PRE← S-r_i //remove lower level role r_i from S
9	$i++$
10	**return** *ORS_PRE*

Algorithm 4   ORS_MER(MER,S)
Input: r_i– a role with MER constraints
       MER–the *MER* constraints of role r_i
       S – a role set which is generated by RHT and satisfied with task requests
Output: *ORS_MER*-- the optimized role set satisfied with MER constraints

1	Initialize $MER\_R_{i=}\varnothing$
2	**Foreach** $r_i (i \in n)$ in S
3	**if** $r_j \subseteq MER(i \neq j)$
4	MER_R_i ← r_j //add mutually exclusive roles with r_i into MER_R_i
5	$i++$
6	**foreach** $r_i (i \in n)$ in S
7	**if** $S \bigcap MER\_R_i \neq \varnothing$ //when there are roles intersection between MER_R_i and S
8	ORS_MER← S-r_i //remove the mutually exclusive role r_i from S
9	$i++$
10	**Return** *ORS_MER*.

ORS algorithm optimize the process of role assignment to satisfy the task requests of workflow system in distributed and parallel computing service, which also take the PRE and MER constraints into consideration, and ensure the cooperated work of workflow.

4   Simulation

In this paper, we simulate the ORS algorithm and MUR algorithm on DPCRBAC model platform builded by the lab. In the simulation, we adjust the task requests number to get the role assignment number needed for the task requests, roles assignment response time and the roles conflicts number. The simulation results of MUR and ORS algorithm are compared and analyzed on the same platform.

In this paper, we simulate the ORS algorithm and MUR algorithm on the distributed parallel computing access control model platform builded by the lab. In the simulation, we adjust the task requests number to get the roles assignment number needed for the task requests, roles assignment response time and the roles conflicts number. The simulation results of MUR and ORS algorithm are compared and analyzed on the same platform.

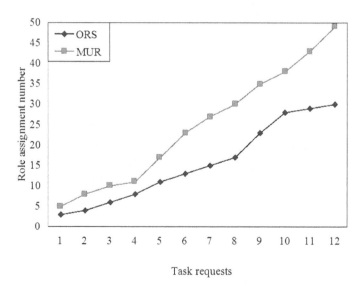

Fig. 2. The relationship of task request and roles assignment number

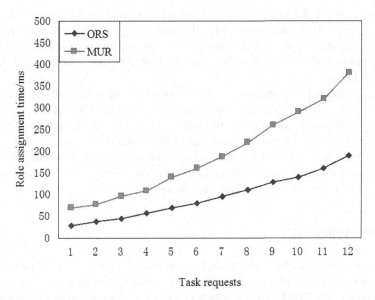

Fig. 3. The relationship of task request number and roles assignment response time

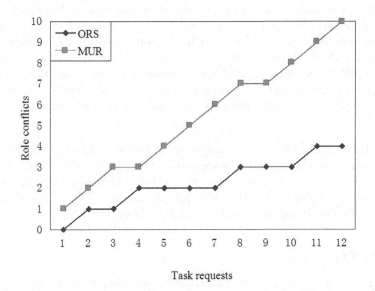

Fig. 4. The relationship of task request and roles conflicts number

Figure 2 shows the comparison of roles assignment number under ORS algorithm and MUR algorithm with the increasing number of task requests. According to Figure 2, we conclude that the roles assignment number under the ORS algorithm and is overall less than that of MUR algorithm when the task request number is the same.

Figure 3 shows the comparison of roles assignment response time under ORS algorithm and MUR algorithm with the increasing number of task requests. According to Figure 3, we conclude that the roles assignment response time under the ORS algorithm and is overall less than that of MUR algorithm when the task request number is the same.

Figure 4 shows the comparison of roles conflicts of roles assignment under ORS algorithm and MUR algorithm with the increasing number of task requests. According to Figure 4, we conclude that roles conflicts of roles assignment under the ORS algorithm and is overall less than that of MUR algorithm when the task request number is the same. With relatively lower roles conflicts, ORS algorithm can ensure the roles assignment in distributed parallel computing environment to meet the task requests and the consistency of security constraints.

5   Summary

In this paper, we introduce the related research and progress on different access control models, especially varieties of RBAC models, and propose a new access control model-DPCRBAC Model, which can meet the task requests of workflow in distributed parallel computing environment.Since the traditional role assignment algorithms cannot satisfy the security constraints requirement in distributed parallel computing service ,We propose a new roles set assignment algorithm-Optimized Roles Set algorithm, and simulate the ORS algorithm and MUR algorithm on the DPCRBAC platform.According to the comparison of the simulation results, the proposed ORS algorithm has overall better performance than the MUR algorithm on the role assignment number , role assignment response time and role conflicts, so it can effectively improve the reliability and safety distributed parallel computing system.

Acknowledgements. This work is supported by The National High-Tech Research and Development Plan of China under Grant (2012AA01A301-01),The National Natural Science Foundation of China (61173036), The National Natural Science Foundation of China(61103047), National Postdoctor Science Foundation of China(20100480936), Hunan Natural Science Foundation(11JJ4052).

References

1. Tanenbaum, A.S., Van Steen, M.: Distributed Systems:Principles and Paradigms, pp. 1–2. Prentice-Hall, Inc. (2002)
2. Karger, P.A.: Authentication and discretionary access control in computer networks. Computer Networks and ISDN Systems 10(1), 27–37 (1985)
3. Thomas, T.A.: Mandatory Access Control Mechanism for the Unix File System. In: Marshall, A. (ed.) Proceedings of the 4th Aerospace Computer Security Applications Conference, pp. 173–177 (1988)
4. Sandhu, R.S., Coyne, E.J., Feinstein, H.L., Youman, C.E.: Role-based access control models. IEEE Computer 29(2), 38–47 (1996)

5. Ferraiolo, D.F., Sandhu, R., Gavrila, S., Kuhn, D.R., Chandramouli, R.: Proposed NIST Standard for Role-Based Access Control. ACM Transactions on Information and System Security 4(3), 224–228 (2001)
6. Sun, Y., Meng, X., Liu, S., Pan, P.: Flexible workflow incorporated with RBAC. In: Shen, W.-m., Chao, K.-M., Lin, Z., Barthès, J.-P.A., James, A. (eds.) CSCWD 2005. LNCS, vol. 3865, pp. 525–534. Springer, Heidelberg (2006)
7. Bertino, E., Ferrari, E., Atluri, V.: The Specification and Enforcement of Authorization Constraints in Workflow Management Systems. ACM Transactions on Information and System Security 2(1), 65–104 (1999)
8. Thomas, R., Sandhu, R.: Towards A Task-Based Paradigm for Flexible and Adaptable Access Control in Distributed Applications. In: Proceedings of the 1992-1993 ACM SIGSAC New Security Paradigms Workshops, pp. 138–142 (1993)
9. KapadiaA: I-RBAC 2000: A Dynamic Role Translation Model for Secure Interoperability (2001)
10. Bertino, E., Bonatti, P.A., Ferrari, E.: TRBAC: A Temporal Role-Based Access Control Model. ACM Trans. Information and System Security 4(3), 191–233 (2001)
11. Joshi, J., Bertino, E., Latif, U., Ghafoor, A.: A Generalized Temporal Role Based Access Control Model. IEEE Trans. Knowledge and Data Eng. 17(1), 4–23 (2005)
12. Liu, Y., Zhuo, T., Renfa, L.: Roles query algorithm in cloud computing environment based on user require. Journal on communications 32(7), 169–175 (2011)
13. Joshi, J.B.D., Bertino, E., Ghafoor, A., et al.: Formal Foundation for Hybrid Hierarchies in GTRBAC. ACM Transactions on Information and System Security (TISSEC) 10(4), 1–39 (2008)
14. Sun, Y., Wang, Q., Li, N., Bertino, E., Atallah, M.J.: On the Complexity of Authorization in RBAC under Qualification and Security Constraints. IEEE Trans. Dependable Sec. Comput. 8(6), 883–886 (2011)
15. Tang, Z., Li, R., Lu, Z.: Request-Driven Role Mapping Framework for Secure Interoperation in Multi-Domain Environments. International Journal of Computer Systems Science and Engineering 23(3), 193–200 (2008)
16. Tang, Z., Wei, J., Li, K., Li, R.: An Access Control Model in Cloud Computing Environment based RBAC. In: The 7th International Conference on Grid and Pervasive Computing, Hong Kong, pp. 11–13 (2012)

Application of Improved Simulated Annealing Optimization Algorithms in Hardware/Software Partitioning of the Reconfigurable System-on-Chip

Yiming Jing*, Jishun Kuang, Jiayi Du, and Biao Hu

College of Information Science and Engineering,
ChangSha. 410082, China
jshkuang@hotmail.com
{jingyiming,maxdujiayi,hubiao}@hnu.edu.cn

Abstract. The hardware/software codedesign technique traditionally is taken to design embedded systems. The hardware/software partitioning is a key problem in hardware/software codedesign. In this paper, we propose Greedy Simulated Annealing Algorithm (GSAA) to implement an approximately optimal or optimal partition on reconfigurable System-on-Chip (SoC) in embedded system. The experimental results on a set of benchmarks show the proposed GSA algorithm can improve the performance by 34.96% and 18.85% on average when comparing with a pure greedy algorithm and a pure simulating annealing algorithm, respectively. So our algorithm is an effective hardware/software partitioning algorithm.

Keywords: Hardware/software Partitioning, Unit Area Speedup Ratio, Greedy Algorithm, Simulated Annealing.

1 Introduction

The logic unit of FPGA is programmable; designers can custom the hardware for the special application. The embedded system with FPGA is a flexible system. So a lot of embedded systems equip the FPGA. The hardware/software codedesign technique traditionally is taken to design embedded systems. The hardware/software partitioning is a key problem in hardware/software codedesign [1]. The hardware/software partitioning problem is a typical combination problem, which has been proved to be NP-hard [2].

Branch Bound Algorithm [3], Integer Liner Programm [4] and Dynamic Programm [5] are generally utilized for the partitioning problem. However, exact algorithms is quite slow for big size inputs. A number of heuristic algorithms have been proposed, such as, Greedy Algorithm, Genetic Algorithm, Particle Swarm Optimal Algorithm, Clustering Algorithm and Simulated Annealing algorithm.

---

* This work is partially supported by 863 Project 2007AA01Z104 and NSFC 61173036.

K. Li et al. (Eds.): ParCFD 2013, CCIS 405, pp. 532–540, 2014.
© Springer-Verlag Berlin Heidelberg 2014

In this paper, we propose a greedy simulated annealing algorithm to get the approximately optimal or optimal solution for hardware/software partitioning problem with area cost constraint. Our target platform is equipped with FPGA. The contributions of our work as follow:

- In our algorithm, we constrain the area which greedy algorithm can use to distribute. The values of area are increased by 0.1 from $0.1A$ to A. A is the area constraint of the hardware.
- Our greedy strategy is based on unit area speedup ratio.
- We take the operation of Simulated Annealing to the initial solution which is produce by greedy algorithm. And then we chose the minimize time cost from ten solutions.
- We also, in our object function, consider the time cost of communication between two nodes which are implemented in different function unit.

The remainder of this paper is organized as follows The target architecture and computation model are presented in Section 3. Section 4 presents GSA algorithm. The experimental results are shown in Section 5 and finally we conclude this paper in Section 6.

2   Related Work

A number of researchers have been proposed for hardware/software partitioning problem. In [6] Luo et al. presented particle swarm optimization and immune clone algorithm. They combined particle swarm optimization with immune clone algorithm. The experimental results show it is an effective algorithm for hardware/software partitioning problem. A 1D Search Algorithms is proposed by Wu et al. [7], and, on the new computing model, they proposed three low-complex algorithms, together with the lower bound of the solution quality, for the hardware/software partitioning problem. Youness et al. proposed a high performance algorithm for scheduling and hardware/software Partitioning on MPSoCs [8]. The optimal scheduling and optimize the number of cores by this algorithm. In [9] Lifa et al. proposed a static algorithm for hardware/software partitioning based on speculative prefetch. Moreover, they intended to develop dynamic prefetching algorithms in the future.

3   Model

In this section, we introduce the target architecture model. Then, we model basic-blocks, which are partitioned to reconfigurable System on Chip (SoC), with Data Flow Graph (DFG).

3.1   Target Architecture Model

In this paper, we target embedded system of reconfigurable SoC with CPU and FPGA as shown in Figure 1. The software task is executed on CPU. And the hardware task is executed on FPGA. CPU and FPGA access share main memory via inter-connection. During the time of design embedded system with FPGA, at the first, designers do not need to determine functions are implemented in hardware or software. In the middle of design, if designers want to improve the performance of this embedded system, they can implement the bottleneck in hardware on FPGA instead of software. The logic unit of FPGA is programmable; designers can custom the hardware for the special application. The embedded system with FPGA is a flexible system. Examples of FPGA products for embedded system include Virtex-II pro, Virtex-IV, Virtex-VII[10], and Strtratix-V[11] etc.

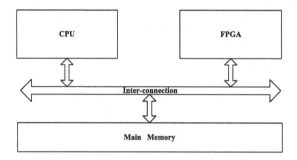

Fig. 1. Hardware Architecture

3.2   Computation Model

In this section, we present the computation model with formal description. In this paper, we take fine Fine-grained partitioning (basic-block levels). Basic-blocks are modeled as Data Flow Graph (DFG) as shown in 2, A DFG $G =< V, E, T, C, X >$ is a node-weighted and edge-weighted Directed Acyclic Graph (DAG). $V =< v_1, v_2, \ldots, v_n >$ is a set of node represents a set of tasks. Set $E =< e_1, e_2, \ldots, e_m > \subseteq V \times V$ represents the dependency among tasks. Node weight $T(v, x_k)$ represents the execution time of a basic-block $v \in V$. And node weight $C(v, x_k)$ represents the execution area cost of a basic-block $v \in V$. When the basic-block is Implemented in software, $C(v, x_k)$ is equal to 0. Edge-weighted $T(e, (u, v))$ represents the communication time cost between node u and node v, if and only if u and v are implemented in different function unit. $X =< x_0, x_1 >$ represents basic-blocks are implemented in which function unit. If $X = x_0$, basic-block is implemented in software, otherwise in hardware.

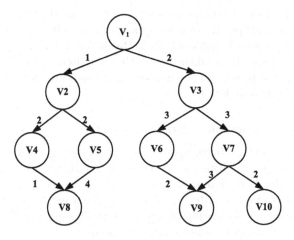

Fig. 2. Data Flow Graph

4   Algorithm

In this section, we first introduce the Greedy Algorithm in section 4.1. and then introduce Simulated Annealing Algorithm in Section 4.2. Finally, in Sectio 4.3 we propose a combination Algorithm to get the approximately optimal or optimal solution.

4.1   Greedy Algorithm (GA)

The algorithm which can solve optimization problems usually has a series of selection steps. However, for most optimization problems, dynamic programming is not the best choice. So we can use a more simple and effective algorithm, greedy algorithm has much concern to the researchers because that it have the features in above [12]. The main idea of the greedy algorithm is that in each step the algorithm selects the local optimum to expect that ultimately the global will be optimum.

The hardware/software partitioning problem in embedded systems can be transformed into the 0-1 knapsack problem. It can be effectively solved by greedy strategy because of its fast convergence as well as the simple structure. The method is widely used to solve all kinds of 0-1 knapsack problems. Section 3.2 describes the time and area overheads when the block is executed on the hardware. The constraints, in this paper, is the hardware area. During the greedy strategy, we must satisfy the following inequality, in which A is the constraint of area:

$$\sum_{i=1}^{n} C(v_i, x_k) \leq A, k \in (0, 1) \tag{1}$$

The traditional greedy strategy usually selects the block of the best fitness value in each iteration and then adds the block to the hardware, until the hardware can not lay down any blocks. Previous research es have shown that the greedy strategy is easy to fall into local optimal, and the optimization results are usually has a large difference compared to other algorithms. In this paper, we use the greedy strategy based on unit area speedup and the rest of the simulated annealing algorithm algorithm is combined to study the partitioning of hardware and software. Section 4.3 will be described it in detail.

4.2 Simulated Annealing Algorithm (SA)

The simulated annealing algorithm is a stochastic search technology based on simulated solid annealing principle, the entire annealing process is a high temperature metal, gradually cooling to achieve the minimum energy crystal structure. The technology is often used to look for the optimal result of the system. The technology is also the formation of the method of solving combinatorial and other problems based on the optimization techniques.

Simulated annealing is a method proposed in 1983 to solve the nonlinear problem [13]. "Simulated Annealing" principle: each point of the solution space is seen as a molecule in the high temperature metal, the energy of the molecules of these metals is their own kinetic energy; every point in the solution space, also has "energy" like metal molecules, which means the point of the problem-solving fitness. The algorithm is Firstly started according to any point in the solution space: every step firstly select a "neighbor", and then calculate the probability of arriving "neighbors" from the existing location [14]. In the simulated annealing algorithm for hardware and software partitioning, most of the researchers firstly will be need to allocate nodes, use random initialization to generate an initial solution, calculate the candidate solutions in the neighborhood, directly bitwise the value of a node (changed from 0 to 1, or 1 to 0), use of the fitness function to evaluate the results of the division result, and then ensure the feasibility of candidate solutions and increase the efficiency of the algorithm. The simulated annealing algorithm has the characteristic of asymptotic convergences, and can be proved to have the probability to obtain a global optimal solution. But its drawback is the slow rate of convergence, in the actual process to solve optimization problems, it is usually combined with other algorithms to speed up the convergence speed or improve the quality of solutions.

4.3 Greedy Simulated Annealing Algorithm (GSAA)

In this section, we present the Greedy Simulated Annealing (GSA) algorithm in detail. In the GSA algorithm, we integrate the greedy algorithm into simulated annealing to solve the hardware/software partition problem in embedded system. The GSA algorithm can get a near-optimal results when satisfies the hardware area constraint without adding the time complexity of the traditional simulated annealing. The GSA algorithm is presented in Algorithm 4.1.

Before presenting the details of GSA algorithm, we define unit area speedup ratio denoted by R in Equation 2.

$$R = ((T(v_i), x_0) - T(v_i, x_1))/C(v_i, x_1) \qquad (2)$$

Algorithm 4.1. Greedy Simulated Annealing Algorithm (GSAA)

Require: A DFG graph $G < V, E, T, C, X >$, and a area constraint A.
Ensure: An approximately optimal or optimal partition for G.
1: Compute R by Equation 2 ← unit area speedup ratio.
2: $\{R_1, R_2, \ldots, R_n\}$ ← for each node.
3: Sort node by descending order of R_i.
4: **for** j ← 1 to 10 **do**
5:    **for** i ← 1 to n **do**
6:       Set $remainArea = (j/10) \times A$.
7:       **if** remainArea is bigger than $C(v_i)$ **then**
8:          $X = x_1$.
9:       **else**
10:          $X = x_0$.
11:       **end if**
12:    **end for**
13:    Find the partition result with greedy algorithm.
14:    Use simulated annealing algorithm to obtain a partition and compute the $cost_j$ by Equation 3.
15:    Find the minimum $cost_j$.
16: **end for**

In traditional greedy algorithm, it just takes or as local optimal solution. It's more accurate to use unit area speedup. We propose the following fitness function for GSA algorithm in Equation 3.

$$cost = \sum_{i=1}^{n}(T(v_i, x_k) - T(e_j, (u, v))), k \in (0, 1) \qquad (3)$$

In the process of annealing simulated, the GSA algorithm will measure the partition results. We suppose there are s edges in the DFG. represents the communication cost when node u and node v assign to the different function unit.

In this paper, our algorithm is combined with Greedy Algorithm and Simulated Annealing Algorithm. As shown in Algorithm 4.1, the time complexity of greedy algorithm is less than $O(n)$. And the time complexity of simulated annealing algorithm is decided by reclusive step. In this paper, m represents the reclusive step. So the operation of simulated annealing takes $O(m)$ time. Therefore, the time complexity of GSA Algorithm is $O(n + m)$.

In the following, we introduce the detail of the GSA algorithm. In steps 1,2,3, Equation 2 is used to compute the unit area speedup ratio R_i for each node. And then order the nodes in the descent according the value of R_i. From steps 5 to 8, the GSA algorithm uses the greedy method based on the unit area speedup ratio to get the partition results. Step 9 makes the partition results as the initial solution for the annealing simulated algorithm, while Equation 3 is used to get the execution time cost with the partition results. Step 10 chooses the optimal solution among the 10 partition results based on greedy algorithm, under which the time execution time cost is minimized when they are simulated annealing.

5 Experimental

The experiments are conducted on a custom simulator which runs on a PC with Intel Core 2Duo T6600 2194.5MHz CPU and 2 GB RAM main memory. Our simulator is developed in Microsoft VS2010 in Windows XP. The benchmark programs are partly from DSPstone which consists a set of Digital Signal Processing applications, and others are randomly generated by the TGFF tool. The data flow graphs are extracted from the gcc compiler and then fed to our custom simulator.

The experimental results show the effectiveness of the Greedy Simulated Annealing (GSA) algorithm by comparing with a pure greedy (GA) algorithm and a pure simulated annealing (SA) algorithm. Table 1 shows the experimental results. As show in table 1, the first column shows the benchmark. The second column shows the number of nodes each benchmark contains. The third column shows the total execution time cost need to finish basic-blocks when using GA algorithm. The fourth column shows the total execution time cost when using SA algorithm. The fifth column shows the time cost by the proposed GSA algorithm. The sixth column represents the improvement by GSA algorithm when comparing it with SA algorithm. The last column shows the improvement by GSA algorithm when comparing it with GA algorithm. From Table 1, we can see the proposed GSA algorithm can improve the performance by 34.96% and

Table 1. Comparison between schedules and data allocation

Benchmark	Node	GA	SA	GSAA	%SA-GS	%GA-GS
allpole	15	244	212	161	24.06%	34.02%
Floyd	16	213	229	169	26.20%	20.66%
4latiir	26	446	340	311	8.53%	30.27%
volt	27	517	424	370	12.74%	28.43%
elliptic	34	602	517	328	36.56%	45.51%
random1	50	1052	658	530	19.45%	49.62%
random2	100	2304	1924	1350	29.83%	41.41%
random3	200	3766	2914	2544	12.70%	32.45%
random4	400	7676	6157	5306	13.82%	30.88%
random5	600	11422	8437	7878	6.63%	31.03%
random6	800	15284	11328	10456	7.70%	31.59%
random7	1000	18740	15104	13234	12.38%	29.38%
random8	2000	39889	31713	26574	16.20%	33.38%
random9	3000	67050	52996	39880	24.75%	40.52%
random10	4000	84718	66323	53151	19.86%	37.26%
random11	5000	116794	95483	66638	30.21%	42.94%
Average improvement					18.85%	34.96%

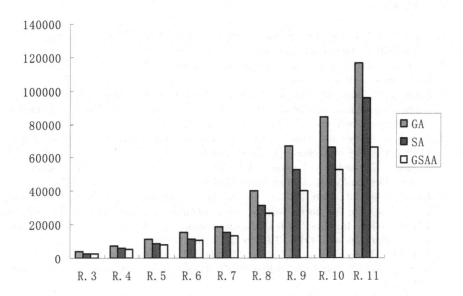

Fig. 3. Experimental results for benchmarks of DFGs

18.85% on average when comparing with a pure greedy algorithm and a pure simulating annealing algorithm, respectively. In the best case, it can improve 36.56% by comparing with SA algorithm and 49.62% by comparing with GA algorithm. To illustrate the results visually, Figure 3 gives the results by parts of DFGs benchmarks.

6 Conclusion

In this paper, we propose an improved simulated annealing algorithm based on the hardware speedup, the Greedy Simulated Annealing (GSA) algorithm. The GSA algorithm can get the better partition results when satisfies the hardware area constraint with the same complexity comparing to the traditional simulated annealing. The problem of hardware/software partition is modeled based on Data Flow Graph (DFG). The unit area speedup based greedy algorithm is used to generate the partitioning results when satisfies the area constraint, and then use simulated annealing to optimize the results. The experimental results on a set of benchmarks show the proposed GSA algorithm can improve the performance by 34.96% and 18.85% on average when comparing with a pure greedy algorithm and a pure simulating annealing algorithm, respectively. In the future work, we will compare the GSA algorithm with more other optimizing algorithm. And more improvement will make on the GSA algorithm itself such as the convergence speed, to get better partition results.

References

1. Ernst, R.: Codesign of Embedded Systems tatus and Trends. IEEE Design & Test of Computers 46(15), 24–34 (1981)
2. Micheli, G.D., Gupta, R.K.: Hardware/Software Co-Design. Proceedings of the IEEE 85(3), 349–365 (1997)
3. Binh, N.N., Imai, M., Shiomi, A., et al.: A hardware/software partitioning algorithm for designing pipelined ASIPs with least gate counts. In: Proc. of 33 Design Automation Conference, LasVegas, pp. 527–532 (1996)
4. Ditzel, M.: Power-aware architecting for data-dominated applications: [PhD thesis]. Delft University of Technology, 70–80 (2004)
5. Madsen, J., Gorde, J., Knudsen, P.V., et al.: LYCOS: The Lyngby co-synthesis system. Design Automation of Embedded Systems 2(2), 195–236 (1997)
6. Luo, L., He, H.J., Liao, C.K., et al.: Hardware/software partitioning for heterogeneous multicore SoC using particle swarm optimization and immune clone (PSO-IC) algorithm. In: Proc. 2010 IEEE International Conference on Information and Automation, pp. 490–494. IEEE Press, Harbin (2010)
7. Wu, J.G., Thambipillai, S., Guang, C.: Algorithmic aspects of hardware/software partitioning: 1D search algorithms. IEEE Transactions on Computers 59(4), 532–544 (2010)
8. Youness, H., Hassan, M., Sakanushi, K.S., et al.: A high performance algorithm for scheduling and hardware-software partitioning on MPSoCs. In: The 4th International Conference on Design & Technology of Integrated Systems, pp. 71–76. IEEE Press, Nanoscal Era (2009)
9. Lifa, A., Eles, P., Peng, Z.B.: Execution time minimization based on hardware/software partitioning and speculative prefetch. Technical reports, Computer and Information Science (2012)
10. Wikimedia Foundation, Inc., http://en.wikipedia.org/wiki/XilinxJan
11. Wikimedia Foundation, Inc., http://en.wikipedia.org/wiki/AlteraJan
12. Cormen, T.H., Leiserson, C.E., Rivest, R.L., et al.: Introduction to Algorithms, 3rd edn. MIT Press, USA (2002)
13. Dimitris, B., John, T.: Simulated Annealing. Statistical Science 8(1), 10–15 (1993)
14. Wikimedia Foundation, Inc., http://en.wikipedia.org/wiki/Simulated_annealing

Large-Scale Parallel Computing
for 3D Gaseous Detonation

Wang Cheng, Bi Yong, Han Wenhu, and Ning Jianguo

State Key Laboratory of Explosion Science and Technology, Beijing Institute of Technology
Beijing, China, 100081
wangcheng@bit.edu.cn

Abstract. In numerical simulation of 3D gas detonation, due to the complexity of the computational domain in high resolution numerical computing negative density and pressure often emerge, which leads to blow-ups. In addition, a large number of grids resulting from relative mesh resolution and large-scale computing domain consume tremendous computing resources, which poses another challenge on the numerical simulation. In this paper, the positivity-preserving high order weighted essentially non-oscillatory (WENO) scheme is constructed without destroying the numerical accuracy and stability, and then the high-resolution parallel code is developed on the platform of Message Passing Interface (MPI). It is used to simulate the propagation of detonation wave in the 3D square duct with obstacles. The numerical results show that high-resolution parallel code can effectively simulate the propagation of 3D gas detonation wave in pipe, and the results also show that density and pressure are not negative in the event of diffraction. Therefore, the high-resolution parallel code provides an effective way to explore the new physical mechanism of 3D gas detonation.

Keywords: WENO scheme, positivity-preserving, parallel computing, detonation.

1   Introduction

Detonation phenomenon is essentially three dimensional, thus some important structural characteristics can not be obtained from two-dimensional simulations. The numerical simulation of 3D detonation requires high grid resolution and algorithm, in particular for unstable detonation [1-4]. If the number of grid does not meet requirements, the front structure of detonation wave and the flow characteristics can not be captured, and the resulting law of detonation propagation wave does not reflect the real physical cases [5]. Furthermore, the 3D detonation wave requires a long computation time and sufficient length of the duct to form a self-sustaining detonation. If computational domain is very small, the boundary will affect the real detonation propagation characteristics. In numerical simulation, computational time and the number of grids occupy very large resource, which far exceeds computing capacity of a single CPU. Therefore, large parallel computing is a key to numerically investigate 3D detonation.

K. Li et al. (Eds.): ParCFD 2013, CCIS 405, pp. 541–552, 2014.

In practical detonation propagation, especially when detonation wave propagates in complex laneway, interaction of detonation wave with the boundaries and the resulting diffraction complicates the detonation propagation mechanism. In numerical simulation, pressure and density are often negative, which results in blow-ups. When density and pressure tend to be negative, they are forced to zero in the simple solution. However, this method damages the numerical accuracy and stability. To ensure pressure and density non-negative without destroying the accuracy and stability, the equations have to be resolved in high-resolution computing of 3D gas detonation.

First order and second order positivity-preserving schemes had already been studied in the reference by Linde [6,7]. Recently, Wang proposed a general framework for constructing arbitrarily high order positivity-preserving discontinuous Galerkin (DG) [8]. Zhang constructed high order positivity-preserving weighted essentially non-oscillatory (WENO) finite difference for 2D Euler equations [9]. However, to construct positivity-preserving high order finite difference WENO schemes for 3D, Euler equations have been seldom researched.

In this paper, we present an extension of 2D positivity-preserving method to construct positivity-preserving high order WENO finite difference schemes for 3D Euler equations with reaction source. And the positivity-preserving limiter is added to WENO finite difference scheme. Design of new limiter can not only preserve the positivity of pressure and density, but also maintain the conservation of conserved variables and high order accuracy of numerical solutions under suitable CFL condition. Based on this, we develop a high-resolution dynamic parallel code of 3D gaseous detonation. According to the computational domain, we dynamically adjust the computation of every process to ensure load balance. By applying the code to simulate the propagation of 3D detonation propagation in duct with obstacles, the numerical results agree well with the physical process.

2   Governing Equations

Reactive-flow Euler equations with a source term are described by

$$\frac{\partial U}{\partial t} + \frac{\partial F(U)}{\partial x} + \frac{\partial G(U)}{\partial y} + \frac{\partial H(U)}{\partial z} = S$$

where, the conserved variable vector U, the flux vectors F, G and H as well as the source vector S are given , respectively, by

$$U = (\rho, \rho u, \rho v, \rho w, \rho E, \rho Y)^T$$
$$F = (\rho u, \rho u^2 + p, \rho uv, \rho uw, (\rho E + p)u, \rho uY)^T$$
$$G = (\rho v, \rho uv, \rho v^2 + p, \rho vw, (\rho E + p)v, \rho vY)^T$$
$$H = (\rho w, \rho uw, \rho vw, \rho w^2 + p, (\rho E + p)w, \rho wY)^T$$
$$S = (0, 0, 0, 0, 0, \omega)^T$$
$$E = \frac{p}{(\gamma-1)} + \frac{1}{2}(u^2 + v^2 + w^2) + \rho qY$$

$$\omega = -K\rho Y e^{-(Ea/T)}$$
$$p = (\gamma - 1)\rho e$$

where, p, ρ, E, T, u, v, w are pressure, density, total energy per unit volume, temperature and velocity, respectively; Y is reactant mass fraction, ω is reaction rate; γ is specific heat ratio, Ea is activation energy; K is pre-exponential factor; q is the heat of reaction; R is gas constant.

3   Positivity-Preserving High Order Finite Difference WENO Schemes

Define the set of admissible states by $G = \{U \mid \rho > 0, p \geq 0\}$, then G is a convex set, p is a concave function of U. We want to construct finite difference WENO schemes producing solutions in set G.

3.1   Positivity-Preserving Condition

For simplicity, we consider 1D Euler equations first,

$$U_t + f(U)_x = S \tag{1}$$

Let $A_{i+1/2}$ denote the Roe matrix[10] of the two states U_{i+1}^n and U_i^n, let $L_{i+1/2}$ and $R_{i+1/2}$ be the left and right eigenvector matrices of $A_{i+1/2}$ respectively, $\alpha = \max \|(|u| + c)\|$.

Let $f^{\pm}(U) = \dfrac{1}{2}\left[U \pm \dfrac{f(U)}{\alpha}\right]$ and $h_{\pm} = R_{\Delta x}(f^{\pm})$. Then we have the cell averages $\bar{h}_{\pm i}^n = f^{\pm}(U_i^n)$. Perform the WENO reconstruction to obtain $(h_+)_{i+\frac{1}{2}}^-, (h_-)_{i+\frac{1}{2}}^+$.

Construct the flux by $\hat{f}_{i+\frac{1}{2}} = \alpha\left[(h_+)_{i+\frac{1}{2}}^- - (h_-)_{i+\frac{1}{2}}^+\right]$, let $\lambda = \dfrac{\Delta t}{\Delta x}$, then we get the finite difference scheme

$$U_i^{n+1} = U_i^n - \lambda\left(\hat{f}_{i+\frac{1}{2}} - \hat{f}_{i-\frac{1}{2}}\right) + \Delta t S(U_i^n, x_i)$$

$$= \frac{1}{2}U_i^n - \lambda\left(\hat{f}_{i+\frac{1}{2}} - \hat{f}_{i-\frac{1}{2}}\right) + \frac{1}{2}U_i^n + \Delta t S(U_i^n, x_i)$$

$$= \frac{1}{2}H^+ + \frac{1}{2}H^- + \frac{1}{2}\tilde{S} \tag{2}$$

where,

$$H^+ = \bar{h}_{+i}^n - 2\alpha\lambda\left[(h_+)_{i+\frac{1}{2}}^- - (h_+)_{i-\frac{1}{2}}^-\right] \tag{3}$$

$$H^- = \bar{h}^n_{-i} - 2\alpha\lambda\left[(h_-)^+_{i+\frac{1}{2}} - (h_-)^+_{i-\frac{1}{2}}\right] \tag{4}$$

$$\tilde{S} = U^n_{ijk} + 2\Delta t S(U^n_i, x_i) \tag{5}$$

Notice that (3) and (4) are finite volume schemes for h_+ and h_-. Obviously, if H^+, H^-, $\tilde{S} \in G$, then $U^{n+1}_i \in G$.

Let $q^+_i(x)$, $q^-_i(x)$ be the polynomials of degree k, such that $q^+_i(x_{i+\frac{1}{2}}) = (h_+)^-_{i+\frac{1}{2}}$, $q^-_i(x_{i-\frac{1}{2}}) = (h_-)^+_{i-\frac{1}{2}}$, the cell average of $q^\pm_i(x)$ is $\bar{h}^n_{\pm i}$.

Let $q^{+,*}_i = \dfrac{1}{1-\hat{w}_N}\displaystyle\sum_{k=1}^{N-1}\hat{w}_k q^+_i(\hat{x}^k_i)$, then

$$\bar{h}^n_{+i} = \frac{1}{\Delta x}\int_{I_i} q^+_i(x)\,dx = \sum_{k=1}^{N}\hat{w}_k q^+_i(\hat{x}^k_i) = \sum_{k=1}^{N-1}\hat{w}_k q^+_i(\hat{x}^k_i) + \hat{w}_N (h_+)^-_{i+1/2} \tag{6}$$

Substituting (6) into (3), then (3) becomes
$$H^+ = (1-\hat{w}_N)q^{+,*}_i + (\hat{w}_N - 2\alpha\lambda)(h_+)^-_{i+1/2} + 2\alpha\lambda(h_+)^-_{i-1/2}$$

Therefore, if $q^{+,*}_i$, $(h_+)^-_{i+1/2}$, $(h_+)^-_{i-1/2} \in G$, $H^+ \in G$ under the CFL condition $2\alpha\lambda \le \hat{w}_N$.

Similarly, if $q^{-,*}_i$, $(h_-)^+_{i+1/2}$, $(h_-)^+_{i-1/2} \in G$, $H^- \in G$ under the CFL condition $2\alpha\lambda \le \hat{w}_N$, where $\hat{w}_1 = \hat{w}_N$. And $\tilde{S} \in G$ is discussed in [8].

From the above, the following theorem is obvious.

Theorem 1. Under the CFL condition $2\alpha\lambda \le \hat{w}_1$, if $q^{+,*}_i$, $(h_+)^-_{i+1/2}$, $(h_+)^-_{i-1/2}$, $q^{-,*}_i$, $(h_-)^+_{i+1/2}$, $(h_-)^+_{i-1/2} \in G$, the finite difference WENO scheme (2) will be positivity-preserving, i.e. $U^{n+1}_i \in G$.

Based on the above, finite difference WENO scheme for 3D Euler equations with source term is given by

$$U^{n+1}_{ijk} = U^n_{ijk} - \frac{\Delta t}{\Delta x}\left(\hat{f}_{i+\frac{1}{2},j,k} - \hat{f}_{i-\frac{1}{2},j,k}\right) - \frac{\Delta t}{\Delta y}\left(\hat{g}_{i,j+\frac{1}{2},k} - \hat{g}_{i,j-\frac{1}{2},k}\right) - \frac{\Delta t}{\Delta z}\left(\hat{h}_{i,j,k+\frac{1}{2}} - \hat{h}_{i,j,k-\frac{1}{2}}\right) + \Delta t S$$

Similarly, it can be written as

$$U^{n+1}_{ijk} = \frac{1}{4}\hat{F} + \frac{1}{4}\hat{G} + \frac{1}{4}\hat{H} + \frac{1}{4}\hat{S}$$

where

$$\hat{F} = U^n_{ijk} - 4\frac{\Delta t}{\Delta x}\left(\hat{f}_{i+\frac{1}{2},j,k} - \hat{f}_{i-\frac{1}{2},j,k}\right)$$

$$\hat{G} = U^n_{ijk} - 4\frac{\Delta t}{\Delta y}\left(\hat{g}_{i,j+\frac{1}{2},k} - \hat{g}_{i,j-\frac{1}{2},k}\right)$$

$$\hat{H} = U_{ijk}^{n} - 4 \frac{\Delta t}{\Delta z} \left(\hat{h}_{i,j,k+\frac{1}{2}} - \hat{h}_{i,j,k-\frac{1}{2}} \right)$$

$$\hat{S} = U_{ijk}^{n} + 4\Delta t S$$

It is straightforward to extend the positivity-preserving results for 1D to 3D.

3.2 Positivity-preserving limiter

(1) At first, modify the density

Let $\bar{h} = (\bar{\rho}, \overline{\rho u}, \overline{\rho v}, \overline{\rho w}, \overline{\rho E}, \overline{\rho Y})^{T}$, for each cell I_{i}, modify the density

$$\hat{\rho}_{i+1/2} = \theta_{i} \hat{\rho}_{i+1/2}^{-} + (1-\theta_{i})\bar{\rho}_{i}$$

where $\theta_{i} = \min\left\{ 1, \left| \frac{\bar{\rho}_{i} - \varepsilon}{\bar{\rho}_{i} - \rho_{\min}} \right| \right\}$, ε is a small number. In practice, we can

choose $\varepsilon = 10^{-13}$.

(2) Then, modify the pressure
Define

$$\hat{u}_{i+1/2}^{-} = \left(\hat{\rho}_{i+1/2}^{-}, \hat{\rho} u_{i+1/2}^{-}, \hat{\rho} v_{i+1/2}^{-}, \hat{\rho} w_{i+1/2}^{-}, E_{i+1/2}^{-}, \rho Y_{i-1/2}^{-} \right)^{T}$$

Let

$$\tilde{u}_{i+1/2}^{-} = \theta_{i} [\hat{u}_{i+1/2}^{-} - \bar{u}_{i}] + \bar{u}_{i}$$

Such that

$$p(\theta_{k}[\hat{u}_{i+1/2}^{-} - \bar{u}_{i}] + \bar{u}_{i}) \geq 0.$$

For each x, find θ_{x} as solution of

$$p(\theta_{x}[\hat{w}_{i-1/2}^{-} - \bar{w}_{i}] + \bar{w}_{i}) = 0.$$

4   Realization of High-Resolution Parallel Program

Computational domain is divided into N sub-domains, and every sub-domain is undertaken by a process. Message communication of the interface between sub-domains is completed by library function of MPI. For example, 5-th order WENO scheme requires three layers of ghost grid outside boundary, and message communication takes lots of time. Therefore, non-blocking communication MPI_ISEND (buf,count,datatype,dest,comm,req) is used for data transmission between sub-domain interfaces, where req denotes status and is used to check the status of message transmission. It is not necessary to return after finishing data transmission. So, overlapping of communication and computing improves the efficiency of program execution [11].

Basic idea of high-resolution parallel steps
(1) Define array A(nx(t),ny(t),nz(t)) for 3D domain, where t is time. Thus sub-domain arrays are Asub(nx(t)/cut_x, ny(t)/cut_y, nz(t)/cut_z)= Asub(nx, ny, nz),

where cut_x, cut_y and cut_z are the number of divisions in x, y and z directions, respectively. Assume cut_x=4, cut_y=4 and cut_z=4, the sub-domain is shown in Fig.1.

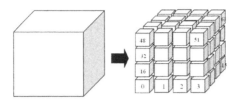

Fig. 1. Three-dimensional cutting of the computational domain

(2) Expand sub-domain arrays Asub(-md:nxm, -md:nym, -md:nzm), where md=3, nxm=nx+md, nym=ny+md, nzm=nz+md.

(3) Number the divided sub-domain

Call library function MPI_Comm_rank(MPI_COMM_WORLD, mpirank, ierr) to achieve numbering sub-domain integer, mpirank is the index of number order, from 0 to cut_x*cut_y* cut_z-1.

(4) The data structure of the communication

Define one-dimensional array send_bufx1(n), send_bufx2(n), and put x-direction variables into send_bufx1(n), send_bufx2(n), where n is total number. Similarly, put y, z-direction variables into send_bufy1(n), send_bufy2(n) and send_bufz1(n), send_bufz2(n) in order.

(5) Data communication between sub-domain interfaces

Fig.2 shows the message transmission in x-direction. Domain 0 sends message in send_bufx1(n), send_bufx2(n) to domain 1 and 3, meanwhile receiving message from domain 1 and 3. Similarly, communication object of domain 3 is domain 0 and 2.

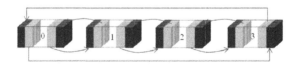

Fig. 2. Sketch of message communication among sub-domains

5   Numerical Simulation of 3D Detonation

5.1   Detonation Diffraction

To verify the positivity-preserving method, we simulate the diffraction behaviour when the 3D detonation propagates from the duct to a free space. The width and height of duct are 5 and 3, respectively. An ignition zone is set on the left of the duct, while the remaining region is filled with un-reacted mixture. The left of the duct is in flow condition, and other boundaries are walls.

Fig.3 shows the pressure and density contour at some time when detonation propagates into free space. As can be seen from Fig.3, a region of low pressure and density can be seen obviously. Minimum value of density and pressure is very small, but the values of pressure and density in this region are not negative. This fully demonstrates that reliance of the positivity-preserving method is very good.

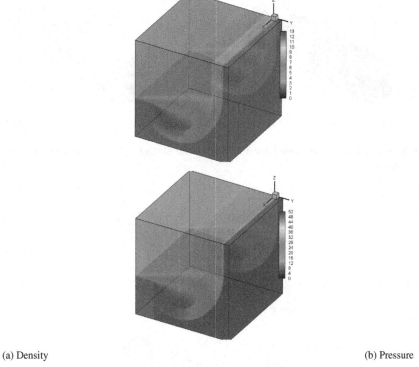

(a) Density   (b) Pressure

Fig. 3. Colored contour of density and pressure

5.2   Effect of Obstacles on Detonation Propagation

Take 3D square duct as computing domain. Its length and width are 126 and 16, respectively. The width of obstacles is 0.6. The heights of obstacles (H) are 2.0, 4.0 and 6.0, respectively. The space of obstacles is 16. The one-dimensional ZND analytical solution is used as initial value. The left of the duct is inflow boundary, and the other is rigid walls[12].

(1) One obstacle

Fig.4 shows the propagation of detonation wave in case of one obstacle. It can be seen from Fig.4(a) that a very low pressure rarefaction zone emerges before the obstacle due to diffracting when detonation wave passes the obstacle. As shown in Fig.4(b), we can observe that the wave passes the obstacle, with pressure on its front decreasing, then is reflected by the walls. The local detonation is formed and the triple-point structure can be seen obviously [13].

Fig.5 shows maximum pressure history on the walls when the obstacle heights are 2.0 and 4.0, respectively. It can be seen that when the obstacle height is 2.0, re-ignition occurs. Cellular detonation can be formed and irregular cells appear on the walls. When the height reaches 4.0, re-ignition can also occur after passing the obstacle[14], as shown in Fig. 5(b).

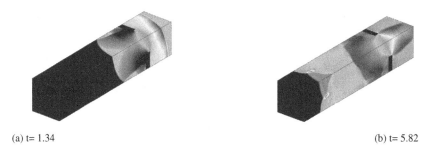

(a) t= 1.34   (b) t= 5.82

Fig. 4. Propagation of detonation wave in case of one obstacle: (A fourth part of total domain along axis line)

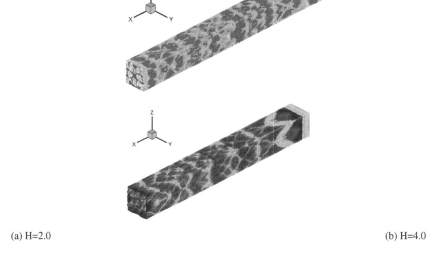

(a) H=2.0   (b) H=4.0

Fig. 5. Maximum pressure history on the walls in case of one obstacle

(2) Two obstacles

Fig.6 shows the propagation of detonation wave in case of two obstacles of H=2.0. It can be seen that at t=1.20, the wave front takes on a spherical characteristics and diffracting wave front collides with the walls and reflection occurs. Thus transverse waves appear on every wall. At t=1.88, transverse waves on the neighboring walls collide each other at wall corner and strong local explosions happen. The resulting energy ignites the un-reacted gas near the corner and gives impetus to the front of local detonation. At t=2.06, the front collides with the second obstacle and rectangular structure is formed. The front contains two pairs of triple-point lines, one of which are parallel to the y-direction and the other parallel to the z-direction. Each pair of the triple-point lines moves in opposite direction parallel to the front. At t=2.85-4.05, the triple-point lines collide at the axis line of the duct and separate each other. Then the triple-point lines split and the number of triple points on every wall increases.

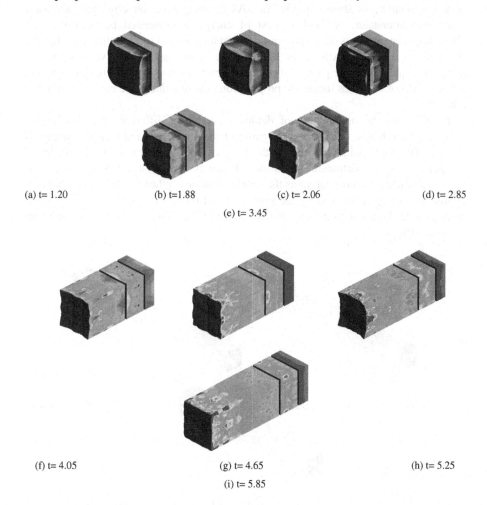

(a) t= 1.20   (b) t=1.88   (c) t= 2.06   (d) t= 2.85

(e) t= 3.45

(f) t= 4.05   (g) t= 4.65   (h) t= 5.25

(i) t= 5.85

Fig. 6. Propagation of detonation wave in case of two obstacles of H=2.0

However, the front still maintains rectangular structure. At t=4.65-5.85, due to instability of detonation the triple-point lines become irregular and detonation cells become irregular too, as shown in Fig. 7(a).

Fig.7 shows maximum pressure history on the walls at different obstacles height. It can be observed that when obstacles height is 2.0, re-ignition behavior can occur. After a low velocity stage, cellular detonation can be formed and irregular cells appear on the walls. It can be seen further that after passing the second obstacle, detonation initially propagates in rectangular mode and slapping waves appear on the walls. Then the mode of detonation transits from the rectangular to the diagonal and slapping waves on the walls disappear. Over time, detonation cell splits and its size becomes smaller, as shown in Fig.7(a). As the height of the obstacles increases, detonation attenuates. At H=4.0, most of energy is consumed between the two obstacles. The result is that re-ignition behavior can not occur after passing the obstacle. At H=6.0, maximum pressure in the walls has become very weak and detonation quenches after passing the second obstacle, as shown in Fig. 7(c). Hence, as the height of obstacles increases, propagation of detonation wave can be effectively inhibited.

Fig.8 shows the propagation of detonation wave at different obstacles height. When obstacle height is 2.0, local re-ignition behavior occurs and local detonation is formed. The triple-point structure on the front can be seen clearly. As the height of obstacles increases, detonation attenuates. It can be seen that a low pressure zone among obstacles becomes larger as the height increases. When the height reaches 6.0, nearly all energy is blocked by the obstacles and the wave has become very weak after passing the second obstacle, as shown in Fig.8(c). The conclusion is consistent with [15, 16].

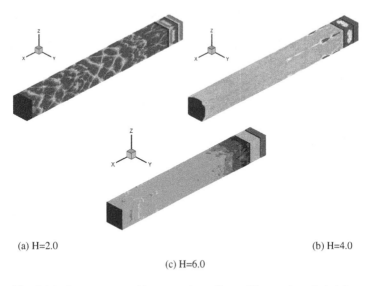

(a) H=2.0   (b) H=4.0

(c) H=6.0

Fig. 7. Maximum pressure history on the walls at different obstacle heights

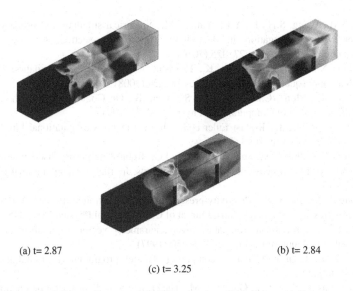

(a) t= 2.87   (b) t= 2.84

(c) t= 3.25

Fig. 8. Propagation of detonation wave at different obstacle heights: (A fourth part of total domain along axis line)

6   Conclusions

A 3D detonation MPI parallel code is developed to investigate the effect of obstacles on the detonation wave based on positivity-preserving high order finite difference WENO schemes. The numerical results show that high-resolution parallel code can effectively simulate the propagation of 3D gas detonation in large-scale tube with obstacles. It can be found that   pressure and density are positive. Numerical results also show that when detonation wave diffracts through obstacles, the propagation of detonation wave can be inhibited by increasing the number of obstacles. As the height of obstacles increases, detonation wave becomes weaker and weaker after passing two obstacles. Additionally, high-resolution parallel code saves communication time of data in interface, and further enhances the computational efficiency. It not only improves the computational efficiency but also the resolution of the detonation wave front. Therefore, it is a means to explore new physical mechanism of 3D gaseous detonation.

References

1. Sharpe, G.J.: The effect of curvature on detonation waves in Type Ia supernovae. Monthly Notices of the Royal Astronomical Society 322, 614 (2001)
2. Hwang, P., Fedkiw, R.P., Merriman, B., Aslam, T.D., Karagozian, A.R., Osher, S.J.: Numerical resolution of pulsating detonation waves. Combustion Theory and Modelling 4, 217 (2000)
3. Wang, G., Zhang, D.L., Liu, K.X., Wang, J.T.: An improved two-dimensional CE/ SE method and its high order schemes. Chinese Journal of Computational Mechanics 25, 741 (2008)

4. Zai, J.M., Wang, S.H., Li, Y.C., Yang, J.M.: Numerical simulation of primary-secondary shock wave propagation in duct with waring cross-section. Chinese Journal of Computational Mechanics 27, 925 (2010)
5. Tsuboi, N., Asahara, M., Eto, K., Hayashi, A.K.: Numerical simulation of spinning detonation in square duct. Shock Waves 18, 329 (2008)
6. Einfeldt, B., Munz, C.D., Roe, P.L., Sjogreen, B.: On Godunov-type methods near low densities. Journal of Computational Physics 92, 273 (1991)
7. Linde, T., Roe, P.L.: Robust Euler codes. In: Thirteenth Computational Fluid Dynamics Conference, AIAA, p. 2098 (1997)
8. Wang, C., Zhang, X.X., Shu, C.W., Ning, J.G.: Robust high order discontinuous Galerkin schemes for two-dimensional gaseous detonations. Journal of Computational Physics 231, 653 (2012)
9. Zhang, X.X., Shu, C.W.: Positivity-preserving high order finite difference WENO schemes for compressible Euler equations. Journal of Computational Physics 231, 2245 (2012)
10. Roe, P.L.: Approximate Riemann solvers, parameter vectors, and difference schemes. Journal of Computational Physics 135, 250 (1997)
11. Dou, Z.H.: High performance computing Parallel programming. Tsinghua University Press, Beijing
12. Knystautas, R., Lee, J.H., Guirao, C.M.: The critical tube diameter for detonation failure in hydrocarbon-air mixtures. Combustion and Flame 48, 63 (1982)
13. Pintgen, F., Shepherd, J.E.: Detonation diffraction in gases. Combustion and Flame 156, 665 (2009)
14. Xu, B.P., Wen, J.X., Tam, V.H.Y.: The effect of an obstacle plate on the spontaneous ignition in pressurized hydrogen release: A numerical study. International Journal of Hydrogen Energy 36, 2637 (2010)
15. Valiev, D., Bychkov, V., Akkerman, V., Law, C.K., Eriksson, L.E.: Flame Acceleration in Channels with Obstacles in the Deflagration-to-detonation Transition. Combust Flame 57, 1012 (2010)
16. Pantow, E.G., Fischer, M., Kratzel, T.: Decoupleing and recoupling of detonation waves associated with sudden expansion. Shock Waves 6, 131 (1996)

Numerical Simulation about Train Wind Influence on Personnel Safety in High-Speed Railway Double-Line Tunnel

Limin Peng[1,2], Ruizhen Fei[1,*], Chenghua Shi[1,2], Weichao Yang[1,2], and Yiting Liu[3]

[1] School of Civil Engineering, Central South University, Hunan Changsha 410075, China
[2] National Engineering Laboratory of High Speed Railway Construction Technology,
Hunan Changsha 410075, China
[3] School of Foreign Languages, Central South University, Hunan Changsha 410083, China
`lmpeng@mail.csu.edu.cn`,
`{csufrzh,csusch,weic_yang,csulyt}@163.com`

Abstract. According to the $100\,m^2$ double-line tunnel cross-section which is generally used in high-speed railway of China, this paper develops a tunnel - air - train simulation model, based on the three-dimensional incompressible Navier - Stokes equations and the standard $k-\varepsilon$ turbulence model. This model can simulate two situations one is that a single train runs through a tunnel normally while the other is that another train runs beside a train parked in the tunnel. Time-history variation rules and space distribution characteristics of train wind are studied respectively at 120 km, 200 km, 250 km, 300 km and 350 km per hour. Furthermore, the authors discuss train wind influence on personnel safety on evacuation passageways. In addition, the authors give out analytically the results of the numerical simulation. The results show that: Train wind is complex three-dimensional flow changing with time and space, so people should avoid activities at dangerous time and places; since personnel safety may be threatened by train wind in the two situations above, therefore, effective measures should be taken to avoid accidents.

Keywords: tunnel aerodynamics, characteristics of train wind, analyses of personnel safety, unsteady three-dimensional flow, numerical analysis.

1 Introduction

The Collinear Operation Mode that high-speed trains ($v \geq 250km/h$) run during day time and medium-speed trains ($160km/h \leq v \leq 250km/h$) run during night time is widely adopted on the initial stage of high-speed railway, while timely and effective track maintenance is the premise and guarantee of punctual, safe and comfortable running of trains, so the situation that one line is in operation while the other is under maintenance may be formed [1], at the same time trains may shut down in double-line tunnel due to reasons such as electrical equipment failure. High speed train wind can

---

* Corresponding author.

K. Li et al. (Eds.): ParCFD 2013, CCIS 405, pp. 553–564, 2014.

be formed within a certain distance around train because of train body friction and air viscous resistance when a train is running at a high speed. Train wind would be a threat to the security of maintenance workers and passengers in the tunnel. To ensure the safety of personnel and train, security measures must be taken.

Foreign and Chinese scholars have done a lot of research about train wind through theoretical studies, model experiments, field measurements, numerical simulations and other methods [2-3], but research about characteristics of train wind and analyses of personnel safety in high-speed railway is rare. At present most of research results are applied only when train's speed is under $300\,km/h$, farther more tunnel contours in each country are different. Based on the $100\,m^2$ double-line tunnel cross-section which is generally used in high-speed railway of China, the authors use three-dimensional incompressible unsteady computational model to simulate two running situations: one is that a single train runs through tunnel normally (hereafter "Normal Situation") while the other is that another train runs beside a train parked in the tunnel (hereafter "Accident Situation"). Time-history variation rules and space distribution characteristics of the train wind are studied respectively at 120 km, 200 km, 250 km, 300 km and 350 km per hour, and the train wind influence on personnel safety is further discussed.

2   Operating Model Design

2.1   Governing Equations

As a large and slender near-earth carrying tool, when a train's speed is under $360\,km/h$, the corresponding Mach Number is not greater than 0.3, so train wind belongs to subsonic flow, which can be dealt with three-dimensional viscous unsteady flow. Since the Reynolds Number Re of high-speed train flow field is commonly greater than 10^6, so train wind can be viewed as a turbulent flow [4]. The three-dimensional incompressible Navier-Stokes equation and standard $k-\varepsilon$ turbulence model are adopted in this paper. The Greek symbols ϕ is set to be a certain flow field parameter, and the flow control equation for any control volume V can be written as the following form [5]:

$$\frac{d}{dt}\int_v \rho\phi dV + \int_s [\rho\phi U - \Gamma_\phi grad\phi]dS = \int_v S_\phi dV \qquad (1)$$

When ϕ is respectively equal to $1,U,e,k,\varepsilon$, equation (1) respectively represents continuous equation, momentum equation, energy equation, turbulent kinetic energy equation and turbulent kinetic energy dissipation rate equation; Γ_ϕ, S_ϕ and ρ respectively represents generalized diffusion coefficient, generalized source term and air density.

Equation (1) is not closed, so it is necessary to introduce thermodynamic equation to complete state equation of ideal gas:

$$\begin{cases} \rho E = P/(\gamma - 1) + \rho(u^2 + v^2 + w^2)/2 \\ \rho H = \rho E + p \\ p = \rho RT \end{cases} \qquad (2)$$

Where E represents the total energy of unit mass gas, P the gas pressure, γ the gas adiabatic index, u、 v、 w are the velocity components on x、 y、 z axis respectively, and R represents the gas constant, T the air thermodynamics temperature.

2.2 Tunnel - Air - Train Model

Based on the double-line tunnel cross-section which is generally used in high-speed railway of China, the authors establish a tunnel - air - train simulation model. Tunnel cross section shape is shown in Fig.1, and its cross-sectional area is $100\,m^2$. When the length of tunnel is about $1360\,m$, the pressure and speed of train wind will have the most unfavorable influence on tunnel [6]. Therefore, the length of tunnel model was set at $1360\,m$, the length of tunnel inlet external air is $200\,m$, and the scope of tunnel inlet external air is three times as large as the area of tunnel cross-section. Train was idealized simulated and set at three carriages, with a total length of $60\,m$, and the type of train is the China High Speed Train (CHR3). A decrease in train length does not alter the essential physical features of the flow as long as the total length remains above the limit suggested by Copper [7]. And parameters of the train are shown in Table 1. Keep train's flow characteristics when establishing the model, and the model and grid of Train CHR3 are shown in Fig.2. Tunnel and the external air are steady parts, while train and surround air are sliding parts.

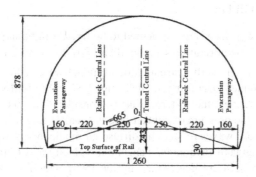

Fig. 1. Contour of double-line tunnel for 300∼350km/h in China

Table 1. Parameters of Train CHR3

Type	Area of Train Cross Section	Length of Train	Width of Train	Height of Train
CRH3	$11.7\,m^2$	$60\,m$	$3.38\,m$	$3.7\,m$

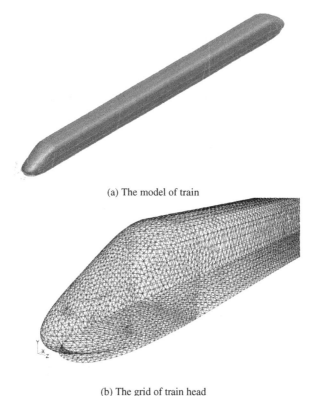

(a) The model of train

(b) The grid of train head

Fig. 2. Model and grid of Train CHR3

2.3   Boundary Conditions

Tunnel walls and train surfaces are considered to be fixed wall boundary surfaces, the normal speed u_n and the normal pressure gradient $\partial p / \partial n$ of air on tunnel walls are equal to zero. There are no eddy currents around tunnel walls, and the roughness of tunnel wall is determined according to the Rough Pipe Wall Model Experiment. Contact Surface of tunnel and external air is considered as the pressure outlet boundary surface, i.e. the pressure of contact face is equal to the initial air pressure, so in this situation pressure waves reflect and diffuse on the boundary surface according to the principle of Riemann Invariants. Tangential Velocity and Entropy of fluid on outflow boundary surfaces are determined by the interpolation of flow field within boundary surfaces, while Tangential Velocity and Entropy of fluid on inflow boundary are determined by free flow field. Make a steady flow field calculation before train running into tunnel and take the convergent flow field as the initial condition of the unsteady flow field. Sliding mesh technology processing has been used in the relative motion of train and tunnel [8].

3   Results and Discussion

3.1   Time-History Variation Rules of Train Wind

In order to study time-history variation rules of train wind, the authors take the 300 m/s condition in Normal Situation as an example for analysis. Two monitoring points are set on the tunnel cross section which is $400\,m$ away from tunnel inlet, and they are respectively on central line of near train evacuation passageway and distant train evacuation passageway and $1.5\,m$ higher than the top of rail. Train wind speed time-history curves in Normal Situation are shown in Fig.3.

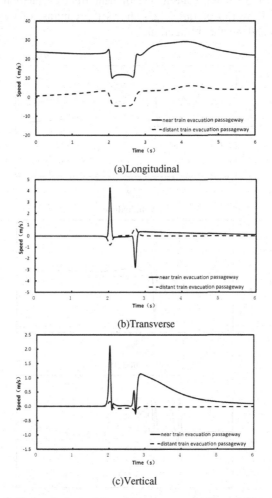

(a)Longitudinal

(b)Transverse

(c)Vertical

Fig. 3. Train wind speed time-history curves in Normal Situation

According to Fig.3: (1) When train head is passing by monitoring points, the speed of longitudinal train wind rises to a maximal value, then quickly drops; when train body is passing by monitoring points, the speed remains nearly unchanged; when train tail is passing by monitoring points, the speed rises again to another maximal value, and piston wind is formed around train tail; (2) When train head and tail are passing by monitoring points, speed of transverse train wind rises rapidly, and directions of transverse train wind are perpendicular to train side wall to left and right; when train body is passing by monitoring points, the speed is nearly equal to zero; (3) Speed of vertical train wind is very small, and direction of vertical train wind is mostly perpendicular to the floor board to upside.

Assuming a train parks in a tunnel $20{\sim}80\,m$ away from the tunnel inlet, the monitoring point is set on the tunnel cross section which is $50\,m$ away from the tunnel inlet, and it is on the central line of near train evacuation passageway and $1.5\,m$ higher than the top of rail. Fig.4 shows the contrast of train wind speed in Normal Situation and Accident Situation.

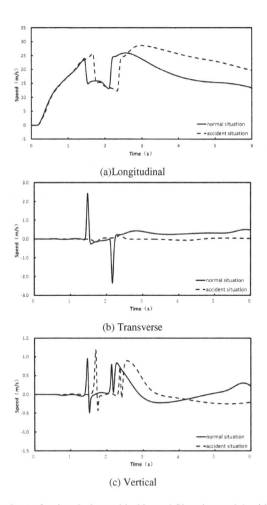

(a)Longitudinal

(b) Transverse

(c) Vertical

Fig. 4. Comparison of train wind speed in Normal Situation and Accident Situation

As Fig.4 shows: (1) Time-history variation rules of train wind in Accident Situation keep nearly unchanged compared with that in Normal Situation; (2) Because of parked train taking up space of tunnel cross section, the speed of longitudinal train wind in Accident Situation is a little higher than that in Normal Situation.

3.2   Space Distribution Characteristics of Train Wind

In order to study space distribution characteristics of train wind, the authors take the $300\,m/s$ condition in Normal Situation as an example for analysis. Monitoring points are set at different mileages along the longitudinal direction of tunnel, they are respectively on central line of near train evacuation passageway and distant train evacuation passageway and $1.5\,m$ higher than the top of rail. The max speeds of longitudinal train wind in Normal Situation are shown in Fig.5.

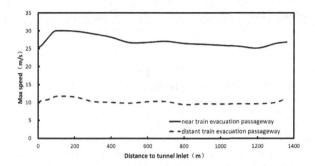

Fig. 5. Maximum speeds of longitudinal train wind at different mileages in Normal Situation

According to Fig.5: (1) The max longitudinal train wind rises to a maximal value near the tunnel inlet, then gradually drops and tends to be stable, but slowly rise near the tunnel outlet; (2) The maximum speed of train wind on near train evacuation is almost 2.6 times as large as that on distant train evacuation.

When a single train runs in tunnel normally (train head is $80\,m$ away from tunnel inlet), which is considered as the Normal Situation. Assuming a train parks in tunnel $50\,m$ away from the tunnel inlet, another train runs by the accident position, which is considered as the Accident Situation. Longitudinal train wind distribution on different height in Normal Situation and Accident Situation are shown in Fig.6.

As can be seen from Fig.6: (1) Variation gradient of longitudinal train wind around train head is large, of which longitudinal distribution range is short, and wind direction is the same as train running direction; (2) Speed of longitudinal train wind on near train evacuation passageway is larger than that of distant train evacuation passageway, and the direction of longitudinal train wind on near train evacuation passageway is the same as train running direction, but that of distant train evacuation passageway is opposite; (3) Variation gradient of longitudinal train wind around train

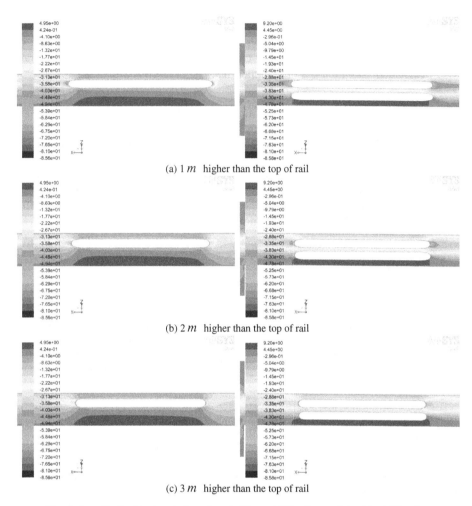

(a) 1 *m* higher than the top of rail

(b) 2 *m* higher than the top of rail

(c) 3 *m* higher than the top of rail

Fig. 6. Longitudinal train wind contour in Normal Situation and Accident Situation

tail is small, of which longitudinal distribution range is long, and the wind direction is the same as train running direction; (4) Longitudinal train wind tends to be unchanged along tunnel vertical; (5) Compared with Normal Situation, the speed of longitudinal train wind around train head and tail in Accident Situation becomes larger, variation gradient becomes smaller, longitudinal distribution range becomes longer. Adverse effect range and time of longitudinal train wind on people becomes larger and longer.

When train moves to tunnel (train head is 80 *m* away from tunnel inlet), transverse train wind distribution characteristics in Normal Situation and Accident Situation are studied. As can be seen from Fig. 7: (1) Due to the crowding-out effect of streamlined train head, air at the front of train flows away from the train head, while air at the rear of train flows to the train tail; (2) The speed of transverse train wind around train body is very low, and the air flow field around train body mainly flows in longitudinal direction; (3) The maximum transverse train wind appears on the surface of train walls, while the minimum transverse train wind appears on the tunnel walls; (4) Compared with Normal Situation, the speed of transverse train wind around train in Accident Situation becomes a little larger.

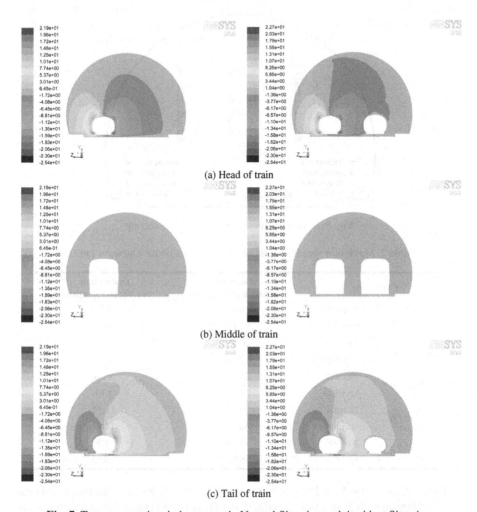

(a) Head of train

(b) Middle of train

(c) Tail of train

Fig. 7. Transverse train wind contours in Normal Situation and Accident Situation

3.3   Analysis of Personnel Safety

Train wind has aerodynamic force on people in high-speed rail tunnel, which changes rapidly with time and space, and it is only about 1 m from the center line of near train evacuation passageway to the train body. Therefore, people on passageways may fall down when a train is running by. In order to understand maximum speeds of train wind on evacuation passageways when train runs through tunnel, eight monitoring points are set on tunnel cross sections at $50\,m$ along tunnel longitudinal, which are respectively $0.5\,m$, $1.0\,m$, $1.5\,m$ and $2.0\,m$ away from the top of rail. As shown in Fig.8. The maximum speeds of train wind on evacuation passageways based on numerical simulation are shown in Table 2.

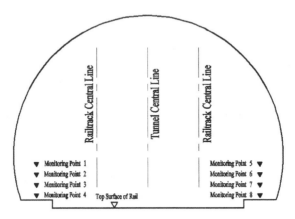

Fig. 8. Monitoring points on tunnel cross-section

Table 2. Maximum speeds of train wind on evacuation passageways (m/s)

Conditions		Near train evacuation passageway	Distant train evacuation passageway
$120\,km/h$	Normal	11.99	3.39
	Accident	12.15	3.88
$200\,km/h$	Normal	20.27	7.85
	Accident	20.68	8.23
$250\,km/h$	Normal	24.17	9.36
	Accident	24.75	9.81
$300\,km/h$	Normal	30.06	11.75
	Accident	30.10	11.91
$350\,km/h$	Normal	35.77	15.88
	Accident	35.81	16.26

There are many kinds of body postures and different angles between people and rail tracks. If human body is precisely simulated, it will cause a too large model and inaccurate results, so human body models haven't been built in this paper. We can calculate aerodynamic force on human body according to train wind by the Formula (3):

$$F = p_w \cdot A_p = \frac{1}{2}\rho v_w^2 A_p \tag{3}$$

Where p_w is pressure of train wind, A_p is stressed area of people and set at $1.02\,m^2$ [9]; ρ is air density and set at $1.225\,kg/m^3$; v_w is speed of train wind.

According to Formula (3), maximum values of air force on people on evacuation passageways are worked out, as shown in Table3.

Table 3. Maximum values of air force on people on evacuation passageways (N)

Conditions		Near train evacuation passageway	Safe or dangerous	Distant train evacuation passageway	Safe or dangerous
120 km/h	Normal	89.81	Safe	7.18	Safe
	Accident	92.23	Safe	9.41	Safe
200 km/h	Normal	256.69	Dangerous	38.50	Safe
	Accident	267.18	Dangerous	42.32	Safe
250 km/h	Normal	364.97	Dangerous	54.73	Safe
	Accident	382.70	Dangerous	60.12	Safe
300 km/h	Normal	564.53	Dangerous	86.25	Safe
	Accident	566.03	Dangerous	88.62	Safe
350 km/h	Normal	799.36	Dangerous	157.55	Dangerous
	Accident	801.15	Dangerous	165.18	Dangerous

Germany and France have put forward $100\,N$ aerodynamic control standard through tank tests, field measurements and so on [10]. China hasn't set this kind of standard, therefore, this paper study personal safety with reference to the control standards of Germany and France.

In Normal Situation and Accident Situation: (1) When the speed of train is $120\,km/h$, and the maximum air force on people who stay on near or distant train evacuation passageways is $92.23\,N$, it is safe; (2) When the speed of train is $200\,km/h$, $250\,km/h$ and $300\,km/h$, and the minimum air force on people who stay on near train evacuation passageway is $256.69\,N$, it is dangerous; while the maximum air force on people who stay on distant train evacuation passageway is $88.62\,N$, it is safe; (3) When the speed of train is $350\,km/h$, and the minimum air force on people who stay on near or distant train evacuation passageways is $157.55\,N$, it is dangerous.

4   Conclusions

The flow of air passed by a simplified high-speed train geometry has been simulated numerically based on the three-dimensional incompressible Navier-Stokes equations and the standard $k-\varepsilon$ turbulence model. Characteristics of the train wind and analysis of personnel safety have been studied as well. Based on the above discussions of results, the following conclusions can be deduced:

(1) Train wind is a complex three-dimensional flow which changes with time and space. The moment train tail runs by people is the most dangerous time, and the evacuation passageway near tunnel inlet is the most dangerous place. People should avoid activities at dangerous time and dangerous places, and guardrails should be installed on the edges of evacuation passageways when necessary.

(2) Maintenance workers should work in tunnel during night time when there is no train running. One line in tunnel is under operation for medium-speed trains during night time, meanwhile, the other line needs maintenance, moving train should slow down to $120\,km/h$ to run through the tunnel, and maintenance workers must stay on distant train evacuation passageway before the train runs by.

(3) Adverse effect range and time of train wind becomes larger and longer when a train is broken down in tunnel. In this situation, to guarantee safety of passengers, moving train should slow down to $120\,km/h$ to run through the tunnel, and passengers must stay in accident train compartments, so they can escape from tunnel when rescue trains arrive to the accident area.

Acknowledgements. This work is financially supported by Natural Science Foundation of China (No. 51008310) and High Speed Railway Basic Research Mutual Funds of China (No. U1134208).

References

1. Lei, M., Zhang, K.: Analysis of maintenance personnel safety in the high-speed railway. Railway Survey and Design (4), 98–101 (2005)
2. Pope, C.W., Johnson, T., Broomhead, S.F.: Aerodynamic and thermal design for the Great Belt Tunnel. In: 6th International Symposium on the Aerodynamics and Ventilation of Vehicle Tunnels, Durham, England, pp. 245–272 (1988)
3. Tian, H.Q.: Research and applications of air pressure pulse from trains passing each other. Journal of Railway Science and Engineering 1(1), 83–89 (2004)
4. Wu, Q.H., Zhou, H.W., Zhu, Y.G.: Research on numerical simulation calculation for high speed train in turbulence field. Journal of the China Railway Society 24(3), 99–103 (2002)
5. Wyczalek, F.A.: Maglev tansit technology in Russia. In: Proceeding of Maglev 13th International Conference on Magnetically-Leviated systems and Linear Runnings, Pairs, pp. 88–93 (1993)
6. Yang, W.C., Peng, L.M., Shi, C.H.: Analysis on the Action Mechanism and the Influencing Factors of the Tunnel Shaft to the Pressure of the Carbody. China Railway Science 30(3), 68–72 (2009)
7. Copper, R.K.: The effect of cross-wind on train. In: Proceedings of Aerodynamics of Transportation, ASMECSME Conference, Niagara, pp. 127–151 (1979)
8. Luo, J.J., Gao, B., Wang, Y.X., Zhao, W.C.: Numerical Simulation of Unsteady Three-Dimensional Flow Induced by High-Speed Train Entering Tunnel with Shaft. Journal of Southwest Jiaotong University 39(4), 442–446 (2004)
9. The State Bureau of Technical Supervision: Human dimensions of Chinese adults (GB10000-88). China Standards Press, Beijing (1988)
10. Xu, H.S., He, D.Z., Wang, H.X.: A Study on the Safe Clearance for Persons from Running Quasi-High-Speed Train. China Railway Science 17(01), 21–31 (1996)

Parallel Computation of Shaped Charge Jet Formation and Penetration by Multi-material Eulerian Method

Tianbao Ma[*], Xiangzhao Xu, and Jianguo Ning

State Key Laboratory of Explosion Science and Technology, Beijing Institute of Technology,
Beijing 100081, China
madabal@bit.edu.cn

Abstract. A parallel version of the PMMIC-3D hydrocode using message passing interface (MPI) standard was developed based on multi-material Eulerian methods which are more suitable for solving elastoplastic hydrodynamics. The data dependence associated with Eulerian methods was investigated for PMMIC-3D parallel hydrocode. By studying the shaped charge jet as useful and practical numerical example, the speedup of the parallel hydrocode was tested with a cluster consisting of 64 cores. Furthermore, the bottlenecks of the parallel hydrocode were analyzed. At last, numerical results of jet formation and penetration show the capability of PMMIC-3D parallel hydrocode in dealing with large scale complex engineering problems.

Keywords: shaped charge jet, Eulerian method, parallel computing, MPI.

1 Introduction

Shaped charge has been widely used in military and civil fields. A shaped charge consists in its simplest form, of an explosive with a conical cavity, lined with metal. With the ignition of explosive a detonation front sweeps the liner causing it to collapse owing to extremely high pressure in gaseous detonation products. The collapse of liner under the high pressures produces a hypervelocity jet, the fastest parts of which can reach typical speeds of 8-12km/s [1]. This hypervelocity jet is used to penetrate targets in both military and industrial applications. It is a complicated physical process for the formation and penetration of shaped charge jet, including explosive detonation, liner deformation, jet formation and elongation, jet moving in the air, jet and detonation products acting on the targets, and so on. Numerical studies for these issues need the hydrocode to treat nonlinear large deformation and multi-material interaction at large scale and long time steps.

Eulerian method is very useful in simulating flows with large distortions such as explosion problems, because it uses a fixed mesh and can eliminate the problems associated with a distorted mesh under Lagrangian method. Based on Eulerian numerical methods, Multi-Material in Cell for 3D (MMIC-3D) hydrocode was

---

[*] Corresponding author.

K. Li et al. (Eds.): ParCFD 2013, CCIS 405, pp. 565–576, 2014.

developed [2]. Owing primarily to the limited processing speed and relatively small size of local memory and storage in single computers, parallel computing has became an indispensable technique for running large-scale simulations, especially in applications such as computing hydrodynamics, bioinformatics and meteorology, where a combination of many millions of grids and many thousands of time steps are involved [3]. Message Passing Interface (MPI) is a library specification for message-passing generally used for parallel computing. It has been adopted by a broad base of vendors and users as the standard for high performance and portability on personal computers, workstations, and almost all parallel machines. In this paper, we developed a parallel version of the MMIC-3D hydrocode using message passing interface (MPI) standard. The Speedup of the hydrocode was tested with a cluster consisting of 64 cores by the numerical examples of shaped charge jet. Furthermore, the bottlenecks of PMMIC-3D parallel hydrocode were analyzed. At last, the numerical example of shape charge jet formation and penetration into steel target was investigated to show the ability of the PMMIC-3D parallel hydrocode in simulating large scale complicated engineering problems.

2   Numerical Method

2.1   Governing Equations

If viscosity and heat conduction are neglected, the Euler equations are obtained which can be written in tensor form as follows [4]:

$$\frac{\partial \rho}{\partial t} + \boldsymbol{u} \cdot \nabla \rho + \rho \nabla \cdot \boldsymbol{u} = 0 \tag{1}$$

$$\frac{\partial \boldsymbol{u}}{\partial t} + \boldsymbol{u} \cdot \nabla \boldsymbol{u} = \frac{1}{\rho} \nabla \cdot \boldsymbol{\sigma} \tag{2}$$

$$\frac{\partial e}{\partial t} + \boldsymbol{u} \cdot \nabla e = \frac{1}{\rho} \nabla \cdot (\boldsymbol{\sigma} \cdot \boldsymbol{u}) \tag{3}$$

where t is time, $\boldsymbol{u}$ is the velocity, $\boldsymbol{\sigma}$ is the Cauchy stress tensor, $\dot{\varepsilon}$ is the strain rate tensor, ρ is the density, and e is the specific internal energy.

The Cauchy stress tensor can be divided into the deviatoric stress and hydrostatic pressure tensor as follows:

$$\boldsymbol{\sigma} = -P\boldsymbol{I} + \boldsymbol{S} \tag{4}$$

where $\boldsymbol{I}$ is the identity tensor, P is the hydrostatic pressure obtained by state equations, and $\boldsymbol{S}$ is the deviatoric stress tensor obtained by constitutive equations.

In the elastic range, the generalization of Hooke's law by the Jaumann rate of Cauchy stress can be written as:

$$\overset{\triangledown}{\boldsymbol{S}} = \dot{\boldsymbol{S}} + \boldsymbol{\Omega} \cdot \boldsymbol{S} - \boldsymbol{S} \cdot \boldsymbol{\Omega} = 2G[\dot{\varepsilon} - (tr\dot{\varepsilon})\boldsymbol{I}] + \boldsymbol{\Omega} \cdot \boldsymbol{S} - \boldsymbol{S} \cdot \boldsymbol{\Omega} \tag{5}$$

where $\dot{\varepsilon}$ is the strain rate tensor and Ω is the spin rate tensor, and they are given by:

$$\dot{\varepsilon} = \frac{1}{2}\left(u\nabla + \nabla u\right) \tag{6}$$

$$\Omega = \frac{1}{2}\left(u\nabla - \nabla u\right) \tag{7}$$

2.2   Operator Splitting Algorithm

All physical quantities including density, specific internal energy, velocity, pressure and deviatoric stress are defined at the center of each grid, while artificial viscosity is defined at the midpoint of grid boundary. The operator splitting method was adopted herein. The governing Eqs. (1-3) can be represented by a general form:

$$\frac{\partial \varphi}{\partial t} + u \cdot \nabla \varphi = H \tag{8}$$

where φ is a solution variable, and H is the source term.

Since the operator splitting method was employed, Eq. (8) can be rewritten as follows:

$$\frac{\partial \varphi}{\partial t} = H \tag{9}$$

$$\frac{\partial \varphi}{\partial t} + u \cdot \nabla \varphi = 0 \tag{10}$$

Eq. (9) and Eq. (10) are called the 'Lagrangian phase' and the 'Eulerian phase', respectively.

In the Lagrangian phase, changes in velocity and internal energy caused by pressure and deviatoric stresses are calculated, and the grid is allowed to distort along with the material. Eq. (9) is updated using a first order finite difference scheme, while the changes in three dimensions are calculated simultaneously by:

$$\tilde{\varphi}^{n+1} = \varphi^n + \frac{\Delta t}{\Delta x}\left(H^n_{i+1/2,j,k} - H^n_{i-1/2,j,k}\right) + \frac{\Delta t}{\Delta y}\left(H^n_{i,j+1/2,k} - H^n_{i,j-1/2,k}\right) + \frac{\Delta t}{\Delta z}\left(H^n_{i,j,k+1/2} - H^n_{i,j,k-1/2}\right) \tag{11}$$

In the Eulerian phase, the transport of mass, internal energy and momentum across the grid edges are calculated, which can be considered as remapping of the displaced grids back to the spatially-fixed Eulerian frame. Although there are many interface reconstruction methods available for the Eulerian phase, such as volume-of-fluid (VOF) methods [5], piecewise linear interface construction (PLIC) methods [6] and level-set methods [7], it is hard to extend these methods to handle multi-material in three dimensional. Thus, we used the fuzzy interface treatment method [2] to dispose the transport of physical quantities. Fuzzy interface treatment can easily dispose mixture grids involving three or more materials in 3D space, and the computational cost is low. While the interface may become fuzzy with the increase of many time-steps, this disadvantage can be overcame with parallel computing by increasing the amount of grids and reducing the corresponding grid size.

2.3   Parallel Algorithm

Domain decomposition method is sub-divided into overlapping and non-overlapping method, as one processor disposes one or multi-subdomains. The non-overlapping method is typically employed in models that use implicit and semi-implicit numerical schemes. Numerical algorithms of these models lead to the necessity of solving a system of linear equations with large sparse matrix, which is split into sub-matrices corresponding to subdomains, making parallel realization relatively complex [8]. The overlapping method is used in PMMIC-3D parallel hydrocode. An example of splitting the two-dimensional computational domains into 4 subdomains and their overlapping is shown in Fig. 1. The gray grids are referred to boundary ghost grids of subdomain.

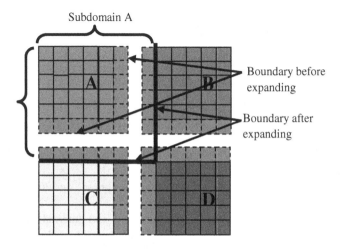

Fig. 1. Two-dimensional subdomains and overlapping

The key issue of parallel algorithm for multi-material Eulerian methods is data dependence analysis, which generally appears on the Eulerian phase. Fuzzy interface method uses 'direction splitting' transport, and the transport of three directions proceeds under a triple loop. Current grid parameters update depending on the surrounding related grid parameters which have been updated, and they affect the surrounding grid parameters update. Therefore, data dependence appears and it affects the whole calculation domain. To eliminate data dependence in transport algorithm of PMMIC-3D, quantities of transport were calculated using original values, but this will reduce calculation precision. To maintain precision, the transport of three directions under a triple loop was changed into three triple loops, and the related variables of all grids were updated after one complete direction transport. The pseudo-code is shown in Table 1, where Keb, Kee, Jeb, Jee, Ieb and Iee are beginning and ending of loops.

Table 1. Pseudo-code of transport

Sequential Code	Parallel Code
	do k=Keb, Kee
	do j=Jeb, Jee
	do i=Ieb, Iee
	x-direction transport
	enddo
	update variables
do k=Keb, Kee	do k=Keb, Kee
do j=Jeb, Jee	do j=Jeb, Jee
do i=Ieb, Iee	do i=Ieb, Iee
x-direction transport	y-direction transport
y-direction transport	enddo
z-direction transport	**update variable**
enddo	do k=Keb, Kee
	do j=Jeb, Jee
	do i=Ieb, Iee
	z-direction transport
	enddo
	update variable

3   Numerical Tests of Shaped Charge Jet Formation and Penetration into Targets

The geometric model of numerical example is shown in Fig. 2. The conical angle of the liner was 60°, and the liner thickness was 2.4 mm. The charge height was 33.2 mm, with a diameter of 60.0 mm [1].

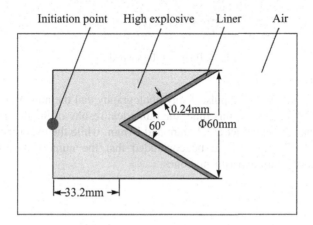

Fig. 2. The geometric model of numerical example

In the simulation, the explosive was composition B, the metal was No.45 steel and the air was treated as an ideal gas. Point initiation was chosen as way of initiation and a simple combustion model was used to simulate the propagation of detonation wave.

Four numerical examples were designed according to grid step. The grid steps were 1.0mm, 0.6mm, 0.4mm and 0.3mm, respectively. The corresponding grid numbers were 80×80×180, 151×151×300, 227×227×480 and 301×301×600, respectively.

Pulse X-ray photography can be used to record fast changing processes occurring in the interior of opaque objects, thus it is widely used to study explosion process. Fig.3 showed the image of the shaped charge, which was placed in an experimental shelter. Two channels of pulse X-ray systems were equipped to take images of the jet at two different times, as shown in Fig.4. In order to improve the accuracy, the experiment was repeated three times, and an average value was applied.

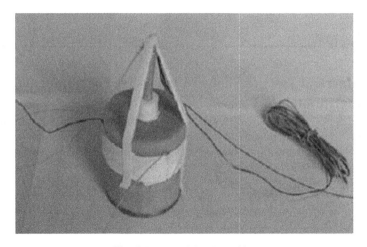

Fig. 3. Image of the shaped jet

The pictures taken with the pulse X-ray photography and the numerical results are shown in Fig.5 at 41.2μs. At this time, the numerical results of the diameter and the length of the shaped charge jet are 4.5mm and 81mm, while the experimental results are 4.2mm and 77.5mm. It can be concluded that the numerical results are in approximate accord with experimental ones.

Fig. 4. Pulse X-ray systems

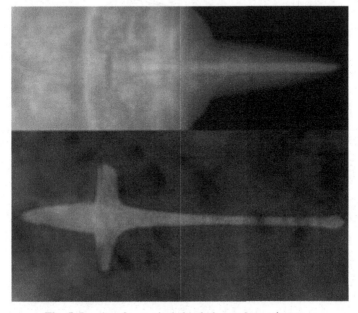

Fig. 5. Results of numerical simulation and experiment

The velocity distribution of jet tip versus time among the four examples is presented in Fig. 6, which indicates that the maximum velocity of the jet tip increases slightly with increasing number of grids. Moreover, the velocity distributions of the four examples are 4000m/s, 4400m/s, 4500m/s and 4700m/s, respectively. Consequently, the numerical results are more accurate with the decreasing of grid step.

Speedup refers to the speed improvement of a parallelized algorithm over the corresponding sequential algorithm, which is defined as:

$$S_n = \frac{T_1}{T_n} \tag{12}$$

where T_1 is the execution time using a single processor and T_n is the execution time of the parallelized code using n processors. If the parallelization is perfect, the speedup should be linear. In reality, linear speedup is limited by factors such as communication between processors, synchronization, and file input/output (I/O). The speedup of the 4th example versus the number of processes is shown in Fig. 7. It shows that the speedup increases as the efficiency decreases when a lager number of processors are used. The speedup of girds 301×301×600 is 19.6 when 64 processors are used.

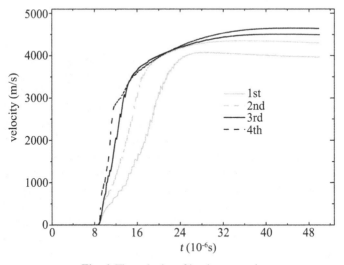

Fig. 6. The velocity of jet tip versus time

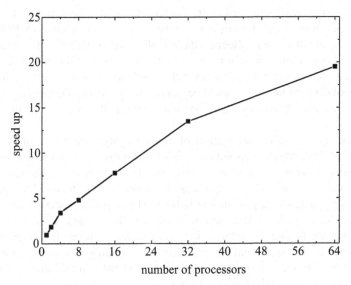

Fig. 7. The speedup versus the number of processors

The scalability of parallel algorithms strongly depends on the communication time. The percentage of communication time to the total computing time for the 4th example (grids 301×301×600) is shown in Fig. 8. When the number of processors exceeds 8, the percent communication time increases rapidly as the communications between processors are completed via network. It is 2.55% using 8 processors, and 48.53% with 64 processors.

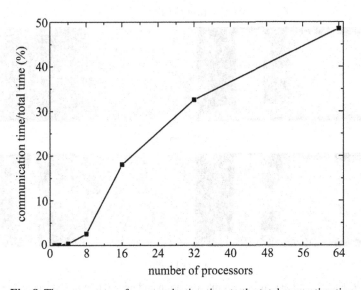

Fig. 8. The percentage of communication time to the total computing time

There are three reasons for scalability bottleneck. Firstly, the variables for volume, mass, velocity, moment and energy are updated in the sub-module of PMMIC-3D hydrocode, where they can influence the variables being updated in the next sub-module, such that communication is crucial and occurs very frequently. Secondly, the cluster nodes are linked by a gigabit network, which has an actual speed of just 35-45 Mb/s. The switch and network should be improved to enhance performance. Thirdly, before the disturbance arrives, there are many idle grids when using the Eulerian method.

Based on the numerical simulation of shaped charge jet formation, the whole process of jet formation and penetration into steel target was numerical simulated. The thickness of the steel target was 35mm, and the distance of the shaped charge to the target was 100mm. The computational region was 120mm×120mm×288mm, which was discretized by a grid step of 0.4mm. The physical processes are shown in Fig.9, which clearly shows the motion of the jet, the jet and detonation products acting on the targets, and the deformation of the target. At time of 35.93μs, the tip of the jet reaches to the target, and the tip velocity is 4794m/s. The jet perforates to the target at 57.39μs, and its tip velocity decreases to 3480m/s. At this time, the diameter of the perforation hole on the target is 14mm.

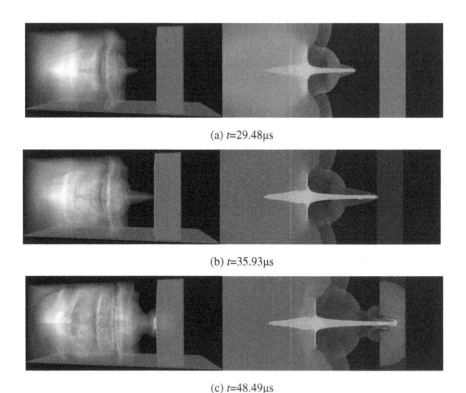

(a) t=29.48μs

(b) t=35.93μs

(c) t=48.49μs

Fig. 9. The 3D and 2D images for the formation and penetration of shaped charge jet.

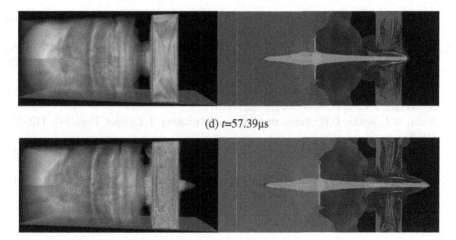

(d) t=57.39μs

(e) t=65.78μs

Fig. 9. (*Continued*)

4   Conclusions

In this study, we investigated the data dependence in designing parallel algorithm using multi-material Eulerian methods. The results indicate that frequent communication between processors and the inherent network limitations contribute to the high communication overhead. Further, hydrocode optimization and communication improvement need to be implemented to improve parallel performance.

The numerical results of shaped charge jet tests reveal that the calculation accuracy increases with decreasing grid step for the PMMIC-3D hydrocode. Although the scalability of PMMIC-3D needs to be improved, we have demonstrated that the parallel algorithm can accelerate calculation and enlarge the computation scale by the numerical example of shaped charge formation and penetration, which make it potentially useful in many engineering applications for explosion and impact problems.

Acknowledgments. This work was supported by National Basic Research Program of China (Grant No. 2010CB832706), the National Natural Science Foundation of China (Grant No. 11172041), and Project of State Key Laboratory of Explosion Science and Technology (Beijing Institute of Technology, Grant No. YBKT14-03).

References

1. Ma, T.B., Wang, C., Ning, J.G.: Numerical study on the shaped charges. International Journal of Modern Physics B 22(31-32), 5749–5754 (2008)
2. Ning, J.G., Chen, L.W.: Fuzzy interface treatment in Eulerian method. Sci. China Ser. E 47, 550–568 (2004)

3. Dongarra, J., Fox, G., Kennedy, K., Torczon, L., Gropp, W.: The Sourcebook of Parallel Computing. Morgan Kaufmann Press (2002)
4. Ma, T.B., Wang, C., Ning, J.G.: Multi-material Eulerian formulations and hydrocode for the simulation of explosions. CMES: Computer Modeling in Engineering and Sciences 33(2), 155–178 (2008)
5. Hirt, C.W., Nichols, B.D.: Volume of fluid method (VOF) for the dynamics of free boundaries. J. Comput. Phys. 39, 201–225 (1981)
6. Rider, W.J., Kothe, D.B.: Reconstructing volume tracking. J. Comput. Phys. 141, 112–152 (1998)
7. Osher, S., Fedkiw, R.: Level Set Methods and Dynamic Implicit Interfaces. Springer, New York (2003)
8. Nesterov, O.: A simple parallelization technique with MPI for ocean circulation models. Parrellel Distrib. Comput. 70, 35–44 (2010)

Calculation of Guide Cone Wall Temperature of Concentric Canister Launcher with Considering Gas Radiation

Xiaolei Hu, Guigao Le, and Dawei Ma

School of Mechanical Engineering, Nanjing University of Science and Technology,
Nanjing 210094, Jiangsu
China,hu0423@126.com

Abstract. To study the thermo-impact of combustion gat jet on guide cone of concentric canister launcher (CCL), dynamic layering method and radiation heat transfer were adopted to simulate fluid-solid coupling heat exchange model between the combustion gas jet and CCL during missile launch. The radiative heat transfer term in energy equation is simulated by Discrete Ordinates (DO) Radiation Model. The flow structure and temperature distribution are obtained. It has been shown that temperature of launcher with radiation heat transfer is higher than without. The guide cone wall temperature is connected with the wall thickness. While the thickness is beyond 20 mm, the guide cone wall temperature changes with no difference. The calculation of gas jet thermo-impact is conformed to related experiment results.

Keywords: numerical simulation, temperature distribution, gas radiation, guide cone.

1 Introduction

CCL (concentric canister launcher) launch technology has the advantages of simple mechanism, high reliability, radar asynchronous and comprehensive emission. It is widely used in ship-borne missile vertical launch system [1]. Guide cone is one of important part in launch system. Its role is to inherit the gas jet impact and ablation, and guide the high temperature and velocity gas jet to the space where is benefit to launch. As the application of composite propellant with high energy, scour and ablation of CCL guide cone, which come from the gas jet, have become increasing important issues. The strength and stiffness of thin wall materials, which are used in concentric cylinder diversion cone shell structure of, decrease obviously under the gas jet thermal impact. This decline will lead guide cone to ablation and fracture, which may cause mission security problem. So it needs to study the thermal-impact of guide cone and provide a theoretical basis for thermal protection.

There are lots of theoretical experiment researches about the thermal-impact of CCL. The temperature and pressure distribution of CCL had been studied by Yagla by the finite difference method and experiment [1]. Jiang Yi studied the methods to reduce the CCL heating effect by installing guide device and changing the rail size

K. Li et al. (Eds.): ParCFD 2013, CCIS 405, pp. 577–588, 2014.
© Springer-Verlag Berlin Heidelberg 2014

[2]. Ma Yanli studied the influence of spacing of inner cylinder of CCL to guide cone by simulation and experiment [3]. Lin Cuilang researched the guide cone distribution by fluid-solid coupled method [4]. These researches did not consider high temperature radiation heat transfer influence of gas jet act on the wall of CCL. For the CCL launch, whether the radiation of high velocity gas jet can be neglected is our research aim.

In present paper Discrete Ordinates algorithm was used to solve the source item of radiative heat transfer equation, while dynamic layering method was used to simulate the missile moving. The fluid-solid coupled method was established to achieve the coupled solving of fluid and solid zone.

2   Numerical Method and Physical Models

2.1   Numerical Method

As the gas jet flow field containing turbulence heat transfer and radiation heat transfer, the temperature and heat flux couldnot be predicted. So the fluid-solid coupling heat transfer should be used [5].

The energy equation for solving the fluid-solid coupling heat transfer as follows:

$$\frac{\partial}{\partial t}(\rho E) + \nabla \bullet (\upsilon(\rho E + p)) = \nabla \bullet (k_{eff} \nabla T) + S_h \tag{1}$$

where k_{eff} is effective thermal conductivity. The right two items of equation (1) is for energy transfer caused by heat conduction and radiation.

The way of heat transfer in solid was given priority to thermal conductivity. At the same time, we should consider radiation heat transfer influence. The solve equation as follows:

$$\frac{\partial}{\partial t}(\rho h) + \nabla \bullet (\upsilon \rho h) = \nabla \bullet (k \nabla T) + S_h \tag{2}$$

where ρ is density, h his enthalpy, k is heat conductivity, T is temperature, S_h is heat source caused by radiation.

The heat source-S_h caused by radiation in equation (1) and equation (2) was solved by radiation equation as follows:

$$\frac{dI(\mathbf{r},\mathbf{s})}{ds} + (a + \sigma_s)I(\mathbf{r},\mathbf{s}) = an^2 \frac{\sigma T^4}{\pi} + \frac{\sigma_s}{4\pi} \int_0^{4\pi} I(\mathbf{r},\mathbf{s}')\phi(\mathbf{s},\mathbf{s}')d\Omega' \tag{3}$$

where $\mathbf{r}$ is position vector, $\mathbf{s}$ is director vector, s' is scattering direction, a is absorbing coefficient, n is refraction coefficient, σ is Stefan-Boltzmann constant (6.672×10^{-8}W/m^2·K^4), I is radiation intensity, T is local temperature, Φ is phase function, Ω' is space solid angle.

The above equations were transformed into space coordinates of the radiation intensity of transport equation based on Discrete Ordinates (DO) Radiation Model.

The number of vector s was equal to the number of transport equation. The method of solving equation was similar to the method of solving fluid equation. Thus, the equation could be expressed as

$$\nabla[I(\mathbf{r},\mathbf{s})\mathbf{s}] + (a + \sigma_s)I(\mathbf{r},\mathbf{s}) = an^2 \frac{\sigma T^4}{\pi} + \frac{\sigma_s}{\pi} \int_0^{4\pi} I(r,s')\phi(s,s')d\Omega' \tag{4}$$

While solving the above equation, the four quadrants each was divided into two quadrants, and the zenith angle and circumference each divided into two equal parts. There were eight spatial positions. Without considering the gas solid particles in scattering, gaseous absorption coefficient used the weighted sum of gray gases model (WSGGM). This model considered mixed gas as a single gas. The absorption coefficient distribution function calculated by mixed gas absorption coefficient was equal to the sum of various components of the gas absorption coefficient. The calculation did not consider scattering. The scattering coefficient set to zero.

According to the fluid-solid coupling heat transfer calculation method, the fluid area and solid area used different control equation. In order to realize the different areas of real-time data exchange, fluid region and solid region in the coupling surface must satisfy the continuity boundary conditions, that was coupling surface temperature equal; heat flow density was given as

$$T_w\big|_{fluid} = T\big|_{solid} \tag{5}$$

$$k_{solid} \frac{\partial T}{\partial n}\Big|_{solid} = k_{fluid} \frac{\partial T}{\partial n}\Big|_{fluid} \tag{6}$$

The fluid-solid coupling heat transfer calculation of solving steps was
1) Assumed coupling boundary on the temperature distribution, it can be gotten heat flow density of fluid coupling boundary from solving the fluid field.
2) Applying equation (6) and assigning the heat flow density to solid coupling boundary, it can be gotten the new temperature distribution of coupled boundary by solving solid thermal conductivity equation.
3) Using equation (1) and assigning temperature of solid coupling boundary to a fluid domain, repeating step (1) ~ (3) and iterating until the convergence.

2.2   Dynamic Layering Method

According to the missile movement characteristics, we chose the dynamic layering method to realize the calculation domain moving. Using Hooke's law, the force on a node could be written as

$$\mathbf{F}_i = \sum_j^{n_i} k_{ij}(\Delta \mathbf{x}_j - \Delta \mathbf{x}_i) \tag{7}$$

where Δx_i and Δx_j are the displacements of node i and its neighbor j, n_i is the number of neighboring nodes connected to node i, and k_{ij} is the spring constant (or stiffness) between node i and its neighbor j is defined as

$$k_{ij} = \frac{1}{\sqrt{|\mathbf{x}_i - \mathbf{x}_j|}} \tag{8}$$

$$\Delta_{i\mathbf{x}}^{m+1} = \frac{\sum_{j}^{n_i} k_{ij}\Delta\mathbf{x}_j^m}{\sum_{j}^{n_i} k_j} \mathbf{v} \tag{9}$$

At equilibrium, the net force on a node due to all the springs connected to the node must be zero. This condition results in an iterative equation was such that

$$\Delta_{i\mathbf{x}}^{m+1} = \frac{\sum_{j}^{n_i} k_{ij}\Delta\mathbf{x}_j^m}{\sum_{j}^{n_i} k_j} \mathbf{v} \tag{9}$$

Since displacements were known at the boundaries (after boundary node positions have been updated), Equation (9) was solved using a Jacobi sweep on all interior nodes. At convergence, the positions were updated such that

$$\mathbf{x}_i^{n+1} = \mathbf{x}_i^n + \Delta\mathbf{x}_i^m \mathbf{v} \tag{10}$$

where n+1 and n are used to denote the positions at the next time step and the current time step, respectively.

If the cells are expanding, their cell heights are allowed to increase until h> (1+ah) h_{ideal}, the cells are split based on the specified layering option: constant height or constant ratio. Where h is the minimum cell height, h_{ideal} is the ideal cell height, and ah is the layer split factor.

2.3   Physical Model

Concentric cylinder launcher is consisting of cap, inner tube and outer tube as shown in figure 1. When the missile engine overcome its gravity and locking force, the gas jet of high temperature, high pressure and high speed exhausted by solid rocket engine impact to cap and bend over $180°$ into the annular space between the cylinder.

Based on the characteristic of two-dimensional symmetry, the mesh diagram of nozzle exit was showed in figure 2.

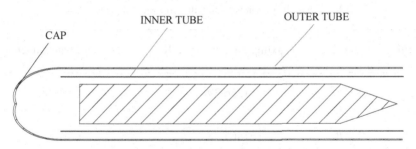

Fig. 1. Schematic of the CCL launcher

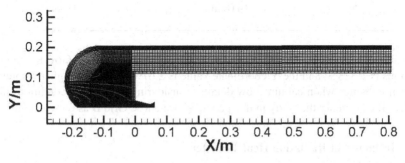

Fig. 2. Mesh diagram of nozzle exit

This article selects the titanium alloy material, which is widely used in aerospace, as the solid material. Material physical parameters include material density, specific heat ratio, thermal conductivity, and emissivity. Here we do not consider the temperature impacting the material thermal physical properties. So we take Ti-6Al-4V in 1200K as titanium alloy material properties, which is shown in table 1.

Table 1. Ti-6Al-4V titanium alloy material properties

Density/(kg/m³)	specific heat ratio /(J/kg·K)	emissivity
4.4	544.25	0.78

The nozzle inlet uses pressure inlet boundary. The pressure of combustion chamber was 9 MPa and gas temperature T was 3190 K.

3   Numerical Method and Physical Models

3.1   Model Examination

Due to the gas jet action time was short when missile launching, the accuracy of fluid-structure coupling temperature calculation depends on grid density. Therefore, it was important to exam the model's validation. In order to select appropriate calculation mesh, we chose three kinds of grid number in this paper to validate which were 683.8 million (grid A), 1.0227 billion (grid B), 1.3569 billion (grid C).We compared peak temperature of the cap and its position at 5 ms . The results of comparison were shown in table 2.

Table 2. Results of comparison with three kind of grids at 5ms

Grid	Number	Maximum temperature/K	Y coordinate value/m
A	68380	1256.39	0.0135
B	102270	1465.78	0.0182
C	135690	1418.56	0.0187

As shown in Table 2, the difference of peak temperature between Grid B and Grid C at 5 ms is 3.328%, and the Y coordinate value is 2.67%. Although higher resolution grid can be better when capture flow details, considering calculation condition limit, the Grid B can satisfy the study in this paper. So we chose Grid B as our calculation.

3.2   Influence of Radiation Heat Transfer

To study whether the radiative influence CCL cap temperature when the missile launch, we chose the 15 *mm* thickness of cap, established the models with/without radiation heat transfer and computed the temperature and heat flux of CCL cap. The calculation results were shown in figure 3 and figure 4.

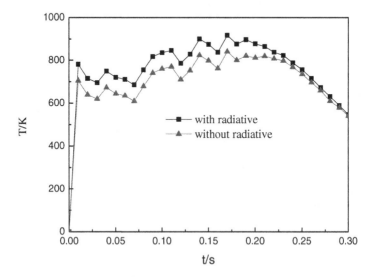

Fig. 3. Temperature change of CCL cap depending on time

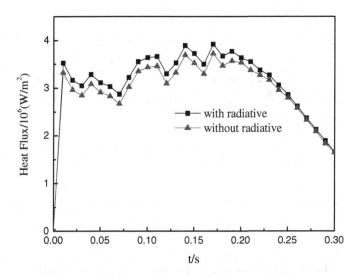

Fig. 4. Heat flux change of CCL cap depending on time

As shown in Figure 3 and Figure 4, we can see the radiative influence the temperature of CCL cap before 0.25 s which was time that all the missile body get out of the tube. After 0.25 s, there was no difference between with/without radiative. This is because the missile nozzle is near the cap, temperature is higher than 2500 K, and the jet can not be ruled out of tube fluently before 0.25 s. During this time, the function of radiation heat transfer is greater than convection heat transfer. The temperature difference between them is 80 K and the maximum heat flux difference is 2×10^6 W/m^2.Also the atmosphere has little impact on the cap. After 0.25 s, as the gas jet ruled out of tube, the pressure in tube is lower than atmosphere, the air is sucked into tube. During that time, the function of radiation heat transfer is greater than convection heat transfer.

3.3   Influence of Different Wall Thickness

In order to study the thermal impact influence of different wall thickness to the CCL cap wall, we chose four cases: 10 mm, 15 mm, 20 mm and 30 mm.

Figure 5 is the temperature changes depending on different cap thickness. From figure 5 we can see that temperature changes are relatively obvious when the wall thickness increased from 10 mm to 15 mm. The maximum temperature difference is 180 K. When the wall thickness increased from 15 mm to 20 mm, the largest temperature difference is 52 K. When the wall thickness increased from 20 mm to 30 mm, temperature change is not obvious. This is because the time that gas jet act on cap is very short.

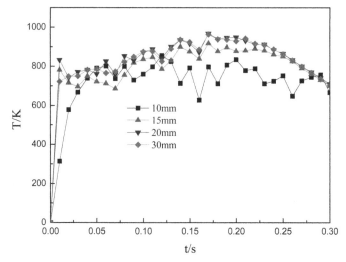

Fig. 5. Temperature changes depending on different cap thickness

Figure 6 is cap temperature distribution at different time with 15 mm thickness. From the chart, we can see the highest temperature of the cap area focus on the area below engine nozzle. This is because the exhausted gas is high under expanded. The area below engine nozzle is the gas jet core region which is mostly directly impacted. So it is the highest temperature.

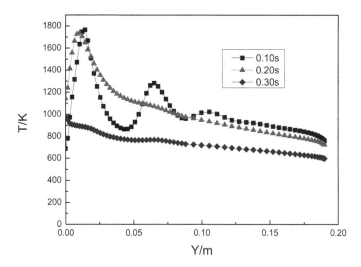

Fig. 6. Cap temperature distribution at different time with 15mm thickness

Figure 6 is temperature field cloud at different time with 15mm thickness. Figure 7 is velocity vector diagram near cap at 0.2 s with 15mm. Figure 7 is Velocity vector diagram near gas cavity at 0.2 s with 15 mm. From the pictures, we can see that the cap guided the gas jet both directions when the jet meets the guide cone. The cap and inner tube are mostly directly impacted. As the missile moved out of tube, the air near tube is drawn back to tube. Both the air and gas mixed in the tube flowed into the cap zone, which leaded to the cap temperature down. From all missiles launching process, we can see the guide cone is always in high temperature. This phenomenon is satisfying with the experiment results [3]. So it is needed to take thermal protection to the guide cap.

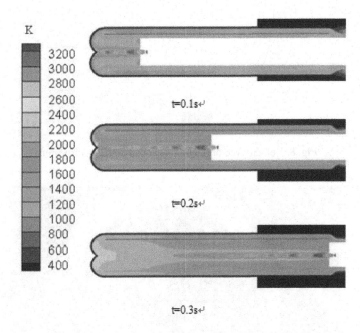

Fig. 7. Temperature field cloud at different time with 15mm thickness

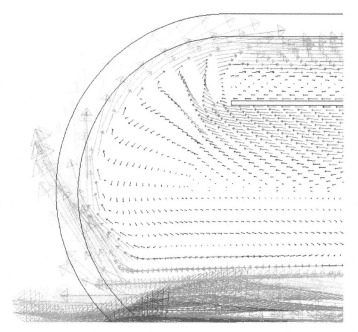

Fig. 8. Velocity vector diagram near cap at 0.2s with 15mm

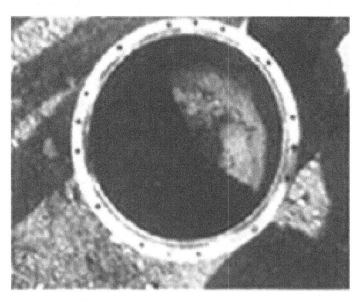

Fig. 9. Ablation of cap with experiment

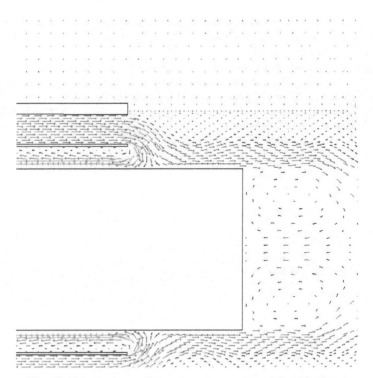

Fig. 10. Velocity vector diagram near gas cavity at 0.2s with 15mm

4   Conclusions

1）The Discrete Ordinates(DO) Radiation Model can use in CCL fluid-solid-heat coupling simulation. Wall temperature with radiative is 180 K higher than without, and heat flux difference is 2×10^6 W/m^2 higher than no radiative.

2）When the cap wall thickness increased from 10 mm to 20 mm, the temperature changed obviously. Exceed 20 mm, the temperature did change significantly.

3）From simulation and experiment results ,we can see the guide cone of cap is mostly directly impacted. It is needed to take thermal protection to the guide cap.

References

1. Yagla, J.J.: Concentric Canister Launcher. Naval Engineer Journal 1, 313–330 (1997)
2. Yi, J., Jiguang, H., Qun, L.: Improvement Measures of Exhausting the Jet in the Concentric Vertical Launching Equipment. Transactions of Beijing Institute of Technology 27, 95–99 (2007)
3. Yanli, M., Yi, J., Weicheng, W.: Study on the impact effect of solid racket motor exhaust plume to the launching platform. Journal of Solid Rocket Technology 34, 140–145 (2011)

4. Cuilang, L., Shihua, B.: Numerical Simulation of Thermal Effect of Missile Combustion-gas Flow for Concentric Canister Launcher. Journal of Projectiles, Rockets, Missiles and Guidance 28, 193–195 (2008)
5. Wenqun, T.: Numerical heat transfer. Jiaotong University Press, Xi'an (2001)
6. Chiwang, S., Osher, S.: Efficient implementation of essentially non-oscillatory shock capturing schemes. Journal of Computational Physics 83, 32–78 (1989)
7. Yi, J., Jiguang, H., Debin, F.: 3D Unsteady Numerical Simulation of Missile Launching. Acta Armamentar 8, 911–915 (2008)

Numerical Optimization of Structural Parameters on GQ-108C Air Reverse Circulation DTH Hammer Bit

Zhiqiang Zhao[1], Lijia Li[1], Xiangtian Huan[2], and Kun Bo[1,*]

[1] College of Construction Engineering, Jilin University, XiMinZhu. 938,
130021 Changchn, China
zzqhn@qq.com, luoyongjiang2008@126.com, bokun@jlu.edu.cn
[2] Beijing Vibroflotation Engineering Co., LTD, WangJingXiYuan. 221,
100102 Beijing, China
dhxt486486@163.com

Abstract. In order to solve the problem that cuttings running out through the annular space between the drill pipe and borehole wall in Reverse Circulation drilling with Down-The-Hole (DTH) hammer, the ejector theory and orthogonal test design as well as Engineering Fluidic Dynamics (EFD) technology were utilized to optimize the structural parameters of the reverse circulation drill bit, including: the diffuser slot depth(H), the diffusion angle (β)of diffuser slot, the diameter of inner injection nozzle (d) ,inclination angle of inner injection nozzle (θ) and the number of suction nozzles (N) of the internal orifice. Research has shown that the H=20mm, β=10°, d=7mm, θ=25°, N=3 is the best configuration when air consumption is 12m^3/min.

Keywords: DTH hammer bit, air reverse circulation, numerical optimization, EFD.

1   Introduction

With the developing of Chinese social and economic, the demands of resources is increasing fastly. Since the past few decades, we have continued exploration of the mineral resources in the eastern region and economically developed areas of China and the total amount of resources have almost been exhausted in these areas. So exploration mineral in the west of China where is arid is particularly important. Because of shortage water, the conventional rope core drilling technology is not suitable drilling in the west of China, and air drilling technology become get extensive application in exploration mineral in these area[1-3].

In the early of 1990s, reverse circulation central sampling technology(RC) had been introduced from abroad, but the technology introduced from abroad can only get powder sample that maybe cause cross-contamination and also need huge drilling rig and complex system and the expensive price. In order to solve the weakness of RC, Run-Through Reverse Circulation DTH Technique which allows grasp the formation

---

* Corresponding author.

K. Li et al. (Eds.): ParCFD 2013, CCIS 405, pp. 589–601, 2014.

variation through observing lithology changes real-time was developed in the 1990s by College of Construction Engineering , Jilin University. And its core recovery rate can get to 95%.

The reverse circulation bit is the more key component in this technique. To achieve suction air from the space formed with the drill pipe and borehole wall and a better reverse circulation, we have used orthogonal design to optimize the structural parameters of the reverse circulation bit. Run-Through reverse circulation continuous coring drilling technology can real-time observation of the surface stratigraphic changes, core recovery can also be more than 98% [4,5]. And all this with performs of the reverse circulation drill closely related to this article through to optimize the structural parameters of the hammer bit to obtain the best air reverse circulation affect, and improve the rock dust collection rate.

2   Gas Ejector Theory and Principle of Run-Through Reverse Circulation of DTH Technique

2.1   Gas Ejector Theory

Ejector has been widely used in chemical, military and other fields. Gas ejector utilize the turbulent diffusion of high-speed jet to bring of two different pressure fluid mixed and exchange energy with each other.

The structure of gas ejector includes: nozzle, receiving room, mixing chamber and diffuser chamber. Its working principle is shown in Fig.1. Ejected flow is entrainment into mixing chamber under the shear force formed by the eject flow which ejected from the nozzle with high-speed and mixing and exchange energy with each other [6-8].

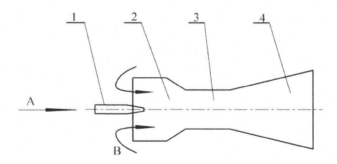

1: nozzle ; 2: receiving room ; 3: mixing chamber ; 4: diffuser chamber
A: eject flow with high pressure ; B: ejected flow with lower pressure

Fig. 1. Schematic diagram of gas ejector

2.2   Principle of Run-Through Reverse Circulation of DTH Technique

Limited to the particularity of the size and function of the drill structure, we can't use the ejector structure directly, but the ejector principle can be applied to the design of reverse circulation hammer bit. The structure of the GQ-108C DTH reverse circulation drill bit was shown in Fig.2.

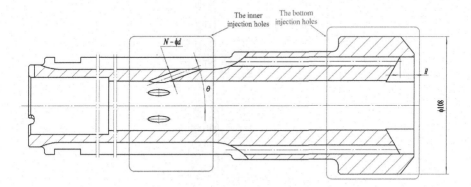

Fig. 2. Structure of GQ-108C air reverse hammer bit

The Fig.3. has shown the principle of run-through reverse circulation of DTH technique. Compressed air with high-speed is discharge through the vent hole at the bottom of the bit after driving the DTH hammer and formation of a low pressure area near the vents, produce a suction effect on the surrounding medium due to the pressure difference. Airflow and pumped media pumped into the center through-hole of the bit through the diffuser slot after reflection by the rock bottom of the hole. The high-speed fluid carries cores, cuttings and pore fluid into the central channel of the drill pipe with the reduction of the flow rate increased pressure and discharge outside the drill hole by dual-channel gas faucet and gooseneck elbow.

2.3   The Optimized Structure Parameters of the Air Hammer Drill Bit

The structure parameters of the reverse circulation bit including: the diffuser slot depth(H), the diffusion angle (β)of diffuser slot, the diameter of inner injection nozzle (d), inclination angle of inner injection nozzle(θ) and the number of suction nozzles (N) of the internal orifice. All structure parameters are shown in Fig.2.and Fig.4.

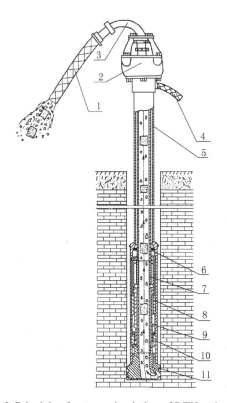

Fig. 3. Principle of reverse circulation of DTH technique

1: discharge pipe ; 2: dual-channel gas faucet ; 3: gooseneck elbow ; 4: air inlet pipe ;
5: dual-wall drill pipe ; 6: check valve ; 7: core tube ; 8: inner cylinder ; 9: piston ; 10: bush ;
11: reverse hammer bit

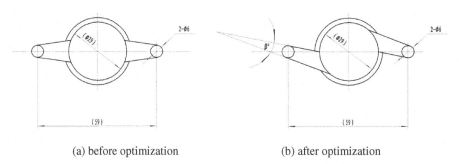

(a) before optimization   (b) after optimization

Fig. 4. Hammer bit bottom lip surface contour shape

3   EFD Simulation

3.1   Mathematical Model

The fluid flow is dominated by the physical law of conservation of basic conservation law: the law of conservation of mass, the conservation of momentum, the law of conservation of energy[9].

The law of conservation of mass :

$$\frac{\partial \rho}{\partial t} + \mathrm{div}(\rho \boldsymbol{u}) = 0 \tag{1}$$

The conservation of momentum :

$$\frac{\partial(\rho u)}{\partial t} + \mathrm{div}(\rho u \boldsymbol{u}) = \mathrm{div}\left(\mu \mathrm{grad} u\right) - \frac{\partial p}{\partial x} + S_u \tag{2}$$

$$\frac{\partial(\rho v)}{\partial t} + \mathrm{div}(\rho v \boldsymbol{u}) = \mathrm{div}\left(\mu \mathrm{grad} v\right) - \frac{\partial p}{\partial y} + S_v \tag{3}$$

$$\frac{\partial(\rho w)}{\partial t} + \mathrm{div}(\rho w \boldsymbol{u}) = \mathrm{div}\left(\mu \mathrm{grad} v\right) - \frac{\partial p}{\partial z} + S_w \tag{4}$$

The law of conservation of energy :

$$\frac{\partial(\rho T)}{\partial t} + \mathrm{div}(\rho \boldsymbol{u} T) = \mathrm{div}\left(\frac{k}{c_p} \mathrm{grad} T\right) + S_T \tag{5}$$

div: divergence ; $\boldsymbol{u}$: velocity vector ; u: the velocity vector of the x-direction; v: the velocity vector of the y-direction, w: the velocity vector of the z-direction ; ρ: fluid density ; μ: dynamic viscosity ; p: pressure ; k: heat transfer coefficient ; c_p: specific heat capacity ; S_u, S_v, S_w is Momentum conservation equation generalized source term[10].

3.2   EFD Model

We use the 3D CAD software Solidworks to model the internal fluid flow region of the hammer bit. To meet the calculation accuracy, the number of EFD model grid control between 30million to 40 million(as shown in Fig.5.).

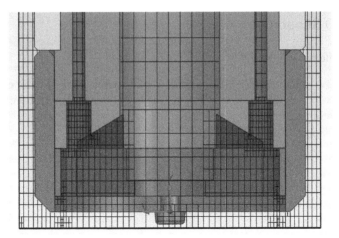

Fig. 5. The meshing grids of the bottom of reverse circulation bit

3.3   EFD Simulation

A three-dimensional model of the reverse circulation bit was established by utilizing the Solidworks, and the eventual theory value would be obtained by the optimized analysis of the bit corresponding to the EFD simulation technology. In order to improve the accuracy of the solution, the grids distributed in the key regions like near the jet suction were particularly refined during the analysis process. The pass lines of flow fields within the reverse circulation bit (as shown in Fig.6.)

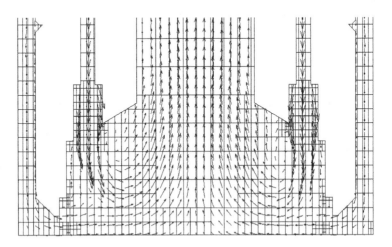

Fig. 6. The pass lines of flow fields within the reverse circulation bit

4   The Design of Orthogonal Design

The influence of air consumption Q on the hammer bit must be additionally considered in the design of the structure of the reverse circulation bit. For example, when every structural parameter with 3 variables was selected, and then the number of simulation models with 6 parameters would be reached to 729 (3^6), which would make it complicate for the EFD computation, statistics, and analysis of the simulation results.

The data statistics would be simplified and the number of simulation models would be significantly reduced while the orthogonal test design was scientifically utilized to conduct the EFD simulation [11, 12].

First of all, a L_8 (2^7) orthogonal table was presented, and 2 variables out of 6 structural parameters of the drill bit was selected. Meanwhile, the primary and secondary relationship of each parameter needed to be confirmed, and the interaction of any two parameters should be simultaneously eliminated. Fortunately, there were no interactions for each parameter of the 15 configurations once the computation analysis was finished.

The 3 levels of orthogonal design with 6 structure parameters was eventually accomplished according to the L_{18} (3^7) orthogonal table (as shown in Table1). In addition, the evaluation index M_s was introduced to represent the air mass sucked in the annulus: when the value of M_s is greater than zero, it represents that the air in the annulus was sucked into the central passage, and the value was a reflection for the suction capacity of the ejector, which would mean that the large value is corresponding to a large suction capacity, in return the reverse circulation would be better. When the value of M_s is equal to zero, it would mean that the compressed air flow outside the annulus was neither sucked into the annulus through the ejector nor be flowed into the annulus. When the value of M_s is less than zero, it would mean that the reverse circulation bit couldn't suck the air outside the annulus and the reverse circulation is in failure, which would be avoided in the design of a drill bit.

5   Analysis for the Results

5.1   Effect of the Diffuser Slot Depth H on the Suction Capacity of Reverse Circulation Drilling

The effect of the variable diffuser slot depth H on the reverse circulation capacity is shown as Fig.7., the velocity of gas sprayed out of the bottom injection nozzle can't be reduced while the depth H of the diffuser slot was smaller, and the air jet would erode against the bottom of the borehole and lead to a crossflow reflection phenomenon, which would make it more difficult for the gas to flow through the central passage. However, the velocity of the compressed air would be reduced and the air in the diffuser slot would suck the low-pressure gas while the depth H is raised.

Table 1. The L_{18} (3^7) orthogonal table in the optimized design of structure of GQ-108C hammer bit

No.	structural parameters							M_s/kg/s
---	Q	H	β	d	Θ	N	Blank column	
1	1	1	1	1	1	1	1	0.0338
2	1	2	2	2	2	2	2	0.0450
3	1	3	3	3	3	3	3	0.0415
4	2	1	1	2	2	3	3	0.0199
5	2	2	2	3	3	1	1	0.0770
6	2	3	3	1	1	2	2	0.0504
7	3	1	2	1	3	2	3	0.0121
8	3	2	3	2	1	3	1	0.0338
9	3	3	1	3	2	1	2	0.0396
10	1	1	3	3	2	2	1	0.0020
11	1	2	1	1	3	3	2	0.0302
12	1	3	2	2	1	1	3	0.0551
13	2	1	2	3	1	3	2	0.0062
14	2	2	3	1	2	1	3	0.0393
15	2	3	1	2	3	2	1	0.0242
16	3	1	3	2	3	1	2	0.0360
17	3	2	1	3	1	2	3	0.0146
18	3	3	2	1	2	3	1	0.0146
K_1	0.147	0.098	0.102	0.120	0.182	0.281	0.185	
K_2	0.205	0.179	0.198	0.214	0.160	0.148	0.135	
K_3	0.151	0.225	0.203	0.168	0.161	0.073	0.183	
k_1	0.049	0.033	0.034	0.040	0.061	0.094	0.062	
k_2	0.068	0.060	0.066	0.071	0.053	0.049	0.045	
k_3	0.050	0.075	0.068	0.056	0.054	0.024	0.061	
Range	0.019	0.043	0.034	0.031	0.017	0.069	0.007	
Sorting	5	2	3	4	6	1	7	
The optimal parameter combination	2	3	3	2	1	1	1	0.0812

The mixed gas would flow back to the surface through the central passage after the exchange of energy. It can be concluded that the suction capacity of the drill bit would be strongest while the value of depth H is 15mm according to Fig.7.

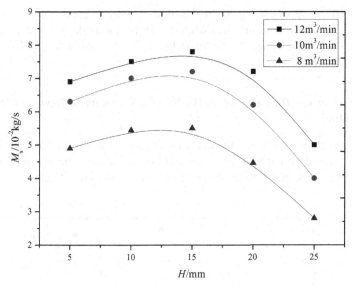

Fig. 7. Diffuser slot depth on the anti-cycling capability

5.2   Effect of Diffusion Angle in the Working Face of Hammer Bit on the Suction Capacity of Reverse Circulation Drilling

It could be implied that when the shape of the working face was changed or deflected, the suction capacity of reverse circulation was enhanced, as shown in Fig.8. It could be analyzed that the air flow with spiral form in the diffuser slot, and simultaneously return to the surface with the suction of air in the bottom of the borehole. Meanwhile, the reverse circulation capacity of the drill bit would be optimized while the diffusion

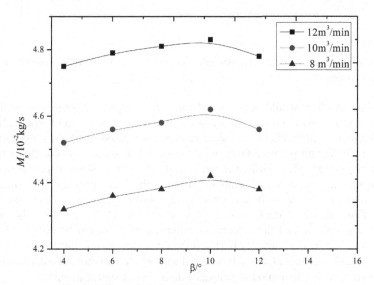

Fig. 8. Different helix angle reverse circulation capacity

angle was 10°, as shown in Fig.8. , the suction capacity of reverse circulation would be declined with a fiercer air crash while the diffusion angle was greater than 10°. Therefore, the diffusion angle of the spiral diffuser slot would be selected as 10° in the design of a drill bit.

5.3   Effect of the Diameter of on the Suction Capacity of Reverse Circulation Drilling

It could be implied that when the diameter D_n was raised from 5mm to 9mm, the value of M_s would primarily have a raise and then a decrease, the all maximum value of M_s would be appeared with the diameter of 7mm, as shown in Fig.9.

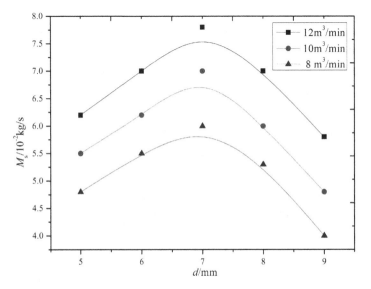

Fig. 9. The effect of diameter of inner injection nozzle on the suction capacity of reverse circulation drilling

The Venturi effect would be produced when the compressed air jet flowed through the suction nozzle with a high velocity, and it could generate an entrainment effect on the low-velocity fluids. Therefore, negative pressure regions would be produced in the bottom of the drill bit working face, and it facilitated air suction outside the annulus to the central passage. Meanwhile, the back pressure of the bottom of piston would be raised while the D_n was too small to increase the local pressure loss of suction nozzles, and the energy of the compressed air couldn't be converted into the impact energy of piston, which leads to an energy dissipation. However, when the value of D_n was large enough and the velocity of compressed air would be decreased, which could reduce the suction capacity for the injection air jet outside the annulus.

Therefore, the value of D_n could be selected appropriately as 7mm in order to obtain the optimized reverse circulation suction capacity during the design of a drill bit.

5.4 Effect of Inclination Angle Θ of Inner Injection Nozzle on the Suction Capacity of Reverse Circulation Drilling

It could be concluded that when the inclination angle was raised from $20°$ to $40°$, the value of M_s could lead to a primary raise and then decrease, as shown in Fig.10. The value of M_s could be reached to the maximum when the θ_s is $35°$.

When the inclination angle is too small and the travel distance of the flow is too long, the linear loss would increase, therefore, the entrainment capacity of high velocity fluid would be decreased. However, when the inclination angle is large enough, the flow jet with high velocity would impact on the inner wall of the core barrel and produce a turbulence flow with crossflow reflection phenomenon, which is adverse to the entrance of air outside the annulus to the central passage.

Therefore, the inclination angle of suction nozzle could be selected as $25°$ during the design of a drill bit.

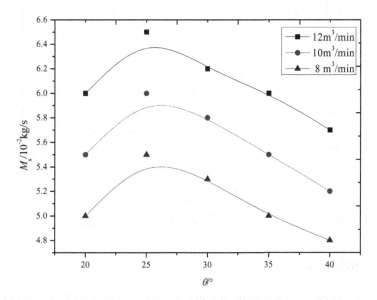

Fig. 10. The effect of inclination angle Θ of inner injection nozzle on the suction capacity of reverse circulation drilling

5.5 Effect of the Number of Suction Nozzles on Reverse Circulation Drilling

It could be concluded that when the number of suction nozzle was raised from 2 to 6, the value of M_s would lead to a primary increase and then a decrease, as shown in Fig.11. While the number of suction nozzle was 3, the M_s would reach to the maximum value.

While the D_n was remained at a constant value and the number of suction nozzle N was increased, the total sectional area of suction nozzle was accordingly increased, and the velocity of compressed air flowed through the suction nozzle was decreased, thereby the entrainment capacity of the eject fluid was decreased. In addition, the jet fluid wouldn't have an interaction with each other, and the low velocity was adverse to the formation of negative pressure region. When the number of suction nozzle N was less, the local pressure loss of the suction nozzle would be increased, leading to a energy loss of the compressed air, which could decrease the suction capacity of the ejecting jet on the air outside the annulus.

Therefore, the number of suction nozzles should be selected as 3 during the design of a drill bit in order to obtain the optimized suction capacity of reverse circulation drilling.

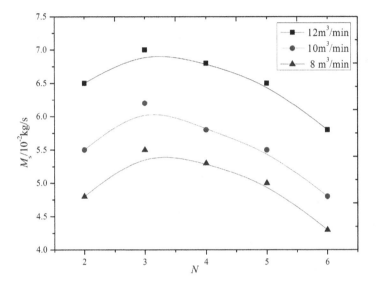

Fig. 11. The effect of numbers of suction nozzle on the reverse circulation capacity of drill bit

6   Conclusion

Steady and reliable reverse circulation effect could be obtained from the optimized hollow reverse circulation drill bit according the results of orthogonal test design and EFD simulation technology.

The primary and secondary relationship for the effect of structure parameters of GQ-108C drill bit on the reverse circulation performance were: the number of inner suction nozzle N, diffuser slot depth H, diffusion angle of spiral diffuser slot β, the diameter of inner suction nozzle d, air consumption Q and the inclination angle of suction nozzle Θ.

When the air consumption Q was12 m³/min, the optimal parameter configuration of drill bit GQ-108C would be: the depth of diffuser slot H was 20mm, the diffusion angle of spiral diffuser slot was 10°, the diameter of inner suction nozzle d was 7mm, the inclination angle of suction nozzle Θ was 25° and the number of suction nozzle was 3. Meanwhile the M_s was 0.0812 kg/s.

References

1. Fan, L., Yin, K., Zhang, Y.: Numerical Investigation of Geometry Parameters On Side-ejector DTH Hammer RC Bit. Journal of Central South University: Science and Technology 42, 220–226 (2011)
2. Zhang, Y.: Application of Reverse Circulation Drilling Technology. Exploration Engineering: Rock & Soil Drilling and Tunneling 9, 46–47 (2007)
3. Yin, K.: Deepen Research on Reverse Circulation Techniques to Promote Development of Drilling and Exploration Science and Technology. Exploration Engineering: Rock & Soil Drilling and Tunneling 3, 1–3 (2006)
4. Bo, K.: Research of Application and Drilling Tool Optimization of Reverse Circulation Drilling Technique with Hollow-through DTH Hammer. Jilin University. College of Construction Engineering (2009)
5. Liu, J.: Researches on the Key Technologies of Hollow-through DTH Used in Gas Drilling. Jilin University. College of Construction Engineering (2009)
6. Yadav, R.L., Patwardhan, A.W.: Design Aspects of Ejectors: Effects on Suction Chamber Geometry. Chemical Engineering Science 63, 3886–3897 (2008)
7. Lucas, C., Koehler, J., Schroeder, A.: Experimentally Validated CO_2 Ejector Operation Characteristic Used in a Numerical Investigation of Ejector Cycle. International Journal of Refrigeration 36, 881–891 (2013)
8. Zhang, K., Xue, F., Pan, W.: Experimental Investigation and Numerical Simulation of High-pressure Gas Ejector. Journal of Thermal Science and Technology 3, 133–138 (2004)
9. Wang, F.: Computational Fluid Dynamics Analysis. Tsinghua University Press, Beijing (2004)
10. Lin, J., Ruan, X., Chen, B.: Fluid mechanics. Tsinghua University Press, Beijing (2005)
11. Li, Y., Hu, C.: Experiment design and data processing. Chemical Industry Press, Beijing (2008)
12. Deng, S., Gong, Z., Cai, Y.: Orthogonal design of technology for electrodeposition nanocrystalline Fe-Ni-Cr alloy foil. Journal of Central South University: Science and Technology 36, 24–29 (2005)

Parallel Conjugate Gradient Method Based on Spline Difference Method for the One-Dimensional Heat Equation

Aijia Ouyang[1], Wangdong Yang[1], Guangxue Yue[2,*], Tao Jiang[2],
Xiaoyong Tang[3], and Xu Zhou[2]

[1] School of Information Science and Engineering, Hunan City University,
Yiyang, Hunan 413000, China
[2] College of Mathematics, Physics & Information Engineering, Jiaxing University,
Jiaxing, Zhejiang 314001, China
guangxueyue@163.com
[3] State Key Laboratory for Novel Software Technology, Nanjing University,
Nanjing, Jiangsu 210093, China

Abstract. A new parallel conjugate gradient method (PCGM) implemented in GPU is presented to solve the one-dimensional heat equation with nonlocal boundary conditions in the paper. It is found that, at the interior nodal points, the method derived by using quartic spline is equivalent to the classical compact difference scheme which is unconditionally stable and the accuracy order is of $O(k^2 + h^4)$, where k and h are the time step length and the space step length, respectively. Both the accuracies of the new difference schemes at the two endpoints to deal with the nonlocal boundary conditions are of $O(k + h^4)$, which is much better than that of the classical finite difference. Finally, a numerical example is given to illustrate the efficiency of our method. Computational times are compared between high-end GPU and CPU systems with speedup of over 7.27 times when applied to one-dimensional heat equation.

Keywords: Quartic spline, Heat equation, Unconditionally stable, Derivative conditions.

1   Introduction

Graphics Processing Units (GPU) technique has been applied to engineering problems [1], shallow water simulations [2], finite difference scheme [3], finite element operator [4], incompressible flow [5], 3D flow simulations [6,7,8], computational fluid dynamics [9,10,11], et al.

We consider the one-dimensional nonclassical heat equation

$$\frac{\partial u}{\partial t} = \alpha \frac{\partial^2 u}{\partial x^2}, \quad 0 < x < 1, \quad 0 < t \le T, \tag{1}$$

---

* Corresponding author.

K. Li et al. (Eds.): ParCFD 2013, CCIS 405, pp. 602–611, 2014.
© Springer-Verlag Berlin Heidelberg 2014

with initial conditions

$$u(x,0) = f(x), \quad 0 \le x \le 1, \tag{2}$$

$$\frac{\partial u}{\partial x}u(1,t) = g(t), \quad 0 < t \le T, \tag{3}$$

and a nonlocal condition

$$\int_0^b u(x,t)dx = m(t), \quad 0 < t \le T, \quad 0 < b < 1. \tag{4}$$

In this problem, $f(x)$, $g(t)$ and $m(t)$ are given functions and α and b are constants. If $b = 1$, Eq. (4) can be differentiated as

$$m'(t) = \int_0^1 u_t dx = \int_0^1 \alpha u_{xx} dx = \alpha u_x(1,t) - \alpha u_x(0,t). \tag{5}$$

The derivation holds only when m and u are differentiable.

The one-dimensional heat equation is a well-known simple second order linear partial differential equation (PDE) [12]-[14]. PDEs like the heat equation very often arise in modeling problems in science and engineering. It is also used in financial mathematics in the modeling of options. For example, the Black-Scholes option pricing model's differential equation can be transformed into the heat equation [15].

Recently nonlocal boundary value problems have been considered in the literature [16]-[20]. Very recently, Dehghan [21] presented a new finite difference technique for solving the one-dimensional heat equation subject to the specification of mass, but the accuracy of their method is only first order. Caglar *et al.* [22] developed a third degree B-spines method to solve the heat equation (1-3) with the accuracy being $O(k^2 + h^2)$, and at the endpoints, the approximation order is second order only.

2   Quartic Splines and Interpolation Errors

Let Π be a uniform partition of $[0,1]$ as follows

$$0 = x_0 < x_1 < \ldots\ldots < x_n = 1, \tag{6}$$

where $x_i = ih$, $h = 1/n$.

The quartic spline space on $[0,1]$ is defined as

$$S_4^3(\Pi) = \left\{ s \in C^3[0,1] : s\big|_{[x_{i-1},x_i]} \in P_4, i = 1(1)n \right\},$$

where P_d is the set of polynomials of degree at most d.

It is easy to know that $\dim S_4^3(\Pi) = n+4$. For any $s \in S_4^3(\Pi)$, the restriction of s in $[x_{i-1}, x_i]$ can be expressed as

$$s(x) = s_{i-1} + hs_{i-1}'t + h^2 s_{i-1}''\frac{t^2}{12}(6 - t^2) + h^2 s_i''\frac{t^4}{12} + h^3 s_{i-1}'''\frac{t^3}{12}(2 - t), \tag{7}$$

where $x = x_{i-1} + th$, $t \in [0,1]$, $s_i = s(x_i)$, $s_i' = s'(x_i)$, $s_i'' = s''(x_i)$, $s_i''' = s'''(x_i)$, $i = 0(1)n$.

This leads to

$$s_i = s_{i-1} + h s_{i-1}' + \frac{5}{12} h^2 s_{i-1}'' + \frac{1}{12} h^2 s_i'' + \frac{1}{12} h^3 s_{i-1}''', \tag{8}$$

$$s_i' = s_{i-1}' + \frac{2}{3} h s_{i-1}'' + \frac{1}{3} h s_i'' + \frac{1}{6} h^2 s_{i-1}''', \tag{9}$$

$$s_i''' = -s_{i-1}''' + \frac{2}{h} \left[s_i'' - s_{i-1}'' \right], \tag{10}$$

for $i = 1(1)n$. Based on the above three equations, we can have

$$\frac{1}{12} s_{i+1}'' + \frac{5}{6} s_i'' + \frac{1}{12} s_{i-1}'' = \frac{1}{h^2} [s_{i+1} - 2s_i + s_{i-1}], \quad i = 1(1)\overline{n-1}. \tag{11}$$

3   Quartic Spline Method

We consider the following heat equation (1) with the initial boundary value conditions (2- 3) and derivative boundary condition (5).

The domain $[0,1] \times [0,T]$ is divided into an $n \times m$ mesh with the spatial step size $h = 1/n$ in x direction and the time step size $k = T/m$, respectively.

Grid points (x_i, t_j) are defined by $x_i = ih$ and $t_j = jk$, where $i = 0(1)n$, $j = 0(1)m$, n and m are integers.

Let $s(x_i, t_j)$ and U_i^j be approximations to $u(x_i, t_j)$ and $M_i(t) = \frac{\partial^2 s(x,t)}{\partial x^2}|_{(x_i,t)}$, respectively.

Assume that $u(x,t)$ is the exact solution to Eq.(1). For any fixed t, let $s(x,t) \in S_4^3(\Pi)$ be the quartic spline interpolating to $u(x,t)$ such that

$$s(x_i, t) = u(x_i, t), i = 0(1)n, \tag{12}$$

$$\frac{\partial^2 s}{\partial x^2}|(x_n, t) = \frac{\partial^2 u}{\partial x^2}|(x_n, t), \tag{13}$$

$$\frac{\partial s}{\partial x}|(x_0, t) + \frac{1}{12} h^2 \frac{\partial^3 s}{\partial x^3}|(x_0, t) = \frac{\partial u}{\partial x}|(x_0, t) + \frac{1}{12} h^2 \frac{\partial^3 u}{\partial x^3}|(x_0, t), \tag{14}$$

$$\frac{\partial s}{\partial x}|(x_n, t) - \frac{1}{12} h^2 \frac{\partial^3 s}{\partial x^3}|(x_n, t) = \frac{\partial u}{\partial x}|(x_n, t) - \frac{1}{12} h^2 \frac{\partial^3 u}{\partial x^3}|(x_n, t). \tag{15}$$

Then it follows from Theorem 1 that

$$\frac{\partial^2 u}{\partial x^2}|(x_i, t) = \frac{\partial^2 s}{\partial x^2}|(x_i, t) + O(h^4), \quad i = 1(1)\overline{n-1}. \tag{16}$$

For any fixed t, by using the Taylor series expansion, Eq.(1) can be discretized at the point (x_i, t_j) into

$$\frac{u(x_i, t_{j+1}) - u(x_i, t_j)}{k} =$$

$$\frac{1}{2}\alpha \left[\left(\frac{\partial^2 s(x,t)}{\partial x^2} \right)_i^j + \left(\frac{\partial^2 s(x,t)}{\partial x^2} \right)_i^{j+1} \right] + O(k^2 + h^4), \tag{17}$$

where $i = 1(1)\overline{n-1}$, $j = 0(1)\overline{m-1}$.

Substituting (17) into spline relation (11) and using Eq.(12), we conclude

$$
\begin{aligned}
&(1 - 6\alpha r)u(x_{i+1}, t_{j+1}) + (10 + 12\alpha r)u(x_i, t_{j+1}) + (1 - 6\alpha r)u(x_{i-1}, t_{j+1}) = \\
&(1 + 6\alpha r)u(x_{i+1}, t_j) + (10 - 12\alpha r)u(x_i, t_j) + \\
&(1 + 6\alpha r)u(x_{i-1}, t_j) + O(k^2 + h^4),
\end{aligned}
\tag{18}
$$

where $r = \alpha\frac{k}{h^2}$.

Neglecting the error term, we can get the following difference scheme

$$
\begin{aligned}
&(1 - 6\alpha r)U_{i+1}^{j+1} + (10 + 12\alpha r)U_i^{j+1} + (1 - 6\alpha r)U_{i-1}^{j+1} = \\
&(1 + 6\alpha r)U_{i+1}^j + (10 - 12\alpha r)U_i^j + (1 + 6\alpha r)U_{i-1}^j, \\
&i = 1(1)\overline{n-1}, \; j = 0(1)m,
\end{aligned}
\tag{19}
$$

with the accuracy being $O(k^2 + h^4)$.

It is clearly that the difference scheme (19) identify to the classical fourth order compact difference scheme in [23], which is unconditionally stable.

4   The Difference Schemes on the Boundary

From the interpolation conditions (13-15) and Theorem 1, for each $t > 0$, we have

$$
\begin{aligned}
\frac{\partial u(x_0, t)}{\partial x} = &\frac{u(x_1, t) - u(x_0, t)}{h} - \frac{1}{12}h\frac{\partial^2 u(x_1, t)}{\partial x^2} \\
&- \frac{5}{12}h\frac{\partial^2 u(x_0, t)}{\partial x^2} - \frac{1}{12}h^2\frac{\partial^3 u(x_0, t)}{\partial x^3} + O(h^4),
\end{aligned}
\tag{20}
$$

$$
\begin{aligned}
\frac{\partial u(x_n, t)}{\partial x} = &\frac{u(x_n, t) - u(x_{n-1}, t)}{h} + \frac{5}{12}h\frac{\partial^2 u(x_n, t)}{\partial x^2} \\
&+ \frac{1}{12}h\frac{\partial^2 u(x_{n-1}, t)}{\partial x^2} + \frac{1}{12}h^2\frac{\partial^3 u(x_n, t)}{\partial x^3} + O(h^4).
\end{aligned}
\tag{21}
$$

Let $t = t_{j+1}$, it follows form Eqs.(1) and (20) that

$$
\begin{aligned}
u_x(x_0, t_{j+1}) = &\frac{u(x_1, t_{j+1}) - u(x_0, t_{j+1})}{h} - \frac{1}{12\alpha}h\frac{u(x_1, t_{j+1}) - u(x_1, t_j)}{k} \\
&- \frac{5}{12\alpha}h\frac{u(x_0, t_{j+1}) - u(x_0, t_j)}{k} - \frac{1}{12}h^2\frac{\partial^3 u(x_0, t_{j+1})}{\partial x^3} \\
&+ O(k + h^4).
\end{aligned}
\tag{22}
$$

From Eqs.(1),(3) and (5), we can get

$$
\frac{\partial^3 u(0, t)}{\partial x^3} = \frac{1}{\alpha}\frac{\partial^2 u(0, t)}{\partial x \partial t} = \frac{1}{\alpha^2}m''(t) - \frac{1}{\alpha}g'(t).
\tag{23}
$$

Substituting (23) into (22) and neglecting the error term, we get the fourth-order difference scheme at $x = x_0$

$$\left(1 - \frac{1}{12r}\right) U_1^{j+1} - \left(1 + \frac{5}{12r}\right) U_0^{j+1} + \frac{1}{12r} U_1^j + \frac{5}{12r} U_0^j =$$
$$hu_x(0, t_{j+1}) + \frac{1}{12} h^3 \left(\frac{1}{\alpha^2} m''(t_{j+1}) - \frac{1}{\alpha} g'(t_{j+1})\right). \quad (24)$$

Similarly, the difference scheme at the other end $x = x_n$ is

$$\left(1 + \frac{5}{12r}\right) U_n^{j+1} + \left(-1 + \frac{1}{12r}\right) U_{n-1}^{j+1} - \frac{5}{12r} U_n^j + \frac{1}{12r} U_{n-1}^j =$$
$$hu_x(1, t_{j+1}) - \frac{1}{12\alpha} h^3 g'(t_{j+1}). \quad (25)$$

5   Parallel Conjugate Gradient Method

5.1   GPU and CUDA

This section is dedicated to the description of the hardware architecture and software environment. A series of experiments are carried out on a dual-processor eight-core 2.3 GHz AMD Opteron 6134 machine with 8 GB main memory. The NVIDIA graphics cards GTX 465 is used to check the scalability of our approach.

The GTX 465 has 11 multiprocessors, 352 CUDA cores, 48 KB of shared memory per block, 607MHz processor clock, 1 GB GDDR5 RAM, 102.6GB/s memory bandwidth, and 802MHz memory clock. For the GPU card, the maximum number of resident blocks per multiprocessor is 8, the maximum number of threads per block is 1024, the maximum number of resident threads per multiprocessor is 1536, the total number of registers available per block is 32768. In software, the testing system is built on top of the Linux (Ubuntu 10.10) operating system, the NVIDIA CUDA Driver version 4.2, and GCC version 4.4.5.

5.2   Parallel Conjugate Gradient Algorithm

One of the fast iterative algorithms for a system of linear equations is the conjugate gradient method (CGM) [24]. The introduction of a preconditioner is applied to accelerate the convergence of the iterative process in the CGM. Preconditioning consists in the fact that the initial system of equations $Ax = b$ is replaced by the system

$$C^{-1}Ax = C^{-1}b. \quad (26)$$

for which the iterative method converges essentially faster. The condition of choosing the preconditioner C is as follows:

$$cond(\tilde{A}) << cond(A), \quad cond(\tilde{A}) = \frac{\tilde{\lambda}_{max}}{\tilde{\lambda}_{min}}, \quad cond(A) = \frac{\lambda_{max}}{\lambda_{min}}, \quad (27)$$

where $cond(A)$ and $cond(\tilde{A})$ are the condition numbers of the matrices A and $\tilde{A}$; λ_{min}, $\tilde{\lambda}_{min}$ and λ_{max}, $\tilde{\lambda}_{max}$ are the smallest and largest eigenvalues of the matrices A and $\tilde{A}$, respectively. For system of equations (37), the conjugate gradient method with preconditioner C has the form:

$$r^0 = b - Ax^0, \quad p^0 = C^{-1}r^0, \quad z^0 = p^0, \tag{28}$$

$$x^{k+1} = x^k + \alpha_k p^k, \quad \alpha_k = \frac{r^k, z^k}{Ap^k, p^k}, \quad r^{k+1} = r^k - \alpha_k Ap^k, \tag{29}$$

$$z^{k+1} = C^{-1}r^{k+1}, \quad p^{k+1} = z^{k+1} + \beta_k p^k, \quad \beta_k = \frac{r^{k+1}, z^{k+1}}{r^k, z^k}. \tag{30}$$

Where, the preconditioner is chosen by the incomplete LUdecomposition of the matrix A. The condition for stopping the CGM iterative process with preconditioner is

$$\frac{||Az^k - b||}{||b||} < \varepsilon \tag{31}$$

6   Experimental Results and Discuss

In this section, our new method is tested on the following problems from the literature [21]. Absolute errors of numerical solutions are calculated and compared with those obtained by using the three degree B-spline method [21,22].

In this example, we consider the following heat equation

$$f(x) = \cos\left(\frac{\pi}{2}x\right), \quad 0 < x < 1, \tag{32}$$

$$g(t) = -\exp\left(-\frac{\pi^2}{4}t\right), \quad 0 < x < 1, \tag{33}$$

$$m(t) = \frac{4}{\pi^2}\exp\left(-\frac{\pi^2}{4}t\right), \quad 0 < x < 1, \tag{34}$$

with

$$u(x,t) = \exp\left(-\frac{\pi^2}{4}t\right)\cos\left(\frac{\pi}{2}x\right) \tag{35}$$

as its analytical solution.

At first, the results with $h = k = 0.01$, 0.05, 0.025, 0.001, using the present method discussed in Section 3 and 4, are shown in Table 1. We present the relative error $abs((U_i^j - u(x_i, t_j))/abs(u(x_i, t_j))$ for $u(0.5, 0.1)$ using the present method. The numerical results are compared with those results obtained by the methods in [18,21,25,26], see Table 1. It is shown from Table 1 that the numerical

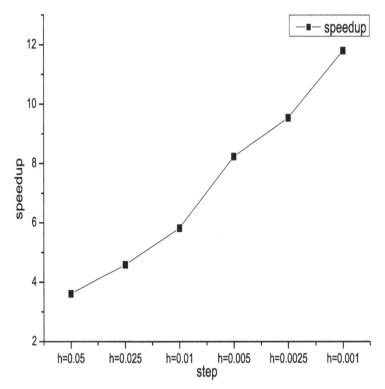

Fig. 1. The speedup of PCGM at various spatial lengths

Table 1. Relative errors at various spatial lengths

Step	Implicit[25]	Galerkin[18]	Keller[26]	RKC[27]	Saulyev[21]	CGM
$h = 0.0500$	9.1×10^{-3}	9.9×10^{-2}	9.4×10^{-2}	9.8×10^{-2}	9.6×10^{-3}	1.2×10^{-4}
$h = 0.0250$	2.3×10^{-3}	3.0×10^{-2}	2.4×10^{-2}	3.7×10^{-2}	2.5×10^{-3}	3.0×10^{-5}
$h = 0.0100$	3.8×10^{-4}	4.9×10^{-3}	4.1×10^{-3}	6.1×10^{-3}	3.9×10^{-4}	4.4×10^{-6}
$h = 0.0050$	9.4×10^{-5}	1.2×10^{-3}	1.0×10^{-3}	1.5×10^{-3}	9.6×10^{-5}	1.1×10^{-6}
$h = 0.0025$	2.3×10^{-5}	3.1×10^{-4}	2.5×10^{-4}	3.5×10^{-4}	2.5×10^{-5}	2.8×10^{-7}
$h = 0.0010$	4.1×10^{-6}	5.0×10^{-5}	4.0×10^{-5}	6.0×10^{-5}	4.3×10^{-6}	4.5×10^{-8}

results of the present method are much better than that in [18,25,26,21]. In [21], Dehghan solved the example by using the Saulyev I's technique with the accuracy being first-order with respect to the space and time variables, and the numerical integration trapezoidal rule is used to approximation the integral condition in (4). However, in this paper, we present a new method to deal with the nonlocal boundary conditions by using quartic splines [28], and the method is very easier than the numerical integration trapezoidal rule[21].

Table 2. The Maximum absolute errors at various step h and k

steps	method[22]	CGM
$h = k = 1/20$	6.1575×10^{-3}	2.7824×10^{-4}
$h = k = 1/40$	1.5751×10^{-3}	6.2456×10^{-5}
$h = 1/40,\ k = 1/60$	9.5842×10^{-4}	3.6223×10^{-5}

Table 3. The speedup of PCGM at various step h

spatial length	C(ms)	C-CUDA(ms)	speedup
$h = 0.0500$	3701.24	1025.27	3.61
$h = 0.0250$	7809.62	1701.44	4.59
$h = 0.0100$	18899.27	3247.30	5.82
$h = 0.0050$	36853.58	4477.96	8.23
$h = 0.0025$	76655.45	8035.16	9.54
$h = 0.0010$	200070.71	16955.15	11.80

7 Conclusion

In this paper, a new parallel method by using quartic splines functions is applied to the one-dimensional heat equation with boundary integral conditions replacing standard boundary conditions. This technique worked well for one-dimensional diffusion with an integral condition which can be transferred to the derivative boundary conditions. Various approaches reported for the numerical solution of diffusion subject to the specification of mass deals with the parabolic partial differential equations whose usual boundary specifications are replaced with integral boundary value conditions. However, no special method to deal with the integral boundary value conditions. In this paper, we construct a special method to approximate the derivative boundary conditions, and the accuracy of this method is fourth order at the end points. The numerical results obtained by using the quartic spline method described in this article give acceptable results and suggests convergence to the exact solution when k and h goes to zero. Computational times are compared between high-end GPU and CPU systems with speedup of over 7.27 times when applied to one-dimensional heat equation.

Acknowledgements. This paper was partially funded by the Key Program of National Natural Science Foundation of China (Grant No.61133005), and the National Natural Science Foundation of China (Grant Nos.90715029, 61070057, 60603053, 61370098 and 61202109), Key Projects in the National Science & Technology Pillar Program the Cultivation Fund of the Key Scientific and Technical Innovation Project, Ministry of Education of China (Grant No.708066), the Ph.D. Programs Foundation of Ministry of Education of China (Grant No.20100161110019), the Program for New Century Excellent Talents in University (Grant No.NCET-08-0177), A Project Supported by the Science and Technology Research Foundation of Hunan Province (Grant No.2013GK3082), and A Project Supported by Scientific Research Fund of Hunan Provincial Education Department (Grant No.12A062 and No.13C333), A Project supported by the Research Foundation of Education Bureau of Hunan Province, China (Grant No.11C0573); Project supported by the Natural Science Foundation of Zhejiang pvovince, China (Grant No.LY12F02019, No.LY12F02047), Project supported by the Science and Technology Foundation of Jiaxing City, China (Grant No. 2012AY1027).

References

1. Kuo, F.-A., Smith, M.R., Hsieh, C.-W., Chou, C.-Y., Wu, J.-S.: GPU acceleration for general conservation equations and its application to several engineering problems. Computers & Fluids 45(1), 147–154 (2011)
2. Brodtkorb, A.R., Stra, M.L., Altinakar, M.: Efficient shallow water simulations on GPUs: Implementation, visualization, verification, and validation. Computers & Fluids 55(15), 1–12 (2012)
3. Tutkun, B., Edis, F.O.: A GPU application for high-order compact finite difference scheme. Computers & Fluids 55(15), 29–35 (2012)
4. Kronbichler, M., Kormann, K.: A generic interface for parallel cell-based finite element operator application. Computers & Fluids 63(30), 135–147 (2012)
5. Storti, M.A., Paz, R.R., Dalcin, L.D., Costarelli, S.D., Idelsohn, S.R.: A FFT preconditioning technique for the solution of incompressible flow on GPUs. Computers & Fluids 74(30), 44–57 (2013)
6. Marrone, S., Bouscasse, B., Colagrossi, A., Antuono, M.: Study of ship wave breaking patterns using 3D parallel SPH simulations. Computers & Fluids 69(30), 54–66 (2012)
7. Borazjani, I., Ge, L., Le, T.: Fotis Sotiropoulos, A parallel overset-curvilinear-immersed boundary framework for simulating complex 3D incompressible flows. Computers & Fluids 1(77), 76–96 (2013)
8. Xiong, Q., Li, B., Xu, J., Wang, X., Wang, L., Ge, W.: Efficient 3D DNS of gas-solid flows on Fermi GPGPU. Computers & Fluids 70(30), 86–94 (2012)
9. Appleyard, J., Drikakis, D.: Higher-order CFD and interface tracking methods on highly-Parallel MPI and GPU systems. Computers & Fluids 46(1), 101–105 (2011)
10. Soni, K., Chandar, D.D.J., Sitaraman, J.: Development of an overset grid computational fluid dynamics solver on graphical processing units. Computers & Fluids 58(15), 1–14 (2012)
11. Lefebvre, M., Guillen, P., Le Gouez, J.-M., Basdevant, C.: Optimizing 2D and 3D structured Euler CFD solvers on Graphical Processing Units. Computers & Fluids 70(30), 136–147 (2012)
12. Carslaw, H.S., Jaeger, J.C.: Conduction of heat in solids. Oxford University Press, Oxford (1959)
13. Widder, D.V.: The heat equation. Academic Press, London (1975)
14. Cannon, J.R.: The one-dimensional heat equation. Cambridge University Press, Cambridge (1984)
15. Wilmott, P., Howison, S., Dewynne, J.: The mathematics of financial derivatives: a student introduction. Cambridge University Press, Cambridge (1995)
16. Ang, W.T.: A method of solution for the one-dimensional heat equation subject to a nonlocal condition. SEA Bull. Math. 26(2), 197–203 (2002)

17. Boutayeb, A., Chetouani, A.: Global extrapolation of numerical methods for solving a parabolic equation with nonlocal boundary conditions. Int. J. Comput. Math. 80, 789–797 (2003)
18. Cannon, J.R., Matheson, A.L.: A numerical procedure for diffusion subject to the specification of mass. Int. J. Eng. Sci. 31(3), 347–355 (1993)
19. Saadatmandi, A., Razzaghi, M.: A Tau method approximation for the diffusion equation with nonlocal boundary conditions. Int. J. Comput. Math. 81(11), 1427–1432 (2004)
20. Wang, S., Lin, Y.: A numerical method for the diffusion equation with nonlocal boundary specifications. Int. J. Eng. Sci. 28(6), 543–546 (1990)
21. Dehghan, M.: The one-dimensional heat equation subject to a boundary intergral specification. Chaos, Solitons Fractals 32(2), 661–675 (2007)
22. Caglar, H., Ozer, M., Caglar, N.: The numerical solution of the one-dimensional heat equation by using third degree B-spline functions. Chaos, Solitons Fractals 38(4), 1197–1201 (2008)
23. Thomas, J.W.: Numericlal Partial Differential Equations: Finite Difference Methods. Springer, New York (1995)
24. Akimova, E.N., Belousov, D.V.: Parallel algorithms for solving linear systems with block-tridiagonal matrices on multi-core CPU with GPU. Journal of Computational Science 3(6), 445–449 (2012)
25. Cannon, J.R., Prez-Esteva, S., van, J.: A Galerkin prodedure for the diffusion equation subject to the specification of mass. SIAM J. Num. Anal. 24, 499–515 (1987)
26. Ewing, R.E., Lin, T.: A class of parameter estimation techniques of fluid flow in porous meida. Adv. Water Resour. 14(2), 89–97 (1991)
27. Makarov, V.L., Kulyev, D.T.: Solution of a boundary value problem for a quai-linear parabolic equation with nonclassical boundary conditions. Different. Equat. 21, 296–305 (1985)
28. Liu, H.-W., Liu, L.-B., Chen, Y.: A semi-discretization method based on quartic splines for solving one-space-dimensional hyperbolic equations. Applied Mathematics and Computation 210(2), 508–514 (2009)

Author Index

Bai, Junqiang   344
Bo, Kun   589

Cai, Jinsheng   185, 252
Caiting, Li   265
Cao, Wei   195
Cao, Zongyan   207
Che, Yonggang   195
Chen, Duan-Duan   383
Chen, Hang   514
Chen, Hao   470
Chen, Jiankui   301
Chen, Xiaoming   403, 440
Cheng, Meng   418
Cheng, Wang   541
Chi, Peng   136
Cui, Dongliang   490

Du, Jiayi   532

Fan, Shuangnan   482
Fei, Ruizhen   553
Feng, Chunsheng   149
Feng, Junhong   221
Feng, Long-long   207
Feng, Xiaoning   54

Gu, Jingzi   54
Gu, Lianjun   100
Gu, Weidong   311
Guanqing, Guo   265
Guo, Meng   311
Guo-hao, Ding   37
Guozhen, Tan   321

Han, Qilong   54
Han, Xiangxi   403
Han, Xu   504
He, Gang   89
Hongyan, Huang   232, 240
Hu, Biao   532
Hu, Huan   287
Hu, Xiaolei   577
Hu, Zhemin   363

Hua, Li   37
Huan, Xiangtian   589
Huang, Danqing   429

Ji, Yu   301
Jiang, Jihai   363
Jiang, Qin   232
Jiang, Tao   602
Jiang, Xi   66, 78
Jianguo, Ning   541
Jian-Xia, Liu   37
Jing, Yiming   532
Jin-Zhi, Fan   37

Kaidi, Zhu   240
Kuang, Jishun   532

Lai, Lin   89
Le, Guigao   577
Lee, Jen-Der   11
Lei, Jing   221
Li, Didi   66, 78
Li, Kenli   1
Li, Lijia   589
Li, Meng   490
Li, Pengyuan   54
Li, Renfa   124, 287
Li, Rui   363
Li, Ting   470
Liang, Jie   354
Liang, Shan   25
Liao, Yingqiang   1
Lin, Nansheng   440
Lin, Ren   514
Lin, Wei   403, 440
Lin, Zhiyong   504
Liu, Qiuhong   185, 252
Liu, Rangsu   1
Liu, Tiegang   393
Liu, Wei   25, 195
Liu, Yiting   553
Liu, Yu   504
Lu, ZhongHua   160
Luo, Congshu   149

Ma, Dawei   577
Ma, Tianbao   565
Ma, WenPeng   160
Ma, Zihui   332
Meng, Chen   207
Meng, Qingliang   66, 78
Meng, Wu   232
Mian, Haris Hameed   11, 418

Ning, Jianguo   565

Ouyang, Aijia   602

Pan, Haiwei   54
Pan, Jingshan   311
Peng, Limin   553

Qin, Haichen   301

Salah, Ahmad   482
Sammut, Karl   403
Shanhong, Li   265
Shen, An   376
Shi, Chenghua   553
Shi, Lin   470
Shu, Shi   149
Sun, Hongling   276

Tang, Xiaoyong   602
Tang, Youhong   403, 440
Tang, Zhuo   100, 522
Tangqi,   265
Tao, Li   232, 240
Tian, Fang-Bao   383
Tian, Min   311
Truong, Tung Khac   482

Wang, Bowen   490
Wang, Chen   344
Wang, Fang   252
Wang, Gang   11, 418
Wang, Guangxue   195
Wang, Long   207
Wang, Qiancheng   221
Wang, Yan   136
Wang, Yongxian   195
Wang, Zheng   393
Wang, Zhenguo   221
Wei, Kai   172

Wei, Qiang   383
Wei, Wei   112
Weihong, Yao   321
Wenhu, Han   541
Wu, Chengtao   124
Wu, Shifeng   450
Wu, Wenkang   522
Wu, Yaogen   301

Xie, Guoqi   100
Xie, Xiaoqin   54
Xu, Chuanfu   195
Xu, Jia   185
Xu, Xiangzhao   565
Xu, Yuan-Qing   383
Xu, Yuming   376, 482

Yang, Wangdong   602
Yang, Weichao   553
Yang, Xiaolong   332
Yang, Yan   276
Ye, Yu   136, 514
Ye, Zheng-Yin   11
Yong, Bi   541
You, Kehua   172
Yu, Feng   232, 240
Yu, Shengjiao   393
Yuan, Li   25, 450
Yuan, Wancheng   172
Yue, Guangxue   602
Yue, Xiaoqiang   149
Yuehui, Yang   321

Zhang, Hao   149
Zhang, Jian   160
Zhang, Ju-Hua   383
Zhang, Lilun   195
Zhang, Yang   344
Zhao, Chengbi   403, 440
Zhao, Xiuxu   363
Zhao, Zhiqiang   589
Zhong, Cheng   112
Zhong, Xiaoqin   66, 78
Zhou, Chuanli   363
Zhou, Jin   89, 504
Zhou, Xu   602
Zhu, Weishan   207
Zhu, Xiangyuan   429, 460
Zu, Wen-Hong   383